The Internet
GIGABOOK™
FOR DUMMIES®

Peter Weverka

**Tony Bove, Mark Chambers, Marsha Collier, Brad Hill,
John Levine, Margaret Levine Young, Doug Lowe,
Camille McCue, Deborah Ray, Eric Ray, Cheryl Rhodes**

WILEY

Wiley Publishing, Inc.

The Internet GigaBook™ For Dummies®

Published by
Wiley Publishing, Inc.
111 River Street
Hoboken, NJ 07030-5774

Copyright © 2004 by Wiley Publishing, Inc., Indianapolis, Indiana

Published by Wiley Publishing, Inc., Indianapolis, Indiana

Published simultaneously in Canada

No part of this publication may be reproduced, stored in a retrieval system or transmitted in any form or by any means, electronic, mechanical, photocopying, recording, scanning or otherwise, except as permitted under Sections 107 or 108 of the 1976 United States Copyright Act, without either the prior written permission of the Publisher, or authorization through payment of the appropriate per-copy fee to the Copyright Clearance Center, 222 Rosewood Drive, Danvers, MA 01923, (978) 750-8400, fax (978) 646-8600. Requests to the Publisher for permission should be addressed to the Legal Department, Wiley Publishing, Inc., 10475 Crosspoint Blvd., Indianapolis, IN 46256, (317) 572-3447, fax (317) 572-4355, e-mail: brandreview@wiley.com.

Trademarks: Wiley, the Wiley Publishing logo, For Dummies, the Dummies Man logo, A Reference for the Rest of Us!, The Dummies Way, Dummies Daily, The Fun and Easy Way, Dummies.com, and related trade dress are trademarks or registered trademarks of John Wiley & Sons, Inc. and/or its affiliates in the United States and other countries, and may not be used without written permission. All other trademarks are the property of their respective owners. Wiley Publishing, Inc., is not associated with any product or vendor mentioned in this book.

For general information on our other products and services or to obtain technical support, please contact our Customer Care Department within the U.S. at 800-762-2974, outside the U.S. at 317-572-3993, or fax 317-572-4002.

Wiley also publishes its books in a variety of electronic formats. Some content that appears in print may not be available in electronic books.

Library of Congress Control Number: 2004109258

ISBN: 0-7645-7415-9

Manufactured in the United States of America

10 9 8 7 6 5 4 3 2 1

1B/ST/QY/QU/IN

Acknowledgments

Wiley Publishing, Inc., gratefully acknowledges the contributions of these authors and contributing writers: Peter Weverka, Brad Hill, Cheryl Rhodes, Doug Lowe, Emily Vander Veer, John Levine, Margaret Levine Young, Marsha Collier, and Tony Bove.

We would like to thank Peter Weverka for editing this book, Virginia Sanders, Teresa Artman, and Jean Rogers for copy editing it, and Linda Morris for serving as project editor. Thanks also go to Jim Kelly for his technical edits, Steve Rath for creating the index, and Rich Tennant for the witty cartoons that you find in this book. We also thank the many page layout technicians, graphic artists, proofreaders, and others in Composition Services who worked to bring this book to fruition.

Peter Weverka wishes to thank Steve Hayes for the opportunity to work on this and other *For Dummies* books for Wiley Publishing, Inc.

Publisher's Acknowledgments

We're proud of this book; please send us your comments through our online registration form. To register this book, go to www.dummies.com, click Contact Us at the bottom of the page, and then click Register Your Book on the page that appears.

Some of the people who helped bring this book to market include the following:

Acquisitions, Editorial, and Media Development

Project Editor: Linda Morris

Acquisitions Editor: Steven Hayes

Copy Editor: Virginia Sanders

Technical Editor: James F. Kelly

Editorial Manager: Leah Cameron

Media Development Supervisor: Richard Graves

Editorial Assistant: Amanda Foxworth

Cartoons: Rich Tennant (www.the5thwave.com)

Production

Project Coordinator: Maridee Ennis

Layout and Graphics: Lauren Goddard, Denny Hager, Joyce Haughey, Stephanie D. Jumper, Michael Kruzil, Jacque Roth, Julie Trippetti

Proofreaders: Laura Albert, Laura L. Bowman, Andy Hollandbeck, Carl Pierce, Charles Spencer, Brian H. Walls

Indexer: Steve Rath

Special Help: Teresa Artman, Jean Rogers

Publishing and Editorial for Technology Dummies

    Richard Swadley, Vice President and Executive Group Publisher

    Andy Cummings, Vice President and Publisher

    Mary Bednarek, Executive Acquisitions Director

    Mary C. Corder, Editorial Director

Publishing for Consumer Dummies

    Diane Graves Steele, Vice President and Publisher

    Joyce Pepple, Acquisitions Director

Composition Services

    Gerry Fahey, Vice President of Production Services

    Debbie Stailey, Director of Composition Services

Contents at a Glance

Table of Contents

Introduction

This book is a general-purpose guide to all things that have to do with the Internet. It takes on a variety of subjects — how to send and receive e-mail, chat online, conduct Internet research, use Yahoo!, shop on eBay, enjoy music with iTunes, and create your own Web pages. Don't look in this book to find out how the Internet works. Look here to find out how you can make the most of the time that you spend on the Internet.

What's in This Book, Anyway?

This book is really six different books wrapped up in one convenient volume. It's jam-packed with tips, advice, shortcuts, and how-to's to help you squeeze the last drop of fun and profit from your computer. It's a reference book. It isn't meant to be read from start to finish. Dip into it when you need to solve a problem, investigate a new use for your computer, or find a better way to do a task. Here's a bare outline of the six parts of this book:

✦ **Book I: The Basics:** Looks into how to choose an Internet service provider, connect your computer to the Internet, handle e-mail, visit newsgroups, chat, and surf the Internet.

✦ **Book II: Google:** Explains how to research by using Google, arguably the best search engine on the Internet. You discover things that you can do with Google that you likely didn't know about, including how to customize Google and use Google as a means of finding shopping bargains.

✦ **Book III: Yahoo!:** Explores how to take advantage of the numerous services that Yahoo! offers, including searching the Internet, using Yahoo! mail, shopping, chatting, playing games, doing financial research, and customizing Yahoo!.

✦ **Book IV: eBay:** Describes how to buy and sell on eBay, the online auction house. You can find many tips in this book for acquiring bargains and selling your own items.

✦ **Book V: iTunes:** Examines iTunes, Apple's online music store. You discover how to buy music from iTunes and use the iTunes software to play music, burn CDs, and organize your music collection.

✦ **Book VI: Creating Web Pages:** Helps you create a Web site with Front-Page 2003 and Dreamweaver. You also find advice here for coding with HTML and designing a Web site that will keep people coming back.

What Makes This Book Special

You're holding in your hands a computer book that's designed to make using the Internet as easy and comfortable as possible. Besides the fact that this book is easy to read, it's different from other books about computers. The following sections tell you why.

Information that's easy to look up

This book is a reference, and that means that I want you to be able to find instructions quickly. To that end, the people who have contributed to this book have taken great pains to make sure that the material in this book is well organized and easy to find. The descriptive headings help you find information quickly. The bulleted and numbered lists make following instructions simpler. The tables make options easier to understand.

A task-oriented approach

Most computer books describe what the software is, but this book explains how to complete tasks with the software. I assume that you came to this book because you want to know how to *do* something — build a Web site, send e-mail, conduct research on the Internet. You came to the right place. This book describes how to get tasks done.

A Greatest-Hits Collection

The material in this book was culled from eight *For Dummies* books published by Wiley Publishing, Inc. You can think of this book as a kind of greatest-hits collection of computer books about the Internet. If you stumble upon a topic in this book that intrigues you and you want to know more about it, I suggest looking into one of the eight books from which this book was created:

✦ *The Internet All-in-One Desk Reference For Dummies,* 2nd Edition

✦ *Mac OS X Panther All-in-One Desk Reference For Dummies,* 2nd Edition

✦ *Google For Dummies*

✦ *Yahoo! For Dummies*

✦ *eBay For Dummies,* 4th Edition

✦ *iPod & iTunes For Dummies*

✦ *Creating Web Pages All-in-One Desk Reference For Dummies,* 2nd Edition

✦ *Office 2003 All-in-One Desk Reference For Dummies*

Foolish Assumptions

Please forgive me, but I made one or two foolish assumptions about you, the reader of this book. I assumed that

✦ You have a Windows-based or Macintosh computer.

✦ Your computer is outfitted with a modem, DSL connection, T1 line, or other means of connecting to the Internet.

✦ You're kind to foreign tourists and small animals.

Conventions Used in This Book

I want you to understand all the instructions in this book, and in that spirit, I've adopted a few conventions.

To show you how to step through command sequences, I use the ⇨ symbol. For example, you can choose File⇨Save to save a file. Using the ⇨ is just a shorthand method of saying, "From the File menu, choose Save."

Where you see boldface letters or numbers in this book, it means to type the letters or numbers. For example, "Enter **25** in the Margin text box" means to do exactly that: Enter the number 25.

Icons Used in This Book

To help you get the most out of this book, I've placed icons here and there. Here's what the icons mean:

Next to the Tip icon, you can find shortcuts and tricks of the trade to make your visit to the Internet world more enjoyable.

Where you see the Warning icon, tread softly and carefully. It means that you're about to do something that you might regret later.

When I explain a juicy little fact that bears remembering, I mark it with a Remember icon. When you see this icon, prick up your ears. You can discover something that you need to remember throughout your computer adventures.

When I'm forced to describe high-tech stuff, a Technical Stuff icon appears in the margin. You don't have to read what's beside the Technical Stuff icons if you don't want to, although these technical descriptions often help you understand how a software or hardware feature works.

For Further Fun Factoids . . .

Check It Out sections appear at the end of some chapters and suggest a cool task or an entertaining project that you might be interested in, so Check It Out!

Book I

The Basics

The 5th Wave   By Rich Tennant

Rothman
Paint Drying Equip.
TV Test Pattern Design
Sap Buckets

"Maybe it would help our Web site if we showed our products in action."

Book 1: The Basics

Chapter 1: Hooking Up with the Right Service

In This Chapter

✔ **Choosing an Internet service provider**

✔ **Deciding between a broadband or dial-up connection**

✔ **Choosing an ISP for hosting a Web site**

*T*his short chapter is for people who want to jump aboard the Internet but haven't chosen an ISP yet. ISP stands for *Internet service provider,* which you need to surf the Internet and send and receive e-mail. This chapter also gets you up to speed on speedy broadband connections and slower dial-up connections. It also explains how to go about finding a company to host your Web site — in case you want to create a Web site of your own.

Selecting an Internet Service Provider

If you intend to surf the Internet, send and receive e-mail, or create a Web site for the Internet, your first task is to choose an ISP. An *ISP* is a company that provides customers access to the Internet, e-mail services, and in some cases, the opportunity to post Web sites. You've probably heard of popular ISPs such as America Online (AOL), MSN, and EarthLink. There are some 5,000 ISPs in the United States. How do you choose which one is right for you?

Here are some considerations to make as you choose an ISP:

✦ **What is the monthly service charge?** Monthly service charges range from $10–$30 (for people who use dial-up modems) to $30 or more per month for a fast digital subscriber line (DSL), cable modem, or T1 connection. (These connections are explained in the upcoming section, "Broadband or Dial-Up?")

✦ **What is the set-up fee?** Most ISPs charge a one-time set-up or enrollment fee. Depending on how many ISPs are located in your area and how stiff the competition among ISPs is, fees vary from no charge to $40.

✦ **Can I dial in without having to call a long-distance number?** If you connect to the Internet by modem, the modem in your computer calls the ISP's computers. If that telephone call is a long-distance call, going on the Internet becomes an expensive proposition because you have to pay long-distance rates for each connection time. National ISPs, such as those run by the major telephone companies, offer regional phone numbers that you can call no matter where you travel. If you travel a lot and have to connect a laptop computer to the Internet from various cities and regions, consider signing on with an ISP that offers what are called *points of presence* (or simply POPs), which are the regional telephone numbers that you can dial to connect to an ISP.

✦ **How many hours of monthly online time are included in the monthly fee?** Nowadays, most ISPs charge a flat monthly rate to go online for as many hours as you want. Still, find out whether the ISP that you're considering charges a flat rate or a by-the-hour rate. That way, you know what to expect from your first bill.

✦ **How much storage space am I allowed for the Web pages I want to post on the Internet?** Some ISPs offer their subscribers the opportunity to post Web sites at no extra charge; others charge an additional fee to subscribers who want to post their Web sites on the Internet. Most ISPs allow from 1–2MB to as much as 50MB of file storage space.

✦ **Do you have spam-blocking and virus protection?** Some ISPs have built-in software that screens out *spam,* which is the Internet equivalent of junk mail. Some ISPs screen all files for viruses as well. On the face of it, spam-blocking seems like a good deal, but some spam-blocking software isn't sophisticated and merely blocks certain kinds of files, such as .exe (executable) files or files that are larger than a certain number of megabytes. You might legitimately receive these kinds of files from co-workers, in which case spam-blocking is not for you.

✦ **Do you have a length-of-service contract?** Anybody who has a cellphone knows that length-of-service contracts can be a real burden. Under these contracts, you have to sign on for a year. If the service doesn't suit you, you can't quit the service during the first year without paying a fee. If an ISP that you're considering requires you to sign a length-of-service contract, make sure you investigate the ISP — especially its billing policies — before you put your name on the dotted line.

✦ **Do you offer technical help?** Typically, ISPs that charge a low monthly rate don't offer very much technical assistance to customers. Even if you go with an expensive ISP, find out how long the company takes to reply to e-mail queries for technical assistance. Find out as well whether the ISP maintains a 24-hour telephone line that you can call if you need technical assistance. (By the way, queries as to what to do about smoke coming from a modem should be directed to the local fire department, which is obliged to respond faster than an ISP.)

Broadband or Dial-Up?

A *broadband connection* is an Internet connection that is always on and is capable of transmitting data very quickly. Broadband services can be delivered over the telephone lines, by way of a private network, by way of a cable modem, or in a wireless network. A *dial-up connection* is one that literally dials a telephone number whenever you connect with the Internet. This type of connection operates over the telephone lines. The only advantage of a dial-up connection over a broadband connection is the cost. At $10–$30 per month, dial-up service costs half as much as broadband service, which is much, much faster. In fact, if you've surfed the Internet using a broadband service, it's hard to go back to the slower dial-up method. What's more, you can simultaneously talk on the telephone while you surf the Internet if you have broadband service. With a dial-up connection, the phone line is occupied, so you can't make a phone call while you're online — nor can anyone call you.

A *modem* (the term stands for *mo*dulator/*dem*odulator) is a hardware device for connecting a computer to the Internet. Data transmission rates for Internet connections are measured in megabits per second (Mbps) or kilobits per second (Kbps). Table 1-1 describes the different Internet connections (these are top speeds, not necessarily the speed at which the connection really runs). The first two entries in the table are dial-up connections; the others are broadband.

Table 1-1		Internet Connection Choices
Modem	*Speed*	*Description*
Internal	28.8–56 Kbps	The modem is plugged into the motherboard of the computer. To connect to the Internet, you plug the phone line into a port on the back or side of your computer.
External	28.8–56 Kbps	The modem is attached to your computer through a parallel, serial, or USB (Universal Serial Bus) port. You plug the modem into your computer and the telephone line into your modem.
ISDN	128 Kbps	This requires installing ISDN (Integrated Services Digital Network) adapters in your computer. The connection is made through high-speed digital cables installed by the phone company or a service provider.
Cable	1.5 Mbps	This type of modem can be an external or internal modem. Through a cable wall outlet, the computer is connected to the cable TV line.
DSL	6.1 Mbps	This type of modem can also be internal or external. It requires a network adapter.

To find out whether a modem is installed on your computer, click the Start button and choose Control Panel. In the Control Panel window, choose Phone and Modem Options. You see the Phone and Modem Options dialog box. On the Modems tab, you see a list of modems installed on your computer. If you connect to the Internet by way of a DSL or ISDN line, no modem will be listed.

Choosing an ISP to Host Your Web Site

If you decide to take the plunge and create a Web site, you need to choose an ISP to host your site. *Hosting* means to put Web sites on a Web server so that people traveling the Internet can find the Web sites. In order for others to find your Web site, it must be hosted on a Web server.

These days, many ISPs host Web sites for their members. Most of them do it at no extra charge or for a small monthly fee. Call your ISP and pop the question, "Can I post my Web site on your Web server?" If your ISP doesn't host

Web sites for its members, or if your Web site is too large or too sophisticated for your ISP's Web server to handle, your next task is to find an ISP that offers Web-hosting services. Some outfits offer Web-hosting for free. What's the catch? Usually, you have to carry an advertisement of some kind on your Web site. Sometimes you meet with narrow restrictions as to how large (in megabytes) your Web site can be. What's more, the Web servers at free sites often work slowly, which causes pages to take longer to download. Book VI, Chapter 2 explores in detail how to find a hosting service.

Paying the extra money each month to host your Web site with the ISP you now use is the way to go if you can afford it. That way, you spare yourself the hassle of signing up with a new ISP. However, if you've never created a Web site and you want to experiment before you decide whether the Web site thing is for you, sign up with a free service. If you get cold feet, you can abandon your Web site without spending any money.

Table 1-2 describes places you can go on the Internet to find ISPs that offer Web-hosting services. Table 1-3 describes where you can go to investigate ISPs that offer Web-hosting services for *free*. You can find hundreds (if not thousands) of Web-hosting sites by going to the Web pages listed in Tables 1-2 and 1-3.

Table 1-2	Web Sites Where You Can Investigate Hosting Services
Web Site	*Address*
GiantWebHost.com	www.giantwebhost.com
HostIndex.com	www.hostindex.com
SMESource.com	www.smesource.com/hosting
The List	www.thelist.com

Table 1-3	Web Sites Where You Can Investigate ISPs that Offer Free Hosting
Web Site	*Address*
FreeHomePage.com	www.freehomepage.com
FreeWebspace.net	www.freewebspace.net

Chapter 2: Managing Your Online Security

In This Chapter

✔ Keeping viruses from infecting your PC

✔ Making sure your kids use the Internet wisely

Many people forget that when you hook up to the Internet, the Internet also hooks up with you. Your computer is suddenly susceptible to virus infections. Graphic images and strange ideas that might not be welcome in your home suddenly appear there. To make sure that you use the Internet safely and wisely, this chapter explains how to prevent your computer from being infected with a virus and how to make sure children get all the advantages of the Internet — but avoid the Internet's disadvantages.

Preventing Viruses from Infecting Your Computer

A computer *virus* is a malignant computer program that infects computers without their owners knowing it. Some viruses simply display a text message; others are more virulent and destroy important computer files. In order to be executed, a virus must ride piggyback on another program or document. These days, the majority of viruses are spread in files that are sent by e-mail, although a number of viruses are still spread on floppy disks that are passed from person to person.

If you trade files on a regular basis with others, you owe it to yourself to get antivirus software. The best are VirusScan (by McAfee) and Norton AntiVirus (from Symantec). Either program does a great job of protecting computers from a virus attack. Figure 2-1 shows Norton AntiVirus at work.

The two most important points to look for in any antivirus program are

✦ **Real-time scanning:** Whatever you run or load, the antivirus program should check it before your PC is exposed. With real-time scanning, you only have to check all the files on your PC once every three months or so instead of once every week.

✦ **Automatic and frequent updates:** Seeing as new viruses are invented every day, no antivirus protection is worth a nickel if it can't be updated. McAfee and Symantec provide at least two updates a month. You can update these programs over the Internet.

 If you think your computer has been struck by a virus, visit the Microsoft Virus Assistance Center at office.microsoft.com/assistance/9798/ antivirus.aspx to find information about viruses and virus prevention. Another good Web site for learning about viruses is VMyths at www.vmyths. com, where you can read about virus hoaxes and virus hoaxsters. The next time someone sends you a panicky e-mail explaining that you were sent a virus, visit this site to see whether the virus is really worth panicking over. So far in my experience (he said, knocking on wood), every virus I am supposed to have received turned out to be a hoax.

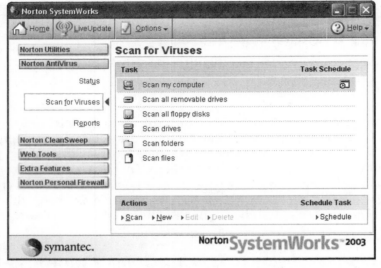

Figure 2-1:
I don't fear viruses with Norton AntiVirus on the job.

Maintaining a Kid-Friendly PC

A kid-friendly PC is one that a child or young adult can use to surf the Internet without running into objectionable material. It's no secret that this kind of material is easy to find on the Internet. Pornography, Web sites that espouse violence, and gruesome pictures and images are easy to come by. These pages explain some of the things parents can do to keep their children from finding this stuff.

Supervising kids' access

The best way to keep children from finding objectionable material is to supervise them when they are traveling on the Internet. Put your computer in a common room in the house — in the living room or family room, for example — where you can keep an eye on who is using it. I strongly recommend against letting children keep computers in their bedrooms. Besides giving them the opportunity to get into all kinds of mischief on the Internet, it discourages kids from playing with their friends and developing all the social skills that they need for a life that is rewarding and fun.

Using filtering software

Filtering software, also known as *blocking software,* is software that keeps inappropriate material from appearing in a browser window. Here are popular brands of filtering software, along with Web sites where you can learn about the software and even download it:

- ✦ **CyberPatrol:** www.cyberpatrol.com
- ✦ **CYBERsitter:** www.cybersitter.com
- ✦ **Net Nanny:** www.netnanny.com
- ✦ **SafeSurf:** www.safesurf.com

Some online services have built-in filtering. With America Online (AOL), for example, you can click in the keyword box, type **parental control**, and press Enter to find out about filtering.

Screening Web content with the Content Advisor

Internet Explorer (IE), the browser made by Microsoft, has a feature that prevents (in theory anyway) objectionable material from arriving by way of the Internet: the Content Advisor. It works like this. Web site developers rate their Web sites using the five-point scale shown in Table 2-1. Meanwhile, also using the five-point scale, you tell Internet Explorer which Web sites you find objectionable, and then those Web sites are not displayed on your computer. The problem with this system is that it relies on Web site developers to install Content Advisor software, rate their Web sites, and rate their Web sites correctly. Not all developers have signed onto the Content Advisor. And the ones who have signed on haven't necessarily described their sites accurately on the five-point scale. Still, the Content Advisor is worth a try. Setting it up and using it is quite easy, as I explain here.

Table 2-1		Rating Levels		
Level	*Language*	*Nudity*	*Sex*	*Violence*
0	Inoffensive slang	None	None	None
1	Mild expletives	Revealing attire	Passionate kissing	Fighting
2	Moderate expletives	Partial nudity	Clothed sexual touching	Killing
3	Obscene gestures	Frontal nudity	Nonexplicit sexual touching	Killing with blood and gore
4	Explicit or crude language	Provocative frontal nudity	Explicit sexual activity	Wanton and gratuitous violence

Setting a password and enabling the Content Advisor

To set up the Content Advisor, you have to supply a password, thereby making you its supervisor. If you're very concerned about screening Web content, be sure to provide a password that's hard to guess or crack. To keep your password secure, you should provide one that contains a completely random combination of letters, numbers, and special characters (such as $ and @ signs).

Never lose your password. You need your password to change any of the settings, including setting a new password. Memorize your password or write it down and store it somewhere secure, such as a fire-resistant safe or a safe-deposit box at a bank.

After you decide on your password, follow these steps to get the Content Advisor up and running:

1. **In Internet Explorer, choose Tools⇨Internet Options and click the Content tab.**

You see the dialog box shown in Figure 2-2.

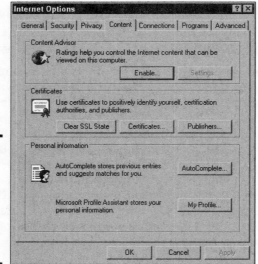

Figure 2-2: Click the Enable button to begin setting up the Content Advisor.

2. **Click the Enable button.**

The first time you attempt to set a password, the Content Advisor dialog box opens and asks you to create a supervisor password. If you've set a password previously and want to change it, skip to the next section, "Changing the Supervisor password."

3. **Click the General tab.**

4. **In the User Options section, select one or both of the following options:**

- **Supervisor Can Type a Password to Allow Users to View Restricted Content:** Select this option if you want anyone with the administrative password to be able to override default settings.

- **Users Can See Sites That Have No Rating:** If you select this option, the Create Supervisor Password dialog box appears. Enter your password in the Password text box and click OK. This enables the Settings button.

Again, be sure to remember your password. Internet Explorer requires it any time you want to change Content Advisor settings.

5. **Click OK to close the Content Advisor dialog box.**

You can now begin using the Content Advisor with its default settings. If you want to change the Ratings and General options in the Content Advisor dialog box, refer to "Modifying the level of the ratings," later in this chapter.

Changing the Supervisor password

If you want to change your Supervisor password, follow these steps:

1. **In Internet Explorer, choose Tools⇨Internet Options and click the Content tab.**

2. **Click the Settings button.**

The Supervisor Password Required dialog box appears.

3. **Type your existing password in the Supervisor Password Required dialog box and click OK.**

The Content Advisor dialog box appears.

4. **Click the General tab, and then click the Change Password button to open the Change Supervisor Password dialog box.**

5. **Type your existing password in the Old Password text box, type your new password in the New Password text box, and type your new password again in the Confirm New Password text box.**

6. **Click OK, enter a hint if necessary, and click OK in the dialog box that acknowledges that you have changed your password.**

Modifying the level of the ratings

When you first enable the Internet Explorer Content Advisor, the ratings are set to the maximum levels of content screening in all four of the following categories: Violence, Nudity, Sex, and Language. Internet Explorer uses the RSAC (Recreational Software Advisory Council) rating system, which has five levels. Level 0 is the most stringent, and Level 4 is the most permissive (refer to Table 2-1).

When you first enable the Content Advisor, all levels are set to the most restrictive (Level 0), by default. To change the level of any of these ratings, follow these steps:

1. **Choose Tools⇨Internet Options; then click the Content tab.**

2. **Click the Settings button, type your password in the Password text box of the Supervisor Password Required dialog box, and then click OK.**

The Content Advisor dialog box appears, with the Ratings tab displayed. A list box contains the four categories: Language, Nudity, Sex, and Violence.

3. **In the list box of the Content Advisor dialog box, click the category for which you want to set the rating levels.**

4. **Drag the slider control to reset the level for that category.**

5. **Repeat Steps 3 and 4 for each category that you want to reset, and then click the Apply button.**

6. **Click OK when you have made all the necessary changes.**

The Content Advisor dialog box closes, and the new ratings settings are put into effect.

Disabling the Content Advisor

You might want to disable the Content Advisor at some point. (Hey, some-day the kids are going to grow up and move away.) Just keep in mind that as soon as you enable the Content Advisor, its Enable button magically toggles into a Disable button. To permanently turn off the cyber-thought police, click the Content tab of the Internet Options dialog box and then click the Disable button. Now you're just a password away from disabling the Content Advisor. You can always use the Enable button at a later time if you find the need to use the Content Advisor again. After you have placed a password on the Advisor, you cannot remove it.

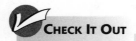

CHECK IT OUT

Finding Out Which Web Sites Have Been Visited

In case you want to find out where your children have been surfing on the Internet, here are ways to see lists of recently visited Web sites:

- In Internet Explorer, click the History button or press Ctrl+H.

- In Netscape Navigator, choose Communicator⇨History or press Ctrl+H.

Chapter 3: America Online

In This Chapter

- ✔ Installing and signing on to AOL
- ✔ Reading e-mail and receiving files
- ✔ Organizing and storing e-mail messages
- ✔ Sending e-mail and files
- ✔ Tracking addresses in the Address Book
- ✔ Surfing the Internet with AOL

A merica Online (AOL) is an online service for surfing the Internet, sending and receiving e-mail, storing addresses, and doing a few other things besides. The cost of the service is $23.90 per month. (AOL usually offers free service for the first month or two.) Chances are that if you bought your computer at a big-time electronics store, it came with the AOL icon on the desktop. Having that icon doesn't mean that you have to subscribe to AOL, but lots of people do. AOL has many fans and many detractors. In general, people who fall on the novice side of computing favor AOL over the heartier, more sophisticated programs for handling the Internet because AOL is easy to use. Starting from one place, you can surf the Internet and trade e-mail messages. AOL's *keywords* (you'll find out more about them shortly) make it possible to visit Web sites without having to enter cumbersome Web site addresses. This chapter explains how to handle e-mail and surf the Internet with America Online.

Installing AOL

If AOL isn't installed on your computer, you can either install it from a CD or download the program from www.aol.com. As part of the installation, you'll be asked for a screen name and a password. You will need this name and password each time you log on to AOL.

If you have trouble with the installation or trouble connecting to the Internet with AOL, call 800-827-6364. If you get frustrated and want to cancel the service, call 888-265-8008. You can learn about AOL's cancellation policy by entering the keyword *Cancel* in the Keyword dialog box.

Signing On to AOL

You must sign on to AOL each time you run the program. To sign on, either double-click the America Online icon on your desktop or click the Start button and choose Programs⇨American Online⇨America Online. You see the Sign On window as shown in Figure 3-1. Choose your screen name if you have more than one, enter your password, and click the Sign On button.

Changing and deleting passwords and screen names

AOL makes it easy to change and delete screen names and passwords. (Who doesn't need another Internet personality now and then?) AOL permits you to have as many as seven different screen names. Follow these steps to manage passwords and screen names:

1. **Press Ctrl+K or click the Keyword button on the Quick Start toolbar.**

   The Keyword dialog box appears.

2. **Enter this keyword:** screen names.

3. **Click the Go button.**

   A dialog box for changing and deleting passwords and screen names appears.

4. **Click the appropriate link and answer the questions in the dialog boxes as they appear.**

   Don't worry — this is real simple stuff.

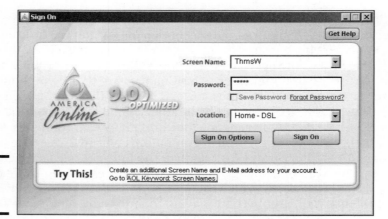

Figure 3-1: Signing on to AOL.

A Short Geography Lesson

When you start AOL, you see a window like the one in Figure 3-2. I wager that the menu bar and row of buttons along the top of the screen are not foreign to you — they are found in lots of computer programs. From left to right, here are the things that might make the AOL screen seem unusual:

✦ **Quick Start window:** This window is designed to help you do things quickly. It includes buttons found elsewhere in the AOL window. Click its Close button if you don't care to see it. To display it after you have closed it, click the Quick Start button.

✦ **Next and Previous buttons:** Click these buttons to retreat to or go forward to windows that you have visited recently either in AOL or on the Internet.

✦ **URL Address box:** Enter a Web address here and click the Go button to visit a Web site. You can click the down arrow and select a site from the drop-down list to revisit a site you visited recently.

✦ **Search button:** Click the Search button to open a new window and search the Internet.

✦ **Favorites:** Click the Favorites button (or its drop-down arrow) to visit a site you bookmarked because you wanted to visit it again.

Next and Previous buttons

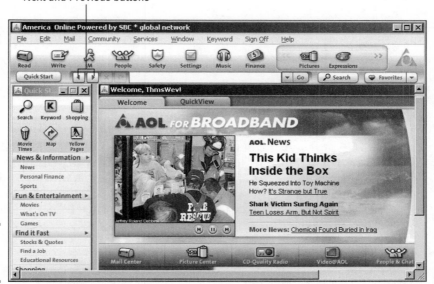

Figure 3-2:
The AOL
screen.

 When you signed up with AOL, you chose a Toolset and Line Up for the Welcome screen that appears when you start AOL. If you would like to rethink those choices, click the Change This Screen link in the lower-left corner of the Welcome screen. You will be presented with a series of dialog boxes for constructing a Welcome screen.

Handling Incoming E-Mail

Mark Twain was wrong when he said that nothing is certain except death and taxes. What is just as certain as those inevitabilities is this: Anyone who has an e-mail account will receive ever-increasing amounts of e-mail. Besides reading this mail, the person will have to devise strategies for sorting and organizing it. These topics are covered in the pages that follow.

Reading incoming mail

When someone sends you an e-mail, you hear the words *You've got mail*, and a flag rises on the Read button in the upper-left corner of the screen. The number beside this button tells you how many messages are waiting to be read. By moving the pointer over the Read button, you can see a drop-down list with senders' names and message topics. To open your Mailbox and read the mail, click the Read button. You see a Mailbox window similar to the one in Figure 3-3.

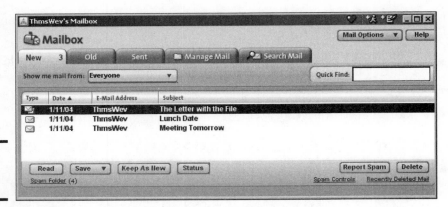

Figure 3-3:
Collecting
the mail.

Here are instructions for reading your mail:

✦ **Reading a message:** Double-click a message or select it and click the Read button to open it. The message appears in the Message window, as shown in Figure 3-4. After you open a message, it is moved to the Old tab. You can read it by opening the Old tab and double-clicking it there. (Click the Keep As New button to move a message from the Old tab back to the New tab.)

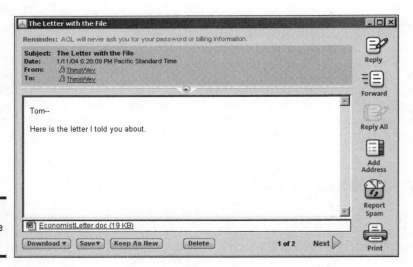

Figure 3-4:
Reading the
mail.

✦ **Deleting a message:** Click the Delete button to remove a message. Messages that you delete are sent to the Recently Deleted folder. To open the Recently Deleted folder, click the Manage Mail tab and select the folder in the My Mail Folder list. To recover a message, open the Recently Deleted folder, select the message, and click the Restore button.

To find a stray message in the Mailbox window, enter a word you remember from the message's title or text in the Quick Find box and then press Enter.

Receiving a file

You can tell when someone has sent you a file because a little page appears behind the standard message icon on the left side of the Mailbox window. The name of the file appears at the bottom of the message window (refer to Figure 3-4).

✦ To download the file now, double-click its name, click Yes when AOL asks whether you really want to download it, and select a folder for storing the file in the Download Manager dialog box.

✦ To retrieve the file later, click the Download button and choose Download Later. When you want to see the file, choose File➪Download Manager. You see the Download Manager window. Select the file you want to open and click the Finish Download button. You can find the file in your `C:\My Documents` folder.

Managing your e-mail

If you receive e-mail from many different parties, I strongly suggest creating e-mail folders for storing your mail. That way, when you want to find a message from someone, you will know where to find it. Here are instructions for creating folders for e-mail and moving e-mail to different folders.

Creating a folder for storing e-mail

To create new folders for e-mail, start by selecting the Manage Mail tab in the Mailbox window. On the left side of this tab is the My Mail Folders list, which lists the folders where your e-mail is stored. Follow these steps to create a new folder:

1. **Click the Saved on My PC folder.**

All new folders become subfolders of this folder.

2. **Click the Setup Folders button and choose Create Folder.**

You see the Create New Folder dialog box.

3. **Enter a folder name and click the Save button.**

Be sure to choose a descriptive name. The name of your new folder appears under Saved on My PC in the folders list.

Moving e-mail messages to different folders

Follow these steps to move an e-mail message to a different folder:

1. **Select the e-mail message.**

2. **Click the Save button and move the pointer over On My PC on the drop-down list.**

You see a list of folders.

3. **Select the folder you want to move the e-mail to.**

21

Composing and Sending E-Mail

In order to get invited to parties, you have to issue a few invitations. And in order to get e-mail, you have to send out e-mail. In this section, you find instructions for composing e-mail messages, replying to or forwarding messages, and sending files.

Writing an e-mail

Follow these steps to compose and send an e-mail message:

1. **Click the Write button or press Ctrl+M.**

You see the Write Mail window, as shown in Figure 3-5.

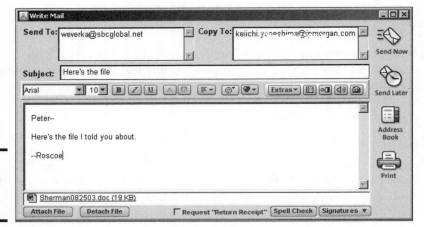

Figure 3-5: Composing an e-mail message.

2. **In the Send To box, enter the address of the person who is to receive the message.**

If the address is on file in your Address Book, all you have to do is type the first two or three letters to see a list of e-mail addresses that begin with those two or three letters. Choose a name from the list to enter the whole address.

To send the same e-mail to more than one person, press Enter to go to the next line of the Send To box, and enter another address there.

Enter an address in the Copy To box if you want to send a copy of the message to someone.

3. **In the Subject line, enter a descriptive subject for the message.**

4. **Enter the body of the message in the text box below the Subject line.**

You can format the message by clicking the Bold or Underline button, for example. However, only people with e-mail software capable of reading formats will see the formatting in your e-mail message.

5. **Click the Send Now button to send the message.**

To postpone sending it, click the Send Later button. You see the Send Later dialog box. Click the Auto AOL button to schedule a time to send the message. To send the message later on your own, click the Read button to open the Mailbox window. Then click the Manage Mail tab and select the Mail Waiting to Be Sent folder in the My Mail Folders list. Finally, select the message and click the Send button.

Replying to and forwarding messages

Replying to and forwarding messages is a cinch. All you have to do is click the Reply, Forward, or Reply All button in the Message window (refer to Figure 3-4). Immediately, a Write Mail window opens with the sender's e-mail address and subject line already entered. Write a reply or scribble a few words at the top of the forwarded message and click either the Send Now or the Send Later button.

Sending a file

Follow these steps to send a file to someone else:

1. **Address and compose the message as you normally would.**

2. **Click the Attach File button in the Write Mail window.**

You will find this button in the lower-left corner of the window. You see the Attached File(s) dialog box.

3. **Select the file or files you want to send and then click the Open button.**

To select more than one file, Ctrl+click the files.

The name of the file or files that you want to send appears on the bottom of the Write Mail window. If you change your mind about sending a file, select it and click the Detach File button.

4. **Click either the Send Now or the Send Later button.**

Maintaining an Address Book

You can keep street addresses and phone numbers as well as e-mail addresses in the AOL Address Book. Keeping e-mail addresses is worthwhile because you don't have to type an e-mail address to address an e-mail message if the address is listed in the Address Book. AOL fills in addresses from the book automatically.

Choose Mail⇨Address Book to open the Address Book. Here are instructions for doing this, that, and the other thing with addresses:

✦ **Entering a new address:** Click the Add button. You see the Address Card for New Contact dialog box, as shown in Figure 3-6. Fill in the pertinent information on the different tabs and click the Save button.

✦ **Changing address information:** Select a name and click the Edit button. You see the Address Card for New Contact dialog box. Change the information there and click the Save button.

✦ **Deleting an entry:** Select a name and click the Delete button.

Sending e-mails to groups

Create a group in the Address Book if you often need to send the same e-mail to several different people at once. For example, if you're the captain of the softball team, you can compose and address messages about upcoming games to all team members. This spares you the trouble of trying to remember to include everyone on each and every e-mail.

Here are instructions for handling group addresses:

✔ **Starting a group:** Click the Add Group button in the Address Book window. You see the Manage Group dialog box. Enter a name for your group. In the Contact List, Ctrl+click to select the names of people you need for the group. Click the Add button and then click Save.

✔ **Changing the group members:** In the Address Book, group names are shown in boldface text. To change a group, select its name and click the Edit button. You see the Manage Group dialog box. Select names and click the Add or Remove button as needed to change the group's members.

✔ **Sending an e-mail to the group's members:** Select the group in the Address Book, click the Send To button, and choose a sending option on the drop-down list. The Write Mail window appears with the addresses of the group members already entered.

✔ **Deleting a group:** Select the group's name and click the Delete button.

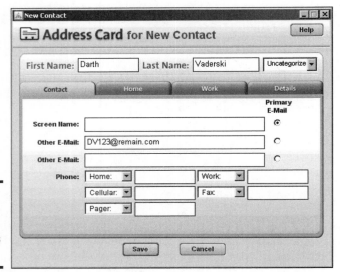

Figure 3-6: Entering an address in the Address Book.

Exploring the Internet in AOL

As well as conventional ways to search the Internet, AOL offers keywords. Instead of typing an unwieldy Web site address, you can enter a keyword. As long as that keyword corresponds to one of AOL's channels, you go to an AOL *channel*, which is a Web site with many links to the subject in question. For example, entering the keyword *autos* takes you to an AOL-maintained Web site with links to many sites that concern cars.

Exploring the Internet by keyword isn't the big advantage it used to be. The Internet is much easier to search and navigate than it was when AOL invented its keyword scheme. AOL subscribers can use Internet Explorer or Netscape

Navigator to search the Internet. I recommend doing just that. Those browsers are much easier to use than AOL's, in my opinion.

You, of course, are entitled to your opinion, and to that end, here are instructions for exploring the Internet with AOL:

✦ **Entering a keyword:** Click the Keyword button on the Quick Start bar and either enter the keyword in the Keyword dialog box or type the keyword directly into the Web site address box. If the keyword is associated with an AOL channel, you go to the AOL Web site. Choose Keyword⇨Explore Keywords to see all the AOL keywords.

✦ **Surfing the Internet:** Enter an address in the Web site address box and click the Go button.

✦ **Searching:** Click the Search button to go to an AOL-maintained site for searching the Internet. (This site is by no means the best place to start an Internet search. Try starting at www.google.com instead. Google is the subject of Book II.)

✦ **Bookmarking your favorite Web sites:** When you come across a Web site you want to revisit, bookmark it. Click the Favorites button; in the Favorite Places dialog box, choose Add to Favorites⇨Favorite Places. The next time you want to visit the Web site, click the Favorites button and choose the Web site's name in the Favorites window.

Don't forget to click the Previous or Next button to go backward or forward, respectively, through Web sites you have visited.

Chapter 4: Browsers and What They Do

In This Chapter

✔ Understanding basic Web concepts

✔ Finding your way around the Web

✔ Using Internet Explorer to navigate the Web

✔ Keeping track of your favorite Web sites

The *World Wide Web* (or *WWW,* or just *the Web*) is a system that uses the Internet to link vast quantities of information all over the world. At times, the Web resembles a library, newspaper, bulletin board, and telephone directory — all on a global scale. "The vision I have for the Web," says its inventor, Tim Berners-Lee, "is about anything being potentially connected to anything." Still very much a work in progress, the Web is destined to become the primary repository of human culture.

This chapter explains all you need to know about the basics of the Web and searching the Web. You find out how to launch Internet Explorer (IE), get to know the elements of the screen, and use a browser to begin your travels on the Web. Now boarding Internet Explorer. The next stop in cyberspace is totally up to you!

ABCs of the Web

To start using the World Wide Web, all you need is an Internet connection and a Web browser, such as Internet Explorer or Netscape Navigator. A *Web browser* displays, as individual pages on your computer screen, the various types of information found on the Web and lets you follow the connections — *hypertext links* — built into Web pages.

Here are some basic Web concepts:

✦ **Hypertext:** A type of electronic document that contains pointers or links to other documents. These links (often called *hyperlinks*) appear in a distinct color or are highlighted when your browser displays the document. When you click a hypertext link, your Web browser displays the document to which the link points, if the document is available.

✦ **Uniform Resource Locator (URL):** The standard format used for hypertext links on the Internet, such as `http://www.microsoft.com`.

✦ **Web site:** A collection of Web pages devoted to a single subject or organization.

+ **Webmaster:** The person in charge of a Web site.

+ **Surfing:** The art and vice of bouncing from Web page to Web page in search of whatever.

Ninety-five percent of Web surfers use Internet Explorer, which is the Web browser that comes with Windows XP.

Web browsers can handle most, but not all, types of information found on the 'Net. You can add software called plug-ins and ActiveX controls to extend your browser's capabilities.

Uniform Resource Locators

One of the key advances that Web technology brought to the Internet is the Uniform Resource Locator, or URL. URLs provide a single, standardized way of describing almost any type of information available in cyberspace. The URL tells you what kind of information it is (such as a Web page or a File Transfer Protocol [FTP] file), what computer it's stored on, and how to find that computer.

URLs (see the following example) are typically long text strings that consist of three parts:

`http://www.microsoft.com/windows/ie/newuser/default.asp`

+ The document access type, followed by a colon and two slashes (://)

+ The host name of the computer on which the information is stored

+ The path to the file that contains the information

Table 4-1 describes the parts of the preceding URL.

Table 4-1	Parts of a URL
Example	*What It Indicates*
`http://`	Indicates a hypertext document (a Web page).
`www.microsoft.com`	Indicates the host computer on which the Web page is stored. (www indicates that the site is located on the World Wide Web.)
`/windows/ie/newuser/default.asp`	Indicates the path and filename of the file.

Common document access types include the following:

+ `http`: For hypertext (the Web)

+ `https`: For hypertext with a secure link

+ `ftp`: For File Transfer Protocol files

+ `mailto`: For e-mail addresses

The following list includes other mysterious things that you see in URLs:

✦ `.html` or `.htm`: The filename extension for a hypertext document. HTML stands for HyperText Markup Language, which is the set of codes used to build Web pages.

✦ `index.html` or `default.html`: The master page or home page of a Web site. (The actual filename depends on the server.) For more on home pages, read Book I, Chapter 5.

✦ `.txt`: A plain-text document without links or formatting.

✦ `.gif`, `.jpg`, `.jpeg`, `.mpg`, `.png`, and `.avi`: Pictures, graphics, or video.

✦ `.mp3`, `.mid` (MIDI), `.wav`, `.snd`, and `.au`: Music files. You can even get a Walkman-size unit that accepts and plays these files.

✦ `.zip`, `.sit`, `.hqx`, `.gz`, `.tar`, and `.z`: Filename extensions for files that have been compressed to save downloading time.

✦ `.class`: A Java applet.

✦ `~george`: As suggested by the tilde (~) character, probably a Unix account belonging to someone with the account name of `george`.

✦ `www`: Short for World Wide Web.

Finding Your Way around the Web

The Web displays pages of information with hypertext links that take you to other pages. Browsers usually highlight the links to make them easy to spot by using a different color for the item and underlining it. By default, the color of a text hyperlink that you've not yet followed is blue. If you return to a page after clicking hyperlinked text, the hyperlinked text color changes from blue to purple. (As the following chapter explains, you can customize the colors that a Web browser uses to indicate links to pages that you've already visited and links to pages that you have yet to view.)

Some links are just areas you click inside an image or photograph. You can always tell when one of these types of graphics contains a hyperlink and when it doesn't by passing the mouse pointer over the picture. Only graphics with hyperlinks cause your mouse pointer to assume the shape of a pointing hand. Figure 4-1 points out some hyperlinks.

You can bring up a page on your browser in ways other than following a link:

✦ Select a page from your browser's list of bookmarks or favorites.

✦ Type a URL in the address field on your browser's screen and press Enter.

✦ If you have the page stored as a file on a hard drive or CD-ROM on your computer, most browsers let you open it by choosing the File⇨Open (or similar) command.

Graphic with hyperlink   Text with hyperlink

Figure 4-1:
Web pages
use both
text hyper-
links and
graphics
hyperlinks.

Web page components that appear in your browser can take on other functions, such as the following:

✦ **File items containing text, pictures, movies, or sound:** If your Web
browser can handle the file, the browser displays or plays the file. If not,
the browser just tells you about the file. If an image or element is missing, the browser displays a broken link icon.

✦ **Search query items that let you type one or more keywords:** A Web
page displays the results of your search.

✦ **Forms you fill out:** The answers are sent as a long URL when you click
Done, Submit, or a similar button on the form.

✦ **Small computer programs called Java applets:** You download and run
them on your computer.

Getting Started with Internet Explorer

Internet Explorer owes its existence to a single type of document — the *Web
page* (also known as an *HTML document*). At first glance, a Web page looks
like any other nicely formatted document containing graphics and text.
What differentiates a Web page from a regular document? In a Web page,
text and graphics elements can be used as hyperlinks. When you click a
hyperlink, you're transported to another Web page.

Launching Internet Explorer

The Windows desktop includes several doorways to the IE browser, as shown in Figure 4-2. Although you could probably hold a contest to find out exactly how many ways Microsoft has provided for starting Internet Explorer, the following three are the most useful:

✦ Double-click the Internet Explorer shortcut on your desktop.

✦ On the Windows taskbar at the bottom of the screen, choose Start⇨ All Programs⇨Internet Explorer.

✦ Click the Launch Internet Explorer Browser button on the Quick Launch toolbar located on the taskbar. (If the Quick Launch toolbar is not displayed, right-click the taskbar and choose Toolbars ⇨Quick Launch.)

Accessing a Web site

After you start IE, you can tell it which Web site you want to go to. If you haven't saved the Web site in your Favorites list (see "Keeping Track of Your Favorite Web Sites," later in this chapter), you must type the Web site's URL or choose it from a list of Web sites you've recently viewed.

Internet Explorer shortcut

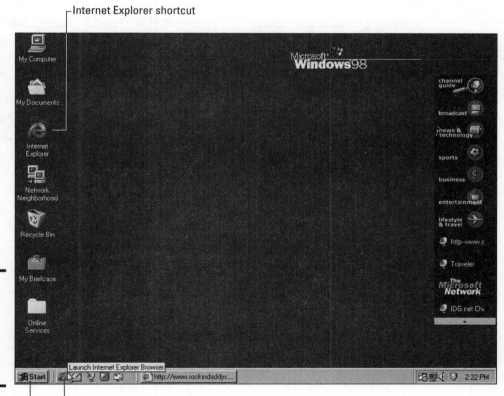

Figure 4-2:
You launch
Internet
Explorer
in several
different
ways.

Launch Internet Explorer Browser button

Start button

To access a Web site, follow these steps:

1. Choose File⇨Open.

The Open dialog box displays.

2. In the Open text box, type the URL of the site you want to visit or click the drop-down arrow and select a site from the list.

3. Click OK.

You also can access a Web site by positioning the cursor in the Address box of the IE window, typing the URL of the Web site you'd like to go to, and pressing Enter or clicking the Go button.

Elements of the Internet Explorer window

Each of the launch methods covered in the preceding section opens Internet Explorer, as shown in Figure 4-3. Table 4-2 provides a rundown of the various parts of the Internet Explorer screen.

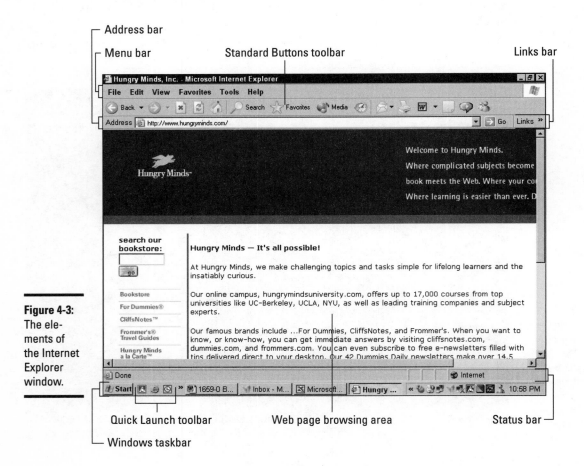

Figure 4-3: The elements of the Internet Explorer window.

Table 4-2	Internet Explorer Screen Elements
Part of the Screen	*What It Is*
Address bar	A text box that displays the URL (Web address) of the current Web page and in which you type the URL that you want to visit. If you click the down arrow on the right of the box, a drop-down list of the addresses you've previously visited appears.
Menu bar	The standard Windows 95/98/XP menu bar with the addition of the Favorites menu.
Standard Buttons toolbar	A set of tools for navigating Web pages and accessing some of the more often used features of IE.
Links bar	The choices on the Links bar of the IE toolbar contain standard links to various pages on the Microsoft Web site.
Windows taskbar	The standard Windows 95/98/XP taskbar contains the Start button and the Quick Launch toolbar, along with icons for all open programs.
Quick Launch toolbar	A set of tools automatically added to the Windows taskbar when you install IE. It provides buttons for launching the browser, minimizing all open windows, viewing channels, and launching Outlook Express.
Web page browsing area	The space where the current Web page actually appears.
Status bar	Provides information on your whereabouts as you travel the Web and also the status of IE as it performs its functions.

The Explorer bar

The Explorer bar is a frame that appears on the left side of the IE screen when you want to perform a search, work with your Favorites list, or display a history of recently viewed Web pages. Click the Search, Favorites, or History button on the Standard Buttons toolbar to display the Explorer bar and additional options for each of these functions. The contents of the current Web page appear in the area (frame) on the right.

The Explorer bar in Internet Explorer comes in four different flavors:

✦ **Search bar:** The Search bar gives you access to the various search engines that you can use to search the Web for particular topics. To open the Search bar, click the Search button, choose View⇨Explorer Bar⇨ Search, or press Ctrl+E. (See "Searching the Web," later in this chapter.)

✦ **Favorites bar:** The Favorites bar contains links to all the Web pages that you have marked as your favorites. To open the Favorites bar, click the Favorites button, choose View⇨Explorer Bar⇨Favorites, or press Ctrl+I. (See "Viewing pages from the Favorites folder," later in this chapter.)

✦ **Media bar:** The Media bar gives you easy access to buttons that let you play music of your choice, whether it be your favorite radio station or CD. You can also use the rest of the bar to read up on the latest audio and video news.

✦ **History bar:** The History bar gives you access to links of all the Web pages that you've visited in the last 20 days. To open the History bar, click the History button, choose View⇨Explorer Bar⇨History, or press Ctrl+H. (See "Viewing Pages from the History Folder," later in this chapter.)

To remove the Explorer bar from the browsing area when you no longer need access to its links, click the Close button (the X) in the upper-right corner of the Explorer bar.

The toolbars

Internet Explorer includes several varieties of toolbars to help you accomplish tasks quickly. The following list describes these toolbars. (Refer to Figure 4-3 to see where these toolbars are located.)

✦ **Menu bar:** As with all standard Windows menu bars, the IE menu bar consists of a group of pull-down menus (File, Edit, View, Favorites, Tools, and Help) that you can click to reveal a list of options and submenus.

✦ **Standard Buttons toolbar:** This toolbar contains the tools that you use most often for navigating and performing tasks, such as the following:

- **Back:** Enables you to return to any Web sites you might have previously visited during your Web session

- **Forward:** Takes you to any available pages in the History listing

- **Stop:** Lets you stop a page from loading

- **Refresh:** Reloads or updates the current Web page

- **Home:** Displays the Web page you designate as the home page

- **Search:** Displays or hides the Search Explorer bar

- **Favorites:** Displays or hides the Favorites Explorer bar

- **Media:** Displays or hides the Media Explorer bar

- **History:** Displays or hides the History Explorer bar

✦ **Address bar:** This bar shows you the URL of the Web page currently displayed in the Internet Explorer browsing area.

As you visit different pages during a Web browsing session, Internet Explorer adds the URL of each site that you visit to the drop-down list attached to the Address bar. To revisit one of the Web pages that you've seen during the session, you can click the drop-down button at the end of the Address box and click its URL or its page icon in the drop-down list.

✦ **Links bar:** This button contains a drop-down list of shortcuts to various Microsoft Web pages — RealPlayer, Customize Links, and various other pages. (If the Links bar is hidden by the Address bar, double-click the word Links to reveal the full Links bar.) You can, however, change the shortcuts listed on the Links bar to reflect the Web pages that you visit most often.

To add a Quick Link button for the Web page that you're currently viewing, drag its Web page icon (the icon that precedes the URL in the Address bar) to the place on the Links bar where you want the Quick Link button to appear. To remove a button from the Links bar, right-click the button and choose Delete from the shortcut menu.

✦ **Discussions bar:** This toolbar appears below the main browsing area when you click the Discuss button on the Standard Buttons toolbar. The Discussions bar contains buttons for taking part in online discussions. You can add your own comments and reply to other people's comments pertaining to the current Web page.

✦ **Quick Launch toolbar:** The Quick Launch toolbar provides one-click access to the IE browser and other applications or features. This toolbar, which appears next to the Start button on the Windows taskbar, includes a variety of buttons, depending on the programs you have on your computer.

You can quickly display or hide toolbars by right-clicking the menu bar and selecting the toolbar that you want to display or hide from the shortcut menu. In this shortcut menu, a check mark appears next to toolbars that are currently displayed.

Searching the Web

The World Wide Web holds an enormous wealth of information on almost every subject known to humanity, but you need to know how to get to that information. To help Web surfers like you locate sites containing the information that you're interested in, a number of so-called *search engines* have been designed. Each search engine maintains a slightly different directory of the sites on the Web (which are mostly maintained and updated by automated programs called *Web crawlers, spiders,* and *robots*).

Starting the search

IE gives you access to all the most popular search engines through the Search bar, which is its special Explorer bar for searching the Web. You can open the Search bar in one of three ways:

✦ Click the Search button on the Standard Buttons toolbar.

✦ Choose View➪Explorer Bar➪Search.

✦ Press Ctrl+E.

In this window, you find a text box where you can type a few words to describe the kind of Web page to look for. After you enter the keyword or words (known affectionately as a *search string* in programmers' parlance) to search for in this text box, you begin the search by clicking the Search button.

IE then conducts a search for Web sites containing the keywords by using the first search engine (the one listed in the Search bar). If that search engine finds no matches, IE then conducts the same search by using the next search engine in its list.

After exhausting the links in the top-ten list, you can display links to the next ten matching pages returned by the search engine by clicking some sort of Next button. Note that in some search engines, this button appears as a page number in a list of the next available result pages at the bottom of the Search bar.

After you're convinced that you've seen all the best matches to your search, you can conduct another search with the same search engine by using slightly different terms. You can also switch to another search engine to see what kinds of results it produces by using the same search string.

Limiting your searches

To avoid getting back thousands of irrelevant (or at the very minimum, uninteresting) search results, you need to consider telling the search engines to return links only to sites that contain all the terms you enter in the search string. For example, say that you want to find sites that deal with koi (the ornamental carp that are very popular in Japan) ponds. If you type the search string **koi ponds** in the Find a Web Page Containing text box, the search engines will return links to Web sites with both *koi* and *ponds* (without any reference to the fish) in their descriptions, as well as sites that contain both *koi* and *ponds* in their descriptions. The problem with this approach is that it can give you far too many extraneous results because many search engines search for each term in the search string independently as well as together. It's as though you had asked for Web sites with descriptions containing koi *and/or* ponds.

The easiest way to tell the search engines that you want links to a Web site returned only when *all* the terms in your search string are matched in their descriptions is to enclose all the terms in double quotation marks. In the case of the *koi ponds* search string, you can find more Web sites that deal only with koi ponds (as opposed to frog ponds or other ponds containing just garden plants), by typing **"koi ponds"** in the Find a Web Page Containing text box. Taking this little extra step often brings you fewer — and more useful — results.

Browsing in full screen mode

One of the biggest drawbacks of Web surfing is the amount of scrolling that you have to do to see all the information on a particular Web page. To help minimize the amount of scrolling, IE offers a full screen mode that automatically minimizes the space normally occupied by the menu bar, Standard Buttons toolbar, Address bar, and Links bar. In full screen mode, only a version of the Standard Buttons toolbar with small buttons is displayed at the top of the screen, as shown in Figure 4-4.

To switch to full screen mode, press F11 or choose View⇨Full Screen. To get out of full screen mode and return to the normal view, press F11 again.

Figure 4-4:
Press F11 to
enter full
screen
mode and
see more of
a Web page.

Displaying Previously Viewed Web Pages

As you browse different Web sites, Internet Explorer keeps track of your progression through their pages. You can then use the Back and Forward buttons on the toolbar, or the equivalent commands on the View⇨Go To submenu, to move back and forth between the pages that you've visited in the current work session.

If you use the Back and Forward buttons on the Standard Buttons toolbar, you get the added benefit of being able to tell in advance which page will be redisplayed when you click the button. Simply position the mouse pointer on the Back or Forward button and hover it there until the title of the Web page appears in a little ToolTip box.

Both the Back and Forward buttons have drop-down lists attached to them. When you display these drop-down lists (by clicking the drop-down arrow to the immediate right of the Back or Forward button), they show a list, in most-recent to least-recent order, of the nine most recent Web pages visited in the work session before (Back) or after (Forward) the current Web page. By using the drop-down list attached to the Back button, you can avoid having to click Back, Back, Back, Back, and so on, to revisit a page that you saw some time ago during the current Web surfing session.

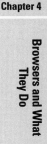

Keeping Track of Your Favorite Web Sites

As you browse the Web with Internet Explorer, you might come across interesting Web sites that you want to revisit later. To make finding a site again easy, you can recall its home page (or any of its other pages) by placing a reference to the page in the IE Favorites folder. You can then revisit the page by selecting its title from the Favorites pull-down menu or from the Favorites bar. (See "Viewing pages from the Favorites folder," later in this chapter.)

Adding Web pages to your Favorites folder

To add a Web page to the Favorites folder, follow these steps:

1. **Go to the Web page that you want to add to your Favorites.**

2. **Choose Favorites⇨Add to Favorites.**

The Add Favorite dialog box opens. The name of the Web page displayed in the title bar of the IE browser window also appears in the Name text box.

3. **(Optional) You can edit the Web page title that appears in the Name text box.**

Keep in mind that this text is listed on the Favorites menu, so you want to make it as descriptive as possible but also keep it brief.

4. **(Optional) To make the Web page that you're adding to your Favorites available for offline browsing, select the Make Available Offline check box.**

5. **(Optional) To add the favorite to a subfolder of Favorites, click the Create In button to expand the Add Favorite dialog box (if the files and folders aren't already displayed in the list box). Then click the appropriate subfolder (see Figure 4-5) or click the New Folder button to create a new folder in which to add your new favorite.**

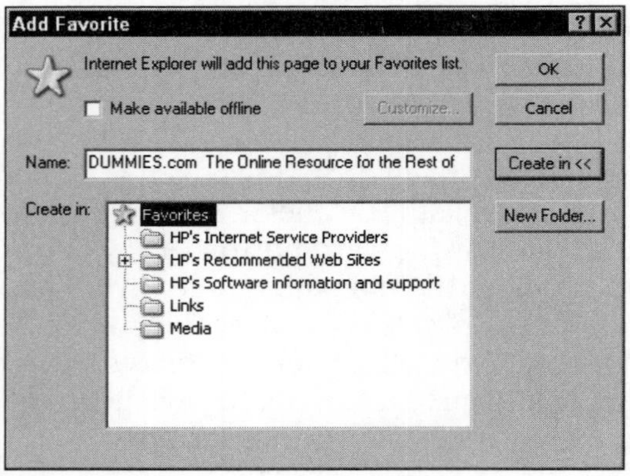

Figure 4-5: You can specify the folder where you want to add your favorite pages.

6. **Click OK to add the Web page to your Favorites.**

If you selected the Make Available Offline check box in Step 4, a synchronization box appears and automatically configures your settings. You're all done!

Viewing pages from the Favorites folder

The Favorites folder contains hyperlinks to all the Web pages that you've marked during your cyberspace travels on the Web as well as all the channels and local folders and files on which you rely. From the Favorites list, you can open Web pages that you want to revisit or go to a channel home page.

To display the links in your Favorites folder, you can select the links directly from the Favorites pull-down menu, click the Favorites button on the Standard Buttons toolbar, or press Ctrl+I. When you click the Favorites button or press Ctrl+I, IE presents the subfolders and links of your Favorites folder in the Favorites bar (a frame on the left side of the screen). The current Web page appears in a frame on the right.

To display the links in one of the Favorites subfolders, click the folder containing the link in the Favorites bar. Then click the desired hyperlink to display a Web page (if it's a Web hyperlink), a list of folders and files (if it's a link to a local disk), or a document in its own program (if it's a link to a particular file).

Organizing your favorites

The Organize Favorites dialog box, as shown in Figure 4-6 (which you open by choosing Favorites⇨Organize Favorites), lets you arrange the links in your Favorites folder (see "Adding Web pages to your Favorites folder," earlier in this chapter), as well as those in your Channels and Links folders.

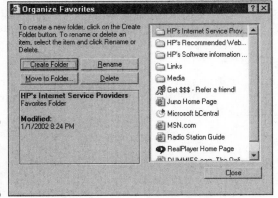

Figure 4-6:
Arrange your links in your folders.

Organizing your favorites and links into folders

One of the best methods for organizing favorites is to group them together into folders — maybe even using subfolders within those folders. After you have a folder structure, you can then move the links to your favorite pages into the appropriate folders, renaming them if you so choose.

Use the following options in the Organize Favorites dialog box to group the links in your Favorites and Links folders:

✦ To create a new folder, click the Create Folder button, type a new name for the folder icon, and press Enter.

✦ To move a link to a favorite page, click its icon to highlight it, and then click the Move to Folder button to open the Browse for Folder dialog box. Click the destination folder in the Browse for Folder dialog box and click OK.

✦ To rename a link to a favorite page, click its icon to select it, and then click the Rename button. Edit the description and press Enter.

✦ To delete a link to a favorite page, click its icon, and then click the Delete button. Then click Yes to confirm the deletion.

Don't delete or rename the Links folder in the Organize Favorites dialog box. Internet Explorer needs the Links folder so that it knows what buttons to display on the Links bar.

Organizing your favorites, channels, and links with drag-and-drop

You can also use the drag-and-drop method to reorganize the links to your Favorites and Links folders from the Favorites Explorer bar in IE. Click the Favorites button on the Standard Buttons toolbar and perform one of the following actions:

✦ To open a folder to display the folder's contents, click its folder icon in the Favorites bar. IE then shows a series of icons for each of the links that it contains. To close a folder and hide its contents, click the folder icon again.

✦ To move an icon to a new position in its folder, drag its icon up or down until you reach the desired position. As you drag, IE shows you where the item will be inserted by displaying a heavy horizontal I-beam. The program also shows you where you can't move the icon by displaying the international No symbol.

✦ To move an icon to another (existing) folder, drag its icon to the folder icon. When the folder becomes highlighted, you can drop the icon and it goes into the highlighted folder.

Viewing Pages from the History Folder

The History folder contains a list of links to the Web pages that you visited within the last 20 days (unless you've changed this default setting). These hyperlinks are arranged chronologically from least recent to most recent, grouped by days for the current week, and then by weeks for all days further back.

To display the links in your History folder, click the History button on the Standard Buttons toolbar or press Ctrl+H. IE shows the folders for each Web site that you visited on a particular day or during a particular week in the History bar (a pane on the left side of the screen). The current Web page appears in a pane on the right.

To revisit a Web page in the History folder, click the Web site's folder icon in the History bar to display the links to its pages; then click the hyperlink for the particular page that you want to go to (see Figure 4-7).

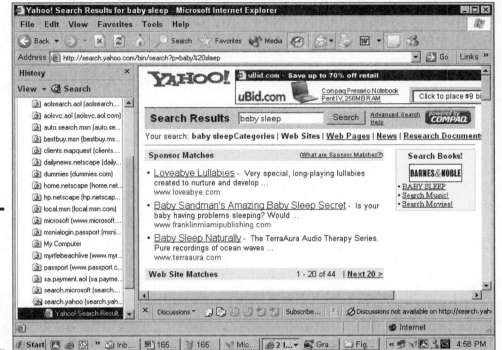

Figure 4-7:
Use the History folder to quickly locate sites that you've recently visited.

CHECK IT OUT

Using Important Internet Explorer Keyboard Shortcuts

Here are three timesaving key combinations that every IE user should know:

✔ **Ctrl+Enter:** If you type the middle part of an address in the Address bar — say, `wiley` — and then press Ctrl+Enter, IE immediately puts `http://www.` on the front and `.com` on the back. Type **wiley** and press Ctrl+Enter, and IE immediately knows to look for `http://www.wiley.com`. (This doesn't work in Internet Explorer 6.1.)

✔ **Ctrl+F5:** If you think that the Web page is "stuck" — it isn't being updated properly, perhaps because it's been put in the cache on your PC — pressing Ctrl+F5 forces Internet Explorer to go out and get the latest copy of the current page. In

theory, the browser even blasts past copies that are cached with your Internet service provider (which can be a real headache if your ISP is slow to update cached pages).

✔ **Shift+click:** When you click a link, sometimes the new page replaces the old window; sometimes the old window stays around, and the new one appears in a window of its own. Usually, the person who designs a Web page decides what happens, but you can take over. To force IE to open a Web page in a new window, hold down Shift while you click the link.

Put a sticky note on your monitor with those three key combinations until they become ingrained in your fingers' little gray cells.

Chapter 5: Customizing Your Browser Settings

In This Chapter

- ✔ Choosing a home page
- ✔ Working with the cache of temporary Internet files
- ✔ Adjusting History settings
- ✔ Speeding up your browser
- ✔ Synchronizing Web pages for offline viewing
- ✔ Using AutoComplete

*I*n preparation for your extensive travels on the World Wide Web via Internet Explorer, you might need to make some minor adjustments. This chapter is the place to look for information on everything from how to change the way Web pages are displayed on your screen to ways to tweak your browser's performance.

Changing Your Home Page

Each time you start the Internet Explorer (IE) browser, it opens a specially designated page, which it calls the *home page*. The home page is also where IE goes when you click the Home button on the toolbar. (For more on IE, read Book I, Chapter 4.)

If your computer isn't connected to the Internet when you click Home, IE loads the home page locally from the cache. The *cache* is an area of a computer's hard drive used to store data recently downloaded from the Internet so that the data can be redisplayed quickly. If the page doesn't happen to be in the cache at the time (because you deleted its files before quitting the browser the last time), IE gives you an error message and displays an empty Web page called `about:blank`. To return to your home page, you must go online again and click the Home button.

To change the home page on your computer, follow these steps:

1. **Launch the IE browser and go to the Web page that you want to make the new home page.**

2. **Choose Tools⇨Internet Options.**

   The Internet Options dialog box appears. Click the General tab if it isn't already selected.

3. In the Home Page section of the dialog box, click the Use Current button to make the current page your new home page.

You can also type the URL of the page that you want to designate as your home page in the Address text box.

4. Click OK to close the Internet Options dialog box.

After you designate the page of your choice as your home page, you can return to that page at anytime by clicking the Home button.

If, for the sake of speed, you want a blank Web page to be used as the home page, click the Use Blank button. IE then enters `about:blank` (the name of its standard blank page) in the Address text box. You also can click the Stop button on the navigation bar as soon as Internet Explorer starts loading the page.

Changing the Way Web Pages Look

A Web page, depending on the computer displaying it, can appear in a variety of fonts and colors and can use various characters and symbols for different languages of the world. The combination of the Web browser settings and the design of the individual pages control how Web pages look in IE.

The changes that you make to the IE settings only affect the way Web pages look on your screen. You don't have to worry that you're actually changing somebody's Web page.

Changing the text size

You can customize your copy of IE so that you get larger, easier-to-read text, or you can choose a smaller font size that lets you see more text at a time on the screen. To change the display size of text in Web pages, follow these steps:

1. Choose View➪Text Size.

A submenu appears with the following size options: Largest, Larger, Medium, Smaller, and Smallest. The Largest, Larger, Smaller, and Smallest font sizes are all relative to the Medium font size (which is the default size used by IE).

2. Choose the Largest or Larger option to make the text on the current Web page appear bigger. Choose the Smaller or Smallest option to make the text appear smaller.

Selecting a different font

Many Web pages do not specify a font for the proportional and fixed-width (or monospaced) text on the Web page, leaving that determination to IE. When you first start browsing the Web with IE, it uses Times New Roman to render nonspecifically defined proportional text and Courier New for all fixed-width text. If you prefer other fonts for rendering the proportional and fixed-width text, you can modify one of the IE character sets (different styles of the alphabet and other symbols).

To choose other fonts, follow these steps:

1. **Choose Tools⇨Internet Options.**

   The Internet Options dialog box appears.

2. **Click the Fonts button on the General tab.**

   The Fonts dialog box opens, as shown in Figure 5-1.

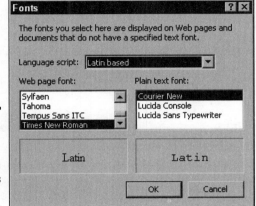

Figure 5-1: You can change the default fonts via the Fonts dialog box.

3. **To change the font used to render proportional text, choose a font in the Web Page Font list box.**

   Your particular choices depend upon which fonts you have installed on the computer.

4. **To change the font used to render fixed-width text, choose a font in the Plain Text Font list box.**

5. **Click OK twice to close the Fonts dialog box and the Internet Options dialog box.**

Changing the text and background colors

If you have problems reading the text on a Web page because of its text color and background, you might be able to modify these colors (assuming that the Web page author hasn't specified his or her own colors). By default, IE chooses black for the text color and battleship gray for the background (page) color. To set custom colors for your Web page background and text, follow these steps:

1. **Choose Tools⇨Internet Options.**

   The Internet Options dialog box appears.

2. **Click the Colors button on the General tab.**

The Colors dialog box appears, as shown in Figure 5-2. In this dialog box, you can set colors for the text and background as well as the colors for visited and unvisited hyperlinks.

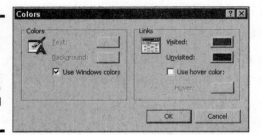

Figure 5-2:
Change the color of Web page text and the background color.

3. **In the Colors section of the Colors dialog box, deselect the Use Windows Colors check box.**

   Deselecting this check box enables you to specify your own colors.

4. **To change the text color, click the Text button in the Colors dialog box to open the Color dialog box, and then select a new color from the Basic Colors palette. Then click OK.**

5. **To change the background color of the page, click the Background button in the Colors dialog box to open the Color dialog box, and then select a new color from the Basic Colors palette. Then click OK.**

6. **When you finish setting the text and background colors that you want to use, click OK twice to close the Colors dialog box and the Internet Options dialog box.**

When the Internet Options dialog box closes, IE displays the current Web page in the text and background colors that you selected. If it doesn't, this means that the author of this Web page has explicitly set a style for the page, which takes precedence over the browser default settings that you set.

Changing the way your browser displays hyperlinks

Hypertext links *(hyperlinks)* are a special form of text that, when clicked, take you to a new location on the current page or to another page altogether. Traditionally, blue underlined text on-screen indicates the hypertext links that you haven't yet followed. When you follow a hypertext link and later return to the original page, IE lets you know that you've followed the link by displaying the same hyperlink in purple underlined text. People often refer to these links as *unvisited* and *visited* links. To modify the color of hypertext links in IE, follow these steps:

1. **Choose Tools⇨Internet Options.**

   The Internet Options dialog box appears.

2. **Click the Colors button on the General tab.**

   The Colors dialog box appears.

3. **To change the color for visited hyperlinks, click the Visited button and choose a new color from the palette in the Color dialog box. Click OK to close the Color dialog box.**

4. **To change the color for unvisited hyperlinks, click the Unvisited button and choose a new color from the palette in the Color dialog box. Click OK to close the Color dialog box.**

   In addition to customizing the visited and unvisited hypertext colors, you can choose to assign a *hover* color: that is, the color that hyperlinked text becomes when you position your mouse pointer over it.

5. **To have text hyperlinks turn a special color whenever your mouse pointer hovers above them, select the Use Hover Color check box. If you don't like the default color of red, click the Hover button and choose a new color from the palette in the Color dialog box. Click OK to close the Color dialog box.**

6. **When you're finished changing the link colors, click OK twice to close the Colors dialog box and the Internet Options dialog box.**

Customizing Toolbars

IE contains several toolbars, which you can customize to your liking. You can change the display size of toolbars, hide toolbars, and add buttons to toolbars. Refer to the Book I, Chapter 4 if you need a refresher on the toolbars included with IE.

Changing the size of toolbars

You can minimize the amount of space that the toolbar takes up by putting Internet Explorer in full screen view. To do so, choose View➪Full Screen or press F11. The full screen view shrinks the amount of space given to the toolbars — IE hides all the toolbars except the Standard Buttons toolbar, which now uses smaller icons.

When IE is in full screen mode, the browser adds an Auto-Hide command to the shortcut menu that appears when you right-click the remaining Standard Buttons toolbar. Selecting the Auto-Hide command causes the entire toolbar to slide up until it's off the screen. To redisplay the toolbar, move the mouse pointer up to the top of the IE window. When the mouse pointer rolls over the area where the toolbar would normally be, the toolbar magically (and temporarily) reappears.

To again fix the Standard Buttons toolbar on the screen, choose the Auto-Hide command from the toolbar's shortcut menu. You can also take IE out of full screen mode by pressing F11.

Hiding and unhiding a toolbar

You can hide the Standard Buttons toolbar, the Address bar, or the Links bar. To do so, choose View➪Toolbars. From the submenu that appears, click to remove the check mark next to the toolbar that you want to hide. You can also right-click any empty area of the toolbar and choose the appropriate name (Standard Buttons, Address bar, or Links) from the toolbar shortcut menu. To display the hidden toolbar again, reverse this procedure.

Adding a button to the toolbar

You can add a button to the Standard Buttons toolbar to make the button's command more accessible. Follow these steps:

1. **Choose View⇨Toolbars⇨Customize or right-click the Standard Buttons toolbar and choose Customize from the shortcut menu.**

The Customize Toolbar dialog box appears.

2. **In the Available Toolbar Buttons list box, click the button you want to add to the toolbar, and then click Add.**

IE adds the button to the end of the list in the Current Toolbar Buttons list box.

3. **(Optional) To change the position of the newly added button on the toolbar, click the button in the Current Toolbar Buttons list box; then click the Move Up button one or more times.**

4. **Click the Close button to close the Customize Toolbar dialog box.**

Changing the History Settings

When you come across a wonderful Web page, you can save the page to your Favorites list or create a shortcut to the page to make returning there easy. (See Book I, Chapter 4 for more details.) However, if you forgot to save a Web page to your Favorites list at the time it was displayed in the IE browsing window, you can still get back to it by finding its link in the History folder.

By default, the Internet Explorer History folder retains links to the pages that you visited during the last 20 days, but you might want to change the length of time that links remain in your History folder. For example, you can increase the time so that you have access to Web pages visited in the more distant past, or you can decrease the time if you're short on hard drive space. You can also purge the links in the History folder to free up space on your hard drive and restore all hyperlinks to pages that you've visited to their unvisited state (and colors).

To change the History settings, follow these steps:

1. **Choose Tools⇨Internet Options.**

The Internet Options dialog box appears.

2. **In the History section, type a new value in the Days to Keep Pages in History text box or click the up or down arrows to select the desired value.**

3. **Click OK.**

To purge the links in the History folder, follow these steps:

1. **Choose Tools⇨Internet Options.**

The Internet Options dialog box appears.

2. **Click the Clear History button on the General tab.**

3. **Click Yes in the Internet Options alert box that appears, which asks whether you want to delete all items from your History folder.**

4. **Click OK to close the Internet Options dialog box.**

Specifying Mail, News, and Internet Call Programs

IE can work with other programs to add to its functionality and capabilities. Microsoft has created certain programs that it intends to work so closely with IE that it refers to them as *members of the Internet Explorer Suite.*

The auxiliary programs that are included with IE as part of the suite depend upon which type of installation you perform:

✦ **Custom:** This installation lets you select which auxiliary programs are installed along with the browser and Outlook Express.

✦ **Minimal:** This installation gives you the Microsoft Internet Connection Wizard along with IE.

✦ **Typical:** This installation includes the browser plus Outlook Express, Windows Media Player, and a few multimedia enhancements.

One of the most practical of these many auxiliary programs is Microsoft *Outlook Express,* which adds e-mail and news-reading capabilities to IE. If you do the typical installation and your computer is equipped with sound and video hardware, such as a microphone and video camera, you can use NetMeeting to make Internet calls or set up video conferencing. Even if you don't have such hardware, you can use Chat (originally known as Comic Chat) as part of NetMeeting to participate in online chat sessions.

To see which programs are configured to run from IE (such as the Mail, News, and Internet call programs) and (if necessary) change them, follow these steps:

1. **Choose Tools⇨Internet Options; then click the Programs tab (see Figure 5-3).**

2. **To change the program listed in the HTML Editor, E-Mail, Newsgroups, Internet Call, Calendar, or Contact List text boxes, select a new program by using the drop-down list boxes.**

3. **After you finish checking over the programs and making any changes to them, click OK.**

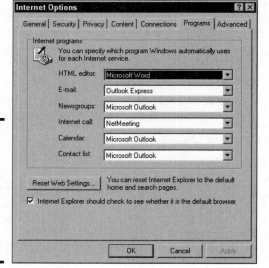

Figure 5-3:
Use the
Programs
tab to view
or select
programs
used with
Internet
Explorer.

If you have installed another Web browser (such as Netscape Navigator) after installing IE, you can click the Reset Web Settings button in this dialog box to restore your original IE default settings for search pages and your home page. Clicking this button also restores the prompt to ask you whether you want to make IE your default browser each time you launch Microsoft's browser.

Speeding Up the Display of Web Pages

You can speed up the display of Web pages on your computer, but unless you do it by getting a faster connection (with a modem upgrade, a DSL or ISDN line, or a cable modem), the increase in speed comes at the expense of hard drive space or viewing content. You can also dramatically speed up the display of Web pages by turning off the display of most pictures, animations, videos, and sounds. To make this kind of change to IE, follow these steps:

1. **Choose Tools➪Internet Options; then click the Advanced tab.**

2. **In the Multimedia section of the Settings list box, deselect the check boxes of as many of the items as you want to disable to get a sufficient speed boost.**

These items include Play Videos, Play Sounds, Smart Image Dithering, Show Pictures, and Play Animations.

3. **Click OK to update the new settings and close the Internet Options dialog box.**

Now when you open new Web pages, weird (but fast) generic icons replace the multimedia contents that you've disabled. If you still see graphics on the Web pages that you visit, click the Refresh button on the Internet Explorer toolbar to remove their display.

After disabling the Show Pictures and Play Videos settings, you can still choose to display a particular graphic or play a particular video. Just right-click the icon placeholder and choose Show Picture from its shortcut menu. IE then downloads and displays the particular graphic or video that you selected.

To restore the multimedia items that you disabled, click the Advanced tab of the Internet Options dialog box again and mark the check boxes to select the desired Multimedia items (or simply click the Restore Defaults button). Then click OK to save your changes and close the Internet Options dialog box. Remember that you have to use the Refresh button on the Internet Explorer toolbar to see and hear multimedia items on pages that were downloaded to the cache when these items were disabled.

Synchronizing Offline Web Pages

To make sure that you have the most current data from an Active Channel or a Favorites Web site that you've made available for browsing offline, you might want to update the contents of your cache — a process known as *synchronization*. To synchronize individual Active Channels or favorite Web sites, follow these steps:

1. **Choose Tools⇨Synchronize.**

The Items to Synchronize dialog box appears.

2. **In the Select the Check Box for Any Items You Want to Synchronize list box, make sure that the check box for each offline Web page you want updated is selected. Deselect the check box of any offline Web page you don't want updated.**

3. **Click the Synchronize button.**

IE then connects you to the Internet and begins the process of checking each selected offline Web page for updated content, which is then automatically downloaded into your computer's cache. Synchronizing enables you to browse the updated contents (using the Favorites Explorer bar) when you're not connected to the Internet.

If you connect to the Internet over a local area network (LAN) or via a cable modem, digital subscriber line (DSL), or Integrated Services Digital Network (ISDN) connection (you can therefore go online at anytime), you might want to specify when and under what conditions particular offline Web pages are synchronized. (Read all about the different Internet connection types in Book I, Chapter 1.) To do this, choose Tools⇨Synchronize. Then with the Offline Web Pages folder selected, click the Setup button. When you click this button, Internet Explorer opens the Synchronization Settings dialog box.

The Synchronization Settings dialog box contains three tabs: Logon, On Idle, and Scheduled:

✦ **Logon/Logoff tab:** Use this tab to select the offline pages that you want synchronized whenever you log onto or log off a networked computer. Select the check boxes for the offline pages to be synchronized when you log onto your computer; then select the When I Log On to My Computer check box.

✦ **On Idle tab:** Use this tab to select the offline pages that you want synchronized whenever your computer is idle for a particular period of time. Select the check boxes for the offline pages to be synchronized when your computer is idle for a particular period, and then select the Synchronize the Selected Items When My Computer Is Idle check box. To specify how long an idle period to use, click the Advanced button and change the settings in the Idle Settings dialog box.

✦ **Scheduled tab:** Use this tab to set up a custom schedule by which selected offline pages are routinely synchronized. To create a new schedule to be used, click the Add button and use the Scheduled Synchronization Wizard to take you through the steps of creating and naming a new custom schedule for certain offline Web pages. To edit the settings for a particular default schedule, click the name of the schedule (such as CNN Desktop Scores Recommended Schedule); then click the Edit button to open a dialog box in which you can modify the current settings. (The name of the dialog box and its tabs and options vary depending on the particular synchronization schedule that you're editing.) This tab is useful for downloading Web sites you like to read when a connection is unavailable, like, for example, when you are on a long plane trip.

Customizing Your AutoComplete Settings

The AutoComplete feature makes it easier to fill out addresses, forms, and passwords by providing a drop-down list of suggestions as you type, based on your previous entries. IE has added the capability to customize the Auto-Complete settings. To customize your AutoComplete settings, follow these steps:

1. **Choose Tools⇨Internet Options and click the Content tab.**

2. **Click the AutoComplete button.**

The AutoComplete Settings dialog box appears.

3. **Select the check boxes for the items for which you want to use AutoComplete.**

Select the Web Addresses check box to have AutoComplete suggest URLs for previously visited Web pages. Select the Forms check box if you want AutoComplete to match the field values from the most recently submitted form. Select User Names and Passwords on Forms if you want Auto-Complete to retain your user ID and password for sites that require them.

4. **(Optional) To delete the form information that AutoComplete retains, click the Clear Forms button. To delete the list of user IDs and passwords that AutoComplete retains, click the Clear Passwords button.**

To delete the list of Web addresses that AutoComplete keeps on file, you must click the Clear History button on the General tab of the Internet Options dialog box.

5. **Click OK twice to close both dialog boxes.**

CHECK IT OUT

Stopping Script Debugging

How many times have you run across a pop-up message that asks whether you want to debug a Web page? Debugging is one of the most annoying so-called features in IE. If there's a bug in a Web page — that is, if the person who created the Web page made a mistake — why would *you* want to fix it? Relax if you're worried that you are at fault for triggering these unwanted Debug messages. You didn't do anything. The messages occur because IE can't figure out how to read a Web page. The person who wrote the Web page screwed up. Not you.

Fortunately, it's easy to turn the blasted error messages off, permanently:

1. **Start Internet Explorer.**

2. **Choose Tools⇨Internet Options⇨ Advanced.**

The Internet Options dialog box appears.

3. **Select the Disable Script Debugging check box (if it's not selected by default), in the Browsing section.**

It's probably not selected, and that's why you see the Do You Wish to Debug? messages.

4. **Deselect the Display a Notification About Every Script Error check box.**

It's probably not selected already, but you should make sure it stays that way.

5. **Click OK.**

You'll never be asked to debug a script again.

Chapter 6: Printing and Saving Web Information

In This Chapter

✔ Printing the contents of a Web page

✔ Saving a Web page or graphic to your hard drive

✔ Copying a Web graphic to your hard drive

✔ Viewing the HTML contents of a Web page

✔ Turning a Web graphic into your desktop's wallpaper

With Internet Explorer (IE), you can print and save all or part of a favorite Web page. You can even save an interesting Web graphic or photo and set it as your desktop's wallpaper. To understand what makes a Web page tick, take a look behind the scenes to examine the HyperText Markup Language (HTML) code used to create the Web page. This chapter provides details on the various aspects of storing and reusing the information that you uncover in your travels with IE.

Printing a Web Page

Although you can save a Web page to your hard drive (as you can discover how to do in the next section, "Saving a Web Page on Your Computer"), you might prefer to just print its contents. Internet Explorer makes it easy to print the contents of the Web page you're currently browsing. Just remember that a Web page (in spite of its name) can produce multiple printed pages because of the amount of information contained on that "page."

When you want to print the contents of the Web page currently displayed in your IE browser, you can choose from a couple of methods:

✦ Click the Print button on the Standard Buttons toolbar.

✦ Choose File⇨Print or press Ctrl+P to open the Print dialog box (see Figure 6-1); then click Print or press Enter.

Before you print from IE, you should check the page settings. You can change page settings from the Page Setup dialog box (see Figure 6-2), which you open by choosing File⇨Page Setup.

To change the page size, select a new size setting from the Size drop-down list. Set the orientation of the printing to either Portrait (vertical) or Landscape (horizontal). To change any or all of the page margins, enter a new value (in inches) in the Left, Right, Top, and Bottom text boxes.

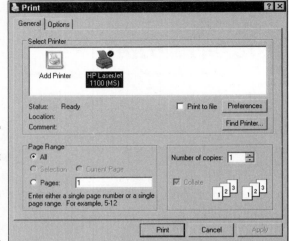

Figure 6-1:
Specify print
settings for
the current
Web page in
the Print
dialog box.

Figure 6-2:
The Page
Setup dialog
box lets you
adjust the
default page
settings.

To change the information that appears at the top of each page as a header
or the bottom of each page as a footer, you need to modify the codes in the
Header and Footer text boxes, respectively. Each of these printing codes
begins with an ampersand (&), followed by a single character. You can use
any of the printing codes shown in Table 6-1.

Table 6-1	Printing Codes
Printing Code	*What It Prints*
&w	Title of the Web page as it appears in the title bar of the browser window
&u	URL (Web address) of the Web page
&d	Current date using the short date format specified in the Regional Settings control panel (for example: 11/6/04)
&D	Current date using the long date format specified in the Regional Settings control panel (for example: Saturday, November 6, 2004)

Printing Code	What It Prints
&t	Current time as specified in the Regional Settings control panel (for example: 9:41:35 PM)
&T	Current time using a 24-hour clock (for example: 21:41:35)
&p	Page number of the current printout
&P	Total number of pages in the printout
&&	Ampersand character (&) in the header or footer text

When setting up a custom header or footer, you can intersperse the preceding printing codes with standard text. For example, if you want the footer to read something like *Page 2 of 3,* you need to intersperse the codes &p and &P between the words *Page* and *of* in the Footer text box, like this:

Page &p of &P

All the printing codes and text that you enter in the Header and Footer text boxes in the Page Setup dialog box are automatically left-justified at the top or bottom of the page. To have some of the text or codes right-justified in the header or footer, type the code **&b&b** immediately before the text and codes that you want to right-justify in the printout. If you want text or codes centered in the text, type **&b**.

To prevent IE from printing a header or footer in the Web page printout, delete all the text and printing codes from the Header and Footer text boxes in the Page Setup dialog box.

Saving a Web Page on Your Computer

You can save to your computer's hard drive any Web page that you visit. Then you use IE to view the page offline. To save a Web page to your hard drive, follow these steps:

1. **Use IE to display the Web page that you want to save to your hard drive; then choose File➪Save As.**

   The Save Web Page dialog box opens.

2. **Select the folder on your hard drive where you want to save the Web page.**

   The folder name appears in the Save In drop-down list box.

3. **(Optional) If you want to change the filename under which the Web page is saved, you need to edit or replace its current name in the File Name text box.**

4. **Click the Save button to close the Save Web Page dialog box.**

   IE downloads the Web page and saves it on your computer's hard drive.

After the Web page is saved on your hard drive, you can view its contents offline by choosing File➪Work Offline and then opening it from the IE Address bar or from the Open dialog box. (Choose File➪Open or press Ctrl+O.)

Saving a Web Graphic on Your Computer

IE makes it easy to save any still graphic images in the GIF or JPG (JPEG) graphics file format. (If you want to save a Web graphic as desktop wallpaper, see "Wallpapering Your Desktop with a Web Graphic," later in this chapter.) To save a Web graphic on your computer, follow these steps:

1. **Use IE to go to the Web page that contains the graphic that you want to save on your computer.**

2. **Right-click the Web graphic to display its shortcut menu and choose Save Picture As.**

   The Save Picture dialog box opens.

3. **In the Save In drop-down list box, select the folder on your hard drive into which you want to save the graphic.**

4. **(Optional) If you want to change the filename that the Web graphic is saved under, you need to edit or replace its current name in the File Name text box.**

5. **(Optional) By default, IE saves the Web graphic in the GIF graphics file format or JPEG graphics file format (depending on which format the Web designer used).**

   To save the graphic in the BMP (bitmapped picture) graphics file format — which Windows uses extensively for such things as buttons and desktop backgrounds — choose Bitmap (*.bmp) in the Save As Type drop-down list box.

6. **Click Save to close the Save Picture dialog box.**

   IE downloads the Web graphic and saves it on your computer's hard drive.

Copying Web Page Information

When surfing the Internet, you might encounter a Web page that contains information that you want to access offline. In those situations, you can use the Windows Copy and Paste features to incorporate the section of Web page text of interest into a document on your hard drive.

To copy text of a Web page into a local document, follow these steps:

1. **With the Web page displayed in the IE browser window, position the I-beam mouse pointer at the beginning of the text that you want to copy; then click and drag through the characters or rows until all the text you want to copy is selected (highlighted).**

   When you drag through the text, all the graphics that appear between or to the side of the paragraphs that you're selecting are highlighted for copying as well. If you don't want to include a particular graphic in your selection, you must copy the text before and after it in separate actions.

   If you want to copy everything on the page (including all text and graphics), choose Edit➪Select All or press Ctrl+A.

2. **Choose Edit⇨Copy or press Ctrl+C.**

   The selected text is copied onto the Windows Clipboard.

3. **Switch to the word processor (for example, Microsoft Word), text editor (such as WordPad or Notepad), or e-mail editor (such as Outlook Express) that contains the destination document or e-mail message into which you want to copy the selected text.**

   If you prefer, you can close IE and launch the word processor, editor, or e-mail program. If you want to copy the selected text into an existing document, open that file with a word processor or text editor. Otherwise, open a new document.

4. **Click the I-beam mouse pointer at the place in the document or e-mail message where you want the selected text to appear, and then choose Edit⇨Paste or press Ctrl+V.**

To copy graphics without surrounding text, you use another copy technique covered in the section, "Saving a Web Graphic on Your Computer," earlier in this chapter.

Depending on the capabilities of the program into which you are pasting the copied Web text, you might find that the copied text retains some or (in rare cases) all of its original formatting (created by using the Web-based computer language, HTML). For example, if you copy a section of text formatted in HTML as a bulleted list into a Word document, Word retains the bullets and properly indents the text items.

When copying text from a Web page, you usually copy hyperlinks that the author has included within that text. Some word processing programs (such as Word) and e-mail editors (such as Outlook Express) retain the correct HTML tags for these hyperlinks, making them functioning links within the destination document. Be forewarned, however, that seldom (if ever) do these hyperlinks work properly when clicked. This problem most often occurs because you don't have the pages to which these links refer copied to your hard drive. You also might end up with extra line breaks or spaces (because of the HTML formatting) when you copy text from a Web page.

When copying information from a table on a Web page, you can retain its tabular format by copying entire rows of the table into Word 2003 documents or Outlook 2003 and Outlook Express e-mail messages. For the best results in copying tables from Web pages, copy the entire table into the Word document or Outlook e-mail message. You can now copy information from a Web table into an Excel 2003 worksheet simply by dragging the copied table cells to the blank worksheet cells and releasing the mouse button!

Viewing the HTML Source of a Web Page

A Web page is no more than a special type of text document that makes extensive use of HTML tags to format its contents. If you're a Web page designer (or have any inclination to become one), you can figure out a lot about Web design by viewing the HTML contents of the really cool pages that you visit.

To see the HTML codes behind any Web page displayed in the Internet Explorer browsing window, choose View⇨Source. When you select this command, IE launches the Windows Notepad utility, which displays a copy of the *HTML source page* (the page containing all the HTML tags and text) for the current Web page, as shown in Figure 6-3.

Figure 6-3: The HTML source code appears in the Notepad window.

You can then print the HTML source page by choosing File⇨Print within Notepad.

Wallpapering Your Desktop with a Web Graphic

IE makes it a snap to copy a favorite graphic from a Web page and use the picture as the background for your Windows desktop. To turn a Web graphic into wallpaper for your desktop, follow these steps:

1. **Use Internet Explorer to go to the Web page containing the graphic that you want to save as wallpaper.**

2. **Right-click the Web graphic to display its shortcut menu and click the Set As Background command.**

As soon as you click Set As Background, IE makes the graphic the wallpaper for your desktop and copies the selected graphic onto your hard drive, placing it in the Windows folder. The graphic is given the filename `Internet Explorer Wallpaper.bmp`.

To remove the Web graphic wallpaper, right-click the desktop and select Properties from the shortcut menu that appears. The Display Properties dialog box opens. On the Desktop tab, choose a new graphic or HTML file for the wallpaper in the Background box. If you no longer want any graphic displayed as the wallpaper, select the (None) option at the top of the list.

Chapter 7: E-Mail Basics

In This Chapter

✔ Getting up to speed on e-mail basics
✔ Understanding e-mail addresses

*E*lectronic mail, or *e-mail*, is without a doubt the most widely used Internet service. Internet mail is connected to most other e-mail systems, such as those within corporations. That means that after you master Internet e-mail, you can send messages to folks with accounts at most big organizations and educational institutions as well as to folks with accounts at Internet providers and online services. This chapter covers the e-mail basics you need to know, such as how to interpret acronyms and emoticons, how to figure out what your e-mail address is, and how to practice proper e-mail etiquette.

Choosing an E-Mail Program

Chances are that if you purchased this book, you have a choice between two e-mail programs made by the mighty Microsoft Corporation: Outlook or Outlook Express (covered in Chapters 8 and 9 of this book). The programs are similar in that they handle incoming mail the same way and store messages the same way. In both programs, messages are stored in folders, and you can move messages from folder to folder to keep track of e-mail. However, Outlook is by far the more sophisticated program. For example, you can schedule tasks and keep a calendar in Outlook.

Unless you are happy with an old-fashioned e-mail program such as Eudora or Netscape Mail, I suggest switching to Outlook or Outlook Express. These programs are very helpful when it comes to sifting through and organizing the barrage of e-mail that most people receive nowadays.

E-Mail Addresses

To send e-mail to someone, you need his or her e-mail address. Roughly speaking, mail addresses consist of these elements:

✦ **Mailbox name:** Usually, the username of the person's account

✦ **@:** The *at* sign

✦ **Host name:** The name of the host's computer (See "Host names and domain names," later in this chapter.)

For example, `elvis@gurus.com` is a typical address, where `elvis` is the mailbox name, and `gurus.com` is the host name.

Internet mailbox names should *not* contain commas, spaces, or parentheses. Mailbox names can contain letters; numerals; and some punctuation characters, such as periods, hyphens, and underscores. Capitalization normally doesn't matter in e-mail addresses.

What's my address?

If you're accessing the Internet through a service provider, your address is most likely

your_login_name@your_provider's_host_name

If you're connected through work or school, your e-mail address is typically

your_login_name@your_computer's_host_name

A host name, however, is sometimes just a department or company name rather than your computer's name. If your login name is `elvis` and your computer is `shamu.strat.gurus.com`, your mail address might look like one of these examples:

```
elvis@shamu.strat.gurus.com
elvis@strat.gurus.com
elvis@gurus.com
```

or even this one:

```
elvis.presley@gurus.com
```

Host names and domain names

Hosts are computers that are directly attached to the Internet. Host names have several parts strung together with periods, like this:

```
ivan.iecc.com
```

You decode a host name from right to left:

✦ The rightmost part of a name is its *top-level domain*, or *TLD* (in the preceding example, `com`). See "Top-level domains," later in this chapter.

✦ To the TLD's left (`iecc`) is the name of the company, school, or organization.

✦ The part to the left of the organization name (`ivan`) identifies the particular computer within the organization.

In large organizations, host names can be further subdivided by site or department. The last two parts of a host name are known as a *domain*. For example, `ivan` is in the `iecc.com` domain, and `iecc.com` is a *domain name*.

For a list of organizations that can register a domain name for you, go to the following URL:

```
www.icann.org/registrars/accredited-list.html
```

Internet service providers (ISPs) often charge substantial additional fees for setting up and supporting a new domain. Shop around.

IP addresses and the DNS

Network software uses the Internet protocol (IP) address, which is sort of like a phone number, to identify the host. IP addresses are written in four chunks separated by periods, such as

208.31.42.77

A system called the *domain name system (DNS)* keeps track of which IP address (or addresses, for popular Internet hosts) goes with which Internet host name. Usually, one computer has one IP address and one Internet host name, although this isn't always true. For example, the Web site at www.yahoo.com is so heavily used that a group of computers, each with its own IP address, accepts requests for Web pages from that name.

The most important IP addresses to know are the IP addresses of the computers at the ISP you use. You might need them in order to set up the software on your computer; if things get fouled up, the IP addresses help the guru who fixes your problem.

Top-level domains

The *top-level domain (TLD),* sometimes called a *zone,* is the last piece of the host name on the Internet. For example, the zone of gurus.com is com. TLDs come in two main flavors:

+ Organizational
+ Geographical

If the TLD is three or more letters long, it's an *organizational name.* Table 7-1 describes the organizational names that have been in use for years.

Table 7-1	Organizational TLDs
TLD	*Description*
com	Commercial organization
edu	Educational institution, usually a college or university
gov	U.S. government body or department
int	International organization (mostly NATO, at the moment)
mil	U.S. military site (can be located anywhere)
net	Networking organization
org	Anything that doesn't fit elsewhere; usually a not-for-profit group

It used to be that most systems using organizational names were in the United States. The com domain has now become a hot property; large corporations and organizations worldwide consider it a prestige Internet address.

Address "haves" and "have-nots" are contesting a plan to add additional top-level domain names to those already in use.

If the TLD is only two letters long, it's a *geographical name*. The two-letter code specifies a country, such as us for the United States, uk for the United Kingdom, au for Australia, and jp for Japan. The stuff in front of the TLD is specific to that country. Often, the letter group just before the country code mimics the style for U.S. organizational names: com or co for commercial, edu or ac for academic institutions, and gov or go for government, for example.

The us domain — used by schools, cities, and small organizations in the United States — is set up strictly geographically. The two letters just before us specify the state. Other common codes are ci for city, co for county, cc for community colleges, and k12 for schools. The Internet site for the city of Cambridge, Massachusetts, for example, is www.ci.cambridge.ma.us.

Port numbers

Internet host computers can run many programs at one time, and they can have simultaneous network connections to lots of other computers. *Port numbers,* which identify particular programs on a computer, keep the different connections straight. For example:

✦ File transfer (FTP) uses port 21.

✦ E-mail uses port 25 and 110.

✦ The Web uses port 80.

Typically, your file transfer, e-mail, or newsgroup program automatically selects the correct port to use, so you don't need to know these port numbers. Now and then, you see a port number as part of an Internet address (URL).

URLs versus e-mail addresses

Uniform Resource Locators (URLs) contain the information that your browser software uses to find Web pages on the World Wide Web. URLs look somewhat like e-mail addresses in that both contain a domain name. E-mail addresses almost always contain an @, however, and URLs never do.

URLs that appear in newspapers and magazines sometimes have an extra hyphen added at the end of a line when the URL continues on the next line. If the URL doesn't work as written, try deleting that hyphen.

E-mail addresses usually are not case-sensitive — that is, capitalization doesn't matter — but parts of URLs are case-sensitive. Always type URLs exactly as written, including capitalization.

Chapter 8: Sending and Receiving E-Mail with Outlook Express

In This Chapter

✔ Collecting your e-mail

✔ Jazzing up your messages

✔ Sending e-mail — now or later

✔ Printing e-mail messages

*I*f you're using Internet Explorer (IE), you have Outlook Express — Microsoft's friendly e-mail program. If you're not sure how to do something in Outlook Express, don't despair. This chapter tells you what you need to know to get up and running quickly and efficiently with this program. This chapter also shows you how to master the basics of composing and sending e-mail, how to get fancy by using color and images in your e-mail, and how to print e-mail messages.

Checking for New Mail

After you start sending messages and giving out your e-mail address, your Inbox will fill up with new mail in no time at all. You need to know how to access all the latest tidbits headed your way and also how to reply to these messages.

Setting Outlook Express to check for mail

Normally, when you launch Outlook Express, the program doesn't automatically tell you when you have new e-mail except when you click the Send/Recv button on the toolbar. However, if you want, you can have Outlook Express automatically inform you of new e-mail anytime you open the program.

If your computer is not connected to the Internet, Outlook Express dials out, connects, and retrieves your mail at this set interval.

To set this up, follow these steps:

1. Launch Outlook Express either by clicking the Launch Outlook Express button on the Windows Quick Launch toolbar or by choosing Start➪Outlook Express.

You need to launch Outlook Express in this manner because you can't change any of the program's settings from a New Message window.

2. **Choose Tools⇨Options from the Outlook Express menu bar.**

   The Options dialog box appears with the General tab selected.

3. **Select the Check for New Messages Every 30 Minute(s) check box. Then, in the associated text box, either replace 30 with the new number of minutes you desire or use the spinner buttons to select this interval value.**

   When you enable the Check for New Messages Every *xx* Minutes check box, Outlook Express automatically checks your mail server for new messages whenever you launch the program and then continues to check at the specified interval as you work in the program.

4. **(Optional) To have Outlook Express play a chime whenever new e-mail messages are downloaded while you're working in the program, select the Play Sound When New Messages Arrive check box.**

5. **Click Apply.**

6. **Click OK.**

   The Options dialog box closes, you return to Outlook Express, and the automatic e-mail checking goes into effect.

After the automatic e-mail checking goes into effect, Outlook Express informs you of the delivery of new e-mail by placing an envelope icon on the Outlook Express status bar (and "dinging" if you enable the Play Sound When New Messages Arrive check box).

This is very nice for those times when you're spending a great deal of time working in Outlook Express. However, don't expect to get this kind of indicator when browsing the Web with IE. The only way to know whether you have any new e-mail when working in this program is by clicking the Mail button on the IE toolbar and then choosing the Read Mail command.

Reading e-mail

When you use Outlook Express as your e-mail program, you read the messages that you receive in an area known as the Inbox. To open the Inbox in Outlook Express and read your e-mail messages from IE, follow these steps:

1. **Open Outlook Express by double-clicking the shortcut on the desktop or by choosing Start⇨Outlook Express.**

   Alternatively, with the IE window active, click the Mail button in the toolbar and then choose Read Mail from the drop-down list that appears.

   After you choose the Read Mail command, Outlook Express opens the Inbox — that is, as long as Outlook Express is configured as your e-mail program.

2. **Click the Send/Recv button on the Outlook Express toolbar to download any new messages.**

   As soon as you click the Send/Recv button, Outlook Express opens a connection to your mail server where it checks for any new messages to download for all e-mail accounts on the computer. New messages are then downloaded to your computer and placed in the Outlook Express Inbox.

Descriptions of any new messages appear in bold in the upper pane of the Inbox, which is divided into six columns: Priority (a red exclamation point); Attachments (a paper clip); Flag Status (a flag); From; Subject; and Received (showing both the date and time that the e-mail message was downloaded to your computer).

Note that mail messages you haven't yet read are indicated by bold type and also by a sealed envelope icon in the From column. Mail messages that you've read are indicated by an opened envelope icon.

3. **To read one of your new messages, click the message in the upper pane of the Inbox.**

   It doesn't matter whether your mouse pointer is located in the From, Subject, or Received column when you click the message.

   The message opens, and the text appears in the lower pane of the Inbox. The From and Subject information appears on the bar dividing the upper pane from the lower pane.

   If you want the message to open in its own window rather than in the lower pane of the Inbox, double-click the message.

4. **When you're finished reading your e-mail, click the Close box in the upper-right corner of the Outlook Express Inbox window.**

Replying to a message

Often, you want to reply to a message right away, especially if the e-mail message uses the High Priority (!) icon. Follow these steps:

1. **To reply to the author of a message, select the message and click the Reply button. To reply to the author and send copies of the reply to everyone copied on the original message, click the Reply All button instead.**

2. **In the message window, type the text of your reply above the text of the original message, and then send the reply by clicking the Send button.**

Forwarding a message

Sometimes, in addition to or instead of replying to the original message, you need to send a copy of it to someone who was not listed in the To or Cc (carbon copy) field. To do so, you *forward* a copy of the original message to new recipients of your choosing. When you forward a message, Outlook Express copies the Subject field and contents of the original message to a new message, which you then address and send.

To forward an e-mail message to another e-mail address, select the message and click the Forward button on the Outlook Express toolbar. Then fill in the recipient information in the To — and if applicable, Cc and Bcc — field(s). Add any additional text of your own above that of the original message, and then click the Send button to send the forwarded message on its way.

Composing E-Mail Messages

Outlook Express makes it easy to compose and send e-mail messages to anyone in the world who has an e-mail address.

Drafting a message

Follow these steps to create a new e-mail message:

1. **In Outlook Express, click the Create Mail button on the toolbar.**

   Alternatively, from the IE toolbar, click the Mail button and then choose New Message from the drop-down list that appears.

   Whichever method you choose, you see an Outlook Express New Message window.

2. **Type the recipient's e-mail address in the text box of the To field and then click OK.**

   If the recipient is already listed in your Address Book, click the word To to open the Select Recipients dialog box. Then in the Name list box, click the name of the recipient and click the To button. If you don't want to send the message to anyone else, click OK.

3. **(Optional) Click somewhere in the Cc field, type the e-mail addresses of everyone you want to add to the list — separated by semicolons (;) — and then click OK.**

   When composing a new message, you can send copies of it to as many other recipients (within reason) as you want. To send copies of the message to other recipients, type their e-mail addresses in the Cc field (if you don't care that they'll see all the other people copied on the message) or in the Bcc (blind carbon copy) field (if you don't want them to see any of the other people copied on the message). To access the Bcc field, click the To or Cc button and indicate Bcc in the Select Recipients dialog box.

4. **Click somewhere in the Subject field and type a brief description of the contents or purpose of the e-mail message.**

   When your message is delivered, the descriptive text that you entered in the Subject field appears in the Subject column of each recipient's Inbox.

5. **(Optional) To set the priority of the message, click the drop-down list next to the Priority button and choose High Priority, Normal Priority, or Low Priority.**

   In Outlook Express, you can change the priority of the e-mail message from normal to either high or low by using the Priority button. When you make a message either high or low priority, Outlook Express attaches a priority icon to the message that indicates its relative importance. (Keep in mind that whether the recipient sees this icon depends on the e-mail program that he or she uses.) The high-priority icon places an exclamation mark in front of the envelope; the low-priority icon adds a downward-pointing arrow.

6. **Click the cursor in the body of the message and type the text of the message as you would in any text editor or word processor, ending paragraphs and short lines by pressing Enter.**

   When composing the text of the message, keep in mind that you can insert text directly into the body of the message from other documents via the Clipboard (using the standard Cut, Copy, and Paste commands). Or, in the case of text or HTML documents, you can choose Insert⇨Text from File and select the name of the file in the Insert Text File dialog box.

7. **(Optional) To spell-check the message, click the cursor at the beginning of the message text and click the Spelling button.**

   When spell-checking the message, Outlook Express flags each word that it can't find in its dictionary and tries its best to suggest an alternative word.

   - **To replace the unknown word** in the text with the word suggested in the Change To text box of the Spelling window, click the Change button. If the suggested edit is a word that occurs frequently in the rest of the text, click Change All.

   - **To ignore the unknown word** and have the spell checker continue to scan the rest of the text for possible misspellings, click Ignore. If it's a word that occurs frequently in the rest of the text, click Ignore All.

8. **To send the e-mail message to the recipient(s), click the Send button on the Outlook Express toolbar.**

Attaching a file to an e-mail message

In Outlook Express, you can attach files to your e-mail messages to transmit information that you don't want to appear in the body of the message. For example, you might need to send an Excel worksheet to a client in another office.

To attach a file to an e-mail message in Outlook Express, follow these steps:

1. **In Outlook Express, click the Create Mail button.**

   Alternatively, from the IE toolbar, click the Mail button and then choose New Message from the drop-down list that appears.

   A New Message window appears in Outlook Express.

2. **Add the recipient(s) of the e-mail message in the To/Cc field(s), the subject of the message in the Subject field, and any message text explaining the attached files in the body of the message.**

3. **Click the Attach button on the message window's toolbar to open the Insert Attachment dialog box.**

4. **In the Look In drop-down list box, choose the folder that contains the file you want to attach. Click the filename in the main list box, and then click the Attach button.**

   Outlook Express adds an Attach field under the Subject field displaying the icon(s), filename(s), and size of the file(s) attached to the message.

5. Click the Send button on the Outlook Express toolbar to send the message to the recipient(s).

If you opened a New Message window from IE after sending your message, the Outlook Express window closes, and you return to the IE window.

Adding an image to your message

If you want to spice up your message even more, consider adding a graphic.

To insert a graphic that appears at the top of your message, choose Insert⇨ Picture. Use the Browse button in the Picture dialog box to select the graphics file that you want to use and then click OK. If the Insert⇨Picture command isn't available, you are sending messages in plain-text format, which doesn't permit graphics to be sent inside messages. To be able to send your graphic, choose Format⇨Rich Text (HTML).

Formatting Your Messages

Want to send your friends and colleagues a message they'll remember — or at least that they'll find attractive? Then consider experimenting with the Formatting toolbar. This toolbar, which separates the header section of the message from the body window, becomes active as soon as you click the cursor in the body of the message. You can then use its buttons to format the text of your message.

 If you don't see this toolbar when you click the message body area, someone has changed the Mail sending format from its default of HTML to Plain Text. (See the following section, "Rich Text (HTML) messages versus Plain Text messages," to see how to change it back.)

Rich Text (HTML) messages versus Plain Text messages

Outlook Express can use one of two file formats for the e-mail messages that you compose. The Rich Text (HTML) format can display all the formatting you see on Web pages on the Internet (including graphics). The Plain Text format can display only text characters (similar to a file opened in the Windows Notepad text editing utility).

When you first install Outlook Express, it uses the Rich Text (HTML) format for any new e-mail messages that you compose. This setting is fine as long as the e-mail program used by the recipient(s) of the message can deal with HTML formatting. (Many older e-mail programs, especially ones running under the Unix operating system, cannot.)

If you send a message using the Rich Text (HTML) format to someone whose e-mail program can't accept anything but plain text, the message comes to the recipient as plain text with an HTML document attached. That way, she can view all the HTML formatting bells and whistles that you added to the original e-mail message by opening the attached document in her Web browser.

To make Plain Text the new default format for Outlook Express, follow these steps:

1. **Launch Outlook Express.**

2. **Choose Tools⇨Options to open the Options dialog box.**

3. **Click the Send tab and then select the Plain Text Settings radio button in the Mail Sending Format area.**

If you don't want Outlook Express to put a greater-than symbol (>) in front of each line of the original message when forwarding it to another recipient, click the Plain Text Settings button to open the Plain Text Settings dialog box. Then deselect the Indent the Original Text With check box.

If you want to change the greater-than symbol (>) to a vertical bar (|) or colon (:), choose the new symbol from the drop-down list to the right.

4. **After making your changes, click OK or press Enter to close the Plain Text Settings dialog box.**

5. **Click OK to close the Options dialog box and put your new settings into effect.**

To change a message you're composing to Rich Text (HTML) format so you can add formatting or a picture to your message, choose Format⇨Rich Text (HTML) in the message window.

Adding bold, italics, underline, and color to your text

The Formatting toolbar in the Outlook Express New Message window makes it easy to add basic HTML formatting to your e-mail message. For example, you can highlight the text that you want to change and then click the Bold, Italics, and Underline buttons to change the way it looks.

In addition to doing basic formatting, you can make your message a little fancier by changing the color of the text. To do so, simply select the text by dragging through it with the mouse pointer and then click the Font Color button on the Formatting toolbar. On the color menu that appears, choose the color that you want the text to be.

Changing the font type and font size

If you really want to make your point, try changing your font type or enlarging its size. To do so, highlight the text you'd like to change, and then choose the type and size you'd like from the two drop-down lists on the left side of the Formatting toolbar.

Sending an E-Mail Message

When you're online (or are about to go online), you can send an e-mail message as soon as you finish writing (and, hopefully, spell-checking). Simply click the Send button in the New Message window (or press Ctrl+Enter or Alt+S) and away it goes, winging its way through cyberspace.

This method doesn't work at all, however, when you're composing an e-mail message while traveling on a plane or train where you might not be able to connect your modem.

For those times when you can't send the message right away, you need to choose File⇨Send Later on the New Message menu bar. When you choose this command, Outlook Express displays an alert box indicating that the message will be placed in your Outbox folder, ready to be sent the next time you choose the Send and Receive command. When you click OK, the e-mail message you just composed goes into your Outbox folder. The next time you connect to the Internet, you can send all the e-mail messages waiting in the Outbox to their recipients by clicking the Send/Recv button.

Printing a Message

Sometimes, you might need to get a hard copy of a message to share with other less fortunate people who don't have e-mail. To print the contents of an e-mail message, choose File⇨Print and then click OK in the Print dialog box. Now you have your hard copy!

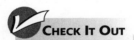

CHECK IT OUT

Arranging Your Outlook Express Desktop

Outlook Express, out of the box, does a pretty good job of hiding the more, uh, flamboyant optional parts of the program. To review and add or remove parts to the Outlook Express layout, choose View⇨Layout. You see the Window Layout Properties dialog box, which offers the following choices:

- **Contacts:** Choose this option to easily start a new, preaddressed message by double-clicking a contact in the Contacts list. If you have more than a few dozen contacts, this option is probably best left deselected.

- **Folders bar:** Deselect this option if you don't want the Folders bar taking up a lot of space.

- **Folder list:** With the Folder list on display, getting around in Outlook Express is easier.

- **Outlook bar:** This one isn't worth the space it occupies on-screen.

- **Status bar:** The strip along the bottom occasionally says something useful.

- **Toolbar:** This displays the icons at the top. You need this one.

- **Views bar:** This drop-down list is useful if you use custom views.

Make your changes in the Window Layout Properties dialog box and click OK.

Chapter 9: Organizing E-Mail Addresses and Messages

In This Chapter

✔ Organizing e-mail messages into folders

✔ Tracking friends, family, and co-workers in an address book

Getting e-mail is great, but it doesn't take long for you to end up with a disorganized mess. If you don't watch it, your Outlook Express Inbox can end up with hundreds of messages, some of which are still unread and all of which are lumped together in one extensive list. This chapter explains techniques for organizing e-mail.

One of the first things you'll want to do is add the names of all the people with whom you regularly correspond to your Outlook Express Address Book. That way, you'll avoid retyping e-mail addresses each time you want to send a message. Instead, you can simply type the name of your intended recipient. This chapter also explains how to keep an address book in Outlook Express.

Organizing Your Messages with Folders

Outlook Express offers a number of methods for organizing your mail, including a handy little feature known as the Inbox Assistant, which can automatically sort incoming mail according to rules that you set.

 Don't forget that the most basic way to organize your e-mail is to sort the messages in the Inbox. To sort all the messages in the Inbox (or any of the other Outlook Express folders, for that matter), click a column heading. For example, if you want to sort the e-mail in your Inbox by subject, click the Subject column heading at the top of the list. And if you want to sort the messages by the date and time received (from most recent to oldest), click the Received column heading at the top of that column.

 Clicking the Received column heading once sorts the messages in ascending or descending order, according to date. Click the column heading again, and the messages appear in the opposite order.

Creating a new folder

Creating a new folder is easy. Just right-click in the Folders list and choose New Folder from the shortcut menu that appears. Type a name for the folder in the Folder Name text box and click OK. Then click the Inbox icon before clicking the OK button. This will place your new folder as a subfolder under Inbox. You can also select other folders to make your new folder a subfolder.

Moving e-mail into a folder

Outlook Express makes easy work of arranging your e-mail messages in folders. To send a bunch of related e-mail messages into a new or existing folder, follow these steps:

1. **Open the Inbox in Outlook Express by clicking the Mail button in Internet Explorer (IE) and then choosing Read Mail from the drop-down list. If you already have Outlook Express running, click the Inbox icon in the Folders pane.**

2. **Select all the messages that you want to put in the same folder.**

   To select a single message, click it. To select a contiguous series of messages, click the first one and hold down the Shift key as you click the last one. To click multiple messages that aren't in a series, hold down Ctrl as you click the description of each one.

3. **After you finish selecting the messages to be moved, choose Edit⇨ Move to Folder from the Outlook Express menu bar.**

4. **Click the plus sign next to the Local Folders icon; then click the name of the subfolder into which you want to move the selected messages.**

5. **Click the OK button in the Move dialog box to move the messages into the selected folder.**

To verify that the items are in the correct folder, click the big Inbox button with the downward-pointing arrow on the bar at the top of the pane with the messages and then select the subfolder on the pop-up outline.

Organizing your e-mail with the Rule Editor

The Rule Editor can automate the organization of your e-mail by using rules that you create in its Rule Editor dialog box. A rule is simply a set of criteria that instruct Outlook Express to route e-mail from particular correspondents to particular folders that you've set up. This saves you the trouble of moving these messages into the folders on your own.

To create a new rule for systematizing your e-mail, follow these steps:

1. **Launch Outlook Express.**

2. **From the menu bar, choose Tools⇨Message Rules⇨Mail.**

3. **If you've previously set up mail rules in your copy of Outlook Express, the Message Rules dialog box opens on your screen; click the New button to open the New Mail Rule dialog box.**

   If this is the first time you've opened the Rule Editor to create a mail rule, the New Mail Rule dialog box opens automatically at this point.

4. **In section 1 of the New Mail Rule dialog box, select a check box or boxes for the condition(s) that must be met by the incoming e-mail.**

5. **In section 2, select a check box or boxes for the action(s) that you want to occur when a message meets the condition(s) you selected in section 1.**

6. **In section 3, click each underlined hyperlink until you have provided all the necessary information that the rule requires.**

The subsequent dialog boxes that open and the information that you are prompted for depend on the options you select in the New Mail Rule dialog box.

As an example, assume that you select Where the From Line Contains People in section 1 and Copy It to the Specified Folder in section 2. In section 3, you click the underlined hyperlink in the Where the From Line Contains People option to open the Select People dialog box. Here, you specify the sender for whom you are establishing the rule. After you type the sender's name, you click the Add button and then click OK. The Select People dialog box closes, and you return to the New Mail Rule dialog box. At this point, you click the hyperlink in the Copy It to the Specified Folder option in section 3, which opens the Copy dialog box. After choosing a folder or clicking the New Folder button to create a new folder, you click OK to exit the Copy dialog box. You return to the New Mail Rule dialog box.

7. **(Optional) Type a descriptive name in the Name of the Rule text box (to replace the generic name) and then click OK.**

The New Mail Rule dialog box closes, and you return to the Message Rules dialog box.

8. **Click the Apply Now button to open the Apply Mail Rules Now dialog box where you choose the folder (most often the Inbox) to which the new rule should be applied.**

9. **Click Close to exit the Apply Rules Now dialog box; then click OK to close the Message Rules dialog box.**

You can set up multiple rules to apply to e-mail messages in the Inbox folder. Just be aware that Outlook Express applies the rules in the order in which they appear on the Mail Rules tab in the Message Rules dialog box. You can use the Move Up and Move Down buttons to rearrange their order.

Deleting and compacting your e-mail

As you get more and more e-mail in your Inbox, you might want to use the File⇨Folder⇨Compact command to compress the messages, thus freeing up valuable disk space. When you have e-mail in all sorts of different folders, you can compact all the messages by choosing File⇨Folder⇨Compact All Folders instead.

To remove messages from the Inbox without permanently deleting them, select the messages and then press the Delete key. The messages instantly disappear from the Inbox window. However, if you ever need any of these messages again, you can display them by clicking the Deleted Items icon in the pane on the left side of the Outlook Express window.

When you have messages (especially those from blocked senders) that you no longer need to store on your computer's hard drive, you can remove them from the Deleted Items folder permanently by selecting them and choosing Edit⇨Delete. Click Yes in the alert dialog box that tells you that you are about to delete the selected messages forever. (Alternatively, you can simply press the Delete key.)

Normally, Outlook Express deletes all messages from your mail server as soon as they are downloaded to your computer. To keep the original messages on the mail server — giving you not only a backup but also the means to retrieve the mail from somebody else's computer — follow these steps:

1. **Launch Outlook Express.**

2. **Choose Tools⇨Accounts; then click the "friendly" name for your mail account and click the Properties button.**

3. **Click the Advanced tab; then, in the Delivery section, select the Leave a Copy of Messages on Server check box.**

   The next time you download messages, these copies will be downloaded to your computer again. Their filenames will be appended with a number to differentiate them from the original copy if it still exists in the same folder.

4. **(Optional) To have the mail left for a set period of time, select the Remove from Server After *xx* Day(s) check box and enter the number of days in the associated text box or use the spinner buttons to select this time period.**

5. **(Optional) To have the mail deleted from the server when you permanently (Ctrl+D) delete them, select the Remove from Server When Deleted from the Deleted Items check box.**

6. **Click OK to close the Properties dialog box; then click Close to make the Internet Accounts dialog box go away.**

Deleting and renaming folders

If you decide that a folder is no longer useful in your organization scheme, deleting the folder is no problem. Simply highlight the folder, press the Delete key, and the folder is gone.

Or you might opt to rename the folder, using a more useful moniker. Click the folder to highlight it, wait a second, and then click again. A rectangular box appears around the folder. Position your cursor inside the box and type your folder's new and improved name.

Adding Entries to Your Address Book

Good news! If you're switching from some other e-mail program (like the one that comes with Netscape Navigator) and you've already created an address book, you can import all those addresses into the Address Book in Outlook Express. No retyping is required; all you have to do is follow the steps in "Importing addresses from somewhere else," later in this chapter.

Creating a new address

You'll want to add all your frequent e-mailees to your Address Book. To add a new recipient, follow these steps:

1. **Open Outlook Express and choose Tools⇨Address Book or click the Addresses button to open the Address Book.**

Alternatively, you can choose File⇨New⇨Contact from the IE menu bar.

2. **Click the New Contact button.**

The Properties dialog box appears, as shown in Figure 9-1.

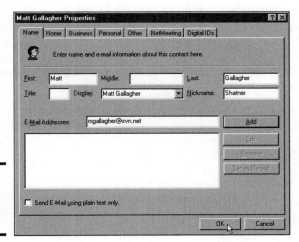

Figure 9-1:
The
Properties
dialog box.

3. **Fill out the name section with information about the new contact. In the E-Mail Addresses text box, type the recipient's e-mail address and then click Add.**

When you click Add, Outlook Express adds the address to the list box and designates it as the default e-mail address for the individual you named.

If the person you're adding to the Address Book has more than one e-mail address (for example, an e-mail account with one address at home and an e-mail account with another address at work), you can add the additional e-mail address by repeating this step.

4. **(Optional) Repeat Step 3 to add an additional e-mail address for the same recipient.**

If you want to make the second e-mail address the default one (that is, the one that Outlook Express automatically uses when you compose a new message to this person), you need to select it in the list box and then click the Set As Default button.

5. **(Optional) If you want, click the other tabs to add more information about your contact.**

The Home tab enables you to add your contact's street address and phone number(s). The Business tab allows you to add information about your contact's work. The Personal tab lets you add your contact's birthday as well as his spouse's and children's names (if applicable).

6. **Click OK to close the Properties dialog box and return to the Address Book.**

Your new contact's display name appears in the Address Book, followed by the default e-mail address.

7. **Click the Close button to close the Address Book.**

Importing addresses from somewhere else

To import into the Address Book addresses from an address book created with Eudora; Microsoft Exchange; Microsoft Internet Mail for Windows; or Netscape Navigator; or stored in a comma-separated text file, follow these steps:

1. **Choose File⇨Import⇨Other Address Book from the Address Book menu bar.**

The Address Book Import Tool dialog box appears, as shown in Figure 9-2.

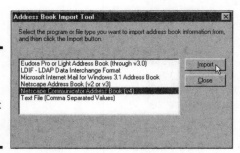

Figure 9-2:
The
Address
Book Import
Tool dialog
box.

2. **Click the type of address book that you want to import in the list box of the Address Book Import Tool dialog box, and then click the Import button.**

Outlook Express imports the names and e-mail addresses of all the contacts in the existing address book if it can locate your address book. If it can't find your address book, you see a dialog box in which to tell Outlook Express where the address book is located.

3. **Click Close after all the information is imported.**

The Address Book Import Tool dialog box closes, and you return to the Address Book dialog box, where the imported contacts now appear.

4. **(Optional) To sort the contacts in the Address Book by their last names, click the Name column heading above the first entry. To sort the contacts by their e-mail addresses, click the E-Mail Address column heading.**

5. **Click OK to close the Address Book.**

 CHECK IT OUT

Reducing Clutter in Your Contacts List

Outlook Express can be overly paternalistic. Case in point: Whenever you send a message to someone, even if it's a reply to a message that was sent to you, the person whom you send the message to is automatically added to your Contacts list. More than that, if you add someone to your Windows Messenger Contacts list and you open Outlook Express with Windows Messenger running, Outlook Express scarfs up the name and puts it in the Contacts list, too.

Follow these steps to keep Outlook Express from adding names to your Contacts list automatically:

1. **Choose Tools➪Options.**

   Outlook Express shows you the Options dialog box.

2. **On the Send tab, deselect the Automatically Put People I Reply to in My Address Book check box.**

3. **Click OK.**

   You probably want to go through your Address Book and get rid of the duplicates. Choose Tools➪Address Book, and be braced for some hard work.

Any time you want to add someone who has sent you a message to your Contacts list, simply right-click the person's name at the top of the message (or in any list of messages, such as the Inbox or the Deleted Items list) and choose Add Sender to Address Book.

Chapter 10: Mailing Lists

In This Chapter

✔ Getting on and off a mailing list

✔ Sending messages to a mailing list

✔ Receiving mailing-list messages

✔ Using filters

✔ Starting your own mailing list

An e-mail *mailing list* offers a way for people with a shared interest to send messages to each other and hold a group conversation. Mailing lists differ from newsgroups in that a separate copy of the mailing list message is e-mailed to each recipient on the list. Mailing lists are generally smaller and more intimate than newsgroups. Comparatively, mailing lists can be very specific, tend to be less raucous, and are less infested with spam.

Imagine a mailing list that would keep you up-to-date in an area vital to your work or one that would let you exchange views with people who share your fondest passions. That list probably already exists. This chapter gives you hints on how to find it and how to start it if it doesn't exist.

Addresses Used with Mailing Lists

Each mailing list has its own e-mail address; on most lists, anything sent to that address is remailed to all the people on the list. People on the list respond to messages and create a running conversation. Some lists are *moderated,* which means that a reviewer (moderator) skims messages and decides which to send out.

Every mailing list, in fact, has *two* e-mail addresses:

✦ **List address:** Messages sent to this address are forwarded to all the people who subscribe to the list.

✦ **Administrative address:** Only the list's owner reads messages sent to this address. Use it for messages about subscribing and unsubscribing. Messages to the administrative address often are processed entirely by a computer, called a *mailing list server, list server,* or *MLM* (mailing list manager). In that case, you have to type your message in a specific format, as described throughout this chapter. ***Note:*** This address might also be called the *request address.*

For matters such as subscribing to or unsubscribing to a list, always send e-mail to the administrative address, not to the list address. If you use the list address, everyone on the list sees your request *except* for the person or computer that needs to act on it. Proper use of the administrative address is the most important thing you need to know about using mailing lists.

You can usually figure out the administrative address if you know the list address:

✦ **Manually maintained lists:** Add *-request* to the list address. If a manual list is named `unicycles@blivet.com`, for example, the administrative address is almost certainly `unicycles-request@blivet.com`.

✦ **Automatically maintained lists:** The administrative address is usually the name of the type of list server program at the host where the list is maintained. Look for the server name in a message header to determine how a list is maintained. The most common list server programs are ListProc, LISTSERV, Mailbase, Mailserve, Lyris, and Majordomo.

✦ **Web-based lists:** A number of companies run Web sites that host mailing lists for free in exchange for placing an ad at the end of each message. These firms accept administrative requests at their Web site, and some allow you to read list messages and archives there, too. Popular Web-based list servers include

- `www.coollist.com`
- `groups.yahoo.com`
- `www.topica.com`

Some mailing list servers don't care whether your administrative request is in uppercase or lowercase, but others might care. In this chapter, I show all commands in uppercase, which generally works with all servers.

Subscribing and Unsubscribing

How you subscribe and unsubscribe depends on how the list is maintained. Subscribing to a mailing list (unlike subscribing to a magazine) is almost always free.

Lists maintained manually

Send a mail message (such as *Please add me to the unicycles list* or *Please remove me from the unicycles list*) to the administrative address. Keep these tips in mind:

✦ Include your real name and complete e-mail address so that the poor list owner doesn't have to pick through your e-mail header.

✦ Because humans read the messages, no fixed form is required.

✦ Be patient. The person maintaining the list is probably a volunteer and might have a life — or might be trying to get one.

Lists maintained automatically

To join a list, send an e-mail message to its administrative address with no subject and the following line as the body of the message:

```
SUBSCRIBE listname your-name
```

Replace *listname* with the name of the mailing list, and *your-name* with your actual name. You don't have to include your e-mail address because it's automatically included as your message's return address. For example, George W. Bush would type the following line to subscribe to the leader_support mailing list:

SUBSCRIBE leader_support George W. Bush

✦ For Mailbase lists, replace SUBSCRIBE with JOIN.

✦ For Majordomo lists, don't include your name.

To get off a list, send an e-mail to its administrative address with no subject and the following line as the body of the message:

UNSUBSCRIBE *listname*

✦ The command SIGNOFF works with most mailing lists, too.

✦ For Mailbase lists, replace UNSUBSCRIBE with LEAVE.

When you're subscribing to a list, be sure to send your message from the e-mail address to which you want list messages mailed. The administrator of the list uses your message's return address as the address she adds to the mailing list.

When you first subscribe to a list, you generally receive a welcome message via e-mail. Keep this message! You might want to keep a file of these messages because they tell you what type of server is being used and how to unsubscribe.

Many list servers e-mail you back for confirmation before processing your request. If you plan to unsubscribe from a bunch of lists before going on vacation — a good idea to keep your mailbox from overflowing — be sure to allow enough time to receive and return the confirmation requests.

Web-based lists

You usually join or leave Web-based lists by going to the list company's Web site, although you can often use e-mail, too. Most services ask you to append -subscribe or -unsubscribe to the list name. For example, send an e-mail to gerbils-subscribe@onelist.com to join the Gerbils list at ONElist.

Sending Messages to a Mailing List

To send a message to a mailing list, just e-mail it to the list's address. The message is automatically distributed to the list's members.

If you respond to a message with your mail program's Reply button, check to see — before you click Send — whether your reply will be sent to the list address. Edit out the list address if you're replying only to the message's author.

Some lists are *moderated* — that is, a human being screens messages before sending them out to everybody else, which can delay messages by as much as a day or two. Mail servers usually send you copies of your own messages to confirm that they were received.

Special Requests to Mailing Lists

Depending on which list server manages a list, various other commands might be available. Read on to find out more about these commands.

Archives

Many mailing lists store their messages for later reference. To find out where these archives are kept, send the following message to the administrative address:

`INDEX listname`

Some lists make their archives available on a Web site. Read the message that you received when you joined the list.

Subscriber list

To get a list of (almost) all the people who subscribe to a list, you can send a message to the administrative address. The content of the message depends on the type of server the list uses. See Table 10-1.

Table 10-1	Getting a List of Subscribers
Server	*Message*
ListProc	RECIPIENTS *listname*
LISTSERV	REVIEW *listname*
Mailbase	REVIEW *listname*
Mailserve	SEND/LIST *listname*
Majordomo	WHO *listname*

Privacy

ListProc and LISTSERV mail servers don't give out your name as just described if you send a message to the administrative address. To find out how to hide your name or show it again, see Table 10-2.

Table 10-2	Setting Your Privacy Preference	
Action	*Server*	*Message*
Conceal your name	ListProc	SET *listname* CONCEAL YES
	LISTSERV	SET *listname* CONCEAL
Unconceal your name	ListProc	SET *listname* CONCEAL NO
	LISTSERV	SET *listname* NOCONCEAL

Going on vacation

If you subscribe to a busy mailing list, you probably don't want mailing list messages to flood your inbox while you're on vacation. To stop messages from a list temporarily and continue receiving messages when you get back, see Table 10-3.

Table 10-3	Managing Messages During Your Vacation	
Action	*Server*	*Message*
Stop messages temporarily	ListProc	SET *listname* MAIL POSTPONE
	LISTSERV	SET *listname* NOMAIL
Resume receiving messages	ListProc	SET *listname* MAIL ACK or
		SET *listname* MAIL NOACK or
		SET *listname* MAIL DIGEST
	LISTSERV	SET *listname* MAIL

Open and Closed Mailing Lists

Most mailing lists are *open,* which means that anyone can send a message to the list. Some lists, however, are closed and accept messages only from subscribers. Other lists accept members by invitation only.

If you belong to a closed list and your e-mail address changes, you must let the list managers know so that they can update their database.

Receiving Digested Mailing Lists

As soon as you join a list, you automatically receive all messages from the list along with the rest of your mail.

Some lists are available in digest form with all the day's messages combined in a table of contents. To get the digest form, send an e-mail message to the list's administrative address with no subject and one of the lines shown in Table 10-4 as the body of the message. Table 10-4 also shows how to undo the digest request.

Table 10-4	Digest Requests	
Action	*Server*	*Message*
Receive digest form	ListProc	SET *listname* MAIL DIGEST
	LISTSERV	SET *listname* DIGEST
	Majordomo	SUBSCRIBE *listname*-digest,
		UNSUBSCRIBE *listname*
Undo digest request	ListProc	SET *listname* MAIL ACK
	LISTSERV	SET *listname* MAIL
	Majordomo	UNSUBSCRIBE *listname*-digest,
		SUBSCRIBE *listname*

Using Filters

Joining even one mailing list can overwhelm your e-mail inbox. Some e-mail programs can sort through your incoming mail and put mailing list messages in special mailboxes or folders that you can look at when you have time.

If you use Eudora, choose Tools⇨Filters, click New, select the Incoming check box, and then copy the From line from the mailing list message and paste it into the first `contains` box. (You also can use the second `contains` box if you want to specify another condition.) Then, in the Action section, specify the mailbox to which you want the messages transferred.

If you use Outlook Express, you can use the Rule Editor to organize your incoming e-mail messages. See the previous chapter for more information on setting up e-mail rules.

Starting Your Own Mailing List

Maybe you've decided that you've got some extra time on your hands (don't you wish!), and you need a new hobby. Or maybe you want to promote your rock band, create a support group for parents, or share your expertise on a topic. Whatever the reason, starting a mailing list might be just what you need.

Here are some tips for starting a new mailing list:

✦ You can start a simple manual list with nothing more than an e-mail program that supports distribution lists (such as Outlook Express, Netscape Messenger, or Eudora). When a message comes in, just forward it to the distribution list.

✦ Put manual distribution lists in the Bcc address field if you don't want every message to include all recipients' names in the header. You can put your own address in the To field, if you want.

✦ You will soon tire of administering your list manually. Some Internet service providers let you use their list server, or you can use one of the ad-supported, Web-based services. (`www.coollist.com`, `groups.yahoo.com`, and `www.topica.com` are all popular.) If someone in your group has a university affiliation, that person might be able to have the list maintained there for free.

✦ Creating a Web page for your list makes it easy to find by using the Internet's search engines.

Chapter 11: Chatting Online

In This Chapter
✔ **Chatting online**
✔ **Using Internet Relay Chat (IRC)**

The Internet lets you communicate with people in a more immediate way than sending electronic mail and waiting hours or days for a reply. You can type something, press Enter, and get a reply within seconds — a process called *chatting*. Chatting is generally done in groups that typically include people whom you don't know. This chapter dishes the dirt on chatting.

Chatting Online

Online chat lets you communicate with people live, just as you would on the telephone, except that you type what you want to say and read the other person's reply on your computer screen. Here are some things that you need to know about chat:

✦ In chat, a window shows the ongoing conversation. You type in a separate box what you want to send to the individual or group. When you press Enter or click the Send button, your message appears in the conversation window, along with any responses.

✦ Chat differs from e-mail in that you don't have to address each message and wait for a reply. Although sometimes a small lag occurs in chatting, communication is nearly instantaneous — even across the globe.

✦ You're usually limited to a sentence or two in each exchange. Instant messages, described in the next chapter, allow longer expressions.

✦ You can select a group or an individual to chat with, or someone can ask to initiate a private chat with you. Many chat venues exist on the Net, including IRC, AOL chat rooms (for AOL users only), Web-based chat, and instant messaging systems like ICQ and AIM (AOL Instant Messenger).

✦ Because tens of thousands of people are chatting at any instant of the day or night, the discussions are divided into groups. Different terms exist for chat groups. AOL and ICQ call them *rooms*. IRC calls them *channels*.

✦ The chat facilities of the value-added service providers are accessible to only that service's members.

✦ People in chat groups can be unruly and even vicious. The online service providers' chat groups usually are tamer because the service provides some supervision.

✦ You can select a special name — called a *screen name, handle,* or *nickname* — to use when you're chatting. This name can and often does differ from your login name or e-mail address.

Although your special chat name gives you some privacy online, someone could possibly find out your real identity, particularly if your online service or Internet service provider (ISP) cooperates. Don't go wild out there.

Following group conversations

Get used to following a group conversation if you want to make any sense of chats. Here's a sample of what you might see. (Screen names and identifying content have been changed.)

```
BrtG221: hey Zeb!
Zebra795: Hello
ABE904: Where is everyone from...I am from Virginia
Zebra795: Hi Brt!
HAPY F: how should I know
Zebra795: Hi ABE
HAPY F: <-Virginia
ABE904: Hi Zebra!!!
BrtG221: so StC... what
Zebra795: <-was from Virginia!
ABE904: Hi HAPY ! Didn't see ya
BrtG221: is going on in FL?
HAPY F: HI ABE
Zebra795: Hap's been on all night!
Storm17: Brt...what?...i miss our heart to hearts
HAPY F: on and off
ABE904: Zeb, and wish you were back here!
DDouble6190: im 26 but i like older women
Zebra795: I was over July Fourth!!
Janet5301: Sorry...DD...call me in 10 yrs...
BrtG221: really DD?... where do you live?
BrtG221: lol.. so talk to me Storm..
ABE904: Gee, you didn't call, didn't write...
```

Here are a few tips for getting started:

✦ When you enter a chat group, a conversation is usually already in progress. You can't see what went on before you entered.

✦ Wait a minute or two for a page full of exchanges to appear on-screen so that you can understand some of the context before you start reading. Then determine with whom you want to converse and whom you want to ignore.

✦ Start by following the comments from a single screen name. Then follow the people whom that person mentions or who reply to that person. Ignore everything else because the other messages are probably replies to messages that went by before you came in.

✦ A few regulars often dominate the conversation.

✦ The real action often takes place in private, one-on-one side discussions, which you can't see.

Safe chatting guidelines

Here are some guidelines for conducting safe and healthy chats:

✦ Many people in chat groups are totally dishonest about who they are. They lie about their occupation, age, locality, and, yes, even gender. Some think that they're being cute, and others are exploring their own fantasies; a few are really sick.

✦ Be careful about giving out information that enables someone to find you, including phone numbers, mailing address, the schools that your kids attend, and the place where you work.

✦ Pick a screen name or handle that's different from your login name; otherwise, you will receive a great deal of unwanted junk e-mail.

✦ Never give out your password to anyone, even if she says that she works for your service provider, the phone company, the FBI, the CIA, or Dummies Press. Never!

✦ If your chat service offers profiles and a person without a profile wants to chat with you, be extra cautious.

✦ If your children use chat, realize that others might try to meet them. Before your kids log on, spend some quality time talking to them about the guidelines. Make sure your kids understand that all is not what it appears to be on the Internet and the kid they are chatting with may really be an adult.

Internet Relay Chat (IRC)

Internet Relay Chat (IRC) is the Internet's own chat service. IRC is available from most ISPs. You can even participate in IRC through most online services although IRC is completely separate from the service's own chat services. You need an *IRC client program* (or just *IRC program*), which is simply another Internet program, like your Web browser or e-mail software. Freeware and shareware IRC programs are available for you to download from the Net. Most Unix systems come with an IRC program. Two of the best shareware IRC programs are mIRC (for Windows) and Ircle (for Macintosh).

You can download updated versions of these programs and get detailed information about installing them from IRChelp.org (www.irchelp.org). They're also available from Tucows (www.tucows.com). Windows XP comes with Windows Messenger. You can download it from www.microsoft.com/downloads.

You use IRC in two main ways:

✦ **Channel:** This is like an ongoing conference call with a bunch of people. After you join a channel, you can read what people are saying on-screen and then add your own comments just by typing them and pressing Enter.

✦ **Direct connection:** This is like a private conversation.

Starting IRC

To start IRC, follow these steps:

1. **Connect to the Internet and run your IRC program.**

   If you're on a value-added service, such as AOL, follow its instructions for connecting to the Internet.

2. **Connect to an IRC server.**

   See the following section, "Picking a server," to find out how to connect.

3. **Join a channel.**

   You're ready to chat! See "IRC channels," later in this chapter, for more about channels.

Picking a server

To use IRC, you connect your IRC program to an *IRC server,* which is an Internet host computer that serves as a switchboard for IRC conversations. Although dozens of IRC servers are available, many are full most of the time and might refuse your connection. You might have to try several servers — or the same one dozens of times — before you can connect. When you're choosing a server, pick one that's geographically close to you to minimize response lag.

To connect to an IRC server in mIRC, choose File⇨Options or press Alt+O to display the mIRC Options window; then click the IRC Servers arrow for the drop-down list. Double-click a server on the list to attempt to connect to it. If you choose All as your IRC Servers, one will be selected randomly.

Issuing IRC commands

You control what is happening during your chat session by typing IRC commands. All IRC commands start with the slash character (/). You can type IRC commands in uppercase or lowercase or a mixture — IRC doesn't care. The most important command for you to know gets you out of IRC:

```
/QUIT
```

The second most important command gives you an online summary of the various IRC commands:

```
/HELP
```

Table 11-1 provides some of the most useful IRC commands.

Table 11-1	**Useful IRC Commands**
Command	*What It Does*
/ADMIN server	Displays information about a server.
/AWAY	Enables you to tell IRC that you will be away for a while. You don't need to leave this type of message; if you do, however, it's displayed to anyone who wants to talk to you.

Command	What It Does
/CLEAR	Clears your screen.
/JOIN *channel*	Joins the *channel* you specify.
/LIST	Lists all available channels.
/NICK *thenameyouwant*	Enables you to specify your chat nickname.
/PART	Leaves the current channel.
/QUERY *nickname*	Starts a private conversation with *nickname*.
/TIME	Displays the date and time in case you can't take your eyes off the screen for even a moment.
/TOPIC *subject*	Changes the topic for the current channel.
/WHO *channel*	Lists all the people on the *channel*. If you type **/WHO ***, you see displayed the names of the people on the channel you're on.

If you use mIRC or Ircle, you can achieve most of the same effects that are controlled by IRC commands by choosing options from the menu bar or clicking icons on the toolbar. These IRC commands work too, however, and some IRC programs don't have menu bar or toolbar equivalents.

IRC channels

The most popular way to use IRC is through *channels*. Most channels have names that start with the # character. Channel names aren't case-sensitive. Numbered channels also exist. (When you type a channel number, don't use the # character.)

Thousands of IRC channels are available. You can find an annotated list of some of the best by visiting www.funet.fi/~irc/channels.html. Each channel listed there has its own linked home page that tells much more about what that channel offers.

Types of channels

Three types of channels are available in IRC:

+ **Public:** Everyone can see them, and everyone can join.
+ **Private:** Everyone can see them, but you can join only by invitation.
+ **Secret:** They do not show up in the /LIST command, and you can join them only by invitation.

If you're on a private or secret channel, you can invite someone else to join by typing

/INVITE *nickname*

If you get an invitation from someone on a private or secret channel and want to join, just type

/JOIN -INVITE

Some people like to write computer programs that sit on IRC channels and make comments from time to time. These programs are called *bots,* short for *robots.* Some people think that bots are cute; if you don't, just ignore them.

Starting your own channel

Each channel has its own channel operator *(chanop)* who can control (to some extent) what happens on that channel. You can start your own channel and become its chanop by typing

`/JOIN #unusedchannelname`

As with nicknames, whoever asks for a channel name first gets it. You can keep the name for as long as you're logged on as the chanop. You can let other people be chanops for your channel; just make sure that they're people you can trust. A channel exists as long as anyone is in it; when the last person leaves, the channel winks out of existence.

Filing a complaint

Compared with AOL and CompuServe, IRC is a lawless frontier. Few rules, if any, exist. If things get really bad, you can try to find out the offender's e-mail address by using the `/whois` command — `/whois badmother@iecc.com`, for example. You can then send an e-mail complaint to the postmaster at the same host name — `postmaster@iecc.com`, in this case. Don't expect much help, however.

Getting more info

You can discover much more about IRC from these sources:

✦ **The official IRC home page:** `irchelp.org` (where IRC was invented)

✦ **The NewIRCusers.com page:** `www.newircusers.com`

✦ **The Usenet newsgroup:** `alt.irc`

Chapter 12: Instant Messaging

In This Chapter

✓ **Instant messaging with AOL Instant Messenger**

✓ **Using MSN Messenger to send and receive instant messages**

*I*f you have teenage children, you probably already know what instant messaging is. Instant messaging is something between chatting online and exchanging e-mail messages. What makes instant messaging so popular with teenagers and others is being able to know which of your friends are online at the same time as you and being able to communicate with all of them at once. Instant messaging gives you the opportunity to have an instant online party — or in a business setting, an instant online meeting.

Instant messaging programs all have a version of the *buddy list,* which is a box that shows which of your friends are online. As soon as the name of someone with whom you want to gossip appears on the list, well, the dirt gets dished, and the party starts flowing. This chapter looks at two of the three most popular instant messaging programs: AOL Instant Messenger and MSN Messenger. The other popular messaging service, Yahoo! Messenger, is discussed in Book III, Chapter 7.

AOL Instant Messenger

If you're one of the 11 million or so AOL subscribers, you probably already know what Instant Messenger is. If you aren't an AOL subscriber, suffice it to say that it's a tool you'll be addicted to in five minutes flat. AOL Instant Messenger (often called *AIM*) has some really neat features. It can tell you when your chat buddies sign on, even before they send you an online "Hello." If your chat buddies sign off, you know that, too. This software is a breeze to use. What's more, it's free to everybody, even people who don't subscribe to America Online.

Becoming a registered user

Before you can chat with someone using Instant Messenger, you have to install the Instant Messenger software and register yourself as a user with a name nobody else has used. To do that, go to the AOL Instant Messenger Web site at this address: www.aim.com. There, click the Download button and complete the form to register yourself.

To log on to Instant Messenger after you've registered, start by

✦ Clicking the AOL Instant Messenger desktop icon, clicking the Start button, and choosing AOL Instant Messenger

or

✦ Clicking the yellow man icon in the notification area (beside the clock in the lower-right corner of the computer screen)

A logon box appears. Replace <New User> in the Name text box with the online name you registered with, enter your password, and click the Sign In button. You see your Buddy List, which looks something like the one in Figure 12-1.

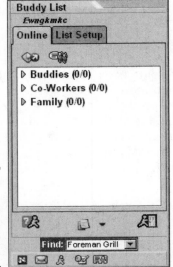

Figure 12-1:
The Buddy List appears after you've successfully signed on.

To avoid having to type the password each time you sign on in the future, you can select the Save Password check box. If you want to automatically log in to Instant Messenger each time you sign on to the Internet, select the Auto-Login check box.

Engaging in a chat session

To initiate a session, either double-click a person's name on your Buddy List or click the Send Instant Message button. In the Instant Message window, type the screen name of the person with whom you want to chat.

If the person you want to chat with is signed on to Instant Messenger, he instantly sees your message on-screen. Your Instant Message window splits into two windows. Type your message in the bottom window and click Send.

To end a chat session, click the Close (X) button in the upper-right corner of the Instant Message window or press Esc.

You can tell which of your buddies is currently signed on by glancing at the Buddy List in your Buddy List window. Click the Online tab in the Buddy List window. The screen names of all those who are currently logged on are displayed there.

Adding and deleting buddies on your Buddy List

The Buddy List within Instant Messenger is like a phone book listing your buddies' screen names, and you can add buddies to the list. To add a buddy to your Buddy List, follow these steps:

1. **Click the Setup button on the Buddy List window.**

2. **Click a folder to select it as the folder to which you want to add your new buddy.**

3. **Click the Add a Buddy button.**

   This creates a *New Buddy* entry within that folder.

4. **Type the Instant Messenger screen name of your buddy and press Enter.**

To delete a buddy from your list, select the name you want to delete, and click the Delete icon.

MSN Messenger

To trade instant messages with MSN Messenger, you need two things: Windows XP and a .NET passport. You need Windows XP because it comes with MSN Messenger software. You need a .NET passport to identify yourself to the Microsoft Network when you go online to instant message. You can obtain the passport at this Web address: `http://register.passport.com`. To obtain it, you provide information about yourself and select a password. Instant messaging with MSN Messenger is free.

Logging on to MSN Messenger

To start MSN Messenger, double-click the MSN Messenger icon in the lower-right corner of the window (near the clock). You see the MSN Messenger dialog box. Click the Sign In button, enter your e-mail address, enter your password, and click OK. You see the MSN Messenger window shown on the left side of Figure 12-2.

Engaging in a chat session

The names of people on your buddy list who are currently signed on to MSN Messenger appear in boldface. To trade messages with one of these people, double-click his or her name. The Conversation window shown on the right side of Figure 12-2 opens. Enter a message and click the Send button.

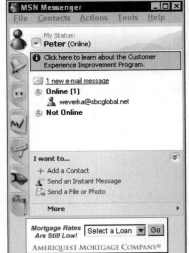 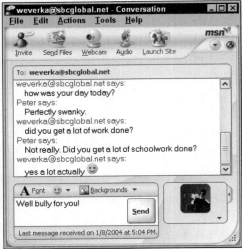

Figure 12-2: The Messenger window (left) and the Conversation window (right).

To defend your privacy and prevent others from knowing when you are connected to MSN Messenger, choose File➪My Status➪Appear Offline. Even if your name is on someone's buddy list, it won't appear there, and your erstwhile friend or bothersome co-worker won't know you are connected.

Adding and deleting buddies

To add a buddy to your list, click the Add a Contact button. In the wizard dialog boxes that appear, either select a name from your MSN Messenger dialog box or enter an e-mail address.

CHECK IT OUT

Disabling MSN Messenger Automatic Sign-In

When you start Outlook Express, it automatically kicks in MSN Messenger (assuming MSN Messenger wasn't running already and you have MSN Messenger). Outlook Express does that so it can show you the status of your Messenger contacts. Of course, as soon as Messenger kicks in, everybody who has you on his or her Messenger Contacts list sees that you've signed in. Many people feel that's an intrusive, time-sapping side effect of starting Outlook Express. If you agree, it's easy to turn off:

1. **In Outlook Express, choose Tools➪ Options to open the Options dialog box.**

2. **On the General tab, deselect the Automatically Log on to Windows Messenger check box.**

    Messenger calls it *sign in,* not *log on,* but what's a little inconsistency among friends?

3. **Click OK.**

    The next time you start Outlook Express, it will not attempt to start MSN Messenger.

Chapter 13: Keeping Up-to-Date with News

In This Chapter

✔ **Getting started with newsgroups**

✔ **Posting articles to newsgroups**

✔ **Reading newsgroups with Google**

✔ **Participating in newsgroups with Outlook Express**

The Internet is chock full of information — you just have to know how to access it. One way that you can delve into some of the most current issues is through newsgroups.

A *newsgroup* is a place on the Internet where people gather to discuss a topic of common interest. A newsgroup resembles an electronic bulletin board on which people post questions or comments, and others respond to these questions and comments. Others then respond to the responses and so on, until a string — or *thread* — of discussion about a topic emerges. At any given time, multiple discussions can be in progress in a particular newsgroup.

Usenet, also known as *network news,* is the worldwide, distributed group-discussion system that feeds information to newsgroups. Internet users around the world submit Usenet messages to tens of thousands of news-groups with names such as `rec.gardens.orchids` or `sci.space`. Within a day or so, these messages are delivered to nearly every other Internet host that wants them for anyone to read.

Newsgroup Basics

Reading Usenet is like trying to take a sip of water from a fire hose. Usenet had more than 55,000 different newsgroups the last time I looked. Here are some tips for maintaining your sanity:

✦ Pick a few groups that really interest you, or use an indexing service, such as Google. (See "Reading Newsgroups with Google," later in this chapter.)

✦ Develop a tolerance for the numerous junk-mail messages that infest many groups.

✦ If you feel that you absolutely have to reply to a comment, save the message and sleep on it. If it still seems urgent in the morning, see "Posting articles to newsgroups," later in this chapter.

✦ Don't get into a flame war; however, if ever you do, let the other guy have the last word. What is a flame war? It's when people on the Internet, operating under the cloak of anonymity, insult each other in a vicious manner. Funny how pseudonyms and facelessness bring out the worst in people.

✦ Don't believe everything you read on Usenet.

To read newsgroup postings, you use a *newsreader* program, or you can use your browser to read newsgroup postings on the Google Web site. To configure your newsreader program, ask your Internet service provider (ISP) for the name of its *news server,* which is the program that stores newsgroup postings for you to download.

Newsgroup "netiquette"

Here are some other suggestions for getting along with others in newsgroups:

✦ Don't post to the whole group if you're sending a follow-up intended solely for the author of the original article. Instead, reply via e-mail.

✦ Be sure that each article is appropriate for the group to which you post it.

✦ Don't post a message saying that another message — a spam ad, for example — is inappropriate. The poster probably knows and doesn't care. The first message wasted enough of everyone's time; your response would waste more. Silence is the best answer.

✦ Never criticize someone else's spelling or grammar.

✦ Make your subject line as meaningful as possible. If your reply is tangential to an article, change the subject line to reflect the new topic.

✦ When you're asking a question, use a question mark:

```
Subject: Meaning of Life?
```

✦ Don't post a 2-line follow-up that quotes an entire 100-line article. Edit out most of the quoted material.

✦ Don't *cross-post;* that is, don't post the same article to multiple newsgroups unless you have a good reason. Be especially careful when you're replying to multiple cross-posted messages; your response might be cross-posted, too.

✦ Watch out for *trolls,* which are messages calculated to provoke a storm of replies. Not every stupid comment needs a response.

✦ Most groups periodically post a list of frequently asked questions (FAQs). Read the FAQ before asking a question. See "Frequently asked questions (FAQs)," later in this chapter.

Newsgroup names

Usenet newsgroups have multipart names separated by dots, such as `comp.dcom.fax`, which is a data communication discussion group about fax machines. Related groups have related names. Groups about data communication, for example, all start with `comp.dcom`. The first part of a newsgroup name is its *hierarchy*. In e-mail addresses and Internet host names, the top-level component (edu, for example) is on the right. In newsgroup names, the top-level component is on the left.

Table 13-1 lists the most popular Usenet newsgroup hierarchies.

Table 13-1	Popular Newsgroup Hierarchies
Newsgroup	*Description*
comp	Computer-related topics
humanities	Discussions relating to humanities
misc	Miscellaneous topics that don't fit anywhere else
news	Topics having to do with the Usenet newsgroup system itself; a few newsgroups with valuable general announcements — otherwise, not very interesting
rec	Recreational groups about sports, hobbies, the arts, and other fun endeavors
sci	Science-related topics
soc	Social groups, both social interests and plain socializing
talk	Long arguments, frequently political
alt	Semiofficial "alternative" to the preceding newsgroup hierarchies (which are often called The Big Eight); alt groups range from the extremely useful to the totally weird

In addition to the popular hierarchies in Table 13-1, you can find regional, organizational, and national hierarchies such as ne for New England, ny for New York, uk for the United Kingdom, and ibm for IBM. If you speak another language, you might be interested in hierarchies that serve languages other than English. For example, de is for German, es for Spanish, fj for Japanese, and fr for French.

New hierarchies are being started all the time. Lewis S. Eisen maintains a master list of Usenet hierarchies (619, at last count) at

www.magma.ca/~leisen/mlnh

Frequently asked questions (FAQs)

Many newsgroups periodically post a list of frequently asked questions and their answers, or *FAQs*. They hope that you read the FAQ before posting a message that they have answered dozens of times before — and indeed you should.

MIT collects FAQs from all over Usenet, in effect creating an online encyclopedia with the latest information on a vast array of topics that is accessible with your Web browser or via FTP, at this URL:

ftp://rtfm.mit.edu/pub/usenet-by-hierarchy

FAQs are often quite authoritative, but sometimes they're just a contributor's opinion. Reader beware!

Posting articles to newsgroups

Standard Usenet dogma is to read a group for a few weeks before posting anything. It's still good advice, although Internet newbies generally aren't big on delayed gratification. Here are some tips on your first posting:

✦ Pick a newsgroup whose subject is one you know something about.

✦ Read the FAQ before you post.

✦ Reply to an article with specific information that you know firsthand or can cite in a reference and that is relevant to the topic being discussed.

✦ Read the entire preceding *thread* (a series of replies to the original article and replies to those replies) to make sure that your point hasn't been raised already.

✦ Edit included text from the original article to the bare minimum.

✦ Keep your reply short, clear, and to the point.

✦ Have your facts straight. Your article should contain more than your opinion.

✦ Check your spelling and grammar.

✦ Stay calm. Don't be inflammatory, use foul language, or call people names.

✦ Avoid Netisms, such as ROFL (rolling on floor laughing). If necessary, use — at most — one smiley : -).

✦ Use a local hierarchy for stuff of regional interest. The whole planet does not need to hear about your school's bake sale.

✦ Save your message overnight and reread it before posting.

Some newsgroups are moderated, which means that

✦ Articles are not posted directly as news. Instead, they're e-mailed to a person or program that posts the article only if he, she, or it feels that it's appropriate to the group.

✦ Because they're unpaid volunteers, moderators do not process items instantaneously, so it can take a day or two for items to be processed.

✦ If you post an article for a moderated group, the news-posting software mails your item to the moderator automatically.

✦ If your article doesn't appear and you really don't know why, post a polite inquiry to the same group.

Remember that Usenet is a public forum. Everything you say there can be read by anyone, anywhere in the world. Worse, every word you post is carefully indexed and archived. However, Google will let you avoid having your material archived if you type **X-No-archive: yes** in the header or first line of the text. If you forget to do this, you can ask Google to remove the message for you or remove the message yourself by using Google's automatic removal tool.

Reading Newsgroups with Google

Google Groups, the area of the Google site that offers newsgroups, is a great place to find answers to problems that you might be having with your computer and its software. You can find a newsgroup for almost every system or program out there, including ones that are obsolete.

Google and Usenet indexes

Usenet has been around almost since the beginning of the Internet and is a bit old and creaky. Google Groups has done much to bring Usenet into the modern Web era. You can use Google Groups to

- ✦ Do a keyword search for newsgroup articles.
- ✦ Look for newsgroups of interest.
- ✦ Read newsgroup articles.
- ✦ Send an e-mail to an article's author.
- ✦ Post a reply article to something you read.
- ✦ Post a newsgroup article on a new topic.

Watch out what you post on Usenet newsgroups because anyone can find your posts later by using Google. A simple search for your name displays your e-mail address and a list of every message that you've posted — at least since 1981. If you include your home address, phone number, kids' names, political opinions, dating preferences, personal fantasies, or whatever in any message, that information also is easily retrieved. You have been warned.

Searching Google Groups

The traditional way to read Usenet is to go to a newsgroup and read the recent messages posted there. With tens of thousands of newsgroups, however, this method has become inefficient. Google Groups enables you to search *all* newsgroups by content. To use Google Groups to search all newsgroups by content, follow these steps:

1. **Open your browser and go to** `groups.google.com`.

   A list of categories appears.

2. **Click a category or type keywords in the Search text box and click Google Search.**

   In the Related Groups area at the top of your search results, you see a list of related newsgroups that include many articles (or contributor's names) with those keywords. The Activity bar to the left of the group name shows how often the groups have been visited. In the Searched Groups For area, you see a list of newsgroup articles that contain your search terms.

3. **Click a group to see a list of specific articles listed by the most recent date, or click an article to read it.**

   To see more search results, click the link that reads <u>Next</u> or <u>Next 25 Threads</u>.

4. **To save an article, choose File⇨Save As in your browser.**

If you don't find what you want in the search results, change your keywords in the Search text box and click the Google Search button.

If you want to do more advanced searching, check out the Advanced Groups Search. Not only can you search by newsgroup, but you can search by subject, author, message ID, language, and message dates as well.

Replying to an article

You can reply to an article in two ways: by sending a message to the poster's e-mail address or by posting a message to the newsgroup. To reply to a newsgroup article via e-mail, find the person's e-mail address in the article and copy it in the To field of your favorite e-mail program. ***Note:*** People often add *nospam* or other text to their e-mail addresses to decrease the amount of spam in their inboxes. Watch for this text to make sure that your message reaches the intended recipient.

To post an article following up on a message, click the <u>Post a Follow-up to This Message</u> link. On the Post a Message page, edit the quoted article to a reasonable size and add your response. You can also edit the list of newsgroups to which your article is posted. Click the Preview Message button to preview your reply. You can make changes by clicking the Edit Message button, or you can post the message by clicking Post Message.

Keep in mind that the first time you post a message, you are taken to a registration page where you're asked for your name, e-mail address, and password. Next, you receive a confirmation message. As soon as you reply, you'll be able to post.

Posting a new article

To post a new message to a newsgroup, at the top of the list of threads, click the <u>Post a New Message to *Newsgroup Name*</u> link. On the Post Message page, type your title in the Subject text box. Type the message in the Your Message box. You can also edit the list of newsgroups to which your article is posted. When the message is ready to send, click either the Preview Message or the Post Message–No Preview button.

Reading Newsgroups with Outlook Express

Outlook Express, the e-mail program that comes with Internet Explorer (IE) and Windows (see Chapters 8 and 9 of this book), also works as a newsreader. You can receive (by subscribing) copies of all the messages being sent by the participants of the newsgroup, or you can peruse the chitchat (by not subscribing to the newsgroup). You must first set up a newsgroup account.

REMEMBER

You can add and remove News Server accounts or make an account your default account by choosing Tools⇨Accounts and clicking the News tab of the Internet Accounts dialog box.

Viewing newsgroup messages before you subscribe

To get a feel for a newsgroup by reading some of its messages before actually subscribing to it, follow these steps:

1. **From the IE toolbar, click the arrow next to the Mail button and choose Read News.**

   Internet Explorer opens the Outlook Express window for the news server that you selected when you set up your News account.

2. **Click Yes to display a list of all available newsgroups in the Newsgroup Subscriptions dialog box.**

   This process might take a few minutes if your connection speed is slow.

3. **Select a newsgroup in the list box of the Newsgroup Subscriptions dialog box by clicking it.**

   If you want to limit the list of newsgroups, you can enter a term or series of terms used in the newsgroup's title (if you know that kind of thing) in the Display Newsgroups Which Contain text box.

4. **Click the Go To button to download all the messages from the newsgroup into the Outlook Express window.**

   You can read through the newsgroup messages just as you do your own e-mail messages.

5. **(Optional) If you want to reply to a particular message, click the message in the upper pane. Then click the Reply button to reply to the author of the message or click the Reply Group button to reply to the entire group.**

6. **To return to the list of newsgroups on your News server, click the Newsgroups button on the Outlook Express toolbar.**

7. **When you finish perusing the newsgroups of interest, click OK to close the Newsgroup Subscriptions dialog box, and then click the Close button in the Outlook Express window.**

Subscribing to a newsgroup

When you find a newsgroup in which you want to regularly participate, you can subscribe to it as follows:

1. **From the Internet Explorer toolbar, click the Mail button and then choose Read News.**

2. **If you see the News Setup Wizard telling you that you haven't subscribed to any newsgroups, click Yes.**

   The Newsgroup Subscriptions dialog box opens.

3. **In the list box, click the name of the newsgroup to which you want to subscribe.**

4. **Click the Subscribe button.**

Outlook Express then adds a newspaper icon in front of the name of the newsgroup to indicate that you are subscribed to it. The program also adds the name of the newsgroup to the Subscribed tab of the Newsgroup Subscriptions dialog box.

5. **Repeat Steps 3 and 4 to subscribe to any other newsgroups of interest.**

6. **When you're finished subscribing, click OK.**

The Outlook Express window appears, where you now see a list of all the newsgroups to which you have subscribed.

7. **To see the messages in a particular newsgroup, select the newsgroup by clicking its name in the Folders pane. To have IE go online and download any new messages for the selected newsgroup, choose Tools⇨Synchronize Account.**

The Synchronize Newsgroup dialog box appears.

8. **Select the Get the Following Items check box, and then select the desired option button: All Messages, New Messages Only (the default), or Headers Only. Click OK.**

After the messages are downloaded, you can get offline and peruse the messages at your leisure.

9. **(Optional) Read and reply to as many of the newsgroup messages as you want. Click the message to display it in the lower pane and then click either the Reply button to reply to the author of the message or click the Reply Group button to reply to the entire group.**

10. **When you're finished looking at the newsgroup messages, click the Close button in the upper-right corner of the Outlook Express window.**

After subscribing to a newsgroup, you can click the Mail button on the IE toolbar and choose Read News to return to the list of newsgroups in Outlook Express. Remember to click the title of a newsgroup to download its current messages.

Unsubscribing from a newsgroup

Should you decide that you no longer want to participate in a newsgroup to which you're subscribed, you can easily unsubscribe by following these steps:

1. **Click the Newsgroups button on the Outlook Express toolbar.**

The Newsgroup Subscriptions dialog box appears.

2. **Click the Subscribed tab and then click the name of the newsgroup to which you want to unsubscribe.**

3. **Click the Unsubscribe button and then click OK.**

Chapter 14: Using Apple Mail

In This Chapter

- Adding and configuring mail accounts
- Receiving and reading e-mail
- Sending e-mail
- Filtering junk mail
- Opening attachments
- Configuring Apple Mail
- Automating Apple Mail

Okay, how many of you can function without e-mail? Raise your hands. Anyone? Anyone at all? I suppose that I *can* function without my Internet e-mail, but why should I? Mac OS X includes a very capable and reliable e-mail client, which has been substantially improved for version 10.3 (affectionately called *Panther* by everyone but Bill Gates).

In this chapter, I discuss the features of Apple Mail and show you how everything hums at a perfect C pitch. However, you'll have to sing out, "You've got mail!" yourself. Personally, I think that's a plus, but I show you how you can add any sound that you like.

Know Thy Mail Window

To begin your epic e-mail journey, click the Mail icon in the Dock. Figure 14-1 illustrates the Mail window. Besides the familiar toolbar, which naturally carries buttons specific to Mail, you'll find the following:

- **Status bar:** This heading bar displays information about the current folder — typically, how many messages it contains, but other data can be included as well. You can hide and show the Status bar from the View menu, or you can press the ⌘+Option+S keyboard shortcut to hide and show it.

- **Message list:** This resizable scrolling list box contains all the messages for the folder that you've chosen. To resize the list larger or smaller, drag the handle on the bar that runs across the window. You can also resize the columns in the list by dragging the edges of the column heading buttons.

  To specify which columns appear in the message list, choose View⇨ Columns. From the submenu that appears, you can toggle the display of specific columns. You can also sort the messages in the message list from the View menu; by default, messages are sorted by the Date Received.

- **Drawer:** The extension to the right of the main Mail window is the Drawer. You can click any of the folders to switch the display in the message list.

The Drawer can be hidden or shown from the View menu by clicking the Mailboxes button on the toolbar, or you can press the ⌘+Shift+M keyboard shortcut to hide and show it. The Drawer is also automatically hidden when you maximize the Mail window.

✦ **Preview box:** This resizable scrolling list box displays the contents of the selected message, including both text and any graphics or attachments that Mail recognizes.

Mail uses the following folders (some of which appear only at certain times):

✦ **In:** Mail you've already received.

✦ **Out:** Messages that Mail is waiting to send.

✦ **Drafts:** Draft messages waiting to be completed.

✦ **Sent:** Mail you've already sent.

✦ **Trash:** Deleted mail. Like the Trash in the Dock, you can open this folder and retrieve items that you realize you still need. Alternatively, you can empty the contents of the Trash at any time by pressing the ⌘+K shortcut or by choosing Mailbox⇨Erase Deleted Messages.

✦ **Junk:** Junk mail. You can review these messages or retrieve anything you want to keep by choosing Message⇨Transfer. After you're sure there's nothing left of value, you can delete the remaining messages straight to the Trash.

✦ **Import:** Messages that you've imported from another e-mail application or an earlier version of Mac OS X Mail.

You can add new personal folders to the Drawer to further organize your messages. Choose Mailbox⇨New Mailbox and then type the name for your new folder in the Name box. Click OK to create the new personal folder.

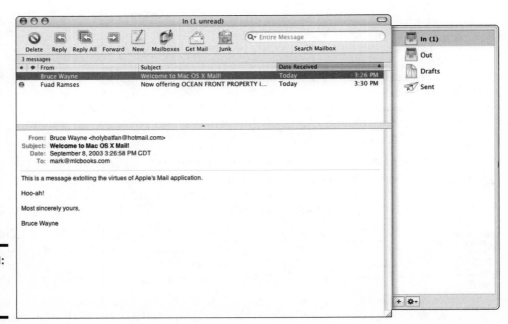

Figure 14-1:
The Apple
Mail
window.

Messages can be dragged from the message list and dropped into the desired folder in the Drawer to transfer them. From the Message list, select the messages that you want to move, choose Message⇨Transfer, and then click the desired destination folder.

Also note that the Search box (upper-right) in the Mail toolbar looks a little different. Click the down arrow in this field, and from the drop-down list that appears, you can specify whether Mail should search for the text that you've entered there within the entire text of a message or just in the From, To, or Subject fields.

Setting Up Your Account

By default, Mail includes one (or more) of these accounts when you first run it:

✦ The account that you entered when you first installed Mac OS X

✦ Your .Mac account

✦ Upgraded accounts

Speaking of the Accounts list, choose Mail⇨Preferences to display the Accounts dialog that you see in Figure 14-2. From here, you can add an account, edit an existing account, or remove an account from Mail. Although most folks still have only one e-mail account, you can use a passel of them. For example, you might use one account for your personal e-mail and one account for your business communications. To switch accounts, just click the account that you want to use from this list to make it the active account.

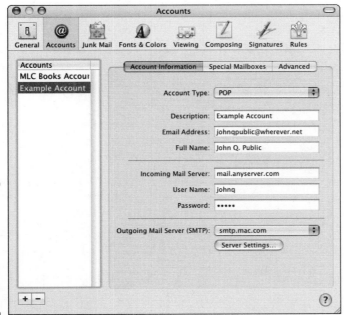

Figure 14-2:
The Accounts list, where all is made clear (about your e-mail accounts).

Adding an account

To add a new account within Mail, click the Add Account button, which carries a plus sign (see bottom left, Figure 14-2), to display the dialog that you see in Figure 14-3. Then follow these steps:

1. **On the Account Information panel, click the Account Type drop-down list box and choose the protocol type to use for the account.**

You can select an Apple .Mac account, a Post Office Protocol (POP) account, a Microsoft Exchange account, or an Internet Message Access Protocol (IMAP) account. If you're adding an account from an Internet service provider (ISP), refer to the setup information that you received to determine which is right. Most ISP accounts are POP accounts.

2. **In the Description field, name the account to identify it within Mail and then press Tab to move to the next field.**

For example, *Work* or *Mom's ISP* are good choices.

3. **In the Email Address field, type the e-mail address supplied by your ISP and then press Tab to move to the next field.**

4. **In the Full Name field, type your full name — or, if this is to be an anonymous account, enter whatever you like as your identity — and then press Tab.**

Messages that you send will appear with this name in the From field in the recipient's e-mail application.

5. **If you're entering a POP or IMAP account: In the Incoming Mail Server field, type the name of the incoming mail server (supplied by your ISP) and then press Tab.**

Figure 14-3: Add an account within Apple Mail.

Add Account

6. **In the User Name field, type the user name supplied by your ISP for login to your e-mail account and then press Tab.**

   This is sometimes different from the user name and password that you use to connect to the Internet.

7. **In the Password field, type the password supplied by your ISP for login to your e-mail account.**

   Again, this might be different from your connection password.

8. **Click the Outgoing Mail Server drop-down list box; if the outgoing server appears in this list, select it.**

   This is often the case if you're adding another new account provided by your ISP.

   If the outgoing mail server doesn't appear in the list, click Add Server in the list, enter the server address provided by your ISP in the Server Options dialog, and then click OK to return.

   Luckily, the defaults for the Outgoing Mail Server settings will work like a charm for 99 percent of us. However, if your ISP or network administrator tells you that you must make changes to your outgoing mail server settings, click the Server Settings button (either while adding or editing an account). You can specify a port number, toggle Secure Sockets Layer (SSL) support, and select your authentication type. Because all that stuff sounds like a medieval Gregorian chant to most computer owners, just enter these server settings if you're told to do so.

9. **Click the Close button.**

   You're done! The new account appears in the Accounts list.

You can specify advanced settings for an account. I cover those in the section "Fine-Tuning Your Post Office," later in this chapter.

Editing an existing account

Need to make changes to an existing account? Choose Mail⇨Preferences and click the account that you want to change. Mail displays the same settings that I explain in the previous section.

Deleting an account

If you change ISPs or you decide to drop an e-mail account, you can remove it from your Accounts list. Otherwise, Mail can annoy you with error messages when it can no longer connect to the server for that account. Display the Mail Preferences window, select the account that you want to delete, and then click the Remove button (which is graced by a minus sign).

Naturally, Mail will request confirmation before deleting the folders associated with that account. Click OK to verify the deletion or click the Cancel button to prevent accidental catastrophe.

Receiving and Reading E-Mail Wisdom

The heart and soul of Mail — well, at least the heart, anyway — is receiving and reading stuff from your friends and family. (Later in this chapter, I show you how to avoid the stuff you get promising free prizes, low mortgage rates, and improved . . . um . . . performance. This is a family-oriented book, so that's enough of that.)

After you set up an account (or select an account from the Accounts list), it's time to check for mail. Use any of these methods to check for new mail:

✦ Click the Get Mail button on the toolbar.

✦ Choose Mailbox⇨Get New Mail in All Accounts or press ⌘+Shift+N.

✦ Choose Mailbox⇨Get New Mail and then choose the specific account to check from the submenu.

This is a great way to check for new mail in another account without going through the trouble of making it active in the Preferences window.

Mail can also check for new messages automatically — more on this in the upcoming section, "Checking Mail automatically."

If you do have new mail in the active account, it appears in the Message list, and the Mail icon in the Dock sports a bright red number indicating how many new messages you've received. As you can see in Figure 14-4, new unread messages appear marked with a dot (it's blue) in the first column. The number of unread messages is displayed next to the In folder icon in the Drawer.

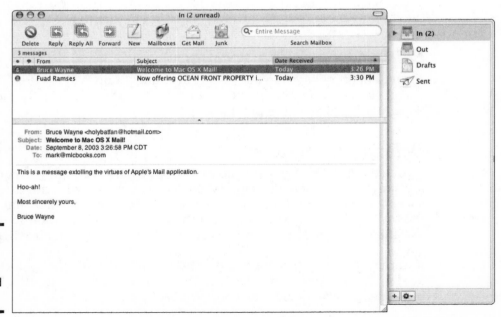

Figure 14-4:
A new message to read . . . and no spam.

Displaying all Mail headers

Mail actually hides the majority of the heading lines that help identify and route an e-mail message to its rightful destination. By default, all you'll see is the *filtered heading,* which includes only the From, Date, To, and Subject fields. This is great unless for some reason you need to display the entire message header in all its arcane madness. If you do, press ⌘+Shift+H. You can toggle back to the filtered heading by pressing the same shortcut.

Mail also displays the number of new messages that you've received on its Dock icon. If you've hidden the Mail window or sent it to the Dock, you can perform a quick visual check for new mail just by glancing at the Dock.

Reading and deleting your messages

To read any message in the message list, you can either click the desired entry (which displays the contents of the message in the preview box) or you can double-click the entry to open the message in a separate message window, complete with its own toolbar controls.

To quickly scan your mail, click the first message that you want to view in the list, and then press the down-arrow key when you're ready to move to the next message. Mail displays the content of each message in the preview box. To display the previous message in the list, press the up-arrow key.

The latest version of Mail allows you to read your messages grouped within threads. A *thread* contains an original message and all related replies, which makes it easy to follow the flow of an e-mail discussion (without bouncing around within your Inbox, searching for the next message in the conversation). Choose View➪Organize by Thread, and the replies in the current folder are all grouped under the original messages and sorted by date. To expand a thread, click the original message to select it; then press the right-arrow key (or choose View➪Expand All Threads). To collapse a thread, select the original message and press the left-arrow key (or choose View➪Collapse All Threads).

To delete a message from the message list, click the desired entry to select it and then click the Delete button in the toolbar (or press the Del key). To delete a message from within a message window, click the Delete button in the toolbar.

Replying to mail

What? Aunt Harriet sent you a message because she's forgotten where she parked her car last night? If you happen to know where her priceless '78 Pinto is, you can reply to her and save her the trouble of retracing her steps.

If Aunt Harriet isn't in your Address Book yet, this is a good time to add her. With the message entry selected in the list, choose Message⇨Add Sender to Address Book or just press the convenient ⌘+Y keyboard shortcut. The person's name and e-mail address are automatically added to your Address Book. To add more information in the Address Book, however, you have to open that application separately.

To reply to a message in Mail, follow these steps:

1. To respond to a message from the message list, click the desired message entry and then click the Reply button on the toolbar.

To respond to a message that you've opened in a message window, click the Reply button on the toolbar for the message window.

If a message was addressed not just to you but also to a number of different people, you can send your reply to all of them. Instead of clicking the Reply button, click the Reply All button on the Mail window toolbar. (This is a great way to quickly facilitate a festive gathering, if you get my drift.)

You can also add carbon copies of your message to other new recipients, expanding the party exponentially; more on carbon copies later in the section, "Raise the Little Flag: Sending E-Mail."

If you'd like to send your reply under a different account, click the Account drop-down list box and choose the account. This is a handy method of re-routing a message that you received in your home e-mail account to your office account.

Mail opens the Reply window that you see in Figure 14-5. Note that the address has been automatically added and that the default Subject is Re: *<the original subject>*. Mail automatically adds a separator line in the message body field that reads `On <day><date>at<time>, <addressee> wrote:`, followed by the text of the original message; this is done so that the addressee can remember what the heck he wrote in the first place to get you so happy/sad/angry/indifferent. The original text is indented and colored blue to set it apart. If you like, you can click in the Subject line and change the default subject line; otherwise, the cursor is already sitting on the first line of the text box, so you can simply start typing your reply.

2. After you complete typing your reply, you can select text in the message body and apply different fonts or formatting.

To change your reply's formatting, click the Fonts button on the message window toolbar. From the window that appears, you can choose the font family, the type size, and formatting such as italic or bold for the selected text. Click the Close button on the Fonts window to continue. (If you like menus, you can also choose Format from the menu and make changes from there.)

To apply color to the selected text, click the Colors button on the message window toolbar and then click anywhere in the color wheel that appears to select that color. You can also vary the hue by moving the slider bar at the right of the Colors window. After you find the color that expresses your inner passion, click the Close button on the Colors window to continue.

3. To add an attachment, click the Attach button on the toolbar.

Mail displays a familiar file Open dialog. Navigate to the to-be-attached file, select it, and click the Open button to add it to the message. (More on attachments in the upcoming section, "Attachments on Parade.")

4. When you're ready to send your reply, you have two options. You can click the Send button to immediately add the message to your Out folder, or you can click the Save As Draft button to store it in your Drafts folder for later editing.

After a message is moved to the Out folder, it is sent either immediately or at the next connection time that you specify in Mail Preferences (more on this in the section "Checking Mail automatically," later in the chapter). However, saving the message to your Drafts folder will not send it. Read the next section for the skinny on how to send a message stored in your Drafts folder.

When you reply to a message, you can also forward your reply to another person (instead of the original sender). The new addressee receives a message containing both the text of the original message that you received and your reply. To forward a message, click the Forward button on the Mail toolbar instead of Reply or Reply to All.

If you don't want to include the text of the original message in a reply, choose Mail➪Preferences➪Composing and disable the Quote the Text of the Original Message check box.

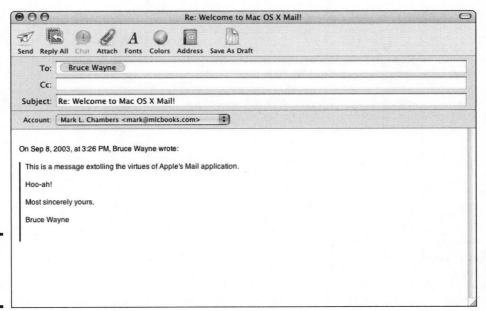

Figure 14-5:
Reply to an e-mail message.

By default, Mail checks your spelling as you type and also underlines any words that it doesn't recognize. (Very Microsoftian.) I like this feature, but if you find it irritating, you can turn it off. Just choose Mail⇨Preferences⇨ Composing and disable the Check Spelling as I Type check box.

Raise the Little Flag: Sending E-Mail

To compose and send a new message to someone else, follow these steps:

1. **Click the New button on the Mail toolbar or choose File⇨New Message (or avail yourself of the handy ⌘+N keyboard shortcut).**

   Mail opens the New Message window that you see in Figure 14-6.

2. **Enter the recipient's (To) address by**

   - Typing it in directly
   - Pasting it in after copying it to the Clipboard
   - Dragging an e-mail address from your Address Book
   - Or (my favorite) clicking the Address button, which shows you the scaled-down version of the Address Book (the Addresses window) that you see in Figure 14-7

   From the Addresses window, click the address that you want to use and then click the To button. To pick multiple recipients, hold down the Shift key while you click the multiple addresses. Click the Close button on the Addresses window to close it and then press Tab.

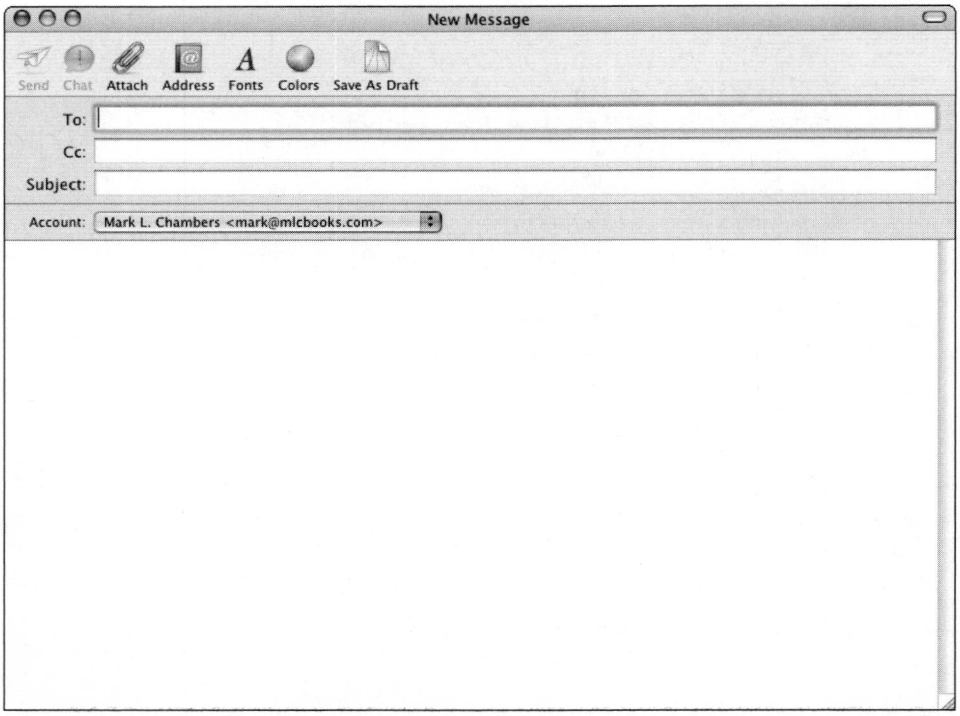

Figure 14-6:
An empty Mail message, waiting to be filled.

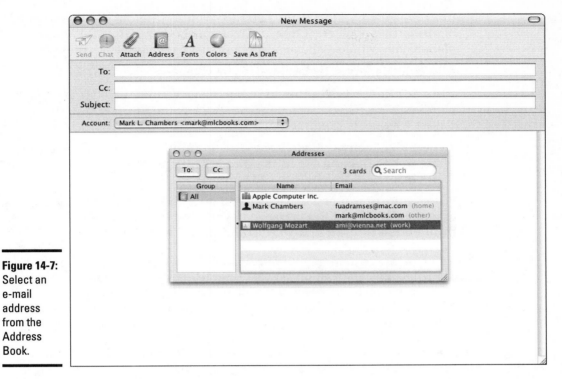

Figure 14-7:
Select an
e-mail
address
from the
Address
Book.

> If you've got a huge number of entries in your Address Book, use the Search field on the Addresses window toolbar, which operates just like the Finder window Search box.

3. When Mail highlights the Cc field (the spot where you can send optional carbon copies of the message to additional recipients), you can type the addresses directly, use the contents of the Clipboard, or display the Addresses window.

If you use the Addresses window, select the addresses that you want to use and click the Cc button. Then click the Close button on the Addresses window and press Tab.

> Looking for the blind carbon copy field? To display it, choose View⇨Bcc Header. (A *blind carbon copy* is a message sent to multiple recipients, just like a regular carbon copy, but the recipients aren't listed when the message is displayed — that way, the other recipients won't know who else got a copy of the message.)

4. In the Subject field, enter the subject of the message and then press Tab.

Your text cursor now rests in the first line of the message text box — type, my friend, type like the wind! It's considered good form to keep this line short and relatively to the point.

5. When you're done typing your message, select any of the text that you've entered and use the toolbar features I describe in the earlier section "Replying to mail" to apply different fonts or formatting.

Click the Fonts button in the message window toolbar to open a window of formatting choices. (Click its Close button to continue.) If you like menus, you can also click Format and make changes from there.

6. **Add color to any selected text, if you like.**

   Just click the Colors button in the message window toolbar and make choices there; when the hue is perfect, click the Close button on the Colors window to continue.

7. **To add an attachment, click the Attach button on the toolbar, navigate to the to-be-attached file in the dialog that appears, select the file, and then click Open to add it to the message.**

8. **When your new message is ready to post, either click the Send button to immediately add the message to your Out folder or click the Save As Draft button to store it in your Drafts folder (without actually sending it).**

To send a message held in your Drafts folder, click the Drafts folder in the Drawer to display all draft messages. Double-click the message that you want to send, which will display the message window — you can make edits at this point, if you like — and then click the Send button on the message window toolbar.

If you don't have access to an Internet connection at the moment, Mail allows you to work offline. This way, you can read your unread messages and compose new ones on the road to send later. After you regain your Internet connection, you might need to choose Mailbox➪Online Status➪Go Online (depending on the connection type).

What? You Get Junk Mail, Too?

Spam — it's the Crawling Crud of the Internet, and I hereby send out a lifetime of bad karma to those who spew it. However, chucking the First Amendment is *not* an option, so I guess we'll always have junk mail. (Come to think of it, my paper mailbox is just as full of the stuff.)

Thankfully, the latest version of Apple Mail has a net that you can cast to collect junk mail before you have to read it. The two methods of handling junk mail are

✦ **Manually:** You can mark any message in the message list as Junk Mail. Select the unwanted flotsam in the message list and then click the Junk button on the Mail window toolbar, which marks the message as you see in Figure 14-8. (Ocean-front property in Kansas . . . yeah, right.) If a message is mistakenly marked as junk but you actually want it, display the message in the preview box and then click the Not Junk button at the top of the preview box.

✦ **Automatically:** Apple Mail has a sophisticated Junk Mail filter that you actually train to better recognize what's junk. (Keep reading to discover how.) After you train Mail to recognize spam with a high degree of accuracy, turn it to full Automatic mode, and it will move all those worthless messages to your Junk folder.

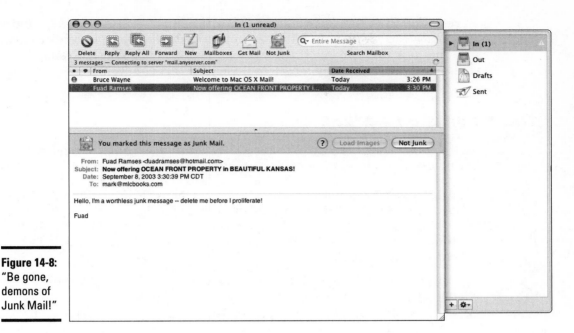

Figure 14-8:
"Be gone, demons of Junk Mail!"

You customize and train the Junk Mail filter from the Preferences dialog (available from your trusty Mail menu); click Junk Mail to show the settings. By default, Mail starts in Training mode, using the When Junk Mail Arrives, Leave It in My Inbox option. This means that it takes its best shot at determining what's junk. When you receive more mail and mark more messages as junk (or mark them as *not* junk), you're actually teaching the Junk Mail feature how to winnow the wheat from the chaff. In Training mode, junk messages are not actually moved anywhere — they're just marked with a particularly fitting, grungy brown color.

After you're satisfied that the Junk Mail filter is catching just about everything that it can, display this submenu and choose the Move It to the Junk Mailbox (Automatic) option. Mail creates a Junk folder and prompts you for permission to move all junk messages to this folder. After you review everything in the Junk folder, you can delete what it contains and send it to the Trash folder. To save a message from junkdom, click the Not Junk button in the preview window and then drag the message from the Junk folder message list to the desired folder in the Drawer.

If you don't receive a lot of spam — or you want to be absolutely sure that nothing gets labeled as junk until you review it — display the Junk Mail submenu and then choose the Off menu item.

By default, Mail exempts certain messages from Junk Mail status based on three criteria: if the sender is in your Address Book, if you've sent the sender a message in the past, or if the message is addressed to you with your full name. To tighten up your Junk Mail filtering to the max, you might want to disable these check boxes as well.

To reset the Junk Mail filter and erase any training that you've done, choose Junk Mail➪Reset. Then click the Yes button to confirm your choice. To display the Junk rule and edit it if necessary, choose Junk Mail➪Advanced. (I discuss filtering rules at length at the end of this chapter.)

Attachments on Parade

Attachments are a fun way to transfer files through e-mail. However, remembering these three very important caveats is imperative:

✦ **Attachments can contain viruses.** Even a message attachment that was actually sent by your best friend can contain a virus — either because your friend unwittingly passed one along or because the virus actually took control of your friend's e-mail application and replicated itself automatically. (Ugh.)

Never send or receive attachments unless you have an up-to-date antivirus scanning application running.

✦ **Corpulent attachments don't make it.** Most corporate and ISP mail servers have a 1–3MB limit for the total size of a message — and the attachment counts toward that final message size. Therefore, I recommend sending a file as an attachment only if it's less than 1MB (or perhaps 2MB) in size. If the recipient's e-mail server sends you an automated message saying that the message was refused because it was too big, this is the problem.

✦ **Not all e-mail applications and firewalls accept attachments.** Not all e-mail programs support attachments in the same way, and others are simply set for pure text messages. Some corporate firewalls even reject messages with attachments. If the message recipient gets the message text but not the attachment, these are the likely reasons.

With that said, it's back to attachments as a beneficial feature. Follow these steps to save an attachment that you receive:

1. **Click the message with an attachment in your message list.**

Having trouble determining which messages have attachments? Choose View➪Columns and then click the Attachments item from the submenu that appears to toggle it on. Now messages with attachments appear with a tiny paper clip icon in the entry.

If Mail recognizes the attachment format, it displays or plays the attachment in the body of the message; if not, the attachment is displayed as a file icon.

2. **To open an attachment that's displayed as a file icon, hold down Control, click the file icon, and then choose Open Attachment from the pop-up menu that appears.**

If you know what application should be used to open the attachment, click the Open With button and choose the correct application from the submenu that appears.

3. **To save an attachment, hold down Control, click the attachment (however it appears in the message), and then choose Save Attachment from the pop-up menu.**

In the Save dialog that appears, navigate to the location where you want to save the file and then click Save.

Fine-Tuning Your Post Office

Like all other Apple software, Mail is easily customized to your liking. In this section, I discuss some of the preferences that you might want to change.

Adding sound

To choose a sound that plays whenever you receive new mail, choose Mail⇨Preferences⇨General. Either click the New Mail Sound drop-down list box and choose one of the sounds that Apple provides or choose Add/Remove from the drop-down list to choose a sound file from the Sounds folder (which, in turn, is located within your Library folder). Choose None from the drop-down list to disable the new mail sound altogether.

Checking Mail automatically

By default, Mail automatically checks for new mail (and sends any mail in your Out folder) every five minutes. To change this delay period, display the General panel in the Preferences dialog, choose the Check for New Mail drop-down list box, and then choose one of the time periods. To disable automatic mail checking, choose Manually; you can click the Get Mail toolbar button to manually check your mail any time you like.

Automating message deletion

If you like, Mail can be set to automatically delete sent mail and Junk messages (as well as permanently erase messages that you relegate to the Trash). To configure these settings, display the Accounts list in the Preferences window, click the desired account, and then click the Special Mailboxes tab.

To delete Sent messages automatically, enable the Erase Copies of Sent Messages When drop-down list box and choose the delay period or action. You can choose to delete mail after a day, a week, a month, or immediately upon quitting Mail. Alternatively, you can leave this field set to Never, and Mail will never automatically delete any messages from the Sent folder.

To delete Junk messages automatically, click the Erase Messages in the Junk Mailbox When drop-down list box and choose the delay period or action. (They're the same as the options available for Sent mail.)

To delete messages from the Trash, click the Erase Deleted Messages When drop-down list box and choose the delay period or action — again, the choices are the same as those for Sent messages.

Adding signatures

To add a block of text or a graphic to the bottom of your messages as your personal signature, follow these steps:

1. **Choose Mail⇨Preferences⇨Signatures.**

2. **From the Signatures pane that appears, click the Add Signature button.**

3. **Type a descriptive name for the signature in the Description box and then press Tab.**

4. **Type the signature itself in the text entry box or copy the signature to the Clipboard and paste it into the text entry box.**

   Because downloading a graphic in a signature takes long — and because some folks still use plain text e-mail — avoid the temptation to include large graphics in your signature.

   If you enter a block of formatted text, click the Make Plain Text button to reduce those fancy fonts to plain text.

5. **Click OK to save the signature.**

6. **If you have multiple signatures, click the Automatically Insert Signature drop-down list to choose which one you want to use or to use them all randomly or in sequence.**

If you use specific signatures for different subjects, you can also enable the Show Signature Menu on Compose Window check box, which allows you to switch signatures from the Compose window.

Changing the status of an account

Sometimes you won't be able to reach one of your accounts. For example, maybe you're on the road with your laptop and you're unable to access your office network. Apple Mail allows you to enable and disable specific accounts without the hassle of deleting an account and then having to add it again.

To disable or enable an account, choose Preferences⇨Accounts and click the desired account; click the Advanced tab and then enable (or clear) the Enable This Account check box as necessary.

If you disable an account, you should also disable the Include When Automatically Checking for New Mail check box to make sure that Mail doesn't display an error message. You can always check any account for new mail by choosing Mailbox⇨Get New Mail and then choosing the desired account name from the submenu.

Automating Your Mail with Rules

Before I leave the beautiful shores of Mail Island — *"GILLIGAN!"* — I'd be remiss if I didn't discuss one of its most powerful features: the ability to create *rules,* which are automated actions that Mail can take. With rules, you can specify criteria that can perform actions such as

✦ Transferring messages from one folder to another

✦ Forwarding messages to another address

✦ Highlighting or deleting messages

To set up a rule, follow these steps:

1. **Choose Mail➪Preferences and then click the Rules button on the toolbar.**

Mail displays the Rules dialog, as shown in Figure 14-9.

Figure 14-9:
The Rules
list.

2. **To duplicate an existing rule, highlight it in the list and then click the Duplicate button. (For this demonstration, however, create a rule from scratch by clicking the Add Rule button.)**

3. **In the Description field, type a descriptive name for the new rule and then press Tab to move to the next field.**

4. **Click the If drop-down list to specify whether the rule will be triggered if *any* of the conditions are met or whether *all* conditions must be met.**

5. **Because each rule requires at least one condition, click the target drop-down list boxes to see the target for the condition.**

These include whom the message is from or to, which account received the message, whether the message is marked as junk, and whether the message contains certain content. Select the target for the condition.

6. **Click the Criteria drop-down list box to choose the rule's criteria.**

The contents of this drop-down list box change depending on the condition's target. For example, if you choose From as the target, the criteria include Contains, Does Not Contain, Begins With, and so forth.

7. **Click in the expression box and type the text to use for the condition.**

For example, a completed condition might read

```
Subject Contains Ocean-Front
```

This particular condition will be true if I get an e-mail message with a subject that contains the string `Ocean-Front`.

8. **Add more conditions by clicking the plus sign button at the right of the first condition.**

To remove any condition from this rule, click the minus sign button next to it. Remember, however, that every rule needs at least one condition.

9. **To specify what actions will be taken after the condition (or conditions) has been met, click the first Perform the Following Actions drop-down list box to see the action that this rule should perform. Then click the second drop-down list box and then select the action for the rule.**

Choices include transferring a message from one folder to another, playing a sound, automatically forwarding the message, deleting it, and marking it as read.

Each rule requires at least one action.

10. **Depending on the action that you select, specify one or more criteria for the action.**

For instance, if I select Set Color as my action, I must then choose whether to color the text or the background as well as what color to use.

Like the plus button next to the conditions, you can also click the plus button next to the first action to perform more than one action. To remove an action, click the minus button next to it.

11. **When the rule is complete, click OK to save it.**

Here's an example of a complex rule:

> If the message was sent by someone in my Address Book AND the Subject field contains the text `FORWARD ME`, forward the message to the e-mail address `fuadramses@mac.com`.

This is a good example of an automated forwarding rule. With this rule in place and Mail running on Mac OS X, any of my friends, family, or co-workers can forward urgent e-mail to my .Mac account while I'm on vacation. To trigger the rule, all the sender has to do is include the words `FORWARD ME` in the message subject. And if the sender isn't in my Address Book, the rule doesn't trigger, and I can read the message when I get home. Mondo *sassy*.

Each rule in the Rules dialog can be enabled or disabled by toggling the Active check box next to the rule. You can also edit a rule by selecting it in the Rules dialog and then clicking the Edit button. To delete a rule completely from the list, select it and then click the Remove button; Mail will prompt you for confirmation before the deed is done.

Chapter 15: Expanding Your Horizons with iDisk

In This Chapter

✔ **Setting up iDisk**

✔ **Using files and folders on your iDisk**

✔ **Using public files**

If you ask the average Mac owner what's available on the Internet, you'll likely hear benefits such as e-mail, Web surfing, and instant communication via iChat AV, the Mac program for chatting with others. What you probably *won't* hear is, "Convenient, trouble-free storage for my files and folders."

You might have tried to use one of the dozens of storage sites on the Internet that allow you to upload and download files from a personal file area via your Web browser. Unfortunately, these Web-based storage sites are slow in transferring files, lacking in convenience, and typically offer only a small amount of space. As a result, most computer owners decide that the idea of online storage is neat . . . but impractical.

In this chapter, I show you what *real* online storage is all about. I'm talking about *iDisk,* which is the online storage feature that's integrated into the Mac OS X Finder. No jury-rigged Web site is necessary (although you can use one if you're not on a Mac). I'll admit that online storage won't replace the hard drives on your Mac, but with a .Mac subscription, you can easily make use of online storage for backups and sharing files with your friends . . . from anywhere on the planet!

So how do you actually use iDisk? That's the simple part! To use iDisk within Mac OS X, just do what comes naturally — it works like any other removable volume's Finder window. You can copy and move files and folders to and from your iDisk, create new subfolders (except in the Backup and Software root folders, which are read-only), and delete whatever you don't need.

Grabbing Internet Storage for Your Mac

To set up iDisk on your Mac OS X system, you'll need a .Mac account. You did create one during the installation of the Big X, right? These trial accounts are limited to 20MB of storage, and the trial account is active for only 60 days. Therefore, if you decide that you like iDisk, you should subscribe to .Mac; a subscription increases your online treasure chest to 100MB of iDisk storage. To subscribe, visit `http://mac.com` and follow the prompts to join from there. (At the time of this writing, the subscription fee is $100 per year.)

Pinning down your iDisk

So where exactly *are* your files kept when you use your iDisk? In earlier versions of Mac OS X, your acre of storage farmland always sat on one of Apple's iDisk file servers — perhaps in Cupertino, perhaps elsewhere. These server computers are especially designed to store terabytes (TB) of information (1TB equals 1,000GB), and they're connected to the Internet via high-speed trunk lines. (And yes, they do have a firewall.)

However, beginning with Panther, you can elect to keep a local copy of your iDisk storage area — usually called a *mirror* — on your Mac's hard drive. (Because Macs have copious hard drives, reserving 100MB is no problem.) Before you scratch your head wondering why you're duplicating your iDisk files on your computer, here's the reason: If you do decide to keep a local copy of your files, you can work on them even when you're not connected to the Internet! Panther automatically synchronizes any files that you've updated locally with your remote iDisk whenever you connect to the Internet. (If you use multiple Macs at different locations, think about being able to access the latest copies of your files from *any* of them, right from the Finder!)

This nifty mirror also greatly speeds up things when you're browsing the contents of your iDisk or perhaps loading and saving an iDisk document; that's because you're working with your local copy, and Mac OS X updates any changes that you make to the corresponding remote file on the iDisk server. You can tell that things are updating when that funky little yin yang, circular doodad — the thing next to your iDisk in the Finder window — is rotating in its animated fashion. (And yes, I have it on good authority . . . that's what the Apple software developers call it, too.)

You're not required to use a mirror, however. To disable the mirroring feature and return to the remote-only operation of old, clear the Synchronize Your iDisk with a Copy on Your Computer check box on the iDisk settings panel to disable it. Remember, though, that with the mirroring feature turned off, you must have an Internet connection to use iDisk, and things will move more slowly because you're accessing everything across the Internet.

With a .Mac account active, iDisk is automatically available. To see how much storage you're using and to configure access to your Public folder, open System Preferences, click the .Mac icon, and then click the iDisk tab to display the settings that you see in Figure 15-1. (You can also click the Buy More button on this panel to subscribe to Apple's .Mac service.)

The iDisk Disk Space bar graph illustrates how much of your current iDisk territory you're using. (Note that the account shown in Figure 15-1 is an evaluation account, so it shows only a total of 20MB.)

You can specify the access privilege level for other .Mac users from this panel as well. Select the Read-Only radio button to prevent any other .Mac user from copying files to your Public folder, or select the Read-Write radio button to allow others to save files there. No matter which privilege level you choose, you can also set a password that other .Mac users must type before they're allowed access to your Public folder. (More on the Public folder in the next section.) If you've already set a password, you can change it by clicking the Password button and typing the new word in the Password box. Retype the word in the Confirm box to verify it; then click the OK button to save the change and return to the .Mac System Preferences panel.

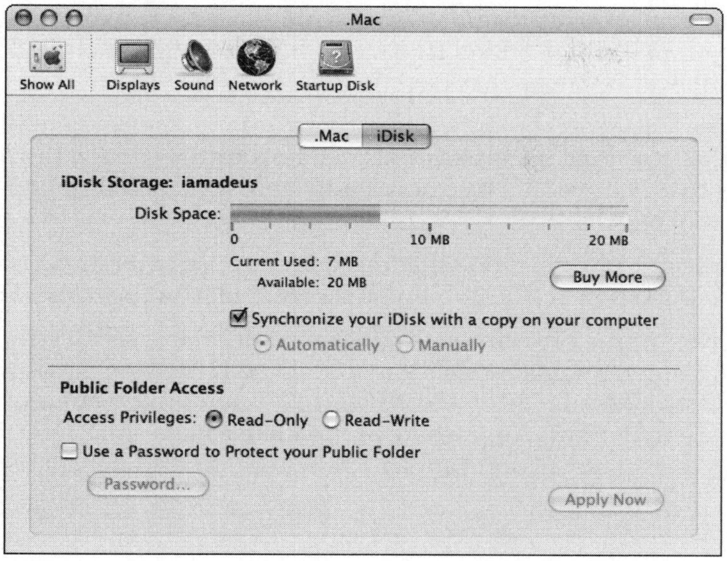

Figure 15-1:
Your iDisk
information
is available
from System
Preferences.

Understanding What's on Your iDisk

Unlike the physical hard drive in your Mac, your iDisk never needs formatting or defragmenting, and you'll never have to check it for errors. However, the structure of an iDisk is fixed, so you can't just go crazy creating your own folders. In fact, you can't create new folders at the *root* — the top level — of your iDisk at all, but you can create new folders inside most of the root folders.

Now that you're thoroughly rooterized, here are the folders that you'll find hanging out in your iDisk:

✦ **Documents:** This folder holds any application documents that you want to store . . . things like spreadsheets and letters. No one but you can access these items.

✦ **Pictures:** This folder is the vault for your JPEG and GIF images, including those that you want to use with iCards or your Web pages.

✦ **Movies:** QuickTime movies go here — again, you can add the movies stored here to your Web pages.

✦ **Public:** This is the spot to place files that you specifically want to share with others, either directly through iDisk or with your Web pages. If you've allowed write access, others can copy files to your Public folder as well.

✦ **Sites:** The Web pages that you store here can be created with Apple's HomePage utility — which is available to all .Mac members — or you can use your own Web page design application and copy the completed site files here.

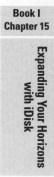

✦ **Music:** This is the repository for all of your iTunes music and playlists — the contents can be added to your Web pages. Mine is stuffed full of Mozart, Scarlatti, and that Bach fellow.

✦ **Backup:** This is a read-only folder that contains the backup files created with the .Mac Backup application. You can, however, copy the files in this folder to a removable drive on your system for an additional level of safekeeping.

✦ **Library:** Another read-only folder. This spot contains the configuration data and custom settings that you've created for other .Mac features.

✦ **Software:** Apple provides this read-only folder as a service to .Mac members; it contains a selection of the latest freeware, shareware, and commercial demos for you to enjoy. To try something out, open the Software folder and copy whatever you like to your Mac OS X Desktop. Then you can install and run the application from the local copy of the files.

Opening and Using iDisk

When you're connected to the Internet, you can open your iDisk in one of the following ways:

✦ **From the Finder menu, choose Go⇨iDisk and then choose My iDisk from the submenu or use the ⌘+Shift+I keyboard shortcut.**

✦ **Add an iDisk button to your Finder window toolbar by clicking View and then choosing Customize Toolbar.**

   After you add the button, you can click it to connect to your iDisk from anywhere in the Finder.

Your iDisk opens in a new Finder window, as shown in Figure 15-2. After you use one of these methods in a Mac OS X session, your iDisk icon appears on the Mac OS X Desktop; Figure 15-3 shows both the iDisk icon and its properties in the Get Info dialog. The iDisk volume icon remains until you shut down or restart your Mac.

If you're using a remote computer with an Internet connection, you can log in to the .Mac page at www.apple.com and use your Web browser to access the contents of your iDisk. (Hey, sometimes this is the only choice you have.)

However, you don't actually need to open your iDisk in a Finder window to use it because you can also load and save files directly to your iDisk from within any application. Simply choose your iDisk as you would any of the hard drives on your system when using the application's Load, Save, or Save As commands.

You can also open an iDisk's Public folder — either yours or the Public folder inside another person's iDisk — as if it were an Internet file server. As I explain earlier, if that person has set a password, you'll need to enter that password to gain access to their Public folder. From the Finder menu, choose Go⇨iDisk⇨Other User's iDisk (or, to jump directly to their Public folder, choose Go⇨iDisk⇨Other User's Public Folder). If you choose the former, Panther prompts you for the other person's member name and password (see Figure 15-4); if you pick the latter, you need only enter the other .Mac member's account name.

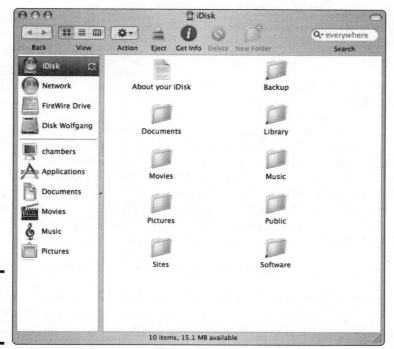

Figure 15-2:
The contents of my iDisk.

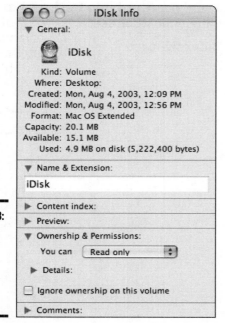

Figure 15-3:
After you open your iDisk, it appears on your Desktop.

Figure 15-4:
You can connect to any iDisk with the right member logon.

After you enter a valid iDisk member name (and password, if required), you'll see the .Mac member's Public folder.

You can also use the server address `http://idisk.mac.com/`*username*`-Public?` to connect to an iDisk from computers running Windows and Linux. Check the Help for your operating system to determine how to connect to a WebDAV server (usually called a *Web folder* in the Windows world). When prompted for your access user name and password, use your .Mac account name and password. If you're using Windows XP, Apple has provided an even easier way to open an iDisk Public folder: Use iDisk Utility for Windows, which you can download from `www.mac.com`.

To connect to your iDisk from within Mac OS 9, follow these steps:

1. **Click the Apple menu and then choose Chooser⇨AppleShare.**

2. **In the dialog that opens, click the Server IP Address button and type** idisk.mac.com **in the Server Address box.**

3. **Click Connect.**

4. **Type your .Mac member name and password into the User Name and Password boxes, respectively; then click Connect.**

5. **Choose your iDisk from the Finder window.**

6. **Click OK.**

Chapter 16: Going Places with Safari

In This Chapter

- Introducing the Safari window and controls
- Visiting Web sites with Safari
- Moving between sites
- Creating and using bookmarks
- Receiving files with Safari
- Saving Web pages to disk
- Protecting your privacy on the Web
- Blocking those irritating pop-ups

When I was designing the Table of Contents for this book, I seriously considered leaving this chapter out — after all, more people use a Web browser now than any other software application. Who really needs a guide to mowing a lawn?

But then again, I suddenly thought of all the hidden features that folks don't know about Apple's Safari browser — for example, the tips and tricks that can help you organize your online visits. It's a little like learning more about the lawn mower itself: Even though you might not need tips on mowing, many people don't know how to remove the spark plug in the winter or how to sharpen the blade so you can handle taller grass. Remember, *magic is nothing more than technology that someone understands.*

In this chapter, I show you how to use those other controls and toolbar buttons in Safari — you know, the ones *besides* the Forward and Back buttons — and you'll discover how to keep track of where you've been and where you'd like to go. (Oh, and did I mention that you'll need an Internet connection?)

Let's Pretend You've Never Used This Thing

Figure 16-1 illustrates version 1.1 of Safari, which runs only under Mac OS X. You can launch Safari directly from the Dock, or you can click the Safari icon within your Applications folder.

Major sections of the Safari window include

+ **The Address bar:** You'll find the most often-used commands on the toolbar for things like navigation, adding bookmarks, and searching Google. Plus, you can type or paste the address for Web sites that you'd like to visit. The Address bar can be hidden to provide you with more real estate in your browser window for Web content. To toggle to hidden mode, press ⌘+| (the vertical bar right above the backslash) or choose View➪Address Bar.

✦ **The Bookmarks bar:** Consider this a toolbar that allows you to jump directly to your favorite Web sites with a single click. I show you later in the section "Adding and Using Bookmarks" how to add and remove sites from your Bookmarks bar. For now, remember that you can toggle the display of the Bookmarks bar by choosing View➪Bookmarks Bar.

✦ **The Content window:** Congratulations! At last, you've waded through all the pre-game show and you've reached the area where Web pages are actually displayed. Like any other window, the Content window can be scrolled; and when you minimize Safari to the Dock, you get a *thumbnail* (minimized) image of the Content window.

The Content window often contains underlined text and graphical icons that transport you to other pages when you click them. These underlined words and icons are *links,* and they make it easy to move from one area of a site to another or to a completely different site.

✦ **The status bar:** The status bar displays information about what the mouse pointer is currently resting upon, like the address for a link or the name of an image; it also updates you on what's happening while a page is loading. To hide or display the status bar, press ⌘+\ (backslash).

Bookmarks bar   Address bar   Content window

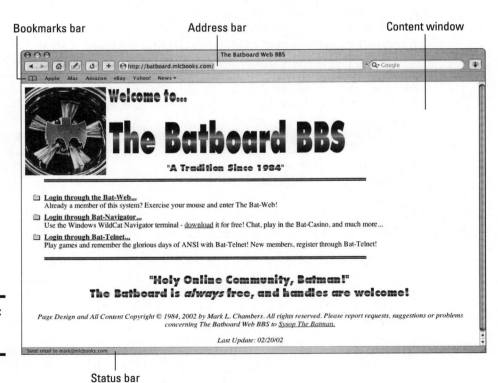

Figure 16-1:
Safari at a
glance.

Status bar

Visiting Web Sites

Here's the stuff that virtually everyone over the age of 5 knows how to do . . . but I get paid by the word, and some folks might just not be aware of all the myriad ways of visiting a site. You can load a Web page from any of the following methods:

✦ **Type (or paste) a Web site address into the Address bar and then press Return.**

If you're typing in an address and Safari recognizes the site as one that you've visited in the past, it helps by completing the address for you. If this is a new site, just keep typing.

✦ **Click a Bookmarks entry within Safari.**

✦ **Click the Home button, which takes you to the home page that you specify.**

More on this in the section, "Setting Up Your Home Page," elsewhere in this chapter.

✦ **Click a page link in Apple Mail or another Internet-savvy application.**

✦ **Click a page link within another Web page.**

✦ **Use the Google box in the Address bar.**

Click in the Google box, type the contents that you want to find, and then press Return. Safari presents you with the search results page on Google for the text that you entered. (In case you've been living under the Internet equivalent of a rock for the last couple of years, *Google.com* is the preeminent search site on the Web — people use Google to find everything from used auto parts to ex-spouses.)

✦ **Click a Safari page icon in the Dock or in a Finder window.**

For example, Mac OS X already has an icon in the default Dock that takes you to the Mac OS X page on the Apple Web site. Drag a site from your Bookmarks bar and drop it on the right side of the Dock. Clicking the icon that you add launches Safari and automatically loads that site.

This trick works only on the side of the Dock to the right of the vertical line.

If you minimize Safari to the Dock, you'll see a thumbnail of the page with the Safari logo superimposed on it. Click this thumbnail in the Dock to restore the page to its full glory.

Navigating the Web

A typical Web surfing session is a linear experience — you bop from one page to the next, absorbing the information that you want and discarding the rest. However, after you visit a few sites, you might find that you need to return to where you've been or head to the familiar ground of your home page. Safari offers these navigational controls on the Address bar:

✦ **Back:** Click the Back button (the left-facing arrow) on the toolbar to return to the last page that you visited. Additional clicks take you to previous pages, in reverse order. The Back button is disabled if you haven't visited at least two sites.

✦ **Forward:** If you've clicked the Back button at least once, clicking the Forward button (the right-facing arrow) takes you to the next page (or through the pages) where you originally were, in forward order. The Forward button is disabled if you haven't used the Back button.

✦ **Home:** Click this button (look for the little house) to return to your home page.

✦ **AutoFill:** If you fill out a lot of forms online — when you're shopping at Web sites, for example — you can click the AutoFill button (which looks like a little text box and a pen) to complete these forms for you. You can set what information is used for AutoFill by choosing Safari⇨Preferences and clicking the AutoFill toolbar button.

To be honest, I'm not a big fan of releasing *any* of my personal information to *any* Web site, so I don't use AutoFill often. If you do decide to use this feature, make sure that the connection is secure (look for the padlock icon in the upper-right corner of the Safari window) and read the site's Privacy Agreement page first to see how your identity data will be treated.

✦ **Stop/Reload:** Click Reload (which has a circular arrow) to refresh the contents of the current page. Although most pages remain static, some pages change their content at regular intervals or after you fill out a form or click a button. By clicking Reload (look for the curvy arrow), you can see what's changed on these pages. (I use Reload every hour or so with CNN.com, for example.) While a page is loading, the Reload button turns into the Stop button — with a little X mark — and you can click it to stop the loading of the content from the current page. This is a real boon when a download takes *foorrevverr,* which can happen when you're trying to visit a very popular or very slow Web site (especially if you're using a dial-up modem connection to the Internet). Using Stop is also handy if a page has a number of very large graphics that are going to take a long time to load.

✦ **Add Bookmark:** Click this Address bar button (which carries a plus sign) to add a page to your Bookmarks bar or Bookmarks menu. (More on this in a tad.)

✦ **Google Search:** As I mention earlier, you can click in this box and type text that you want to find on the Web via the Google search engine. Then press Return to display the results. To repeat a recent search, click the down arrow in the Google Search box and select it from the drop-down list.

✦ **Bug:** A rather strange creature, the Safari Bug button (top right) makes it easy to alert Apple when you encounter a page that doesn't display properly in Safari. (Software developers call such glitches *bugs* — hence the name.) When you click the Bug button, you'll see a sheet with the settings shown in Figure 16-2; take time to enter a short description of the problem that you're having. (I also enable the Send Screen Shot of Current Page and the Send Source of Current Page check boxes to give the Apple folks more to work with while they're debugging Safari.) Then click the Submit button to send the bug report to Apple.

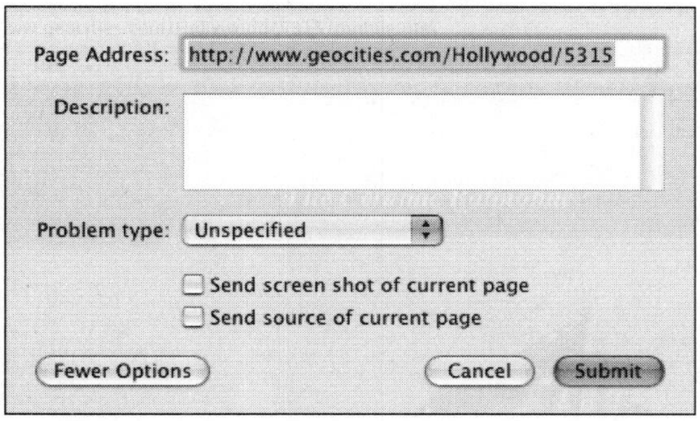

Figure 16-2: Have at thee, troublesome buggy page!

Page Address: http://www.geocities.com/Hollywood/5315

Description:

Problem type: Unspecified

☐ Send screen shot of current page
☐ Send source of current page

Fewer Options   Cancel   Submit

Remember, not all these buttons and controls might appear on your Address bar. To display or hide Address bar controls, toggle them on and off from the View menu.

Setting Up Your Home Page

Choosing a home page is one of the easiest methods of speeding up your Web surfing, especially if you're using a dial-up modem connection. However, a large percentage of the Mac owners whom I've talked to have never set their own home page, simply using the default home page provided by their browser! With Safari running, take a moment to follow these steps to declare your own freedom to choose your own home page:

1. **If you want to use a specific Web page as your new home page, display it in Safari.**

   It's a good idea to select a page with few graphics or a fast-loading popular site.

2. **Choose Safari⇨Preferences or press ⌘+, (comma).**

3. **Click the General button.**

   You'll see the settings shown in Figure 16-3.

4. **Click the Set to Current Page button.**

5. **Alternatively, click the New Windows Open With drop-down list box and click Empty page if you want Safari to open a new window with a blank page.**

   This is the fastest choice of all for a home page.

6. **Press ⌘+Q to exit the Preferences dialog.**

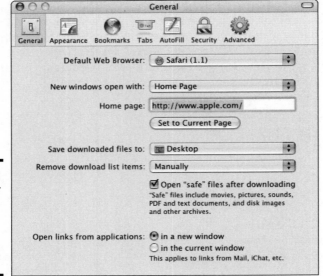

Figure 16-3:
Adding your own home page is an easy change you can make.

Visit your home page at any time by pressing the Home button on the Address bar.

Adding and Using Bookmarks

No doubt about it: Bookmarks make the Web a friendly place. As you collect bookmarks in Safari, you're able to immediately jump from one site to another with a single click on the Bookmarks menu or the buttons on the Bookmarks bar.

To add a bookmark, first navigate to the desired page and then do any of the following:

✦ **Choose Bookmarks➪Add Bookmark.**

✦ **Press the ⌘+D keyboard shortcut.**

Safari displays the sheet that you see in Figure 16-4, where you can enter the name for the bookmark and select where it will appear (on the Bookmarks bar or the Bookmarks menu).

✦ **Drag the Web address from the Address bar to the Bookmarks bar.**

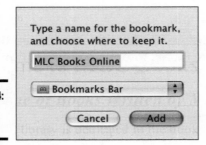

Figure 16-4:
Adding a bookmark.

You can also drag a link on the current page to the Bookmarks bar, but note that doing this only adds a bookmark for the page corresponding to the link — not the current page.

To jump to a bookmark:

+ **Choose it from the Bookmarks menu.**

    If the bookmark is contained in a folder, which I discuss later in this section, move your mouse pointer over the folder name to show its contents and then click the bookmark.

+ **Click the bookmark on the Bookmarks bar.**

    If you've added a large number of items to the Bookmarks bar, click the More icon on the edge of the Bookmarks bar to display the rest of the buttons.

+ **Click the Show All Bookmarks button (which looks like a small opened book) on the Bookmarks bar and then click the desired bookmark.**

    The Bookmarks window that you see in Figure 16-5 appears, where you can review each collection of bookmarks at leisure.

The more bookmarks that you add, the more unwieldy the Bookmarks menu and the Bookmarks window become. To keep things organized, choose Bookmarks⇨Add Bookmark Folder and then type a name for the new folder. With folders, you can organize your bookmarks into *collections,* which appear in the column at the left of the Bookmarks window (or as separate submenus within the Bookmarks menu). You can drag bookmarks within the new folder to help reduce the clutter.

To delete a bookmark or a folder from the Bookmarks window, click it and then press Delete.

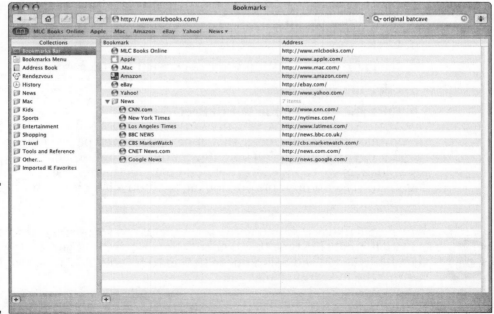

Figure 16-5:
The Bookmarks window puts all your bookmarks in easy reach.

Downloading Files

A huge chunk of the fun that you'll find on the Web is the ability to download images and files. If you've visited a site that offers files for downloading, typically you just click the Download button or the download file link, and Safari takes care of the rest. You'll see the Downloads status window as shown in Figure 16-6, which keeps you updated on the progress of the transfer. While the file is downloading, feel free to continue browsing or even download additional files; the status window helps you keep track of what's going on and when everything will be finished transferring.

Figure 16-6: Monitor downloads with the status window.

By default, Safari saves any downloaded files on your Mac OS X Desktop, which I like and use. To specify the location where downloaded files are stored — for example, if you'd like to scan them automatically with an antivirus program — follow these steps:

1. **Choose Safari⇨Preferences or press ⌘+, (comma).**

2. **Click the General tab and then click the Save Downloaded Files To drop-down list box.**

3. **Click Other.**

4. **Navigate to the location where you want the files stored.**

5. **Click the Select button.**

6. **Click the Close button to exit Preferences.**

To download a specific image that appears on a Web page, move your mouse pointer over the image and hold down Control while you click. Then choose Download Image to Disk from the pop-up menu that appears, as shown in Figure 16-7. Safari prompts you for the location where you want to store the file.

Luckily, Safari has matured to the point that it can seamlessly handle virtually any multimedia file type that it encounters. However, if you've downloaded a multimedia file and Safari doesn't seem to be able to play or display it, try loading the file within QuickTime.

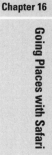

Figure 16-7:
Download single image files from a Web page.

Using Subscriptions and History

To keep tabs on where you've been, you can display the History list by clicking the History menu. To return to a page in the list, just click it from the History menu. Safari also searches the History list when it fills in an address that you're typing — that's the feature I mentioned in the earlier section, "Visiting Web Sites."

I show you how to clear the contents of the History file in the upcoming section, "Handling ancient history."

Saving Web Pages

If you've encountered a page that you'd like to load later, you can save it to disk in its entirety. Follow these steps:

1. **Display the desired page.**

2. **Choose File⇨Save As.**

3. **In the Save As text field, type a name for the saved page.**

4. **From the Where field, navigate to the location where you want to store the file on your system.**

To expand the sheet to allow navigation to any location on your system, click the button with the downward arrow.

5. **Click Save to begin the download process.**

After the Save file has been created, double-click it to load it in Safari.

A quick word about printing a page within Safari: Some combinations of background and text colors might conspire together to render your printed copy practically worthless. In a case like that, use your printer's grayscale setting (if it has one). Alternatively, you can simply click and drag to select the text on the page, press ⌘+C to copy it, and then paste the text into Word or AppleWorks, where you can print the page on a less offensive background (while still keeping the text formatting largely untouched). You can also save the contents of a page as plain text, as I just demonstrated.

Protecting Your Privacy

No chapter on Safari would be complete without a discussion of security, both against outside intrusion from the Internet and prying eyes around your Mac. Hence this last section, which covers protecting your privacy.

Although diminutive, the tiny padlock icon that appears in the top-right corner of the Safari window when you're connected to a secure Web site means a great deal! A *secure site* encrypts the information that you send and receive, making it much harder for those of unscrupulous ideals to obtain things like credit card numbers and personal information.

Yes, there are such things as bad cookies

First, a definition of this ridiculous term: A *cookie,* a small file that a Web site automatically saves on your hard drive, contains information that the site will use on your future visits. For example, a site might save a cookie to preserve your site preferences for the next time or — in the case of a site such as Amazon.com — to identify you automatically and help customize the offerings that you see.

In and of themselves, cookies aren't bad things. Unlike a virus, a cookie file isn't going to replicate itself or wreak havoc on your system, and only the original site can read the cookie that it creates. However, many folks don't appreciate acting as a gracious host for a slew of little snippets of personal information. Also, if you do a large amount of surfing, cookies can occupy a significant amount of your hard drive space over time. (Not to mention that some cookies have highly suggestive names, which could lead to all sorts of conclusions. End of story.)

You can choose to accept all cookies — the default — or you can opt to disable cookies altogether. To change your *Cookie Acceptance Plan* (or CAP, for those who absolutely crave acronyms), follow these steps:

1. **Choose Safari⇨Preferences.**

2. **Click the Security toolbar button.**

   Safari displays the preference settings shown in Figure 16-8.

3. **Select the Never radio button to block cookies entirely, or select the Always radio button to accept all cookies.**

Personally, I use the default option, Only from Sites You Navigate To, which allows sites like Amazon.com to work correctly without allowing a barrage of illicit cookies.

4. **To view the cookies currently on your system, click the Show Cookies button.**

The site that used that cookie will forget any information that it stored in the file, meaning that you might have to take care of things manually, like providing a password on the site that used to be read automatically from the cookie.

5. **Click the Close button to save your changes.**

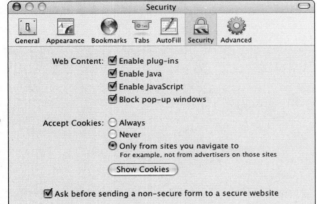

Figure 16-8:
Exploring the contents of my cookie jar.

Cleaning your cache

Safari speeds up the loading of Web sites by storing often-used images and multimedia files in a temporary storage, or *cache,* folder. Naturally, the files in your cache folder can be displayed (hint), which could lead to assumptions (hint, hint) about the sites you've been visiting (hint, hint, hint). (Tactful, ain't I?)

Luckily, Safari makes it easy to dump the contents of your cache file. Just click Safari on the menu and click Empty Cache; then click Empty to confirm that you want to clean up your cache.

Handling ancient history

As you might imagine, your History file leaves a very clear set of footprints indicating where you've been on the Web. To delete the contents of the History menu, choose History⇨Clear History.

Another built-in security feature can also help save your sanity: Safari can block those incredibly irritating pop-up advertisement windows that are automatically displayed by some Web sites. (I rank such Webmasters at the same social level as spammers!) Click Safari and choose Block Pop-Up Windows or press ⌘+K. In case you're visiting a site that actually uses pop-up windows to your advantage, you can toggle off the block feature temporarily.

Book II

Google

The 5th Wave   By Rich Tennant

"This is amazing. You can stop looking for Derek. According to a Google search I did, he's hiding behind the dryer in the basement."

Book II: Google

Chapter 1: Think You Know Google?

In This Chapter

✔ **Getting an overview of Google's many services**

✔ **Exploring Google's search realms**

✔ **Uncovering Google's hidden features**

✔ **Understanding why Google is the best**

1 know what you're saying: You've already discovered Google. Who hasn't? Not since the early days of the Web have people flocked so unanimously to a single, dominant search engine as they do to Google. A recent marketing survey reported that Google was a more recognized brand name than Coca-Cola and Starbucks. No online activity has become as deeply embedded in our culture and language as Googling.

Google is far more than just a search engine and has become more important than other general search engines. Google's value is partly due to its amazingly accurate search results and its no-fluff presentation. Not to be forgotten are Google's supporting services — many of which are covered in this book and outlined in this chapter.

Thanks to Google, general searching of the Web has become standardized. Anybody who wants to find an online destination follows this three-step process:

1. Go to Google at `www.google.com`.

2. Type a few words related to the search goal and press Enter.

3. Click the search results to visit relevant Web sites.

What You Can Do with Google

The World Wide Web was developed to bring order to the chaotic Internet, which academia and the government had been using since the 1960s. Because people regarded the Internet as primarily an information source — more than an entertainment medium or a community space — it was natural to imagine the quick construction of a universal, all-inclusive online library. Through the years, I often heard people mistakenly speak of the Internet as an information realm in which one could find anything, read any book, and access all knowledge.

But the truth splintered away from that ideal. First, the Web became a distinct and autonomous entity with its own content. Second, regular folks who stormed into the new virtual playground were interested in other, more recreational pursuits than learning.

I'm not going to tell you that Google single-handedly presents an Alexandrian library of human knowledge. (Yet.) However, because Google search results are so accurate, Google offers an amazing scope of knowledge. Want to know something? Google is the modern recipe for discovery in this information-saturated age.

Find all sorts of stuff

In addition to traditional Web searching, Google offers refined areas that you can search by using the same basic keyword process. The Google home page offers the following additional tabs to the right of the Web tab:

✦ **Images:** As Chapter 2 of Book II explains, you can search for photographs and drawings on Google.

✦ **Groups:** Chapter 4 of Book II explains that Google is a means of searching more than 30,000 newsgroups. Through Google, you can establish an identity and post messages to newsgroups, all through your Web browser.

✦ **Directory:** As Chapter 3 of Book II explains, Google presents a topical directory for browsing, and you can search it separately from the basic Web search.

✦ **News:** Chapter 3 of Book II explains that Google News presents continually updated links to established news sources in dozens of countries.

✦ **Froogle:** As Chapter 10 of Book II explains, Froogle (the word is a pun on "frugal") is a shopping directory that can be searched by keyword.

Explore the hidden strengths of Google

You might be surprised to find what Google can be for you. Google is all of the following things:

✦ **A shopping portal:** Google offers two main shopping services: Google Catalogs and Froogle. Use Froogle to find shopping bargains. Google Catalogs offers a paper-free ability to access the mail-order universe. See Chapter 10 of Book II.

✦ **A document repository:** Most people, most of the time, search for Web pages. But many other types of viewable (or listenable) pieces of content are available on the Internet. For example, almost every modern computer comes with the ability to view PDF files. Google includes documents other than Web pages in its general search results and also lets you narrow any search to a specific file type. See Book II, Chapter 5.

✦ **A translator:** Google is multilingual. You can dump foreign text into an on-screen box for instant conversion to the language of your choice. See Book II, Chapter 8.

✦ **A government and university tracker:** Google reserves distinct portions of its search engine for university domains and for government domains. See Book II, Chapter 8.

Get answers from real people

One problem with the Web as an information resource is the question of authenticity. Anybody can put up a Web site and publish information that might or might not be true. True expertise is difficult to verify on the Web.

Google Answers is . . . well, the answer. Staffed by a large crew of freelance researchers in many subjects, Google Answers lets you ask questions and receive customized answers — for a price. How much? That's up to you; Google Answers uses an auction system whereby you request an answer for a specified price and individual researchers either take on your question or not, as Chapter 9 of Book II explains.

Take Google with you

Doesn't everyone deserve a personal hard-working search engine? You can rip the Google engine right out of its site (so to speak) and take it with you while traipsing around the Web in two ways:

✦ **Google Toolbar:** If you're aware of the Google Toolbar, you're probably using it. If not, you're missing out. The Google Toolbar bolts right onto your browser, near the top where your other toolbars reside. As Chapter 6 of Book II explains, it enables you to launch a Google search without surfing to the Google site.

✦ **Google browser buttons:** Perhaps even snazzier than the Google Toolbar, the browser buttons attach to your browser's existing toolbar, where they inscrutably await your mouse clicks. I explain them in Book II, Chapter 6.

The Greatness of Google

In this chapter, I serve a sample platter of Google's buffet of services. But one central question remains: What makes Google so great in the first place? How did it become so rampantly popular that it nearly eradicated other general search engines? Google's success depends to some extent on the size of its index, which has long passed the billion-page mark — Google claims to have the largest Web search index in the world.

But the big index is hardly the entire story. More important is a certain intelligence with which the index interprets keywords. Google's groundbreaking innovation in this department is its capability to not only find pages but also rank them based on their popularity. The legendary Google page rank is determined largely by measuring how many links to a page exist on other sites all over the Web. The logic here is simple and hard to refute: Page A links to page B for one reason only, and that is because page B contains something worthwhile. If pages C, D, E, F, and G also link to page B, odds increase that page B has something important going for it. If 500,000 pages link to page B, it is without question truly important in some way. The use of back-links logic is the advantage that makes Google search results so fantastic.

Every day, Google answers more than 200 million search queries. Google calmly digests keywords in almost 90 languages. At this writing, only a third of Google's search requests come from the United States. Googling is the one activity that unites the entire Internet citizenry, and Google has forever altered the Internet landscape.

Chapter 2: Improving Your Google Searches

In This Chapter

- ✓ Choosing keywords and searching the Web
- ✓ Interpreting and using the search results page
- ✓ Understanding advanced searching
- ✓ Discovering the convenience and power of search operators
- ✓ Searching for images

This chapter is where you get down to the business of searching for sites, finding files, wrangling with search results, and generally raiding Google for all it's worth. You might be thinking, "I know how to search Google. You type a few words, press Enter, blink rapidly, and view the results." I won't comment on disturbing facial tics, but that process is essentially correct. In this chapter, however, I show you just how powerful Google is for searching the Internet.

Basic Web Searches

One of the nicest aspects of Google is how cut and dried the Google home page is. As Figure 2-1 shows, there's no mistaking where to enter the keywords of your search. Google has embraced the purity of searching with an ad-free home page that leaves no doubt that searching is the task at hand. These days, for most people, to search is to Google.

When you arrive at the Google home page, the mouse cursor is already waiting for you in the keyword search box. Type a word, multiple words, or a sentence. Press Enter or click the Google Search button. The results come up on your screen within seconds.

 Note the I'm Feeling Lucky button next to the Google Search button. Clicking it instead of the Google Search button takes you directly to the top search result's Web page instead of to the search results page. Only Google could dare to invite its users to skip the search results page and make it work out so well, so often.

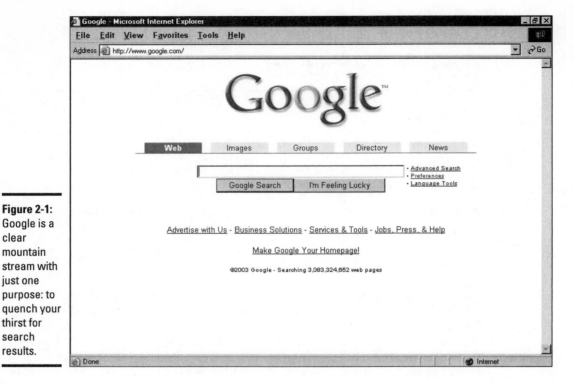

Figure 2-1:
Google is a clear mountain stream with just one purpose: to quench your thirst for search results.

Clicking the tabs above the keyword box — Web, Images, Groups, Directory, News — takes you to the main pages of those sections. If you're on a search results page and click a tab, however, you get results for that section instantly.

Choosing the right keywords

Google is possibly the most forgiving search engine ever created. You can type just about any darn thing into it and get good results. Sometimes you can even get away with sloppy spelling. Google often catches the misspelled word and suggests the correct spelling.

The golden rule for Internet searching is that more keywords deliver fewer results. So pile them on to narrow your search. With that technique, however, you run the risk of having conflicting or unclear keywords, creating a mixed bag of search results. Ideally, you want to concisely convey to Google what you need. I've found that two is the golden number of keywords to use in Google searches. At my Web sites, the tracking software tells me which search queries get to my pages, and invariably the two-word strings reach my best stuff.

On the other hand, many people get good results by typing entire sentences or questions in the keyword box. Google always eliminates certain little words such as *what* and *why,* which might seem to devalue questions but doesn't in practice.

Beware of words that have more than one meaning, especially if you search for one keyword at a time. For example, a search for *bridge* yields Web sites about a card game, a supportive structure, and dental work.

For power searching, in which the goal is not more results but fewer, better results, use the Advanced Search pages or the search operators, both of which I describe later in this chapter.

Understanding the Google Results Page

Every Google search results page for a Web search includes at least three basic types of information:

✦ A summary of the search results

✦ The search results themselves

✦ A few things that you can do with the results

As you can see in Figure 2-2, the results summary is located on the right side in the shaded bar above the results list. The summary tells you how many total results for your keywords exist in the Google index and how long the search took. (Rarely does a Google search require more than two seconds.)

On the left side of the summary bar, your keywords are displayed as links. When you click one of those links, you go to Dictionary.com for a definition of the word. This seems a bit gratuitous — if you didn't know what a word means, why would you use it as a keyword? But don't underestimate the variety of ways that people use Google, including as a dictionary. Dictionary.com also functions as a thesaurus, so if a certain keyword isn't delivering good results, perhaps a synonym will. Note that the links to Dictionary.com appear only when Google's language is set to English — naturally enough, because Dictionary.com is an English dictionary.

Book II
Chapter 2

**Improving Your
Google Searches**

Figure 2-2:
A Google
Web search
results
page.
Notice the
suggested
spelling
correction.

The search results consist of the page name, which is hyperlinked to the page itself. Below that is a short bit of relevant text from the page. Below the text you can see the page's URL, which is there for information value and is not a link. Next to the URL is a number indicating the size of the page. Glancing at the page size helps you decide whether or not to visit it. Pages more than 50K (that's 50 kilobytes) are too large for a quick visit if you don't have high-speed Internet access.

The Google staff doesn't compose the page title or the accompanying text, which explains why they're a little goofy sometimes and incoherent other times. The page developer creates the page title as part of the HTML code underlying all Web pages. Some page designers forget how important the page title is, or they pack in lots of words to try and get the page higher on the search results pages of search engines such as Google.

Note: The result link doesn't identify where on the target page your keywords are located. Not uncommonly, you link to a page and must then search in that page for relevant information — a headache when the page is long. Of course, you can always use your browser's Find feature to locate specific words on any Web page, or the highlight feature on the Google Toolbar (which I explain in Chapter 6 of Book II).

Breaking Down Web Search Results

Other elements on the search results page enable you to understand the result, continue the search, narrow the search, or avoid Internet traffic jams when seeing the target page. Some of these features are present on every search result, and some exist occasionally.

Page description

Although the Google staff doesn't compose the search result text, sometimes part of the accompanying text *is* so composed. If Google Directory (which is built by humans) has an entry for a target page, the brief description that appears in the Google Directory is imported to the Web search result. It's set apart from the snippets of page text by the Description heading.

Directory category

When a target page appears in Google Directory, its directory category is presented next to a Category heading under the page name. The category is a link, and you can proceed directly to that page of Google Directory by clicking the link. Figure 2-3 shows a search whose first result is a directory listing.

There's little difference between this method and starting your search in Google Directory. But the Category link on the Web search results page is helpful in a surprising way: When you want to see pages similar to the target page, Google Directory is better than the Similar Pages feature (which I describe in "Similar pages"). If your experience mirrors mine, the more you try the Category link, the more you'll come to rely on it for high-quality, related results. The handpicked Google Directory houses more stable sites than an index search is likely to house.

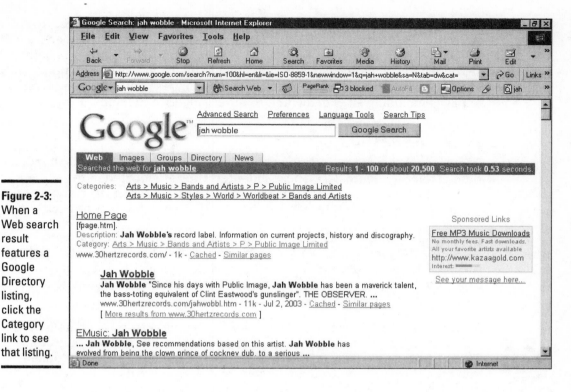

Figure 2-3:
When a
Web search
result
features a
Google
Directory
listing,
click the
Category
link to see
that listing.

The Google cache

A *cache* (pronounced the same as the word *cash*) is a storage area for computer files. Google maintains an enormous cache of Web pages. Don't confuse the cache with the index. (Actually, for practical purposes, whether you confuse them or not doesn't matter, but they are different.) The index is a database of Web-page content that's stripped of its formatting. The cache contains the pages themselves. By and large, clicking the Cached link that appears under each search result provides a quicker display of the target page because you're getting it from Google's computer instead of the Internet at large.

So why would you ever *not* use the Cached link instead of the main page title link? Well, the cached page is not necessarily up to the minute, especially with pages that change frequently. If you view the cached version of a page that you know is changed frequently and dated, such as the front page of a newspaper site, you can see that Google's cache is about three days behind. For users without high-speed Internet access, it's more convenient to pull from the cache when looking for a big page (about 50K or so) that doesn't change much.

Similar pages

The Similar Pages link is interesting although not always tremendously useful. Clicking this link starts a new search for pages that somehow resemble the original search result. Sorry to be vague, but Google isn't very talkative about its Similar Pages formula.

The results are interesting and more diverse than you might expect. You'd think the search would yield a narrowed set of results, but my experience is to the contrary. Search for Kelly Clarkson, for example, and you get a solid set of results, including fan sites and official *American Idol* destinations. Click a Similar Pages link under a target page, and you get a far-ranging assortment of pages including sites dedicated to other singers and bands.

Indented results

Some search results are offset from the main body of results with an indentation (refer to Figure 2-2). These indented sites are located in the same domain (such as www.kellyclarksonweb.com) as the target page above them. They're indented to tell you that it might be redundant to click both.

Google refrains from listing all the pages in a single domain that match your keywords. However, you can see more results from that domain by clicking the More Results from www.*domain*.com link in any indented search result. Doing so is a great way to perform a mini-search within any domain that has already proved useful to you.

Searching in a large Web site (also called a *domain*) can be accomplished another way: by using a special search operator called the *site* operator. This operator tells Google to apply your keywords to a specified domain. You type the *site* operator, the domain, and the keywords in a single glop of instructions. For example, if you want to search www.kellyclarkson.com for the keyword *idol,* you could do so with a single entry:

```
site:www.kellyclarkson.com idol
```

You can reverse the order of the syntax, placing the keyword(s) before the *site* operator and domain, without affecting the search results.

Conducting an Advanced Search

Later in this chapter, I cover the use of special query terms (similar to the *site* operator), general search operators that you can use with keywords, and searching for specified types of documents. All these tricks and more are consolidated on the Advanced Search page, shown in Figure 2-4. To get to this page, click the Advanced Search link on the Google home page.

Use Advanced Search for any of the following three reasons:

+ You want to focus a search more narrowly than a general keyword search.

+ You don't want to bother with the complexity and thorny syntax of search operators.

+ You want to combine more than one search operation.

As you see in Figure 2-4, the Advanced Search page bundles many keyword boxes and drop-down lists to launch a finely targeted search. You don't have to use everything that this page has to offer. In fact, you may conduct a simple, one-keyword search from here, although that would be like using a racecar to buy groceries.

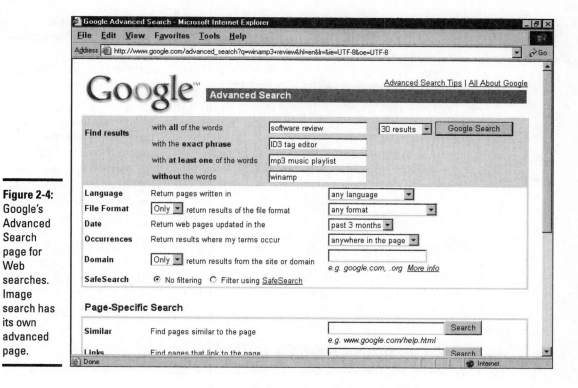

Figure 2-4:
Google's
Advanced
Search
page for
Web
searches.
Image
search has
its own
advanced
page.

Following is a review of the Advanced Search features. After setting any combination of these features, click the Google Search button to get your results.

Using multiple keywords

At the top of the Advanced Search page are a series of keyword boxes grouped in a shaded area called Find Results (see Figure 2-4). You use the four keyword boxes in this area to tell Google how to manage multiple keywords. If you have just one keyword, type it in the top keyword box. The instructions next to each keyword box correspond to *Boolean operators,* typed shorthand instructions that I cover in "Searching Shorthand: Using Operators," later in this chapter. The Advanced Search page gives you the laser exactness of Boolean searching without all the typing.

Use these keyword boxes in the following ways:

✦ **With all of the Words:** Tells Google to scour for pages that contain every word with no exceptions. This option has the effect of narrowing search results. For example, if you use the keywords *alan greenspan federal reserve,* you don't see irrelevant pages that contain only *alan* or only *federal.*

✦ **With the Exact Phrase:** Delivers pages that contain your keywords in the exact order and with the exact spelling that you type. You might use this option for people's names *(david hyde pierce),* sport teams with their cities *(los angeles dodgers),* and colloquial phrases *(jump the shark).*

✦ **With at Least One of the Words:** Widens the search results. This option is useful when you're less picky about matching your words. For example, if you're conducting broad research about building string instruments, you might use the keywords *violin cello viola* in this text box and *instrument building* in the top text box.

✦ **Without the Words:** Eliminates matches that contain certain words. This command is useful when one of your keywords is often undesirably associated with other words. It has the effect of narrowing search results and making them more accurate. For example, if you're looking for pages about giants in fairy tales, you can stack words into this box that eliminate pages about certain sports teams, such as *new york san francisco baseball football.* At the same time, you need to place the *giants* keyword in the top box and *fairy tale* in the exact phrase box.

Here's something to keep in mind: Google's general search results are so accurate that Boolean commands are usually unnecessary. It all depends on your level of searching. If, during a general search, you find yourself looking beyond the first page of results (given 30 or fewer results per page), the Advanced Search keyword boxes might speed your searches along.

Other Advanced Search features

The central portion of the Advanced Search page contains six settings designed to narrow your results. They are

✦ **Language:** Similar to the Search Language setting on the Preferences page (see Chapter 5 of Book II), this drop-down list instructs Google to return search results only in the specified language. The default setting is any language.

✦ **File Format:** Google recognizes certain distinct file formats, such as Microsoft Word documents (which end in the .doc extension) and Adobe Acrobat (.pdf) files. You can use the File Format setting to include or exclude selected file formats.

✦ **Date:** Google's index crawler can determine when a page was last changed. (Google's crawlers sweep through the Web gathering information about Web sites.) A page update might be as trivial as changing one word, or it might involve a massive content revision. The drop-down list for this feature doesn't give you fine control over the update time — you may select pages updated in the past three months, past six months, and past year.

✦ **Occurrences:** This powerful and useful setting whisks away questionable search results and gives you control of how important your keywords are to the matched page. The purpose is not to determine where your keywords exist in the page's text (that is, how near to the top of the page they occur), nor is it to help you avoid scrolling the page. This feature culls pages in which your keywords appear in the page title, in the page URL, or in the page's incoming links.

✦ **Domain:** Like the Occurrences setting, you can use this setting to include or exclude matches with certain properties. In this case, you're allowing or eliminating a certain domain, which is the portion of a site's URL after www. When typing the domain, you may type the **www** or leave it out. So, for *The New York Times* domain, you could type **www.nytimes. com** or **nytimes.com**. Use the first drop-down list to select Only (includes the selected domain and no others) or Don't (excludes the selected domain and admits all others).

✦ **SafeSearch:** The default position of this setting turns off SafeSearch if you have it turned on in your Preferences (see Chapter 5 of Book II). You can activate SafeSearch on a per-search basis by using this feature of the Advanced Search page.

Following are the two Page-Specific Search features found on the Advanced Search page:

✦ **Similar:** Identical to the Similar Pages link on the search results page, this feature finds pages related to the URL that you type in the keyword box.

✦ **Links:** This one is addictive and shows off Google's extreme network awareness. The *link* operator tells Google to find Web pages that contain links to a page that you specify. The URL of your specified page is the keyword that you type in the text box. Because most large sites link to their own home pages from every other page, these searches yield a lot of tedious results from within the domain. However, it's fun to try with an inner page from a site.

Searching Shorthand: Using Operators

You don't need to detour to the Advanced Search page if you know about the keyword modifiers called *search operators*. Standard search operators are not unique to Google; most search engines understand them and require the same symbols and syntax when typing them. Search operators are typed with the keywords right in the keyword box. You do have to type neatly and make sure that you don't add spaces in the wrong places or use the wrong case (small letters instead of capital letters in some instances).

The four major Boolean operators work in Google's keyword boxes as follows:

✦ *AND:* Forces Google to match the search results against *all* your keywords. The operator is signified by a plus sign (+). The effect is to narrow search results, giving you fewer and more accurate hits. Place the plus sign immediately before any word(s) that you want to force into the match, without a space between the symbol and the word (for example, *dog +chew +toy +slobber*). Keep in mind that Google naturally attempts to match all keywords without being commanded to. It always lists complete matches first, followed by Web pages that match fewer keywords. So the *AND* operator is best used in combination with other operators or in combination with words that aren't preceded by an operator.

✦ *NOT:* Excludes words that might otherwise bring up many undesirable page matches. The effect is to narrow search results. The symbol is a minus sign (-). Like the *AND* operator, place the symbol immediately before a word. When using it, think of anti-keywords that thwart the mission of your pro-keywords. For example, "giants NOT football" gets information about the San Francisco Giants baseball team, but not the New York Giants football team.

✦ *OR:* Divides a search along two concurrent avenues of exploration. It's not as wishy-washy as you might think: The *OR* operator is helpful when using obscure keywords that might not return much of value if used singly. This operator has no symbol; simply type **OR** (use capital letters) before a keyword and leave a space between the operator and the following keyword.

✦ *quote:* Finds text sequences identical to what you enter. This is the same as the With the Exact Phrase feature of the Advanced Search page. Whatever you type within the quotes is interpreted and matched identically by Google.

If you forget to close the quotation at the end of the quotes-applied keywords, Google extends the *quote* operator to the end of your keyword string, possibly reducing your matches to zero.

A Picture Is Worth a Thousand Keywords

Image searching in Google is less complex than Web searching and is fun in different ways. For example, you can search for pictures of people that you haven't seen in years, for postcard-like images of travel destinations, or for pictures of yourself.

Google's task is a tricky one. It must match your keyword(s) with pictures — a far harder task than matching words with text. At best, Google can make educated guesses about the identity or subject matter of a picture based on the filename of the picture, the URL address of the image, the surrounding text, and any caption. So the results are bound to be erratic. Fortunately, Google errs on the side of abundance, delivering truckloads of possible photos and other images in response to your keywords.

Simple searches are identical to Web searches. From the Google home page, click the Images tab, enter a keyword or two, and press Enter. You can even use the operators that I describe in the previous section when searching for images.

It's in the search results that Image and Web searches differ. Image results come in the form of *thumbnails* — small versions of images. Click any thumbnail to see the image along with the Web page on which it resides. As you see in Figure 2-5, Google reproduces the image above the Web page that contains the image — arguably a big waste of space. (Click the Remove Frame link in the top-right corner if you want to get rid of it.) This second reproduction of the image is usually also a thumbnail. You may click this thumbnail to see a full-size version of the picture. Or you can scroll down the page to see the picture in context.

Figure 2-5:
Google's
display of
a search
image and
its Web
page.

Advanced Image Searching

As with Web searches, Google provides a collection of enhanced search tools on the Advanced Image Search page. (See Figure 2-6.) Follow these steps to reach that page:

1. **Go to the Google home page.**

2. **Click the Images tab.**

3. **Click the Advanced Image Search link.**

The Find Results portion of the Advanced Image Search page is nearly identical to the Find Results portion of the Advanced Search page for Web searches. (See "Conducting an Advanced Search," earlier in this chapter.) The difference is that the keyword modifiers here relate to images by matching filenames, captions, and text surrounding the images. Use the keyword boxes to add search modifiers to your keywords, but don't expect exact textual matches as with a Web search because images are not text.

Below the Find Results portion of the Advanced Image Search page are five settings that determine the type and location of your sought images:

✦ **Size:** Use the drop-down list to restrict your search to images of certain sizes. Admittedly, the choices are vague: icon-sized, small, medium, large, very large, and wallpaper-sized. By themselves, these choices are nearly meaningless.

157

✦ **Filetypes:** Use this drop-down list to select JPG, GIF, or PNG files. As a practical matter, these file formats are nearly interchangeable. Whatever you plan to do with your found images, you can probably do equally well with any one of those three types.

✦ **Coloration:** Here you can choose to locate black-and-white pictures, grayscale images, or full-color art. Full-color images usually have the largest file sizes.

✦ **Domain:** Use this keyword box to specify a Web domain that you want to search for images. This is a helpful way to search online newspaper graphics.

✦ **SafeSearch:** With the three SafeSearch options, you can determine the level of filtering that Google applies to your image search. The choices are identical to the SafeSearch preference settings (see Chapter 5 of Book II), but apply to only one search at a time.

In nearly all cases, the images that you find through Google are owned and implicitly copyrighted by other people. There is some buzz among copyright scholars about the capability of search engines to display other people's property on demand. Google itself puts a little copyright warning on the display page that you get when you click a thumbnail image. If you're wondering whether you can download and apply a photo as desktop wallpaper, for example, the quick legal answer is no in most cases. The search results are meant to be informational, and Google isn't intended as a warehouse of downloadable images.

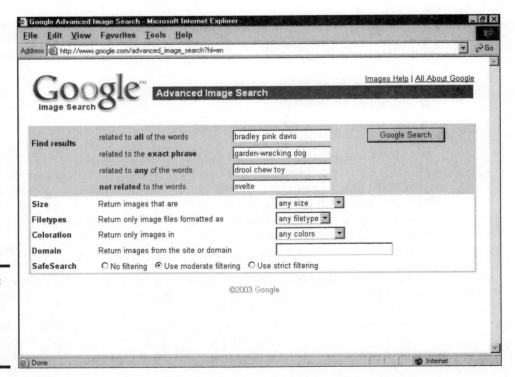

Figure 2-6: The Advanced Image Search page.

How you choose to approach online intellectual property is your business, but respect for property of others strengthens the online community. Besides, with Google at your disposal, you can easily find images whose owners invite downloads. Try using the keywords *public domain* or *free download* on the Advanced Image Search page to find images that you can legally reuse.

CHECK IT OUT

The Special Google Operators

Google understands standard search operators that have been in common use for years, but it also provides special operators for Google only. These unique keyword modifiers take advantage of Google's extraordinary index and bring to life Google's under-the-hood power. Google-specific operators use a colon to separate the command from the keyword string. The format is like this: *operator:keyword string.*

Some Google operators require that you leave no space between the colon and the first keyword, as in the preceding example. It doesn't matter with other operators. Because I don't want to remember which is which, I always crush the first keyword up against the operator's colon. (That sounds like a medical condition.)

Nine Google-specific operators exist:

- ✔ **stocks:** If you put one or more stock ticker symbols in the keyword string, preceded by the *stocks* operator, Google throws you over to one of several financial sites to display the stock's quote. It seems cool at first, but I never use this operator because it doesn't reach into the Google index to do its work. The default destination is Yahoo! Finance, and you can switch to one of four other sites represented by tabs near the top of the page.

- ✔ **cache:** If you know the Web page address, use this operator to pull up Google's cache of that page. By itself, it's not too useful. But the *cache* operator has an intriguing hidden feature. If you type a keyword after the page URL, Google highlights that word throughout the cached document that it displays. For example, try *cache:www. lycos.com music.*

- ✔ **link:** This operator performs the same function as the Links feature on the Advanced

Search page, finding pages that contain a link to whatever URL you specify.

- ✔ **info:** A nearly pointless operator, you use *info* by pairing it with a URL keyword. The result is the Google index entry for that page, plus links to view the cached page, similar sites, and pages that link to that URL. For information about the Google home page, for example, try *info:www. google.com.*

- ✔ **site:** Use this operator in your keyword string to limit results to a specified domain. It's a good way to search online newspapers (for example: *alan greenspan site:www.usatoday.com*). Combined with quotations, you can get pretty specific results in a newspaper site (for example: *"axis of evil" site:www.nytimes.com*). The *site* operator even works with domain extensions, such as `.gov` and `.edu`, without using a domain. Knowing this, you can search for keywords matching university or government pages (for example: *"code orange" site:gov*).

- ✔ **intitle** and **allintitle:** These operators restrict your results to pages in which one or more of your keywords appear in the page title. The *intitle* operator affects the single keyword (or group of keywords in quotes) immediately following the operator. All other keywords following the first might be found anywhere on the page. For example, *intitle:"tiger woods" golf* assures that result pages are about Tiger Woods, not Bengal tigers. The *allintitle* operator forces Google to match all your keywords with page titles. This operator can severely narrow a search. For example, the last time I checked, the *allintitle:"carrot top" nobel prize* search string returned no results.

CONTINUED

☞ ***inurl*** and ***allinurl:*** These function similarly to *intitle* and *allintitle* (see the preceding entry) but restrict search results to pages that contain one or more of your keywords in the page's URL (or Web site address). The result is a drastic narrowing of search results, but it's an effective way to discover new sites with great domain names. For example, *inurl:diaper* returns `www.dog-diaper.com` as the first result. Another example is *allinurl:purple elephant,* which displays results, believe it or not. Note that using *allinurl* with two or more keywords is likely to match pages deep within Web sites with very long URLs.

You may use Boolean operators in the keyword string when the string is preceded by a Google operator, like this: *allintitle:new times –york.*

Power Googling is all about knowing the operators and skipping the Advanced Search page. The more authority over the Google index that you can wield on the home page in its simple keyword box, the quicker you can get great search results.

Chapter 3: Ogling the News

In This Chapter

✔ **Browsing and searching the directory**

✔ **Understanding Google Directory**

✔ **Visiting Open Directory Project**

✔ **Submitting a site to the directory**

✔ **Browsing and searching the astounding Google News**

Most users know Google primarily as a search engine, but it offers two services that provide superb browsing:

✦ **Google Directory:** A fastidiously crafted catalogue of good Web sites that is broken into hundreds of topical categories.

✦ **Google News:** The world's first international newsstand enhanced by Google technology.

In a way, these two portions of Google are exactly opposed. Google Directory is completely hand-built, and Google News is completely automated. No site can be listed in the directory without human approval, but posted articles in Google News are untouched by human hands.

The directory represents the ultimate in human cooperation and virtual cataloguing. Google takes its basic listings from the Open Directory Project database, which is created by a large volunteer organization determined to assemble the largest and most useful classified index of Web sites. More than 20,000 editors evaluate and select Web sites for this project, which was started in 1998. Certain other Web directory sites, including Google Directory, use the listings that are created by Open Directory Project. To the raw Open Directory Project database, Google adds its PageRank formulas, creating an enhanced directory experience.

This chapter covers Google Directory and Google News. You might be less familiar with the directory than with the increasingly popular News section, but consider reading through both halves of the chapter. They contain tips that can turn your life around and save you from imminent perdition. Well, let me back down from that statement. The chapter contains tips for getting more out of Google.

Relaxing into Browsing Mode

After a hard day of Googling, you can take comfort in putting on comfy slippers, lighting up a pipe, and cruising around Google Directory. And if that scenario isn't weirdly retro-tech enough for you, throw in a dog bringing you the newspaper.

Browsing *is* more relaxing than searching, though. Trolling the directory leads to unexpected discoveries as opposed to the routine precision of Google's Web search. Google's search index is so precise and uncannily helpful that you could easily lose track of the directory entirely. Don't. The directory is truly fun. Browsing the directory is like shining a giant spotlight on broad topic areas of Web content. Search the index to be productive; browse the directory for fun.

Understanding Google Directory

First things first. Google Directory, like most other directories, is self-explanatory on the face of it. You just need to visit the front page to get started. Here it is:

```
http://directory.google.com
```

Alternatively, click the Directory tab on the main Google home page or use the Google Toolbar (see Book II, Chapter 6) to go straight there. Figure 3-1 shows the home page of Google Directory.

Click any of the main category links or any of the subcategory links to get started. Many more subcategories exist in directory strata beneath the front page. However, you needn't dig deep before encountering results: Most main category pages list primary Web sites for that category in addition to the first level of subcategories for that topic.

Figure 3-1: The Google Directory home page. Start exploring by clicking a category or sub-category.

When you search the Web within the directory, you're not searching the entire Google Directory. You're shifting your search over to the Web index, which is separate. To search the entire Google Directory, go to the directory home page and use the keyword box.

You might think that searching in a narrow subcategory is pointless because a quick scroll down the page shows you what sites are listed. But when Google searches a category, it doesn't match your keywords against only the words on the category page; it searches the *content* of the listed pages. This throws the door wide open, but in a small topic area. Searching in a narrow directory category results in extremely rewarding hits.

Figure 3-2 shows a subcategory page, in this case a second-level page in the News category. Two items on subcategory pages are worth noting:

Book II Chapter 3

Ogling the News

✦ The directory path is displayed above the Categories banner. Figure 3-2 shows a second-level page with a short path. Lower-level pages have longer paths, and each step you climb down is linked so that you can leap back up along the path.

✦ The Related Categories section, located under the Categories banner, links to directory categories that share some degree of topicality with your current category.

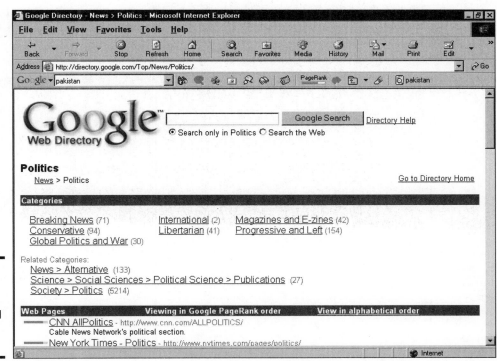

Figure 3-2: A subcategory page with related categories listed.

Submitting a Web Page to the Directory

Anyone may submit a site for inclusion to Google Directory or offer corrections of currently listed sites and their descriptions. When doing so, you deal not directly with Google but with Open Directory Project, from which Google obtains its listings. Google provides links for interacting with the Open Directory Project submission forms, but I think it's easier to operate from the Open Directory Project site.

Most people don't sit in front of their computers trying to find interesting sites that aren't represented in Google Directory. If you do find yourself burning hours that way, you might consider becoming an Open Directory Project editor. (Click the Become an Editor link at the bottom of any Google Directory page.) Site submissions are usually made by site owners hoping to get more exposure for their pages. Nothing's wrong with that, but be aware that Open Directory Project is a handpicked, edited directory, and Google isn't obligated to list a submitted site.

You submit a site by filling in an on-screen Open Directory Project application that asks for the site URL, a description, the proposed directory category for inclusion, and your contact information. Google provides links to this application at the bottom of all directory pages. Look for the Submit a Site link at the bottom of the page.

Go to this URL for the Open Directory Project home page:

```
www.dmoz.org
```

Figure 3-3 shows the Open Directory Project home page with its top-level categories. They're the same categories as in Google Directory, but the layout is different.

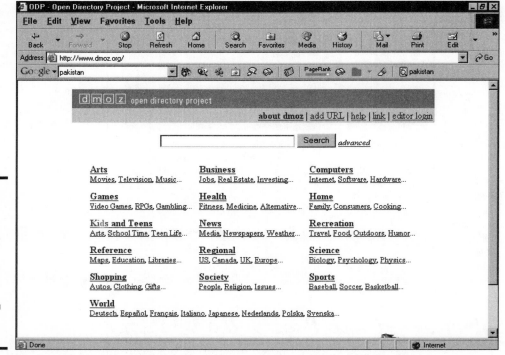

Figure 3-3: The home page of Open Directory Project. Start your site submission project here.

As you drill into the directory, keep an eye on the upper-right corner of the page. Notice that some pages carry no reference to adding or correcting a URL, but other pages offer the Add URL link, the Update URL link, or both. Figure 3-4 shows a third-level directory page with both links. Click the Add URL link to see the application for that subcategory.

Generally, the broad categories closer to the top of the directory are unavailable for new submissions. Open Directory Project is particular about where new listings are placed, and it receives your submission better if you take the time to research appropriate categories.

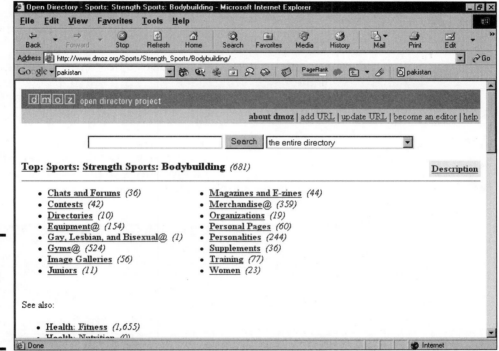

Figure 3-4:
Check for links to add or update in Open Directory Project.

Googling the Day's News

Google News is simply incredible. After you get a taste for Google's news delivery style, you'll go back for more throughout the day. The front page (see Figure 3-5) is the first place that I turn to for headlines or in-depth current events. And I don't mean just among Web sites. I prefer Google News to TV, radio, newspapers, and magazines. Nothing on the planet approaches its global scope, intelligent organization, and searchability.

Start at the beginning — the front page. It contains five main features:

✦ **Searching:** As in each of Google's main information areas, Google News presents a keyword box for searching. (I cover searching further in the next section.) Use the Search News button to confine the search to Google News. Use the Search the Web button to toss your keywords over to the Web index.

✦ **News categories:** The left sidebar contains seven main news categories: World, U.S., Business, Sci/Tech, Sports, Entertainment, and Health. Each of these subject divisions has its own portion of the front page — scroll down to see them. Clicking a sidebar link takes you to a dedicated news page for that news topic.

✦ **Top story categories:** Top current event items of each category crowd the entire front page. The first section is devoted to Top Stories. The seven main news sections have their top stories further down the page. A More Top Stories section lurks at the bottom.

✦ **Headlines:** When you click a headline, the source page opens. Your browser's performance when displaying Google News stories varies depending on the source's capability to serve the page when you click it. Slowdowns can also be the result of attempting to display a publication from halfway across the world.

✦ **Related stories:** Click any related link after a headline to see an amazing range of publications covering that story. The related articles are listed on as many pages as it takes to fit them all (often hundreds), and each listing includes the first line or two of the published story.

Unlike Google Directory, your Google Preferences apply to Google News. This means that if you have Google Web search set to open a new window when you click a search result (which I recommend in Chapter 5 of Book II), Google News likewise opens articles in new windows.

Figure 3-5:
The Google News home page updates every few minutes.

If you prefer a less graphic presentation of news, find the Text Version link on the left side of the front page. This format has the same features as the graphic version but without any photographs or columns.

Searching for News

You search Google News with the same set of tools for searching the Web that I describe in Chapter 2 of Book II. Keywords go in the keyword box. (Click the Search News button or press Enter to begin the search.) Google attempts to streamline your results by filtering similar articles and presenting the top-ranked hits for your keywords.

Figure 3-6 illustrates a News search results page. Note that at the bottom of the page, Google offers to repeat the search without filtering.

A final word about Google News: If the default U.S. version doesn't pertain to your geography or nationality, try one of the other national editions linked at the bottom of the front page. More country-specific versions are in development.

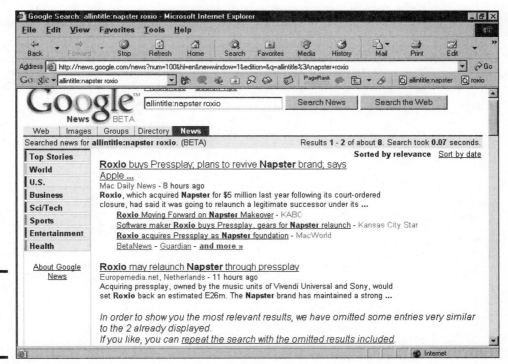

Figure 3-6:
Search
results in
Google
News.

CHECK IT OUT

Tracking a Story over Time

Using the related stories feature, you can track the evolution of a current event in Google News. Here's how:

1. **On the Google News front page, click the related story link after any headline.**

2. **On the next page, click the Sort by Date link in the upper-right corner.**

3. **After the page reloads, scroll to the bottom and click the last result page listed.**

4. **On the last page, view the oldest headlines related to the story.**

   To move forward in time, click the Previous link at the bottom of each page.

Chapter 4: More Than You Care to Know

In This Chapter

- ✔ Getting to know Usenet newsgroups, the Internet's bulletin board system
- ✔ Discovering essential Google Groups terms
- ✔ Browsing and searching the Groups archive
- ✔ Using standard and Groups-specific search operators
- ✔ Reading and posting messages
- ✔ Using advanced searching in Google Groups

*I*f you're unfamiliar with Usenet, this chapter might seem like a big nuisance. I implore you to mellow any such harsh attitude and ease into these pages with an open mind. Usenet is incredible. Google Groups is magnificent. The encompassing newsgroup culture is, to my mind, an indispensable part of online citizenship.

But what the heck *are* Usenet and its newsgroups, anyway? Read on. This chapter gives you a bit of history and then moves to the practical stuff of using Google Groups to begin — or, for the more experienced, to enhance — your Usenet participation.

Welcome to the Pre-Web

Usenet is the original bulletin board system of the Internet. It consists of posted messages, many millions of them in fact, left over the years by prophets crying in the wilderness and lonely souls who needed company. You're probably familiar with some type of online message board. If a favorite Web site includes a discussion forum, you've probably read or posted messages in that format.

This is what Usenet is all about:

- ✦ **Usenet is public:** Anybody with Internet access on any computer can view and participate in Usenet. Google makes it easy to stay connected with Usenet.

- ✦ **Usenet is threaded:** On a threaded message board, you can see at a glance who is responding to whom. Many Web-based forums are flat and unthreaded.

✦ **Usenet is unregulated:** Nobody owns Usenet and nobody even tries to regulate it. Message board behavior is uncontrolled and often vulgar. Usenet is not a place for children. People can be mean, kind, ill-tempered, good-humored, stupid, smart, inarticulate, eloquent — and you see it all on Usenet. Language is spicy. Hundreds of groups are dedicated to pornography. Fortunately, the Usenet realm is organized, and avoiding undesirable newsgroups is easy.

A Usenet glossary

You, too, can know what you're talking about when the conversation turns to newsgroups. The following are some essential terms regarding Usenet and newsgroups, in particular:

✔ **alias:** See *screen name.*

✔ **article:** Traditionally, a newsgroup message is called an article. This terminology is a holdover from the days when newsgroups were about news and academic discourse.

✔ **binaries:** Media files posted to Usenet. Discussion newsgroups usually discourage posting binaries such as pictures, music files, and video files. Even HTML posting is frowned on — plain text is the preferred format. But thousands of newsgroups are devoted to binary postings, from music to movies to software to pornography. These groups are usually identified by the word *binaries* somewhere in the Usenet address.

✔ **cross-post:** A message sent to more than one newsgroup simultaneously. Generally speaking, cross-posting is bad form. If you do it, acknowledge the cross-post in the message.

✔ **expired messages:** Usenet messages stay on their servers, available for viewing, for a certain amount of time and then they expire. The amount of time varies from server to server and even from group to group on one server depending on the group's traffic. When messages expire, Google Groups swings into action by archiving the content that would otherwise be lost.

✔ **flame:** A message posted with the intent to hurt. Flames are personal attacks, launched sometimes in response to spam or other behavior contrary to community interests or just because somebody is in a bad mood.

✔ **frequently asked questions (FAQs):** Many newsgroups maintain an *FAQ file,* which is a long message spelling out the customs and basic facts of the group. Google Groups can also locate FAQs for individual groups — just search for FAQs within a group. Ignore the FAQs at your peril.

✔ **lurking:** Reading without posting. In any message board community, lurkers greatly outnumber active participants. There's nothing illicit about lurking; newsgroups are for recreational reading as well as conversation.

✔ **message:** Similar to an e-mail message and often composed in an e-mail program, a Usenet message is posted to a newsgroup, where it can be read by anyone in the group.

✔ **newsgroup server:** Usenet newsgroups are distributed through a network of autonomous, networked computers called *servers.* That's how the entire Internet works, in fact, and newsgroup servers are a specialized type of Internet computer. Each newsgroup server administrator decides which newsgroups to carry as well as the duration of messages in the groups.

✔ **newsgroups:** Topical online communities operating in message board format. Newsgroups don't necessarily have anything to do with news; many groups are purely social.

✔ **newsreader:** A stand-alone program interface to Usenet often paired with e-mail functions. Outlook Express, primarily an e-mail program, is the best-known newsreader.

✔ **post and posting:** Posting a message (often called a post) places it on the public message board. Usenet software, operating behind the scenes, positions the post in correct thread order as long as you don't change the thread title.

✔ **screen name:** The online identity of a Usenet participant, the *screen name* is also called an *alias*. You find a great deal of anonymity in newsgroups — and also lots of real names out in the open.

✔ **spam:** One message, usually promotional in nature, posted (or e-mailed) to many destinations simultaneously. Less formally, any repetitive and self-serving behavior is regarded as spam.

✔ **subscribe:** Bookmarking a newsgroup in a newsreader is called subscribing. Unlike a newspaper subscription, newsgroups are free of charge and nothing is delivered to your screen.

✔ **thread:** A series of messages strung together into a single newsgroup conversation. Sometimes called a *string*. A thread might consist of two messages or hundreds. Initiating a new conversation on a newsgroup message board is called *starting a thread*.

✔ **troll:** Newsgroup disrupter. Trolls post deliberately offensive or off-topic messages in an apparent desire to get noticed at any cost.

The Usenet system contains more than 30,000 newsgroups. The Google Groups archive holds about 800 million messages and is expanding daily. Size isn't everything, though, and the issue is really what value Usenet has, or could have, in your life. I find newsgroups irresistible in four major ways:

✦ **Community:** Usenet can connect like-minded people without regard to geography, time zone, or any other factor that keeps people from meeting face to face. A newsgroup has been created for practically every area of human discourse, from philosophy to specific television shows. Finding a home in one of these groups and getting to know people from the inside out can be a unique experience.

✦ **Expertise:** When I have a technical question, especially about computers, Usenet is the first place that I turn. Thousands of people hang out in the *comp.* groups (and others) for no purpose other than to help answer questions and share knowledge about computers.

✦ **Recreation:** Newsgroups are just plain fun — the rants, the humor, the childishness, the astuteness, the complex threads. I browse through Google Groups sometimes, searching on various keywords that come to mind, just to get out of my well-worn newsgroup ruts and see what people are saying in other parts of the vast Usenet landscape.

✦ **Learning:** Besides getting technical questions answered, I regularly read certain newsgroups to eavesdrop on professional chatter. I have an amateur's interest in physics and cosmology — quarks and black holes and other unseemly phenomena. It's fascinating to listen to conversations among people who really know what they're talking about.

Browsing and Searching Google Groups

Just as with the Web, Directory, and News portions of the site, Google Groups allows you to browse its content in directory style or search it with keywords. You can merge the two approaches by searching in a single part of the directory. And with so many newsgroups named cryptically, searching for a group is part of the browsing experience.

Google organizes newsgroups by Usenet top-level address types. The largest and best-known of these is the *alt.* collection of newsgroups. Google Groups carries ten of these major divisions plus many minor ones that aren't represented on the Groups home page (see Figure 4-1) but can be found by searching.

Start browsing from the home page by clicking the Groups tab. Each subsequent page lists 50 groups in alphabetical order. You can see one of these subsequent pages in Figure 4-2. Google applies its PageRank system to evaluating the popularity and importance of newsgroups. The familiar horizontal green bars indicate how popular a newsgroup is, saving you much trial and error.

However, PageRank or no PageRank, browsing is difficult. Google does its best to help you navigate through thousands of groups by providing a dropdown list (see Figure 4-2) that you can use to leapfrog ahead in the alphabetical list. That's fine, but at this point, resorting to keywords is the way to go. In fact, you can safely skip this second-level directory page entirely and start with a keyword on the home page. The benefit of launching your keyword search from the *alt.* page (or whichever page you're on) is that you can restrict your search to the *alt.* division.

Follow these steps to search Google Groups:

1. **From the Google Groups home page, click the link for the newsgroup division that you want to search.**

   To follow along with the example, click the alt. link.

2. **In the keyword box, type your search words.**

   I'm assuming that you have a passion for anything related to *Star Trek* and want to read postings about it. So type **star trek** in the keyword box.

3. **Decide whether you want to search all groups or just a division and select the correct radio button.**

   Three options appear below the keyword box. (Skip the Web option and stay in Groups.) To follow along, select the Search Only in alt.* option. (The asterisk, also called a *wildcard*, represents any words following the *alt.* division.)

4. **Click the Google Search button.**

Accessing newsgroups on and off the Web

Some people use Google Groups as their only interface to Usenet for reading and posting messages, but I recommend performing most of your active Usenet participation with a standalone newsgroup reader. This program might not be the same as your e-mail program. (They're not the same for AOL users.) Outlook Express, probably the most popular e-mail program, offers full newsgroup functionality. In addition, many dedicated newsreaders are available as freeware and shareware downloads. The Netscape browser/e-mail/newsgroup program is free and quite advanced. X-News is another good (and free) one. You can download it at www.cnet.com.

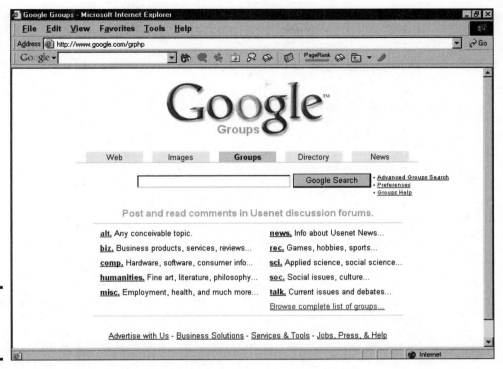

Figure 4-1:
The Google Groups home page.

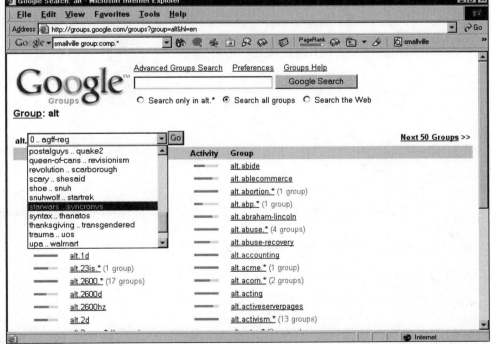

Figure 4-2:
The familiar Google PageRank indicates the popularity of newsgroups.

Figure 4-3 shows the result of this search. A few notable features of the search results page are itemized in the following sections.

Using the group operator

Notice in Figure 4-3 how the keyword string is now presented in the keyword box on the results page:

```
star trek group:alt.*
```

This syntax is an introduction to a new search operator specific to Google Groups: the *group* operator. Using it forces Google to match your keyword(s) against newsgroups in one division. You can use this operator to ferret out newsgroups in minor divisions that don't appear on Google's home page. For example, when searching for a Windows 95 support group in the Microsoft newsgroups, this keyword string is effective:

```
windows 95 group:microsoft.*
```

The result of this search is illustrated in Figure 4-4. Under the Related Groups banner, no direct match to the keywords (*windows 95*) exists in the newsgroup names — but Google determines that win95 and windows95 (without a space) are relevant hits. Google's capability to make smart choices on your behalf based on comprehensive searches of content is as pronounced in the Groups sections as in the Web search section.

Figure 4-3:
A search results page in Google Groups. In addition to individual messages, Google gives you related groups.

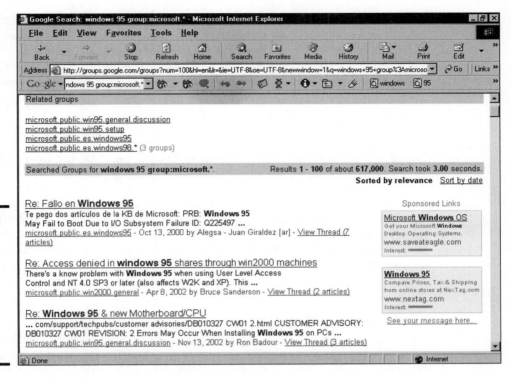

Figure 4-4:
Searching with the group operator yields targeted and intelligent results.

When using the *group* operator, always place a period and asterisk after the division name that you're searching for if you know (or you're guessing) an exact division. Neglecting the period and wildcard combination leads to quirky and less specific results. And another tip — use the *group* operator only when searching all Google groups. If the search engine is set to search only the *alt.* division, for example, and you use the *group* operator and specify the *soc.* division, your computer shoots lasers into your eyes. Kidding. Google handles the confusion rather well by simply adding the two divisions. But don't tempt the wrath of the Googlebeast.

Operators usually work in reverse as well. (See Book II, Chapter 2.) Such is the case with the *group* operator and the *-group* operator. The *group* operator immediately preceded by a minus sign (no space) tells Google to exclude groups in the newsgroup division that follows. Suppose you want to find discussions about Windows 95 and want to avoid Microsoft-sponsored newsgroups. The following string is productive:

```
windows 95 -group:microsoft.*
```

Understanding related groups

Many search results pages, typified previously in Figure 4-3, contain a Related Groups banner under which are newsgroups that Google has determined contain relevant search results. You can see those groups represented if you scroll through all the search results. The list is for reference only; you may click any group in that list, but doing so doesn't carry your keyword search into that group. Instead, you merely see the display page for that group, and the most recently posted message is at the top.

In some cases, Google uses the wildcard (*) in the Related Groups list to indicate clusters of related newsgroups. Click the *alt.startrek.* * cluster, for example, to see a new page containing the complete list of groups that fulfill the wildcard, as shown in Figure 4-5. Note that wildcards can be found in this list, too, representing newsgroups whose names contain yet another *dot-extension* — that is to say, another period followed by another word. Newsgroup names can be quite long and cryptic.

When confronted with a long list of related groups, glance at the PageRank indicators to quickly determine which groups might be the best to browse.

Whenever you're on a directory or results page for a single newsgroup or a cluster of groups, you have the option of restricting your next search to that group or cluster. This option doesn't exist on a search results page showing posts from many groups; naturally, Google wouldn't know how to restrict subsequent searches. When in doubt, just look below the keyword box for options that enable you to search all Google Groups or a subset of groups.

Sorting search results

I don't have too much to report on the subject of sorting. Google usually sorts search results by relevance according to the mysterious and profound Google formulas. Use the Sort by Date link to switch to a chronological order of posts. The chronology goes in reverse with the most recent result at the top of the list.

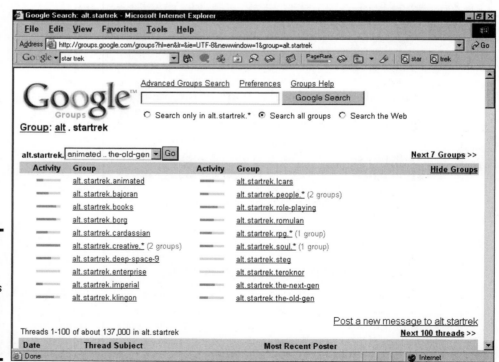

Figure 4-5: A complete list of newsgroups related to a search result newsgroup.

Interpreting search results

Search results contain the following six elements:

✦ **Thread title:** Every message title carries the name of its parent thread. All message titles in a thread (except the first one) are preceded by *Re:*. The *Re:* prefix is standard practice in most newsgroup readers. Click the message title to read the message and see how it fits in the thread.

✦ **Message excerpt:** Google snips sentences that contain your keywords. The small excerpt is sometimes enough to determine whether you want to click over to the full message.

✦ **Newsgroup name:** Click this link to see a straight, unmatched display of the newsgroup.

✦ **Date:** The date represents when the message reached Google's newsgroup server. If you display the entire message (by clicking the thread title), Google shows you the time — down to the second — that the message hit the server and was archived.

✦ **Screen name:** This is the screen name of the message's author.

✦ **View Thread:** Clicking this link, which indicates how many messages await you in the thread, displays the entire single message and links to others in the thread.

Reading Messages and Threads

When you click a thread title, Google throws you into a different sort of page that shows an entire newsgroup message (finally!) and various options that affect how you perceive and interact with the entire thread. It's from this page that you can post a message (see the following section for info on posting).

Figure 4-6 shows a full Usenet post from a search on the keyword *borg* in the group *alt.startrek.* *. Note that the keyword is highlighted throughout the message.

Just poking around might be the best way to get acquainted with the message page. Besides the message text itself, check out the following major elements:

✦ **Keyword box:** As always, the keyword box sits atop the page, ready to launch a new search in the current newsgroup or in all newsgroups.

✦ **Sponsored links:** These are advertisements.

✦ **Message header:** In the large gray banner, you see details about the message. These details include the author, his or her e-mail address, the thread title, the newsgroup(s) to which it was posted, the date and time, the position of this message on your search results page, and links for seeing an alternate format and the entire thread.

✦ **Post a reply:** Click the Post a Follow-Up to This Message link to compose a message in response to the message that you're reading.

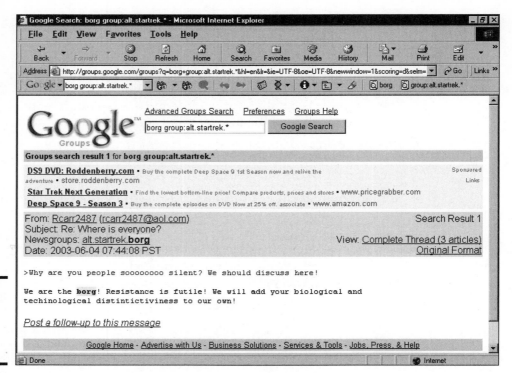

Figure 4-6:
A Google Groups message page.

If you look more closely at the gray message header in Figure 4-6, you see several elements and links. The following is a breakdown of their functions:

✦ **Author:** The message author's screen name is linked to a list of that person's Usenet posts in Google's archive. In some cases, the author is responsible for many thousands of posts. The author archives are organized by e-mail address, which is changeable.

✦ **Author's e-mail:** This bit of information is also linked. Clicking it displays a New Message window in your default e-mail program. This makes it easy to contact Usenet authors privately.

✦ **Newsgroups:** Click this link (or one of these links, if the message was cross-posted) to see a straight, unmatched view of the newsgroup.

✦ **Complete Thread:** This link leads to the most comprehensive view of the message and its place in the thread. Figure 4-7 shows this view, which is split into two frames. The left frame displays a link to every message in the thread in a format that makes it clear who responded to whom. Rather than use message titles in this list (they would all be the same), Google shows the author screen names and posting dates.

✦ **Original Format:** Click this link to see the message in raw text format, without any Web page formatting around it.

In the Complete Thread view, the relative sizes of the frames are adjustable. Position your mouse cursor over the border between the two frames until the double arrow appears, and then click and drag to the left or right. When dealing with long and complex threads that are sharply indented, the left frame needs to be widened to view the entire thread.

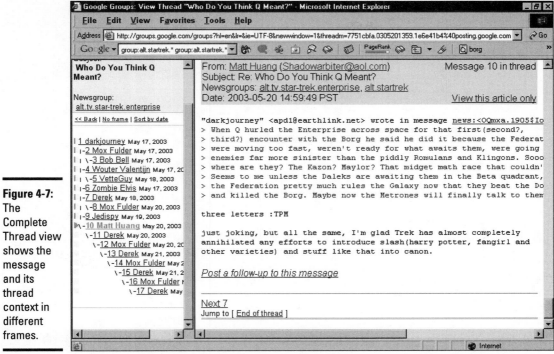

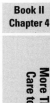

Figure 4-7:
The Complete Thread view shows the message and its thread context in different frames.

A special Google search operator lets you troll the Groups index for messages written by a single person. The operator in question is the *author* operator. It's useful when searching within a single newsgroup or across Usenet globally. The operator needs to be paired with an e-mail address, *not* with a screen name. (You can, however, search for a screen name without any operator.) As usual with Google operators, don't put a space between the operator and the address. Here's the correct syntax:

```
author:name@email.com
```

Posting Messages through Google Groups

Google allows posting to newsgroups, but you must register as a Google Groups user to do so. The main reason that you must register is to establish a screen name for identifying your posts. Registration is not required to browse, search, or read newsgroups through Google Groups. In fact, Google doesn't encourage or even display a path toward registration until you first attempt to reply to a newsgroup message or start a new thread.

In order to post messages, you must have a Google account. Follow these steps to register to post messages in newsgroups:

1. On any newsgroup page, click a message header link.

2. At the bottom of any message to which you want to respond, click the Post a Follow-Up to This Message link. (See Figure 4-8.)

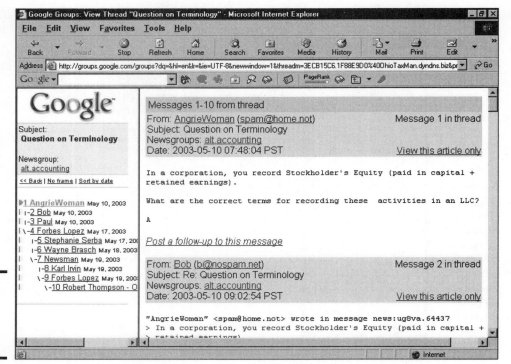

Figure 4-8:
Google
refers to
replies as
follow-ups.

3. **On the sign-in page, enter your e-mail address, enter your password, and click the Sign In button.**

4. **Enter your name in the Your Name text box.**

Your name can be any combination of characters that isn't already registered at Google Groups. Pause here to think. The first choice is whether to use your real name or some variant of it that doesn't hide you. Many people keep their identities out in the open. The other choice is to make up an alias.

5. **Read the terms and conditions, using the scroll bar to see the entire document.**

6. **Click the Acceptance button.**

Now you have an established Groups name. The next page allows you to post your reply.

The newsgroup name and subject header are automatically filled in when replying to a message. (If you change the subject header, your message is posted as a new thread, disrupting the continuity of the current thread.) Notice, also, that the message you're responding to appears in the Your Message text box. This repetition is a standard Usenet practice called *quoting* or *quoting back,* and it reminds readers what you're responding to, exactly.

Due to the decentralized distribution of Usenet messages, not all threads are filled in at the same time for all readers, so quoting back fills in the gaps for anyone who's missing a message in their newsreader. Feel free to highlight and delete all but the most pertinent part of the quote, and then respond either above or below the quote, as shown in Figure 4-9.

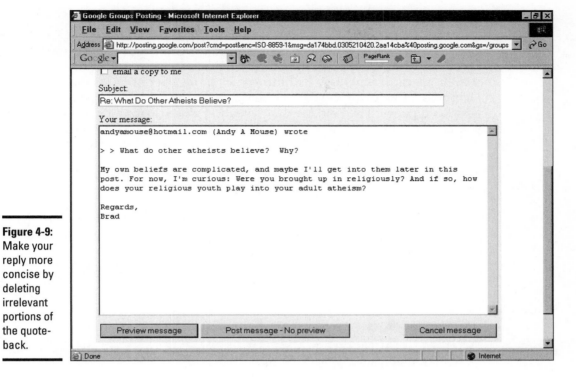

Figure 4-9:
Make your reply more concise by deleting irrelevant portions of the quote-back.

After you compose your message, click the Preview Message button to see what it looks like (and get one more chance to edit it) or go straight for the Post Message — No Preview button. Your message might not show up in the group immediately, but the question of when it shows up is meaningless because different readers see it at different times depending on the erratic course of Usenet server distribution.

Fun and flames: Newsgroup etiquette

To a greater extent than other portions of the Internet (except perhaps chat rooms), Usenet embodies a distinct, autonomous culture. Embarking on a Usenet journey is like visiting another country. You might know the language, but that doesn't mean you know the customs. It's easy to make gaffes. And unlike polite society in many countries, Usenet citizens don't hesitate to pound your virtual self to the ground when you make a mistake. Rudeness? Yes, but it's more than that; Usenet is ancient by Internet standards and proud of its traditions. An unspoken requirement is that newcomers find out the local ways before opening their mouths.

Perhaps the most important rule is this: Lurk before you leap. Even if you've been around online communities before, get to know any individual group before jumping in with your own posts. Read the board for a few weeks to get the flow of inside jokes, to understand its topical reach, and to discover the personalities and social power structures of the group. Google Groups can compress this process by allowing you to read back in time, covering a lot of ground quickly.

Advanced Searching

Google provides an Advanced Search page for Groups as it does for its other indexes. And as with the others, it offers a user-friendly way to employ search operator functions without knowing the operators. As you can see in Figure 4-10, the Advanced Groups Search page looks very much like the other advanced pages. The Find Messages section works just as it does with a Web search. (See Book II, Chapter 2.) Use the four keyword boxes in this section in combination, forcing Google to treat your keywords in certain ways.

The Advanced Groups Search page also includes the following search parameters exclusive to Google Groups:

✦ **Newsgroup:** Use this keyword box to specify a particular newsgroup or even part of a newsgroup name for searching. Feel free to include the asterisk if you don't know the entire name.

✦ **Subject:** Use this keyword box for words that you want to appear in the thread title.

✦ **Author:** Use this keyword box to specify an author's screen name or e-mail address.

✦ **Message ID:** This rarely used feature searches for a Usenet Message ID, which you can glean from a message header.

✦ **Language:** Usenet is international, just like the Web. Use the drop-down list to specify a language.

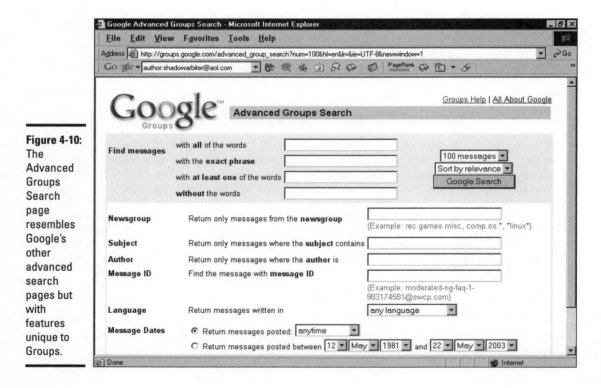

Figure 4-10: The Advanced Groups Search page resembles Google's other advanced search pages but with features unique to Groups.

✦ **Message Dates:** This is da bomb. Here's where the real advanced action is at in Google Groups. The Groups archive is precisely historical in a way that the Web index can't be because each one of the 800 million catalogued Usenet posts is stamped with a date and time. Use these drop-down lists to specify a date range for your search. Google Groups stretches back to 1981, although not all newsgroups are that old.

✦ **SafeSearch:** This feature applies the same content filter as in Web searches. (See Book II, Chapter 2.)

You can throw a Web search into Google Groups by clicking the Groups tab above any Web search results list. It's a quick way to siphon the information flow in a new direction.

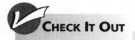

Keeping Your Posts out of the Groups Archive

You can restrict Google from including your Usenet posts in the Groups archive in two ways: Prevent Google from archiving a post to begin with or remove an archived post.

You can use the Usenet software to prevent archiving by typing a single line of code either in the message header or in the first line of the message body:

```
X-No-archive: yes
```

The line must be typed exactly as it appears here, with a single space between the colon and yes. Placing the line in a message header is less conspicuous than positioning it in the message body but much harder for most folks to accomplish. So, when posting a message that you want to keep out of the archive, just place that line in the message itself. Make sure it is the *first* line, above the quote-back that Google places in all response messages.

Removing an already archived post is more complicated. Follow these steps:

1. From the Google Groups home page, click the Groups Help link.

The Google Groups Help page appears.

2. Click the question, How can I remove articles from Google's archive?

An *article* is a posted message.

3. Click the Automatic Removal Tool link.

4. Create an Automatic Removal Tool account.

Yes, another account. Please note that this one isn't the same as the Google Groups account that establishes your screen name. After creating your Automatic Removal Tool password (which can be the same as your Groups password), Google sends you a confirmation e-mail.

5. Click the link in your confirmation e-mail.

A browser page pops up showing the Automatic Removal Tool. Note that you can use it to remove not only Usenet posts from the Groups index but also URLs from Google's Web index.

6. On the Remove Your URL or Google Groups Post page, click the Remove Your Usenet Posts from Google Groups link.

Chapter 5: Setting Your Preferences

In This Chapter

- ✔ Finding the Google Preferences Page
- ✔ Choosing your language settings
- ✔ Filtering out objectionable material
- ✔ Choosing how many search results to display

Many people breeze through Google umpteen times a day without bothering to set their preferences — or without even being aware that preferences exist. A recent Internet study asked users whether they would rather set Google preferences or get bathed in chocolate syrup. Sentiment was overwhelmingly against setting Google preferences. But I'm here to tell you that the five settings on the Preferences page (see Figure 5-1) enhance the Google experience far more than the effort required to adjust them. This short chapter explains everything that a mere mortal needs to know about Google preferences.

Visiting the Preferences Page

Figure 5-1 shows the Google Preferences page. To adjust Google preferences, click the Preferences link on the Google home page or go here:

```
www.google.com/preferences
```

If you set your preferences and later return to the Preferences page by manually entering the preceding URL, your browser displays an unadjusted Preferences page (without your settings). That's because *your* Preferences page has a distinct URL with your preferences built into it. For example, after selecting English as Google's default language for your visits, the URL appears like this:

```
www.google.com/preferences?hl=en
```

Your best bet for reaching the Preferences page after first setting your preferences (when you want to readjust them, for example) is to use the Preferences link on the home page.

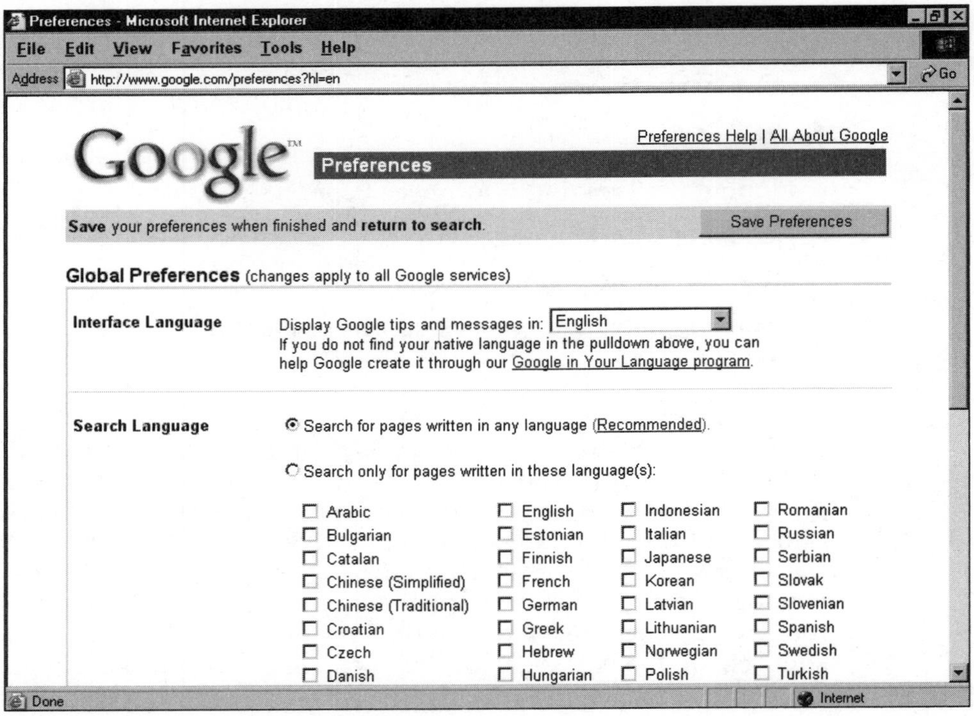

Figure 5-1:
Part of the Google Preferences page. Its settings enhance the Google experience.

How Google remembers your preferences

When you set preferences in Google, the site is customized for you every time you visit it as long as you're using the same computer through which you set the preferences. To provide this convenience, Google must place a *cookie* (a small information file) in your computer. The site and the cookie high-five each other whenever you visit Google, and the site appears according to your settings. For this system to work, cookies must be turned on in your browser.

Some people are militantly anti-cookie, claiming that the data files represent an invasion of computer privacy. Indeed, some sites plant cookies that track your Internet movements and identify you to advertisers.

The truth is, Google's cookie is fairly aggressive. It gets planted when you first visit the site, whether or not you visit the Preferences page. Once planted, the Google cookie records your clicks in Google and builds a database of visitor behavior in its search results pages. For example, Google knows

how often users click the first search result and to what extent they explore results lower on the page. Google uses this information to evaluate the effectiveness of its service and to improve it.

As to privacy, Google does indeed share aggregate information with advertisers and various third parties and even publicizes knowledge about how the service is used by its millions of visitors. The key word is *aggregate*. Google's privacy policy states that individual information is never divulged except by proper legal procedure, such as a warrant or a subpoena, or by individual consent. The privacy policy is published on this page:

```
www.google.com/privacy.html
```

I have no problem with the Google cookie or with cookies in general. The convenience is helpful, and I don't mind adding to the aggregate information. It's rather comforting being a data droplet in Google's information tsunami.

A single basic process changes one or several preferences. Just follow these steps:

1. **Go to the Preferences page by clicking the Preferences link on the Google home page.**

2. **Use the drop-down lists, check boxes, and option buttons to make your adjustments.**

3. **Click the Save Preferences button, which appears at the top and bottom of the screen.**

   A confirmation window appears, telling you that your preferences are saved.

4. **Click OK.**

   You then return to Google's home page.

The rest of this chapter describes what you can accomplish on the Preferences page.

The International Google

If you're reading the English-language edition of this book, you probably enjoy Google in its default English interface. If you're reading the Icelandic edition of this book, please send me a copy — I want to see whether my jokes are any funnier in a chilly language. Whatever your native language, you can get Google to appear in one of dozens of languages.

Interface Language is the first Google preference setting, and changing this setting adjusts the appearance of certain pages — specifically, the home page, Preferences page, Advanced Search page, and many Help pages and intrasite directories.

Changing the Interface Language doesn't alter the language on the search results page or the search results themselves. (To change the language on those pages, use the Search Language preference, which I describe in the following section.)

Interface Language changes the Interface Language list in the drop-down list. If you choose an obscure language that uses an unfamiliar alphabet while playing around (it's irresistible), you might have trouble finding your way back to the mother tongue again. Do you know how to say "English" in Urdu?

Searching for Non-English Pages

After you have the Google interface speaking your language, you can turn your attention to searching for Web pages written in certain languages. The language you search *for* doesn't need to match the language you search *in*.

In other words, the first two preferences, Interface Language and Search Language, can be set to different languages. Furthermore, you can select more than one language in the Search Language setting, whereas the Interface Language preference, naturally, can be only one language at a time.

Use Search Language to narrow your search results by language. Choosing French, for example, returns Web pages written only in French. Use the check boxes to select as many languages as you want.

If you don't select any languages, leaving the Search Language preference in its default setting, your search results do not discriminate based on language. You're likely to see an international array of pages if you rummage through enough results.

G-Rated Searching

Google uses a filter called SafeSearch to screen out pornography from Web-page and image searches. In its default setting, Use Moderate Filtering, SafeSearch applies fairly strict filtering to image searches and leaves Web search results unedited. Change the setting to Use Strict Filtering for harsher filtering of images and clean Web-page searches. You can turn off the filter entirely for an unbiased search session. You select the filtering strength on the Preferences page, as shown in Figure 5-2.

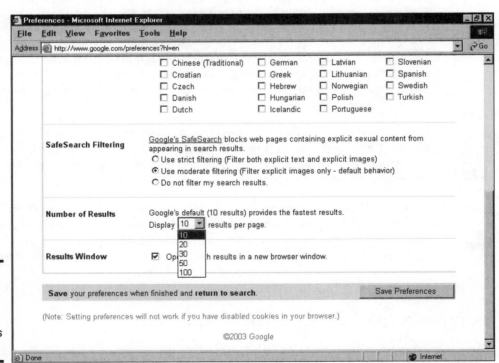

Figure 5-2: The bottom portion of Google's Preferences page.

SafeSearch operates automatically but can be modified manually by the Google staff. They accept suggestions of sites and images that should be subject to the adult-content filter. If you come across any objectionable material through a Google search, feel free to send a link to the offending page or image to the following e-mail address:

safesearch@google.com

Opening the Floodgates

Using the Number of Results drop-down list, you can increase the number of search results that appear on the page, raising it from the default ten results. It's a good idea, I think; I keep my preference set at the maximum — 100 results per page.

Google reminds you that shorter pages are displayed more quickly, which is a good point for people who hit the site for lightning-quick searches many times a day. Google's results are so startlingly accurate that you might not often need more than ten results. Still, I like the higher number because the long page of search results arrives more rapidly than shorter pages at competing search engines.

Google is fast no matter how many results per page you request. The only thing that might hold you back is your modem speed. If you access the Internet with a high-speed connection (cable modem, DSL, corporate connection, or university connection), you might as well set the results number to 100 and be done with it.

New Windows

The Results Window setting consists of a single check box which, when selected, tells Google to open Web pages in new windows when you click a search result. This is a useful way of staying anchored in the search results page, from which you might want to sample several Web pages that match your keywords. Without this preference, your browser opens the Web pages in the same window that Google is in, forcing you to Back-button your way back to Google if you want to see the search results again.

If you dislike multiple browser windows cluttering your desktop, leave the Results Window box deselected. If you prefer a hybrid experience in which you sometimes want to anchor at Google while exploring several search hits, leave the box deselected and get in the habit of right-clicking search result links when you want a new window. Choose Open in New Window from the pop-up menu that your browser displays.

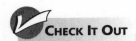

CHECK IT OUT

Google's Rather Bizarre Language Choices

Google is nothing if not occasionally silly. The Interface Language drop-down list on the Google Preferences page offers a handful of must-try languages:

- **Elmer Fudd:** Capriciously changes all *rs* and *ls* to *ws*. On the home page, Groups becomes Gwoups, and Directory has been cartoonized to Diwectowy. The I'm Feeling Lucky button is denatured to I'm Feewing Wucky.

- **Hacker:** Changes alphabet letters to numerals and symbols wherever possible (pretty much everywhere), rendering a semicoherent page best comprehended after several bags of potato chips and a six-pack of soda.

- **Interlingua:** This vaguely Euro blend of tourism-speak is roughly understandable by nearly everyone.

- **Klingon:** If I have to explain it, you don't watch enough *Star Trek*.

- **Pig Latin:** You nowkay owhay histay orksway.

Chapter 6: Using the Google Toolbar

In This Chapter

✔ **Installing the Google Toolbar**

✔ **Choosing the Toolbar options that suit you**

✔ **Letting AutoFill enter your personal information**

✔ **Blocking pop-up ads**

✔ **Putting Google buttons on your browser toolbar**

*E*ven if you think Google is the best thing since sliced bread, visiting the home page for every little search is an undeniable inconvenience. Wouldn't it be great if you could access all of Google's amenities without visiting the Google home page? Well, you can do just that.

Every browser has built-in toolbars near the top of the browser window. They contain navigation buttons, a Web address bar, and other perks that help you move around online with a minimum of hassle. In addition, you can attach third-party toolbars to some browsers. Google's add-on Toolbar absolutely rocks.

This chapter explains how to install and use the Google Toolbar, as well as how to put special Google buttons on a toolbar in your Web browser.

All browsers are not created equal

Most people use some version of the Microsoft Internet Explorer (IE) browser. And only a minority of those folks uses a version that precedes version 5, much less version 4. That big majority of IE4+ users can proceed to install Google browser buttons and the default browser search engine with no trouble. IE5+ users can do all that plus install the Google Toolbar smoothly. It's clear sailing for AOL7+ users, too, if they use the default Web browser.

As for everyone else, Google maintains a Web page with detailed instructions pertaining to each type of browser. You can find the Web page here:

```
www.google.com/options/
defaults.html
```

Installing the Google Toolbar

If you're not (yet) using the Google Toolbar, I suggest that you start using it right away. It both deepens and streamlines your relationship to Google. Figure 6-1 shows the Google Toolbar installed, ready for action. (Your Google Toolbar might look a little different, depending on the settings that you chose, your browser, and your screen resolution.)

Figure 6-1:
The Google
Toolbar.

The Toolbar installation process is almost completely automated. You just click your way through a few buttons before Google takes over. Follow these steps:

1. **Go to this page:**

   `http://toolbar.google.com`

2. **From the drop-down list, scroll down and select a language.**

3. **Click the Download Google Toolbar button.**

   The File Download dialog box appears.

4. **Click the Open button.**

   You see the Welcome to the Google Toolbar Installer dialog box with its Terms and Conditions agreement. This agreement specifies that Google owns the Toolbar, that Google isn't responsible if it blows up your computer (it won't), and that you can't try to make money from the Toolbar (for example, by charging admission to watch you Google with it, which sounds a little bit disgusting).

5. **Click the Agree button.**

   Now comes yet another notice involving Google's privacy policy. This one you must read. It explains that installing the Google Toolbar with advanced features, including the PageRank indicator, allows Google to collect anonymous information about your Web surfing. Google uses this information to calculate accurate PageRanks, thereby improving the performance of the entire service. However, you may opt out of the advanced features on this page if the thought of surfing feedback clashes with your sense of privacy. Furthermore, after installation, you can visit the Toolbar Options page to activate certain advanced features while still disabling PageRank feedback.

6. **At the bottom of the page, click the Enable Advanced Features button or the Disable Advanced Features button, and then click Next.**

Using the Google Toolbar on other computers

One of the traditional advantages of add-on browser toolbars, such as Yahoo! Companion Toolbar (which, in *Yahoo! For Dummies,* Brad Hill recommends with the same verve that I recommend Google's Toolbar here), is that you can transfer your settings to any computer when traveling. This convenience holds in the case of the Yahoo! Companion Toolbar, which stores the user's Internet bookmarks and other settings on the Yahoo! computers. The happy result is that you can load all your destinations to the browser of any computer with Web access.

The Google Toolbar doesn't work that way. It's meant to assist you in searching, not in storing your links or other personal information. You certainly can configure the Toolbar to your preferences (see "Choosing Toolbar Options"), but those settings are stored in your computer, not Google's. So if you uninstall the Toolbar and then reinstall it, you must reset your preferences. Likewise, when traveling, you may install the Toolbar onto a strange computer's browser, but it doesn't remember you or your home preferences.

7. In the next window, select the Google site that corresponds to the place where you live.

8. Click the Next button.

The Google Toolbar downloads and installs itself on your computer. The installation takes five to ten seconds over a high-speed connection; phone modems might require a minute or two. When the process is finished, you see the Toolbar attached to your browser.

You're ready to go. You can try a search immediately by typing a keyword in the keyword box and pressing Enter. It's that easy.

To turn off the Google Toolbar, right-click any empty place on any toolbar and deselect the Google option on the pop-up menu that appears. To remove the Google Toolbar, do it as though you were removing a computer program and start in the Control Panel.

Choosing Toolbar Options

The Google Toolbar comes with a host of options that fine-tune the Toolbar's appearance and functionality. To see these options, click the Options button on the Toolbar or click the Google button and choose Options on the menu. You see the Toolbar Options dialog box shown in Figure 6-2. The following sections explain these options.

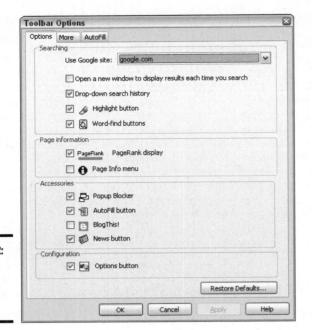

Figure 6-2:
Choosing
Google
Toolbar
options.

When you adjust your Google Toolbar options, remember that they don't affect — nor are they affected by — your Google Preferences (see Chapter 5 of Book II). The Google Preferences influence your search experience at the Google site. Toolbar options affect Toolbar searching only.

Options tab choices

Beginning with the Options tab of the Toolbar Options dialog box (refer to Figure 6-2), here are your choices:

✦ **Open a new window to display results each time you search:** Leaves the original browser window anchored at its current site while Google search results are displayed in a fresh window.

✦ **Drop-down search history:** Allows you to open the Search text box drop-down list and select a search word that you entered before.

✦ **Highlight button:** Highlights keywords, each in a different color, on Web pages that appear after you conduct a search. This option is extremely useful for finding keywords on Web pages.

✦ **Word-find buttons:** Places a button on the Toolbar for each of your keywords. (They appear after you launch the search, not as you type the words.) If you have your options set to deliver search results in a new window, the word-find buttons follow you to the new window. Furthermore, they stay with you when you click search results, *even* if your Google Preferences cause yet another window to be opened.

✦ **PageRank display:** Lets you see the Google ranking of Web pages that you visit. Knowing a page's rank is, to be honest, marginally valuable at best. I leave it on most of the time, because . . . well, why not? And I enjoy glancing at the page rank from time to time.

✦ **Page Info menu:** Puts the Page Info button on the Toolbar. By selecting this option, you can open a drop-down list with options for seeing pages that are similar to the one you're viewing, a cached version of the page, pages that are linked to the page, or an English translation of the page.

✦ **Pop-up Blocker:** Prevents free-floating ads from sprouting atop and behind your browser. In certain conditions, this blocker doesn't touch the ads streamed directly to the desktop in Windows XP. The feature does block ads that are associated with Web sites, which spoils the sites in many cases. (See "Pop-Up Blocker," later in this chapter, for more information.)

✦ **AutoFill button:** Fills in online forms with one click — a tremendous timesaver. (See "AutoFill," later in this chapter.)

✦ **BlogThis!:** Enables users to post an entry to their Weblogs that automatically refers to the Web page currently displayed. This is for users of Blogger (www.blogger.com), Google's recently acquired Weblog service.

✦ **News button:** Takes you directly to Google News, the essential current events portal of the Internet.

✦ **Options button:** Places the Options button on the Toolbar so that you can quickly open the Toolbar Options dialog box.

More tab choices

The More tab choices in the Toolbar Options dialog box are as follows:

✦ **Save the search history across browser sessions:** Permanently saves the list of Web pages that you visit. Permits you to open the Search text box drop-down list and select a search word that you entered previously. (You can always clear your search history manually by choosing the Clear Search History option on the Google menu button on the Toolbar.)

✦ **Automatically search when you select from the search history:** Forces Google into action when you select a previous search. You don't have to press Enter or click the Search Web button.

✦ **Remember last search type:** Keeps you from having to click the Web Search button and tell Google what kind of search you want. Google merely searches with the search type that you chose previously.

✦ **Use Google as my default search engine in Internet Explorer:** Causes a Google screen to appear when you click the Search button in Internet Explorer.

✦ **Include special searches on search menu:** Adds these five options to the Search Web button's drop-down list: Linux, BSD Unix, US Government, Apple Macintosh, and Microsoft.

✦ **Web buttons:** Places the following four buttons on the Google Toolbar: Up, Next & Previous, Category, and Voting.

✦ **Extra search buttons:** Places the following buttons on the Google Toolbar so you don't have to access these commands from Toolbar menus: Search Site, I'm Feeling Lucky, Search Images, Search Groups, Search Directory, and Search Froogle.

✦ **Button text labels:** Lets you decide what text to put on buttons.

✦ **Automatically highlight fields that AutoFill can fill:** Highlights fields such as name and address fields that can be filled in automatically by clicking the AutoFill button. (See "AutoFill," later in this chapter.)

✦ **Play a sound when blocking pop-ups:** Emits a little beep when a pop-up advertisement has been blocked. (See "Pop-Up Blocker," later in this chapter, for more information.)

✦ **Fix PageRank through proxies:** Displays ranking estimates to people who are on intranets that are protected by a firewall and can't properly see Google page rankings.

✦ **Hide popup blocker count:** Hides the counter that shows how many pop-ups have been blocked.

AutoFill tab information

Enter your personal information here if you want to use the Toolbar's AutoFill feature, which permits you to fill in online forms in a matter of seconds. I explain this feature in the following section of this chapter.

AutoFill

If you register at as many sites and shop online as much as I do, filling out online forms is a tedious hassle. The AutoFill function in the Google Toolbar invites you to fill in your crucial information just once and then let the Toolbar handle any forms that you encounter.

Use the AutoFill tab of the Toolbar Options dialog box to enter your information, as shown in Figure 6-3. You may add your name, e-mail address, phone number, two mailing addresses, and one credit card. (AutoFill would become much more useful if it accepted multiple credit cards.) Credit card information is protected by a password — and all Toolbar information, including AutoFill, is stored on your computer, not on an Internet computer.

Conveniently, the Toolbar highlights the portions of an online form that it's capable of filling in. You may proceed to fill them in manually if you choose, or just click the AutoFill button on the Toolbar to complete those fields all at once. AutoFill never fills in user name and password fields, which can change from site to site. Not so conveniently, AutoFill takes the extra step of telling you what it's about to do instead of just doing it. That confirmation window gives you a chance to review your information in a concise format, which gets annoying after a while.

Figure 6-3: AutoFill accepts your personal information and supplies it to site registrations, shopping carts, and other online forms.

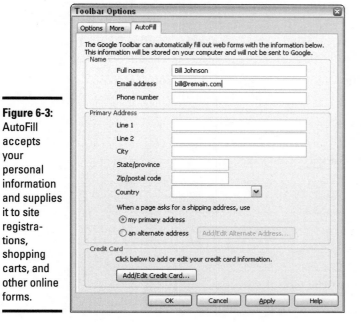

Pop-Up Blocker

Google's new ad-blocker feature on the Toolbar is stable, effective, and flexible — an outstanding little utility. After you add the pop-up blocker to the Toolbar (you can remove and add it at will by using the Toolbar Options dialog box), the blocker destroys pop-up browser advertisements before they hit your screen, makes a proud little noise for each blocked ad, and keeps track of the total number of killed pop-ups.

If you want to allow pop-ups from a certain site, simply click the Pop-Up Blocker button after you arrive at that site. Google reloads the page, this time allowing the ads to pop up. The button changes appearance to notify you that pop-ups are enabled for that site and keeps track of your selection. Any time you return to that site, pop-ups are allowed and the button tells you so. When you surf away from the liberated site, the button reverts to its original appearance and ads are blocked as normal.

Pushing Google's (Browser) Buttons

If the Google Toolbar seems a bit complex and overpowering for your needs, you might find the Google browser buttons more appealing. Three buttons are available, each of which attaches to your browser's toolbar (not the Google Toolbar). As shown in Figure 6-4, the three buttons are

✦ **Google.com:** This simple navigation button takes you to the Google home page.

✦ **GoogleScout:** Click this button to activate the Similar Pages feature, calling up a search results page of sites related to the current page.

✦ **Google Search:** Highlight any single word or group of words on a Web page, and then click the Google Search button to run a Web search.

Figure 6-4:
You can put Google buttons on your browser's toolbar.

Follow these steps to get the Google browser buttons:

1. **Go to this page:**

    www.google.com/options/winexplorer.html

2. **Follow the instructions to prepare your browser for receiving Google buttons.**

3. **Click and drag each button you want to the Links bar of your browser.**

A Security Alert window might pop up, warning you that adding the link might not be safe and asking whether you want to continue. Click Yes.

If you don't see your Links toolbar, right-click any toolbar in your browser and choose Links to display it.

The truth is that the Google buttons don't offer any joy that you can't get through the Google Toolbar. One-click access to Google's home page is available on the Toolbar, as is the Similar Pages feature (under the Page Info button). Google Search is the most interesting browser button, but even that function — instant searching on a text string highlighted in the Web page — is accomplished two different ways in the Toolbar. The first method is highlighting words and clicking the Google Search selection in the right-click menu. The second way is highlighting one or more words and dragging the highlighted excerpt up to the Google Toolbar, which launches a search.

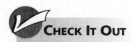
CHECK IT OUT

Launching a Search on Highlighted Words

I recommend understanding all the methods of highlighting keywords and launching a search to match them because searching for keywords derived from a Web page is one of Google's most engaging features. First, get comfortable with the three methods of highlighting text in a Web page:

✔ Double-click any single word to highlight it.

✔ In Internet Explorer, triple-click any sentence to highlight the entire sentence.

✔ To highlight a group of neighboring words that don't form a complete sentence, single-click one word and drag the mouse cursor to highlight other words before or after the first word.

After the text is highlighted, you can launch a search on those keywords in one of three ways:

✔ Click and drag the text to any spot on the Google Toolbar and release the mouse button (my favorite method, just because I think it's so cool). The highlighted words appear in the keyword box.

✔ Right-click the highlighted text and select Google Search.

✔ Click the Google Search button if it's on your Links toolbar.

**Book II
Chapter 6**

Using the Google Toolbar

Chapter 7: Googling in Tongues

In This Chapter

⊯ Seeing Google in other languages

⊯ Searching for non-English Web sites

⊯ Finding Web sites located in other countries

⊯ Translating Web sites

The global Google has risen. Nobody will be unaffected for long. Google's internationalism is a profound mission that seeks to provide every literate person with a friendly path into the information matrix. This chapter consolidates all Google language initiatives, some of which are also mentioned in other chapters.

Google presents non-English content in three broad areas:

✦ **Interface:** The familiar Google main pages can be displayed in dozens of languages.

✦ **Web pages:** Google can limit a search to Web pages written in any of dozens of languages and even to sites residing in certain countries.

✦ **Ad hoc translating:** Google is always ready to translate text that you entered by typing or posting.

Google in Your Native Tongue

As shown in Figure 7-1, Google headquarters for most language tasks is the Language Tools page at this URL:

```
www.google.com/language_tools
```

You can also access the Language Tools page by clicking its link on the main Google page and indicating its importance in the buffet of Google services. In the screen shot shown in Figure 7-1, I scrolled down a bit so that you could see the main interactive tools on the page. But I want to start lower on the page, where you select an interface language.

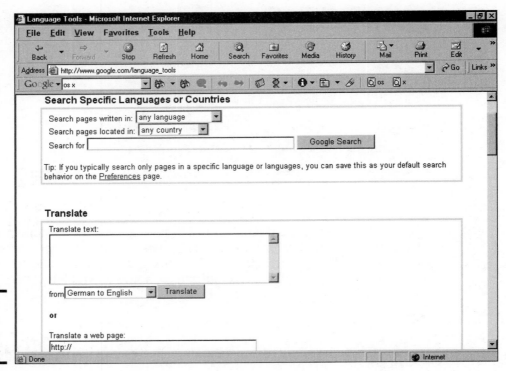

Figure 7-1:
Part of the
Language
Tools page.

Google's interface language can be set on the Preferences page as well as on the Language Tools page. (See Chapter 5 of Book II for details about the Preferences page.) This dual placement of the interface language selection is not just duplication. The setting on the Preferences page is more powerful than the setting on the Language Tools page. The Language Tools links allow you to audition Google in different languages, after which you can return to the Language Tools page to try a new one.

Trying a new interface language from the Language Tools page doesn't change your language setting on the Preferences page. You remain in your newly chosen language as you surf from page to page in Google, but when you leave Google or shut down your browser, subsequent visits to Google return you to the language set on the Preferences page. In fact, simply selecting the Google home page on the Google Toolbar knocks out the language that you chose on the Language Tools page and releases Google to your Preferences language.

Although the interface language doesn't affect Web search results, Google does translate Google's Cached and Similar Pages links on the search results page, as well as other artifacts of the Google interface that appear on results pages. Figure 7-2 shows a results page in the French interface.

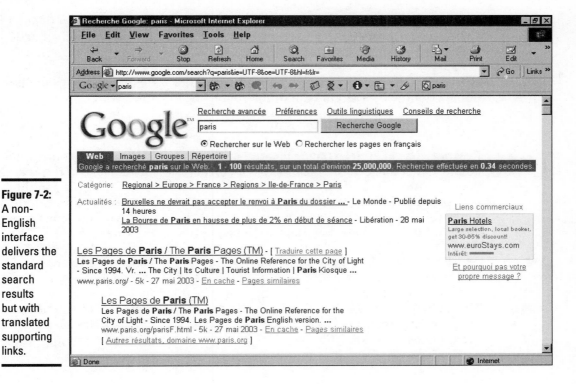

Figure 7-2:
A non-English interface delivers the standard search results but with translated supporting links.

Searching Around the World

No matter what language you choose for the Google interface, you can apply language requests to search results. Not only can you search for Web pages written in certain languages, you can also have Google find pages located in certain countries, regardless of the page's language. These two features are interesting individually — and even more so when combined.

These language controls are near the top of the Language Tools page (refer to Figure 7-1). Operate them using the Search Pages Written In and Search Pages Located In drop-down lists. You may use both menus together or either one on its own. Below them is a keyword box for launching the search. Here you may use any applicable search operator (see Chapter 2 of Book II) in your keyword string.

Your computer's capability to display languages that use non-Latin alphabets depends on your browser — Google has nothing to do with it. If you want to read Chinese pages, for example, you might need to download a Chinese plug-in for your browser. Consult your browser's Help menu for instructions. If some non-Latin-based pages display part of the text but leave the rest as gibberish symbols, it's because the displayed text is part of a graphic.

Assuming that you're not a linguist, you can get good results by searching in your native language (for this example, I assume it's English) for Web pages in another country. To search in a specific country, use the Search Pages Located In drop-down list on the Language Tools page. This tactic has

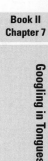

the marvelous effect of narrowing the search results while targeting them in some way that relates to your keywords. For example, try searching pages in France for *wine bordeaux*.

More productive still, you can get away from the widespread biases of your home country by searching in other countries. Try this string:

```
alan greenspan filetype:pdf
```

Restrict your search to pages located in Great Britain, Japan, or some other country. Just make sure that you specify English as the language in the Search Pages Written In drop-down list. Limiting the results to PDF files (as in the *alan greenspan filetype:pdf* string) brings up a lot of academic papers about America's role in macroeconomics and sheds light on the perception of Federal Reserve Chairman Alan Greenspan outside the United States.

As with the interface language, using the Language Tools page to select search languages and countries doesn't make your choice permanent. In fact, you can't make a permanent selection of the country — the Language Tools page is the only interface page that offers a country selection. If you want to permanently select a results language, set that language on your Preferences page. (See Chapter 5 of Book II for more Preferences page info.)

Translating on-the-Fly

Google provides machine translation for blocks of text and entire Web pages. Both features are located on the Language Tools page.

You can copy the entire page from a foreign Web page and paste it into the Translate Text form. However, when it comes to Web pages, I find letting Google get the page and then redisplay it in English easier and more satisfying. Here's how that works:

1. **Find a Web page in a language that you don't understand.**

You can wait until you encounter one by accident or you can search for one by using the Language Tools page (see "Searching Around the World").

2. **Highlight the page's URL in the Address bar of your browser.**

3. **Press Ctrl+C to copy the URL.**

4. **Go to the Language Tools page.**

You can also open a new browser window and go to Language Tools there if you want to remain anchored on the original non-English page.

5. **Click in the Translate a Web Page text box to place your curser there, and then press Ctrl+V to paste the URL.**

6. **Select a translation from the drop-down list.**

7. **Click the Translate button.**

Making happy of translate by automatic

How good is machine translation? The title of this sidebar gives you an idea of the sort of mangling that you can expect. I recently used Google to translate (to English) a long interview from a German Web site. I did the translation as a favor for a friend of mine, who was the interview subject. We laughed ourselves silly over the result, which made my friend sound like a parody of bad English. Nevertheless, the translation conveyed the gist, and that's what you can expect from Google's auto-translate feature. If you don't know the language, Google certainly gets the main points across.

The translated page appears with a horizontal frame above it, indicating that it's a Google translation and offering a View Original Web Page link. (When clicked, that link displays the original page in a new browser window.) Figure 7-3 shows a translated page. Note that words incorporated in graphics and banners (for example, About This Site, New Additions, and the entire top logo) remain untranslated; only text is recognized by Google as translatable.

Now, here's the great part. Click any link on the translated page, and Google continues translating. You can move through the entire site, reading it in the language of your choice. Figure 7-3 illustrates an English-to-French translation so that English-speaking readers can see how the translation works. Normally, though, an English-speaking user would translate a non-English page into English and then click around that site, continuing to read in English.

Book II
Chapter 7

Googling in Tongues

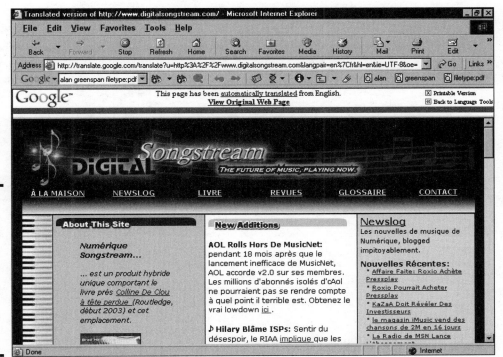

Figure 7-3:
A Google-translated Web page (English to French). Words in graphics remain untranslated.

Both the autotranslate feature that I describe here and the method of sending Google out to translate pages enhance the value of the language selection feature described in the preceding section. As long as you stick with a language that Google can translate into English (currently German, French, Italian, Spanish, and Portuguese), searching for pages in those languages is a fantastic way to broaden and internationalize your Internet experience.

The following steps describe a streamlined way that an English-speaking user can search for foreign sites and read them in English:

1. **On the Language Tools page, use the Search Pages Written In drop-down list to select a language to search.**

   For this example, the language should be French, German, Italian, Spanish, or Portuguese.

2. **Type one or more keywords.**

   For a true cultural experience, search for something related to the language or its country.

3. **Click the Google Search button.**

4. **On the search results page (see Figure 7-4), click the Translate This Page link next to any item that you want to read.**

When translating Web pages from search results lists, remember that Google assumes that you want the translation to be made in the language that you chose as the Google interface language. It doesn't matter whether you've set the language on the Language Tools or Preferences page, that's the language Google translates to.

Figure 7-4:
Translate Web pages without displaying the originals directly from the search results page.

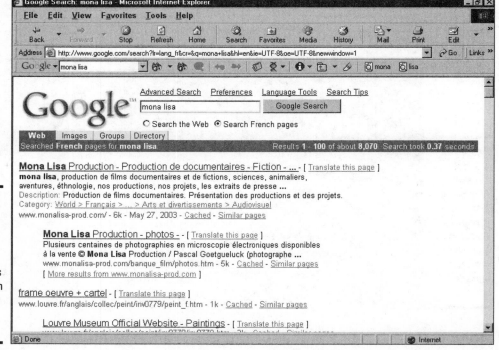

Chapter 8: Searching for Specialty Items

In This Chapter

✔ Finding your way to Google specialty searches

✔ Discovering tips for using the U.S. government search engine

✔ Exploring the Linux and BSD worlds

✔ Using the Apple Macintosh and Microsoft search engines

✔ Searching university sites

*T*ake Google's hand and let it lead you into a specialized universe or two. Or three, or four, or five. Google has created alternate search engines whose results are limited to certain subject areas. Google accomplishes this topical restriction by choosing source sites that effectively contribute to search results. On the technical side, Google has isolated the worlds of Linux, BSD, Apple Macintosh, and Microsoft. Each of these areas enjoys a dedicated engine that searches sites that are provided by these organizations or related to them.

To me, the most interesting specialty search is the one devoted to the U.S. government and related fields of military, local government, and global government. Rounding out the specialty categories is a large group of university-specific search engines, each of which prowls through a single college or university Web site.

Finding the Specialty Searches

Following its quiet tradition of refusing to promote its fringe features, Google buries its specialty services, perhaps discouraging regular use. You can get to the search engines that I describe in this chapter through the main Google home page, but you have to know where to click, and the procedure is tiresome. This section provides some tips for quickly reaching the government, BSD, Linux, Mac, Microsoft, and university search pages.

The direct Web addresses are so easy to remember (with the exception of the university page) that your preferred method might be to simply type the URL in your browser's Address bar. Here are the addresses, which point self-evidently to their respective search pages:

```
www.google.com/bsd
www.google.com/linux
www.google.com/unclesam
www.google.com/mac
www.google.com/microsoft
www.google.com/options/universities.html
```

Another way to get to the specialty search pages is to start at the Google home page, click More, and click Special Searches.

U.S. Government Searches

Arguably, the most useful of Google's specialty search areas is the one devoted to the U.S. government. Actually, this distinct search engine is both larger and smaller than the name implies. This engine is global in reach. At the same time, it reaches below federal government sites to the state and municipal level.

You might think that this entire search engine merely replaces the *site:.gov* operator:keyword combination that I describe in Chapter 2 of Book II. Not so. In fact, *site:.gov* remains quite useful in the search because the results pages dish up a hearty mix of .gov, .mil (for military), and .com sites that bear some relation to government, public policy, law, defense, and other fields of administration, the judiciary, and the legislature. All domain extensions are represented here.

Use the results of your search to find Web sites that you can later search with the *site* operator. You can perform such a search in a general or advanced Web search. In fact, some of these discovered sites might make it to your bookmark list for regular visitation. The following are some examples of interesting sites that turn up in searches:

```
http://speaker.house.gov
http://freedom.house.gov
http://democraticleader.house.gov
http://memory.loc.gov
http://gop.gov
```

Searching on issues and hot phrases can reveal who in the government (individuals, agencies, committees) is involved in that issue. Some examples include

```
pledge of allegiance
fcc deregulation
abortion legislation
```

These searches display sites of agencies and members of congress, in addition to more general information pages.

All the specialty search engines recognize the same search operators that you use in a normal Web search (see Chapter 2 of Book II). I often use the *filetype* operator to search for PDF files in the U.S. government area, plumbing a rich trove of Congressional hearing transcriptions, court judgments, and other official documents that are customarily posted online in PDF format. Using *filetype:pdf* transforms any search; try adding it after any keyword string. For example:

```
music hearings filetype:pdf
housing starts filetype:pdf
```

```
testimony military filetype:pdf
consumer confidence filetype:pdf
```

Linux and BSD Searches

These search engines are for searching exclusively in Web sites that offer information about Linux and operating systems that fall under the Berkeley Software Distribution (BSD) heading.

Linux is an open-source operating system that has been making waves for the past few years. Linux loyalists regard their operating system as a dynamic competitor of Microsoft Windows. Nobody owns Linux, but several companies own their respective operating system products based on Linux. Accordingly, Linux really refers to a family of operating systems, all built on the same foundation and with similar features.

Berkeley Software Distribution (BSD) is also an open-source family of operating systems, based on Unix. BSD got its start at the University of California at Berkeley. BSD has less prominence in the consumer marketplace than Linux does, but BSD servers (operating systems for Internet and intranet computers) are in fairly wide use.

Mac and Microsoft Searches

Apple Macintosh and Microsoft Windows: two operating system behemoths representing a fundamental polarity in the computer world. Nobody can claim that the Mac is a behemoth in terms of market share — Apple sells less than 5 percent of all new computers. But when it comes to ferocious loyalty and PR stamina, Apple has world-class clout. Google has assembled a trove of Web sources relating to each system and segregated them into distinct search engines.

University Searches

High school seniors take note: Google has your search engine. The University specialty searches let you rummage through a single university's Web site with the power of Google's search algorithms and operators.

University searches operate differently than the other specialty searches that I describe in this chapter. Google doesn't aggregate many university sites for searching. This is not a search engine for getting information *about* universities in general. Instead, Google has actually created hundreds of small search engines, each dedicated to a single university Web domain.

Useful? Well . . . this specialized search helps if you repeatedly search in a certain college site. Or, if you use the URL syntax that I divulge in the first section of this chapter, you can seamlessly surf around from one specialty university engine to another.

Here's how to approach the university specialty search sites the way Google intended:

1. **Go to the following page:**

```
www.google.com/options/universities.html
```

2. **Click the university link that you want to search.**

All the universities links are contained on this single, long page. Scroll down or click an alphabet link to leap ahead.

3. **On the resulting search page, launch your search in the regular fashion.**

All resulting links point to pages in that university's Web site.

The university search engines aren't affiliated with the universities. Go directly to the university Web site for a glossier presentation of the school.

You can avoid the inconvenient trip to Google's university search pages by using the *site* operator, assuming you know a university URL. Virtually all university site domains end with the .edu extension, so you need to know the primary domain name, which is often easy to guess. Suppose you want to search for keywords matching inside Princeton's site. A simple (and correct) guess of Princeton's domain is princeton.edu. So this keyword string

```
applying admission site:www.princeton.edu
```

gets you the links you want from the Google home page or Toolbar.

Not all colleges and universities are represented in these search engines — not by a long stretch. I sometimes visit Rollins College in Winter Park, Florida, and am disappointed that it's missing from Google's college list. But this situation is when using the *site* operator is handy: Because I know the Rollins domain is rollins.edu, I can search it from Google's home page or the Toolbar at any time.

Remember also that you can conduct a more general search across all educational domains by using the .edu extension with the *site* operator, like this:

```
undergraduate stress site:edu
```

Chapter 9: Getting Answers (From Human Beings!)

In This Chapter

✔ Creating a Google Answers account

✔ Posting and canceling questions

✔ Adding comments and joining conversations

✔ Clarifying questions and evaluating answers

✔ Writing effective questions and setting appropriate prices

As if Google weren't already a fount of knowledge, a service called Google Answers goes a step further and provides custom research. Google Answers lets you set the price for expert advice, facts, and linkage.

This chapter covers every aspect of Google Answers — from creating an account to posting a question and from setting a price to rating the answers. Don't blow off this chapter no matter how against the Google grain it might seem. Even if you're a veteran Googler who never needs research assistance, knowing your way around Google Answers (if only its directory archive of previously posted queries) can be invaluable. And if you're a budding researcher with no interest in paying someone else, this chapter shows you how you can sharpen your skills by observing Google Answers in action.

Paying for Google Expertise

In the background, behind your screen, next to the heaving mass that is the living Google index, resides a freelance staff of human researchers approved by Google to track down the answers to specific queries. Whereas keyword search queries display automated search results — basically page after page of links — Google Answers queries result in conversations and expert answers.

Google rigorously screens this staff of researchers for informational agility and communicativeness. They are paid 75 percent of the fees assigned by users to their posted questions. Google gets the other 25 percent. Researchers aren't assigned to certain questions; they claim questions based on areas of expertise and willingness to tackle the query's needs.

The next section establishes how you create a Google Answers account. Creating an account allows you to participate in one free aspect of Google Answers: posting comments to questions. (Later in the chapter, I offer guidelines for this type of participation.) Creating the account doesn't obligate you to pay a research fee or post a question. In fact, you aren't required to provide credit card information until you post your first question, at which point you're prompted for it.

Creating an Account and Logging In

The main purpose (at first, anyway) of creating a Google Answers account is to get an ID. The ID enables you to post a comment to somebody's question and be recognized by the system. Then, when you're ready, you can add payment information to your account and post your own questions. To get the ID, you must have already obtained a Google account. Follow these steps to get a Google Answers account ID:

1. **Go to the Google Accounts page at this address:**

    www.google.com/accounts/newaccount

2. **Enter your e-mail address, your password, and your password confirmation.**

   The password must contain at least six characters.

3. **Click the Terms of Use button.**

   The Terms of Use is a standard set of agreements: you won't use Google for commercial purposes; you won't troll the index with automated software searchers; Google isn't responsible for what you might find in a search; and Google isn't responsible if a terrible heat wave causes your geraniums to wither.

   The Privacy Policy (which I also explain in Chapter 5 of Book II) divulges that Google places software trackers called cookies in your computer; that the cookies send anonymous usage data to Google; that Google shares or publishes the collected information but doesn't release your personal information; and that Google promises not to rummage through your underwear drawer.

4. **Click the Create My Account button.**

   Google now sends an e-mail verification notice to the address that you entered, verifying that it is indeed *your* e-mail address. The e-mail looks at first glance like a piece of spam, so be careful of your deletions when looking for it.

5. **Click the link provided in the body of the e-mail that Google sent you.**

6. **Back in the browser, which has changed to a different page, click the Click Here to Continue link.**

   Your e-mail program might open a new browser window, depending on your settings.

7. **On the Google Answers: Sign Up page, type a nickname and select your e-mail notification level.**

   Your e-mail choices are to receive a notice whenever any activity occurs on a question you've asked, a single daily notice whether or not any activity has occurred, or nothing.

8. **Click the I Accept button, indicating your agreement with the Google Answers Terms of Service.**

This is a paid service, and you might want to read the TOS more diligently than you do those pertaining to free services. The statement includes warranty information, details on how your account is billed, the refund policy, a lot of disclaimers about the nonprofessional nature of the service's financial and medical information, and a declaration that, should you become stupider by using Google Answers, Google won't supply you with smart drugs. Click your browser's Back button to return to the Google Answers: Sign Up page.

9. **Click the Create My Google Answers Account button.**

Your account is activated at this point, and you're deposited on the Google Answers: My Questions page.

The Google Answers: My Questions page (see Step 9) is accessible with the My Account link on any Google Answers page.

Note: Whenever your Google Answers nickname appears on the screen, the following hyphenated suffix is attached to it: -ga. So if your chosen nickname is mynickname, your on-screen nickname is mynickname-ga. This alteration identifies you in the Google Answers portion of your Google Account, which covers a few different services.

Creating a Google Answers account doesn't authorize Google to collect fees from you. Note that in the preceding steps Google doesn't require your credit card information to establish the account. However, you can't post a question (see the following section) without providing payment information.

Posting and Canceling Questions

Posting a question to Google Answers is simple enough, but never free. For putting a question in play, the minimum charges are

✦ A $0.50 listing fee

✦ A fee between $2.00 and $200.00, determined by you and paid to the researcher

So the least you can pay to get a question on the board is $2.50. The listing fee is credited to Google at the time of posting. The researcher's fee is charged when an expert answers your question — no answer, no payment.

Your credit card is charged on a schedule determined by your balance and the time of month. If you run up listing fees and researchers' fees of $25.00 or more, Google hits your credit card for the full amount right away. If your due balance stays under $25.00, Google collects the dough once a month. Remember, researchers' fees come due not when you ask a question, but when you get an answer.

When you created your Google Answers account (see the preceding section) you didn't provide credit card information or any other way for Google to bill you. Google Answers fees are always paid by credit card. You can't post a question without providing that information. There's no point in providing it *before* you ask a question, so the following steps assume that you've sat down at the computer, opened up your browser, and want to post your first question to Google Answers.

1. **Go to the main Google Answers page at** `http://answers.google.com`, **or, on the Google Toolbar, click the Google button and choose Google Links➪Google Answers.**

2. **Click the Log In or Create a Google Account link.**

3. **Assuming that you have a Google Account (see the preceding section if you need to create one), log in with your e-mail address and password.**

4. **On your account page, click the Ask a Question link near the upper-right corner of the page.**

You can also begin setting up your payment information by clicking the My Profile link. But proceeding directly to Ask a Question takes you through the credit card process, too.

5. **On the Ask a Question page (see Figure 9-1), fill in the Subject, Question, and Price fields, and then select a Category.**

This seems a lot like work, doesn't it? It's worth it. For more about how to fill in these fields and maximize your chances of getting the answer you need at the price you want to pay, see the following section of this chapter.

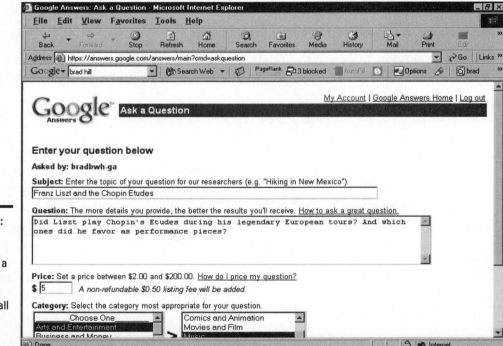

Figure 9-1: Ask your question, title it, set a price, and choose a category all on this page.

6. Click the Continue to Payment Information button.

You might be asked to enter your Google Account password again. No need to include the -ga suffix.

7. On the Google Answers: Enter Payment page, fill in your credit card and billing information.

8. Click the Pay Listing Fee and Post Question button.

If you click this button, the listing fee of 50 cents immediately becomes collectible by Google. You may also use the Go Back and Edit Question button to reword your query or set a different price. The preview posting of your question as currently worded and priced is displayed below the buttons.

That's it — your question is immediately posted. Click the View Your Question link on the confirmation page to see what you did. Figure 9-2 shows a posted question. Note that the time of posting and the expiration date are both listed. Questions remain posted, unanswered, for one month. Answered questions remain in the Google Answers directory permanently.

The View Question page contains enough features to warrant a closer look:

◆ You might see sponsored links on your View Question page. (See Figure 9-2.) Other Googlers see them, too. Google's AdWords program positions these paid links throughout the service, not just on the search results page, where they're prevalent.

◆ Use the Edit Question Parameters button to adjust the wording of your question or the price that you're offering for an answer. You may continue to tweak your words and price until the moment that a Google researcher claims the question. Once claimed, the question is locked in place.

◆ Use the Clarify Question button to add information to your question that would help a researcher better answer it. You can do so at any time.

◆ Use the Close Question button if you change your mind and no longer want to receive a paid-for answer. On the following page, simply click the Yes, Close Question button. Or if you're truly indecisive and now want to keep your question alive, click the No, Keep Question button. If you close the question, it remains posted, but researchers can't claim it. And although you don't have to pay for an answer, you do still owe Google 50 cents for posting the question in the first place.

◆ Below your posted question is space for the answer (which, when it comes in, is publicly viewable, as is your question) and space below that for comments from other Googlers. You don't pay for comments from the peanut gallery.

You may post as many questions as you like. Manage your questions, billing profile, and invoice information on your Google Answers account page, which is available through the My Account link on every Google Answers page. Figure 9-3 illustrates a posted question with a researcher's request for clarification.

Book II
Chapter 9

Getting Answers
(From Human Beings!)

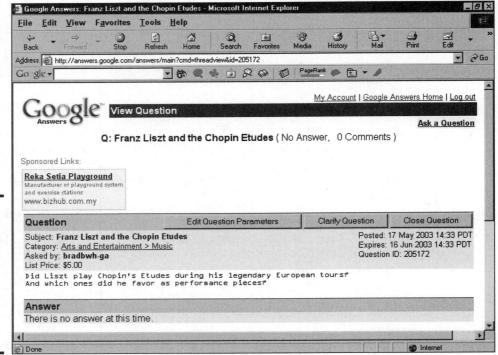

Figure 9-2:
A question
posted to
Google
Answers,
viewed on
the poster's
View
Question
page.

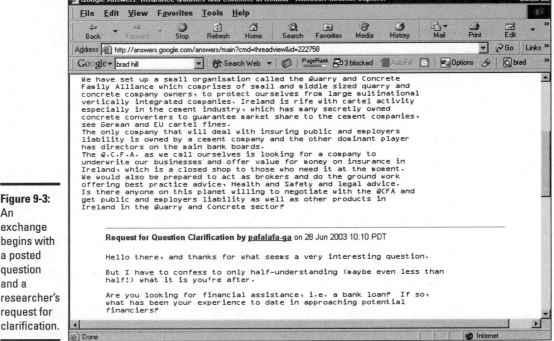

Figure 9-3:
An
exchange
begins with
a posted
question
and a
researcher's
request for
clarification.

Comments and Conversations

A lot of clarifying goes on in Google Answers, both before and after a researcher gets hold of a question. The system is devised to encourage conversation and cooperation between user and researcher; it's not *Jeopardy!* Flexibility is built into the system to increase the chance of satisfaction on both sides. The conversational nature of the Google Answers system combined with Google researchers' eagerness to share knowledge makes it possible to find the information that you want (or some of it) without getting a formal answer to your posted question.

Anybody can add a comment to a posted question, and the authors of added comments aren't identified as researchers or regular users. The result is an information milieu in which people share what they know. The trick is to distinguish between good information and bad information — an issue that can be universally applied to the Internet. Many Google Answer comments and nearly all official answers are documented with links to research sites, which helps establish their authenticity.

Your question might sometimes be essentially answered by comments without an official researcher's answer. This development is somewhat rare in the case of specific, data-oriented questions, which researchers jump on with dizzying speed. But it's not so uncommon when a question requires deep research or has multiple answers.

If you're satisfied with the posted comments that your question has attracted and no longer need an official answer, feel free to close the question by following these steps:

1. **Click the My Account link on any Google Answers page.**

2. **Click the link to your question.**

   You might have more than one posted question. If necessary, use the Show My drop-down list and select the Questions Awaiting Answers option to narrow the number of links.

3. **On your question's page, click the Close Question button (refer to Figure 9-2).**

   The page reloads with a confirmation notice at the top, asking whether you're sure that you want to close the question.

4. **Click the Yes, Close Question button.**

   After closing a question, that question appears on your Google Answers account page with CLOSED in the Status column, as shown in Figure 9-4.

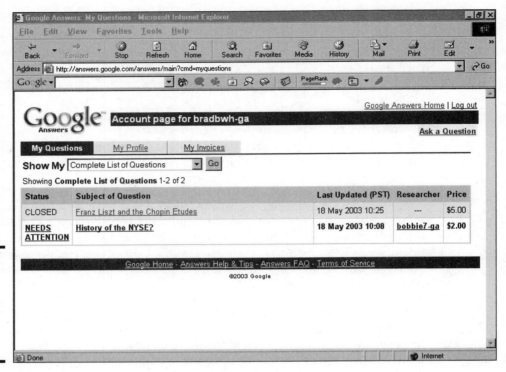

Figure 9-4:
Closed
questions
still appear
on the
account
page.

Refunds and repostings

In the rare event that a Google Answers expert lets you down completely, your recourse is to apply for a price refund. You have two options:

✔ Apply for a refund. Getting a refund closes the question to all further activity, including comments.

✔ Apply for a credit for the amount of your expert payment, plus a reposting of the question. Getting the credit reposts the question for research by a different expert. The second 50-cent listing fee is waived.

Both options are included in one online form. You must go to this page:

```
http://answers.google.com/
    answers/main?cmd=refundrequest
```

If you don't want to copy that rather long URL, find the link by clicking the Answers FAQ link, which is listed at the bottom of every Answers page.

Choose Repost My Question or Request a Refund radio button and explain why you think either option should happen. You need to include the question ID, which is located on the question's page, not your account page.

Good Questions at the Right Prices

The best way to maximize your Google Answers experience is to ask the right question at the right price. Asking a difficult, multipart question and offering $2.00 for its answer might not attract the best — or any — researchers. Offering $30.00 for the answer to a simple question creates a researcher feeding frenzy but leaves you feeling ripped off. Additionally, posting an unclear question (even though it can be corrected with the Clarify feature) is liable to generate time-wasting clarifying conversations, perhaps leading to the researcher feeling ripped off or you feeling obligated to tip heavily.

Good questions equal good answers

First off, certain types of questions head straight into a dead end because of Google's legal restrictions. In some cases, Google even deletes the question from public view. So don't do the following:

✦ **Don't place any personal contact information in your question.** Don't ask researchers to phone you or e-mail you privately, for example.

✦ **Don't ask for help doing something questionably legal or outright illegal.** For example, requesting assistance in making unauthorized music downloads will probably get your question removed or at least incite warning comments from researchers.

✦ **Don't spam.** If you try to use the Google Answers space to promote your Internet business or sell products, Google bumps you off for sure.

✦ **Don't get X-rated.** References to porn, and especially links to it, are over the line.

✦ **Don't cheat on your tests.** Google Answers encourages student use while doing homework, but getting a researcher to answer a test question is against the rules. A fine line separates the two uses, to be sure, and questions stay or go at Google's discretion.

Questions spawn related questions all too easily. Asking multipart questions isn't against the rules, but know what you're doing. Don't ramble on with every query that enters your head. Be aware, too, that you're essentially bidding for a researcher's time, and the more complex your question(s), the more money you should offer.

Exploring the Google Answers directory

The Google Answers directory is a virtual laboratory of questions, comments, and answers. It allows you to discover what works and what doesn't. Surf the directory by following these steps:

 1. **Go to the Google Answers home page by clicking the Google Answers Home link on any Answers page or, on the Google Toolbar (see Chapter 7 of Book II), by clicking the Google button and choosing Links⇨ Google Answers.**

2. **Scroll down the page to see the Answers directory topics.**

   You can drill into the directory from two angles. Either click a subject area in the Browse Previously Asked Questions section or click a question from the Recently Answered Questions column. To follow along with this example, enter the directory through a subject heading, as shown in Figure 9-5.

3. **Click any subject category.**

4. **On the category page, click a question, click a subcategory, or scroll down the page to view a summary of comments, answers, and prices in that category.**

You can discover a lot just by glancing down a main category page. Many question titles are fairly explanatory, the price is right there in the far-right column, and you can see the Comment and Answer traffic that each question has attracted. Click a few questions, too, to see how researchers handle various types of questioning. You might be amazed at the detail and depth of the answers. Pay particular attention to the star-rated answers — most ratings are five stars, signifying an extremely successful transaction between seeker and expert. Asking a good question is half that equation.

Creating a descriptive heading for your question and placing the query in an appropriate category are both as important as good phrasing of the question itself. When creating the query title, don't worry about crafting a good sentence. You can even word the title as if it were a Google search string. (While you're at it, you might want to try Googling your query before posting to Google Answers.) Do whatever it takes to convey the subject of your query precisely.

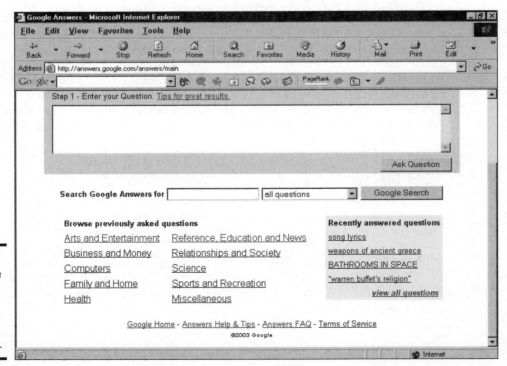

Figure 9-5:
Get into the Answers directory from the Answers home page.

Putting your money where your query is

Setting a price for the Google Answers service might seem awkward. I recommend avoiding the temptation to bottom-line your every query. Likewise, don't pay too much for simple questions simply because you're reluctant to appear cheap. Google recommends estimating how long it will take to research your question and then pricing it accordingly. This advice, although relevant to the researchers, is nearly pointless to regular users who aren't information experts and can't anticipate the type of research needed. A better bet is to gauge, roughly, how demanding your question is based on two factors:

✦ **Speed:** Do you have a deadline, or are you just impatient? If so, paying more for a quick answer is worth your while.

✦ **Complexity:** If your query contains more than one part or more than three sentences, chances are you're requesting more than $2.00 of expertise.

If you have plenty of time, one pricing strategy is to start at the bottom and work your way up. Post a $2.00 question and see what it brings in. Interested users post comments regardless of price because they're not getting paid. If your $2.00 post doesn't get the attention you want, raise the stakes to $5.00, and so on.

**Book II
Chapter 9**

**Getting Answers
(From Human Beings!)**

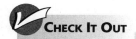 **CHECK IT OUT**

The Google Phone Book

One of the great, under-recognized features of Google is the built-in phone and address book. This isn't a link-over deal like maps or stock prices. Like the White Pages, the Google index embodies address and phone number information. In my experience, Google does a better job culling this information from its index than do the high-profile online directories.

Activating the Google phone and address book is a somewhat hit-and-miss affair, but Google takes the hint as easily here as it does with the mapping function. Type a first name, a last name, and a ZIP Code in the keyword box, and if that person's address is in the index, Google displays it above the regular search results (along with the phone number). Don't know the ZIP Code? Who does? Replace it with the U.S. state abbreviation — that works fine. No commas are necessary in the keyword string.

 Google provides a specialized search operator (a keyword modifier) that hooks into the phone book. Unsurprisingly, it's the phonebook operator. Use it without any spaces between the colon and the first keyword (see Book II,

Chapter 2 for more on using Google's operators), like this:

```
phonebook:smith ny
```

The volume of results sometimes requires multiple pages, just as with a Web search. Another difference in this results page is just below the keyword box. After Google dips into its phone book, it presumes that you might want to stay there for a while and gives you a choice of applying your next keywords to the phone book or to a Web search.

You can narrow your phone book searches to residential only or business only by using variants of the plain *phonebook* operator:

↪ Use *rphonebook* for residential listings

↪ Use *bphonebook* for business listings

Using the *bphonebook* operator, Google turns into one heck of a fast Yellow Pages directory. Looking for a Chinese restaurant in your neighborhood? Lay down the keyword string with your ZIP Code:

```
bphonebook:chinese restaurant
10010
```

Chapter 10: Shopping with Froogle and Google Catalogs

In This Chapter

✔ Introducing the Google shopping portal

✔ Searching and browsing in Froogle

✔ Putting special Froogle search operators to work

✔ Using advanced searching in Froogle

✔ Introducing the dazzling Google Catalogs

Google, the world's most intelligent search engine, has an academic, ivory-tower sheen. The science behind its index and the insightfulness of its results lend Google an otherworldly feeling, except when it comes to . . . shopping! Shopping is the common denominator of the Web — everybody likes to buy stuff. Google turns its all-seeing eye to the swarming, steamy jungle of e-commerce.

Yes, Google is a shopping portal, but not of the sort that you might be familiar with in AOL and Yahoo!. Google provides two shopping directories and applies its insightful, destination-ranking intelligence to them. The result is a sharp, objective, results-oriented, virtual-window-shopping experience.

This chapter covers the details of Froogle, a keyword-empowered shopping directory, and Google Catalogs, an online mail-order browsing environment.

Google's Approach to Online Shopping

The main difference between Google's shopping services and those in other major portals is that Google doesn't get its hands on the money. You don't buy anything through Google. Both Froogle and Google Catalogs function purely as directories to products, sending you elsewhere to get your hands on the goods. Google has no revenue-sharing association with e-commerce retailers (in Froogle) or mail-order companies (in Google Catalogs). The search results that you get in both services are pure; preferred placement in the search results lists is not for sale by Google.

Google isn't (currently) interested in handling purchase transactions, taking payment information, or hosting stores. The Google shopping portal is a search engine that separates products from stores to deliver targeted search lists. Furthermore, it uses similar evaluations as in its Web searches to determine which products matching your keywords are most important and should be listed first. The results aren't quite as startling as with a Web search, which often seems to know what you want before you do.

When it comes to buying through Google, *through* is the right word (as opposed to *from*). Froogle search results are like Web search results insofar as they link you to target sites (in this case, e-commerce sites with their own shopping carts and payment systems). Google Catalogs provides mail-order phone numbers and — where possible — links to Web sites.

Searching and Browsing in Froogle

Your Froogle experience starts on the Froogle home page. You can get there starting at the Google home page by clicking the Froogle link or by going to this Web address:

`www.froogle.com`

As you can see in Figure 10-1, Froogle is a search engine for finding merchandise. It looks and works much like Google itself. Enter a keyword to find an item you want to buy.

Search results in Froogle

Eventually, you reach a Froogle product page similar to the one in Figure 10-2. The product page is where you see individual items for sale. They're for sale only through their host sites — not through Google. The product page contains six main features:

- ✦ **Keyword box:** You may launch a new search from any Froogle directory or product page.

- ✦ **Summary bar:** This familiar feature tells you how long the search took and how items were found.

- ✦ **Price Range:** Specify a price range and click the Go button.

- ✦ **Show All Products:** Froogle normally lists one search result per store. Click the Show All Products link for a more complete list. I find this option unproductive — for any item, you can drill into its store to see all matching products.

- ✦ **Product name:** The product name is the main link to its page in the host store. You may also click the picture.

- ✦ **Product description:** Here you find the basic stats: price, store name, and short product description.

Froogle notices and obeys your general Google settings on the Preferences page (see Chapter 5 of Book II). If you've set Google to display the maximum 100 listings per results page, Froogle displays 100 listings. Also, if you follow my recommendation and set Google to open a new browser window for the target page, Froogle does so when displaying an online store that carries the product that you clicked. Doing so keeps you anchored at Froogle while you shop around in the target site.

Froogle search operators

Froogle adds to Google's arsenal of search operators. Book II, Chapter 2 introduces Google-specific *search operators* — words in your keyword string that tell Google how to interpret your keywords. Standard operators that work in all search engines (*AND, OR, NOT,* and the exact phrase operator) mix with Google-specific operators listed in Chapter 2 of Book II to yield highly targeted search results.

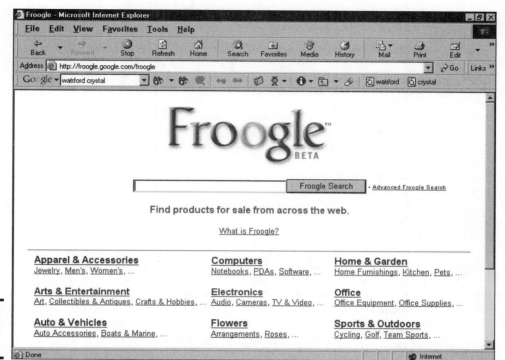

Figure 10-1:
The Froogle home page.

Figure 10-2:
Froogle's product page contains thumbnails, descriptions, and ways to narrow the search.

In Froogle, three operators (one of them peculiar to Froogle) narrow your shopping search with great effectiveness:

✦ *store:* The *store* operator limits matches to particular stores.

✦ *allintext:* The *allintext* operator limits matches to product description text.

✦ *allintitle:* The *allintitle* operator limits matches to product names.

store

The *store* operator is special to Froogle and is one powerful little rascal. Using it, you can instantly browse one store's inventory in any product category. To find items from BestBuy, for example, type

```
"digital camera" store:bestbuy
```

The *store* operator is designed to work when the keyword following it is mashed up against it. Don't put a space between the operator and the keyword.

To effectively use the *store* operator, you must know the Internet domain name of the store. Froogle doesn't understand store names per se if they differ from the domain names. For example, Home Shopping Network has an e-commerce Web site, and its URL is www.hsn.com. Froogle doesn't know anything about Home Shopping Network as a store name, but it does recognize hsn as a keyword related to the *store* operator.

allintitle

The *allintitle* operator forces Froogle to match your keywords to product names. I find this more useful when using descriptive keywords than when using identifying keywords. For example, the identifying keywords *digital camera* are likely to be in relevant results titles anyway. But if I'm searching for a certain type of digital camera, using this search string narrows the results beautifully:

```
allintitle:4 megapixel
```

In fact, the preceding search string is all you need to get a nicely targeted list of digital cameras because *megapixel* is a term so closely related to digital cameras. You can further narrow the search to a single store like this:

```
allintitle:4 megapixel store:zones
```

This string yields two 4-megapixel digicams currently on sale at www.zones.com.

allintext

The *allintext* operator works similarly to *allintitle* but forces Google to look in the product description when matching your keywords. Going for the text instead of the title widens the search and lengthens your results. Use it when you're using keywords that describe product features and those features aren't likely to be part of the product name.

Note that many retailers squeeze lots of information into their product headers in an attempt to get a higher position on search results lists because Google and other engines are swayed to some extent by whether keywords appear in titles. So when using *allintext*, your keywords might appear both in the text and in the title. Don't be frustrated — this reality merely encourages you to associate more esoteric keywords with the *allintext* operator.

Think in plain English when you're considering *allintext* keywords. Imagine that you're talking to a salesperson in the store, describing features that you want to see in a product.

Froogle Advanced Search

If you prefer avoiding the use of search operators typed by hand but want to make your searches more powerful, go to the Froogle Advanced Search page, as shown in Figure 10-3. To get there, click the Advanced Froogle Search link on the Froogle home page. The first section of the page, shaded in green and labeled Find Products, operates identically to the Advanced Web Search page that I describe in Chapter 2 of Book II. This section employs standard search operators to include, exclude, and group keywords in certain ways.

The final six Advanced Search features jockey your keywords in ways that I describe earlier in this chapter:

✦ Use the Price fields to define a price range within which products must fall to enter your search results.

✦ Use the Occurrences drop-down list box to specify whether your keywords need to appear in the product name *and* description (the default selection), or just one or the other (the *allintitle* or *allintext* operator, respectively).

✦ Use the Category menu to limit searches to a single Froogle directory category.

✦ Use the Stores options to group the search results by product or by store.

✦ Use the View options to display results in a grid or in a long list.

✦ Use the SafeSearch options to determine the level of filtering Google will apply to your image search. The choices are identical to the SafeSearch preference settings (see Chapter 5 of Book II), but apply to only one search at a time.

About Google Catalogs

Most of Google's great ideas depend on behind-the-scenes technology that works invisibly to precisely meet information needs. But one Google service relies more on hard work and continual maintenance than great programming: Google Catalogs, a searchable directory of mail-order catalogs, is brilliant in conception and execution. Keeping it going must require a monumental effort of scanning on Google's part.

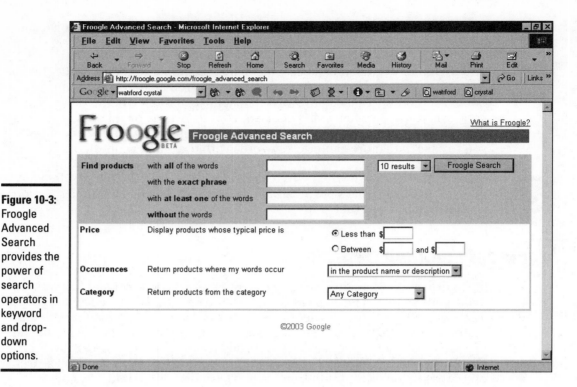

Figure 10-3:
Froogle
Advanced
Search
provides the
power of
search
operators in
keyword
and drop-
down
options.

Unlike Google's Web index, which crawls through Web sites and reduces their content to a tagged database controlled by retrieval algorithms, the Google Catalogs index leaves the content in its original format. What you see in this directory are scanned catalog pages laid out exactly as they would appear at home.

Merely presenting scanned catalog pages would be interesting but ultimately frustrating and unproductive. However, Google can search every word of the scanned catalog pages, deliver targeted results, and even contrive to highlight your keywords when they appear on the pages. Google has also designed a control bar for thumbing through the catalogs, turning your browser into a specialized e-zine reader.

Searching Google Catalogs

As in Froogle, Google Catalogs presents a topical directory and keyword searching. After you get into the directory, you can limit further searching to that directory category or launch a global Catalogs search. Start at the Google Catalogs home page (see Figure 10-4):

```
http://catalogs.google.com
```

The directory tempts users by listing a few mail-order companies in each main category. Feel free to leap into the directory by clicking a catalog or a topic on the home page. Google presents each catalog with its cover, title, short description, date, and Web link. Google maintains an archive of past catalogs, which can gum up the works when browsing the directory. The Advanced Search page (which I describe shortly) lets you specify current catalogs, but some of them are a bit dusty, too.

Click any catalog cover to see its directory page. Searching by keyword provides a somewhat different experience. For each result, you get the catalog cover, a thumbnail of the page matching your keywords, and a zoomed-in shot of the portion of that page containing your keyword, as shown in Figure 10-5.

Note the rectangular highlighting on the middle page, indicating the portion zoomed on the right. This, ladies and gentlemen, is fantastic search technology, blowing away the search engine for scanned documents at ProQuest, an expensive research service. Each of these three images is a thumbnail; click for a larger view. (The second and third thumbnails give you the same large view.)

You can request the addition of any catalog that you don't find in Google Catalogs. Before requesting additions to the Google Catalogs index, be sure that your request doesn't already exist in the index. Don't count on browsing or haphazard search results — search directly for the catalog by name. In fact, searching for catalogs, not products, is a good way to review all recent issues of that catalog. Use the following online request form to request a catalog:

```
http://catalogs.google.com/googlecatalogs/add_catalog.html
```

Figure 10-4:
The Google Catalogs home page. Search by product keyword or browse by mail-order house.

Advanced Catalogs searching

The truth is, advanced searching in Google Catalogs isn't as powerful as other Advanced Search pages. The reason for the simplicity of advanced searching is that the Google Catalogs search engine doesn't offer any special search operators. So the Advanced Catalogs Search page is useful mostly for invoking standard search operators without having to know them. Chapter 2 of Book II describes these operators (*AND, OR, NOT,* and the exact phrase operator) in detail.

Zoomed image

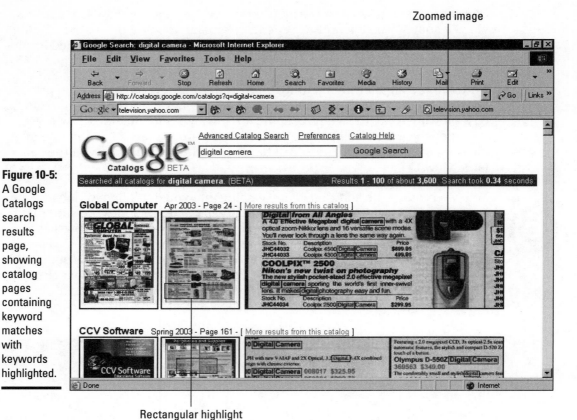

Figure 10-5:
A Google
Catalogs
search
results
page,
showing
catalog
pages
containing
keyword
matches
with
keywords
highlighted.

Rectangular highlight

CHECK IT OUT

Comparison-Shopping with Froogle

Froogle can become a handy price-comparison search engine if you know the brand and model number of the item that you're shopping for. Even if you don't know that information going in, Froogle can help you compare prices of any product that you find while searching. Here's how it works:

1. **On the Froogle home page (www.froogle.com), start a search for some type of product.**

2. **On the search results page, identify a product that you're interested in (for example, the Sony Cybershot DSC-P9 digital camera).**

3. **In the keyword box, type the product brand and model number.**

   To follow along with the example, type **Sony Cybershot DSC-P9.**

4. **Press Enter to launch your search and view the results.**

Scanning down the list gives you a good idea of the range of retail prices. You can further hone the results by identifying a small price range in the Price fields. Unfortunately, Froogle doesn't (yet) enable you to sort search results by price.

Chapter 11: Raising Your Visibility with Google

In This Chapter

✔ **Understanding the Google crawl**

✔ **Preparing your site for the Google spider**

✔ **Avoiding Google's wrath**

✔ **Keeping Google (and other search engines) out**

From the inception of the Web, every person with even the most modest Web page has wanted to attract visitors. Advertising, reciprocal linking, word of mouth, getting listed in directories — all have been tools in the mad scramble for traffic. In the Google era, getting into the index has become the single most important task of Webmasters large and small.

Search engine listing has always been crucial. Page owners have spent hours submitting requests to innumerable directories and engines. Coding a page in a way that attracts a search engine crawler and puts the page high on the search results list became a crafty art form in the late 1990s. Google has become so dominant in the search field that if your page can't be Googled, it might as well not exist — that's today's presumption.

Getting your site into the Google index requires patience and networking skill, but it's not hard. Improving your *position* in the index — how high your site places on search results lists — is another matter. Old coding tricks don't work in Google, which means bad news and good news. The bad news is that no shortcuts to prominence exist in Google. The good news is that the index is utterly democratic, affording any Web site, large or small, a chance to gain good positioning based on merit. In this way, Google is different than, and superior to, other search engines.

This chapter covers how Google crawls the Web, how a new page can get into the index, and how a new or established site can improve its position in Google's search results.

The Google Crawl

As with most search engines, Google's work has two parts: searching the Web and building an index. When you enter a search request, Google doesn't really go onto the Web to find matching sites. Instead, it searches its index for matches. Google is special at both ends of its work spectrum: first in the scope of its Web searching (and therefore the size of its index), and second in the method by which it matches keywords to Web pages stored in the index.

Most search engine indexes start with an automatic, wide-flung search of the Web, conducted by automated software fancifully called a *spider* or *crawler*. Google's crawl is farther flung than most, resulting in an index that includes between three and four billion Web pages, as of this writing.

Google performs two levels of Web crawl. The main survey, often referred to as Google's *deep crawl,* is conducted once a month. Google's spider takes slightly more than a week to accomplish its profound examination of the Web. Then, as a bonus, Google launches a so-called *fresh crawl* much more frequently. The fresh crawl is an experimental update to Google's index that began in mid-2002 and runs almost every day at the company's discretion. Naturally, the fresh crawl is shallower than the deep crawl and is designed to pick up new material from sites that change often. Material gleaned from the fresh crawl is added to the main Google index, though the schedule for the incorporation of new pages is a company secret.

Webmasters can see the fresh crawl in action by searching for their new content in the main Google index. The continual index shifting (sometimes called the *Everflux*) is all part of the Google dance. Eager Webmasters should never forget that the Everflux is unpredictable, and one should never pin one's hopes on the Google dance. No guarantees exist in the Google index, not even one saying that any particular site must be included in the daily crawl. Hold fast to persistence and patience. The daily crawl is by no means designed to provide the Google index with a daily comprehensive update of the Web. Its purpose is to freshen the index with targeted updates.

Getting into Google

You can get your site into the Google index in two ways:

✦ Submit the site manually

✦ Let the crawl find it

Both these methods lead to unpredictable results. Google offers no assurance that submitted sites will be added to the index. Google doesn't respond to submissions, and it doesn't promise to add or discard the site within a certain time frame. You may submit the site, or you may just wait for the crawl. You may submit *and* wait for the crawl. Submitting doesn't direct the crawl toward you, and it doesn't deflect it. Google is impassive and promises nothing. But Google *does* sometimes add sites that aren't linked on other pages, and would probably not be found by the crawl.

If you have added a new page to a site already in the Google index, you don't need to submit the new page. Under most circumstances, Google finds it the next time your site is crawled. But you might as well submit an entirely new site, even if it consists of a single page. Do so at this URL:

```
www.google.com/addurl.html
```

Checking your status

How do you know whether your site is in the Google index? Don't try searching for it with general keywords — that method is hit-and-miss. You could search for an exact phrase located in your site's text, but if it's not a unique phrase, you could get tons of other matches.

The best bet is to simply search for the URL. Make it exact and include the www prefix. If you're searching for an inner page of the site, precision is likewise necessary, and remember to include the htm or html file extension if it exists.

The *link* operator (see Chapter 2 of Book II) is invaluable for checking the status of your incoming links, and, by extension, the health of your PageRank. Use the operator followed immediately by the URL, like this: *link:www.bradhill.com*. The search results show every page containing a link to your URL. When you try this operator with an inner page of your site, remember that you most likely link to your own pages with menus or navigation bars, and Google regards those links as incoming links, artificially inflating your incoming link count. Incoming links within a domain don't contribute to PageRank. You need to get other sites linking to you.

The submission form could hardly be simpler. Enter your URL address, and make whatever descriptive comments you feel might help your cause. Then click the Add URL button — which is a bit misleading. Submitting a site is not the same as adding it to the index! Only the Google crawler or a human Google staffer can make additions to the index.

Luring the spider

The key to attracting Google's spider is getting linked on other sites. Google finds your content by following links to your pages. With no incoming links, you're an unreachable island as far as the Google crawl is concerned. Of course, anybody can reach you directly by entering the URL, but you won't pluck the spider's web until you get other sites to link to you.

In theory, any single page currently crawled by Google (that is, in the index) that links to your page or site is enough to send Google's spider crawling toward you. In practice, you want as many incoming links as possible, both to increase your chance of being crawled (sounds a little uncomfortable, doesn't it?) and to improve your PageRank after your site is in the index.

Keep your pipes clean and don't make life difficult for Google's spider. In other words, host your site with a reliable Web host and keep your pages in good working order. The Google crawl attempts to break through connection problems, but it doesn't keep trying forever. If it can't get through in the monthly deep crawl and your site isn't included in the fresh crawl, you could suffer a longish, unnecessary delay before getting into the index.

Don't expect instant recognition in Google when you add a page to your site. If your site is part of the fresh crawl, new page(s) show up fairly quickly in search results, but no firm formula exists for the frequency of the fresh crawl or the implementation of its results. If the spider hits your site during the deep crawl, the wait for fresh pages to appear in the index is considerably longer. The same factors apply if you move your site from one URL address to another (although not if you merely change hosts, keeping the same URL). Complicating that situation is that your site at the old address might remain cached (stored) in Google's index even while search results are matching keywords to your site at the new address. This confusion is one reason that some Webmasters don't like the Google cache — when they make a change to a site or its address, they don't want the old information living on in the world's most popular search index.

Spider-friendly tips

Getting into the Google index is largely a waiting game, in which preparation, persistence, and patience are the tools of success. However, several techniques incline Google's spider to look on you more favorably:

✦ **Place important content outside dynamically generated pages:** A *dynamic page* is one created on the fly based on choices made by the site visitor. Examples include search results pages and dynamic maps that are produced after the user submits an address. This method of page generation works fine when the visitor is a thinking human (or even a relatively thoughtless human). But when an index robot hits such a site, it can generate huge numbers of pages unintentionally (assuming that robots ever have intentions), sometimes crashing the site or its server. The Google spider picks up some dynamically generated pages, but generally backs off when it encounters dynamic content. Weblog pages do not fall into this category — they are dynamically generated by *you,* the Webmaster, but not by your visitors.

✦ **Don't use splash pages:** *Splash pages* (which Google calls *doorway pages*) are content-empty entry pages to Web sites. You've probably seen them. Some splash pages employ cool multimedia introductions to the content within. Others are mere static welcome mats that force users to click again before getting into the site. Google doesn't like pointing its searchers to splash pages. In fact, these tedious welcome mats are bad site design by any standard, even if you don't care about Google indexing, and I recommend getting rid of them. If you give Google and your visitors meaningful content from the first click, you're rewarded with happier visitors and better placement in Google's index.

✦ **Use frames sparingly:** Frames have been generally loathed since their introduction into the HTML specification early in the Web's history. They wreak havoc with the Back button, and they confuse the fundamental format of Web addresses (one page per address) by including independent page functions within one Web page.

✦ **Divide content topically:** How long should a Web page be? The answer differs depending on the nature of the page, the type of visitor that it attracts, how heavy (with graphics and other modem-choking material) it is, and how on-topic the entire page is. Long pages are sometimes the result of lazy site building; it takes effort to spin off a new page, address it, link to it, and integrate into the overall site design. From Google's perspective, and in the context of securing better representation in the index, breaking up content is good as long as it makes topical sense. If you operate a fan page for a local music group and the site contains bios, music clips, concert schedules, and lyrics, Google could make more sense of it all if you devote a separate page to each of the content groups. Google also likes to see page titles relating closely to page content. Keeping your information bites mouth-sized helps Google index your stuff better.

On your own

Creating the Google index is an automated procedure. The Google spider crawls through more than three billion pages in its surveys of the Web. Some sites (small ones in particular) might be tossed around by the Google dance, even to the extent of dropping out of the index for a month at a time and then reappearing. PageRank can fluctuate, influencing a site's position in search results. Some sites have trouble breaking into the index in the first place.

Although Google receives and attends to URL submissions, as I describe in this chapter, the company doesn't provide customer service in the traditional sense. Google doesn't offer customer contact for indexing issues. The positive aspect of this corporate distance is that the index is pure — nobody, regardless of corporate size or online clout, can obtain favorable tweaking in the index. The downside is that you're on your own when navigating the surging tides of this massive index. Patience and diligent networking are your best allies.

✦ **Keep your link structure tidy:** Google's spider is efficient, but it's not a mind reader. Nor does it make up URL variations, hoping to find hidden content. The Google crawler is a slave to the link. If you want all your pages represented in the index, make sure each one has a link leading to it from within your site. Many site-building programs contain link-checking routines and administrative checks to diagnose linkage problems. Simple sites might not warrant such firepower; in that case, check your navigation sidebars and section headers to make sure that you're not leaving out anything.

The Folly of Fooling Google

For as long as search engines have crawled the Web, site owners have engineered tricks to get the best possible position on search results pages. Traditionally, these tricks include the following:

✦ **Cloaking:** In which important, crawl-attracting keywords are hidden from the view of site visitors but remain visible to spiders.

✦ **Keyword loading:** Related to cloaking, in which topical words are loaded into the page's code, especially in page titles and text headers.

✦ **Link loading:** Through which large numbers of incoming links are fabricated.

Spider manipulating tricks have worked to some extent in the past thanks to the automated nature of search crawling. Google is highly automated, too, but is more sophisticated than most other spiders. And as a company policy, Webmaster chicanery is dealt with harshly. Obviously, you're not breaking any laws by coding your pages in a certain way, even if your motive is to fool Google. But Google doesn't hesitate to banish a site from the index entirely if it determines that its PageRank is being artificially jiggered. No published policy states when or if a banished site is reinstated. Google is serious about the integrity of PageRank.

The best rule is this: Create a site for people, not for spiders. Generally, the interests of people and Google's spider coincide. A coherent, organized site that's a pleasure to surf is also a site that's easy to crawl. Keeping your priorities aligned with your visitors is the best way to keep your PageRank as high as it can get.

Keeping Google Out

Your priorities might run contrary to this chapter in that you want to *prevent* Google from crawling your site and putting it in the Web search index. When you think about it, it does seem pushy for any search engine to invade your Web space, suck up all your text, and make it available to anyone with a matching keyword. Some people feel that Google's cache is more than just pushy: They feel that it infringes copyright regulations by caching an unauthorized copy of a site.

If you want to keep the Google crawl out of your site, get familiar with the robots.txt file, also known as the Robots Exclusion Protocol. Google's spider understands and obeys this protocol.

The robots.txt file is a short, simple text file that you place in the top-level directory (the root directory) of your domain server. (If you use server space provided by a utility ISP, such as AOL, you probably need administrative help placing the robots.txt file.) The file contains two instructions:

✦ User-agent: This instruction specifies which search engine crawler must follow the robots.txt instructions.

✦ Disallow: This line specifies which directories (Web page folders) or specific pages at your site are off-limits to the search engine. You must include a separate Disallow line for each excluded directory.

A sample robots.txt file looks like this:

```
User-agent: *
Disallow: /
```

This example is the most common and simplest robots.txt file. The asterisk after User-agent means *all* spiders are excluded. The forward slash after Disallow means that *all* site directories are off-limits.

The name of Google's spider is Googlebot. ("Here, Googlebot! Come to Daddy! Sit. Good Googlebot! Who's a good boy?") If you want to exclude only Google and no other search engines, use this robots.txt file:

```
User-agent: Googlebot
Disallow: /
```

You may identify certain directories as impervious to the crawl, either from Google or all spiders:

```
User-agent: *
Disallow: /cgi-bin/
Disallow: /family/
Disallow: /photos/
```

Notice the forward slash at each end of the directory string in the preceding examples. Google understands that the first slash implies your domain address before it. So, if the first `Disallow` line is found at the `www.bradhill.com` site, the line is shorthand for `http://www.bradhill.com/cgi-bin/`, and Google knows to exclude that directory from the crawl. The second forward slash is the indicator that you're excluding an entire directory.

To exclude individual pages, type the page address following the first forward slash and leave off the ending forward slash, like this:

```
User-agent: *
Disallow: /family/reunion-notes.htm
Disallow: /blog/archive00082.htm
```

Each excluded directory and page must be listed on its own `Disallow` line. Don't group multiple items on one line.

You may adjust the `robots.txt` file as often as you like. It's a good tool when building out fresh pages that you don't want indexed while still under construction. When they're finished, take them out of the `robots.txt` file.

Book III

Yahoo!

The 5th Wave   By Rich Tennant

©RICHTENNANT

"I have to say I'm really impressed with
the interactivity on this car wash Web site."

Book III: Yahoo!

Chapter 1: Introducing Yourself to Yahoo!

In This Chapter

✓ Creating a Yahoo! ID

✓ Making a public profile

✓ Searching the Yahoo! Member Directory

Yahoo! began as a mere Web site, though an important one. Yahoo! was one of the first attempts to index the Web when the Web was little more than a small, quirky, mostly noncommercial network of personal pages. Because you could search the Yahoo! index, the site was everyone's favorite launching point for a night of Web surfing.

That was then. Yahoo! grew, adding features to its core index and search service. In time, Yahoo! began to resemble a distinct network of sites that covered a wide range of interests, such as sports, finances, entertainment, chatting, and more. The growth and evolution continued. When certain Internet-measuring firms began keeping track, they found that the vast and rapidly expanding Yahoo! was one of the most popular destinations on the entire Web. Now, with many millions of registered users and an astonishing number of Web pages displayed each day, Yahoo! is clearly a full-fledged online service. Great content and a vibrant community add up to one of the dominant and most-visited domains in cyberspace. Do you think you know Yahoo!? Prepare to be amazed.

Because Yahoo! is a Web-based service that's equally available to all Internet users, it doesn't require membership, but it does encourage it. In fact, Yahoo! withholds certain functions from nonmembers. Getting a Yahoo! membership is simple and free. The process amounts to filling in a few bits of information and clicking a button. Yahoo! members are defined by their Yahoo! IDs, which are like on-screen membership badges that I refer to repeatedly throughout this minibook. Your Yahoo! ID is your screen name when using any of the many community and interactive features.

This chapter explains how to set up your ID (it takes only a minute or so); how to create a public profile; and how to search for other member profiles.

Getting Your Yahoo! ID

Frequent Yahoo! users almost always end up establishing a Yahoo! identity (ID). Each Yahoo! ID is paired with a password, and you must know both to sign in and view your personalized settings. Many services are available only to people with Yahoo! IDs — in particular, the interactive services that allow you to create something within Yahoo!.

You need a Yahoo! ID to buy something in a Yahoo! store; make travel reservations; build a Web site at GeoCities; place a Yahoo! Classifieds or Yahoo! Personals ad; play games; open a Yahoo! Mail account; use Yahoo! Messenger; personalize the service with My Yahoo!; create a stock portfolio; post a message; use the calendar; make a Yahoo! profile; and take advantage of other functions and services.

Joining Yahoo! with an ID and a password is entirely free. Your membership gives you access to many interactive portions of Yahoo! and doesn't cost a dime, ever. You have no limit on how much you can use your ID. Everyone in your family can have his or her own Yahoo! ID, with its own set of personalized features, and never incur charges.

If you explore Yahoo! enough, you're bound to encounter invitations to join. The following steps work no matter where you start from:

1. Type the following URL in your browser:

`http://login.yahoo.com`

The Welcome to Yahoo! page appears.

2. Click the Sign Up Now link.

The sign-up page appears, as shown in Figure 1-1.

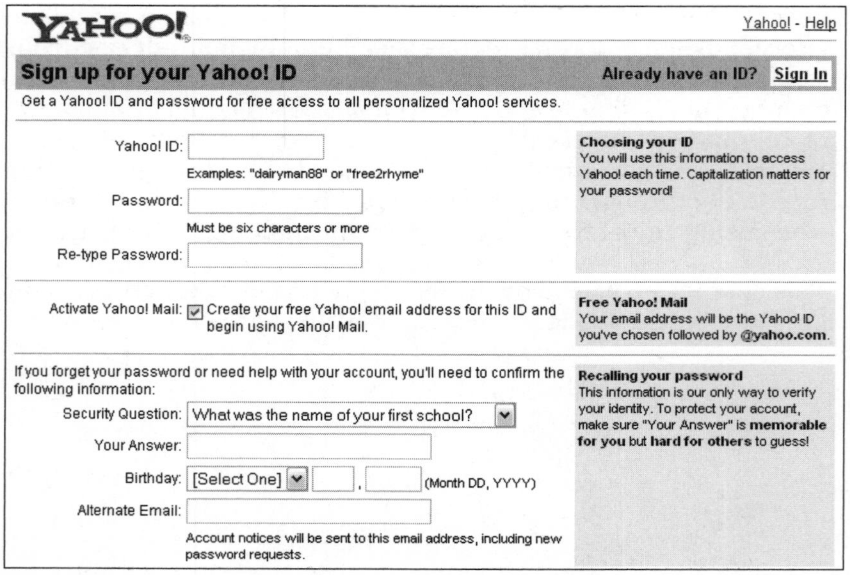

Figure 1-1:
The sign-up page for creating a Yahoo! ID and password.

> **YAHOO!** Yahoo! - Help
>
> **Sign up for your Yahoo! ID** Already have an ID? **Sign In**
>
> Get a Yahoo! ID and password for free access to all personalized Yahoo! services.
>
> Yahoo! ID: [_____]
> Examples: "dairyman88" or "free2rhyme"
>
> Password: [_____]
> Must be six characters or more
>
> Re-type Password: [_____]
>
> **Choosing your ID**
> You will use this information to access Yahoo! each time. Capitalization matters for your password!
>
> Activate Yahoo! Mail: ☑ Create your free Yahoo! email address for this ID and begin using Yahoo! Mail.
>
> **Free Yahoo! Mail**
> Your email address will be the Yahoo! ID you've chosen followed by @yahoo.com.
>
> If you forget your password or need help with your account, you'll need to confirm the following information:
>
> Security Question: [What was the name of your first school? ▼]
>
> Your Answer: [_____]
>
> Birthday: [Select One ▼] [__] , [__] (Month DD, YYYY)
>
> Alternate Email: [_____]
> Account notices will be sent to this email address, including new password requests.
>
> **Recalling your password**
> This information is our only way to verify your identity. To protect your account, make sure "Your Answer" is **memorable** for you but hard for others to guess!

Signing in and out

When you sign in to Yahoo! with your ID and password, you stay signed in for the duration of your session. You have to sign out manually (by using a Sign Out link, which appears on almost every page of the service) or shut down your browser to end your session. However, there's no harm in remaining signed in, even if you're elsewhere on the Web and not using Yahoo!. You're not incurring any charges by being signed in. Normally, signing in to Yahoo! is the first thing I do when I go online, and I never have a reason to sign out.

The Sign Out links are useful if your computer lives in a household with more than one Yahoo! user, each with an individual Yahoo! ID. (Because the service is free and Yahoo! isn't your Internet service provider, there's no limit to how many IDs can be initiated from a single computer.) Every Yahoo! ID in your household can have its own identity, e-mail account, Personals mailbox, My Yahoo! pages, and so on.

3. **In the Choosing Your ID section, fill in the text boxes.**

   You choose your own user name (Yahoo! ID) and password. If you choose an ID name that's already in use, Yahoo! prompts you to choose another after you submit the form. You must complete all the fields in this section.

4. **In the Free Yahoo! Mail section, select the check box if you want to use the Yahoo! mail services.**

   Chapter 3 of Book III explains e-mailing by way of Yahoo!. You don't have to sign up for the e-mail service now. In Chapter 3, I show you how to do it.

5. **In the Recalling Your Password section, fill in all text boxes.**

   You can select from a list of questions that Yahoo! will ask if you ever forget your password. This section is important, especially for the people who keep multiple IDs.

6. **In the Customizing Yahoo! section, consider filling in the fields.**

   This section is optional and is important only if you don't personalize the service manually. Chapter 2 of Book III describes how to create a My Yahoo! page, which I recommend for getting the most out of the service.

   By the way, don't leave the special offer boxes selected unless you want to receive more marketing e-mail, otherwise known as spam.

7. **In the Word Verification text box, type the word that Yahoo! provides.**

   Typing a word is a security mechanism to prevent computer robots from signing up for Yahoo!.

8. **Click the Submit This Form button.**

That's it! You now have a Yahoo! ID. A page appears with that crucial bit of information — it's a good idea to write it down along with your password somewhere or commit these items to your flawless photographic memory.

Signing In to Yahoo!

After you have a Yahoo! ID and password, you can sign in to Yahoo! by following these steps:

1. Go to the Yahoo! home page by following a browser bookmark or using the following URL:

   www.yahoo.com

2. Click the My button or the Personalize link in the upper-left corner of the page.

   The Welcome to My Yahoo! page appears.

3. Enter your Yahoo! ID and password, and then click the Sign In button.

   If you select the Remember My ID on This Computer check box, Yahoo! places your sign-in information on your computer's hard drive, where Yahoo! can find it. From then on, clicking the My button in Step 2 signs you in and takes you to your My Yahoo! page.

Creating a Profile

The Yahoo! profile tells other Yahoo! members a bit about you. How much you reveal is up to you. Every Yahoo! ID has a corresponding profile that's created automatically when you establish the ID. These default profiles contain nothing more than the basic information that you supply when creating your ID. You can elaborate on that stripped-down profile, or not, as you choose.

Many user-enhanced profiles remain basic, including the member's name, perhaps a general location, and nothing else. But if you really get motivated, you can put in your gender, location, age, marital status, real name (not your ID name), occupation, e-mail address (different from your Yahoo! e-mail), a statement of your interests, personal news, a favorite quote, a home page URL, and links to other Web sites that you enjoy visiting. Oh — and a picture if you have one scanned.

You must have a Yahoo! ID to create a profile. After you establish your ID, follow these steps:

1. After you sign in with your Yahoo! ID, go to the Member Directory page at the following URL:

   http://profiles.yahoo.com

2. Click the View My Profiles link at the top of the page.

   The Public Profiles for *YourID* page appears.

3. **Click the Edit link next to the Yahoo! profile that you want to adjust.**

   If you have more than one Yahoo! ID assigned to a single password, choose from the list of profiles. You can start from scratch with a new profile by clicking the Create New Public Profile button. Creating a new profile adds it to the list shown on this page.

4. **On your Profile page, click the link representing the portion of the page that you want to change.**

   As you can see in Figure 1-2, you can edit your basic profile information, your picture, your voice greeting, and your page colors.

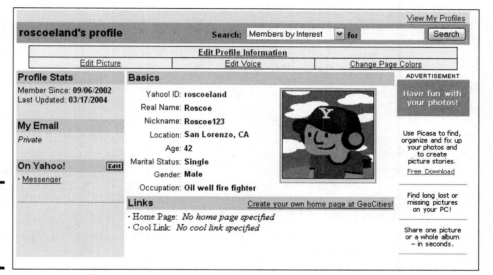

Figure 1-2:
Start here to edit your Yahoo! profile.

The following sections describe how to adjust the four main portions of your Yahoo! profile.

The basic you

Your most essential information is displayed in the central portion of your Yahoo! profile. On your Profile page, click the Edit Profile Information link to add, remove, or alter this information.

The Edit Public Profile page presents several information fields, each of which is optional. Fill in only what you want to fill in. You could include your name and still leave out your gender or age. Or perhaps if you're interested in meeting a significant other, you could include your age, marital status, and gender. You might not want to display your non-Yahoo! e-mail address — visitors can always write you easily enough at your Yahoo! ID address. (See Book III, Chapter 3 for a thrilling play-by-play account of Yahoo! Mail.)

Near the bottom of the page is a check box for adding your profile to the Member Directory. Doing so allows other Yahoo! members to find your profile by matching keyword or interest. Leave the check box deselected if you don't want to be found.

The photogenic you

Any profile can contain a photo of you or some other picture. If you don't select or upload a picture for display, the photo space of your profile remains blank. Most people upload a photo, use one of the Yahoo! cartoon characters, or leave the space blank.

If you have a photo of yourself scanned and residing on your computer, and you'd like to show the world what you look like, follow these steps:

1. **On your Profile page, click the Edit Picture link in the upper-left corner (refer to Figure 1-2).**

   The Upload a Picture page appears.

2. **Click the Browse button.**

   You can also enter a URL link to a photo of yourself that currently resides at a Web location — for example, in your server space at Yahoo! GeoCities (a great service that I describe in Book III, Chapter 9). Quite possibly, you have photos of yourself stored in Yahoo! Photos, and you can link your profile's photo to that space also. If you decide to pursue one of these options, click the appropriate link on this page.

3. **In the Choose File dialog box, double-click a photo file from your hard drive's folders.**

4. **In the Enter Confirmation Code section, enter the word that appears.**

5. **Click the Upload button.**

   It might take a minute or two for your photo to upload, depending on its size and your connection speed. After the upload is complete, your Profile page appears with the photo in place (refer to Figure 1-2). Every photo is compressed into the available space on the Profile page, which is not large. You can see a full-sized version of the photo (and anyone else's photo on other profiles) by clicking the photo itself.

The voluble you

If you have recorded a voice greeting of some kind, you can make it a part of your profile and enable others to hear your voice. You can do that, I hasten to add, if the recording is stored at a Web site. Yahoo! accepts the following file formats for recordings: AIF, MP3, MPEG, RM, MIDI, MOV, or WAV.

Follow these steps to upload a voice recording for your profile:

1. **On your Profile page, click the Edit Voice link.**

2. **On the Edit Voice for *YourID* page, enter the URL of the voice recording.**

3. Click the Finished button.

You return to the Profile page.

4. Click the Hear My Voice link to test your recording.

This link is found below the picture area.

The colorful you

Yahoo! Profile pages are simple and rather sparse in design, like every Yahoo! page. You do have some choice, however, in the color scheme of headings, subheadings, and the background. Click the Change Page Colors link on your Profile page and then select the color scheme that you prefer. When you click the Finished button, your Profile page appears with the new colors. You can change them as often as you like.

Cruising the Profiles

You can become acquainted with other Yahoo! members by searching their public profiles. Searching is also a way to get ideas for your own profile. Here's what to do:

1. Enter the following URL in your browser:

```
http://profiles.yahoo.com
```

The Yahoo! Member Directory page appears.

2. Use the keyword text box and drop-down list to search the Yahoo! public profiles.

If you know a person's Yahoo! ID, for example, select Yahoo! ID from the drop-down list and enter the ID. Select Real Name from the list to search for a person by his or her real name, which might or might not be entered in that person's profile information.

3. Click the Find People button.

The Profile Search Results page appears.

4. Click any Yahoo! ID to see that profile.

If you get too many search results, you might want to try a power version of the profile search engine. Use your browser's Back button to return to the Yahoo! Member Directory page, and then click the Advanced Search link. The page that appears gives you several more searching options, including the ability to search for only profiles with pictures, profiles indicating one gender, or profiles within a certain age range.

Every search results page in the Yahoo! Member Directory comes with its own Refine Member Search form at the bottom of the page. This duplication is handy because you can initiate a new search without backtracking to the original Yahoo! Member Directory page from which you started.

CHECK IT OUT

Declaring Your Interests in Your Profile

You can make your profile show the topics that you're interested in by visiting the Interests section and declaring an interest. This way, people with similar interests can find you more easily on Yahoo!. Here's how to proceed:

1. **On the Yahoo! Member Directory page, click any topic link under the Browse Interests heading and begin drilling into the Interests directory.**

2. **On any Interests directory page, click the Join This List link to put that interest on your Yahoo! profile.**

   When you take this step, you go to a Join the *Interest* List page.

3. **Click the Add to My Interests button.**

   Your profile shows the interest as a link that visitors can click to go to the directory page.

Each directory page of the My Interests section contains a list of every Yahoo! member who has added that interest. Click any member name to see that person's profile.

Using My Interests is a superb way to meet people with shared interests and find their profiles. This service is far more effective than roaming around chat rooms or message boards hoping to find somebody with whom you have common ground.

Chapter 2: Customizing Your Yahoo! Experience

In This Chapter

✓ Understanding the customization process

✓ Changing the look and content of a My Yahoo! page

✓ Choosing subject matter for your My Yahoo! page

This chapter instructs you in choosing and configuring your personal Yahoo! choices. It explains how you can change the Yahoo! interface — in other words, the way Yahoo! looks on your screen. Yahoo! has a name for the personal customization that you make — My Yahoo!. You do have limits to how you can change its appearance, and some large portions of Yahoo! are off-limits to customization, but the important point is that, through My Yahoo!, you're empowered to create your own custom Web pages of Yahoo! features.

If I were to write detailed explanations of every feature that's available in My Yahoo!, this book would deal with nothing else, and a scandal would ensue. So instead, I offer a quick rundown of all the features and recommend certain choices as good starting points. That doesn't mean that I discourage you from making any of the available selections — I just like to see people get started on the right foot.

By the way, some users ignore My Yahoo!, and indeed, you don't have to use it. The design of Yahoo! makes it pretty easy to click your way anywhere without much delay. But I feel certain that any Yahoo! user who creates a My Yahoo! page (or two) will quickly become dependent on it (or them). Give it a try.

Customizing This and That

Yahoo! is vast. The service is massive, prodigious, and colossal. It has features within features, and still more features within those features. The sheer magnitude of Yahoo! is what makes the My Yahoo! feature so useful in getting a grip on it all. At the same time, you can't possibly squeeze the whole shebang onto a few customized pages. Yahoo! doesn't even let you try. In almost every case, you're customizing just the tip of an iceberg, with plenty of depth waiting to be explored.

Following are the main types of content that you can gather together by using My Yahoo! and the instructions in this chapter:

✦ **Web searching:** Mapping the Internet is Yahoo!'s traditional function — the service started as a simple directory and search engine. (See Book III, Chapter 4 for an explanation of these terms and a guide to using the features.) In My Yahoo!, you can place the Yahoo! directory or a variation of it on your personal page. You can also place the Yahoo! keyword-entry form on your page for searching by word, phrase, or name.

✦ **Finances:** Yahoo! Finance is a major realm unto itself — one of the most popular and trafficked money sites on the Web. (Book III, Chapter 11 gets deep into the heady atmosphere of high finance.)

✦ **News:** News headlines can take up a major portion of your personalized page. My Yahoo! offers all kinds of news categories, and you can even set up clipping folders (a service called News Clipper) based on keywords, names, or places.

✦ **TV and movies:** If you're willing to part with a bit of personal information — namely, the ZIP Code of your residence — you can get some real-time, local entertainment information.

✦ **Sports:** Yahoo! delivers sports news with the same attention to detail that you find in *USA Today* and other publications.

✦ **Community:** My Yahoo! lets you place links to favorite message boards, clubs, and chat rooms on your personalized page.

✦ **Tips and tidbits:** There's no reason your personal page shouldn't be fun. You can sprinkle lottery results, recipes, and other nuggets through your My Yahoo! design.

✦ **Weather:** I read recently that America is the only country whose citizens take weather beyond mere small talk and establish it as an important news topic in daily life. Yahoo!, being an American company, must resonate with this priority, because it puts the weather on My Yahoo! as a default item.

✦ **Travel:** Yahoo! runs an online travel agency whose reservation pages (for flights, hotels, and rental cars) can be linked to your My Yahoo! page.

✦ **Organization:** Keeping your feet on the ground and your mind neatly compartmentalized is part of the value in personalizing Yahoo!. You can keep your e-mail address book and interactive calendar on your page. The calendar is especially useful and flexible.

✦ **Daily features:** Like a newspaper, My Yahoo! can enliven your page with an array of items whose content changes daily.

Choosing What Appears on Your My Yahoo! Page

Although you can customize the look and content of My Yahoo! pages, they all have the same fundamental design. Figure 2-1 shows a My Yahoo! page as it appears before customization. Notice that it has two columns of features. You can lay out your My Yahoo! page in two or three columns.

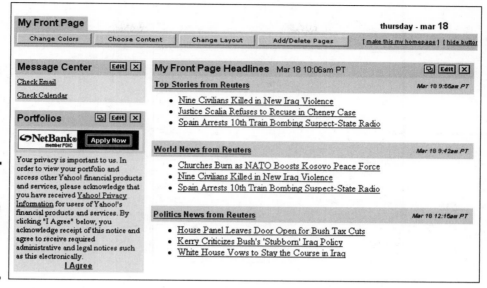

Figure 2-1:
Every My Yahoo! page shares the same basic layout design.

The My Yahoo! features are modules that you plug into and out of your page and arrange in whatever order you please. Each column can be extended as far as you like down the page. A page can be as long as you want, although at some point, it makes more sense to create another page.

My Yahoo! always starts out with preselected content modules in place. You can keep them, edit them, or discard them. Then you can move around what remains to the order that you prefer. The following sections walk you through the details of setting up your page's substance and appearance.

Deciding on the content

The first step is to decide what content goes on your My Yahoo! page. After you finish this task, you can start choosing the subject matter. For example, after you tell Yahoo! that you want to see comic strips on your My Yahoo! page, you can decide which comic strips you want to see. (I explain how to do so later in this chapter, in the section "Choosing Subject Matter for Your My Yahoo! Page.") Follow these steps to choose the content that you want:

1. **On your My Yahoo! page, click the Choose Content button.**

The Personalize Page Content page appears, as shown in Figure 2-2.

2. **In the Page Name text box, type a name for your page.**

Your page name may be 20 characters long (including spaces between words). In general, shorter looks better.

3. **Select check boxes to indicate the content that you want for your page.**

Notice that each selection is marked N or W, indicating whether it's a narrow (right-side) or a wide (left-side) feature. Just select the check box next to any feature that you want to include. Preselected check boxes currently exist as default content on your page — deselecting them removes them from the page.

4. **Click the Finished button.**

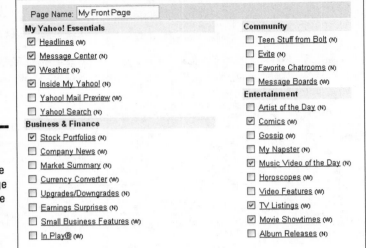

Figure 2-2:
Set your
Page Name
on this page
and browse
among the
content
modules.

Another way to select content for your My Yahoo! page is to scroll to the bottom of the My Yahoo! page and make selections in the two drop-down lists, as shown in Figure 2-3.

Figure 2-3:
Adding
content
modules.

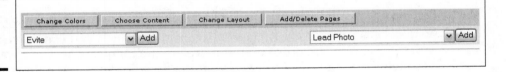

Here are the basic facts about adding content by using the drop-down lists:

✦ You have two drop-down lists, for left-side and right-side features.

✦ The two sets of features don't overlap, and you can't make any of them switch sides.

✦ Each list has a scroll bar for browsing the entire list of features.

✦ You may add 20 features to your page but only 1 feature at a time. Click the Add button after selecting a module from either drop-down list. After the page reloads, add another feature to either side.

✦ You may stack features on either side of the page, up to the limit of 20 overall.

As your modules get plugged into your page, you get a better sense of what they are. The drop-down lists give you only a broad clue; you need to see the modules to decide whether you want them. Keep reading to find out how to customize within the modules and what to do if you don't want them.

Choosing a color scheme

The next step is to select a color scheme for your My Yahoo! page. To do so, click the Change Colors button on your My Yahoo! page. You see the Personalize Theme and Settings page. From here, you can choose a predefined theme or take out your paint brush and apply colors on your own:

✦ **Customized colors:** Click the Customize Theme link in the Current Theme section, and on the Personalize Custom Colors page, select option buttons to describe the color scheme that you want.

✦ **Theme:** Click a link in the Theme Directory and keep clicking until you find a theme that you like.

Click the Finished button when you're done.

Choosing a layout

After you decide on the content and a color scheme, it's time to arrange them in the order that you prefer. Of primary importance is moving to the top whatever features you want displayed when you *first* enter My Yahoo!. It's nice to make the important stuff visible without scrolling down the page.

You can't mix and match narrow and wide column features. They're locked to their respective columns.

Starting on the My Yahoo! page, follow these steps to arrange your page's layout:

1. **Click the Change Layout button.**

The Personalize Layout page appears, as shown in Figure 2-4.

2. **In the Narrow Column list box, click to select any content module listed.**

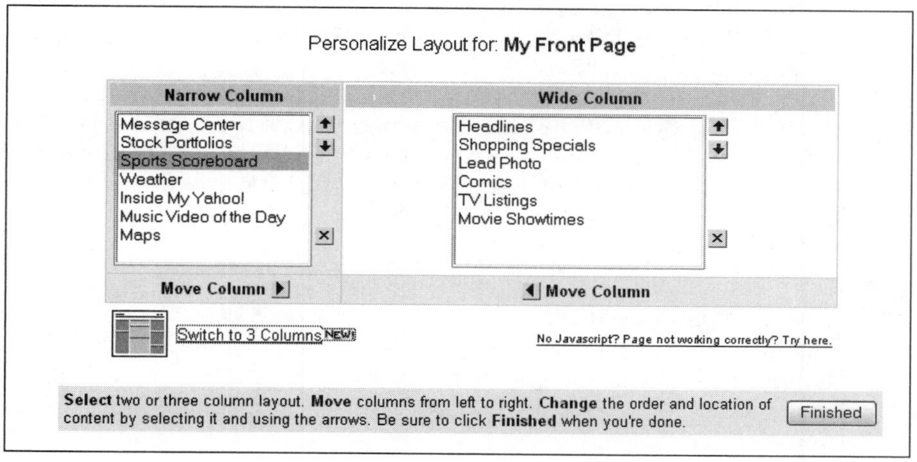

Book III
Chapter 2

Customizing Your
Yahoo! Experience

Figure 2-4: The Personalize Layout page lets you move content features up and down the page and reverse the columns.

Personalize Layout for: **My Front Page**

Narrow Column	**Wide Column**
Message Center	Headlines
Stock Portfolios	Shopping Specials
Sports Scoreboard	Lead Photo
Weather	Comics
Inside My Yahoo!	TV Listings
Music Video of the Day	Movie Showtimes
Maps	

Move Column ▶   ◀ Move Column

Switch to 3 Columns NEW!   No Javascript? Page not working correctly? Try here.

Select two or three column layout. **Move** columns from left to right. **Change** the order and location of content by selecting it and using the arrows. Be sure to click **Finished** when you're done.   [Finished]

3. **Use the up and down arrow buttons to move the selected module higher or lower on your page, or use the X button to eliminate it.**

   You can move any module as many steps up or down as you like. Just keep clicking the arrow button of your choice.

4. **Repeat Steps 2 and 3 for the Wide Column list box.**

5. **Use the Move Column buttons to switch the position of the wide and narrow columns.**

6. **Click the Finished button.**

You could also use a three-column layout (the contents of the narrow column are divided into two narrow columns), but I don't recommend this option if you have a small monitor or use a screen resolution of either 640 x 480 or 800 x 600. Those conditions make the three-column layout too crowded to use easily. If you have a large monitor or run the screen at a high resolution, however, the three-column layout can shorten a long page, making it easier to navigate. Click the Switch to 3 Columns link. As with the two-column layout, you can adjust the position of the columns on the page.

Choosing Subject Matter for Your My Yahoo! Page

After you choose the content modules for your My Yahoo! page (see "Deciding on the content" earlier in this chapter), your next task is to tell Yahoo! what subject matter you want. Do so with these buttons on the My Yahoo! page:

✦ **Edit:** The function of the Edit button varies depending on the module. Click it to discover what specific content features are available for that module and to choose among them.

✦ **Remove:** The button with an X in it deletes the module from your page.

✦ **Detach:** The button with two little squares in it whisks the content module right off your page and establishes it in a new, small browser window. You can resize the window to whatever dimensions are best.

When you detach a content module into its own window, it remains on your main My Yahoo! page as well. So, when you're ready to get rid of the dedicated window, just close it as you would any window on your screen. No need to add the content again to My Yahoo!. It's still there.

Chapter 3: The Yahoo! All-Mail Revue

In This Chapter

- Setting up a Yahoo! Mail account
- Getting to your mail and writing letters
- Creating an address book
- Setting up a distribution list

Guess what the most-used feature of the Internet is. Go on, guess. Okay, I'll tell you — it's e-mail. E-mail is used more than the Web.

Built-in e-mail accounts — you know, the kind that you have to pay for — are convenient and are usually accessed with dedicated e-mail programs, such as Outlook Express, Netscape Messenger, or Outlook. In the last few years, though, *Web-based e-mail* services like the one that Yahoo! provides have become popular. For one thing, they're free. And you can access a Web-based e-mail account no matter where you are.

Each of your Yahoo! IDs has its own e-mail box. This chapter explains how Yahoo! Mail works and unravels its most important features.

Getting Ready for Yahoo! Mail

Setting up your Yahoo! Mail account is an easy matter, especially if you've already created a Yahoo! ID. If not, now is a good time to set one up — you can't have Yahoo! Mail without an ID. You get one Yahoo! mailbox per password. Different IDs accessed by one password all share a single mailbox. You may use those different IDs as distinct e-mail addresses, each with the @yahoo.com suffix. However, all incoming mail lands in the single mailbox that's assigned to the first ID you created. You can access that mailbox while you're signed in to any of the IDs.

Follow these steps to set up your Yahoo! mailbox:

1. **At the top of the Yahoo! home page, click the Mail button.**

The Welcome to Yahoo! Mail page appears.

2. **Fill in your ID and password, and then click the Sign In button.**

The Set Up Yahoo! Mail page appears.

If you don't have a Yahoo! ID yet, click the Sign Up Now link and continue from there or get some help from Book III, Chapter 1.

You land in your Yahoo! Mail page (pardon the advertisements), as shown Figure 3-1.

Figure 3-1:
The Yahoo!
Mail page.

E-Mail Coming and Going

I'm a much more active correspondent in the realm of e-mail than I ever was with paper letters. This discrepancy could be due to my latent fear of post offices, but more likely it's because e-mail is so easy. No envelope. No stamp. And best of all, no delivery delays. E-mail is fast, and I have fun chatting with friends and acquaintances throughout the day.

Checking and reading your Yahoo! mail

Here's how to check your mail:

1. **On the Yahoo! home page, click the Mail button at the top of the page.**

If it has been a while since you last checked your mail, you might have to enter your password. If you're not signed in to your Yahoo! account ID, you definitely need to enter both it and your password.

2. **On the Yahoo! Mail page, see whether any unread messages are waiting for you.**

On the page, look at the number in parentheses next to the Inbox link to see how many unread messages are crying out for your attention.

3. **Click the Check Mail button or the Inbox link.**

Your Inbox page appears (see Figure 3-2), showing all mail in the Inbox, both read and unread. Read mail is in Roman type and is shaded; unread mail is shown in bold type.

4. **Click the subject of any letter to read it.**

Figure 3-3 illustrates what a letter (albeit an extremely brief one) looks like in Yahoo! Mail.

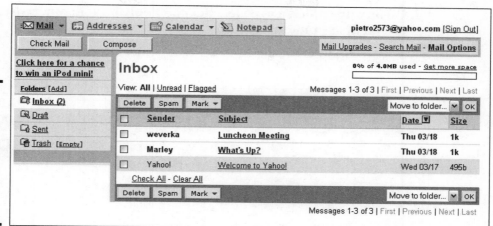

Figure 3-2:
The Inbox
page
displays all
letters, read
and unread.
E-mail that
you've read
is shaded.

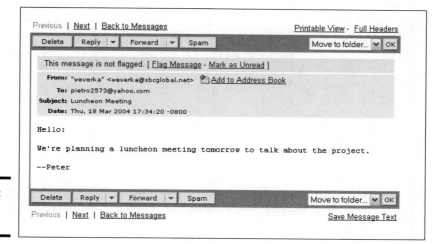

Figure 3-3:
A Yahoo!
e-mail.

I recommend bookmarking your Yahoo! Mail page or the main service page at the following URL:

`http://mail.yahoo.com`

That URL (or *bookmark*) takes you to your personal mail page or sign-in page (if you haven't checked your mail for a while) when you're signed in to your Yahoo! ID.

Composing and replying to e-mail

If you want to reply to an e-mail message, you've got it made. All you have to do is click the Reply button in the e-mail message that was sent to you, and Yahoo! addresses the e-mail message for you. Composing an e-mail message is somewhat different because you have to provide the address. Follow these steps to compose or reply to an e-mail message:

1. On any Read Message page, click the Reply button; otherwise, click the Compose button.

The Compose Mail page appears (see Figure 3-4).

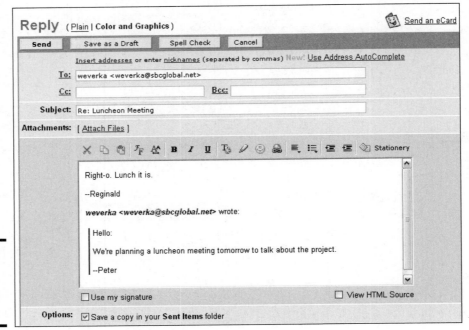

Figure 3-4:
Use this page to respond to e-mail.

2. To enter an address (if one isn't entered already), type the address in the To text box or click the To link and select an address from your Address Book.

Later in this chapter, "Your Virtual Black Book" explains the Address Book.

3. Use the large text-entry box to type your letter.

Notice that the text of the letter that you're replying to is placed in the text-entry box. In all e-mail formats, it's typical to *quote back* the letter that you're responding to so that the recipient doesn't have to remember what the conversation is about. Typically, you type your response above the quote. Quoting back isn't a requirement, though, so feel free to highlight and delete the quoted letter before sending your reply.

4. Click the Send button.

If you're not ready to send the letter yet, but you're tired of working on it (or can't think of how to finish your missive), click the Save As a Draft button. The letter in progress is placed in your Draft folder. (Every mailbox has a Draft folder — you don't have to create it.)

5. To keep a copy of your reply after sending it, select the Save a Copy in Your Sent Items Folder check box.

As with the Draft folder, the Sent folder already exists.

While writing long e-mails, use the Save Draft button to occasionally save the letter in progress to the Draft folder. Then if your computer crashes and you lose your screen, you don't have to start from scratch upon your return to Yahoo! Mail.

You can use the Spell Check feature on outgoing messages. On the Reply (or Compose Mail) page, click the Spell Check button before sending the mail.

Sending a file

In e-mail jargon, sending a file to someone is called *attaching* it. To attach a file to an e-mail message, follow these steps:

1. Click the Compose button (or the Reply button), and on the Compose Mail (or Reply) page, address and write your message as you normally do.

Earlier in this chapter, "Composing and replying to e-mail" explains the Compose Mail page.

2. Click the Attach Files link.

You see the Attach Files page shown in Figure 3-5.

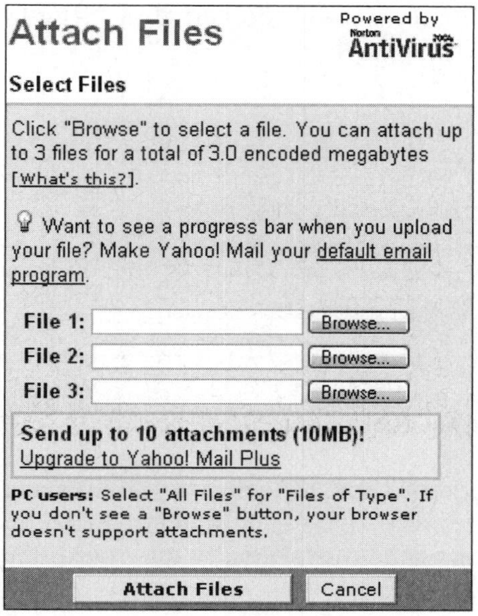

Attach Files

Powered by
Norton
AntiVirus 2004

Select Files

Click "Browse" to select a file. You can attach up to 3 files for a total of 3.0 encoded megabytes [What's this?].

💡 Want to see a progress bar when you upload your file? Make Yahoo! Mail your default email program.

File 1: [   ] [Browse...]
File 2: [   ] [Browse...]
File 3: [   ] [Browse...]

Send up to 10 attachments (10MB)!
Upgrade to Yahoo! Mail Plus

PC users: Select "All Files" for "Files of Type". If you don't see a "Browse" button, your browser doesn't support attachments.

| Attach Files | Cancel |

Figure 3-5:
Attaching a file to an e-mail message.

3. For each file that you want to send, click the Browse button, locate the file in the Choose File dialog box, and click Open.

4. Click the Attach Files button.

You see the Attachments page, which lists each file that you want to send with your e-mail message. If you change your mind about sending a file, click the Remove link beside its name.

5. Click the Done button.

You return to the Compose page. It lists the files that you want to send. If you change your mind about sending a file at this point, click the Remove link beside the filename.

Receiving a file that someone sent to you

You can tell when someone sent you a file because the file icon (a paper-clip) appears beside the subject of the message in the Inbox. To handle the file, click the file icon or click the subject of the message and scroll to the bottom of the Read Message page. Either way, you see the Attachment options shown in Figure 3-6. Your choices are three:

✦ **Scan and Download Attachment:** Scans the file with Norton AntiVirus software and presents the file in the Scan Results dialog box. Click the Download Attachment link. The File Download dialog box appears. Click the Open button to open the file; click the Save button to save it on your computer.

✦ **Scan and Save to your My Yahoo! Briefcase:** Scans the file for viruses and saves it to your Yahoo! Briefcase, an online storage area that Yahoo! maintains. (The Briefcase isn't covered in this book, but you can explore it at `http://briefcase.yahoo.com`.)

✦ **View Attachment:** Opens the file so that you can view it right away. (This option works only with HTML files.)

Figure 3-6: Handling a file that was sent to a Yahoo! Mail address.

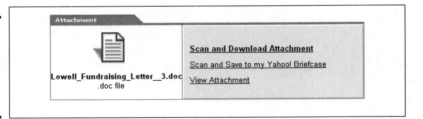

Organizing your mail

If you're an active e-mailer, you know how letters can pile up and how the ol' Inbox can become a cluttered mess. One way to get around this problem is to create folders and organize e-mail messages by moving them into the different folders.

Here's how to create a new folder in Yahoo! Mail:

1. In Yahoo! Mail, click the Folders link.

You land in the Folder page. The default folders — Inbox, Draft, Sent, Bulk, and Trash — are already listed.

2. In the Name text box, enter a folder name.

3. Click the Add Folder button.

Your Folders page reloads, this time listing your new folder. Whenever you return to this page, you can click a link to delete or rename one of your folders.

Immediately after you create your first personal folder, incoming mail still goes directly to your Inbox. From there, you can move it to any folder, default or personal. Here's how:

1. On your Inbox page, select the check box next to any message that you want to move.

2. From the Move to Folder drop-down list, select the folder that you'd like to use to hold the selected letter.

This drop-down list is located in the upper- and lower-right corners of the Inbox list area, as shown in Figure 3-7.

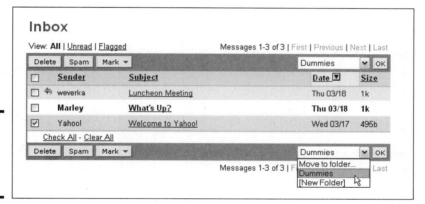

Figure 3-7: Moving a message to another folder.

3. Click the OK button.

The Inbox page reloads with your selected message no longer present in your Inbox list. To view the contents of any of your folders, click the desired link in the left sidebar.

Your Virtual Black Book

Making friends in Yahoo! through chatting, the message boards, and Yahoo! Messenger is so easy that you might quickly develop a large and varied correspondence. Keeping your contacts' e-mail addresses on paper becomes impractical. The best system is to have an online address book. Yahoo! Mail provides such a thing. Here's how to get it started:

1. In Yahoo! Mail, click the Addresses link.

You see an Address Book page similar to the one in Figure 3-8.

2. Click the Add Contact button.

The Add Contact page appears.

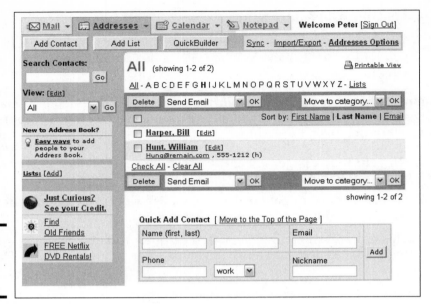

Figure 3-8:
A working
address
book.

3. Fill in the fields.

All that's really necessary is a name and an e-mail address. You don't
need to use the Yahoo! Address Book to keep track of phone numbers
and company names if you don't feel so inspired.

4. Click the Save button.

Figure 3-8 illustrates an address book with a few entries. This option-packed
page has several features:

✦ Use the Search Contacts text box to find a name or part of a name if
your address book is large and you've lost someone. The search engine
is pretty smart — you can enter a name, a nickname as entered in the
address book, a fraction of a name, an e-mail address, or a portion of an
e-mail address, such as the domain name.

✦ Select the check boxes next to names, turning them into recipients of
your outgoing mail when you select Send Email from the drop-down list
and click the OK button. You may select as many as you like.

✦ Click any letter to see address book entries for that letter only.

✦ Click the First Name, Last Name, or Email link to sort the list by that
criterion, alphabetically.

✦ Click any name to see all the information that you entered for that
contact.

✦ Use the Edit link to change the information for any contact.

You might want to organize your names into group lists if you mail repeatedly to certain groups of names in your address book. Here's how to create your first group:

1. On your Address Book page, click the Add List button.

The Edit List page appears.

2. Enter a name for the distribution list in the Name of List text box.

3. In the Category list box, Ctrl+click to select the names that you want for your list.

4. Click the Add button.

Your selected names move, as if by psychic powers, to the New List list box.

To eliminate names from your list, select the names and click the Remove button.

5. Click the Save button.

In the Yahoo! Address Book, distribution list names are shown in italics. By addressing an e-mail message to a distribution list, you can send the e-mail to many people at once.

Chapter 4: Serious Searching at Yahoo!

In This Chapter

✔ Getting an overview of the Yahoo! directory

✔ Becoming a directory power user

✔ Adding a Web site to the Yahoo! directory

✔ Understanding the Yahoo! search engine

The Yahoo! directory and the related search engine remain core features of the entire online service. The directory is an astounding menu of Web sites, and the search engine is a great way to navigate it. When you want an overview of Web destinations on a certain topic — general and detailed, good and bad, corporate and personal, famous and obscure — the Yahoo! directory is the place to turn.

Although the directory and search engine aren't difficult features to use, they represent a massive catalogue of content that can be intimidating. Luckily, navigating this catalogue succumbs nicely to a few tricks and shortcuts. That's the purpose of this chapter. Here I tackle Yahoo!'s sprawling, magnificent information menu, which played a huge part in popularizing the Internet and still provides a daily virtual map to millions of online citizens.

Understanding the Yahoo! Directory

I might have titled this section "Understanding the Toaster" because the Yahoo! directory is somewhat easier to comprehend than piloting an airliner. This isn't brain surgery or even a relatively simple appendectomy. But this *is* where the tricks and shortcuts come in. I guide your mouse through the points and clicks of the Yahoo! directory, adding my tips along the way.

Start with the main directory page, as shown in Figure 4-1. Get there by using the primary Yahoo! URL and scrolling down the page a bit:

www.yahoo.com

The home page displays a Search the Web text box above the directory topics, but ignore that for the time being. Scroll down to those big, fat directory topics — Arts & Humanities, News & Media, and the twelve others. These are the *top-level,* or *first-level,* directory topics. Each one is a link leading to a *second-level* directory page. Each second-level page contains subtopic links leading to *third-level* pages, and so it goes for several levels. How many levels, exactly? It depends on the topic. Some subjects reach down eight levels.

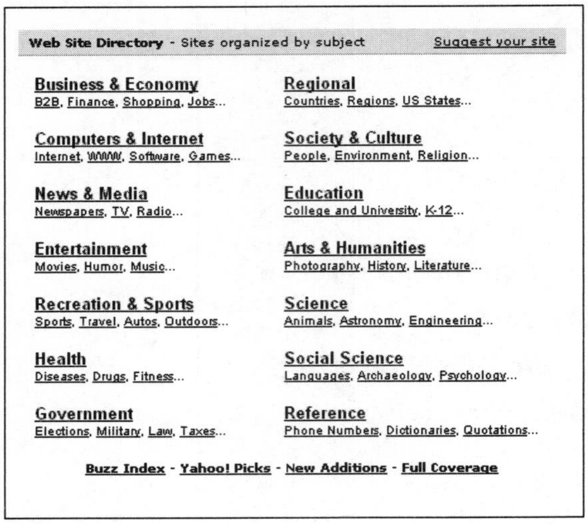

Web Site Directory - Sites organized by subject   Suggest your site

Business & Economy
B2B, Finance, Shopping, Jobs...

Regional
Countries, Regions, US States...

Computers & Internet
Internet, WWW, Software, Games...

Society & Culture
People, Environment, Religion...

News & Media
Newspapers, TV, Radio...

Education
College and University, K-12...

Entertainment
Movies, Humor, Music...

Arts & Humanities
Photography, History, Literature...

Recreation & Sports
Sports, Travel, Autos, Outdoors...

Science
Animals, Astronomy, Engineering...

Health
Diseases, Drugs, Fitness...

Social Science
Languages, Archaeology, Psychology...

Government
Elections, Military, Law, Taxes...

Reference
Phone Numbers, Dictionaries, Quotations...

Buzz Index - **Yahoo! Picks** - **New Additions** - **Full Coverage**

Figure 4-1:
The main
Yahoo!
directory
page.

Site links versus directory links

Site links and directory links work together to bring sparkle and joy to many directory pages. Well, they work together, anyway. I mention site links versus directory links to draw a distinction between when you're linking to a Web site (leaving Yahoo! to visit another site) and when you're linking to a lower-level page in the Yahoo! directory.

Some directory pages have only directory links; some have only site links. (They're lower-level pages representing highly specific topics and containing links to other sites on those topics.) The middle ground is populated with pages that have both directory and site links, and in those cases, the directory links are always above the site links and are displayed in bold type.

Figure 4-2 shows a hybrid directory page. The figure illustrates the Trivia portion of the Entertainment topic. Trivia subcategories are placed above the site links. Clicking a subcategory leads to another directory page (a third-level page in this case), and clicking a site link takes you to that site, outside Yahoo!.

The numbers next to directory links throughout the Yahoo! directory give you an indication of how many site links are within that topic and its subtopics. Next to the Chats and Forums link in Figure 4-2, for example, three site links are indicated.

Fun with shortcuts

When I was a kid, I cut through a neighbor's yard on the way to school, trampling flowerbeds in my haste to educate myself. Who knew that a life of juvenile crime would prepare me to be a famous author? Or even an obscure one? Anyway, Yahoo! lets you take shortcuts for the sake of education, too.

Getting your bearings

Near the top of every Yahoo! directory page is a succession of links, the leftmost of which is a Directory link, which takes you to the Yahoo! directory main page. The links get more topic-specific as you track them to the right. Moving up to a higher-level directory page is as simple as clicking any of the links.

You might be tempted to think that the string of links represents a trail of your journey into the directory,

but in fact it doesn't always work that way. As you navigate through the directory, you might notice that the entire string changes from one page to another, even when you expect only the last link to be added to the previous string. This discrepancy is due to the cross-referencing of the directory, wherein some very specific topics might be listed in more than one main topic's directory pages.

If you look back at Figure 4-1, you see a few links in small type beneath the main topic categories. Each link takes you directly to a third-level directory page, skipping over the second level with the same blithe spirit that I felt when thrashing through tulips as an eager young lad. Yahoo! attempts to place the most popular, in-demand subcategories as these shortcut links.

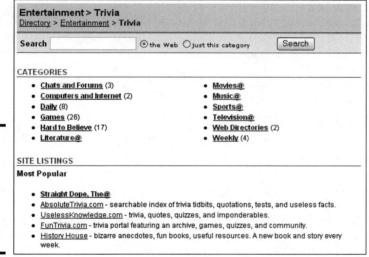

Figure 4-2: A Yahoo! directory page showing directory links above site links.

Steroid-Infused Tips

As the preceding section makes clear, the Yahoo! directory is a marvel of organization and complexity. It contains an astounding number of topics, subtopics, and directory pages. Navigating within the directory isn't hard after you grasp the multilayered architecture of the thing. (All Web directories are structured in essentially the same way.)

This section highlights two tricks for any would-be power Yahoo! user. The following points are habits that I've incorporated in my constant quest for more, faster, and better content.

Use multiple windows

One important detail that can escape the attention of Internet newcomers — and even folks of greater experience — is that you can open multiple browser windows. In Internet Explorer or Netscape Navigator, just press Ctrl+N.

When using the Yahoo! directory, I usually open new browser windows in the process of clicking a link. Both Explorer and Navigator give you the option of opening a link in a new window by using the right-click menu. Here's how it works:

1. **When you find a link to a site that you'd like to visit, place your mouse cursor over it and right-click.**

   A menu appears beside the mouse cursor.

2. **Choose Open in New Window.**

   The targeted site appears in a new browser window.

3. **Resize the window if necessary.**

   You can switch back and forth between the site and the directory page.

Opening multiple browser windows helps you avoid getting lost. Keep in mind that finding good stuff through the Yahoo! directory is a hit-or-miss business. The directory exposes you to a gigantic range of sites on almost any topic, and bouncing back and forth between Yahoo! and outside sites is commonplace. That bouncing is a lot easier if you keep one browser window dedicated to the directory page that you're linking from.

Bookmark your Favorites

If you're the adventurous sort, the Yahoo! directory is made for you. During your explorations, you will no doubt investigate many a terrific Web site. One common downfall of surf-loving folks is forgetting to bookmark sites and then never finding them again.

The Navigator browser has its Bookmark feature, and Explorer uses lists called Favorites. Although the two browsers implement these features somewhat differently, they both serve the same essential function, which is to put reminder links to sites in the browser itself, so you don't have to track them down the hard way a second time. Both Bookmarks and Favorites allow you to accumulate many such links and organize them into named folders.

The rule is bookmark first, sort later. If you go into a site that looks halfway decent and might possibly be worth a second visit sometime, just add it to your Bookmarks or Favorites list immediately. It's a lot easier to remove a bookmark than to find an obscure site a second time.

Adding a Site to the Yahoo! Directory

Yahoo! is a highly interactive online service. You might be surprised to discover that the directory relies on its visitors for additions to its extensive menu of sites. The Yahoo! editors perform a small portion of the selecting and reviewing of new directory sites, but most additions result from the suggestions of users.

If you have a Web page of your own, submitting it to the Yahoo! directory doesn't take much time and it's free as long as the Web site isn't a commercial one. You must follow a certain procedure, however, or you'll get bogged down in error messages. When sending in the name and URL of a site, you must also select a subcategory page where you think the link should be. You must submit a subcategory, not one of the 14 main topic areas that appear on the Yahoo! home page. Note, though, that the Yahoo! Surfers (the Yahoo! team) might change the location before adding your site.

Although you have no assurance that a site will be added to the Yahoo! directory, Yahoo! isn't in the business of turning sites away from the directory. As long as you have a legitimate URL and follow the procedure, it should get added within a reasonable time. (It sometimes takes a few weeks.)

 When looking for your site's listing in the Yahoo! directory, search the directory by keyword. Don't just look in the subcategory that you selected; the editors at Yahoo! might have decided that your page fit better elsewhere. If after two months you're convinced your site hasn't been added to the directory, resubmit it.

 Choosing a good subcategory page for your site submission increases your chances of getting the site added — and added quickly. For that reason, choosing the subcategory is probably the most important part of the entire process. Don't slight it by taking a hasty or ill-informed guess at where your site belongs. Digging around the directory until you find the best spot is worth the time.

Following are a few pointers for finding the best subcategory:

✦ **Look for site links:** When choosing a subcategory, the first thing you should look for is the presence of site links on the subcategory directory page. (I explain the difference between site links and directory links earlier in this chapter.) If the page has only directory links leading to more specific subtopics, you're still too high in the directory and need to dig deeper to find your subcategory.

✦ **Search for sites that are similar to your own:** When examining a possible subcategory directory page, look for sites that serve the same purpose as the one you're submitting. You might even want to visit a few. Sometimes you can tell immediately by reading the site title whether it's the Web page for you.

✦ **Determine whether your site is personal or topical:** When assessing where your site belongs, distinguish between a *personal* site and a *topical* site. By this I mean, is your site about yourself or about other subjects? Is it an online personal scrapbook, or is it about a hobby? If it's along some specific subject line, it's a topical site. All personal sites get listed in the Society & Culture: People: Personal Home Pages category. Topical sites fit into other directory subcategories.

After you go to the directory page where you believe your site should be listed, follow these simple steps:

1. **Click the Suggest a Site link.**

The link appears on every directory page in the upper-right corner.

2. **On the next page, click the Standard Consideration button.**

3. **Click the Continue button.**

After following the preceding steps, Yahoo! tosses you into a forum for describing the site.

4. **Fill in the Site Title, URL, Graphic Location, and Description text boxes.**

Follow the instructions below each text box. The title doesn't need to be the page title exactly as it appears in the title bar of a browser visiting that page, but it's probably less confusing to visitors if you keep them the same. In the Description form, take the time to write a concise, positive description of the site. Remarkably, most submissions don't contain descriptions. A short blurb encourages users to link to your site.

5. **Fill in your contact information.**

This information tells Yahoo! who you are (in a perfunctory way; you don't have to discuss your troubled childhood), and how you can be contacted.

6. **If you have any alternate category suggestions for the site, enter them in the Additional Information text area.**

7. **Click the Submit button.**

You're finished! Have patience as Yahoo! checks out your site.

Starting the Yahoo! Search Engine

You've probably heard the slightly intimidating phrase, *search engine*. Sounds like something you don't want to get your hands dirty on. Actually, search engines are extremely sanitary and useful. They help you find things on the Internet without spending all night browsing through directories.

If browsing directories is like window shopping, using a search engine is like striding into a store, plastic in hand, with intent to purchase. Browsing goes for the haystack; searching goes for the needle. (My Bachelor of Metaphor degree is really coming in handy.)

The remaining portion of this chapter describes how Yahoo! differs from other search engines and explains how to use keywords in Yahoo! to find stuff on the Net.

Yahoo! searching secrets revealed

Yahoo! became famous several years ago as an Internet directory with a search engine attached. This chapter describes how searching in Yahoo! works, but it's important to distinguish between two types of search engines that you can find on the Web. Many search engines use automated software to continually troll the Net, learning about new sites. Those sites then become part of a massive, searchable index of Internet destinations.

Yahoo! operates differently, without any such automated indexing software (sometimes called *spiders, robots,* or just *bots*). The Yahoo! search engine performs only within the Yahoo! directory. (See the first portion of this chapter to find out more about the directory.) The difference between the Yahoo! search engine and others might seem subtle — after all, a directory is nothing more than a big index. Although that's true, a fairly big difference exists in how different indexes are compiled. For example, automated Web-trolling software picks up individual pages of multipage sites, whereas Yahoo! — which relies on site owners to submit their URLs to the directory — might contain only the main page of a site.

Each search engine is different and produces distinctive search results for any given query. Yahoo! is unique in that its directory is gigantic and targeted to main pages of sites. On the other hand, if a site owner hasn't submitted his or her site to Yahoo! for inclusion in the directory, it doesn't exist on Yahoo!'s radar. Search engines that run automatically might well turn up that same site, thanks to the work of their tireless software robots.

Sleuthing with keywords

Keywords are clues. Computers, being the dense creatures they are, need all the clues they can get. Keywords are cryptic hints that lead you to specific topics on the Internet.

Using keywords to search in Yahoo! is the reverse of using the directory, which gives *you* keywords. As shown in Figure 4-3, typing your own keywords in the Search the Web text box lets you cut to the chase by zooming directly to Web sites and directory pages on highly specific topics. What's more, you can click the Images tab to see images of the item that you're looking for, or click the Yellow Pages, News, or Products tab to get results from those categories. Figure 4-4 shows the tabs.

A keyword can be anything related to what you're looking for. You may also enter more than one keyword, called a *keyword string*. A certain craft is involved in determining what keyword(s) will give you the best results. This part of the chapter gets you started on the right foot for the Yahoo! search engine and provides some helpful tips.

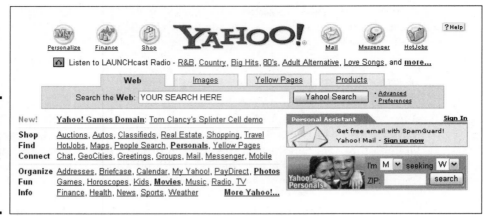

Figure 4-3:
The Yahoo!
search form
is located at
the top of
the home
page.

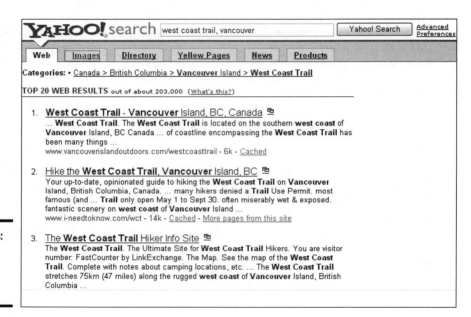

Figure 4-4:
A Yahoo!
search
results
page.

You need to remember a few basic points if you're just starting to use keywords in Yahoo!. The following might seem obvious, but I get to the more sophisticated stuff later in this chapter:

✦ **No caps:** Capital (uppercase) letters aren't important when searching in Yahoo!. It doesn't hurt your search to use them, but there's no point knocking yourself out unnecessarily. The search engine isn't *case sensitive*. Even when using proper names as your keywords, feel free to use lowercase letters, as in *kevin costner.*

✦ **Don't forget the spaces:** Yahoo! may be literal, but it can't understand multiple keywords if you don't have a space between each word. You can enhance your search by inserting things in those spaces. I get to them later in this chapter, in "Getting precise with search operators."

✦ **Watch your spelling:** Spelling counts when searching. You can get away with sloppy spelling in just about every other aspect of the Net — e-mail, chat rooms, message boards — but it usually kills a search. All is not lost, however, because Yahoo! sometimes suggests correct spellings if it encounters what it thinks is a misspelled word.

You can always start over in the midst of any Yahoo! search. At the top and bottom of every search results page is a keyword search text box. Yahoo! remembers your previous keywords, but you can type over them to begin a new search. By the same token, you can begin a search from any directory page — the keyword search text box is located near the top of each of them.

Advanced searching

From any search results page or from the Yahoo! home page, you can opt for a more sophisticated set of options for your keywords by clicking the Advanced link. You see the Advanced Web Search page shown in Figure 4-5. On this page, you can conduct *AND* searches, *OR* searches, and even searches for an exact phrase. You can also search within sites and domains and for Web pages written in a certain language.

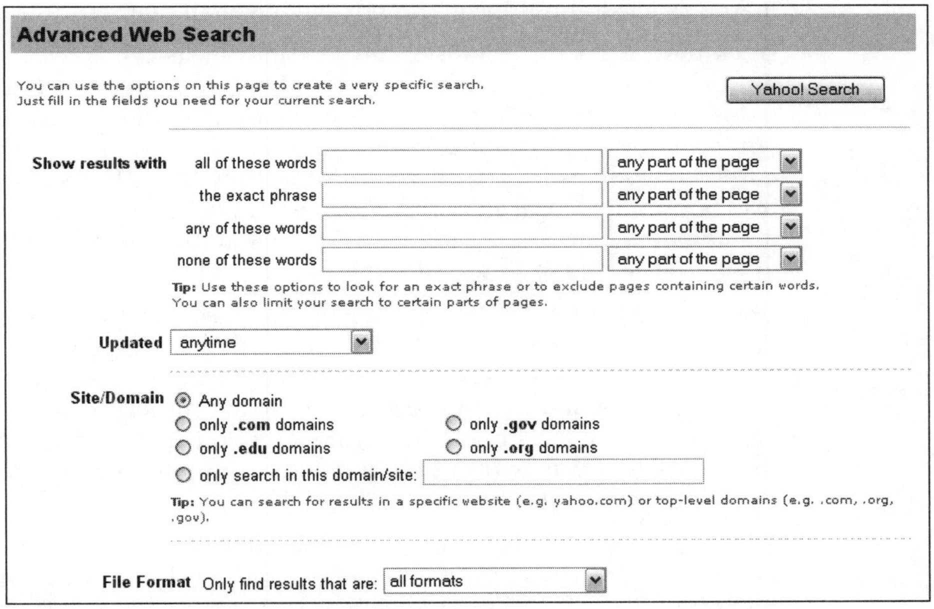

Advanced Web Search

You can use the options on this page to create a very specific search. Just fill in the fields you need for your current search.

[Yahoo! Search]

Show results with
all of these words		any part of the page ▼
the exact phrase		any part of the page ▼
any of these words		any part of the page ▼
none of these words		any part of the page ▼

Tip: Use these options to look for an exact phrase or to exclude pages containing certain words. You can also limit your search to certain parts of pages.

Updated [anytime ▼]

Site/Domain
- ● Any domain
- ○ only **.com** domains   ○ only **.gov** domains
- ○ only **.edu** domains   ○ only **.org** domains
- ○ only search in this domain/site: [   ]

Tip: You can search for results in a specific website (e.g. yahoo.com) or top-level domains (e.g. .com, .org, .gov).

File Format Only find results that are: [all formats ▼]

Figure 4-5: Conducting an advanced search.

Getting precise with search operators

Search operators are words or symbols that you add to your keyword string to tell Yahoo! how to interpret your request. On the Advanced Web Search page, the All of These Words and Any of These Words options refer to two basic search operators that instruct the search engine to find matches for *all* keywords *(AND)* and *any* keywords *(OR)*. You can bypass the Advanced Web Search page by becoming acquainted with the search operators and typing them manually into your search string.

In Yahoo!, symbols and single-letter abbreviations indicate search operators. As always when dealing with simple-minded computers, you must be literal and use the correct spelling and syntax — the symbols must not be varied or positioned in the wrong place. This section summarizes the search operators that are recognized by Yahoo! and specifies how to type them:

✦ **AND:** The *AND* search operator is symbolized with the plus sign (+), and you place it immediately before any keyword that must be included in the search results. This operator tends to narrow the search, delivering fewer, better-targeted results. An example of its use is the search string *baltimore +orioles,* which eliminates sites about the city of Baltimore that don't include a reference to its baseball team, the Orioles. If you're concerned about getting sites about birds, you could extend the string to *baltimore +orioles +baseball* which would force Yahoo! to return sites that include all three words.

✦ **NOT:** This operator, the equivalent of the None of These Words option on the Advanced Web Search page, excludes keywords from being matched and is symbolized by the minus sign (-). As with the *AND* operator, place the *NOT* symbol immediately before any word that you want to exclude from matching. An example is *orioles -baseball,* which would match to sites about birds but not the baseball team.

✦ **Document titles only:** Yahoo! can restrict the search to Web site titles only, disregarding descriptions and URLs. To do so, enter **t:** immediately before a keyword or keyword string. (If you're using multiple keywords, you need enter only one **t:** in front of the whole string.) An example is *t:anthony hopkins,* which searches for sites with Anthony Hopkins in the title but not necessarily in the site description or URL. At the same time, it eliminates matches of Anthony Hopkins in the description if his name doesn't also appear in the title.

✦ **Document URLs only:** As a reverse of the preceding search operator, Yahoo! can limit the search to URLs, excluding Web page titles and descriptions. This is a great option for zooming in on specific Web sites. Simply enter **u:** in front of the keyword string (or single keyword). Try it when searching for a company name. A good experiment is to search on the company name without the *u:* operator and then with it and then compare the results.

✦ **Exact phrases:** The Advanced Web Search page allows you to specify exact phrase matches, and you can do the same thing by using quotation marks ("...") around the keyword string. If you're searching for a person's name (such as Jack London), and the first and last name could be mistaken for words with other meanings, the phrase operator comes in handy. Try the *"jack london"* keyword string.

✦ **Wildcard:** This search operator lets you get away with not knowing how to spell something and is also an easy way to broaden a search. The symbol is an asterisk (*), and it must be placed immediately after a word or partial word. An example is *paris*,* which matches up with Paris and Parisian.

Search operators can be combined! Stay calm; don't get too excited. I know this is good news. You can mix and match the preceding operators in any way that remains logical. Here are two examples based on keywords that I already used:

✦ If you want to find sites about the Baltimore Orioles baseball team but specifically exclude bird information, try

baltimore +orioles +baseball -birds

✦ If you want pages about Anthony Hopkins, but don't care to read about the *Silence of the Lambs* movie, try

anthony +hopkins -"silence of the lambs"

Generally, when you combine search operators with the number of keywords, you can drastically enlarge or shrink your search results. Here are two rules:

✦ To get fewer hits, add keywords and use the *AND* search operator.

✦ To get more hits, subtract keywords and use the *NOT* operator on the Advanced Web Search page.

Chapter 5: Finding People and Businesses

In This Chapter

- ✔ Searching for old friends in People Search
- ✔ Registering so that you can be found
- ✔ Navigating the personal ads
- ✔ Opening the Yahoo! White Pages

The Internet might seem like a galaxy of colorful Web pages (billboard heaven?), but actually it's all about people. What started out as the information highway has a more personal destiny than merely feeding data faster and more overwhelmingly than ever before. Ultimately, the Web will fulfill its potential only if it brings people closer together. It's already step-ping into that destiny in a few ways.

E-mail, for all its seeming impersonality, is actually the servant of closer relationships. And I know from personal experience that e-mail has the power to bridge the chasms of time, geography, and neglect. Have you ever thought of tracking down an old friend through e-mail? This chapter explains how Yahoo! contributes to that goal.

Personal ads also thrive on the Internet. This fact might make the Web seem like nothing more than a digitized meat market. But the truth is that information databasing, when applied to the problem of human loneliness, can improve the human condition. (Didn't think I'd get quite this deep in a *For Dummies* book, did you? Don't worry — I emerge from the philosophical mist soon.) Yahoo! Personals opens up one of the most popular meeting places for people looking for companionship of all sorts, and I cover it in this chapter. Keep reading to see how your Yahoo! account helps you find old friends and make new ones.

Finding an E-Mail Address

To find regular folks, look in the phone book; to find a business, look in the Yellow Pages. To find an e-mail address, what can you do? The Web has several e-mail directories, and one of them is in Yahoo!.

Keeping an e-mail directory is a thorny challenge for a few reasons. First, people often have multiple addresses: office e-mail, home e-mail, and Web-based e-mail. In the early days of the Internet, a single e-mail address defined a person's virtual location — like a street address in the offline world. The contemporary online scene, however, doesn't have a single, irrefutable identifier. People are spread among many addresses.

The second reason that e-mail directories are problematic is that even though many people might have a main address, it's liable to change fairly often. Every time your long-lost high-school buddy switches Internet providers, the e-mail address changes. Directories try to keep up, but not one of them provides a really stellar, reliable service.

Yahoo! People Search offers e-mail address searching from a different angle. The idea is not to attempt a database of all current e-mail addresses. Instead, the service is a registry of information about people who *want to be found.* The directory finds *only* those people who have registered a free listing in the directory. As such, it's not a general-purpose e-mail White Pages. People Search is designed to help people find old friends and invites everyone to include a bit of personal history to help past acquaintances locate them.

To begin searching for e-mail addresses, click the People Search link on the Yahoo! home page or go directly to

```
http://people.yahoo.com
```

Figure 5-1 illustrates the People Search page. Follow these steps to conduct a search:

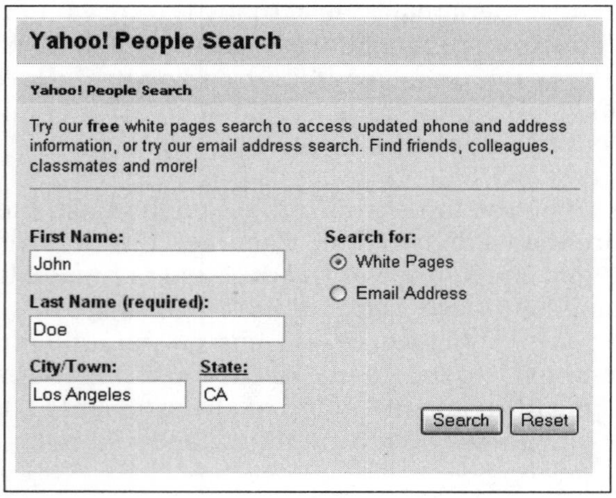

Figure 5-1:
The People Search page, from which you can find e-mail addresses and phone numbers.

Yahoo! People Search

Yahoo! People Search

Try our **free** white pages search to access updated phone and address information, or try our email address search. Find friends, colleagues, classmates and more!

First Name:
John

Last Name (required):
Doe

City/Town: State:
Los Angeles   CA

Search for:
⦿ White Pages
○ Email Address

[Search] [Reset]

1. **On the Yahoo! People Search page, fill in the Name text boxes.**

Either text box is optional, but filling in both (first and last name) makes it easier to find someone. Entering only one or the other is likely to overwhelm you with results. Clicking the Reset button clears both fields of any text.

2. **If you know or suspect that you know the city and state where your long-lost friend resides, enter the city and state as well.**

3. **Select the White Pages radio button to search for a snail-mail address. For an e-mail address, select the corresponding radio button.**

For this example, select the Email Address radio button.

4. Click the Search button.

The Email Search Results page appears.

5. Click any link in the Name column or the Email column.

Clicking the e-mail links opens up a window of your default e-mail program, ready to send a note to the selected address. Clicking name links provides as much information about that person as he or she provided to the database.

Notice these amenities on the Email Search Results page:

✦ Click the Add to Address Book link to add the e-mail address to your Yahoo! Address Book. (See Book III, Chapter 3 for more on Yahoo! Mail.)

✦ Click the Map link to visit a Yahoo! Maps page showing where your long-lost friend resides. This link is next to the person's city and ZIP Code.

Getting Yourself Registered

While you're using People Search, why not participate in both directions? That is to say, instead of just searching in the database, register yourself so that people can find *you*. As long as you're registered with Yahoo!, you can enter your name so that others can find you. Here's how:

1. On the Yahoo! People Search page, click the Edit/Create My Listing link.

If you haven't signed in to Yahoo!, you will be asked to do so now.

2. On the Create Your Yahoo! People Search Listing page (could they have thought of a longer page name?), fill in your name and any other info that you want to add to the searchable database.

Filling in text boxes is optional, but the more information you plug in, the easier it is for people to find you. Under the Internet Address(es) banner, remember that it's not enough to simply fill in addresses — you must also select the radio button next to the address that you want added to the directory.

3. Click the Finished button at the bottom of the page.

Searching the Yahoo! Personals

Been looking for love in all the wrong places? Don't despair: Yahoo! runs one of the most popular personal classified services on the Web. The classified service is only moderately sophisticated, but it has two great advantages over slick competing online personals sites. First, it's free. Putting up an ad, browsing, contacting someone — it's all free of charge. Second, it's fast. You can cover a lot of ground in your search for Mr. or Ms. Right without spending all night at it. After all, what you *really* want to spend all night doing is getting to know someone, not searching for his or her e-mail address.

To search the personal ads, it pays to be registered with Yahoo!. This way, you can conduct more thorough searches. Assuming that you're registered and signed in with Yahoo!, you can start browsing Yahoo! Personals by clicking the Personals link on the Yahoo! home page or going directly to the following URL:

`http://personals.yahoo.com`

On the Yahoo! Personals page, conduct your search by using one of these methods:

✦ **Quick search:** Fill in the text boxes and click the Find My Match button.

✦ **Advanced search:** Click the Advanced Search link. You see the My Advanced Search page shown in Figure 5-2. Using the drop-down lists and check boxes, describe your ideal mate, and then click the Find My Match button.

✦ **Keyword search:** Click the Keyword Search link, and, in the form that appears, enter a search term and click the Find My Match button.

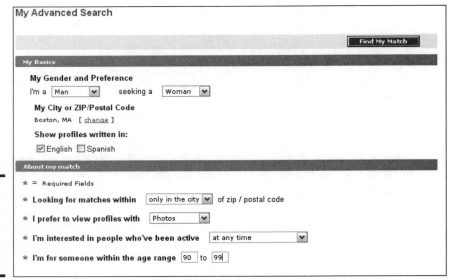

Figure 5-2:
Looking more thoroughly for Ms. or Mr. Right.

If a search yields any results, you see a list of profiles that have descriptions and in some cases photos that you can view and ponder as love mates.

If you go to the trouble to construct a search that works for you, save it. That way, you can run it again. To save a search, click the Save My Search button. To run the search later on, click the My Saved Search link and then the Run My Saved Search button. Everyone is allowed to save one search. The buttons are located at the bottom of the search page.

You can also save a profile and be able to view it later. To save a profile, click the Save Profile link. Click the My Saved Profiles link to see profiles you have saved.

Placing a Personal Ad

Browsing, writing responses to ads, and hoping for replies are all well and good, but you can cut to the chase with a more assertive approach. Consider placing your own Yahoo! personal. To do so, sign in to Yahoo! and follow these steps:

1. **On the Yahoo! Personals main page, click the Create a Free Profile link.**

   The link takes you to the five-part Create a Profile questionnaire shown in Figure 5-3.

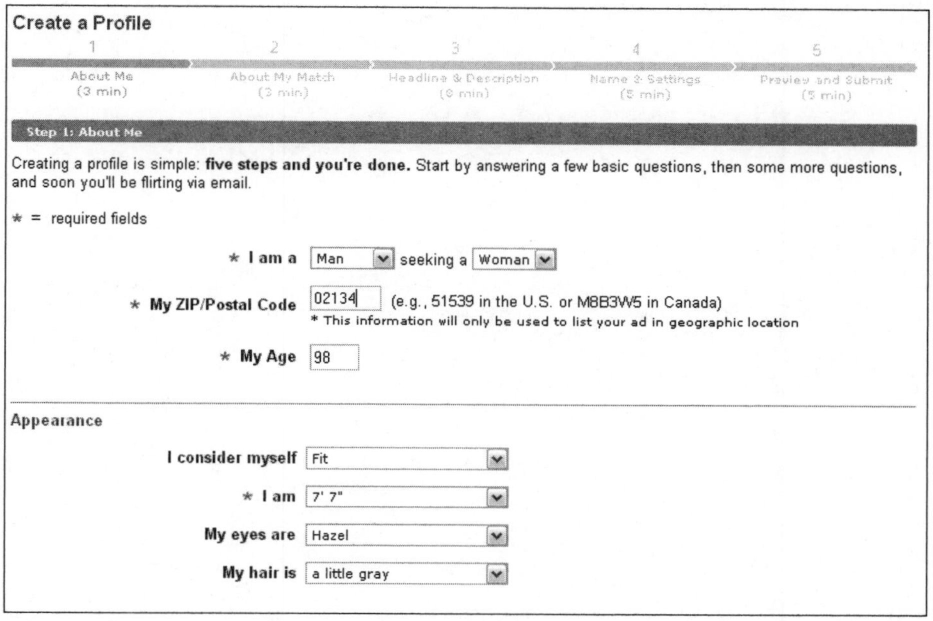

Create a Profile

1	2	3	4	5
About Me (3 min)	About My Match (3 min)	Headline & Description (8 min)	Name & Settings (3 min)	Preview and Submit (5 min)

Step 1: About Me

Creating a profile is simple: **five steps and you're done.** Start by answering a few basic questions, then some more questions, and soon you'll be flirting via email.

* = required fields

* **I am a** [Man ▾] seeking a [Woman ▾]

* **My ZIP/Postal Code** [02134] (e.g., 51539 in the U.S. or M8B3W5 in Canada)
  * This information will only be used to list your ad in geographic location

* **My Age** [98]

Appearance

I consider myself [Fit ▾]

* **I am** [7' 7" ▾]

My eyes are [Hazel ▾]

My hair is [a little gray ▾]

Figure 5-3: Fill in all the required fields to place an ad.

2. **Fill in all the required information fields, plus whatever optional information you want to share.**

   You fill out five questionnaires in all.

3. **Click the Submit Profile button.**

   After Yahoo! reviews it, your ad is automatically positioned in the geographical directory that best matches your ZIP Code.

Responses to your personal ad go directly and automatically to your Personals Mailbox. They aren't mixed with your Yahoo! Mail. Some people set up a separate Yahoo! ID for Personals communications to ensure that all Personals correspondence remains separate from other letters. You can access your Personals Mailbox in a few different ways, including from My Yahoo!. You can also click the Personals Mailbox link on the Yahoo! Personals main page.

CHECK IT OUT

Looking Up a Phone Number

Yahoo! has a nationwide (U.S. only) White Pages for looking up phone numbers. This service is separate from the e-mail search, even though you initiate both from the same page. No registration is required — Yahoo! gets its database information from the phone companies. Here's how to find a number:

1. On the Yahoo! home page, click the People Search link.

2. Enter the name of the person whose phone number you need and make sure that the White Pages option is selected.

3. Click the Search button.

With any luck, you see a list of people with the name that you entered, their addresses, and their phone numbers.

Chapter 6: And That's the Way It Is: News Searching

In This Chapter

✔ Using the main Yahoo! News directory

✔ Browsing and searching for news

✔ Telling Yahoo! what kind of news you want to see

"Information wants to be free" is the motto of the Internet. Whether information actually has desires is a question beyond my metaphysical capacity, but Yahoo! does seem to adhere to the sentiment. Free news is provided in almost embarrassing wealth. Big, sloppy buckets of news. Up-to-the-second, comprehensive news. You can get a broad overview or drill deeply into a topic.

Best of all, Yahoo!'s plain, straightforward display style makes the experience fast and generally without hassle. Unlike other news magazines on the Web that force you to load graphics-intense, feature-laden pages, Yahoo! gets a lot of its news from wire services and keeps the stark headline style that characterizes those sources. It's not that Yahoo! News pages are unattractive, but neither are they unnecessarily encumbered with fancy borders, pictures, and advertisements. The viewing experience is clean. Yahoo! gathers news photos into separate areas for people who want to take the time to view them.

This chapter walks you through the sometimes labyrinthine hallways of the Yahoo! news room.

Finding the Front Page

Getting started is perhaps the trickiest part of enjoying news, Yahoo! style. The Yahoo! home page doesn't make a big deal of the rich news resources that await you, so your mouse might circle the page a bit before knowing how to proceed. Here's the solution:

1. **On the Yahoo! home page, click the News link.**

You can find this link in the Info heading, and if you can't find it, try going directly to the Yahoo! News main page, shown in Figure 6-1, with this link:

```
http://news.yahoo.com
```

Figure 6-1: The Yahoo! News main page.

2. **On the Yahoo! News main page, click any story headline from the center of the page or any topic on the left side of the page.**

   Clicking a news topic takes you to a Yahoo! News topical front page. The topical pages are the *real* front pages, and in my view, they're the ones to bookmark for the future. I dissect the topical pages in "Filling the Tank with High-Octane News."

You can angle into the Yahoo! News main page in other ways as well:

✦ On the Yahoo! home page, select a story from the In the News panel. This panel is found on the right side of the screen.

✦ Conduct a normal search, and on the search results page, select the News tab, as shown in Figure 6-2. Yahoo! turns up news stories related to the subject that you entered for your search.

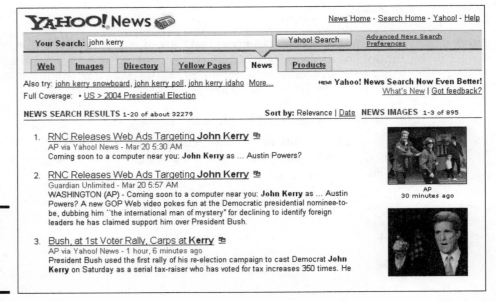

Figure 6-2: Searching for news on the News tab.

Here are some hints for productive news searching:

✦ Remember that Yahoo! News searching is literal and detailed. Every word of every story is compared to your keyword(s), including the writer's name. So a search for *o.j. simpson* might deliver an unrelated story written by Ian Simpson, the writer for Reuters news service.

✦ The Yahoo! News search engine finds every matching story in its archived database, which goes back ten days. If you want to avoid scrolling through page after page of results — going further and further back in time — select keywords that deliver narrower results. (See Book III, Chapter 4 for keyword help.)

✦ Very general searches that deliver hundreds of results aren't particularly useful — you're better off browsing your way through the Yahoo! News pages to find current headlines and stories. General searches for photos, however, work nicely.

✦ Search results in Yahoo! News are displayed on a general Yahoo! search results page, which includes links to search results (for your keywords) among Yahoo! directory categories, Web Sites, Web Pages, Related News, and Net Events. The upshot is an integrated result to your search that covers categories of Web sites, Web sites themselves, and scheduled Internet events — all related to your search query.

Filling the Tank with High-Octane News

Notice in Figure 6-3 the topics on the left side of the Yahoo! News main page. No matter where you go in Yahoo! News, you see these topic links. Click any topic to see more news stories on the topic. For the sake of illustration, I clicked the Business link. Figure 6-3 shows the Business news directory page. Notice the subtopics displayed under Business.

Figure 6-3:
The Yahoo!
Business
page is a
topical
news
destination.

Each news topic presents a slightly different front page, but some elements appear on most of them:

✦ **Headlines:** The meat of every Yahoo! News topical front page, the headlines stretch down the main portion of the page, including the first line from each story. Click any headline to see the full story.

✦ **Topic menu:** The main Yahoo! News topics are presented on the left side of the page. Click a topic to view news in a different category.

✦ **Full Coverage:** Full Coverage, a link found haphazardly on many different news pages, is a place where information from multiple sources about major news stories and subtopics is gathered in one place.

✦ **Audio/Video News:** Some topic pages have an Audio News section in the left sidebar, featuring links to *netcasts* (radio broadcasts for the Web) that you can listen to with RealPlayer or Windows Media Player. In most cases, the links go directly to the audio file, so a minimum of clicking is necessary. You might not even have to leave the Yahoo! page to hear the netcast.

✦ **Source Links:** To the right of the main headlines are links to the news sources that contribute to the topic you're looking at. Wire services are almost always included.

Local news isn't given quite the same status as U.S. and international news in Yahoo!, but the service does take a stab at state-level information for Americans, including news on a handful of major cities. Take a look for yourself:

1. **On a Yahoo! News main page, click the Local link in the Topic menu.**

2. **From the Select an Area drop-down list, select a U.S. metropolitan area.**

You get headlines from the area that you select.

Personalizing the Yahoo! News Page

As long as you're registered and signed in to Yahoo!, you can personalize the news page to make it present the news that you're interested in. After you sign in to Yahoo!, go to the Yahoo! News main page and click the Personalize News Home Page link. You see the Personalize the Yahoo! News Front Page page shown in Figure 6-4. It offers the following tabs for customizing your Yahoo! News main page:

✦ **Change Colors:** Choose which colors adorn the news page.

✦ **Choose Content:** Choose the kind of news that you want.

✦ **Order Sections:** After you've chosen news topics, prioritize them.

✦ **Weather:** Tell Yahoo! where you live so that local weather information can appear on the Yahoo! main page.

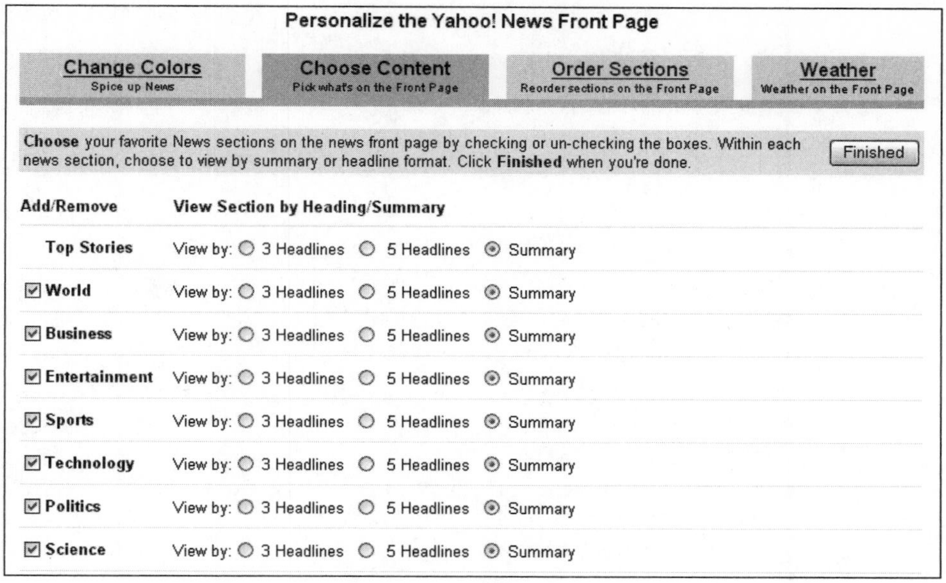

Personalize the Yahoo! News Front Page

Change Colors	Choose Content	Order Sections	Weather
Spice up News	Pick what's on the Front Page	Reorder sections on the Front Page	Weather on the Front Page

Choose your favorite News sections on the news front page by checking or un-checking the boxes. Within each news section, choose to view by summary or headline format. Click **Finished** when you're done.   [Finished]

Add/Remove   **View Section by Heading/Summary**

   Top Stories   View by: ○ 3 Headlines   ○ 5 Headlines   ◉ Summary

☑ **World**   View by: ○ 3 Headlines   ○ 5 Headlines   ◉ Summary

☑ **Business**   View by: ○ 3 Headlines   ○ 5 Headlines   ◉ Summary

☑ **Entertainment**   View by: ○ 3 Headlines   ○ 5 Headlines   ◉ Summary

☑ **Sports**   View by: ○ 3 Headlines   ○ 5 Headlines   ◉ Summary

☑ **Technology**   View by: ○ 3 Headlines   ○ 5 Headlines   ◉ Summary

☑ **Politics**   View by: ○ 3 Headlines   ○ 5 Headlines   ◉ Summary

☑ **Science**   View by: ○ 3 Headlines   ○ 5 Headlines   ◉ Summary

Figure 6-4:
Deciding the news that's fit for you.

Chapter 7: Instant Messaging with Yahoo! Messenger

In This Chapter

✔ **Downloading and launching Yahoo! Messenger**

✔ **Finding and chatting with friends**

✔ **Using Messenger as a Yahoo! control center**

*L*et me state it right up front: Yahoo! Messenger is one of the great features of cyberspace. For Yahoo! users, it's an invaluable software gadget that centralizes much of the Yahoo! experience. Messenger is free, small, and doesn't take much screen space, but this powerful little instant-messaging application keeps you in contact with friends, lets you search the Web, delivers e-mail alerts, tracks your stock portfolio, and integrates beautifully with your browser.

Messenger is the Yahoo! answer to the online passion for *instant messaging*, which is one-to-one and one-to-many chatting and file sharing. You can exchange messages and files with anyone else running Messenger and even get groups together for chatting.

Yahoo! designed Messenger to stay running all the time, and while that might seem excessive, I've found that it's exactly what works best for me. It's the first thing that I boot up when I go online, and I never turn it off.

Getting Ready to Run Yahoo! Messenger

It seems that everyone wants to get into the act. Yahoo! Messenger is Yahoo!'s instant-messaging program. It works much like AOL Instant Messenger and Windows Messenger. (Do you ever get the impression that the Internet is just a bunch of copycats?) To take Yahoo! Messenger for a spin, you must have a Yahoo! ID (it's free), and you must have downloaded the Yahoo! Messenger program:

✦ To get a Yahoo! ID, go to `www.yahoo.com`, click the Sign In link, and on the Web page that appears, click the Sign Up Now link. (Book III, Chapter 1 explains how to sign up with Yahoo!)

✦ To download Yahoo! Messenger, go to the Web page at this address: `http://messenger.yahoo.com`.

Messenger starts as a small window, but you can resize it to any dimension that you like, as shown in Figure 7-1. Keeping it compact for viewing online friends and chatting is convenient, but widening the window is helpful when using the information features that I describe in this chapter.

Figure 7-1:
Changing
the size
of the
Messenger
window.

By the way, if you want to uninstall Yahoo! Messenger, do so as if you were uninstalling any computer program. Go to the Control Panel, select Add or Remove Programs, select Yahoo! Messenger, and click the Add/Remove button.

Logging On to Yahoo! Messenger

To start running Yahoo! Messenger, double-click the Yahoo! Messenger icon in the notification area (the lower-right corner of the screen next to the clock), or click the Start button and choose All Programs⇨Yahoo! Messenger⇨Yahoo! Messenger. You see the Login dialog box, where you enter your Yahoo! ID and password.

Training Messenger

You can make Messenger behave properly when you turn on your computer and appear the way you want while you're using it. To do so, choose Login⇨ Preferences and select the General category. In the General category are check boxes related to basic operating selections, as shown in Figure 7-2. Use the check boxes to do the following:

✦ **Automatically Start Yahoo! Messenger:** Selecting this check box puts Messenger in your startup folder, from which it boots automatically when you turn on your computer and load Windows.

✦ **Stand By and Wait until I Connect to the Internet:** Whether you set Messenger to launch automatically or not, this setting determines whether Messenger attempts to connect with Yahoo! even if your computer isn't yet online. Select this check box to put the brakes on, forcing Messenger to wait until you manually connect with the Internet.

✦ **Keep Yahoo! Messenger on Top of All Other Applications:** Select this check box if you want Messenger to be visible on your screen at all times. If you find running in this mode inconvenient (it blocks your view of other on-screen windows), you can deselect it at any time.

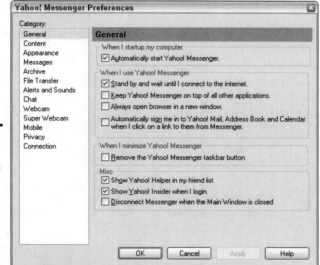

Figure 7-2:
General preferences determine how Messenger behaves when started.

Book III
Chapter 7

Instant Messaging
with Yahoo! Messenger

✦ **Always Open Browser in a New Window:** I like to leave this check box selected. When Messenger uses your browser for something — getting news stories or sports scores, for example — this selection ensures that a fresh browser pops open so that you don't lose whatever you're looking at in the current browser window.

✦ **Automatically Sign Me In to Yahoo! Mail, Address Book and Calendar When I Click on a Link to Them from Messenger:** Select this check box if you want your ID and password to apply to other areas of Yahoo!. This way, you don't have to enter your ID and password all over again.

✦ **Disconnect Messenger When the Main Window Is Closed:** Shuts down Messenger when you close the Messenger window. This saves you the trouble of disconnecting manually from Yahoo! Messenger.

If you're not sure what you did and want to start again from scratch, click Cancel to close the Preferences window, open it again, and begin anew. After you make your selections, click OK.

Making New Friends

Friends are at the heart of Yahoo! Messenger. You can use Messenger to search for new friends and of course to get to know current friends better. Follow these steps to find new friends on Messenger:

1. With Yahoo! Messenger connected, click the Add button (refer to Figure 7-1).

The Add a Friend dialog box appears.

2. Select an option button that describes how you want to search for your friend.

Depending on which option you choose, you see a dialog box with fields to fill in, as shown in Figure 7-3.

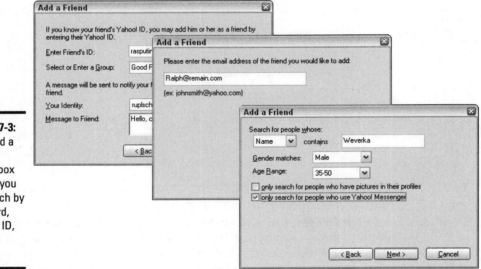

Figure 7-3:
The Add a Friend dialog box allows you to search by keyword, Yahoo! ID, or real name.

3. Fill in the dialog box and click Next.

If Yahoo! can find a match, the next dialog box gives you an opportunity to invite the person to be on your friends list.

4. Enter a message to the person and click Finish.

Yahoo! sends an invitation to your prospective friend. If he or she agrees to be on your friends list, the name appears in your Yahoo! Messenger window.

Of course, you can use Messenger's Add button to include friends in your group after meeting them in some other fashion. You can also encourage friends that you know outside Yahoo! to get Messenger and join the party.

The time is bound to come when you want to remove a friend from your group. It's not necessarily an insult (although if a fellow Trekkie called you a Denubian slime devil, you should dump that person immediately).

Sometimes keeping a friend on your list isn't worthwhile because the friend is rarely online. Whatever reason motivates the removal of a friend, it's easily accomplished:

1. When Yahoo! Messenger is connected, right-click the name of any friend.

If Messenger is set to display only friends who are currently connected, choose the View menu and deselect Show Only Online Friends.

2. Choose Delete.

A small window opens, asking whether you're sure you want to make like Tony Soprano and delete this person.

3. Click the OK button.

After a second, the deleted name disappears from your list of friends.

Chatting with Friends

You can chat with other Messenger users in three ways:

✦ **Online text chatting:** This is traditional chatting, using an Instant Message window to trade lines of typed text with another connected user.

✦ **Offline text chatting:** You can send an instant message to anyone on your Friends list even if that person is not presently connected. If your friend is unconnected, the message is stored until he or she next connects to Messenger.

✦ **Online group chatting:** You can pull more than one friend into a chat, which is then called a *conference*. Conferences operate in both text and voice mode simultaneously. It's outrageously cool.

The most typical way of beginning a Messenger chat is to send an instant message to a connected friend. You open an Instant Message window in three ways:

✦ Double-click any friend's name. (The friend can be connected or unconnected, but don't expect an instant response if he or she is offline.)

✦ Right-click a friend's name and choose Send a Message.

✦ Click a friend's name and then press Ctrl+S.

Whichever way you open an Instant Message window, Figure 7-4 illustrates what it looks like. The Instant Message window is easy enough to use — at the most basic level, you just type a message and click Send (or hit the Enter key). The text of your online conversation can be seen in the top half of the window.

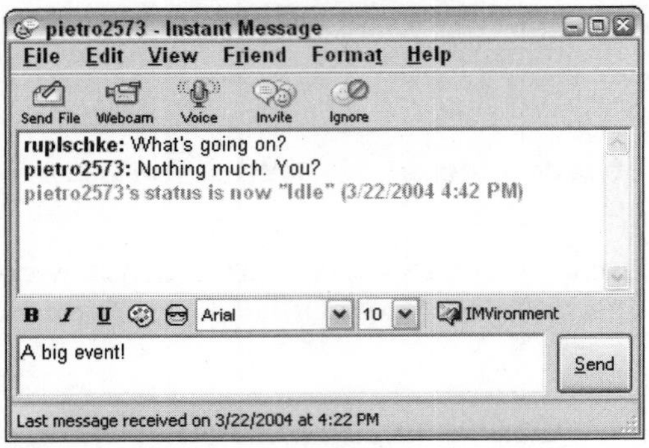

Figure 7-4:
The Instant
Message
window,
where chats
take place.

The Messenger Control Center

Although many people are satisfied with Yahoo! Messenger as a social tool,
it's far more than just a mobile chat room. Seven tabs at the bottom, plus a
hidden search engine, unlock its information resources. The tabs aren't
identified with text, but they divulge their identities when you run your
mouse cursor over them. Here's what those seven tabs do:

✦ **Friends:** The leftmost tab opens the area that I describe in most of
the previous sections of this chapter. This is where your Friends
groups appear and where you initiate instant messages and voice chat
sessions.

✦ **Stocks:** The Stocks tab, second from the left, displays any stock prices
that you selected in the Stock Portfolios of My Yahoo!. (It doesn't display the more advanced portfolios from Yahoo! Finance.) If you haven't
created a stock portfolio in My Yahoo!, this tab displays a simple default
selection of stock prices. To adjust your portfolio, visit your My Yahoo!
page and click the Edit button in the Portfolios module.

✦ **Calendar:** This tab opens your Yahoo! Calendar, where you can schedule tasks and appointments.

✦ **News:** As with the Stocks tab, the News section links to your settings in
My Yahoo! and displays the same headline links, as shown in Figure 7-5.
In this tab, Messenger provides an Edit button for making alterations,
which get applied to both My Yahoo! and Yahoo! Messenger. When you
click a headline link in Messenger, your browser displays the full story.

✦ **Weather:** Clicking this tab shows you a bare-bones weather report.

✦ **Address Book:** This tab shows addresses you entered for your Yahoo!
friends.

✦ **Overview:** The rightmost tab provides a recap of what's happening in
your account. The list notifies you of new e-mail that's arrived at your
Yahoo! address, new messages in your Yahoo! Personals Mailbox, alerts
from your Yahoo! Calendar settings, stock alerts if you've established
alert parameters in your My Yahoo! portfolio, and a Friends Online
summary.

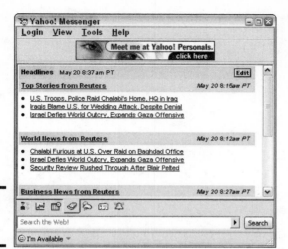

Figure 7-5:
The
News tab.

Chapter 8: Passing the Time at Yahoo! Games

In This Chapter

✔ Joining and watching games

✔ Creating your own game tables

Yahoo! isn't *all* fun and games, but one portion is devoted to pure interactive recreation, and that's Yahoo! Games. If you don't care for the violence of computer games, you have nothing to worry about. The most violent thing that transpires at Yahoo! Games is a checkmate. Yahoo! Games features board and card games that you can play with other Yahoo! members (or against the Yahoo! computer in some cases) in real time. This chapter walks you through one game, illustrating the basic gaming software common to most of the games.

The bantering that goes on in some of the game rooms is, shall we say, uncouth. If you are offended by foul language and all-around rudeness, think twice about playing some of these games. And if you don't want your children to be exposed to this kind of thing, steer them clear of Yahoo! game rooms.

Playing a Game

To visit the Yahoo! game room, click the Games link on the Yahoo! home page or go to this URL:

`http://games.yahoo.com`

Scroll down the screen to see a list of all the games that Yahoo! offers, as shown in Figure 8-1.

Most Yahoo! Games operate in basically the same way but with variations due to the different natures of the games themselves.

The following steps take you through the process of beginning a game of checkers (or watching a game without playing). Other games differ in cosmetic details, but the same basic windows apply to them all:

1. **On the Yahoo! Games main page, click the Checkers link.**

The Checkers game page appears. Each game page lists several rooms that you can enter immediately. On some game pages, rooms are grouped by playing level: Beginner, Intermediate, and Advanced. The number in parentheses beside game names indicates how many games are currently being played.

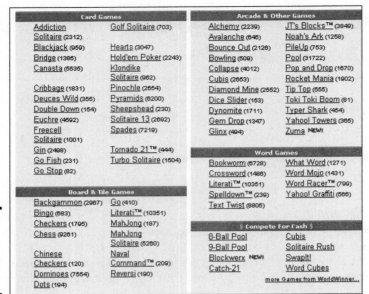

Figure 8-1:
Games list
in the
Yahoo!
game room.

2. **Click a room (or a level of play first and then a room).**

A Java applet download starts, which might take a minute or two to complete through telephone modems or a few seconds through a cable modem. The next thing that you see is a room window, independent of your browser window. Figure 8-2 shows the Checkers room window.

3. **Click any Watch button to observe a game in progress, or click any Join button to play.**

A new window opens — the game window — independent of both the room window and your browser window. In two-person games, such as checkers, clicking a Join button matches you with the listed opponent, and you begin the game by each clicking a Start button. In group games, such as Poker, the Join button gets you a seat at the table — you can also click the Watch button to observe the table and then click the Join button from there.

Rules for the games can be found on most of the game pages in your browser window. Generally, Yahoo! Games assumes a basic familiarity with the rules and with navigating the game window. To play board games, click and drag pieces from one position to another. The poker game window supplies preset buttons for calling, raising, and folding.

The room window contains the more complex set of features of the two Java windows. As you can see in Figure 8-2, the room window packs a busy screen into a small space. (You can resize the window.) Here are some important points about this window:

✦ **Color-coded for your convenience:** The color-coded ratings in the left sidebar are maintained automatically in Yahoo! Games. Whenever you enter a game room for the first time, you are given a provisional rating that moves up and down as you win and lose games. Notice how each name in the Name column has a rating color next to it.

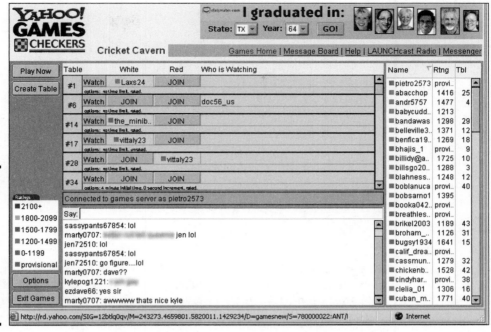

Figure 8-2:
A Checkers room window, where you select a partner to play with or a game to watch.

✦ **Set the table:** The Create Table button lets you establish a new playing station, which other people can join and to which you can invite anyone to play.

✦ **Organize the columns:** Look at the Name, Rtng, and Tbl columns. A small arrow appears next to one of these columns at all times. Click the header of any column to organize the names according to that column's criterion, and the arrow moves next to the column header. This feature is especially helpful in listing potential players in order of their rating.

✦ **Link away:** All the items on the link menu near the top of the room window (except for Messenger) open browser windows to various Yahoo! locations. For example, the Games Home link takes you to the Yahoo! Games main page. The Message Board link surfs your browser to the relevant board in Yahoo! Messages.

✦ **Get player info:** Double-click a player's name to pop open a Player Information window (see Figure 8-3) that tells you the player's game history and rating. You can also send an instant message to that person. Select the Ignore check box if you don't want to receive an instant message from that person. Clicking the Ping button sends a data pulse to that person's server and back to your server — a sort of Internet radar. The Ping test is for determining how much delay exists between two network points. Why have the Ping test in Yahoo! Games? Because when playing timed games, it's important that a quick network connection exists between the two players. If the Ping test results in a delay of more than a few seconds, frustrating lags might slow a game with that person. Clicking the Profile button opens a browser window displaying that person's Yahoo! Profile.

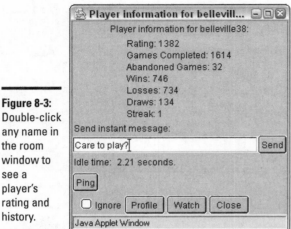

Figure 8-3: Double-click any name in the room window to see a player's rating and history.

You can get involved in a game in two ways: Join someone's table or create your own table. You accomplish both in the room window. Click the Join button of any room that needs a player or click the Create Table button in the left sidebar to establish a new game.

Playing a Checkers Game

Creating your own table is the only way to set the game timer (if one exists for that game) and invite particular players to join you. The following list continues in the Checkers windows, but the steps are essentially the same for the other games:

1. In the room window, click the Create Table button.

A game window opens (see Figure 8-4). In some games, a pop-up box asking for timing and other settings precedes the game window.

2. Using the Table Type drop-down list, select Public, Protected, or Private.

Public tables can be joined by anyone who wants to play and can be watched by anyone who wants to observe a game in progress. Protected tables can be watched by anyone, but players can join only by invitation. Private tables are invisible to other members and can be joined or observed only by invitation.

3. Click the Set Timer button to establish a time limit for games.

The default timer setting for checkers is unlimited time for the complete game, with a limit of five minutes per move. (It takes deep strategic thinking to ponder a checkers move for five minutes. Falling asleep helps, too.) Clicking the Set Timer button pops open a Set Timer window. The Initial time setting is an overall time limit for a game. The Increment is the number of seconds added to each player's clock after every move. (Called a *Fisher clock* in chess, this timing feature prevents a quick-moving player from ever running out of time.) Select the check box to set a five-minute-per-move deadline. After entering your settings, click OK.

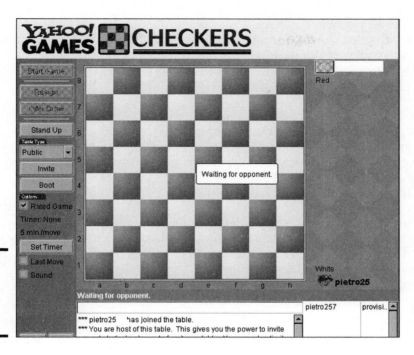

**Book III
Chapter 8**

Passing the Time at Yahoo! Games

Figure 8-4:
A newly
created
Checkers
table.

4. **Select the Sound check box.**

   This way, a bell notifies you when it's your turn to play.

5. **Click the Invite button to ask another player to your table.**

   A pop-up window appears with a list of players currently in the game
   room. As in the room window, you can sort the names by rating — just
   click the Rtng column header. If a player has a table number next to his
   or her name, that player might be engaged in a game. Click a player's
   name once and then click the Invite button. A pop-up window appears
   on that player's screen with an invitation to join you. The invited player
   then clicks the Accept or Decline button.

6. **Click a Sit button to take your place at the table.**

   In checkers (and other board games), you get your choice of color. In
   multiplayer card games, you get your choice of position around the
   table. Click the Stand Up button to relinquish your place at the table.

The Boot button doesn't simulate your slamming a shoe on the table. It
does give you the power to remove a player from your table. Click any
player's name and click the Boot button to give that person the heave-ho.
The expelled person receives a "You have been removed from the table"
notice, and the game window disappears from that person's screen. Be
careful! It's actually possible to boot yourself from your own table — an
ego-bruising experience.

Throughout Yahoo! Games, you might see *Ladder rooms*. This feature brings
an element of competitiveness to the game rooms. Ladders are session
rankings for people who want to see how they match against other players
in the room. As you play games, Yahoo! moves you up and down the room

ladder as you win and lose. It's a fun feature, especially if you plan to play several quick games during a single session. However, don't confuse Ladders with rankings. Rankings are adjusted in all rooms and carry over from one session to another. Ladders exist only in marked rooms and apply to only a single session.

Feeling antisocial? Do you prefer solitary games? The Yahoo! Crossword (click the Crossword link on the Yahoo! Games main page) is a single-person game. Additionally, you can play Hearts against computerized opponents. From any Hearts room window, create a table by clicking the Create Table button and invite three robots to play with you. Robots are identified as *~robot1, ~robot2,* and *~robot3.*

Scroll down the main games page to see more games that you can play. Of particular interest is Baseball, which is a fantasy game based on statistics, in which you can join a league and let Yahoo! manage all the statistical accounting and bookkeeping for you.

Chapter 9: Posting Your Web Page through GeoCities

In This Chapter

✓ **Starting your free GeoCities account**

✓ **Designing a Web page quickly with PageWizards**

✓ **Constructing a Web page easily with PageBuilder**

✓ **Becoming a power Webmaster**

What defines your online home? Your e-mail address? Your Yahoo! ID, which identifies you in Messenger? Your My Yahoo! page? In the physical world, your home defines your permanent presence. What's the comparable home in the virtual world?

Nothing quite says cyber-home like a Web site. A site may be a single page or a complex labyrinth of linked pages. Yahoo!, complete online provider that it is, offers a free service for establishing your Web-based home. This service is called Yahoo! GeoCities, and this chapter takes you through getting started in GeoCities and building a Web page.

Creating a GeoCities-Hosted Web Site

GeoCities began as an independent community whose members enjoyed free page-hosting services. Yahoo! left the basic idea intact when it acquired GeoCities and then repackaged the service into a clearer, more coherent interface. Yahoo! GeoCities is still free (for the basic service) and provides all the help that you need to build a simple or complex online home.

All you need is a Yahoo! ID (also free, as I describe in Chapter 1 of Book III) to establish your space in GeoCities. What exactly do you get? Primarily, some server space. *Server space* is computer memory on the GeoCities computers, in which you store your pages and the files (such as pictures) that your pages use. Everybody gets 15MB (megabytes) of server space, free of charge.

The first thing to do is establish your free GeoCities account. Then, whenever you're ready, use the later sections of this chapter to help you build a page or three. You must be signed in to your Yahoo! ID to use GeoCities. First, follow these steps to begin your account:

1. **On the Yahoo! home page, click the GeoCities link.**

   You can also go to GeoCities directly at the following URL:

   ```
   http://geocities.yahoo.com
   ```

   You see the Welcome page, which explains the different services for creating a Web site that you can get from Yahoo! Geocities. This book focuses on the free service.

2. **Look for the Free link and click it.**

   You can find this link in the Get Started area on the left. The link whisks you to the Yahoo! GeoCities Free page, which explains free Web site hosting in more detail.

3. **Click the Sign Up link.**

4. **From the list, select which kind of advertisements will appear on your Web site, and then click Continue.**

   Your Web site is free, but you still have to pay the piper in the form of advertisements that appear on your site.

5. **Click the Build Your Web Site Now link.**

   You see the Welcome to Yahoo! GeoCities page shown in Figure 9-1. Now you're getting somewhere! This page shows the URL of your new Web site:

   ```
   www.geocities.com/your Yahoo! ID
   ```

Figure 9-1:
The starting point for building and improving upon a GeoCities Web site.

Building Your GeoCities Web Site

At any time, you can get to your Yahoo! GeoCities page for building Web sites (refer to Figure 9-1) by going to the Yahoo! home page, signing in, and clicking the GeoCities link.

You might think that you need to know about HTML, the underlying language of all Web pages, to have a Web page of your own. But it ain't so. (By the same token, you don't need good grammar to write books, apparently.) Yahoo! GeoCities provides the following methods of creating pages, both of which are available on your Yahoo! GeoCities page for building Web sites:

✦ **Yahoo! PageWizards:** This method of page building is the easiest. The PageWizards let you choose a basic design from a preset selection, and then you slap together a simple page on the basis of a few pieces of information supplied by you.

✦ **Yahoo! PageBuilder:** PageBuilder is a Java program that lets you drag text and graphic boxes around the page, and then it publishes the result with all the correct HTML code in the background. The program is reasonably powerful and very easy to operate if you have some experience using computer software.

A Quick and Easy Page

When you want to get started fast, when you want to get a basic page up on the Web without fuss, who you gonna call? PageWizards! Remember, this service is absolutely free — free of charge and free of hassle. Within 15 minutes from the time you first surf into Yahoo! GeoCities (signed in with your ID), you can have a Web site published and ready to show your friends — even if you have absolutely no Web-page experience.

Using PageWizards is probably the best way for novices to start. If it seems too limiting, you can always move your work to PageBuilder, which offers many more tools and options. The following is the simplest path to your first Web page. After Step 4, the details of the process may vary depending on which PageWizard you choose.

1. **Go to your Yahoo! GeoCities page at the following address:**

    http://geocities.yahoo.com

2. **Click the Yahoo! PageWizards link.**

   The PageWizards page displays several templates from which to choose the basic design of your page. Each design is a separate PageWizard. The Quick Start templates are slightly easier than the Popular Themes templates.

3. **Click any PageWizard.**

   A new PageWizard window opens with simple instructions for proceeding.

4. **Click Begin.**

Book III
Chapter 9

Posting Your Web Page
through GeoCities

As you move through the PageWizard's instruction pages, you can back up at any time by clicking Back. Clicking the Preview button on any page opens a Web browser window and displays your site in progress. Clicking Cancel gets you out of the wizard entirely and doesn't save your page.

5. Select a look for your page, and then click Next.

I know what you're thinking — you already chose a look on the main PageWizards page. That's true, and now you have a chance to change your mind. Click any option button to see that style.

6. Enter a page title and any text that you want on the page, and then click Next.

This is your only opportunity to write some text, so make it Pulitzer-worthy. (Actually, immortal prose isn't as important as basic information.)

7. Select a picture for your page, type a caption, and click the Next button.

This is the picture page. In the PageWizards, you may place only one picture on the page. You can use the default picture that comes with the style or upload a photo from your hard drive. If you have a scanned picture of yourself, that's a possibility. The PageWizards accept pictures in JPG and GIF formats. Click the Upload New Image button, which opens a small window, and then click the Browse button to select a file from your computer — the PageWizard uploads it automatically.

8. Enter some links and their names in the appropriate text boxes, and then click Next.

You don't need to have links on your page, but doing so is a long-standing Web tradition. The PageWizard comes with default links, and guess what? They all lead to Yahoo! destinations. (See Figure 9-2.) That's a surprise! Feel free to take those links out and replace them with your own favorites. You must know the URL of your links for this feature to work correctly for visitors.

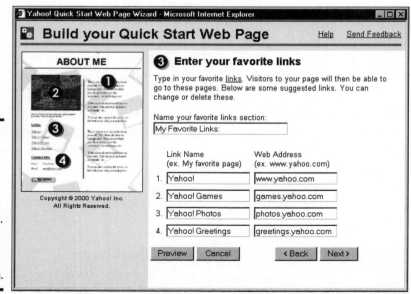

Figure 9-2: The Page Wizard window on which you assign links for your site. Feel free to remove the default Yahoo! links.

9. **Enter your personal information, and then click Next.**

This page is where you put your name and e-mail address if you want that information to appear. You also have the option of placing the I'm Online indicator on the page — this icon, which appears throughout the community portions of Yahoo!, lets your page visitors know when you're signed in to Yahoo! through Messenger or Yahoo! Chat.

10. **Name your page and then click Next.**

The name that you select here becomes the last part of your URL.

11. **Click Done.**

This final page spells out your new site's URL as a link, which you can click to see your page.

The information fields that you fill in during the PageWizard process are optional. You can always leave them blank and move onto the next page. Of course, if you do that too often, you end up with one mighty boring Web page. But the point is that nothing is mandatory — you're not required to upload a picture, assign links, or enter your contact information.

The result of your PageWizard work is a simple, informative personal page. (See Figure 9-3 for an example.) Note the little Y!GeoCities window in the upper-right corner of the page. That's an ad. You (and any other visitor to your page) can remove it by clicking the small X in the corner, but it always reappears when someone surfs to your page, even if that person removed it the last time. You can't remove this small promotion at the code level, but you can get it off your page by using the GeoGuide, which I describe later in this chapter.

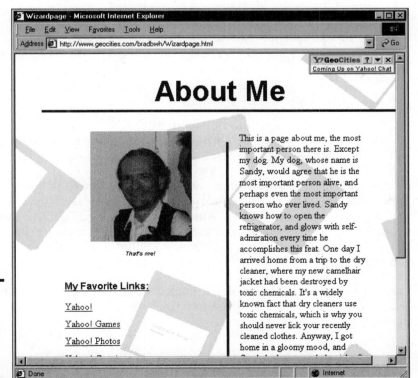

Figure 9-3:
A simple site built with Yahoo! Page Wizards.

You can't add anything extra to your page within PageWizards, though you can change your text, links, picture, and personal information at any time. You can't add a second picture, place a new text box, or put new headings on the page. If you get ready to bring your site to the next level, move to Yahoo! PageBuilder. See the next section for a profoundly meaningful discussion of that program.

Page Construction Made Easy

Yahoo! PageBuilder is an intermediate tool — much more sophisticated than PageWizards but still sparing the rigors of HTML code. Moving from PageWizards to PageBuilder is a natural progression, and the slight learning curve rewards users with much greater power and flexibility. Pages that you design in PageBuilder can be far more interesting and varied than PageWizard pages.

You can use PageBuilder to start a page from scratch or to upgrade any page originally built with a PageWizard. You can start a new PageBuilder page even if you created PageWizard pages and want to leave them as they are.

The following steps get you started with Yahoo! PageBuilder:

1. **On the Yahoo! GeoCities main page, click the Yahoo! PageBuilder link.**

2. **On the next page, select a theme or click the Launch PageBuilder link.**

   PageBuilder provides pre-built templates within which you can enter your content, just as PageWizards do. The PageBuilder templates (sometimes called *themes*) are more complex than PageWizard templates, and they can be much more flexibly adjusted. If you click a theme link, that template is displayed — if you open PageBuilder from that page, it automatically starts with that template ready to be filled in. If you launch PageBuilder without clicking a template link, the program starts off with a blank page.

   One way or the other, launch PageBuilder at this point. A small window with the heading Yahoo! PageBuilder Running pops open. Don't close that small window while working in PageBuilder.

Yahoo! PageBuilder might take as long as five minutes to download to your computer if you have a 28.8K modem. After it opens (see Figure 9-4), PageBuilder operates just like a Windows application. The first thing that you see is a blank page (if you didn't select a template and this is the first time you've used PageBuilder), a template page (if you selected a template), or one of your previously edited pages (if you've used PageBuilder before).

To start a new page in PageBuilder, click the New icon on the toolbar. To work on a page that you've already created, either in PageBuilder or PageWizards, follow these steps:

1. In PageBuilder, click the Open icon on the toolbar.

The Open Page window displays a list of all the pages that you've created in the GeoCities account of your current Yahoo! ID.

2. In the Open Page window, double-click any page.

That page opens in PageBuilder. Everything on the page is translated to PageBuilder's underlying language, so you can manipulate page elements in PageBuilder fashion (see the following section) even if you didn't create the page in PageBuilder.

You should know about two things in PageBuilder right away and remember them as you work. First, the Preview button is your new best friend. Use this button at any time to see what your page looks like in a Web browser. Using the Preview button is the only way to find out how some of the interactive elements actually work. Second, save your work frequently. If you undergo a computer crash or lose your Internet connection, your page in progress isn't automatically saved. Click Save to name your page and save it.

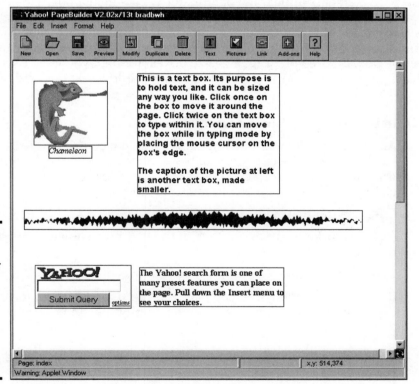

Figure 9-4:
A Yahoo!
PageBuilder
work in
progress.
You can
drag each
element
around the
screen.

Dragging stuff around in PageBuilder

Unlike the PageWizards system, Yahoo! PageBuilder doesn't walk you through the creation of a page. The tools are easy to use, but you must initiate the placement of every page element. Those elements include

✦ Portions of text

✦ Pictures

✦ Buttons and bullets

✦ Horizontal and vertical lines for borders

✦ Games

✦ Animated images

✦ Information elements, such as a clock, a page-hit counter, and a search form

✦ A message board

✦ Interactive forms that allow visitors to send information to you

All the elements offered in the program, with the exception of text, are pre-built. No expertise is required to add a game or a message board to your page. Just select it from the menu (keep reading this part of the chapter to find out how) and plug it in.

All page elements appear in PageBuilder enclosed in a box. This box is PageBuilder's unique feature and enables you to design your page without worrying about HTML code. You can drag around every box on the page and drop them somewhere else on the page. Furthermore, you can resize every box. Before you drag or resize boxes, though, you need to place at least one element on the page. Here's how to add a text box and put text into it:

1. In PageBuilder, choose Insert⇨Basics⇨Text.

An empty rectangular box appears on the page. (See Figure 9-5.) At the same time, the PageBuilder toolbar changes to a text-formatting toolbar with buttons and drop-down lists for changing the font, size, boldness, color, and other qualities of the displayed text.

2. Click inside the text box.

A place-marking cursor appears in the text box, showing that it's ready to receive text.

3. Type your text.

Be as brief or verbose as you like. You can use text boxes for major expositions, simple picture captions, or anything in between.

4. Click anywhere outside the text box.

The box changes to a single, thin blue line, ready to be moved or resized.

Inserting text requires more work from you than inserting any other element. That's because you must type the text. You can't copy and paste text from another program.

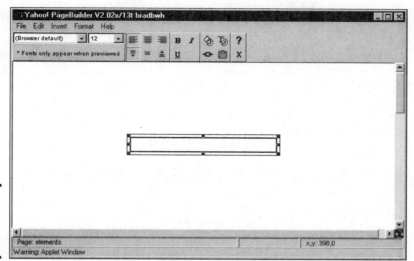

Figure 9-5:
An empty
text box in
PageBuilder.

After you have a text box with text in it (or any other type of element), you're ready to move it around and resize it. The following steps walk you through both procedures, illustrating how to move a text box from above a horizontal divider to below it, and then showing how to resize the text box to the width of the divider. The divider is in a box, too, just like any other element, but it remains in place during these steps.

1. **Click any text box, holding the mouse button down.**

The text box changes to thicker lines with eight small squares spaced around it, as shown in Figure 9-6. You use those little squares to resize the box.

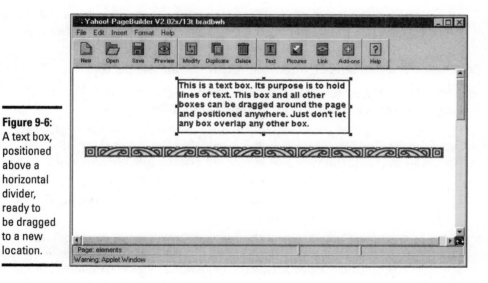

Figure 9-6:
A text box,
positioned
above a
horizontal
divider,
ready to
be dragged
to a new
location.

2. Still holding down the mouse button, drag the box below the horizontal divider.

When passing across the horizontal divider, a bright red grid appears in the area of overlap. Never let two boxes remain in an overlapped position — no red grids should be showing in the final version of your page. Overlapped boxes make for gobbledygook on the page, as some material is obscured. Figure 9-7 shows the text box in its new position below the horizontal divider.

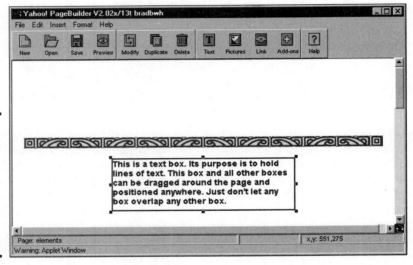

Figure 9-7:
The text box after being dragged to its new position below the horizontal divider.

3. Position the mouse cursor over one of the small squares on the right edge of the text box.

When the mouse is positioned correctly, the cursor displays a short line with an arrow at each end. That cursor is your sign that you can grab the box's edge by clicking and holding the mouse button.

4. Click the small square and hold down the mouse button.

5. Drag the right edge of the text box to the right until the edge is aligned with the edge of the horizontal divider.

Of course, you can stop dragging at any point — I'm aligning with the edge of the divider for illustrative purposes. Note that the text in the box adjusts to fit the new box size. Text always fills out the width of a larger box, leaving room at the bottom.

6. Drag the left edge of the text box to the left until the edge is aligned with the edge of the horizontal divider.

At this point, the lower half of the text box has a lot of room because the text has adjusted upward into the larger width. (See Figure 9-8.) You can drag the bottom edge upward to close that space or leave it alone. Leaving the space there creates a buffer into which no other page element can be placed without overlapping boxes. (You can also type more text by clicking your mouse cursor inside the text box and typing.)

7. Click anywhere outside the text box to remove the resizing squares.

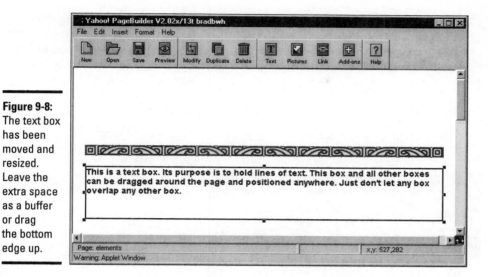

Figure 9-8:
The text box has been moved and resized. Leave the extra space as a buffer or drag the bottom edge up.

When you resize a graphic element box, the picture inside stretches or squashes to fit the new box size. This adjustment distorts clipart, so it's generally a good idea to leave those boxes at their original size. Of course, you can move them around the page just like text boxes without distorting them.

You can't perform a cut-and-paste or copy-and-paste operation by using the Windows or Mac Clipboard with PageBuilder. In other words, you can't copy text from another Windows or Mac program into a PageBuilder text box. This limitation is because PageBuilder is a Java program, not a Windows or Mac program. PageBuilder has its own Clipboard, however, and you can cut text from one text box and paste it into another text box. You lose the formatting (font, size, and color) of the text when you paste it, but you can always reformat it. Doing so is easier than typing the text all over again in a new text box, which would also require formatting.

You can delete any element on your page. Just click that element and then click the Delete button on the toolbar. (You can also press Delete.)

Choosing stuff for your page

Yahoo! PageBuilder puts quite a bit of designer content up for grabs. Diving deep into the Insert menu reveals a large library of graphics and interactive elements. I can't comprehensively cover PageBuilder's content without devoting the entire book to this one program. Instead, this section explores the high points of the three categories of content in the Insert menu.

Basics

Basics cover the basics. You can easily create an entire Web site by using only the choices in the Basics portion of the Insert menu. This is where you find text boxes, picture boxes, border lines, backgrounds, buttons and bullets, and a page-hit counter. I describe the operation of text boxes in the preceding section.

PageBuilder dishes up plenty of pictures, both of the clipart and photographic variety. You can also upload your own picture files and place them on your page. If you have no pictures of your own but want to spice up your page with graphics, PageBuilder rushes to the rescue with an extensive library of free choices. Here's how to browse in that graphics library:

1. **In PageBuilder, choose Insert⇨Basics⇨Pictures.**

The Select Picture dialog box appears, as shown in Figure 9-9.

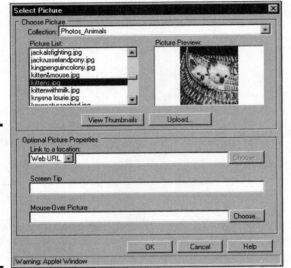

Figure 9-9: You can select from several libraries of graphic photos and clipart. It's all free.

2. **In the Collection drop-down list, select a picture group.**

3. **In the Picture List area, select any picture file.**

A small version of the picture appears in the Picture Preview pane. You can view thumbnail versions of all the pictures in the currently selected Collection by clicking the View Thumbnails button. Clicking any thumbnail displays a slightly larger view in the Picture Preview pane.

4. **Click OK.**

The Select Picture dialog box disappears, and your selected picture appears on the page that you're currently building. You can move it around the page; resizing is usually a bad idea because it distorts the picture.

Three other features appear under Optional Picture Properties in the Select Picture dialog box, as shown previously in Figure 9-9. They are

✦ **Link to a Location:** Activating this feature turns the picture into a hyperlink on your page. That means if a visitor clicks the link, something happens. Use this property to determine what happens. Use the drop-down list to link the picture to any URL on the Web, your e-mail address, or another of your Yahoo! GeoCities pages. The Choose button is active when you link to another one of your pages.

+ **Screen Tip:** This feature displays a small pop-up flag when a visitor runs the mouse cursor over your picture. Enter text in this field to determine what that pop-up flag says.

+ **Mouse-Over Picture:** This feature lets you choose a second picture that appears when a visitor runs the mouse cursor over your first picture. The second picture flashes into the same space that's occupied by the first picture. The first picture returns when the visitor moves the mouse cursor away. Click the Choose button to select the second picture from the Select a Picture dialog box.

Uploading a picture from your computer is fairly simple:

1. In PageBuilder, choose Insert⇨Basics⇨Upload Picture.

The Upload Image dialog box appears.

2. Click the Browse button.

The Choose File dialog box appears.

3. Select a picture file in GIF or JPG format to upload, and then click Open.

Alternatively, you can just double-click the picture file to upload.

4. Click the Upload button.

PageBuilder copies the picture file from your computer to your GeoCities server space and adds the picture as an element on your page in progress.

When uploading pictures to your page, copies of the pictures are stored in your Yahoo! GeoCities server space. You have 15MB of space, which can hold a lot of pictures in most cases. If you do lots of uploading or if your picture files are large (hundreds of kilobytes), you can fill up your available memory. Use File Manager to manage your server space.

Other portions of the Basics menu include the following:

+ **Background:** A background can be a simple color selection of a design. Some backgrounds contain a left-hand border. PageBuilder provides a large selection of backgrounds, which you can preview and select just like you do pictures.

+ **Background music:** You can set music to play when a visitor arrives at your page. As of this writing, PageBuilder provides the menu selection but no music selections. Possibly by the time you read this, PageBuilder will be equipped with MIDI and small WAV files to choose from.

+ **Buttons and bullets:** You may use these small graphic elements to offset and emphasize text.

+ **Horizontal and vertical lines:** These are custom-designed graphic dividers with which you can organize your page.

+ **Counter:** This automatic gadget counts the number of visitors to your page and displays the result. Most people put their counters near the bottom of their pages.

Instant Info

The Instant Info selection in the Insert menu contains information modules that deliver some time-sensitive data to your visitors. You can add a clock, a stock charter, a Yahoo! search form, a birthday countdown, a mortgage calculator, and a few other gadgets. These info perks are easy to place on your page. Simply select one from the menu, and it appears. The modules don't actually work within PageBuilder — you can't, for example, call up a stock chart — but they appear just as they do on the Web page. When your site goes live, these things work just fine.

Forms and Scripts

The final category of the Insert menu invites you to place interactive text-entry forms, check boxes, and radio buttons on your site. When visitors use these features, an e-mail containing their entries is automatically sent to the e-mail address listed in your Yahoo! profile for the ID currently in use as your GeoCities identifier. (That's a bit complex. Basically, whatever ID you used to sign in to GeoCities gets the e-mail containing text entries and check box results.)

These forms, which use invisible segments of code called *scripts,* are great for compiling a mailing list or running a survey. If you know HTML or want to copy a script from another page, choose HTML code.

Two more points to remember about Yahoo! PageBuilder. First, you can't use the program to construct pages that reside anywhere outside GeoCities. You simply can't save a page to any location except your GeoCities server space. Second, remember that the PageBuilder templates provide a good starting point, and you can edit and alter them with all the power and flexibility that you have when starting from scratch.

Chapter 10: Going, Going, Gone to Yahoo! Auctions

In This Chapter

✔ Finding an auction and bidding

✔ Snapping up the best bargains

Millions of people have discovered the odd, unique, exhilarating kick of winning an online auction.

When you think about it, you might find it strange that buying something through an auction is called *winning*. Is it a sign of the sweepstakes-oriented, consumer-intensive culture? Certainly, buying through an auction can be a victory when you get a bargain. Some products sold in this fashion, though, don't have fixed prices, and in those cases it's not clear whether you've secured a bargain or participated in an expensive garage sale.

Two types of Internet auction sites are available. *House auctions* provide the merchandise and accept bids on it. These sites stock their own inventory, which can range from new products to second-run items, overstocked merchandise, and used or refurbished equipment. *User-to-user auctions* simply provide the cyberspace and the software for bidding and selling — the visitors supply the goods. Yahoo! Auctions is this second type of auction house. You can use it to buy from other individuals or sell your own stuff in an auction format. (eBay, the other user-to-user auction house on the Internet, is the subject of Book IV.)

In this chapter, I provide the details on bidding on items and selling stuff in your own auction.

Finding Auctions and Bidding

The first step is to find the Yahoo! Auctions main page. Easy enough. Just click the Auctions link on the Yahoo! home page or go directly to

```
http://auctions.yahoo.com
```

You need a Yahoo! ID to buy or sell in Yahoo! Auctions.

Yahoo! Auctions is organized in directory fashion (no surprise), like most other portions of Yahoo!. The Yahoo! Auctions main page, which is shown in Figure 10-1, presents a directory of auction categories in the left sidebar. Featured auctions are shown in the center portion of the page. You get involved by either browsing or searching for an auction. If you're wandering around for the first time or you're new to Internet auctions in general, you might want to take the directory route. Just click a main topic area to begin prowling around the directory.

Figure 10-1:
The Yahoo!
Auctions
main page.

Some directory topics extend several layers down before you see any auction listings. Subcategory pages get you close to specific types of objects being sold. Figure 10-2, the auction page for Buffalo nickels, shows a sixth-level page of the auctions directory. You can tell how many levels deep you are by looking at the categories along the top of the page.

Search forms are located on every directory page in Yahoo! Auctions. Use them to enter specific items that you're looking to buy, such as *keyboard synthesizers, baby clothes,* or *whitney houston cd.* (As you can see in these examples, you don't need to use capital letters when you search.) Be aware, though, that Yahoo! matches your keywords against the descriptive text of the auction pages, not just the auction titles, and also that sometimes just one keyword is matched. I often search with the keywords *cd collections,* hoping to scarf up lots of music from somebody liquidating his or her collection. Inevitably, the search results match with computer systems for sale with CD drives.

The auction directory pages (refer to Figure 10-2) show you the auction name, the current bid, the remaining time in the auction, and the number of bids if anyone has done any bidding at all. (Because Yahoo! Auctions holds so many auctions, many transpire without a single bid.) Lack of bids can indicate a too-high minimum price or a great bargain that has become lost in the crowd. To see an auction page in progress, click any auction title.

The auction page, shown in Figure 10-3, presents a bundle of information plus an opportunity to place a bid. Here are the major points to look for:

✦ Look at the Seller Info area on the left for the types of payment accepted and shipping information.

✦ Click the Seller's Current Auctions link (or the seller's name) to go to a page with all the seller's auctions. (Many sellers are auction dealers or other small-business people who have migrated their retail operations to Yahoo! Auctions.)

✦ Click the Comments about Seller link to read comments made by buyers and check out the seller's rating. Every seller is ranked on a point system based on buyer feedback at previous auctions.

✦ Click the Ask Seller a Question link to query the seller about the auction item and read any previous dialogue that's been posted.

✦ In the Auction Info area, click the Bid History link to see a log of the bidding so far.

Figure 10-2: Some of the listed auctions for Buffalo nickels.

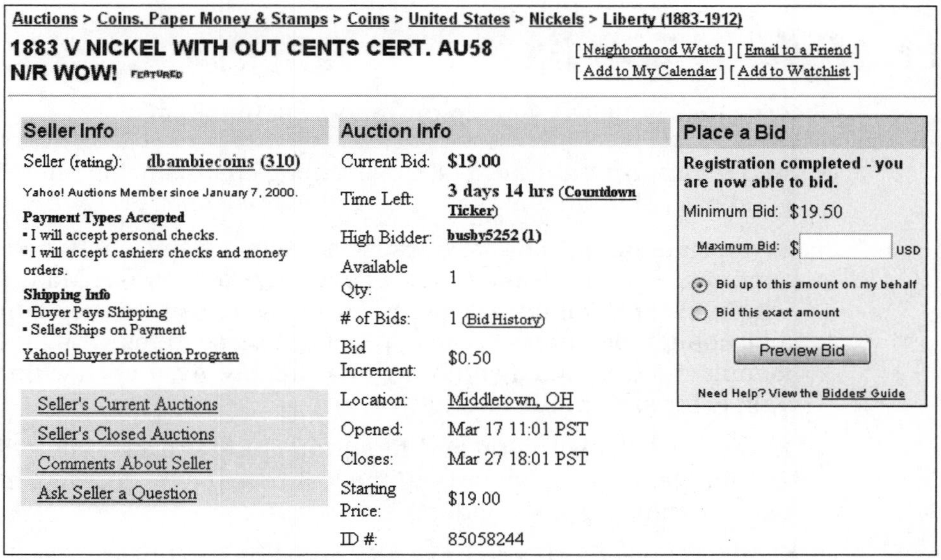

Figure 10-3: An auction page, where you get info about the seller and place a bid.

Bidding on Items

Use the Place a Bid box on the right to participate in the auction. Enter your maximum bid amount. Use the radio buttons to determine whether Yahoo! should bid you up to your maximum amount during the auction or simply bid the exact amount that you entered right away. When you're finished, click the Preview Bid button.

Yahoo! Auctions uses a system called Automatic Bidding. Yahoo! understands that if you enter a bid higher than $1 above the current winning bid, you want the system to manage your bidding for you. Yahoo! monitors the auction and bids up your figure to remain just above any new bids. Automatic Bidding continues in this fashion until your limit (the amount that you typed in the Maximum Bid text box) is reached. If someone tops your maximum amount, you're out of the auction. Until then, you're kept on top of the heap. With the system helping everyone in the same fashion, popular auctions quickly reach the highest maximum bid. You can always enter an auction again if you're pushed out by higher bids.

What happens if you win? Yahoo! brings you together with the seller and steps out of the picture. The seller contacts you by e-mail and arranges the details of your transaction. Each auction page indicates what forms of payment the seller accepts. Small-business sellers often take credit cards, but individuals running auctions as a hobby usually take checks or money orders and may implement precautions such as not shipping until the check clears. Each seller determines individual shipping and handling costs.

To see a list of all auctions in which you're participating, as a bidder or a seller or both, click the My Auctions link on the Yahoo! Auctions main page.

A Few Rules to Live By

Observe these rules as you bid on Yahoo! auction items:

+ **Avoid impulse bidding.** Yes, the beanbag chair is being offered at a good price, but do you really need a beanbag chair?

+ **Investigate the price.** Just because an item is being auctioned at Yahoo! auctions doesn't mean that it's a good buy. ***Remember:*** Many people who auction at Yahoo! are merely reselling items that they purchased at a discount. Sometimes you can purchase these items straight from the manufacturer yourself and buy them cheaply. After all, a wide variety of stuff is for sale on the Internet.

+ **Know what the shipping and handling charges are.** Some sellers who auction items cheaply make up the lost revenue by charging exorbitant fees for shipping and handling.

+ **Contact the seller if you have any questions**. Yahoo! makes it easy to contact a seller. On the item's auction page, click the Ask Seller a Question link. A message form appears so that you can send an e-mail to the seller.

✦ **Investigate the seller.** On the item's auction page, you can click the Comments about Seller link to see a summary of the seller's transactions and ratings.

✦ **Ask yourself how difficult the item is to assemble if it needs assembling.** Not everyone can interpret the complicated directions that come with items that you have to put together yourself. Not everyone can wield a screwdriver. Because purchases are delivered by mail, they need assembling more often than other purchases. If you're not good at assembling things, make sure that the items you buy are already assembled.

**Book III
Chapter 10**

Going, Going, Gone
to Yahoo! Auctions

Chapter 11: From Wall Street to Your Street: Yahoo! Finance

In This Chapter

✓ Touring the Finance section of Yahoo!

✓ Getting up-to-the-15-minute stock quotes

✓ Tracking your holdings with an online portfolio

The Yahoo! Finance main page is an anchor site for millions of online investors. What was once primarily a stock quote server has blossomed into a data hub and information resource. Yahoo!'s no-nonsense, fast-moving pages really come in handy for online traders who value quick, reliable information. What's more, the range of editorial services has rounded out what was once a fairly dry set of features.

Yahoo! doesn't maintain an in-house staff of writers like some other investment sites. Instead, Yahoo! licenses the articles and columns of other Web-based publications and presents them in the Yahoo! format.

One other feature treated lightly by Yahoo! is the stock chart. Yahoo! Finance does display stock charts along with price quotes, but the charts don't hold a candlestick to the elaborate interactive price graphs that you can find at some other sites.

These supposed imperfections notwithstanding, Yahoo! Finance is superb in what it does best, and uncountable online investors consider it their home base on the Web for good reason. For gathering fundamental information about a company, no site does the job faster or more thoroughly than Yahoo! Finance.

This chapter runs down the most important features of Yahoo! Finance, including getting stock quotes and creating an online portfolio.

A Basic Map of Yahoo! Finance

Following is a quick tour of the main content features of the Yahoo! Finance main page. As you can see in Figure 11-1, the main page has one heck of a lot of links — even more when you scroll down that page. Many links lead to deeply informative sites that would be worth a chapter by themselves. Because I can't do justice to the whole thing, this section provides a map of the page's basic topography so that you don't miss anything important. I describe stock quotes and portfolios in separate sections later in this chapter.

Figure 11-1:
The Yahoo!
Finance
main page.
Scroll down
for a feast
of links.

To get to Yahoo! Finance, click the Stock Quotes link on the Yahoo! home page or go directly to this URL:

```
http://quote.yahoo.com
```

Market overview

Most people who follow the financial markets check in periodically throughout the business day to get a snapshot of stock and bond activity. For most people, that snapshot is provided by the major index prices. You've probably heard them quoted on radio and TV stock market reports: "The Dow is up (or down) for the day, and the Nasdaq Composite has rallied (or slumped) throughout the afternoon. The yield on the 10-year Treasury bond is at an all-time high (or low)." Those statistics are presented at the very top of Yahoo! Finance, in real time (unlike individual stock quotes, which are delayed). If you continually click your browser's Reload or Refresh button, you can see the prices changing.

As you can see in Figure 11-1, the three index benchmarks for measuring stock market performance in the United States are

✦ **Dow:** The Dow Jones Industrial Average is a measure of large-company performance consisting of 30 big companies from the New York Stock Exchange.

✦ **Nasdaq:** The Nasdaq stock exchange composite average is generally considered a measure of technology companies because of the many such companies traded on the Nasdaq exchange.

✦ **S&P 500:** The Standard and Poor's index of 500 large and mid-sized companies is widely considered the most accurate barometer of broad stock market performance.

Trading volume numbers for the New York Stock Exchange (NYSE) and Nasdaq are displayed, plus the yield (but not the price) for the 10-year Treasury bond, the benchmark bond product used to evaluate the entire bond marketplace.

Click the index name for a detailed quote of that index's price, including the day's range and the 52-week range. The 10-Yr Bond link divulges the bond yield in basis points.

Data for investors

Yahoo! Finance is a data-rich resource, and it knows no boundaries. From Asian stock markets to currency exchange rates, Yahoo! has it. Several major sections contain links to data about the U.S. markets and those abroad.

Under the Investing heading on the left side of the window (you might have to scroll down to see it) are links that you can click to get international investor data, do stock research, and do any number of things. Under Today's Markets, for example, you can find links that take you to pages with information about the day's most active stocks. Click the Indices link under International to see how stock indices abroad are performing. Under Mutual Funds, you find a basic fund screener, performance statistics, and news headlines.

News and commentary

Current news headlines are located in the middle column of the Yahoo! Finance main page. This vortex of financial news is one of the most dynamic headline feeds on the Web. Constantly changing, you can best appreciate it by clicking your browser's Reload or Refresh button every few minutes. That's not practical, of course, but the point is that the news is up to the minute, no matter when you check in.

Getting Stock and Mutual Fund Quotes

To get a stock quote or mutual fund quote from Yahoo! Finance, follow these steps:

1. **On the Yahoo! Finance main page, type a stock or mutual fund symbol in the Enter Symbol(s) text box at the top of the page.**

   If you know the company or mutual fund name but not its ticker symbol, click the Symbol Lookup link. On the Symbol Lookup page, enter the company or mutual fund name (or part of it) and then click the Look Up button to find the symbol.

2. **Click Go.**

   You go to the Quotes & Info page, as shown in Figure 11-2.

Book III
Chapter 11

From Wall Street
to Your Street:
Yahoo! Finance

Figure 11-2:
Quotes and information about a stock.

Yahoo! Finance offers a varying amount of data along with the simple stock price. The chart selection (shown in detailed quotes) includes a few links for altering the time period of the chart and the size of its display.

Price quotes are just the beginning at Yahoo! Finance. By clicking links in the panel on the left side of the window, you can investigate the stock or mutual fund in many ways:

✦ **Quotes:** Examine the stock or mutual fund's value in different time periods.

✦ **Charts:** Create charts for gauging the investment's performance.

✦ **News & Info:** See news headlines, greatly expanding the small selection visible on the quote page. Click any headline to get the full story. You can also see what people are saying about the stock or mutual fund on the Yahoo! Message Board.

✦ **Company:** Read the company profile, its SEC filings, and other pertinent data.

✦ **Analyst Coverage:** See what Smith Barney, JPMorgan, and others say about the company.

✦ **Ownership:** Get information about the company's owners. The Insider Trading link is especially revealing. You can see who inside the company is unloading their stock.

✦ **Financials:** Get data about a company's profits and losses.

Creating Portfolios

If you own stocks or mutual funds, creating an online portfolio is a way to track your holdings that beats monthly brokerage reports and daily newspapers hands down. If you're accustomed to following your investments more casually, with an occasional glance at the newspaper stock listings and a monthly perusal of your brokerage statement, you might discover the fun of minute-by-minute portfolio fluctuations. Fun? Some might call it an obsession. Fanaticism isn't required, but keeping your stocks listed in Yahoo! Finance at least gives you a quick way to check your bottom line and your individual holdings whenever you want.

You have another reason to create an online portfolio. If you're considering becoming an online trader — the popular high-risk hobby of new-millennium investing — paper trade first. *Paper trading* means buying and selling stocks in a virtual portfolio, without money. Yahoo! Finance isn't a brokerage, and you can't open an account in it. So the service doesn't know or care whether your portfolio reflects actual holdings or pretend holdings. Many beginning online investors practice virtual trading through an online portfolio before putting any real money into play.

One final reason to try a Yahoo! Finance portfolio is that it's a great consolidator of stocks that interest you, even if you don't hold them. Throwing those stocks into an on-screen portfolio gathers all the information associated with each price quote (which I describe in the preceding section) into one place. You can track news releases, price fluctuations, and constantly shifting per-share valuations for the whole basket of stocks whenever you want.

Creating your portfolio

Yahoo! Finance throws a lot of portfolio features in your face, but you don't have to use them all. You can fashion a simple list of stocks or develop a complex tool including upper- and lower-price-alert limits, notes on each holding, commission rates to be subtracted from capital gains, and so on. You can set up a portfolio to track stocks generally (as if you didn't own them) or to track ownership of certain numbers of shares that are purchased at a certain price (whether you own the stock or are just pretending).

You must have a Yahoo! ID to create a portfolio and you must be signed in to follow along with the steps below. See Chapter 1 of this minibook for information about registering as a Yahoo! member.

Whether you want to create a wannabe portfolio with investments that you don't own but want to track, or you want to track investments you own, follow these steps to describe and track investments with Yahoo!:

1. **On the Yahoo! Finance main page, click the Create link.**

This hard-to-find link is in the upper-right corner near the word *Portfolio.* You see the Create New Portfolio page.

2. **To track investments that you don't own but want to follow, click the Track a Symbol Watch List link. To track investments that you own, click the Track Your Current Holdings link.**

No matter which option you choose, you see the Create Your Portfolio page shown in Figure 11-3.

**Book III
Chapter 11**

From Wall Street
to Your Street:
Yahoo! Finance

Create your portfolio

Name your portfolio, customize your settings and then click 'Continue' to start recording the number of shares owned and price paid.

Step 1: Portfolio Basics

Portfolio Name: `My Investments`

Portfolio Currency: `U.S. Dollar` ▾   • Overrides default where supported

Step 2: Ticker Symbols

Enter symbols for the stocks, mutual funds and indices you want to track.

Symbols (look up symbol):

`MCD TOY DIS WOGSX`

Add all ticker symbols separated by spaces.

- If you don't know the symbol for something you want to track, you can look up any stock, mutual fund, or market index by name.

- Or, try our alphabetical listing (stocks and funds only).

- Use the backspace key to delete or re-order symbols.

Example Market Indices	Symbol
☑ Dow Jones Industrial	^DJI
☐ NASDAQ Composite	^IXIC
☐ S&P 500	^GSPC
☐ S&P 100	^OEX

Figure 11-3: Describing investments on the Create Your Portfolio page.

3. **On the Create Your Portfolio page, type a name for the portfolio in the Portfolio Name text box.**

Because you might establish a number of portfolios, name this one something that indicates what is in it or give it a number. (Why am I being so pushy? Name it whatever you want.)

4. **In the Portfolio Currency drop-down list, select the currency that you want to use.**

Yahoo! converts the native currency of the exchange where your stocks are located to whatever currency you *would* use if you were to buy the stock. This feature is only for tracking; it has nothing to do with whether you plan to actually buy your selected stocks.

5. **Under the Ticker Symbols banner, enter the stock symbols that you want listed in your portfolio.**

Put a space between all your symbols. If you don't know a stock symbol, use the Look Up Symbol link. Enter ticker symbols in either uppercase or lowercase letters.

6. **Under Example Market Indices, select the check boxes next to any indices that you want in your portfolio.**

You can choose as many indices as you like. If the one(s) you want aren't on the short list, click the More U.S. Indices link or the More International Indices link.

7. **Scroll below the Basic Features banner and select the check boxes if you'd like your stocks listed alphabetically and if you want a small-type display.**

If you deliberately entered your stock symbols in the order that you want them to appear, ignore the alphabetical option. The small font is useful if you choose any display option other than Basic. All the other options contain more information than can fit into most browser windows. (Although that depends on your screen size, screen resolution, and how wide you keep your windows.) I routinely use small fonts.

8. **Using the drop-down list, select a profile view.**

   The views determine how much information is stuffed into your portfolio. The views correspond to the quote views that you get when ordering a stock quote from the Yahoo! Finance main page. Basic view contains the least information and is good for quickly getting the gist of your portfolio's activity. The views get more detailed as you move down the list. Don't agonize over this decision; you can change views on the Portfolio page and also return to this page to edit your configuration at any time.

9. **Click the Finished button if you're creating a watch list portfolio. If you're tracking your investments, click the Continue button, and on the next page, describe the shares that you own in the text boxes, and then click the Finished button.**

   Your portfolio is displayed, as shown in Figure 11-4.

Figure 11-4:
A stock portfolio in Performance view.

Portfolio for rupls - My Investments — Customize Finance

Enter symbol(s): e.g. YHOO, ^DJI [____] Go | Symbol Lookup | Finance Search

Views: Basic - DayWatch - **Performance** [edit] - Real-time Mkt - Detailed - [Create New View]

Symbol	Last Trade		Chg	Volume	Shrs	Value	Value	Change	Paid	Gain		Related Information
^IXIC	5:16pm	1,909.48	+7.68	N/A	-	-	-	+0.40%	-	-	-	Chart, **more...**
^N225	2:01am	11,364.99	0	N/A	-	-	-	0.00%	-	-	-	Chart, **more...**
DIS	4:00pm	24.77	-0.33	8,576,700	-	-	-	-1.31%	-	-	-	Chart, Messages, Profile, **more..**
MCD	4:01pm	27.70	-0.06	3,455,100	-	-	-	-0.22%	-	-	-	Chart, Messages, Profile, **more..**
TOY	4:04pm	15.26	-0.32	2,622,500	-	-	-	-2.05%	-	-	-	Chart, Messages, Profile, **more..**
WOGSX	Mar 23	33.54	-0.14	N/A	-	-	-	-0.42%	-	-	-	Chart, Profile, **more...**
6 symbols				Total(USD):		$0.00	$0.00	N/A		$0.00	N/A	

**Book III
Chapter 11**

From Wall Street
to Your Street:
Yahoo! Finance

To edit your portfolio, look above the Portfolio banner on the Yahoo! Finance main page, next to your currently displayed portfolio name, and click the Manage link. That takes you to the Edit Portfolios page, where you can click an Edit link to return to the Edit Your Portfolio page and rearrange your portfolio.

Viewing a portfolio in different ways

To view a portfolio you created, go to the Yahoo! Finance main page and click the portfolio's name. Yahoo! offers five ways to examine a portfolio. By clicking the Basic, Daywatch, Performance, Real-Time Mkt, or Detailed link, you can examine investments in different ways. You can find these links along the top of the portfolio grid.

CHECK IT OUT

Comparing Investments

One of the neatest features of Yahoo! Finance is being able to compare two investments in a chart. The chart shows quite plainly which investment is performing better, and you can also compare investments to indices such as the Dow Jones Industrial Average or Nasdaq. Follow these steps to compare investments:

1. Generate a chart of one investment on the Finance main page or in your portfolio.

If you need to, enter the investment's ticker symbol in the Enter Symbol(s) text box, click Go, and on the investment's Quotes & Info page, generate the chart. You don't need to enter the ticker symbol if you're working with an investment that you entered in a portfolio. Simply click the symbol and generate the chart.

2. In the Compare text box, enter the ticker symbol of the investment that you want to compare.

You can also select an index check box — S&P, Nasdaq, or Dow — to compare your investment to a stock index.

3. Click the Compare button.

Lines on the chart compare the investments to one another and show clearly which is performing better. Click one of the Range links if you want to change the time period in which the investments are compared.

Book IV

eBay

The 5th Wave   By Rich Tennant

"Guess who found a Kiss merchandise eBay Store while you were gone?"

Book IV: eBay

Chapter 1: Getting a Grip on eBay Auctions

In This Chapter

✔ Finding out about eBay

✔ Getting the scoop on types of auctions

eBay has emerged as *the* marketplace of the 21st century. In July 2003, *Wired* magazine reported that eBay's promise is that "retailing will become the national pastime." eBay is a safe and fun place to shop for everything from collectibles to clothing, all from the comfort of your home. eBay is also a marketplace for new merchandise. It's no longer just the destination for collectibles and old china patterns. These days you can purchase new and useful items, such as alarm systems, fancy electronic toothbrushes, light bulbs, clothing, cars, homes — just about anything you can think of.

In this chapter, I tell you what eBay is and how it works. eBay is the perfect alternative to spending hours wandering through antique shops or swap meets looking for the perfect doohickey. It can also be your personal shopper for gifts and day-to-day items. Not only can you buy and sell stuff in the privacy of your home, but you can also meet people who share your interests. The folks who use the eBay site are a friendly bunch, and soon you'll be buying, selling, swapping stories, and trading advice with the best of them.

What Is eBay, and How Does It Work?

eBay is a place where buyers and sellers can meet, do business, share stories and tips, and have fun. It's like one giant online potluck party — but instead of bringing a dish, you sell it! However, eBay *doesn't* sell a thing. Instead, the site does what all good hosts do: It creates a comfy environment that brings people with common interests together. You can think of eBay like you think of the person who set you up on your last blind date — except the results are often a lot better. eBay puts buyers and sellers in a virtual store and lets them conduct their business safely within the rules that eBay has established.

All you need to do to join eBay is fill out a few forms online and click. Congratulations — you're a member, and you didn't have to pay a big fee or use a secret handshake. After you register, you can buy and sell anything that falls within the eBay rules and regulations.

The eBay home page, shown in Figure 1-1, is your first step to finding all the cool stuff that you can see and do at eBay. You can conduct searches, find out what's happening, and get an instant link to the My eBay page, which helps you keep track of every auction item that you have up for sale or have a bid on.

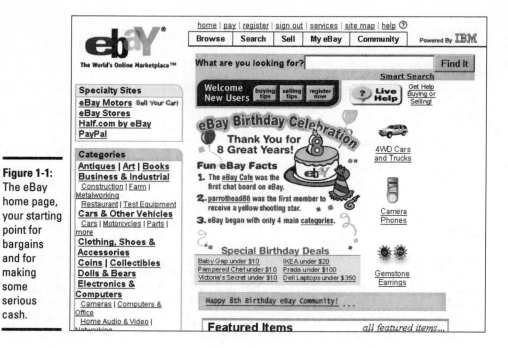

Figure 1-1:
The eBay home page, your starting point for bargains and for making some serious cash.

Yikes! What happened? The eBay home page on your computer looks nothing like the one in Figure 1-1? Don't rub your eyes — even squinting hard won't help; eBay has a different version of the home page for people who have never registered on eBay. Even if *you* have never registered, someone else who uses the computer might already have. Take a look at Figure 1-2 and see whether it's a closer match.

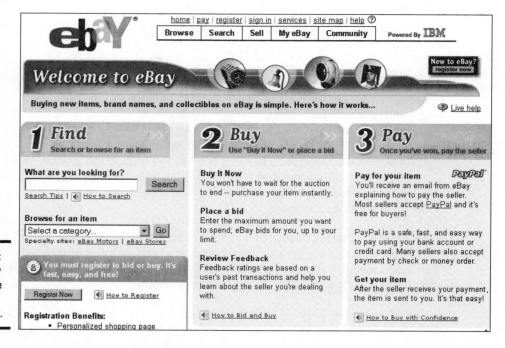

Figure 1-2:
The "eBay Lite" home page for new users.

All About Auctions

The value of an item is determined by how much someone is willing to spend to buy it. That's what makes auctions exciting. eBay offers several kinds of auctions, but for the most part, they all work the same way. An *auction* is a unique sales event where the exact price of the item for sale is unknown. As a result, there's an element of surprise involved — not only for the bidder (who might end up with a great deal) but also for the seller (who might end up making a killing). Here's how an auction works from a seller's and a bidder's perspective:

✦ **Seller:** A seller pays a fee, fills out an electronic form, and sets up the auction, listing a *minimum bid* that he or she is willing to accept for the item. Think of an auctioneer at Sotheby's saying, "The bidding for this diamond necklace begins at $5,000." You might *want* to bid $4,000, but the bid won't be accepted. Sellers can also set a *reserve price* — sort of a financial safety net that protects them from losing money on the deal. I explain how this stuff works later in this section.

✦ **Bidder:** Bidders in auctions duke it out over a period of time (the minimum is one day, but most auctions last a week or even longer) until one bidder comes out victorious. Usually, the highest bidder wins. The tricky thing about participating in an auction (and the most exciting aspect) is that no one knows the final price of an item until the last second of the auction.

eBay auctions

Unlike traditional live auctions that end with the familiar phrase "Going once, going twice, sold!" eBay auctions are controlled by the clock. The seller pays a fee and lists the item on the site for a predetermined period of time; the highest bidder when the clock runs out takes home the prize.

Reserve-price auctions

Unlike a minimum bid, which is required in any eBay auction, a *reserve price* protects sellers from having to sell an item for less than the minimum amount they want for it. You might be surprised to see a 1968 Jaguar XKE sports car up for auction at eBay with a minimum bid of only a dollar. It's a fair bet that the seller has put a reserve price on this car to protect himself from losing money. The reserve price allows sellers to set lower minimum bids, and lower minimum bids attract bidders. Unfortunately, if a seller makes the reserve price too high, and it isn't met by the end of the auction, no one wins.

eBay charges a fee for sellers to run these auctions. Nobody knows (except the seller and the eBay computer system) what the reserve price is until the auction is over. When you're dealing with a reserve-price auction, the auction page tells you as much. You see the words *Reserve Not Met* if bids have not reached the reserve price, or the words *Reserve Met* if the bid exceeds the reserve price.

Charity auctions: All for a good cause

A *charity auction* is a high-profile fundraising auction where the proceeds go to a selected charity. Most people don't wake up in the morning wanting to own the shoes that Ron Howard wore when he put his footprints in cement at Mann's Chinese Theater in Hollywood, but one-of-a-kind items like that are often auctioned off in charity auctions. (In fact, someone did want those shoes badly enough to buy them for a lot of money at eBay.) Charity auctions became popular after the NBC *Today Show* sold an autographed jacket at eBay for over $11,000 with the proceeds going to Toys for Tots. Charity auctions are run like most other auctions at eBay, but because they're immensely popular, bidding can be fierce, and the dollar amounts can go sky high. Many famous celebrities use eBay to help out their favorite charities.

Live Auctions

If you yearn for that traditional, going-going-gone (highest bidder wins) sort of auction, you can participate in auctions that are running live at a gallery in real time. In *eBay Live Auctions,* you can bid via eBay's Internet hook-up just as if you were sitting in a chair at the auction house. These auctions are usually for unique and interesting items that you're not likely to find in your locality. Figure 1-3 shows the Live Auctions home page located at www.ebay.com/liveauctions.

Figure 1-3: The Live Auctions home page lists current and upcoming auctions and provides links to view their item catalogs.

Restricted-access auctions

If you're over 18 years of age and interested in bidding on items of an adult nature, eBay has an adults-only (Mature Audiences) category, which has restricted access. Although you can peruse the other eBay categories without having to submit credit card information, you must have a credit card number on file at eBay to view and bid on items in this category. Restricted-access auctions are run like the typical timed auctions. To bid on adult items, you first need to agree to a Terms of Use page after entering your User ID and password. The Terms of Use page pops up automatically when you attempt to access this category.

Private (shhh-it's-a-secret) auctions

Some sellers choose to hold private auctions because they know that some bidders might be embarrassed to be seen bidding on a box of racy neckties in front of the rest of the eBay community. Others might go the private route because they're selling big-ticket items and don't want to disclose their bidders' financial statuses. Private auctions are run like the typical timed auctions except that each bidder's identity is kept secret. At the end of the auction, eBay provides contact info to the seller and to the high bidder, and that's it.

Multiple Item auctions

Multiple Item auctions (also called *Dutch* auctions) have nothing to do with windmills, wooden shoes, or sharing the check on a date. A *Multiple Item auction* allows a seller to put multiple, identical items up for sale. Instead of holding 100 separate auctions for 100 pairs of wooden shoes, for example, a seller can sell them all in one listing. As a buyer, you can elect to bid for 1, 3, or all 100 pairs.

Buying It Now at eBay

You don't have to participate in an auction at eBay to buy something. If you want to make a purchase — if it's something that you *must* have — you can usually find the item and buy it immediately. Of course, using Buy It Now (*BIN* in eBay speak) doesn't come with the thrill of an auction, but purchasing an item at a fraction of the retail price without leaving your chair or waiting for an auction to end has its own warm and fuzzy kind of excitement.

If you seek this kind of instant gratification on eBay, visit eBay Stores. Visiting eBay Stores is as easy as clicking the eBay Stores link from the home page. Thousands of eBay sellers have set up stores with merchandise meant for you to Buy It Now. eBay Stores are classified just like eBay, and you can buy anything from socks to jewelry to appliances. Figure 1-4 shows the eBay Stores hub page.

More and more sellers are selling items with a Buy It Now option or at a fixed price. This enables you to buy an item as soon as you see one at a price that suits you.

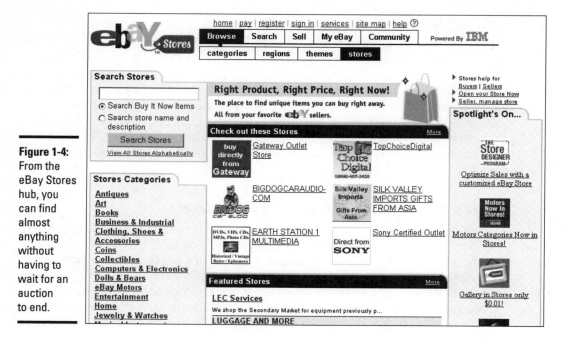

Figure 1-4:
From the
eBay Stores
hub, you
can find
almost
anything
without
having to
wait for an
auction
to end.

eBay's Role in the Action

Throughout the auction process, eBay's computers keep tabs on what's going on. When the auction or sale is over, eBay takes a small percentage of the final selling price and instructs the seller and buyer to contact each other through e-mail. At this point, eBay's job is pretty much over, and eBay steps aside.

Most of the time, everything works great, everybody's happy, and eBay never has to step back into the picture. But if you happen to run into trouble in paradise, eBay can help you settle the problem, whether you're the buyer or the seller.

eBay regulates members with a detailed system of checks and balances known as *feedback,* which I describe in Chapter 4 of this minibook. The grand plan is that the community polices itself. Don't get me wrong — eBay does jump in when sketchy activity comes to light. But the people who keep eBay most safe are the community members, the buyers and sellers who have a common stake in conducting business honestly and fairly. Every time you sell something or win an auction, eBay members have a chance to leave a comment about you. You should do the same for them. If they're happy, the feedback is positive; otherwise, the feedback is negative. Either way, your feedback sticks to you like glue.

Building a great reputation with positive feedback ensures a long and profitable eBay career. Negative feedback, like multiple convictions for grand-theft auto, is a real turnoff to most folks and can make it hard to do future business at eBay.

Chapter 2: The Bucks Start Here: Signing Up at eBay

In This Chapter

✔ Using eBay's easy forms (the shape of things to come)

✔ Getting to know eBay rules and regulations

✔ Getting up close and personal about privacy

Compared to finding a prime parking space at the mall during the holidays, signing up at eBay is a breeze. About the toughest thing that you have to do is type in your e-mail address correctly.

In this chapter, you find out everything you need to know about registering at eBay. You get tips on what information you have to disclose and what you should keep to yourself. Don't worry — this is an open-book test. You don't need to memorize state capitals, the periodic table, or multiplication tables.

Registering at eBay

You don't have to wear one of those tacky *Hello, My Name Is* stickers on your shirt after you sign in, but eBay needs to know some things about you before it grants you membership. You and several million other folks will be roaming around eBay's online treasure trove; eBay needs to know who's who.

The only hard-and-fast rule at eBay is that you have to be 18 years of age or older. Don't worry, the Age Police won't come to your house to card you; they have other ways to discreetly ensure that you're at least 18 years old. (**Hint:** Credit cards do more than satisfy account charges.)

---

eBay internationale!

eBay has Web sites in the United States, Argentina, Australia, Austria, Brazil, Belgium, Canada, China, France, Germany, Ireland, Italy, Korea, Mexico, The Netherlands, New Zealand, Singapore, Spain, Sweden, Switzerland, Taiwan, and (whew) the United Kingdom. The vast majority of eBay users that you trade with are from the United States, but the international membership is growing.

Registering Is Free and Fun (And Fast)

To register, start by typing **www.ebay.com** in the address box of your browser and pressing Enter. Your next stop is the eBay home page. Right there, where you can't miss it, is the Register Now link. Click the link and let the sign-up process begin.

Clicking the Register Now link takes you to the Registration form, where you go through a four-step process. Here's an overview:

1. Enter the basic required info.

2. Read and accept the User Agreement.

3. Confirm your e-mail address.

4. Breeze through (or past) the optional information.

The following sections fill you in on all the details.

So, what's your sign? Filling in your required information

After you click the Register link, you're taken to the heart of the eBay Registration pages. To get started, follow these steps:

1. **At the top of the first registration page, eBay shows the steps of the registration process and asks you to fill in some required information (see Figure 2-1).**

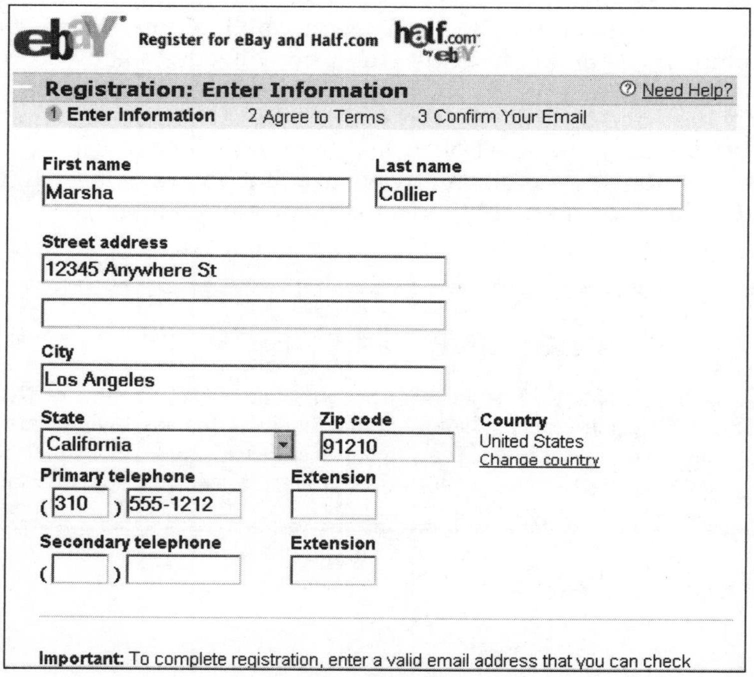

Figure 2-1: Some of the required information for your eBay registration.

eBay Register for eBay and Half.com half.com by eBay

Registration: Enter Information ⑦ Need Help?
① **Enter Information** 2 Agree to Terms 3 Confirm Your Email

First name
Marsha

Last name
Collier

Street address
12345 Anywhere St

City
Los Angeles

State
California

Zip code
91210

Country
United States
Change country

Primary telephone
(310) 555-1212

Extension

Secondary telephone
( )

Extension

Important: To complete registration, enter a valid email address that you can check

Here's what eBay wants to know about you:

- Your full name, address, and primary telephone number. eBay keeps this information on file in case the company (or a member who is a transaction partner) needs to contact you.

- You can also include, if you want, a secondary phone number.

- Your e-mail address (*yourname@myISP.com*).

If you register with an *anonymous e-mail service* such as Yahoo! Mail or Hotmail, you're taken to a page that requires additional information for authentication. You must provide valid credit card information for identification purposes. Your information is protected by eBay's privacy policy, and your credit card won't be charged.

After you input your personal information, you're ready to create your eBay persona.

2. **Scroll down the page and create your new eBay User ID.**

3. **Choose a permanent password, enter it in the Create Password text box, and then type it a second time in the Re-Enter Password text box to confirm it.**

4. **Select your unique secret question and enter the answer.**

    eBay uses the secret question that you select here to identify you if you ever have problems signing in. If you're registering with an anonymous e-mail address, this is where you enter your credit card information.

5. **Enter in your date of birth by using the drop-down lists.**

6. **Click the Continue button to move on to the next screen.**

If you make a mistake, eBay gives you the opportunity to correct the information by using the Edit Information button.

Do you solemnly swear to . . . ?

After you click the Continue button, you're taken to a page that has the eBay User Agreement and Privacy Policy. At this page, you take an oath to keep eBay safe for democracy and commerce.

Be sure to read the User Agreement thoroughly when you register. So that you don't have to put down this riveting book to read the legalese right this minute, I provide the nuts and bolts here:

- ✦ You understand that every transaction is a legally binding contract. (Click the User Agreement link at the bottom of any eBay page for the current eBay Rules and Regulations.)

- ✦ You agree that you must pay for the items you buy and the eBay fees that you incur.

- ✦ You understand that you're responsible for paying any taxes.

✦ You're aware that if you sell prohibited items, eBay can forward your personal information to law enforcement for further investigation.

✦ eBay makes clear that it is just a *venue,* which means it's a place where people with similar interests can meet, greet, and do business.

Before you can proceed, you must select the two check boxes to indicate that you really, really understand what it means to be an eBay user. Because I know that you, as a law-abiding eBay member, will have no problem following the rules, go ahead and click the I Agree to These Terms button at the bottom of the page, which takes you to a screen stating that eBay is sending you an e-mail. You're almost done.

The next step is confirming your e-mail address, which I cover in the following section.

It must be true if you have it in writing

After you accept the User Agreement, it takes eBay less than a minute to e-mail you a confirmation notice. When you receive the eBay registration confirmation e-mail, print it out. What's most important is the confirmation code. If you lose that number, click the link in your e-mail to get the confirmation number.

With your confirmation number in hand, head back to the eBay Registration page by clicking the link supplied in your e-mail. If your e-mail doesn't support links, go to this address:

```
http://pages.ebay.com/register
```

After you reconnect with eBay and it knows your e-mail address is active, you'll be heartily congratulated, as shown in Figure 2-2.

Figure 2-2:
It's time
to start
shopping!

Getting to know you: Optional information

Now that you're a full-fledged, officially registered member of the eBay community, you might see an eBay pop-up window, giving you the option to provide more information about yourself. These optional questions allow you to fill in your self-portrait for your new pals at eBay.

Don't tell anyone, but your info is safe at eBay

eBay keeps most personal information secret. The basics (your name, phone number, city, and state) go out only to answer the specific request of another registered eBay user (if you're involved in a transaction with that person), law enforcement, or members of the eBay Verified Rights Owner Program (eBay's copyright-watchdog program). Other users might need your basic access info for several reasons — a seller might want to verify your location, get your phone number to call you regarding your auction, or double-check who you really are. If somebody does request your info, you get an e-mail from eBay giving you the name, phone number, city, and state of the person making the request. You need to keep your information up to date. If you don't, you risk being banished from the site.

Although eBay doesn't share member information with anyone, you don't have to answer the optional questions if you don't want to.

The following points show you the optional questions that eBay asks. You decide what you feel comfortable divulging and what you want to keep personal. eBay asks for this information because the company wants a better picture of who is using its Web site. In marketing mumbo-jumbo, this stuff is called *demographics* — statistics that characterize a group of people who make up a community. In this case, it's the eBay community. Here is the optional information that you can provide:

✦ **Annual household income:** Fill this in if you want to (eBay states that this info is kept anonymous), but I think this information is too personal. If you're not comfortable with it, skip it.

✦ **Your highest completed education level:** Again, if this is too personal, leave this area blank.

After selecting your responses from the drop-down list box, you can click Submit. If you're not in the mood right now, you can click the Answer Later link. (This pop-up box reappears for your response later in your eBay dealings.) If you don't want to answer any of the demographic queries, click the Please Don't Ask Me Again link at the bottom of the pop-up window.

Chapter 3: Just Browsing: Navigating eBay

In This Chapter

✔ **Getting the lay of the land**

✔ **Getting the first word on searches**

✔ **Using the eBay home page's links and icons**

The writer Thomas Wolfe was wrong: You *can* go home again — and again. At least at eBay you can! Month after month, millions of people land at eBay's home page without wearing out the welcome mat. The eBay home page is the front door to the most popular auction site on the Internet.

Everything that you need to know about navigating eBay begins right here. In this chapter, I give you the grand tour of the areas that you can reach right from the home page with the help of links.

What Is the Home Page?

The eBay home page is shown in Figure 3-1 and includes the following key areas:

✦ A navigation bar at the top of the page with five eBay links that can zip you straight to any of the many eBay areas, as well as seven additional — and powerful — links right above the navigation bar

✦ A search box that — like the Search link in the navigation bar — helps you find items by title keywords

✦ A list of links to auction categories

✦ Links to eBay's specialty sites, featured auctions, fun stuff like charity auctions, and information about what else is happening at eBay

Do not adjust your computer monitor. You're not going crazy. You might notice that a link is on the eBay home page one day and is gone the next day. The links on the eBay home page change often to reflect what's going on — not just on the site, but in the world as well. (Remember that new, unregistered visitors to eBay see a different home page than the one shown in Figure 3-1.)

Figure 3-1:
The home page, your jumping-off point for fun and values.

Sign In, Please

Sign In is possibly the most powerful of all the links on the eBay pages, and it should be your first stop if you plan on doing any business at eBay (see Figure 3-2). By going to the Sign In page and signing in, you don't have to enter your User ID when you bid or post items for sale.

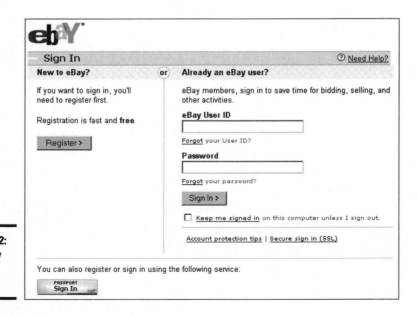

Figure 3-2:
The eBay Sign In page.

Here's how to get to the eBay Sign In page and sign in:

1. **Click the Sign In link above the navigation bar on any eBay page.**

2. **On the next page, enter your User ID and password.**

If you're the only one who uses your computer, be sure to select the Keep Me Signed In check box. This way, you're always signed in to eBay every time you go to the site. The Sign In process places a *cookie* (a techno-related thingy) on your computer that remains a part of your browser until you sign out. If you don't select the check box, you're signed in only while you're on the site. If there's no activity for 40 minutes — or if you close your browser — the cookie expires, and you have to sign in again.

3. **Click the Sign In button.**

If you prefer to use your Microsoft Passport for eBay, click the Passport Sign In button and then enter your Passport e-mail address and password. When you're prompted, enter your eBay User ID and password. Your Passport is then activated for use on eBay until you sign out.

A fast way to get to the Sign In page (refer to Figure 3-2) is to click the My eBay button on the eBay home page. Doing so takes you straight to the Sign In page.

This Bar Never Closes

The *navigation bar* is at the top of the eBay home page and lists five eBay links that take you directly to any of the different eBay areas. Using the navigation bar is kind of like doing one-stop clicking. You can find this bar at the top of every page that you visit at eBay. When you click one of the five links, you get a subnavigation bar with specific links to other related important places.

Here are the five navigation bar links and where they take you:

✦ **Browse:** Takes you to the page that lists Featured Items and all the main eBay categories. From here, you can click category names and drill down deeper until you find items that truly interest you.

✦ **Search:** Takes you to the eBay main Search page. Because over 10 million items are up for auction at any given time, finding just one (say, an antique Vermont milk can) is no easy task.

✦ **Sell:** Takes you to the Sell Your Item form that you fill out to start your auctions. I explain how to navigate this form in Chapter 13.

✦ **My eBay:** Takes you to your personal My eBay page, where you keep track of all your buying and selling activities, account information, and favorite categories (more about My eBay in Chapter 4).

✦ **Community:** Takes you to a page where you can find the latest news and announcements, chat with fellow traders in the eBay community, find charity auctions, and find out more about eBay.

Exploring Your Home Page Search Options

There's an old Chinese expression that says, "Every journey begins with the first eBay search." Okay, the expression is a bit updated. Very wise words nonetheless. You can start a search from the home page in one of two ways:

✦ **Use the search text box.** It's right there at the top of the home page next to the phrase "What are you looking for?" and it's a fast way of finding item listings.

✦ **Use the Search button on the navigation bar or the Smart Search link below the search text box on the home page.** These links take you to the Basic Search page, where you can do all kinds of specialized searches.

Both options give you the same results. The instructions that I offer in the next two sections about using these search methods are just the tip of the eBay iceberg. For the inside track on how to finesse the eBay search engine to root out just what you're looking for, visit Book IV, Chapter 5.

Peering through the home page search text box

To launch a title search from the home page, follow these steps:

1. **In the search text box, type no more than a few keywords that describe the item that you're looking for.**

Refer to Figure 3-1 to see the search box.

2. **Click the Find It button.**

The results of your search appear on-screen in a matter of seconds.

You can type just about anything in this box and get some information. Say that you're looking for *Star Trek* memorabilia. If so, you're not alone. The television show premiered on September 8, 1966, and even though it was canceled in 1969 because of low ratings, *Star Trek* has become one of the most successful science-fiction franchises in history. If you like *Star Trek* as much as I do, you can use the search text box on the eBay home page to find all sorts of *Star Trek* stuff.

When you search for popular items at eBay (and a classic example is *Star Trek* memorabilia), you might get inundated with thousands of auctions that match your search criteria. Even if you're traveling at warp speed, you could spend hours checking each auction individually. If you're pressed for time like the rest of us, eBay has not-so-mysterious ways for you to narrow down your search so that finding a specific item is much more manageable. Turn to Chapter 5 of Book IV for insider search techniques.

Going where the Search button takes you

One of the most important buttons on the navigation bar is the Search button. When you click this button, you're whisked away to the main Search page, which promptly presents you with five search tabs. Although

Chapters 5 and 6 of this minibook tell you all that you need to know about searching eBay, the following list explains some other searches that you can perform from the Search page:

✦ **Basic Search:** Search by keywords or item number. Type in the keywords that describe an item (for example, **Superman lunchbox** or **antique pocket watch**) and click Search, and you can see how many are available at eBay.

✦ **Advanced Search:** Enables you to define your search without using a bunch of code. It works pretty much the same as the Basic Search method, but you can exclude more features from your search. You can also take advantage of eBay's regional trading and find items for sale in your neighborhood. Figure 3-3 shows the Advanced Search options.

✦ **By Seller:** Every person at eBay has a personal User ID (the name that you use to conduct transactions). Use a By Seller search if you liked the merchandise from a seller's auction and want to see what else the seller has for sale.

✦ **By Bidder:** For the sake of practicality and convenience, User IDs help eBay keep track of every move that a user makes at eBay. If you want to see what a particular user (say, a fellow *Star Trek* fan) is bidding on, use the By Bidder search.

✦ **Stores:** If you're looking for a particular eBay Store, eBay provides a search text box that allows you to search for a store by name (or part of the name).

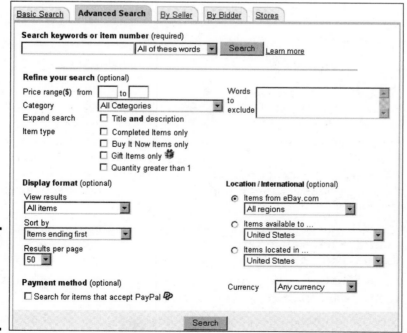

Figure 3-3: The Advanced Search page and its options.

Book IV
Chapter 3

Just Browsing: Navigating eBay

Home Links, the Next Generation

If you look carefully, you can see several other links on the home page. These links give you express service to several key parts of the site. Here are the highlights:

✦ **Specialty Sites:** Here's where clicking a link gets you to eBay's new specialty sites. A click on the eBay Motors link brings you to `http://ebaymotors.com`, an area dedicated to the sale of almost everything with a motor and wheels. eBay Stores (`http://stores.ebay.com`) takes you to a separate area of eBay that's loaded with thousands of stores from eBay sellers. eBay Stores are filled with items that you can purchase without bidding.

✦ **Featured Items:** Visit the featured items. (Translation: Sellers paid more to have them featured in this section.)

✦ **Global Sites:** This links to eBay's international auction sites.

Maneuvering through Categories

So how does eBay keep track of the millions of items that are up for auction at any given moment? The brilliant minds at eBay decided to group items into a nice, neat little storage system called *categories*. The home page lists most of the main categories, but currently eBay lists tens of thousands of subcategories, ranging from Antiques to Writing Instruments. And don't ask how many sub-subcategories (categories within categories) eBay's got — I can't count that high.

Here's how to navigate around the categories:

1. **Click the category that interests you, such as Books or DVDs & Movies.**

You're transported to the category's page. You see categories and subcategories listed next to each heading. Happy hunting.

If you don't find a category that interests you among those on the home page, simply click the Browse button on the navigation bar, and you're off to the main categories page. You can also click the See All eBay Categories link on the main category page to get a comprehensive list of all categories.

2. **After the category page appears, find a subcategory that interests you underneath the main category title. Click the subcategory and keep digging through the sub-subcategories until you find what you want.**

3. **When you find an item that interests you, click the item and the full Auction page pops up on your screen.**

Congratulations — you've just navigated through several million items to find that one TV-collectible item that caught your attention. You can instantly return to the home page by clicking the Home link at the top of the page (or return to the Listings page by repeatedly clicking the Back button at the top of your browser).

Near the bottom of every subcategory page, you can see a link list of numbers. The numbers are page numbers, and you can use them to fast-forward through all the items in that subcategory. So if you feel like browsing around page 8 without going through 8 pages individually, just click number 8, and you're presented with the items on that page (their listings, actually). Happy browsing.

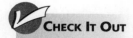

CHECK IT OUT

The eBay Quick Links

At the top of almost every eBay page, you find six small (but powerful) links that are just as important as the links on the navigation bar:

- **Home:** Takes you right back the home page. Use this link from any other page when you need to get back to the home page right away.

- **Pay:** Takes you to a page that shows the last few items that you've won and haven't paid for.

- **Sign In/Sign Out:** This link, which toggles between Sign In and Sign Out depending on your sign-in status, lets you sign in to eBay or quit the place.

- **Services:** Takes you to the eBay Services Overview page. Here you can find links to pages that tell you all about buying and

selling, registration pages, the Feedback Forum, and other eBay programs.

- **Site Map:** Provides you with a bird's-eye view of the eBay world. Every *top-level* (or main) link available at eBay is listed here. If you're ever confused about finding a specific area, try the Site Map first. If a top-level link isn't listed here, it's not at eBay — yet.

- **Help:** Opens the eBay Help Center. If you get turned around, confused, or just can't find the answer to your question, you can find eBay's old Help Center at `http://pages.ebay.com/help/index.html` (for now). It might be helpful in a pinch.

Chapter 4: It's All About You: My eBay

In This Chapter

- Making the My eBay page a space to call your own
- Keeping tabs on what you're buying and selling
- Rolling with your feedback

I know that eBay is a sensitive kind of company because it gives all users plenty of personal space. This space is called the My eBay page, and it's your private listing of all your activities on eBay — sort of a "This is your eBay life." I think it's the greatest organizational tool around, and I want to talk to somebody about getting one for organizing my life outside of eBay.

In this chapter, you find out how you can use the My eBay page to keep tabs on what you're buying and selling, find out how much money you've spent, and add categories to your own personalized list so that you can get to any favorite eBay place with just a click of your mouse. You gain knowledge of the ins and outs of feedback — what it is, why it can give you that warm, fuzzy feeling, and how to manage it so that all that cyber-positive reinforcement doesn't go to your head.

Getting to Your My eBay Page

Using your My eBay page makes keeping track of your eBay life a whole lot easier. Everybody who is registered with eBay gets a My eBay page. After you sign in to eBay, click the My eBay link to go to your My eBay page, shown in Figure 4-1.

The My eBay page consists of five categories along with their subcategories, where you can view different areas of your eBay business. Table 4-1 gives you the scoop on these categories.

Table 4-1	Categories on Your My eBay Page
Category	**What's There**
My Summary	Items you're bidding on, items you've won, and items you're watching, as well as announcements from eBay.
All Buying	Every auction you're currently bidding on and items you've won, as well as auctions you're watching and auctions you've lost.

(continued)

Table 4-1 *(continued)*

Category	What's There
Selling	Every auction in which you're currently selling items. You also have a list of the items you've sold.
All Favorites	Your favorite categories, searches, sellers, and stores.
My Account	What you currently owe eBay and links to locations where you can get information on payment terms, fees and credits, and refunds. It also links to your PayPal account, your preferences, and your feedback.

Don't confuse the My eBay page with the About Me page. The About Me page is a personal Web page that you can create to let the world know about you and your eBay dealings. (You don't have to have an About Me page if you don't want to — but they're free for the taking and are fun to share.)

When you finally get to your My eBay page, save yourself a lot of work and time by using your browser to bookmark your My eBay page as a favorite. Doing so saves you a lot of keystrokes later on. If you want to send a shortcut to your desktop, in Internet Explorer choose File⇨Send⇨Shortcut to Desktop. This way, you can open your browser directly onto your My eBay page. Some folks also make their My eBay pages their browser home pages so that their My eBay pages appear the minute they log on. That's dedication.

Figure 4-1: Your My eBay page, the hub for your eBay activities.

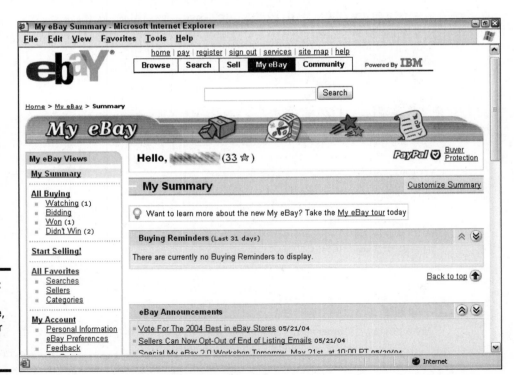

Choosing Your My eBay Preferences

One of the most important areas of your My eBay page is Preferences. eBay created this feature to help you avoid having to type your password every time you do certain activities, such as bid, check your account balance, and participate in auctions.

After you sign in and set up your My eBay page, you can change any of your preferences by scrolling to the My Account category and clicking the eBay Preferences link. You see the Web page shown in Figure 4-2. As you scroll down the page, you can click the Change link and make changes in the following areas:

✦ **eBay Preferences:** You can tell eBay how you want to be notified when someone outbids you, when you make a bid, and when someone has bid on an item in your Watch List.

✦ **eBay Sign In Preferences:** For security purposes, you can tell eBay for which activities you want to enter your password and e-mail address. For example, you can sign out automatically when you leave the eBay Web site and be required to enter your password again when you return, or you can remain signed in when you leave eBay and not have to enter your password when you return.

✦ **Seller Preferences:** For sellers, you can decide how to display the Pay Now button, your shipping preferences, and unsuccessful bidder notices.

✦ **My eBay Preferences:** You can customize how your My eBay page appears in your browser.

Figure 4-2: Even more eBay activities that you can control from your My eBay Preferences page.

Setting Up Your Account

The eBay folks don't set up an account for you until you list something to sell. That way, they can keep track of the fees charged for listing items on the site. Even if the items don't sell, eBay keeps the fee. It doesn't cost you a nickel in fees to look around or sign up — or even to buy.

Even though you've already become a registered eBay user (if you haven't registered, see Book IV, Chapter 2), you don't have to submit your credit card information until you list an item for auction or until you bid in an auction that has special rules requiring a credit card. You can provide eBay with this credit card information right from your My Account page, which you access by clicking the Personal Information link on your My eBay page.

After you start selling, your Accounts page becomes very powerful. You can look up every detail of your account history, as well as make changes to your personal preferences (such as how and when you want to pay fees). If you think that eBay owes you money, you can submit a refund request from here as well.

The Account-Related Links area at the bottom of the Accounts page relates to your financial dealings with eBay. The Payment Terms link is for telling eBay how you want to pay your bill. You can place your credit card on file, pay by PayPal, pay eBay directly, or pay by check or money order. See Table 4-2 to find out when the different payments are charged to your account.

Table 4-2	eBay's Automatic Payments		
Billing Cycle	*Invoice*	*Deducted from Checking Account*	*Credit Card Charged*
15th of month	Between 16th and 20th	5th of the next month	5–7 days after receipt of invoice
Last day of month	Between 1st and 5th of next month	20th of next month	5–7 days after receipt of invoice

What's that thingy?

For the first 30 days after you register or change your User ID, eBay gives you an icon that stays next to your User ID every time it appears on eBay (when you bid, run an auction, or post a message on any of the chat boards).

So why the icon? eBay calls the graphic of a beaming robot-like critter the *new ID* icon. It's sort of a friendly heads-up to others that you're a new user. You still have all the privileges that everybody else has on eBay while you're breaking in your new identity. The icons are nothing personal — just business as usual.

If you're about to hit your credit limit or you don't want eBay making monthly charges on your credit card, you can make a one-time payment. Check out the Pay Your eBay Seller Fees area to make a one-time payment. To pay by check, you need an eBay payment coupon, which you can get by clicking the Mail In a Check or Money Order link, printing out the coupon page, and following the directions. If you want to make a one-time credit card payment, click the Pay with Your Credit Card link; or to write a virtual e-check from your bank account, click the Pay with Your Checking Account link. You arrive at an SSL-secured area where you can type in your information. Click Submit to send the stuff to eBay for processing. It's just that easy.

Getting Your Favorites Area Together

Part of the fun of eBay is searching around for stuff that you'd never in a million years think of looking for. Wacky stuff aside, most eBay users spend their time hunting for specific items — say, Barbie dolls, Elvis memorabilia, or U.S. stamps. That's why eBay came up with the Favorites area of your My eBay page. Whenever you view your My eBay Favorites page, you see a list of your favorite searches, four of your favorite categories, and a list of your favorite sellers and stores. But because eBay isn't psychic, you have to tell it what you want listed.

Choosing your favorite categories

You can choose only four categories to be your favorites, and with over 30,000 categories to choose from, you need to make your choices count. If you're having a hard time narrowing down your category picks, don't worry: Your choices aren't set in stone. You can change your Favorites list whenever you want. (Chapter 3 of Book IV offers details on eBay categories.)

To choose your favorite categories and list them on your All Favorites page, follow these steps:

1. **Click the All Favorites link on your My eBay page and scroll to the My Favorite Categories area.**

2. **Click the Add New Category link (next to the My Favorite Categories head).**

   You see four windows, each containing category listings for four of your category favorites. These windows contain all of eBay's categories, sub-categories, sub-subcategories, and sub-sub-subcategories.

3. **In the far-left column, select the category that you want.**

   The column to the right automatically changes to reflect more choices based on the main category that you selected. Be sure to highlight the categories and subcategories that you want, as shown in Figure 4-3.

4. **Continue across from left to right.**

   Depending on your choices, you might have to scroll through each window to find the subcategory that you're looking for. After you complete your choice, a number appears in the window at the top. That's your category number.

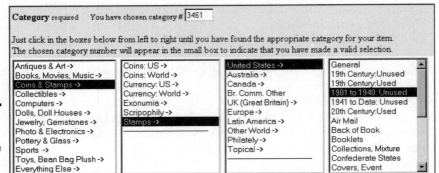

Figure 4-3:
Selecting
your favorite
categories.

5. **Repeat this process for Favorites Category 2 through Category 4.**

   If you don't want to use all four choices, just delete any numbers in the chosen category window.

6. **Click the Submit button at the bottom of the page.**

   You get an acknowledgment that your changes have been made. Click the My eBay link at the top of the page to see your new favorite categories.

How specific you get when selecting your favorites depends on how many items you want to see. The narrower your focus, the fewer items you have to wade through. The more general your favorites, the broader the range of items you have to view.

Your favorite searches and sellers

If you shop eBay like I do, you look for similar things and sellers over and over again. The My Favorite Sellers area allows you to make note of your favorite searches and sellers. You can perform these searches and visit these stores with a click of your mouse.

Favorite searches

You have the opportunity to list a maximum of 100 searches on the page. When you want to repeat one of these searches, just click the search name to search for the items. eBay will even e-mail you when new items are listed for up to 30 of your favorite searches.

To add a search to your favorites, perform a search. (For details on how to perform a search, see Book IV, Chapter 5.) When the search appears on your screen, click the Add to Favorite Searches link in the upper-right corner of the window. The search is now transported to your My eBay Favorite Searches preferences area for that particular search, as shown in Figure 4-4. If you want to be notified by e-mail when new items are listed, select the check box and the time frame next to Email Preferences.

Favorite sellers

When you find a seller whose merchandise and prices are right up your alley, and you'd like to occasionally check out the seller's auctions, you can list the seller in the My Favorite Sellers/Stores area:

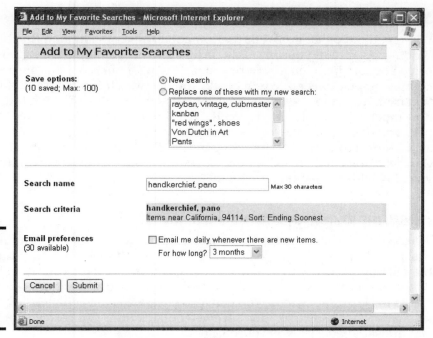

Figure 4-4:
The Adding
a Favorite
Search
details
page.

1. **When you've shopped eBay and found a seller that you're happy with, make note of the seller's store name or User ID.**

2. **Go to your My eBay Favorite Sellers area and click the Add New Seller or Store link.**

3. **Type in the seller's User ID or store name and click the Save Favorite button.**

The seller or store now appears on your My Favorite Sellers area. To view the seller's current auctions or visit his or her store, click the View link to the right of the seller's name.

Got the time? eBay does. Click the eBay Official Time link. (You can find it on any search results page or in the far-left column of the Site Map.) The eBay clock is so accurate that you can set your watch to it. And you might want to, especially if you want to place a last-second bid before an auction closes. After all, eBay's official time is, um, *official.* Here's a quick link to the eBay current date and time:

```
http://cgi3.ebay.com/aw-cgi/eBayISAPI.dll?TimeShow
```

Following the Action on Your Bidding/Watching Area

I have the most fun at eBay when I'm shopping. Shopping at eBay is exciting, and I can find a zillion great bargains. Fortunately, eBay gives us a place to keep all our shopping information together: on the All Buying page. To visit this page, click the All Buying link on your My eBay page.

Seeing the Items I'm Bidding On

When you bid on an item, eBay automatically lists the item in the Items I'm Bidding On area of your My eBay page. If you're winning the auction, the price appears in green; if you're losing, it appears in red. Multiple Item and completed auctions appear in black. You can watch the progress of the auction from here and see the number of bids on the item, the high bid, and how much time is left until the end of the auction. All this information can help you decide whether you want to jump back in and make a bid. eBay also keeps a total of all your active bids at the bottom of this area in the Current Totals: Items I'm Winning section — which should hopefully help you stay within your spending limits.

Keeping track of Items I've Won

When you've won an auction or purchased an item in a store, it appears in the Items I've Won area. From here, you can visit the auction to print out the auction page or double-check it. You can also pay for your item through PayPal directly from here. If you've already paid, you can check the current status in Next Step/Status. You can also click a Leave Feedback link here to leave feedback. However, don't leave feedback until you receive your item and are satisfied with your purchase.

Sleuthing with Items I'm Watching

Items I'm Watching is my most active area of my All Buying page (see Figure 4-5). This is the place for you to work on your strategy for getting bargains without showing your hand by bidding. In this area, you can watch the auction evolve and decide whether you want to bid on the item. You can list several auctions for the same item and watch them all develop and then bid on the one that gives you the best deal. You can track the progress of up to 30 auctions in your Items I'm Watching area.

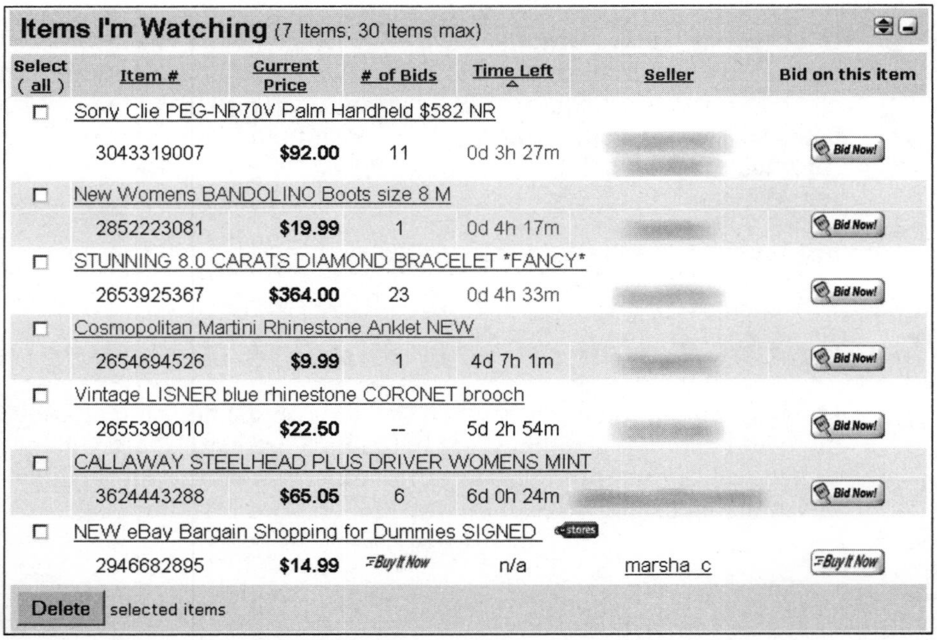

Select (all)	Item #	Current Price	# of Bids	Time Left	Seller	Bid on this item
☐	Sony Clie PEG-NR70V Palm Handheld $582 NR					
	3043319007	**$92.00**	11	0d 3h 27m		🔍 Bid Now!
☐	New Womens BANDOLINO Boots size 8 M					
	2852223081	**$19.99**	1	0d 4h 17m		🔍 Bid Now!
☐	STUNNING 8.0 CARATS DIAMOND BRACELET *FANCY*					
	2653925367	**$364.00**	23	0d 4h 33m		🔍 Bid Now!
☐	Cosmopolitan Martini Rhinestone Anklet NEW					
	2654694526	**$9.99**	1	4d 7h 1m		🔍 Bid Now!
☐	Vintage LISNER blue rhinestone CORONET brooch					
	2655390010	**$22.50**	--	5d 2h 54m		🔍 Bid Now!
☐	CALLAWAY STEELHEAD PLUS DRIVER WOMENS MINT					
	3624443288	**$65.05**	6	6d 0h 24m		🔍 Bid Now!
☐	NEW eBay Bargain Shopping for Dummies SIGNED ⊏stores					
	2946682895	**$14.99**	⇂Buy It Now	n/a	marsha c	⇂Buy It Now

Items I'm Watching (7 Items; 30 Items max)

Delete selected items

Figure 4-5: The Items I'm Watching area of the All Buying page.

Moving auctions into this area is easy. When you've found an auction that you want to keep track of, look for the Watch This Item (Track It in My eBay) link next to the item title (on the right). If you click this link, the item is transported to your Items I'm Watching area.

Surveying Your Sales on Your My eBay Selling Page

Your Selling page supplies you with the tools to keep track of items that you're selling on eBay. The Selling page works very much the same as the Bidding page, but this time you're making the money — not spending it! Your current auction sales are listed in the Items I'm Selling area. The items with bids on them appear in green, and the ones without bids are in red. At the bottom, you have a dollar total of the current bids on your auctions.

Items I'm Selling

Very much like the Items I'm Bidding On section of the All Buying page, the Selling area keeps track of your ongoing auctions at eBay. You can observe the auction action in real time (or at least every time you refresh the page). You can see how many bids have been placed, when the auction closes, and the time left in the auction.

Items I've Sold

When the sale is final, the items go into the Items I've Sold area (shown in Figure 4-6). Here's where you can keep track of the sale. You can check whether the buyer has paid with PayPal and what the transaction status is. If the buyer has completed checkout, you can get his or her information by clicking the Next Steps/Status link. If the buyer hasn't completed checkout, you can click the Send Invoice button to send the buyer an invoice. Very handy!

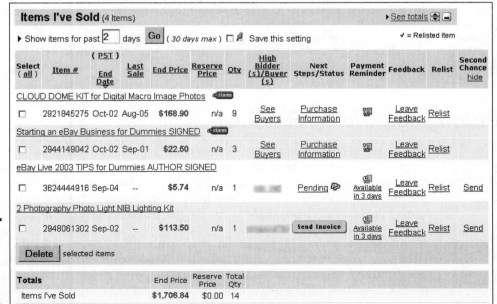

Figure 4-6: The Items I've Sold area and all its options.

Your secret seller tool — Second Chance!

Those cagey great minds at eBay have come up with another great selling implement. Say that you have multiples of a single item (you *did* sell that set of Minton china one piece at a time, didn't you?) or the winning bidder backs out of the transaction without paying. Second Chance gives you the opportunity to offer the item to one of the underbidders (okay, the losers) at their high bid price. The Second Chance opportunity is available for up to 60 days after the sale ends.

You can offer the item to only one of the underbidders at a time and make this personal offer good for one to seven days. The bidder receives an e-mail regarding the offer and can access it on the site through a special link. It is visible only to you and the other bidder for the duration of the offer.

The best part is that eBay doesn't charge any additional listing fees for this feature, but you're charged the Final Value Fee after the transaction is complete.

Keeping Track of Your Transactions

Yes, I bug you about printing stuff out — not because I'm in cahoots with the paper industry but because I care. The best way to protect yourself is to keep good records on your own. Don't depend on eBay to cover you — not that eBay doesn't care. But this is your money, so keep a close eye on it.

Now don't become a pack rat and overdo it. To help point you in the right direction, here's a list of important documents that I think you should print and file whether you're a buyer or a seller:

+ Auction pages as they appear when they close

+ Bank statements indicating any payment you receive that doesn't clear

+ Insurance or escrow forms

+ Refund and credit requests

+ Receipts from purchases that you make for items to sell on eBay

Always, always, *always* save every e-mail message that you receive about a transaction, whether you buy or sell. Also save your *EOAs* (End of Auction e-mails) that eBay sends.

Getting and Giving Feedback

You know how they say that you are what you eat? At eBay, you're only as good as your feedback says you are. Your feedback is made up of comments — good, bad, or neutral — that people leave about you (and you leave about others). In effect, people are commenting on your overall professionalism. These comments are the basis for your eBay reputation.

When you get your first feedback, the number that appears next to your User ID is your feedback rating, which follows you everywhere you go at eBay, even if you change your User ID or e-mail address. It sticks to you like glue. Click the number next to any User ID and get a complete look at the user's feedback profile. You wouldn't be caught dead in a store that has a lousy reputation, so why on Earth would you want to do business on the Internet with someone who has a lousy reputation?

You're not required to leave feedback, but because it's the benchmark by which all eBay users are judged, whether you're buying or selling, you should *always* leave feedback comments. Get in the frame of mind that every time you *complete a transaction* — the minute the payment arrives safely if you're a seller or when an item that you've bid on and won arrives — you should go to eBay and post your feedback.

Every time you get a positive comment from a user who hasn't commented on you before, you get a point. Every time you get a negative rating, this negative cancels out one of your positives. Neutral comments rate a zero — they have no impact either way. Anyone with a –4 rating has his or her eBay membership terminated. eBay even has what it calls the Star Chart, shown in Figure 4-7, which rewards those with good-and-getting-higher feedback ratings.

Figure 4-7: The eBay feedback achievement Star rating.

Home > Services > Feedback Forum > **Member Profile**

Member Profile: ▨▨▨ (33 ☆)

Feedback Score:	**33**
Positive Feedback:	**100%**
Members who left a positive:	33
Members who left a negative:	0
All positive feedback received:	36

Learn about what these numbers mean.

Recent Ratings:

	Past Month	Past 6 Months	Past 12 Months
⊕ positive	0	11	15
⊙ neutral	0	0	0
⊖ negative	0	0	0

Bid Retractions (Past 6 months): 0

Member since: Apr-04-00
Location: United States
▪ ID History
▪ Items for Sale

[Contact Member]

The Feedback page

When you click the Feedback link of your My eBay page (you can find it under the My Account link), you see all the tools that you need for feedback. Think of your feedback profile as your eBay report card. Your goal is to get straight *A*s — in this case, all positive feedback. Unlike a real report card, you don't have to bring it home to be signed.

When someone clicks the feedback number next to your User ID, they see the following information (see Figure 4-8):

Figure 4-8: The feedback profile report card — there's one on every member.

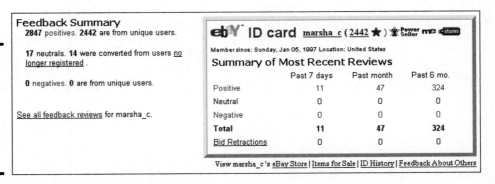

Feedback Summary
2847 positives. **2442** are from unique users.

17 neutrals. **14** were converted from users no longer registered .

0 negatives. **0** are from unique users.

See all feedback reviews for marsha_c.

ebY ID card marsha_c (2442 ★) ⚡Power Seller me estores

Member since: Sunday, Jan 05, 1997 Location: United States

Summary of Most Recent Reviews

	Past 7 days	Past month	Past 6 mo.
Positive	11	47	324
Neutral	0	0	0
Negative	0	0	0
Total	**11**	**47**	**324**
Bid Retractions	0	0	0

View marsha_c 's eBay Store | Items for Sale | ID History | Feedback About Others

✦ **Your User ID:** Your eBay nickname appears, followed by a number in parentheses — the net number of the positive feedback comments that you've received minus any negative feedback comments you've gotten (but that wouldn't happen to you . . .).

✦ **Your overall profile makeup:** This area sums up the positive, negative, and neutral feedback comments that people have left for you.

✦ **Your eBay ID card with a summary of most recent comments:** This area is a scorecard of your feedback for the last six months. At the bottom of the feedback tote board is a summary of your bid retractions — the times that you've retracted bids during an auction.

Reading your feedback

Your eBay reputation is at the mercy of the one-liners that buyers and sellers leave for you in the form of feedback comments. Each feedback box contains these reputation-building (or -trashing) ingredients:

✦ The User ID of the person who sent it. The number in parentheses next to the person's name is his or her own feedback rating.

✦ The date and time the feedback was posted.

✦ The item number of the transaction that the feedback refers to. If the item has closed in the past 30 days, you can click the transaction number to see what the buyer purchased.

✦ Seller or Buyer — Seller if you were the seller, and Buyer if you were the buyer in the transaction.

✦ Feedback comes in different colors: praise (in green), negative (in red), and neutral (in black).

✦ The feedback the person left about you.

Extra, extra, read all about it

Normally, I believe in the adage, "Keep your business private." But not when it comes to feedback. The default setting is for public viewing of your feedback. This way, everyone at eBay can read all about you.

If you want to make your feedback a private matter, you need to go to the Feedback Forum (click the Services link on the navigation bar and then click the eBay Feedback Forum link), and click the Hide Your Feedback link.

Hiding your feedback is a bad idea. You want people to know that you're trustworthy; being honest and upfront is the way to go. If you hide your feedback profile, people might suspect that you're covering up bad things. It's in your best interest to let the spotlight shine on your feedback history.

It's your reputation, your money, and your experience as an eBay member. Keep in mind that all three are always linked.

You have the last word — responding to feedback

After reading feedback that you've received from others, you might feel compelled to respond. If the feedback is negative, you might want to defend yourself. If it's positive, you might want to say thank you. To respond to feedback, follow these steps:

1. **In the Feedback section of your My eBay page, click the Reply to Feedback Received link.**

   You're transported to the Review and Respond to Feedback Comments Left for You page.

2. **When you find the feedback that you want to respond to, click the Respond link.**

3. **Type in your response.**

Don't confuse *responding* to feedback with *leaving* feedback. Responding doesn't change the other user's feedback rating; it merely adds a line below the feedback with your response.

Giving feedback

Several ways are available to leave feedback comments:

✦ If you're on the user's Feedback page, click the Leave Feedback link. The Leave Feedback page appears.

✦ In the Items I've Won area of your My eBay page, click the Leave Feedback link next to the auction.

✦ Go to your auction and click the Leave Feedback icon.

✦ In the Feedback Forum, click the Leave Feedback about an eBay User — See All Pending Comments at Once link to see a list of all your completed auctions from the last 90 days for which you haven't yet left feedback.

✦ Click the Services link in the main navigation bar and then click Feedback Forum. On the next page that appears, click the Go Directly to the Feedback Forum link.

To leave feedback, follow these steps:

1. **Enter the required information.**

   Note that your item number is usually filled in, but if you're placing feedback from the user's Feedback page, you need to have the number at hand.

2. **Choose whether you want your feedback to be positive, negative, or neutral.**

3. **Click the Leave Feedback button.**

CHECK IT OUT

eBay Will Consider Removing Feedback If . . .

✔ eBay is served with a court order stating that the feedback in question is slanderous, libelous, defamatory, or otherwise illegal. eBay will also accept a settlement agreement from a resolved lawsuit submitted by both attorneys and signed by both parties.

✔ A certified arbitrator to whom both parties agreed to submit the issue for binding arbitration requests that the feedback be removed.

✔ The feedback in question has no relation to eBay — such as comments about transactions outside of eBay or personal comments about users.

✔ The feedback contains a link to another page, picture, or JavaScript.

✔ The feedback is composed of profane or vulgar language.

✔ The feedback contains any personal identifying information about a user.

✔ The feedback refers to any investigation, whether by eBay or a law-enforcement organization.

✔ The feedback is left by a user who supplied fraudulent information when registering at eBay.

✔ The feedback is left by a person who can be identified as a minor.

✔ The feedback is left by a user as a part of harassment.

✔ The feedback is intended for another user, when eBay has been informed of the situation and the same feedback has been left for the appropriate user.

Chapter 5: Information Is Power: Researching

In This Chapter

✔ Searching on eBay for items that interest you

✔ Conducting a special item search at eBay

✔ Getting solid online buying advice

Think of walking into a store and seeing thousands of aisles of shelves with millions of items on them. Browsing the categories of auctions at eBay can be just as pleasantly boggling without the prospect of sore feet. Start surfing around the site and you instantly understand the size and scope of what's for sale there. You might feel overwhelmed at first, but the clever eBay folks have come up with lots of ways to help you find exactly what you're looking for. As soon as you figure out how to find the items that you want to bid on, you can protect your investment-to-be by making sure that what you find is actually what you seek.

Of course, searching is easier if you have an idea of what you're looking for. In this chapter, I give you tips for using the eBay turbo search engine from a buyer's perspective. The best advice that you can follow as you explore any free-market system is *caveat emptor* — let the buyer beware. Although nobody can guarantee that every one of your transactions will be perfect, research items thoroughly before you bid so that you don't lose too much of your hard-earned money. I offer advice for researching items on the Internet at the end of this chapter.

Looking to Find an Item? Start Your eBay Search Engine

The best part about shopping on eBay is that you can find just about everything from that esoteric lithium battery to new designer dresses (with matching shoes) to pneumatic jackhammers. New or used, it's all here — hiding in the over 14 million daily listings. However, finding the nuggets (deals) can be like searching for the proverbial needle in the haystack. The search secrets in this section will put you head and shoulders above your competition for the deals.

eBay has lots of cool ways for you to search for items. These are the four main options:

✦ Search Title (Basic or Advanced Search)

✦ Search by Seller

◆ Search by Bidder

◆ eBay Stores

You can access the four search options by clicking the Search link on the navigation bar, which appears at the top of any eBay page where you can customize your search. Each search option can provide a different piece of information to help you find the right item from the right seller at the right price.

If you want to be thorough in your eBay searches, I recommend that you conduct searches often by saving them in your My eBay All Favorites page area (see Book IV, Chapter 4 to find out how). And when you find a particularly juicy item or subcategory, bookmark it, or if it's an item, click the Watch This Item link (which appears on the auction page just under the item number), or use your All Favorites page.

Using the eBay Search page

When you click the Search link on the navigation bar, the Basic Search page appears. It's the most basic of searches (with a few options) and the one you'll use the most.

When you use any of the search options on eBay, the search engine looks for every listing (auction or fixed price) that has the words you're looking for in the title or the description (if you specify so). The title (as you might expect) is just another word or group of words for what you call the item. For example, if you're looking for an antique sterling iced-tea spoon, just type **sterling iced tea spoon** into the search window (see Figure 5-1). If someone is selling a sterling iced-tea spoon and used exactly those words in his or her title or description, you're in Fat City.

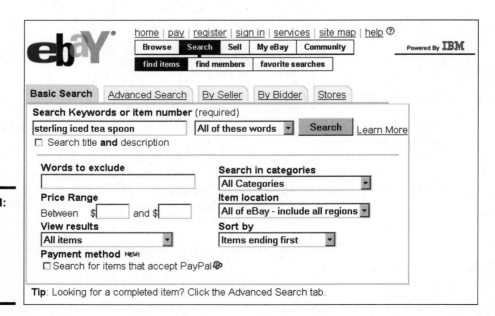

Figure 5-1:
Using
Search
to find a
sterling
iced-tea
spoon.

Before you click the Search button, narrow down your search further. When you type in your search title, you have the option of choosing how you want the search engine to interpret your search entry. You can have the search engine search the title and description for

✦ All the words that you type

✦ Some of the words that you type

✦ The exact phrase in the order that you've written it

In addition, you can select other criteria:

✦ **What price range you want to see:** Type in the price range that you're looking for, and eBay searches the specific range between that low and high price. If money is no object, leave these text boxes blank.

✦ **Words to exclude:** If you want to find a sterling iced-tea spoon, but you don't want it to be plated silver, exclude the word *plated*.

✦ **The payment:** You can restrict your search to items that accept PayPal.

✦ **Within a category:** Use this option if you want to limit your search to a particular main (or *top-level*) category, for example, instead of searching all eBay categories.

✦ **The item location:** You can narrow your search into one of over 50 eBay Local Trading regions.

✦ **The order in which you want your results to appear:** If you indicate Items Ending First, the search engine gives you the results so that auctions closing soon appear first on the list. Newly Listed Items First lists all the newly listed auctions. Lowest Prices First and Highest Prices First list them just that way.

✦ **Whether you want the search engine to check through item titles alone or check both item titles *and* item descriptions:** You get more hits on your search if you select the Search Title and Description check box, but you might also get too many items that are out of your search range. See "Narrowing down your eBay search," later in this chapter, for some solid advice.

Okay, *now* click the Search button. In a few seconds, you see the fruits of all the work that you've been doing. (Wow, you're not even perspiring.)

When running the search for sterling iced-tea spoon, I came up with 29 items. But some people might call them *ice tea spoon*. So, using one of the search tricks that I show you in Table 5-1 (later in this chapter), I changed my search to *sterling (ice,iced) tea spoon* and got 50 items. See Figure 5-2 for those results.

Next to item listings, you often see pictures, or *icons*. A golden yellow rising sun picture means that the listing is brand new (this icon stays on for the first 24 hours that an item is listed), a small camera means that the seller has included a digital picture along with the item description, and a picture frame indicates that the item is listed with a photo in the Gallery.

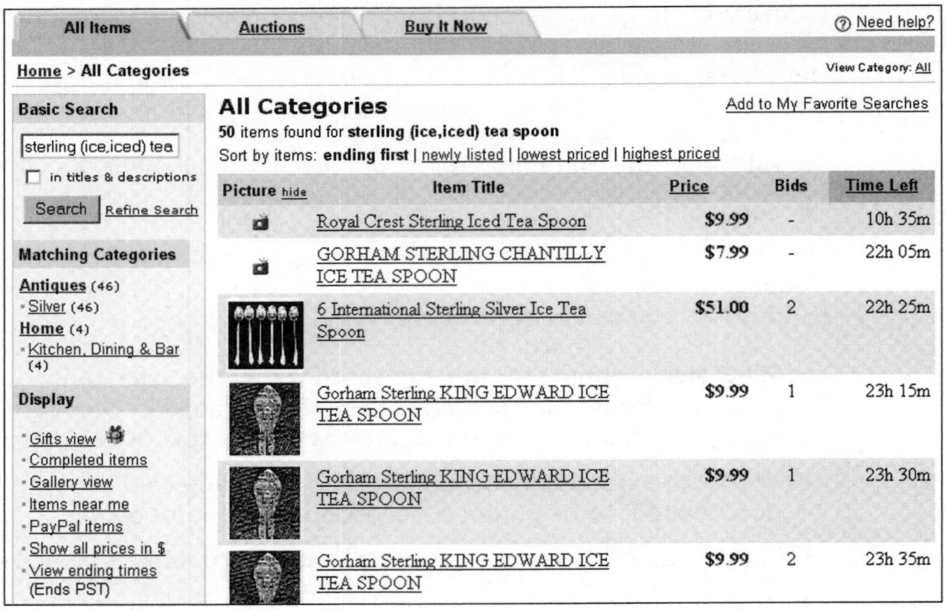

Figure 5-2:
The results of a quest for a sterling iced-tea spoon, using search tricks.

eBay's Advanced Search

The Advanced Search tab of the search area throws quite a few more options into the package. Don't be intimidated by this area; you need to understand just a few important bells and whistles.

A Completed Items Only search

A Completed Items Only search returns results of auctions that have already ended. This is my favorite search option at eBay because you can use it as a strategic bidding tool. How? If you're bidding on an item and want to know if the prices are likely to go too high for your pocketbook, you can use this search option to compare the current price of the item to the selling price of similar items from auctions that have already ended.

You can also use this tool if you want to sell an item and are trying to determine what it's worth, how high the demand is, and whether this is the right time to list the item. (Book IV, Chapter 12 offers the nuts, bolts, and monkey wrenches that you need to set up your auction.)

Type in your keyword criteria and scroll down the page to the Completed Items Only check box. Step by step, here's how to do a Completed Items Only search:

1. **In the Search Keywords or Item Numbers text box, type in the title name or the keywords of the item you want to find.**

2. **Select the Completed Items Only check box to see completed listings as far back as the eBay search engine permits.**

   Currently, you can go back about two weeks.

3. Tell eBay how you want the results arranged.

In the Sort By drop-down list box, select one of the following four options:

- **Items Ending First:** Include completed auctions starting with the oldest available (about two weeks).

- **Newly Listed First:** List the most recently completed auctions first.

- **Lowest Prices First:** List auctions from the lowest price attained to the highest price paid for an item.

- **Highest Prices First:** List completed items from highest to lowest. (This is very useful when you're searching for a 1967 Camaro and you want to buy a car and not a Hot Wheels toy.)

4. Click the Search button.

The search results appear in just a few seconds.

An international search

You can select any country (from Afghanistan to Zimbabwe, no kidding!) or narrow your search to the United States or Canada. Don't forget that you have to pay for shipping, so if you don't want to pay to ship a heavy Victorian-style fainting sofa from Hungary to Hoboken, New Jersey, stick close to home. The Location/International Search option is pretty much an international version of Search, and it's done the same way. You also have the choice of narrowing down your country search with the following options:

- ✦ **Items Available To:** The search engine looks for items within your own country or from international sellers who are willing to ship to you.

- ✦ **Items Located In:** The search engine looks for items from the specific country you entered in the list box.

A seller search

The By Seller tab of the search area, shown in Figure 5-3, gives you a list of all the auctions that a seller is running, and it's a great way for you to keep a list of people you have successfully done business with in the past. The By Seller page is also a strategy that eBay users use to assess the reputation of a seller.

View all items by a single seller

To use the By Seller search option to search for all of a single seller's items, follow these steps:

1. In the Single Seller search text box, type the eBay User ID of the person you want to find out more about.

2. On the Include Bidder Emails line, tell eBay whether you want to see the e-mail addresses of other people who are bidding on auctions posted by the person that you're searching for.

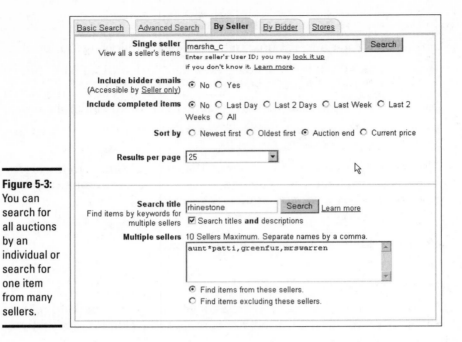

Figure 5-3:
You can
search for
all auctions
by an
individual or
search for
one item
from many
sellers.

If you're the seller and want to view these addresses from this page, select Yes. Note that to protect each member's privacy, e-mail addresses are available to you only if you're involved in a transaction with the other person.

3. **If you don't want to see auctions that this specific seller has conducted in the past, select No on the Include Completed Items line.**

   You can choose to see all current and previous auctions, as well as auctions that have ended in the last day, last two days, last week, or last two weeks.

   eBay keeps past auction results active for only 30 days; if you're looking for something auctioned 31 days (or longer) ago, sorry — no dice.

4. **On the Sort By line, select an option to control how you want the results of your search to appear on-screen.**

   If you want to see the auctions that are closing right away, select the Auction End option.

5. **From the Results per Page list box, select the number of results that you want to see per page.**

   If the person you're looking up has 100 auctions running, you can limit the number of results to a manageable 25 listings on four separate pages. Doing so allows you to narrow down what you want to see.

6. **Click the Search button next to the Single Seller text box.**

   The list of sellers appears on-screen.

Finding items by keywords for multiple sellers

If you're looking for a specific item from a group of sellers, you can fill the search information in the bottom half of the By Seller search page, as shown earlier in Figure 5-3. You might need to perform this type of search after you settle into shopping on eBay and have several sellers that you like doing business with. (Alternatively, you can exclude sellers you prefer not to do business with.) With this method, you can limit the search for a particular item to just the sellers that you want, rather than tens of thousands of sellers.

When you find a seller that you want to continue doing business with, you can add his or her link to your My eBay All Favorites area. Just go to your My eBay page and, in the All Favorites area, click the Add New Seller or Store link. You can add up to 30 sellers in this area and can search their sales with a click of your mouse!

A bidder search

The By Bidder search option is unique because sellers and buyers alike use it when an auction is going on — to figure out their best strategies. After all, money is the name of the game. For information on conducting a By Bidder search, take a look at Book IV, Chapter 7.

Narrowing down your eBay search

After you become familiar with each of eBay's search options, you need a crash course in what words to actually type into those nice little boxes. Too little information and you might not find your item. Too much and you're overwhelmed with information. If you're really into bean-bag toys, for example, you might be looking for Tabasco the Bull from Ty. But if you just search for *Tabasco,* you'll get swamped with results ranging from hot sauce to advertisements.

Some simple tricks can help narrow your eBay search results when you're searching from pages other than the main Search page (where you don't find all the searching bells and whistles). Table 5-1 has the details.

Table 5-1	Symbols and Keywords for Conducting Searches with the eBay Search Engine	
Symbol	**Impact on Search**	**Example**
No symbol, multiple words	Returns auctions with all included words in the title	**reagan letter** might return an auction for a mailed message from the former U.S. president, or it might return an auction for a mailed message from Boris Yeltsin to Ronald Reagan.
Quotes ""	Limits the search to items with the exact phrase inside the quotes	**"Wonder Woman"** returns items about the comic book/TV heroine. Quotes don't make the search term case sensitive. Using either upper- or lowercase in *any* eBay search gets you the same results.

(continued)

Table 5-1 *(continued)*

Symbol	Impact on Search	Example
Asterisk *	Serves as a wildcard	**budd*** returns items that start with budd, such as Beanie Buddy, Beanie Buddies, or Buddy Holly.
Separating comma without spaces (a,b)	Finds items related to either the item before or after the comma	**(gi joe,g.i. joe)** returns all G.I. JOE items no matter which way the seller listed them.
Minus sign –	Excludes results with the word after the –	Type in **box –lunch**, and you'd better not be hungry because you might find the box, but lunch won't be included.
Minus sign and parentheses	Searches for auctions with words before the parentheses but excludes words inside the parentheses	**midge –(skipper,barbie)** means that auctions with the Midge doll won't have to compete for Ken's attention.
Parentheses	Searches for both versions of the word in parentheses	**political (pin,pins)** searches for political pin or political pins.

Here are additional tips to help you narrow down any eBay search:

✦ **Don't worry about capitalization:** You can capitalize proper names or leave them lowercase — the search engine doesn't care.

✦ **Don't use *and, a, an, or,* or *the:*** Called *noise words* in search lingo, these words are interpreted as part of your search. So if you want to find something from *The Sound of Music* and you type in **the sound of music,** you might not get any results. Most sellers drop noise words from the beginning of an item title when they list it, just as libraries drop noise words when they alphabetize books. So make your search for **sound music.** An even more precise search would be **"sound of music"** (in quotes).

✦ **Search within specific categories:** This type of search narrows down your results because you search only one niche of eBay — just the specific area that you want. For example, if you want to find Tabasco the Bull, start at the home page and, under the Categories heading, click Toys and Bean Bag. The only problem with searching in a specific category is that sometimes an item can be in more than one place. For example, if you're searching for a Mickey Mouse infant snuggly in the Disney category, you might miss it because the item might be listed in infant wear.

Finding eBay Members: The Gang's All Here

With millions of eBay users on the loose, you might think that tracking folks down is hard. Nope. eBay's powerful search engine kicks into high gear to help you find other eBay members in seconds.

Here's how to find people or get info on them from eBay:

1. **From the main navigation bar at the top of most eBay pages, click the Search link.**

This action takes you to the main Search page where three links pop up on the subnavigation bar: Find Items, Find Members, and Favorite Searches.

2. **Click the Find Members link on the subnavigation bar.**

This link takes you to the main Find Members page, where you can search for specific About Me pages. Here you can also get a look at the feedback profile of a user (see Book IV, Chapter 4 for details about feedback), find User ID histories of fellow eBay members (which comes in handy when you're bidding on items, as Book IV, Chapter 7 avows), or get contact information when you're involved in a transaction.

3. **Fill in the appropriate text boxes with what you're looking for and click the Search (or, in some cases, the Submit) button to get the info that you want.**

If you're looking for User ID histories or contact information, and you haven't signed in, you have to do so at this point.

Clicking the Favorite Searches link on the subnavigation bar takes you to your My eBay All Favorites page. You can tell eBay about the items that you're looking for, and it does automatic searches for you. You can also have eBay e-mail you when auctions that match your descriptions crop up.

Doing More Research Online

Hey, the experts have been buying, selling, and trading merchandise items for years. But just because you're new to eBay doesn't mean you have to be a newbie for decades before you can start bartering with the collecting gods. I wouldn't leave you in the cold like that — and neither would eBay. You can get information on items that you're interested in, as well as good collecting tips, right at the eBay Web site. To visit the Category-Specific Discussion Boards, click the Community link on the navigation bar and click the Discussion Boards link on the page that appears. You can also search the rest of the Web or go the old-fashioned route and check the library. (Yes, libraries are still around.)

Keep in mind that there are truly several prices for an item. The retail price (the manufacturer's suggested retail price — MSRP), the book value (the cost recommended by an objective third party), the secondary market price (the price charged by resellers when an item is unavailable on the primary retail market), and the eBay selling price. The only way to ascertain the price an item will go for on eBay is to research completed auctions.

Searching sites online

If you don't find the information that you need at eBay, don't go ballistic — just go elsewhere. Even a site as vast as eBay doesn't have a monopoly on information. The Internet is filled with Web sites and Internet auction sites that can give you price comparisons and information about cyber-clubs.

Your home computer can connect to powerful outside servers (really big computers on the Internet) that have their own fast-searching systems called *search engines.* Remember, if something is out there and you need it, you can find it right from your home computer in just a matter of seconds. Here are the addresses of some of the Web's most highly regarded search engines or multi-search-engine sites (the last two on this list are the subjects of Books II and III):

+ AltaVista (www.altavista.com)

+ Dogpile (www.dogpile.com)

+ Excite (www.excite.com)

+ Google (www.google.com)

+ Yahoo! (www.yahoo.com)

The basic process of getting information from an Internet search engine is pretty simple:

1. **Type the address of the search-engine site in the Address box of your Web browser.**

You're taken to the Web site's home page.

2. **Find the text box next to the button labeled Search or something similar.**

3. **In the text box, type a few words indicating what interests you.**

Be specific when typing in search text. The more precise your entry is, the better your chances are of finding what you want. Look for tips, an advanced search option, or help pages on your search engine of choice for more information about how to narrow your search.

4. **Click the Search (or similar) button or press Enter on your keyboard.**

The search engine presents you with a list of the Internet pages that have the requested information. The list includes brief descriptions and links to the first group of pages. You find links to additional listings at the bottom if your search finds more listings than can fit on one page (and if you ask for something popular, like *Harry Potter,* don't be surprised to get millions of hits).

Always approach information on the Web with caution. Not everyone is the expert that he or she would like to be. Your best bet is to get lots of different opinions and then boil 'em down to what makes sense to you. And remember — *caveat emptor.* (Is there an echo in here?)

If you're researching prices to buy a car on eBay, look in your local newspaper to get a good idea of prices in your community. Several good sites are on the Internet. My personal favorite is www.nadaguides.com. I've had many of my friends (and editors) visit the various sites, and we've settled on this one because it seems to give the most accurate and unbiased information.

Finding other sources of information

If you're interested in collecting a particular item, you can get a lot of insider collecting information without digging too deep:

✦ **Go to other places at eBay.** eBay's chat rooms and message boards are full of insider info. The eBay community is always willing to educate a newbie.

✦ **Go to the library.** Books and magazines are great sources of info. At least one book or one magazine probably specializes in your chosen item. For example, if old furniture is your thing, *Antiquing For Dummies,* by Ron Zoglin and Deborah Shouse (Wiley Publishing, Inc.), can clue you in to what antiques collectors look for.

If you find an interesting specialty magazine at the library, try entering the title in your search engine of choice. You might just find that the magazine has also gone paperless: You can read it online.

✦ **Go to someone else in the know.** Friends, clubs, and organizations in your area can give you a lot of info. Ask your local antiques dealer about clubs that you can join and see how much info you end up with.

CHECK IT OUT

Taking Advantage of Misspellings

As you search for items on eBay, use the asterisk symbol (*) as a wildcard character to help you locate misspelled listings. I've found some great deals by finding items incorrectly posted by the sellers. Here are a few examples:

✔ **Rodri*:** In this search, I look for items by the famous Cajun artist George Rodrigue. His *Blue Dog* paintings are world renowned and very valuable. By using this search, I managed to purchase a signed *Blue Dog* lithograph for under $200. (I resold it on eBay later that year for $900!)

✔ **Alumi* tree:** Remember the old aluminum Christmas trees from the '60s? They've

had quite a resurgence in popularity these days. You can buy these pseudo-antiques in stores for hundreds of dollars . . . or you can buy one on eBay for half the price. You can find them even cheaper if the seller can't spell *aluminum.* . . .

✔ **Cemet* plot:** If you're looking for that final place to retire, eBay has some great deals. Unfortunately, sellers haven't narrowed down whether they want to spell it *cemetery* or *cemetary.* This search finds both.

After studying these examples, I'm sure that you can think of many more instances in which your use of the asterisk can help you find the deals.

Chapter 6: Bidding Basics

In This Chapter

✓ Getting your plan together before you bid

✓ Knowing the ins and outs of the item page

✓ Watching an auction

✓ Knowing the seller

✓ Retracting your bid

*B*rowsing different categories of eBay, looking for nothing in particular, you spot that must-have item lurking among other Elvis paraphernalia in the Collectibles category. Sure, you *can* live without that faux gold Elvis pocket watch, but life would be so much sweeter *with* it. And even if it doesn't keep good time, at least it'll be right twice a day.

When you bid for items on eBay, you can get that same thrill that you would get at Sotheby's or Christie's for a lot less money, and the items that you win are likely to be *slightly* more practical than an old Dutch masterpiece that you're afraid to leave at the framer's.

In this chapter, I give you the lowdown about the types of auctions that are available on eBay and a rundown of the nuts and bolts of bidding strategies. I also share some tried-and-true tips that can give you a leg up on the competition.

The Auction Item Page

Because at any given point, you have more than a million pages of items that you can look at on eBay, auction item pages are the heart (better yet, the skeleton) of eBay auctions. All item pages on eBay — whether auctions, fixed-price items, or Buy It Now items — look about the same. For example, Figure 6-1 shows a conventional auction item page, and Figure 6-2 shows a fixed-price sale. Both item pages show the listing title at the top, bidding or buying info in the middle, and seller info on the right. Below this area, you find a complete description of the item, along with shipping information.

Of course, the two auction types have some subtle differences. (With a venue as big as eBay, you gotta have some flexibility.) Some auctions feature a picture at the top of the page, and some don't, depending on how the seller sets up his or her sale page. Some auctions have set item specifics in the description (as shown in Figure 6-2). This area is set up by eBay and filled in by the seller to give you a snapshot description of the item for sale. If the item that you come to after your search is a fixed-price sale, you just see the words Buy It Now (also shown in Figure 6-2). But overall, the look and feel of these pages are the same.

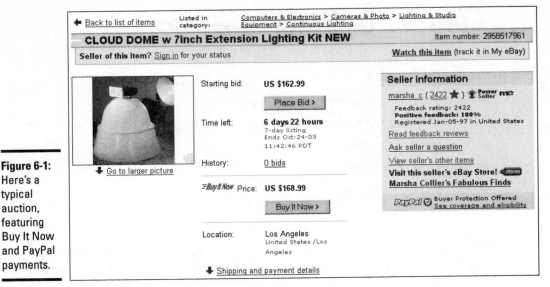

Figure 6-1:
Here's a typical auction, featuring Buy It Now and PayPal payments.

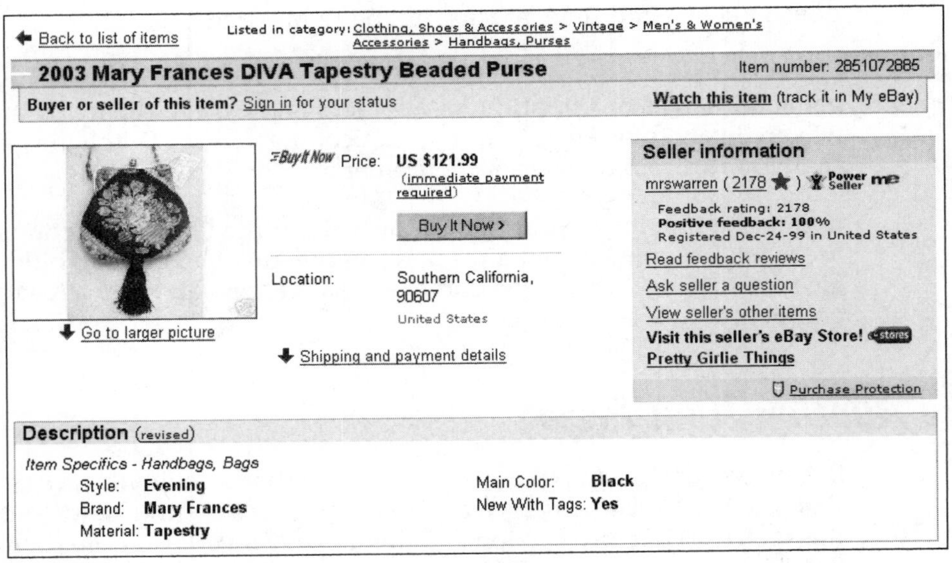

Figure 6-2:
This is a fixed-price sale with item specifics.

Here's a list of stuff that you see as you scroll down on a typical auction item page:

✦ **Item title and number:** The title and number identify the item. Keep track of this info for inquiries later on. If you're interested in a particular type of item, take note of the keywords used in the title (you're likely to see them again in future titles). Doing so helps you in narrowing down your searches.

✦ **Item category:** Located just above the item title and number bar, you can click the category listing and do some comparison shopping.

✦ **Current Bid:** This line indicates the dollar amount that the bidding has reached, which changes throughout the auction as people place bids. If no bids have been placed on the item, this line is called Starting Bid.

Sometimes, next to the current dollar amount, you see *(Reserve not met)* or *(Reserve met)*. This means the seller has set a *reserve price* for the item — a secret price that must be reached before the seller will sell the item. If you don't see this note on an auction item page, don't be alarmed. Not all auctions have reserve prices. The majority don't.

✦ **Buy It Now price:** If you want the item immediately and the price quoted in this area is okay with you, click the Buy It Now link, which takes you to a page where you can complete your purchase.

✦ **Quantity:** This line appears only in a multiple item fixed-price sale or Multiple Item auction (also called a Dutch auction). It tells you how many items are available. If you see a number other than 1 on this line, you're looking at a Multiple Item auction, which is explained later in this chapter.

✦ **Time Left:** Although the clock never stops ticking at eBay, you must continue to refresh your browser to see the time remaining on the official clock. When the item gets down to the last hour of the auction, you see the time expressed in minutes and seconds.

✦ **History:** This line tells you how many bids have been placed. To use the number of bids to your advantage, you have to read between the lines. You can determine just how hot an item is by comparing the number of bids that the item has received over time. Based on the amount of interest in an item, you can create a time strategy (which I talk about later in this chapter). The starting bid is listed in light gray next to the number of bids. If you click the number of bids, you can find out who is bidding and what date and time bids were placed on this item. The dollar amount of each bid is kept secret until the end of the auction.

✦ **High Bidder:** This line shows you the User ID and feedback rating of the current high bidder. Bidding is more an art than a science. Sometimes an item gets no bids because everyone's waiting until the last minute. You see a flurry of activity as bidders all try to outbid each other (called *sniping,* which Book IV, Chapter 7 explains). But that's all part of the fun of eBay.

✦ **Location:** This line tells you at the very least the country where the seller is located, and you might also see more specific info, such as the city and geographic area where the seller is. (What you see depends on how detailed the seller wants to be.) Factor in the geographic location of a seller when you consider bidding on an item. Knowing exactly where the item is can help you quickly calculate what the shipping charges will be — and how long it will take for the item to get to you.

✦ **Watch This Item:** Click this link, and the item is magically added to the Items I'm Watching area of your My eBay page so that you can keep an eye on the progress of the auction — without actually bidding.

✦ **Seller Information box:** This area gives you information about the seller, as shown in Figure 6-3. See the sidebar "Know thy seller" for more information.

✦ **Description banner:** Below this light blue shaded banner is the item description. Read all this information carefully before bidding. Read on to find out how to use this information.

**Book IV
Chapter 6**

Bidding Basics

Know thy seller . . .

Know thy seller ranks right after *caveat emptor* (let the buyer beware) as a phrase that pays at eBay. As I tell you nearly a million times in this minibook, *read the feedback rating!* Human beings come in all shapes, sizes, and levels of honesty, and like any community, eBay has its share of good folks and bad folks. Your best defense is to read the seller's feedback. You can see several things in the Seller Information box (refer to Figure 6-3):

✔ **Feedback Rating:** This is the same number that's to the right of the seller's name in parentheses. Click the number next to the seller's ID to view his or her eBay ID card and entire feedback history just below it. Read, read, and reread all the feedback (hey, we're one closer to a million!) to make sure that you feel comfortable doing business with this person.

✔ **Positive Feedback:** The eBay computers cipher this percentage. It's derived from all the positive and negative feedback that a user receives.

✔ **Registered:** This line lists the date the seller registered on eBay and the country in which he or she registered.

✔ **Read Feedback Reviews:** Clicking this link does the same thing as clicking the Feedback Rating number.

✔ **Ask Seller a Question:** Clicking this link hooks you up with eBay's e-mail system. You can ask the seller a question regarding the item here.

✔ **View Seller's Other Items:** Clicking this link takes you to a page that lists all the seller's current auctions and fixed-price sales.

If the seller has an eBay Store, a link to it appears here as well. I give you a step-by-step guide on how these links work elsewhere in this chapter.

If the seller accepts PayPal, that option is indicated in a shaded area. Also, if the seller qualifies for Buyer Protection, this is also indicated here, as shown in Figure 6-3.

Figure 6-3:
Lots of data on the seller here.

Below the seller's description area, you can find some other important data on the typical auction item page:

✦ **Shipping and Payment Details:** Check here to see the details on shipping. If the item weighs more than a pound, the seller might have conveniently included eBay's shipping calculator in this area. Just type in your ZIP Code, and you're presented with the shipping cost to your location.

✦ **Payment Methods Accepted:** This field tells you the payment methods that the seller accepts: checks, money orders, credit cards, or PayPal. Often, it tells you to read the item description for more details. I explain how to read item descriptions later in this chapter.

✦ **Email This Item to a Friend:** You can tip off a friend on a good find, get some advice from an antiques or collecting expert, or run the auction by a friend who's been around the eBay block a few times and ask for strategy advice. (You find this link below the shipping and payment areas.)

Be sure to use the Watch This Item feature. Organization is the name of the game at eBay, especially if you plan to bid on multiple auctions while you're running auctions of your own. I figure you're in the bidding game to win, so start keeping track of items now.

Beating the Devil in the Details

As with any sale — whether you find it at Joe's Hardware, Bloomingdale's, or Target — carefully check out what you're buying. The item page gives you links to help you know what you're bidding on and who you're potentially buying from. If you take advantage of these features, you won't have many problems. But if you ignore these essential tips, you might end up unhappy with what you buy, who you buy it from, and how much you spend.

Read the item description carefully

The *item description* is the most critical item on the auction item page. This is where the seller lists the details about the item being sold. Read this page carefully and pay very close attention to what is, and *isn't,* written.

Don't judge a book by its cover — but do judge a seller by his or her item description. If the sentences are succinct, detailed, and well structured, you're most likely dealing with an individual who planned and executed the auction with care. It takes time and effort to post a good auction. If you see huge lapses in grammar, convoluted sentences, and misspellings, *you may be gonna get burnt!*

If a picture is available, take a good look. The majority of eBay sellers jazz up their auctions with photos of their items. The seller should answer a few general questions in the item's description. In particular, make sure that you get answers to questions like these:

✦ Is the item new or used?

✦ Is the item a first edition or a reprint? An original or a reissue?

✦ Is the item in its original packaging? Does it still have the original tags?

✦ Is the item under warranty?

✦ Is this item the genuine article or a reproduction, and if it's the real deal, does the seller have papers or labels certifying its authenticity?

✦ What size is the item? (That life-size fiberglass whale might not *fit* in your garage.)

If you win the item and find out that the seller lied in the description, you have the right to request to return the item. But if you win the item and discover that *you* overlooked a detail in the description, the seller isn't obligated to take the item back.

Get the scoop on the seller

I can't tell you enough that the single most important way you can make an auction go well is to *know who you're dealing with.* Apparently, the eBay folks agree; they enable you to get info on the seller right from the auction item page. I recommend that you take advantage of the links offered there. (Book IV, Chapter 5 demonstrates how to conduct a thorough By Seller search.) To get the full scoop on a seller, here's what you need to do:

✦ Click the number beside the seller's User ID to get his or her feedback history. Click the Me link (if there is one) next to the seller to view the seller's *About Me* page. It frequently gives you a good deal more information about the seller.

✦ Make note if you see the PowerSeller icon next to the seller's name. It means that he or she is an eBay seller who has met certain stringent certifications.

View the seller's other auctions

To find out what other auctions the seller has going at eBay, all you have to do is click the corresponding link on the item page; you're whisked away to a list of the other auction pies that the seller has a finger in. If the seller has no other auctions going and has no current feedback, you might want to do a more thorough investigation and conduct a By Seller search that will show you all that person's completed auctions in the last 30 days. (See Book IV, Chapter 5 for details.)

Ask the seller a question

If anything about the auction is unclear to you, remember this one word: *ask.* Find out all the details about that item before you bid. If you wait until you've won the item before you ask questions, you might get stuck with something that you don't want. To ask a seller a question, simply click the Ask Seller a Question link on the item page and fill in the message area.

If you're bidding on a reserve-price auction, don't be afraid to e-mail the seller and ask what the reserve is. Yeah, reserves are mostly kept secret, but there's no harm in asking — and many sellers gladly tell you.

Extend your scam antennae if a seller's reply to your question comes from an e-mail address that's different from the one that you sent your question to. The seller should include an explanation for a difference in addresses. If you don't receive an explanation, ask for one. Fraudulent sellers often use several e-mail addresses to hide their true identity.

Factoring In the Extras

Before you think about placing a bid on an item, factor in the financial obligation that you have to make. In every case, the maximum bid that you place won't be all that you spend on an item. I recommend that you look closely at the payment methods that the seller is willing to accept as well as the shipping costs, insurance costs, and escrow costs (if any).

Payment methods

Several payment options are available, but the seller has the right to refuse some forms of payment. Usually, the accepted forms of payment are laid out in the item's description or in the Shipping and Payment Details area below the item description. The following forms of payment are available to you:

✦ **Credit card:** Paying with a credit card is a favorite payment option — one that's mainly offered by businesses and dealers. I like paying with credit cards because they're fast and efficient. In addition, using a credit card offers you another ally (namely, your credit card company) if you're not completely satisfied with the transaction.

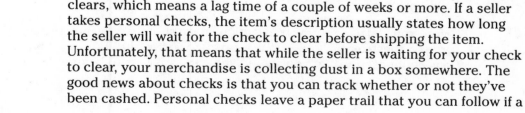

Sometimes sellers use a friend's company to run credit card payments for eBay auctions. So don't be surprised if you buy a vintage Tonka bulldozer and your credit card is billed from Holly's Hair-o-Rama.

✦ **PayPal:** I pay for almost all my eBay purchases through PayPal. Owned by eBay, PayPal is the largest Internet-wide payment network. Sellers who accept PayPal are identified with a special icon in the Seller Information box (as well as a large PayPal logo in the Payment Methods area below the description) and accept American Express, Visa, MasterCard, and Discover as well as electronic checks and debits. The service is integrated directly into eBay auctions, so paying is a mouse click away.

After you register with PayPal to pay for an item, PayPal debits your credit card or your bank checking account (or your PayPal account — if you have earned some money from sales) and sends the payment to the seller's account. PayPal doesn't charge buyers to use the service. Buyers can use PayPal to pay any seller within the United States (and around the world in over 35 countries). For more details, check out the PayPal Web site (www.paypal.com).

✦ **Money order:** My second-favorite method of payment — and the most popular at eBay — is the money order. Sellers love money orders because they don't have to wait for a check to clear.

✦ **Personal or cashier's check:** Paying by check is convenient but has its drawbacks. Most sellers don't ship you the goods until after your check clears, which means a lag time of a couple of weeks or more. If a seller takes personal checks, the item's description usually states how long the seller will wait for the check to clear before shipping the item. Unfortunately, that means that while the seller is waiting for your check to clear, your merchandise is collecting dust in a box somewhere. The good news about checks is that you can track whether or not they've been cashed. Personal checks leave a paper trail that you can follow if a

Book IV
Chapter 6

Bidding Basics

385

problem occurs later on. The bad news about checks is that you're revealing personal information, such as your bank account number, to a stranger.

Most business at eBay is conducted in U.S. dollars. If you happen to buy an item from an international seller, you might need to convert American dollars into another currency. eBay has a currency converter. Type the following URL in your browser:

```
http://pages.ebay.com/services/buyandsell/currencyconverter.
html
```

Just select your choice of currency, type in the amount, and click the Perform Currency Conversion button.

Using an escrow service

Even though most sales at eBay are for items that cost $100 or less, using an escrow service comes in handy on occasion — like when you buy a big-ticket item or something extremely rare. *Escrow* is a service that allows a buyer and seller to protect a transaction by placing the money in the hands of a neutral third party until a specified set of conditions are met. Sellers note in their item descriptions if they're willing to accept escrow. If you're nervous about sending a lot of money to someone you don't really know (like a user named Clumsy who has only two feedback comments and is shipping you bone china from Broken Hill, Australia), consider using an escrow company.

Using an escrow company is worthwhile only if the item you're bidding on is expensive, rare, fragile, or traveling a long distance. If you're spending less than $200 for the item, I recommend that you purchase insurance from your shipper instead — just in case. Remember, with purchases under $200, you're also protected against fraud through eBay. (You might be protected up to $500 if you pay through PayPal — see "Payment methods," earlier in this chapter.)

eBay has a partnership with Escrow.com that handles eBay auction escrow sales in Canada and the United States. After an auction closes, the buyer sends the payment to the escrow company. After the escrow company receives the money, it e-mails the seller to ship the merchandise. After the buyer receives the item, he or she has an agreed-on period of time (normally two business days) to look it over and let the escrow service know that all's well. If everything's okay, the escrow service sends the payment to the seller. If the buyer is unhappy with the item, he or she must ship it back to the seller. When the escrow service receives word from the seller that the item has been returned, the service returns the payment to the buyer (minus the escrow company's handling fee).

Before you start an escrow transaction, make sure that you and the seller agree on these terms. (You can use e-mail to sort it out.) Here are three questions about escrow that you should know the answers to before you bid:

✦ Who pays the escrow fee? (Normally, the buyer does, though sometimes the buyer and seller split the cost.)

✦ How long is the inspection period? (Routinely, it's two business days after receipt of the merchandise.)

✦ Who pays for return shipping if the item is rejected? (The buyer, usually.)

 If you use a credit card or bank wire, you can pay return shipping costs right from your computer. If you're not comfortable giving your credit card number online, you can print out the escrow company's credit card form and fax it to the company.

Shipping and insurance costs

Don't let the sale go down with the shipping. Most auction descriptions end with "buyer to pay shipping charges." If the item isn't an odd shape, excessively large, or fragile, experienced sellers calculate the shipping based on Priority Mail at the U.S. Postal Service, which is the unofficial eBay standard. Expect to pay $3.85 for the first pound and another $0.45 for tracking the item.

It has also become somewhat routine for the seller to add about a dollar for packing materials like paper, bubble wrap, tape, and such. A dollar or so is a reasonable handling charge because the cost of these items adds up over time. You might come across sellers trying to nickel-and-dime their way to a fortune by jacking up the prices on shipping to ridiculous proportions. If you have a question about shipping costs, ask before you bid on the item.

eBay transactions sometimes involve two types of insurance that might have an impact on your pocketbook:

✦ **Shipping insurance:** This insurance covers your item as it travels through the U.S. Postal Service, UPS, FedEx, or any of the other carriers. Some savvy sellers have signed up with a company called Package In-Transit Coverage, which insures all their packages through an annual policy. This way the seller doesn't have to stand in line at the post office to get the insurance stamp from the clerk. The seller logs the packages and reports on them on a monthly basis. Sellers will let you know that they use this service when they ship your item.

✦ **Fraud insurance:** eBay's Fraud Protection Program provides some nominal insurance against fraud. eBay's Fraud Protection insurance pays up to $175 (a maximum of $200 minus a $25 deductible). So if you file a $50 claim, you get $25. If you file a $5,000 claim, you still only get $175. Remember that if you pay via PayPal, you might be covered for purchases up to $500.

Placing Your Bid

Okay, you've found the perfect item to track (say, a really classy Elvis Presley wristwatch), and it's in your price range. You're more than interested — you're ready to bid. If this were a live auction, some stodgy-looking guy in a gray suit would see you nod your head and start the bidding at, say, $2. Then some woman with a severe hairdo would yank on her ear, and the Elvis watch would jump to $3.

When you're ready to jump into the eBay fray, you can find the bidding form (shown in Figure 6-4) at the bottom of the auction item page (or click the Place Bid button at the top of the auction page). To fill out the bidding form and place a bid, follow these steps:

1. **Enter your maximum bid in the appropriate text box.**

The bid needs to be higher than the current minimum bid.

Figure 6-4:
You can find the bidding form at the bottom of every auction page.

Ready to bid or buy?

~ Author SIGNED eBay for Dummies NEW 3rd Ed ~

Place a Bid		**or**	Buy It Now

Starting bid: US $19.99

Your maximum bid: US $ _____ (Enter US $19.99 or more)

[Place Bid >]

eBay automatically bids on your behalf **up to** your maximum bid.
Learn about bidding.

Buy It Now price: **US $20.99** (immediate payment required)

[Buy It Now >]

Purchase this item now without bidding.
Learn about Buy It Now.

The seller requires you to make immediate payment to claim this item. You will be asked to do so with PayPal on the next page. Learn more.

TIP

You don't need to put in the dollar sign, but do use a decimal point — unless you really *want* to pay $1,049.00 instead of $10.49. If you make a mistake with an incorrect decimal point, you can retract your bid. (See "Retracting a Bid," later in this chapter.)

2. **If this is a Multiple Item auction, enter the quantity of items that you're bidding on.**

(If it's not a Multiple Item auction, the quantity is always 1.) Figure 6-5 shows a Multiple Item auction bidding form.

Figure 6-5:
The Multiple Item auction bidding form requires you to enter the quantity of the items.

Ready to bid?

Villeroy & Boch Amapola Cereal Bowl 8/Dutch

Current Bid: US $22.00

Your maximum bid: US $ _____ (Enter US $22.50 or more)

Quantity: x [1]

[Place Bid >]

3. **Click the Place Bid button.**

The Review Bid page appears on your screen, filling it with a wealth of legalese. This is your last chance to change your mind: Do you really want the item, and can you really buy it? The bottom line is this: If you bid on it and you win, you buy it. eBay really means it.

4. **At this point, you have to sign in if you haven't already. If you're signed in, go to Step 5.**

5. **If you agree to the terms, click Submit.**

After you agree, the Bid Confirmation screen appears.

After you bid on an item, the item number and title appear on your My eBay All Buying page, listed under (big surprise) Items I'm Bidding On. Meanwhile, eBay sends you an e-mail confirming your bid. The Items I'm Bidding On list makes tracking your auction (or auctions, if you're bidding on multiple items) easy.

eBay considers a bid on an item to be a binding contract. You can save yourself a lot of heartache if you make a promise to yourself — *never bid on an item that you don't intend to buy* — and keep it. Before you go to the bidding form, be sure that you're in this auction for the long haul and make yourself another promise — *figure out the maximum that you're willing to spend* — and stick to it.

Bidding to the Max: Proxy Bidding

When you make a maximum bid on the bidding form, you actually make several small bids — again and again — until the bidding reaches where you told it to stop. For example, if the current bid is up to $19.99 and you put in a maximum of $45.02, your bid automatically increases incrementally so that you're ahead of the competition — at least until someone else's maximum bid exceeds yours. Basically, you bid by *proxy,* which means that your bid rises incrementally in response to other bidders' bids.

No one else knows for sure whether you're bidding by proxy, and no one knows how high your maximum bid is. And the best part is that you can be out having a life of your own while the proxy bid happens automatically. Buyers and sellers have no control over the increments (appropriately called *bid increments*) that eBay sets. The bid increment is the amount of money by which a bid is raised, and eBay's system can work in mysterious ways. The current maximum bid can jump up a nickel or a quarter or even an Andrew Jackson, but there is a method to the madness, even though you might not think so. eBay uses a *bid-increment formula,* which uses the current high bid to determine how much to increase the bid increment. For example:

✦ A 5-quart bottle of cold cream has a current high bid of $14.95. The bid increment is $0.50 — meaning that if you bid by proxy, your proxy will bid $15.45.

✦ A 5-ounce can of top-notch caviar has a high bid of $200. The bid increment is $2.50. If you choose to bid by proxy, your proxy will bid $202.50.

Table 6-1 shows you what kind of magic happens when you put the proxy system and a bid-increment formula together in the same cyber-room.

**Book IV
Chapter 6**

Bidding Basics

Table 6-1			**Proxy Bidding and Bid Increments**	
Current Bid	*Bid Increment*	*Minimum Bid*	*eBay Auctioneer*	*Bidders*
$2.50	$0.25	$2.75	"Do I hear $2.75?"	Joe Bidder tells his proxy that his maximum bid is $8. He's the current high bidder at $2.75.
$2.75	$0.25	$3	"Do I hear $3?"	You tell your proxy your maximum bid is $25 and take a nice, relaxing bath while your proxy calls out your $3 bid, making you the current high bidder.
$3	$0.25	$3.25	"I hear $3 from proxy. Do I proxy hear $3.25?"	Joe Bidder's proxy bids $3.25, and while Joe Bidder is out walking his dog, he becomes the high bidder.

A heated bidding war ensues between Joe Bidder's proxy and your proxy while the two of you go on with your lives. The bid increment inches from $0.25 to $0.50 as the current high bid increases.

$7.50	$0.50	$8	"Do I hear $8?"	Joe Bidder's proxy calls out $8, his final offer.
$8	$0.50	$8.50	"The bid is at $8. Do I hear $8.50?"	Your proxy calls out $8.50 on your behalf, and having outbid your opponent, you win the auction.

Retracting a Bid

Maybe you're used to going into a shopping mall and purchasing something that you're not sure you like. What's the worst that could happen? You end up back at the mall, receipt in hand, returning the item. Not so on eBay. Even if you realize that you already have a purple feather boa in your closet that's just like the one that you won yesterday on eBay, deciding that you don't want to go through with a transaction *is* a big deal. Not only can it earn you some nasty feedback, but it can also give you the reputation of a deadbeat.

Remember, many states consider your bid a binding contract, just like any other contract. You can't retract your bid unless one of these three outstandingly unusual circumstances applies:

✦ If your bid is clearly a typographical error (you submitted a bid for $4,567 when you really meant $45.67), you may retract your bid. If this occurs, you should reenter the correct bid amount immediately. You won't get any sympathy if you try to retract an $18.25 bid by saying that you meant to bid $15.25, so review your bid before you send it.

✦ You have tried to contact the seller to answer questions on the item, and he or she doesn't reply.

✦ If the seller substantially changes the description of an item after you place a bid (the description of the item changes from "can of tennis balls" to "a tennis ball," for example), you may retract your bid.

If you've made an error, you must retract your bid prior to the last 12 hours of the auction. Before the 12-hour mark, a retraction removes all bids that you have placed in the auction. Mistakes or not, when you retract a bid that was placed within the last 12 hours of the listing, only the most recent bid that you made is retracted — your bids placed prior to the last 12 hours are still active.

Here's how to retract a bid while the auction is still going on:

1. **Click the Services link on the main navigation bar.**

2. **Scroll down to the Bidding and Buying Services banner and click the Retract My Bid link.**

   You might have to sign in again, and after you do, the Bid Retraction page appears.

3. **Read the legalese and scroll down the page. Enter the item number of the auction that you're retracting your bid from. Then open the drop-down list and select one of the three legitimate reasons for retracting your bid.**

4. **Click the Retract Bid button.**

   You receive a confirmation of your bid retraction via e-mail. Keep a copy of it until the auction is completed.

After the auction: Side deals or personal offers?

If a bidder is outbid on an item that he or she really wants or if the auction's reserve price isn't met, the bidder may send an e-mail to the seller and see whether the seller is willing to make another deal. Maybe the seller has another similar item or is willing to sell the item directly rather than run a whole new auction. You need to know that this could happen — but eBay doesn't sanction this outside activity.

If the original auction winner doesn't go through with the deal, the seller can make a Second Chance offer. This is an eBay-sanctioned second chance for underbidders (unsuccessful bidders) who participated in the auction.

Any side deals other than Second Chance offers are unprotected. My friend Jack collects autographed final scripts from hit television sitcoms. So when the curtain fell on *Seinfeld,* he had to have a script. Not surprisingly, he found one on eBay with a final price tag that was way out of his league. But

he knew that by placing a bid, someone else with a signed script to sell might see his name and try to make a deal. And he was right.

After the auction closed, he received an e-mail from a guy who worked on the final show and had a script signed by all the actors. He offered it to Jack for $1,000 less than the final auction price at eBay. Tempted as he was to take the offer, Jack understood that eBay's rules and regulations wouldn't help him out if the deal turned sour. He was also aware that he wouldn't receive the benefit of feedback (which is the pillar of the eBay community) or any eBay Fraud Protection insurance for the transaction.

If you even think about making a side deal, remember that not only does eBay strictly prohibit this activity, but eBay can also suspend you if you're reported for making a side deal. And if you're the victim of a side-deal scam, eBay's rules and regulations don't offer you any protection. My advice? Watch out!

Book IV Chapter 6

Bidding Basics

Chapter 7: Getting Foxy with Bidding Strategies

In This Chapter

✔ **Knowing your competition**

✔ **Finding the hidden secrets in the bidding history**

✔ **Placing a token bid**

✔ **Using canny strategies to win your auction**

1 speak to many people who find an item at eBay, bid on it, and at the last minute — the last hour or the last day — are outbid. Sad and dejected, they feel like real losers. You're not a loser if you lost at eBay. You just don't know the fine art of sneaky bidding. Sneaky bidding is my way of saying *educated* bidding.

Sports teams study their rivals, and political candidates scout out what the opposition is doing. Bidding in competition against other bidders is just as serious an enterprise. Follow the tips in this chapter and see whether you can come up with a strong bidding strategy of your own. Feel free to e-mail me with any scathingly brilliant plans; I'm always open to new theories.

Get to Know the High Bidder

For an auction in progress, the User ID of the high bidder is listed on the auction item page (assuming someone has bid on the item). Take a look at this name because you might see it again in auctions for similar items. If the high bidder has lots of feedback, he or she might know the ropes — and be back to fight if you up the ante.

You can use the By Bidder search option, shown in Figure 7-1 on the eBay Search page, to find out the bidder's recent auction experience. If you're bidding on an item, conducting a bidder search can be a valuable asset: You can size up your competition.

Figure 7-1:
Use a By
Bidder
search to
get an idea
of the
compe-
tition's
bidding
patterns.

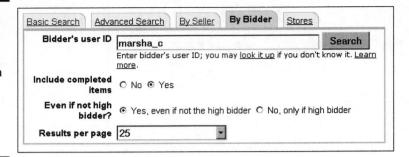

To get the skinny on a bidder, here's the move:

1. **Type in the User ID of the bidder you want to search for.**

2. **If you want to see auctions that this user has bid on in the past, select the Yes option on the Include Completed Items line.**

You should check completed auctions. They give you a sense of how often and at what time of day the user participates in auctions.

Remember that eBay has a 30-day limit on the auction information that it returns, so don't expect to see results from a year ago. By clicking the item number in your search results, you can see at what times your main competition tends to bid and then bid when you know those folks aren't looking.

3. **Tell eBay whether you also want to see the person's bid even if he or she isn't the high bidder.**

Selecting Yes means that you want to see the bidder's activity in every auction, even if the person isn't the *current* high bidder. Selecting No limits the search to auctions where the bidder is the current top dog. I recommend checking all of the bidder's auctions to see how aggressively he or she bids on items.

4. **Select the number of items that you want to see per page.**

5. **Click Search.**

You might be tempted to try to contact a bidder you're competing with so that you can get information about the person more easily. This is not only bad form, but could also get you suspended. Don't do it.

Find Out an Item's Bidding History

The bidding *history,* shown on the auction item page, lists everybody who is bidding on an item. You can see how often and at what time bids are placed, but you can't see *how much* each bidder bids until the auction ends. Look at Figure 7-2 to see a typical bidding history list. You can see bid amounts because this auction has ended.

Figure 7-2:
The bidding history tells you the date and time of day at which the bidders placed their bids.

Strategies to Help You Outsmart the Competition

Your two cents does matter — at least at eBay. Here's why: Many eBay members tend to round off their bids to the nearest dollar figure. Some choose nice, familiar coin increments like 25, 50, or 75 cents. But the most successful eBay bidders have found that adding two or three cents to a routine bid can mean the difference between winning and losing. So I recommend that you make your bids in oddish figures, like $15.02 or $45.57, as an inexpensive way to edge out your competition. For the first time ever, your two cents might actually pay off!

That's just one of the many strategies to get you ahead of the rest of the bidding pack without paying more than you should. ***Note:*** The strategies in this section are for bidders who are tracking an item over the course of a week or so, so be sure that you have time to track the item and plan your next moves. Also, get a few auctions under your belt before you throw yourself into the middle of a bidding war.

Multiple Item auction strategy

Multiple Item auctions (which I explain in Chapter 1 of Book IV) are funky. Yes, that's a technical term that means that a Multiple Item auction strategy is a little different. After all, each winner pays the same amount for the item, and Multiple Item auctions don't have a super-secret reserve price. But *winning* a Multiple Item auction isn't all that different from winning other auctions. Therefore, wait until the closing minutes of the auction to bid and then follow my sage advice for optimum success.

Pirates of the Caribbean . . . or Carribean?

Just before the movie *Pirates of the Caribbean* premiered, Disneyland gave out exclusive movie posters to their visitors. My daughter, savvy eBayer that she is, snagged several copies to sell on the site. She listed them (one at a time) when the movie opened and couldn't get more than the starting bid of $9.99 for each of them.

When we searched eBay for *pirates poster*, we found that the very same posters listed with a misspelled title, *Pirates of the Carribean,* were selling for as high as $30 each. After selling out her initial stock, she found another seller that had 10 for sale — in one auction — with the proper spelling. She bought those as well (for $5.00 each) and sold them with misspelled titles on the site for between $15 and $27!

Here are the key things to remember about a Multiple Item auction:

✦ **The seller must sell all the items at the** *lowest winning price* **at the end of the auction, no matter what.**

✦ **Winners are based on the** *highest* **bids received.** If you up the ante, you could win the auction and pay only the *lowest winning price,* which might be lower than your bid. Confused yet? Say the minimum bid for each of ten Elvis watches is $10, and 20 people bid at $10, each person bidding for one watch. The first ten bidders win the watch. But suppose you come along at the end of the auction and bid $15 as the 21st bidder. You get a watch (as do the first nine people who bid $10), *and* you get the watch for the lowest successful bid — which is $10! Get it?

✦ **Know where you stand in the pecking order.** You can see a list of high bidders (and their bids) on the auction page, so you always know where you stand in the pecking order.

✦ **Avoid being the lowest or the highest high bidder.** The highest bidder is sure to win, so the usual bidding strategy is to knock out the lowest high bidder. The lowest high bidder is said to be *on the bubble* and on the verge of losing the auction by a couple of pennies. To avoid being the bidder on the bubble, keep your bid just above the second-lowest winning bid.

✦ **If you want to buy more than one of an item up for auction, make sure you have that number of successful high bids as the auction draws to a close.** Huh? Remember, winners are based on the *highest* bids. If you're in a Multiple Item auction for ten items and place five $15 bids, nothing guarantees that you'll win five of the item. Nine other people who want the item could bid $20 apiece. Then they each win one of the items at $15, and you end up with only one of the item. (At least you still pay only $15 for it.)

Bidding strategies eBay doesn't talk about

Here's a list of do's and don'ts that can help you win your item. Of course, some of these tips *are* eBay-endorsed, but I had to get you to notice what I had to say somehow.

✦ **Don't bid early and high.** Bidding early *and* high shows that you have a clear interest in the item. It also shows that you're a rookie, apt to make mistakes. If you bid early and high, you might give away just how much you want the item. Of course, a higher bid does mean more bucks for the seller and a healthy cut for the middleman. So it's no big mystery that many sellers recommend it. In fact, when you sell an item, you might want to encourage it, too.

✦ **Do wait and watch your auction.** If you're interested in an item and you have the time to watch it from beginning to end, I say that the best strategy is to wait. Mark the auction for your Items I'm Watching list on your My eBay All Buying page and remember to check it daily. But if you don't have the time, go ahead — put in your maximum bid early and cross your fingers.

✦ **Don't freak out if you find yourself in a bidding war.** Don't keel over if, at the split second you're convinced that you're the high bidder at $45.02, someone beats you out at $45.50. You can increase your maximum bid to $46.02, but if your bidding foe also has a maximum of $46.02, the tie goes to the person who put in the highest bid first. Bid as high as you're willing to go, but bid at the very end of the auction.

✦ **Do check the item's bidding history.** If you find yourself in a bidding war and want an item badly enough, check the bidding history and identify your fiercest competitor; then refer to the earlier section "Get to Know the High Bidder" for a pre-auction briefing. To get a pretty exact picture of your opponent's bidding habits, make special note of the times of day when he or she has bid on other auctions. You can adjust your bidding times accordingly.

Time Is Money: Strategy by the Clock

You can use different bidding strategies depending on how much time is left in an auction. By paying attention to the clock, you can find out about your competition, beat them out, and end up paying less for your item. This section explains how to make the clock work for you when it comes to bidding on items at eBay.

Using the lounging-around strategy

Sometimes the best strategy at the beginning of an auction is to do nothing at all. That's right; relax, take off your shoes, and loaf. Go ahead. You might want to make a *token bid* (the very lowest that you're allowed) or mark the page to watch on your Items I'm Watching list. I generally take this attitude through the first six days of a week-long auction I want to bid on, and it works pretty well. Of course, I check in every day just to keep tabs on the items that I'm watching, and revise my strategy as time goes by.

The seller has the right to up his minimum bid — if his auction has received no bids — up to 12 hours before the auction ends. If the seller has set a ridiculously low minimum bid and then sees that the auction is getting no action, the seller may choose to up the minimum bid to protect his sale. By placing the minimum token bid when you first see the auction, you can foil a Buy It Now from another bidder (because Buy It Now is disabled after a bid has been placed) or prevent the seller from upping the minimum. If it's important enough, you can see whether the seller has done this in the past, by searching the Seller's completed auctions (see "Get to Know the High Bidder," earlier in this chapter, to find out how to do this search). All pre-closing changes are available for public view; just click the Revised button next to the word *Description* on the item page. See Figure 7-3 for a sample of an Item Revisions summary.

Figure 7-3: This page shows the revisions made by the seller during this auction.

Item Revisions summary for item #2949092959

The seller has revised the following item information:

Date	Time	Revised Information
Sep-02-03	19:16:13 PDT	Description
Sep-02-03	19:17:32 PDT	Buy It Now Price Minimum Bid Price
Sep-02-03	19:19:12 PDT	Description

If you see an item that you absolutely must have, mark it to watch on your My eBay All Buying page (or make that token bid) and plan and revise your maximum bid as the auction goes on. I can't stress enough how important this is.

Using the beat-the-clock strategy

Rev up your bidding strategy during the final 24 hours of an auction and decide, once and for all, whether you really *have* to have the item that you've been eyeing. Maybe you put in a maximum bid of $45.02 earlier in the week. Now's the time to decide whether you're willing to go as high as $50.02. Maybe $56.03?

No one wants to spend the day in front of the computer (ask almost anyone who does). You can camp out by the refrigerator or at your desk or wherever you want to be. Just place a sticky note where you're likely to see it, reminding you of the exact time that the auction ends. If you're not going to be near a computer when the auction closes, you can also use an automatic bidding software program to bid for you.

In the last half hour

With a half hour left before the auction becomes ancient history, head for the computer and dig in for the last battle of the bidding war. I recommend that you sign in to eBay about 10 to 15 minutes before the auction ends. The last thing you want to have happen is to get caught in Internet gridlock and not get access to the Web site. Go to the items that you're watching and click the auction title. With 10 minutes to go, if there's a lot of action on your auction, click Reload or Refresh every 30 seconds to get the most current info on how many people are bidding.

Sniping to the finish: The final minutes

The rapid-fire, final flurry of bidding is called *sniping*. Sniping is the fine art of waiting until the very last seconds of an eBay auction and then outbidding the current high bidder just in time. Of course, you've got to expect that the current high bidder is probably sniping back.

With a hot item, open a second window on your browser (by pressing Ctrl+N); keep one open for bidding and the other open for constant reloading during the final few minutes. With the countdown at 60 seconds or less, make your final bid at the absolute highest amount you will pay for the item. The longer you can hold off — I'm talking down to around 20 seconds — the better. It all depends on the speed of your Internet connection, so practice on some small auctions so you know how much time to allow when you're bidding on your prize item. Keep reloading or refreshing your browser as fast as you can and watch the time tick to the end of the auction.

If you want to be truly fancy, you can open a third window (see Figure 7-4) and have a back-up high bid in case you catch another sniper swooping in on your item immediately after your first snipe. You can avoid the third window routine if you've bid your highest bid with the first snipe. Then if you're outbid, you know that the item went for more than you were willing to pay. I know; it's some consolation, but not much.

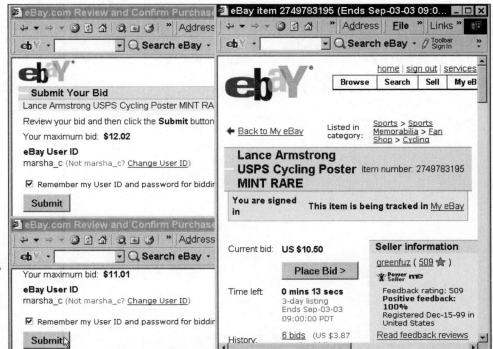

Figure 7-4: My personal sniping procedure in action!

Some eBay members consider the practice of sniping highly unseemly and uncivilized. I say that sniping is an addictive, fun part of life at eBay. And it's a blast. So my recommendation is that you try sniping. You're likely to benefit from the results and enjoy your eBay experience even more — especially if you're an adrenaline junkie.

Here's a list of things to keep in mind when you get ready to place your last bid:

✦ Know how high you're willing to go.

✦ Know how fast (or slow) your Internet connection is.

✦ Remember, this is a game, and sometimes it's a game of chance, so don't lose heart if you lose the auction.

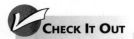

CHECK IT OUT

Auction Sniping

Auction sniping means to outbid competitors at the last possible moment in an eBay auction. If the auction ends at high noon, the successful auction sniper makes the final, highest bid at 11:59.59. If you spend any time on eBay, you're bound to be sniped sooner or later. eBay maintains an article about auction sniping at this address:

```
http://pages.ebay.com/help/basics
    /g-sniping.html
```

Most people don't have the spare time to be an auction sniper, but several Internet services will do it for you — for a fee, of course. After registering for these services, you tell the service which eBay item you're bidding on, set your price, and let the automatic auction sniper place the bid for you at the last moment. Here are some auction sniping services and the addresses of Web sites where you can find out more about them:

✔ **Auction Sniper:** The cost is 1 percent of the auction price, with a minimum fee of $0.25 and a maximum fee of $5. www.auctionsniper.com

✔ **Auction Chief Stealer:** The cost is $6 to $9 per month, depending on how long you enroll. http://auctionchief. auctionstealer.com/home.cfm

✔ **Bidnapper:** The cost is between $4 and $6 per month, depending on how long you enroll. www.bidnapper.com

✔ **HammerSnipe:** The cost is $6 to $9 per month, depending on how long you enroll. http://hammertap. auctionstealer.com/home.cfm

Chapter 8: After You Win

In This Chapter

✔ **Getting yourself organized**

✔ **Talking turkey with the seller**

✔ **Ironing out the details and sending out your payment**

The thrill of the chase is over, and you've won your first eBay item. Congratulations — now what do you do? You have to follow up on your victory and keep a sharp eye on what you're doing. The post-auction process can be loaded with pitfalls and potential headaches if you don't watch out. Remember, sometimes money, like a full moon, does strange things to people.

In this chapter, you can get a handle on what's in store for you after you win the auction. I clue you in on what the seller's supposed to do to make the transaction go smoothly and show you how to grab hold of your responsibilities as a buyer. I give you info here about following proper post-auction etiquette, including the best way to get organized, communicate with the seller professionally, and send your payment without hazards. I also brief you on how to handle an imperfect transaction.

eBay Calling: You're a Winner

The Items I'm Bidding On section of your My eBay All Buying page highlights the titles of auctions that you've won and indicates the amount of your winning bid. If you think you might have won the auction and don't want to wait around for eBay to contact you, check out the Bidding/ Watching section for yourself and find out — are you a winner?

Throughout the bidding process, dollar amounts of items that you're winning appear in green on your Items I'm Bidding On list. If you've been outbid, they appear in red. After the auction ends, there's no marching band, no visit from Ed McMahon and his camera crew, no armful of roses, and no oversized check to duck behind. In fact, you're more likely to find out that you've won the auction from the seller or the Items I'm Bidding On list of your My eBay All Buying page than you are to hear it right away from eBay. eBay tries to get its End of Auction e-mails (EOAs) out pronto, but sometimes there's a bit of lag time. For a look at all the contact information in the End of Auction e-mail, see Figure 8-1.

Figure 8-1:
Everything that you need to know about contacting your buyer or seller is included in eBay's End of Auction e-mail.

Getting Your Paperwork Together

Your auction page shows the amount of your winning bid, the item's description, and other relevant information. The second you find out that you've won the auction, print *two* copies of the auction page if you're mailing the payment to the seller. Keep a copy for your files. Send the second copy to the seller along with your payment; doing so is not only efficient but also polite.

eBay displays auctions for only 30 days in the Bidder search, so don't put off printing out that final auction page for your records. If you save your End of Auction e-mails that you get from eBay, you can access the auction for up to 90 days if you use the link in the e-mail.

Here's a list of the items that you should keep in your auction purchases file:

✦ A copy of your EOA e-mail from eBay. *Don't* delete the EOA e-mail — at least not until you print a copy and keep it for your records. You might need to refer to the EOA e-mail later, and there's no way to get another copy.

✦ Printed copies of any e-mail correspondence between you and the seller that details specific information about the item or special payment and shipping arrangements.

✦ A printed copy of the final auction page.

Getting Contact Information

The eBay rules and regulations say that buyers and sellers must contact each other by e-mail within three business days of the auction's end. Most sellers contact auction winners promptly because they want to complete the transaction and get paid. Few buyers or sellers wait for the official eBay EOA e-mail to contact each other.

If you need to contact the seller before sending payment, you have several ways to find contact information:

✦ Click the Ask Seller a Question link on the auction page, which takes you to the Ask Seller a Question form.

✦ Click the Site Map link, located in the top-right corner of every eBay page, and then click the Search for Members link.

✦ Click the Search link on the main navigation bar, and then click the Find Members link on the submenu.

Within the first three business days after an auction or a Buy It Now transaction, limit yourself to using the Ask Seller a Question form. The seller (if signed in) sees the buyer's e-mail address on the item page after the sale is closed.

So, What's Your Number?

If you don't hear from the seller after three business days, and you've already tried sending an e-mail, you need to get more contact information. Remember back when you registered and eBay asked for a phone number? eBay keeps this information for times like this.

To get an eBay member's phone number, go back to the Find Members page and fill out the Contact Info form by entering the seller's User ID, your User ID, and the number of the item that you're trading with the other member; then click the Submit button. If all the information is correct, you automatically see a request-confirmation page, and eBay automatically generates an e-mail to both you and the other user, as shown in Figure 8-2.

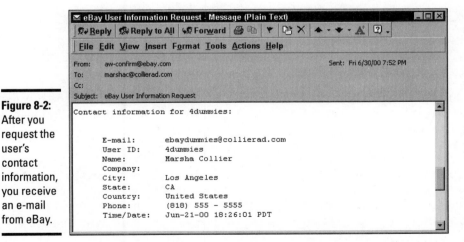

Figure 8-2: After you request the user's contact information, you receive an e-mail from eBay.

eBay's e-mail includes the seller's User ID, name, company, city, state, and country of residence, as well as the seller's phone number and date of initial registration. eBay sends this same information about you to the user you want to get in touch with.

Checking Out

When you buy something in a store, you need to check out to pay. eBay isn't much different. eBay's Checkout is a very convenient way to pay for your completed auctions or Buy It Now sales with a credit card or eCheck through PayPal. You may also use Checkout to exchange your information with the seller and pay for your item by some method other than PayPal (such as by money order, check, or another payment service that the seller accepts).

Checkout is integrated directly onto the item page so that you can win and pay for an item in less than a minute. Some sellers indicate in their description that they will send you a link to their private checkout page. When the sale is over, the item page has checkout information, as shown in Figure 8-3.

Figure 8-3:
Click the Pay Now button to pay for the item through PayPal or to indicate your payment preferences.

When you click the Pay Now button, you're taken step by step through the checkout process. You pay for the item, and the seller is notified. You also get an e-mail confirming your payment, along with the seller's e-mail address.

You can make an immediate payment only if the seller chooses to accept PayPal. If the seller chooses to accept other forms of payment, such as personal checks or money orders, you can still go through the process to send the seller your shipping information (but not your actual payment). If the shipping cost is based on your ZIP Code, the seller can also use this information to send you an invoice or to update the checkout information on the item page. When that's done, you can go ahead and send payment.

Using PayPal, a Person-to-Person Payment Service

Book IV, Chapter 6 covers the pros and cons of using PayPal to pay for your auctions. Here's where I show you why PayPal is the safest way to pay on eBay. eBay sees to it that PayPal is incredibly easy to use because PayPal is the official payment service at eBay. PayPal is my favorite payment option for another reason: PayPal has a buyer protection program that covers your purchases over and above the $200 supplied by eBay's Fraud Protection plan.

When the auction is over, you can click the Pay Now button to check out and enter the PayPal site. If you don't pay immediately from the item page, click the Pay link in the eBay navigation bar or just type **www.paypal.com** in your browser. If you go direct to the PayPal site, follow these steps:

1. **If this is your first visit to the PayPal site, register.**

   If you're already a registered user, go ahead and log on by following the steps that appear on-screen.

2. **Click the Auction Tools tab and then scroll down and click the Pay for eBay Items link.**

PayPal takes you step by step through the process of filling out a payment form to identify the auction you're paying for as well as your shipping information. You're all done. Your credit card information is held safely with PayPal, and the payment is deposited into the seller's PayPal account. The seller receives notice of your payment and notifies you about how quickly he or she will ship your item.

By paying with PayPal, you can instantly pay for an auction without hassle. Your credit card information is kept private, and your payment is deposited into the seller's PayPal account.

You can always view your checkout status by going to the Items I've Won area on your My eBay All Buying page, shown in Figure 8-4. Click the link in the Next Steps/Status column for the item in question.

Figure 8-4:
Click the link in the Next Steps/Status column to verify the status of your payment.

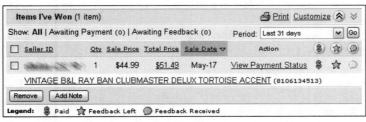

Using Escrow

If you and the seller have agreed to use escrow to complete your transaction, you must first register your auction for an escrow transaction. To sign up for escrow from any eBay page, step right up:

1. Click the Services link on the main navigation bar.

You're taken to the Services Overview page.

2. Under Payment, click the Escrow Services link.

You're taken to the Escrow help page.

3. Click the Start New Transaction button.

You're taken to the beginning of the escrow process. Input the item number of the transaction in question.

4. Click the Continue button.

You're presented with a summary of the item. Be sure that everything is correct and read the terms and conditions; this is your last chance to cancel the process. eBay sends the information to the Internet escrow company for processing.

5. Click the I Agree button.

Your escrow is in the works, and the escrow company calls or e-mails you with information regarding the details of this transaction.

You Get the Item (Uh-Oh, What's This?)

The vast majority of eBay transactions go without a hitch. You win, you send your payment, you get the item, you check it out, you're happy. If that's the case — a happy result for your auction — skip this section and go leave some positive feedback for the seller!

On the other hand, if you're not happy with the item that you receive, the seller might have some 'splaining to do. E-mail or call the seller immediately and politely ask for an explanation if the item isn't as described. Some indications of a foul-up are pretty obvious:

✦ The item's color, shape, or size doesn't match the description.

✦ The item is scratched, broken, or dented.

✦ You won an auction for a set of candlesticks and receive a vase instead.

 A snag in the transaction is annoying, but don't get steamed right away. Contact the seller and see whether you can work things out. Keep the conversation civilized. The majority of sellers want a clean track record and good feedback, so they respond to your concerns and make things right. Assume the best about the seller's honesty, unless you have a real reason to suspect foul play. Remember, you take some risks whenever you buy something that you can't touch. If the item has a slight problem that you can live with, leave it alone and don't go to the trouble of leaving negative feedback about an otherwise pleasant, honest eBay seller.

Of course, although I can give you advice on what you *deserve* from a seller, you're the one who has to live with the item. If you and the seller can't reach a compromise, and you really think you deserve a refund, ask for one.

If you paid the U.S. Postal Service to insure the item, and it arrives at your home pretty well pulverized, call the seller to alert him or her about the problem. Find out the details of the insurance that the seller purchased. After you have all the details, follow the seller's instructions on how to make a claim. If the item was shipped through the post office, take the whole mangled shebang back to the post office and talk to the good folks there about filing a claim.

Chapter 9: Privacy: To Protect and to Serve

In This Chapter

✔ Digging up what eBay knows about you

✔ Determining how safe your information is at eBay

✔ Protecting your privacy

*O*n the Internet, as in real life, you should never take your personal privacy for granted. Sure, you're ecstatic that you can shop and sell at eBay from the privacy of your home, but remember: Just because your front door is locked doesn't mean that your privacy is being protected. If you're new to the Internet, you might be surprised to find out what you reveal about yourself to the world no matter how many precautions you take. (Yes, we all know about that neon blue exfoliating mask that you wear when you're bidding . . . just kidding . . . honest.)

In this chapter, you find out how much eBay knows about you and who eBay shares your information with. I explain what you can do to protect your privacy and tell you some simple steps that you can take to increase not only your Internet privacy, but also your safety.

What (And How) eBay Knows about You

The irony of the Internet is that although you think you're sitting at home working anonymously, third parties such as advertisers and marketing companies are secretly getting to know you. While you're busy collecting World's Fair memorabilia and antique toasters, eBay is busy collecting nuggets of information about you. eBay gets some of this information from you and some of it from your computer. All the data that eBay gets is stored in the mammoth eBay memory bank.

What you tell eBay

eBay gets much of what it knows about you *from* you. When you sign up, you voluntarily tell eBay important and personal information about yourself. Right off the bat, you give eBay these juicy tidbits: your name, e-mail address, snail-mail address, phone number, and password. "Okay, that's no big deal," you say, but if you're using your credit card to settle your eBay fees, you're also giving out the following personal financial information:

✦ Credit card number

✦ Credit card expiration date

✦ Credit card billing address

✦ Credit card history

If you make a one-time payment with a personal check, register to pay by check through PayPal, or apply for ID Verify (see Chapter 10 of Book IV), you give eBay even more information about yourself. eBay instantly knows your bank's name and your checking account number. The bottom line is that *every time* you pay by check, you give away personal info about yourself. eBay carefully locks up this information (in a high-tech Alcatraz, of sorts), but other companies or individuals might not be so protective. Before you put the check in the mail, make sure that you're comfortable with where it's going.

What cookies gather

Web sites collect information about you by using *cookies.* Cookies are nothing more than small files that companies (such as eBay) put on your hard drive to store data about your surfing habits. Most Web site designers install cookies to help you navigate their sites. Sometimes the cookie becomes sort of an admission ticket so that you don't need to register every time you sign in. Cookies can't steal information from other files on your computer. A cookie can access only the information that you provide to its Web site.

eBay has partnerships with companies that provide page-view and data-tracking technology and with advertisers who display advertising banners on eBay pages, whether you want to see the banners or not. If you click a banner, a cookie from that particular advertiser *might* go onto your computer, usually to prevent you from seeing it again. You can find out more about cookies at www.cookiecentral.com/faq.

DoubleClick, a major player in the cookie-tracking field, says that it uses your information to limit the number of times that you see the same advertisement. DoubleClick also measures the kinds of ads that you respond to and tracks which member Web sites you visit and how often. The bottom line is that DoubleClick is just trying to sell you stuff with ads based on your personal interests. The upside is that you get to see stuff that you might like.

Your eBay sign-in cookie

When you visit eBay and sign in, eBay gives you a special kind of cookie — not pecan shortbread — but an *end of session* or *permanent* cookie:

+ **End of session:** This cookie type remains on your computer as long as you remain on the eBay site. It also disappears if you haven't been active on the site for over 40 minutes.

+ **Permanent:** This flavor is perfect if you don't share your computer with anyone else; it permits your computer to always remain signed in to eBay.

eBay's sign-in cookie is a good thing. It prevents the previously repetitive task of typing your User ID and password at every turn. This cookie simplifies your participation in chats, bidding, watching items, viewing e-mail addresses, and so on. Because you don't have to sign in every time you do business at eBay, it's a real timesaver.

Web beacons

Web beacons are clear, 1 pixel x 1 pixel images that are placed in the HTML (or Internet page code) for individual pages. Web beacons, like cookies, are used mainly for collecting marketing information. They track the traffic patterns of users from one page to another.

Web beacons are sneaky little things. They're invisible as cookies, but they're incorporated into Web pages without your knowing. Turning off cookies won't disable them. However, Web beacons are not as ominous as they might seem because the information collected is not personally identifiable.

What Web servers collect

Every time that you log on to the Internet, just like Hansel and Gretel, you leave an electronic trail of information breadcrumbs. eBay, like zillions of other Web sites, uses *servers,* which are immense programs that do nothing but collect and transfer bits (and bytes) of information day and night. Your Internet connection has a special address that identifies you to all servers when you surf the Net. This is called an Internet Protocol (IP) address and is often used to track people whose shenanigans wreak havoc on Web sites or other users.

Web servers all over the Internet track some or all of the following information:

+ The Web site that you came in from
+ The Internet service provider (ISP) that you use
+ The auctions that you're running
+ The Web sites that you linked your auctions to
+ Your favorite Web sites (if you link them to your About Me page)

eBay collects the following information while you visit the eBay site (after you sign out, the server discards the data):

+ What you do while signed in to the site
+ What times you sign in and sign out

Like incredible Internet archivists, eBay's servers keep a record of everything that you bid on, win, and sell, which is great news if you have a problem with a transaction and need eBay to investigate. Also, eBay couldn't display feedback about you and other users if its servers didn't store all the feedback you write and receive. Have you ever sent an e-mail to eBay? eBay's servers record it and keep it in some murky recess of eBay's memory. Remember, we live in the age of electronic commerce, and the people at eBay run a serious business that depends on e-commerce. They have to keep everything in case they need it later.

To see a chart on what personal information is accessible by third parties, check out this address:

`http://pages.ebay.com/help/policies/privacy-appendix.html`

Cookie removal–ware

The other day, my daughter complained that her computer was getting slower and slower. I also noticed that it was opening extra windows and accessing the Internet inconsistently. After checking to see whether she had a virus (no, she didn't), I went to the Internet to obtain spyware-removal software. Perhaps her problem was that too many people had inserted information-gathering cookies on her computer. That was certainly the case. After installing and running the software, I found that she had over 350 cookies pulling information from her computer as she surfed. After we deleted them, her computer ran much faster.

She certainly didn't give these people permission to spy on her comings and goings on the Internet. These cookies were placed on her computer without her knowledge. If you want to purge these uninvited spies from your computer, download any of the free spyware or malware software from the Internet. Two good free ones are Ad-aware from `www.lavasoftusa.com/software/adaware` and Spybot - Search & Destroy, available from `www.security.kolla.de`.

Spam — Not Just a Tasty Treat

Although you can find plenty of places to socialize and have fun at eBay, when it comes to business, eBay is . . . well, all business. eBay's policy says that requests for registration information can be made only for people with whom you're transacting business on eBay. The contact information request form requires that you type in the item number of the transaction that you're involved in as well as the User ID of the person whose contact info you want. If you're not involved in a transaction as a bidder or a seller in the specified item number, you can't access the user information.

When it comes to e-mail addresses, your secret is safe until you win an auction or buy an item on eBay. The End of Auction notice contains your e-mail address so that the person on the other end of the transaction can contact you. After the other user has your e-mail address, eBay rules state that the user can use it only for eBay business.

Here's a list of "business" reasons for e-mail communication that are generally accepted by all at eBay:

+ Responding to feedback that you left

+ Responding to feedback that you received

+ Communicating with sellers or buyers during and after transactions

+ Using the Mail This Auction to a Friend feature to suggest an item to another eBay member

+ Leaving chat room comments

+ Discussing common interests with other members, such as shared hometowns, interesting collections, and past or current auctions

Sending spam versus eating it

Sending e-mail to other members is a great way to do business and make friends. But don't cross the line into spam. *Spam,* once solely a Hormel canned meat product (I've given Spam its own sidebar), now has an alternate meaning. When you spell it with a small *s, spam* is unsolicited e-mail — most often, advertising — sent to multiple e-mail addresses gleaned from marketing lists. Eventually, it fills up your inbox the way that "Spam, Spam, Spam, and Spam" filled up the menu in an old *Monty Python* restaurant skit. Think of spam as the electronic version of the junk mail that you get via snail mail. Spam might be okay for eating (if you're into that kind of thing), but sending it can get you banned from eBay.

If you send an e-mail that advertises a product or service to people you don't know, you're guilty of spamming.

Trashing your junk mail

Sometimes spam can come in the form of mail from people you know and expect mail from. Your closest friend's computer might have been abducted by some weird Internet virus, and it replicated the virus to everyone in his or her e-mail address book. Obviously, this is not a good thing for those who receive and open the e-mail.

Don't open e-mail from anyone you don't know, especially if a file is attached to it. Sometimes, if a spammer is really slick, it's hard to tell that you've received spam. If you receive an e-mail with no subject line, however — or if the e-mail has an addressee name that isn't yours, or is coming from someone you never heard of — delete it. You never know; it could be just annoying spam — or worse, it could contain a computer virus as an attachment, just waiting for you to open and activate it.

Speaking of e-mail, if you're new to the technology, I recommend getting a good antivirus program that can scan e-mail attachments and rid your system of some annoying — and increasingly dangerous — computer bugs.

Spam I am

Spam, the unwanted electronic junk mail, is named after Spam, the canned meat product. (Spam collectibles at eBay are another matter entirely.) According to the Spam Web site (www.spam.com), more than 5 billion cans of Spam have been consumed worldwide. (By the way, Hawaiians eat more Spam than any other state in the union.) Spam is made from a secret recipe of pork shoulder, ham, and special spices. It was first produced in 1937 and got its name from the *SP* for *spiced* and the *AM* from *ham.*

It's widely believed that spam (junk e-mail) got its name from the old *Monty Python* sketch because the refrain "Spam-Spam-Spam-Spam" drowned out all other conversation, and one of the participants kept saying, "I don't want any Spam. I don't like Spam." Others say that it came from a bunch of computer geeks at USC who thought that junk e-mail was about as satisfying as a Spam sandwich. Perhaps they've never enjoyed a Spam luau in Hawaii under the moonlight — aloha!

E-mail spoofing

E-mail spoofing has become the bane of the online community and can really wreak havoc. *Spoofing* is accomplished when crafty techno-geeks send out e-mail and make it appear to come from someone other than themselves — someone you know and expect e-mail from. Most often, this type of e-mail is programmed to invade your privacy or, even worse, bilk you out of confidential information.

A spate of e-mails have purportedly been sent from eBay, PayPal, and other major e-commerce sites, claiming that your membership has been suspended — or that your records need updating. The opportunistic e-mail then asks you to click a link to a page on the site, which then asks you to input your personal information. Don't do it!

Most sites *never* ask you to provide sensitive information through e-mail, so don't do it. If you receive an e-mail saying that your "account has been suspended," close the e-mail and go directly to the site in question — *without* using the supplied link in the e-mail. You'll know soon enough whether there's a problem with your account.

If you get this sort of e-mail from eBay and want to confirm whether it is really from eBay, visit this eBay security page:

```
http://pages.ebay.com/help/confidence/isgw-account-theft-
    spoof.html
```

To help eBay in its investigation of these information thieves, send a copy of the e-mail (along with all identification headers) to spoof@ebay.com. When forwarding the e-mail, do not alter it in any way.

Chapter 10: Reporting Abuses and Fraud

In This Chapter

- ✔ Keeping eBay members safe
- ✔ Staying away from eBay no-no's
- ✔ Filing complaints against eBay bad guys
- ✔ Closing the deal through escrow

Millions of people transact daily at eBay. If you're new to the Internet, however, you might need a reality check. With around ten million items selling every day, the law of averages dictates that you're bound to run into some rough seas. If you do, know that you can get the answers you need from eBay's SafeHarbor. In this chapter, I take you through the SafeHarbor resources — from reporting abuses to resolving insurance issues. This chapter explains how eBay enforces its rules and regulations, shows how you can use third-party escrow and mediation services, and even points out how to go outside eBay for help if you run into some really big-time problems.

Keeping eBay Safe

The eBay Security Center is where eBay focuses on protecting the Web site from members who aren't playing by the rules, as shown in Figure 10-1. At the Center, eBay issues warnings and policy changes — and in some cases, it gives eBay bad guys the old heave-ho.

To go to the eBay Security Center for tips on current security issues on eBay, click the Security Center link that you can find at the bottom of most eBay pages. The Center page provides more than just a link to policies and information. It also connects you with a group of eBay staffers who handle complaints, field incoming tips about possible infractions, and dole out warnings and suspensions. The folks here investigate infractions and send out e-mails in response to tips. eBay staffers look at complaints on a case-by-case basis in the order that they receive them. Most complaints that they receive are about these problems:

- ✦ Shill bidders (see "Selling abuses" in this chapter)
- ✦ Feedback issues and abuses (see "Feedback abuses" in this chapter)

Keep in mind that eBay is a community of people, most of whom have never met each other. No matter what you buy or sell at eBay, don't expect eBay transactions to be any safer than buying or selling from a complete stranger. If you go in with this attitude, you can't be disappointed.

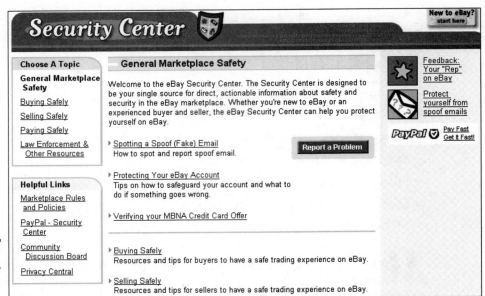

Figure 10-1:
The Security Center.

Another helpful page is the User Agreement FAQs page, which explains the legalese in clearer English. To find it, go to

`http://pages.ebay.com/help/policies/user-agreement-faqs.html`

If you plan on being an active eBay member, it's probably worth your while to opt-in for eBay's User Agreement update e-mail. Go to your My eBay page, click the My Preferences link, and then click the View/Change link next to Notification Preferences. At this point, you're asked to type in your password — this is to protect your security on eBay. Then you go to the magic page, where you can change *all* your eBay preferences, as well as the User Agreement update.

Abuses You Should Report

Before you even consider blowing the whistle on the guy who (gasp!) gave you negative feedback by reporting him, make sure that what you're encountering is actually a misuse of eBay. Some behavior isn't nice (no argument there), but it *also* isn't a violation of eBay rules — in which case, eBay can't do much about it. The following sections list the primary reasons that you may start SafeHarbor investigations.

Selling abuses

If you're on eBay long enough, you're bound to find an abuse of the service. It might happen on an auction you're bidding on, or it might be one of the sellers who compete with your auctions. Be a good community member and be on the lookout for the following:

✦ **Shill bidding:** A seller uses multiple User IDs to bid or has accomplices place bids to boost the price of his or her auction items. eBay investigators look for these telltale signs of a shill bidder:

- A single bidder who puts in a really high bid

- A bidder with really low feedback but a really high number of bids on items

- A bidder with low feedback who has been an eBay member for a while but who has never won an auction

- Excessive bids between two users

✦ **Auction interception:** An unscrupulous user, pretending to be the actual seller, contacts the winner to set up terms of payment and shipping in an effort to get the buyer's payment. This violation can be easily avoided by paying with PayPal directly through the eBay site.

✦ **Fee avoidance:** A seller reports a lower-than-actual final price and/or illegally submits a Final Value Fee credit. (For more on fees, see Book IV, Chapter 12.)

✦ **Hot bid manipulation:** A user, with the help of accomplices, enters dozens of phony bids to make the auction appear to have a lot of bidding action. Let the experts at eBay decide on this one, but you might wonder if loads of bids come in rapid succession but the price moves very little.

Bidding abuses

If you want to know more about bidding in general, see Book IV, Chapter 6. Here's a list of bidding abuses that eBay wants to know about:

✦ **Bid shielding:** Two users working in tandem: Bidder A, with the help of accomplices, intentionally bids an unreasonably high amount and then retracts the bid in the closing moments of the auction — leaving a lower bid (which the offender or an accomplice places) as the winning bid.

✦ **Bid siphoning:** Users send e-mails to bidders of a current auction to offer the same merchandise for a lower price elsewhere.

✦ **Auction interference:** Users warn other bidders through e-mail to stay clear of a seller *during a current auction,* presumably to decrease the number of bids and keep the prices low.

✦ **Bid manipulation (or Invalid Bid Retraction):** A user bids a ridiculously high amount, raising the next highest bidder to maximum bid. The manipulator then retracts the bid and rebids *slightly* over the previous high bidder's maximum.

✦ **Non-paying bidder:** I call them deadbeats. The bottom line is that these people win auctions but never pay up.

✦ **Unwelcome bidder:** A user bids on a specific seller's auction despite the seller's warning that he or she won't accept that user's bids (as in the case of not selling internationally and receiving international bids). This practice is impolite and obnoxious. If you want to bar specific bidders from your auctions, you can exclude them.

Feedback abuses

All that you have at eBay is your reputation, and that reputation is made up of your feedback history. eBay takes any violation of its feedback system very seriously. Because eBay's feedback is now transaction-related, unscrupulous eBay members have less opportunity to take advantage of this system. Here's a checklist of feedback abuses that you should report to the Security Center:

✦ **Feedback extortion:** A member threatens to post negative feedback if another eBay member doesn't follow through on some unwarranted demand.

✦ **Personal exposure:** A member leaves feedback for a user that exposes personal information that doesn't relate to transactions at eBay.

✦ **–4 feedback:** Any user reaching a net Feedback Score of –4 is subject to suspension.

Identity abuses

Who you are at eBay is as important as what you sell or buy. eBay monitors the identities of its members closely — and asks that you report any great pretenders in this area to Rules & Safety. Here's a checklist of identity abuses:

✦ **Identity misrepresentation:** A user claims to be an eBay staff member or another eBay user, or he or she registers under the name of another user.

✦ **False or missing contact information:** A user deliberately registers with false contact information or an invalid e-mail address.

✦ **Under age:** A user falsely claims to be 18 or older. (You must be at least 18 to enter into a legally binding contract.)

✦ **Dead/invalid e-mail addresses:** When e-mails bounce repeatedly from a user's registered e-mail address, chances are good that it's dead, Jim — and it's doing nobody any good. There's usually return e-mail indicating that the address is unknown.

✦ **Contact information:** One user publishes another user's contact information on the eBay site.

Operational abuses

If you see somebody trying to interfere with eBay's operation, eBay staffers want you to tell them about it. Here are two roguish operational abuses:

✦ **Hacking:** A user purposely interferes with eBay's computer operations (for example, by breaking into unauthorized files).

✦ **Spamming:** The user sends unsolicited e-mail to eBay users.

Reporting Abuses to Rules & Safety

If you suspect someone of abusing eBay's rules and regulations, or you encounter any of the abuses in this chapter, go to the Security Center (a link is at the bottom of every eBay page) and click the green Report a Problem button. You're then presented with the form shown in Figure 10-2. From this page, click the appropriate link for your issue.

The Security Center can give you a lot of good general information that can help you prevent something from going wrong in a future auction. Feel free to use these pages as a resource to help prevent problems.

If you've got a troubled auction and need to launch a report, follow these steps:

1. **Read all the information on the Security Center page before filing a new complaint.**

To get to the Security Center, click the Security Center link at the bottom of most eBay pages.

2. **Click any of the many Report links.**

No matter which link you click, you're taken to an area that instructs you further and provides information about what offenses eBay can and cannot investigate.

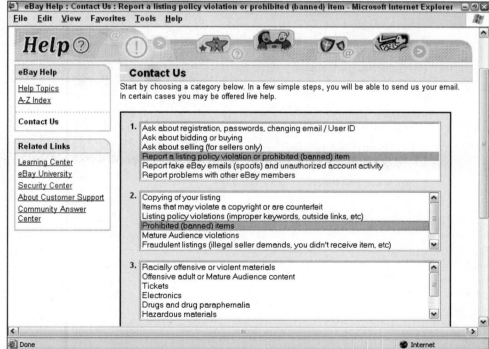

Figure 10-2:
The handy-dandy, encompass-it-all form allows you to report any violations directly to the Security Center of eBay.

3. **If you've found out that you have a legitimate case that should be investigated, click the Contact Rules & Safety link.**

You go to the handy form shown previously in Figure 10-2.

After selecting the items that relate to your situation, click Continue. eBay might present you with a page full of links to teach you about their policies and some possible solutions to your issue. After reviewing them, scroll to the bottom of the page and click Contact Support.

4. **You're now at the Rules & Safety Support Send Message form. (Whew.)**

Figure 10-3 shows you the form. Just type in the item number (or numbers if they're all part of a related problem) and give a thorough description of what transpired.

Before you send your message to Support, be sure to review what you've written to confirm that your report is accurate.

5. **Send the report by clicking Submit.**

Be sure that you send only one report per case — and one case per report.

If you file a report, make your message clear and concise by including everything that happened, but don't editorialize. (Calling someone a "lowdown, mud-sucking cretin" doesn't provide any useful info to anyone who can help you, and it doesn't reflect well on you either.) Keep it businesslike — just the facts, ma'am. Do include all pertinent documentation, such as e-mails, receipts, canceled checks — and (of course) the auction number.

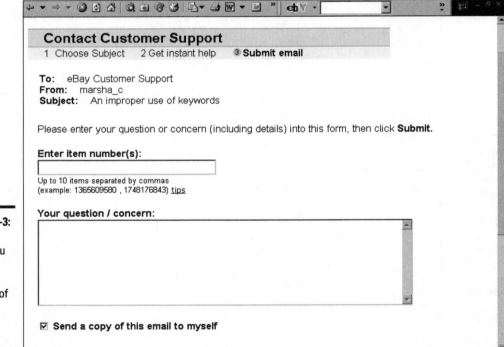

Figure 10-3: Here's where you spill the beans on violators of policy to Rules & Safety.

Here's a checklist of what you should include in your report to Rules & Safety:

✦ Write only the facts as you know them.

✦ Attach any pertinent e-mails with complete headers. (*Headers* are all the information found at the top of an e-mail message.) SafeHarbor uses the headers to verify how the e-mail was sent and to follow the trail back to the author.

✦ Be sure that the subject line of your report precisely names the violation.

After eBay receives your report, you usually get an automatic response that your e-mail was received — although in practice, several days could go crawling by before eBay actually investigates your allegations. (They must look at a *lot* of transactions.)

Depending on the outcome of the probe, eBay might contact you with the results. If your problem becomes a legal matter, eBay might not let you know what's going on. The only indication that you might get that some action was taken is that the eBay member you reported is suspended — or NARU (Not A Registered User).

If your complaint doesn't warrant an investigation by the folks at Rules & Safety, they pass it along to someone at the overworked Customer Support staff, who then contacts you. (Don't bawl out the person if the attention you get is tardy.)

Unfortunately, NARU members can show up again on the eBay site. Typically nefarious sorts such as these just use a different name. In fact, this practice is fairly common, so beware! If you suspect that someone who broke the rules once is back under another User ID, alert Rules & Safety. If you're a seller, you can refuse to accept bids from that person. If the person persists, alert Customer Support with an e-mail.

As eBay has grown, so has the number of complaints about slow response from Customer Support. I don't doubt that eBay staffers are doing their best. Although slow response can get frustrating, avoid the temptation to initiate a reporting blitzkrieg by sending reports over and over until eBay can't ignore you. This practice is inconsiderate, and it just slows down the process for everyone — and won't endear the e-mail bombardier to the folks who could help. It's better to just grin and bear it.

Using Mediation and Dispute Resolution Services

Even the best of friends sometimes have misunderstandings that can escalate to all-out war if they don't resolve their problems early enough. If the going gets tough, you need to call in the heavy artillery: a *mediator*. Just as pro boxing has its referees, auctions might need a level head to intervene in a squabble. eBay partners with SquareTrade, an online problem-solving service, and the service is available through the eBay Web site (or directly at www.squaretrade.com). Acting as a third party with no axe to grind, a mediator such as SquareTrade can often hammer out an agreement or act as judge to resolve disputes.

To find SquareTrade at eBay, click the Dispute Resolution link on the Services page.

Resolving a transaction dispute

If you file a complaint through the SquareTrade link, the service asks you to supply information regarding the offending transaction on an online form. SquareTrade then sends an e-mail to the offending party, outlining the situation. Both the complaint and the response from the other party appear on a secure Web page that only the offender, the mediator, and you can access.

SquareTrade uses a patent-pending technology to help smooth the mediation process. The mediator listens to both points of view and, if the parties can't reach an agreement, suggests a solution that he bases on the rules of fair play and good conduct. The use of a mediator doesn't, however, preclude the use of a lawyer if things truly hit an impasse.

Negative feedback can be removed!

You might find yourself in a situation where you've received unjustified feedback (as in the case of the nervous Nellie who left a negative because the item hadn't arrived but it was just hung up in the mail). If the problem gets resolved between the two of you, you can get that feedback removed. eBay has agreed that if the two parties go through a SquareTrade mediation with a live mediator, and both parties agree that the feedback was unwarranted, the feedback will be expunged from your record.

You need to file an online Dispute Resolution with SquareTrade and request a mediator. There is a $15 charge to involve a live mediator. (eBay pays the balance of SquareTrade's fee.) The process can take from two to six weeks, depending on how fast the other party responds to their SquareTrade e-mails. If the two of you agree ahead of time on the process, it can speed along quickly.

Toss 'em a Life Saver: Insurance

One thing's for sure in this world: Nothing is for sure. That's why insurance companies exist. Several types of insurance are available for eBay users:

✦ Insurance that buyers purchase to cover shipping (see Book IV, Chapter 15)

✦ eBay's Fraud Protection, which I discuss in this chapter

✦ eBay Motors Limited Warranty

✦ Warranties on electronics

✦ PayPal's Buyer Protection

To cover loss from fraud, eBay has its own Fraud Protection Program. The insurance covers money that you pay for an item you never receive (as a result of fraud, not shipping problems) or receive but find to be materially different from the auction item's description. eBay insurance pays up to $175 (a maximum of $200 coverage minus a $25 deductible) for a single claim. So if you file a $50 claim, you get $25. If you file a $5,000 claim, you still get only $175. (Hey, it's better than nothing.)

Here's the checklist to qualify for an eBay insurance payment:

✦ The buyer and seller must be in good standing (no negative feedback ratings).

✦ The buyer must have proof that the item costs more than $25.

✦ The buyer must prove that the payment was sent.

✦ The buyer must prove that the seller didn't send the item.

   OR

✦ The buyer must prove that the item sent is substantially different from the auction description.

To be eligible for insurance, you must register a complaint with the Fraud Reporting System no sooner than 30 (and no later than 60) days after the auction closes. eBay then e-mails the seller that a complaint has been lodged. eBay hopes that by the time the 60 days are up, the differences are resolved and you can withdraw your complaint.

Extended warranties on electronics

eBay has teamed up with N.E.W. Customer Service Companies, a leading provider of extended service plans, to offer buyers of new, refurbished, or used electronics on eBay a 100 percent, one-year warranty. If you purchase this extended warranty, and your product breaks during the warranty period, N.E.W. repairs it — parts and labor are 100 percent covered. If an item requires more than three repairs, the no-lemon guarantee replaces the item for free.

For more information on how this plan works, and how to purchase a policy, go to

`http://pages.ebay.com/help/warranty/buyer_overview.html`

eBay Motors Limited Warranty

Another beneficial eBay venture is its teaming up with 1Source Auto Warranty to offer a *free* limited warranty to anyone who purchases a car on eBay. To qualify (this is the easy part), the car you purchase must be fewer than 10 years old, have fewer than 125,000 miles on it, and have no mechanical modifications. Qualified cars are identified in the listing description in the Item Specifics box, with the words *Free Limited Warranty*.

The warranty covers up to $10,000 in repairs with a $500 deductible per visit. You must redeem the warranty during the checkout process. You can find more information at eBay Motors:

`http://pages.ebay.com/ebaymotors/services/warranty.html`

PayPal Buyer Protection

Aside from safety, PayPal offers an even better reason to pay through their service. If you've purchased your item through a PayPal-verified seller, you're covered for your purchase with an additional $300 of insurance. (Combined with the eBay insurance, that brings your total coverage to $500!)

Buyer Protection covers you only for non-delivery of tangible items and tangible items that are received significantly not as described — not if you are disappointed with the item. This insurance kicks in after you have filed for eBay Fraud Protection and your item exceeds the $200 cap.

If you've paid with a credit card through PayPal, be sure to make a claim with eBay first and *then* with PayPal. Do *not* make a claim with your credit card company. PayPal Protection is for PayPal purchases, and you aren't covered if you've made a claim with your credit card company.

Launching a Fraud Report

The second that you complain about a seller who has taken money but hasn't delivered the goods, a security investigation automatically starts. To file an initial Fraud Alert for misrepresented or non-delivered items prior to eBay's 30-day waiting period, go to

http://pages.ebay.com/help/confidence/programs-fraud.html

and click the Buyer Protection on eBay - Details link. Scroll down the page to the Report Suspicious Activity entry in the table and click the appropriate link to lodge your complaint.

To file an insurance claim with eBay, you must register a fraud report no sooner than 30 days and no later than 60 days after the close of the auction. Be careful not to jump the gun and register a complaint too soon. I suggest waiting about two or three weeks before you register your complaint; double-check first to make sure that your e-mail is working and that you have the correct address of the person with whom you're having difficulties. After all, neither eBay nor your ISP is infallible.

Even if your insurance claim isn't worth a nickel after 30 days, you can still register a fraud report and help the investigation of a lousy, terrible, *allegedly* fraudulent eBay user. That's payment enough, ain't it?

After you register a complaint, eBay informs the other party that you're making a fraud claim. eBay says it will try to contact both parties and help reach a resolution. *Registering* the complaint isn't the same thing as *filing* an insurance complaint. Registering starts the process; filing for insurance comes after a month-long grace period if the situation isn't resolved by then.

If you've clearly been ripped off, use eBay's Fraud Reporting program to file a complaint. Just follow these steps:

1. **Open your browser and go to the Online Fraud Complaint Reporting form at this address:**

   `http://crs.ebay.com/aw-cgi/ebayisapi.dll?crsstartpage.`

2. **Read the step-by-step directions.**

   You're asked whether you want to file a complaint and insurance claim, and the page offers some ideas on how to resolve the problem.

3. **Click either the Submit a New Complaint button or the View a Complaint in Progress button.**

   You're forwarded to an ominous page that reads `Do you feel another eBay member has defrauded you?` If you've made it this far, I assume that you feel this way, so click Yes.

4. **On request, enter your User ID and password and click the Sign In button to move to the next page.**

   Even if you're permanently signed in to eBay, you have to type in your password at this point — for your own protection.

5. **Verify your name, address, and contact info.**

   If it's wrong, click the appropriate button to correct the information.

6. **At this point, enter the item number and click the I Was Bidder button.**

7. **After you finish, print out the final page with the provided claim number.**

If the accusation that you're registering refers to a clear violation, eBay gives you information on the kind of third-party assistance that you can get to help resolve the problem. If eBay deems the problem a violation of the law, it reports the crime to the appropriate law-enforcement agency.

Docking with Escrow

Escrow is a relatively new concept for online trading. Escrow services act as the go-between between the seller and the buyer. The details of using escrow are spelled out in Book IV, Chapter 6. eBay has a direct link to an online escrow service. Click the Services link on the navigation bar, and then scroll down and click the Escrow Services link and click it. This action takes you to the Escrow Overview page. On this page, click the Frequently Asked Questions link and follow the directions on the page that appears next.

Trimming in the Sales: Authentication and Appraising

Despite eBay's attempts to keep the buying and selling community honest, some people just refuse to play nice. After the New York City Department of Consumer Affairs launched an investigation into counterfeit sports memorabilia sold on the Web site, errant eBay outlaws experienced some anxious moments. I can always hope they mend their ways, while at the same time advising *Don't bet on it.* Fortunately, eBay is offering a proactive approach to preventing such occurrences from happening again.

**Book IV
Chapter 10**

**Reporting Abuses
and Fraud**

Topmost among the countermeasures is easy member access to several services that can authenticate specific types of merchandise. The good news here is that you know what kind of item you're getting; the bad news is that, as does everything else in life, it costs you money.

Before you spend the money to have your item appraised and authenticated, ask yourself a few practical questions (regardless of whether you're buying or selling):

✦ **Is this item quality merchandise?** Am I selling/buying merchandise whose condition is subjective but important to its value? Is it really well-loved or just busted? Is this item graded by some professionally accepted standard that I need to know?

✦ **Is this item the real thing?** Am I sure that I'm selling/buying a genuine item? Do I need an expert to tell me whether it's the real McCoy?

✦ **Do I know the value of the merchandise?** Do I have a good understanding of what this item is worth in the marketplace at this time, considering its condition?

✦ **Is the merchandise worth the price?** Is the risk of selling/buying a counterfeit, a fake, or an item that I don't completely understand worth the cost of an appraisal?

ID Verify

During the later years of the Cold War, Ronald Reagan said, "Trust but verify." The president's advice made sense for dealing with the old Soviet Union, and it makes good sense with your dealings at eBay, too! (Even if you're not dealing in nuclear warheads.)

To show other eBay members that you're an honest type — and to get special privileges when you're a newbie at eBay, you can buy a "trust but verify" option, known as *ID Verify,* from eBay for five bucks. The giant credit verification service, VeriSign (www.verisign.com), verifies your identity by asking for your wallet information, including the following:

✦ Name

✦ Address

✦ Phone number

✦ Social Security number

✦ Driver's license information

✦ Date of birth

VeriSign matches the info that you give to what's in its database and presents you with a list of questions from your credit file that only you should know the answers to. VeriSign might also ask you about any loans you have or what kinds of credit cards you own and how many.

Becoming ID-verified can be a bonus for new users. By making sure that the community knows you're really who you say you are, you can get the green light for some higher-level activities:

✦ **Run Auctions with the Buy It Now option.** Ordinarily you need a feedback rating of 10 to run a Buy It Now auction. This privilege might be worth the price of the verification, but honestly, how hard is it really to get your first ten feedbacks? Besides, the experience will be priceless.

✦ **Open an eBay Store.** Although eBay requires a feedback rating of only 20 to open a store — I suggest you have much more. An eBay Store (see Book IV, Chapter 14 for more information) requires a bit more eBay savvy than the newbie seller can muster.

✦ **Run fixed-price auctions offering multiple items (and Multiple Item auctions).** Ordinarily, an eBay seller must have a feedback rating higher than 30 to perform this type of sale. I've spoken to several eBay veterans and they rarely participate in these types of sales.

✦ **Bid on items over $15,000.** Some form of verification is usually required even of eBay's old timers when bidding this high!

✦ **Sell items in the Mature Audiences category.** This category is for selling sex-related material.

VeriSign sends only the results of its Identity Test to eBay (whether you pass the test or fail) and *not* the answers to the private financial questions that it asks you. VeriSign doesn't modify or add the information that you provide to any of its databases.

VeriSign's questions are meant to protect you against anyone else who might come along and try to steal this information from you and assume your identity. The questions aren't a credit check, and your creditworthiness is never called into question. This info simply verifies that you are who you say you are.

If you pass the test and VeriSign can verify that you are who you say you are (and not your evil twin), you get a cool icon by your name for a year. If, after a year, you like the validation that comes from such verification, you can pay another fee and renew your seal.

Although you can feel secure knowing that a user who's verified is indeed who he or she claims to be, you still have no guarantee that he or she isn't going to turn out to be a no-goodnik (or, for that matter, a well-meaning financial airhead) during auction transactions.

Even if an eBay member gets VeriSign verification, this program is controversial for two reasons:

✦ Many members object to giving out Social Security numbers. They see it as an unwarranted invasion of privacy.

✦ Some users also fear that this system creates a two-tiered eBay system, with verified users occupying a sort of upper class and anyone who's not verified stuck in the lower class. They're afraid that sellers might refuse to do business with *un*verified users.

You should consider all of eBay's current and future programs for protecting you from problematic transactions and people, but I think the undisputed heavyweight champ for finding out who someone *really is* (and keeping you out of trouble) is the first program that eBay created. That's right, folks, *feedback* can show you other eBay members' track records and give you the best information on whether you want to do business with them or take a pass. Feedback is especially effective if you analyze it in conjunction with eBay's other protection programs. I suggest taking the time to read all about feedback in Book IV, Chapter 4.

CHECK IT OUT

Getting Items Appraised

If you need items appraised, consider using an appraisal agency. Most agencies offer their services at discount to eBay members. eBay offers links to various appraising agencies:

- ✔ The **PCGS** (Professional Coin Grading Service) and **NGC** (Numismatic Guaranty Corporation) serve coin collectors. You can visit PCGS at www.pcgs.com.

- ✔ **PSA/DNA** (a service of Professional Sports Authenticators) and **OnlineAuthentics.com** authenticate your autographs. Both keep online databases of thousands of certified autographs for you to compare your purchases against. Their respective online addresses are www.psadna.com and www.onlineauthentics.com.

- ✔ **PSE** (Professional Stamp Experts) authenticates your postal stamps and can be found at www.psestamp.com.

- ✔ **CGC** (Comics Guaranty) grades and restores comic books, and you can find it at www.cgccomics.com/ebay_comic_book_grading.cfm.

- ✔ **IGI** (International Gemological Institute) grades, authenticates, and identifies loose gemstones and jewelry. Visit IGI at www.e-igi.com/ebay.

- ✔ **PSA** (Professional Sports Authenticators) and **SGC** (Sportscard Guaranty) help guard against counterfeiting and fraud with sports memorabilia and trading cards. Their respective addresses are www.psacard.com and www.sgccard.com.

Even if you use an appraiser or an authentication service, do some legwork yourself. Often, two experts can come up with wildly different opinions on the same item. The more you know, the better the questions you can ask.

If a seller isn't sure whether the item that he or she is auctioning is authentic, you might find an appropriate comment (such as *Cannot verify authenticity*) in the auction item description. Knowledgeable eBay gurus always like to share what they know, and I have no doubt that someone on the appropriate chat board might be able to supply you with scads of helpful information. But be careful — some blarney artist (one of *those* is born every minute, too) might try to make a sucker out of you.

Chapter 11: Yada, Yada: Message Boards, Announcements, and Chat

In This Chapter

✔ **Looking at announcements and other important messages**

✔ **Using eBay message boards**

✔ **Finding help when you need it**

✔ **Chatting it up**

*e*Bay is more than just an Internet location for buying and selling great stuff. eBay wants the world to know that it has created (and works hard to maintain) a community. It's not a bad deal actually — prime real estate in *this* community costs only pennies! As in real-life communities, you participate as much as works for you. In real life, you can get involved in all sorts of neighborhood activities, or you can just sit back, mind your own business, and watch the world go by. eBay works exactly the same way.

As you've probably heard by now, one of the main ways to participate in the eBay community is through feedback (which I explain in detail in Book IV, Chapter 4). In this chapter, I show you some other ways to become part of the community. You can socialize, get info from other members, leave messages, or just read what everybody's talking about through eBay's message boards, chat boards, and the corporate Announcements Board. Along the way, I include tips on how to use all these places to your benefit.

News and Chat, This and That

It's not quite like *The New York Times* ("All the News That's Fit to Print"), but you can find all the news, chat boards, and message boards links from the Community Overview page. Figure 11-1 shows you what the page looks like. To get there, click the Community link on the navigation bar.

Here's a list of all the major headings of the main Community page. Each heading offers you links to the following specific eBay areas:

✦ **Talk:** A click on these links whisks you to eBay's discussion boards, chat rooms, or the Answer Center.

✦ **News:** This area contains links to the General Announcements page, which covers General News, Policy Changes, Technology Updates, System Announcements, and *The Chatter*, eBay's Newsletter.

✦ **Events:** Click one of these links to find out what's going on at eBay.

✦ **People:** This is where you can get really social, join Groups, find out about Community Values, and get stories from eBay members about their bidding adventures.

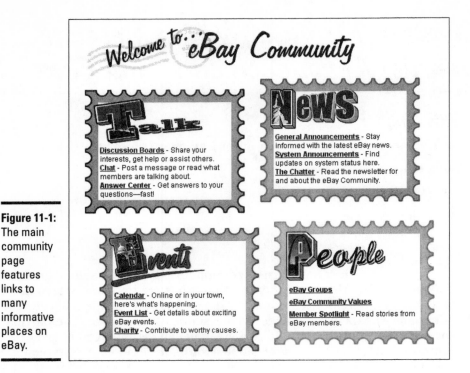

Figure 11-1: The main community page features links to many informative places on eBay.

Hear Ye, Hear Ye! eBay's Announcements Boards

If you were living in the 1700s, you'd see a strangely dressed guy in a funny hat ringing a bell and yelling, "Hear ye, hear ye!" every time you opened eBay's Announcements Boards. eBay's Announcements Boards are the most important places to find out what's going on (directly from headquarters) on the Web site. (And no one even needs to ring a bell!)

You have your choice of two boards. First, the General Announcement Board is where eBay lists any new features and policy changes. Visiting this page is like reading your morning eBay newspaper because eBay adds comments to this page almost every day. You find out about upcoming changes in categories, new promotions, and eBay goings-on. Reach this page at www2.ebay.com/aw/marketing.shtml. Figure 11-2 shows you eBay's General Announcement Board with information that could affect your auctions.

eBay also tips you off to the System Status (in case you wonder whether the glitch is on your computer or on the eBay system). The System Announcement Board at www2.ebay.com/aw/announce.shtml is where eBay reports outages and critical changes in policies and procedures. eBay also uses this board to update users on glitches in the system and when those might be rectified.

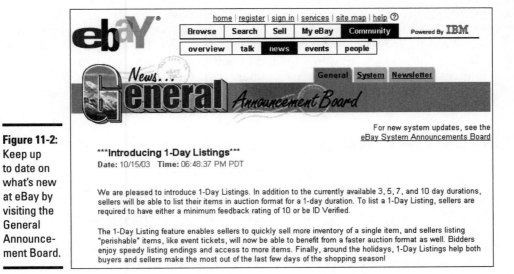

Figure 11-2:
Keep up
to date on
what's new
at eBay by
visiting the
General
Announce-
ment Board.

Help! I Need Somebody

If you ever have specific eBay questions to which you need answers, several eBay Discussion Help boards on the Community: Chat page can help you. You can also go directly to the chat rooms to pose your question to the eBay members currently in residence.

Boards work differently than chat rooms. Chat rooms are full of people who are hanging out talking to each other all at the same time, whereas users of Discussion Boards tend to go in, leave a message or ask a question, and pop out again. Also, on a message board, you need to start a thread by asking a question. Title your thread with your question, and you'll no doubt get an answer to your query posted swiftly. Take a look at the Technical Issues Board in Figure 11-3.

Figure 11-3:
One of the
handy
Discussion
Boards on
eBay, the
Technical
Issues
Board.

Most questions can be answered by going to eBay's Answer Center, which you can get to by clicking the Answer Center link in the Talk area. You then see boards covering almost any topic that you can think of regarding auctions at eBay. Just post your question and hopefully some kind eBay member will suggest an answer. However, remember to take that advice with a grain of salt, just as you would any advice from someone with unknown credentials.

Community Chat Rooms

Because sending e-mail to eBay's Customer Service people can be frustratingly slow if you need an answer right away (they get bombarded with a gazillion questions a day), you might want to try for a faster answer by posting your question on one of the Community message boards.

Knowledgeable veteran eBay members or Customer Service folks (if they're around) generally answer posted questions as best as they can. The answers are the opinions of members and are certainly not eBay gospel. But you get a fast and honest answer; often you get more than one response. Most questions are answered in about 15 minutes. If not, repost your question. Make sure that you post your question on the appropriate board because each board has a specific topic of discussion.

Members who post on these boards often share helpful tips and Web sites and alert other members to scams. *Lurking* (reading without posting) on some of these boards can help newbies find out more about how eBay works. Occasionally, an eBay staffer shows up, which is kinda like inviting Bill Gates to a Windows XP new users' meeting. eBay staff members are usually hounded with questions.

One cardinal rule for eBay chat boards and message boards exists: no business. No advertising items for sale! Not now. Not ever. eBay bans any repeat offenders from participating on these boards.

User-to-User Discussion Boards

eBay has some other boards that take a different tack on things. They're *discussion* boards as opposed to *chat* boards, which basically means that the topics are deliberately open-ended — just as the topics of discussions in coffee houses tend to vary depending on who happens to be there at any given time. Check out these areas and read ongoing discussions about eBay's latest buzz. It's a lot of fun and good reading. Post your opinions to the category that suits you. Each discussion board carries as many topics as you can imagine. Here are few of my favorites:

✦ **The eBay Town Square** is a potpourri of various subjects and topics.

✦ **The Soapbox** is the place to voice your views and suggestions to help build a better eBay.

- ✦ **Night Owls Nest** is the fun locale for creatures of the night and their unique postings. (As I'm writing this, for example, there's a thread with spirited advice to a Community Member who needs help with his gassy cat.)
- ✦ **The Park** is an interesting place where Community Members join in for fun ideas and threads.

Category-Specific Chat Boards

Want to talk about Elvis, Louis XV, Sammy Sosa, or Howard the Duck? Currently, over 20 category-specific chat boards enable you to tell eBay members what's on your mind about merchandise and auctions. You reach these boards by clicking Community on the main navigation bar and then clicking Chat in the Talk area.

Of course, you can buy and sell without ever going on a chat board, but you can certainly find out a lot from one. Discussions mainly focus on merchandise and the nuts and bolts of transactions. Category-specific chat boards are great for posting questions on items that you don't know much about.

These boards are also great for finding out where to go for more research and information on specific items. You can also find helpful sources for shipping information about items in that category (such as large furniture on the Antiques & Art chat board or breakable items on the Glass chat board).

Chapter 12: Trash to Treasure: Selling on eBay

In This Chapter

✔ Staying out of trouble — what you can't sell at eBay

✔ Paying the piper with eBay fees

✔ Keeping the taxman happy (or at least friendly)

Finding items to sell can be as easy as opening up your closet and as challenging as acquiring antiques overseas. Either way, establishing yourself as an eBay seller isn't that difficult when you know the ropes. In this chapter, you find out how to figure out what items are worth and turn them into instant cash. But before you pick your house clean (I know eBay can be habit-forming, but, please, keep a *few* things for yourself!), read up on the eBay rules of the road — like how to sell, when to sell, and what *not* to sell. If you're interested in finding out how to set up your auction page, get acquainted with Book IV, Chapter 13.

Know Thy Stuff

I bet Socrates would have said, "Know thy stuff," if he'd been an eBay seller. Haven't had to do a homework assignment in a while? Time to dust off those old skills. Before selling your merchandise, do some digging to find out as much as you can about it.

Getting the goods on your goods

Here are some ideas to help you flesh out your knowledge of what you have to sell:

✦ **Hit the books.** Check your local library for books about the item. Study price guides and collector magazines. Even though collectors still use published price guides when they put a value on an item, so much fast-moving e-commerce is on the Internet that price guides often lag behind the markets that they cover. Take their prices with a grain of salt.

✦ **Go surfin'.** Conduct a Web search and look for info on the item on other auction sites. If you find a print magazine that strikes your fancy, check to see whether the magazine is available on the Web by typing the title of the magazine into your browser's search window.

✦ **When the going gets tough, go shopping.** Browse local stores that specialize in your item. Price it at several locations. When you understand what the demand for your product is (whether it's a collectible or a commodity) and how much you can realistically ask for it, you're on the right track to a successful auction.

✦ **Call in the pros.** Need a quick way to find the value of an item that you want to sell? Call a dealer or a collector and ask his or her advice. The merchant will likely give you a current selling price.

✦ **eBay to the rescue.** eBay offers some guidance for your research on its category pages. eBay offers special features for each main category. Click the Browse link on the navigation bar and select your favorite category. As you scroll the page, eBay places links to stories and features specifically for this category. Also, eBay has category-specific chat rooms where you can read what other collectors are writing about items in a particular category. See Book IV, Chapter 11 for more on eBay's chat area.

Spy versus spy: Comparison selling

Back in the old days, successful retailers like Gimbel and Macy spied on each other to figure out ways to get a leg up on the competition. Today, in the bustling world of e-commerce, the spying continues, and spying on the competition is as easy as clicking your mouse.

Say that you're the biggest *Dukes of Hazzard* fan ever and you collect *Dukes of Hazzard* stuff, such as VHS tapes from the show, General Lee models, and lunchboxes. Well, good news: That piece of tin that holds your lunchtime PB and J might very well fetch a nice sum of money. To find out for sure, you can do some research at eBay. To find out the current market price for a *Dukes of Hazzard* lunchbox, you can conduct a Completed Items search on the Search page (as I describe in Book IV, Chapter 5) and find out exactly how many *Dukes of Hazzard* lunchboxes have been on the auction block in the past couple weeks. You can also find out their high selling prices and how many bids the lunchboxes received by the time the auctions were over. And repeating a completed auction search in a week or two isn't a bad idea so that you can get at least a month's worth of data to price your item. Figure 12-1 shows the results of a Completed Items search sorted by highest prices first.

Figure 12-1: Use the Completed Items search to find out what an item is selling for and how many have been for sale recently.

eBay makes saving a search easy. Just click the Add to My Favorite Searches link in the top-right corner (you can see it in Figure 12-1) to add the current search to your favorite searches. Then it's on your My eBay All Favorites page, and you can repeat the search with a click of your mouse.

Sure enough, when I tried this tactic, I found a considerable number of additional listings for a *Dukes of Hazzard Lunch Box (lunchbox, "lunch box")*. Coincidentally, when I changed my search (remember, sellers *do* make mistakes) to **dukes (hazzard,hazard) (lunchbox, "lunch box")**, my search results went from 34 lunchboxes to 49! The best deals for buyers (and for sellers to resell) are always when the seller misspells a name or brand in the title. Lunchboxes have always been a hot item at eBay. Check out Figure 12-2 to see some top sellers.

Look at the individual auction item pages for each item that your Completed Items search turns up. That way, you can confirm that the items (lunchboxes, for example) are identical to the one that you want to sell. And when you do your research, factor in your item's condition. Read the individual item descriptions. If your item is in better condition, expect (and ask for) more money for it; if your item is in worse condition, expect (and ask for) less. Also, note the categories the items are listed under; they might give you a clue about where eBay members are looking for items just like yours.

If you want to be extremely thorough in your comparison selling, go to a search engine to see whether the results of your eBay search mesh with what's going on elsewhere. If you find that no items like yours are for sale anywhere else online, and are pretty sure people are looking for what you have, you might just find yourself in Fat City.

Figure 12-2:
A completed items search for *lunchbox* and *lunch box*.

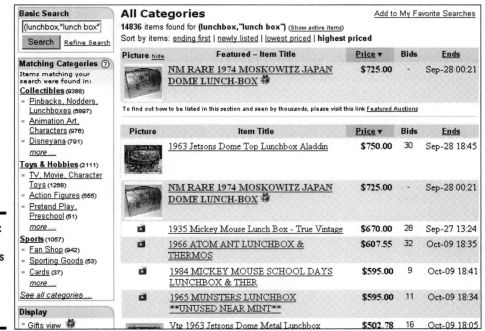

**Book IV
Chapter 12**

Trash to Treasure: Selling on eBay

Know What You Can (And Can't) Sell

The majority of auctions found at eBay are aboveboard. But sometimes eBay finds out about auctions that are either illegal (in the eyes of the state or federal government) or prohibited by eBay's rules and regulations. In either case, eBay steps in, calls a foul, and makes the auction invalid.

eBay doesn't have rules and regulations just for the heck of it. eBay wants to keep you educated so that you don't unwittingly bid on — or sell — an item that has been misrepresented. eBay also wants you to know what's okay and what's prohibited so that if you run across an auction that looks fishy, you'll help out your fellow eBay members by reporting it. And eBay wants you to know that getting your auction shut down is the least of your worries: You can be suspended if you knowingly list items that are prohibited. And I won't even talk about criminal prosecution.

You need to know about these three categories at eBay:

+ **Prohibited** lists the items that may *not* be sold at eBay under any circumstances.

+ **Potentially Infringing** lists the types of items that may be in violation of copyrights, trademarks, or other rights.

+ **Questionable** lists the items that may be sold under certain conditions.

The items that you absolutely *cannot* sell at eBay can fit into *all three* categories. Those items can be legally ambiguous at best, not to mention potentially risky and all kinds of sticky. To find a detailed description of which items are prohibited, potentially infringing, or questionable, go to this eBay Web page:

http://pages.ebay.com/help/sell/item_allowed.html

Because eBay's base of operations is in California, United States law is enforced — even if both the buyer and seller are from other countries. Cuban cigars, for example, are legal to buy and sell in Canada, but even if the buyer *and* the seller are from Canada, eBay says, *"No permiso,"* and shuts down auctions of Havanas fast. Figure 12-3 shows an auction that was shut down soon after I found it.

Ignorance is no excuse. If you list an item that's in any way prohibited on eBay, eBay ends your auction. If you have any questions, always check eBay's Rules & Safety department at http://pages.ebay.com/help/sell/item_allowed.html.

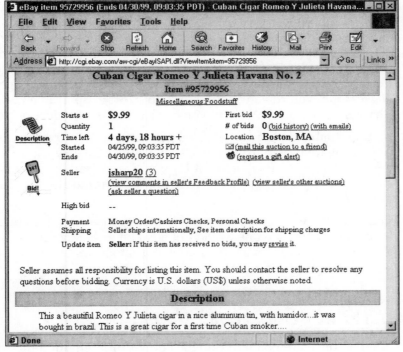

Figure 12-3:
I found this auction for a Cuban cigar before the eBay police did (and cancelled it) in 1999.

Forbidden Auctions

The folks at eBay didn't just fall off the turnip truck. eBay staffers have seen just about every scam to get around paying fees or following policy guidelines. Chances are good that if you try one of these scams, you'll get caught. eBay cancels the auction and credits you for the listing fee. Do it once, and shame on you. Do it a lot, and you're out of eBay.

The following items are definitely forbidden:

+ **Raffles and prizes:** You need to sell something in your auction; you can't offer raffle tickets or chances for a giveaway.

+ **Want ads:** If you want something, you have to search for it. Don't try to run your needs as an ad thinly disguised as an auction.

+ **Advertisements:** An eBay auction isn't the place to make a sales pitch (other than attractive copy describing your item, that is). Some eBay bad guys list an auction name and then use the auction to send bidders to some other auction or Web site. The Real Estate category is one exception. You can run an ad there for your property.

+ **Bait-and-switch tactics:** These are a variation on the ugly old sales technique of pretending to sell what you're not really selling. Some eBay users who are selling an unfamiliar brand of item try to snag bidders by putting a more familiar brand in the title. For instance, writing *Designer Chanel purse — not really, but a lot like it!* is a fake-out. eBay calls it *keyword spamming.* I call it lousy.

✦ **Choice auctions:** These are like Multiple Item (Dutch) auctions gone crazy. Normally, sellers can offer only one item per auction in a regular auction and multiples of the same item in a Multiple Item auction. Choice auctions offer a mishmash of multiple items from which bidders choose. For example, if you're selling T-shirts, an auction can be for only one particular size per sale. If you want to list small, medium, and large sizes, I suggest that you run an auction for one size and open an eBay store (see Chapter 14 of Book IV) where you can list single sales for each size.

✦ **Mixing apples with oranges:** This gambit tries to attract more bidders to view an item by putting it in a high-traffic category where it doesn't belong. Forget it. eBay moves it for you if necessary, but keeping that rutabaga recipe book *away* from the list of automotive repair manuals is more considerate.

✦ **Catalogs:** "Buy my catalog so you can buy more stuff from me!" Uh-huh. I don't know why anyone would put a *bid* on a catalog (unless it's a Sears-Roebuck antique). If it's only a booklet that shows off all the cool junk you're selling, you can't offer it as an auction item.

eBay Fees? What eBay Fees? Oops . . .

The Cliché Police are going to raid me sooner or later, but here's one I'm poking a few holes in this time around: *You gotta spend it to make it.* This old-time business chestnut means that you need to invest a fair amount of money before you can turn a profit. Although the principle still holds true in the real world (at least most of the time), at eBay you don't have to spend much to run your business. This is one reason why eBay has become one of the most successful e-commerce companies on the Internet and a darling of Wall Street. eBay keeps fees low and volume high.

eBay charges the following types of fees for conducting auctions:

✦ Regular auction Insertion Fees ($0.30 to $4.80).

✦ Real Estate Listing Fees. These can vary because you have the choice of listing your property as an ad rather than an auction. Because eBay real estate auctions are *non-binding* (due to legalities), you might be better off running an ad. eBay charges different prices for different types of real estate:

- **Timeshares and Land**

  Auctions: 3-, 5-, 7-, or 10-day listing ($35); 30-day listing ($50)

  Ad format: 30-day listing ($150); 90-day listing ($300)

- **Residential, Commercial, and Other Real Estate**

  Auctions: 3-, 5-, 7-, or 10-day listing ($100); 30-day listing ($150)

  Ad format: 30-day listing ($150), 90-day listing ($300)

✦ Automotive Fees ($40). Motorcycles are only $30.

✦ Additional Reserve Auction Fees, which are refundable if your item meets the reserve and sells ($0.50 to $1; auctions with reserves over $100, 1 percent of the reserve with a maximum of $100).

✦ Final Value Fees (a percentage of the sales price).

✦ Optional fees (vary).

To examine the most up-to-date fees that eBay charges, go to this eBay Web page:

```
http://pages.ebay.com/help/sellerguide/selling-fees.html
```

Insertion Fees

Every auction is charged an Insertion Fee. There's no way around it. The Insertion Fee is calculated on a sliding scale that's based on the *minimum bid* (your starting price) or on the *reserve price* (the secret lowest price that you're willing to sell your item for) of your item. (Later in this chapter, I explain how the reserve price affects what you eventually have to pay.) Take a look at Table 12-1 for eBay's Insertion Fee structure.

Table 12-1	Insertion Fee Charges
If Your Minimum Bid Is . . .	*The Insertion Fee Is . . .*
$0 to $.99	*No fee*
$1.00 to $9.99	$0.35
$10.00 to $24.99	$0.60
$25.00 to $49.99	$1.20
$50.00 to $199.99	$2.40
$200.00 to $499.99	$3.60
$500.00 to gazillions	$4.80

If you're running a reserve-price auction (which I explain in detail in Chapter 13 of Book IV), eBay bases its Insertion Fee on the reserve price, not the minimum bid. eBay also charges a fee to run a reserve-price auction.

Here's a snapshot of how a reserve price affects your Insertion Fee. If you set a minimum bid of $1 for a gold Rolex watch (say what?) but your reserve price is $5,000 (that's more like it), you're charged a $4.80 Insertion Fee based on the $5,000 reserve price plus a $50 (refundable if the item sells) reserve fee.

In a Multiple Item auction (which I explain in Book IV, Chapter 13), the Insertion Fee is based on the minimum bid — as in a regular auction — but then eBay multiplies the minimum bid by the number of items that you list. So if you set a minimum bid of $1 for 300 glow-in-the-dark refrigerator magnets, you pay a $3.60 Insertion Fee for the listing.

So what does the Insertion Fee buy you at eBay?

✦ A really snazzy-looking auction page of your item that millions of eBay members can see, admire, and breathlessly respond to. (Well, I can hope.)

✦ The use of eBay services, such as the SafeHarbor program, that somewhat ease your auction experience.

**Book IV
Chapter 12**

Trash to Treasure: Selling on eBay

Final Value Fees

If you follow the movie business, you hear about some big A-list stars who take a relatively small fee for making a film but negotiate a big percentage of the gross profits. This is known as a *back-end deal* — in effect, a commission based on how much the movie brings in. eBay does the same thing, taking a small Insertion Fee when you list your item and then a commission on the back end when you sell your item. This commission is called the *Final Value Fee* and is based on the final selling price of your item.

In real life, when you pay sales commissions on a big purchase like a house, you usually pay a fixed percentage. eBay's Final Value Fee structure is different: It's set up as a three-tiered system, as Table 12-2 explains.

Table 12-2	Final Value Fees
Closing Bid	*How to Find Your Final Value Fee*
$.01 to $25	Multiply the final sale price by **5.25%**. If the final sale price is $25, multiply 25 by 5.25%. You owe eBay $1.31.
$25.01 to $1,000	You pay $1.31 for the first $25 of the final sale price (which is 5.25%). Subtract $25 from your final closing bid and then multiply this amount by **2.75%**. Add this total to the $1.31 you owe for the first $25. The sum is what you owe eBay. If the final sale price is $1,000, multiply 975 by 0.0275. (**Hint:** The answer is $26.81.) *Now,* add $26.81 and $1.31. You owe eBay $28.12.
$1,000.01 and over	You owe $1.31 for the first $25 of the final sale price (which is 5.25%). But you also have to pay $26.81 for the remainder of the price between $25.01 through $1,000 (which is 2.75%). The current total is $28.12. *Now,* subtract $1,000 from the final sale price (you've already calculated those fees) and multiply the final sale amount that is over $1,000 by 1.5%. Add this amount to $28.12. The sum is the amount that you owe eBay. If the final sales price is $3,000, multiply $2,000 by **1.5%**. (**Hint:** The answer is $30.) Add $28.12 to $30. The sum, $58.12, is what you owe eBay. Don't worry: You won't be graded on this.

When selling a vehicle (car, truck, or RV) through eBay Motors, you're getting a great deal. Although you pay a $40 fee to list your item, when it sells, the Automotive Fee is only $40.

If you try to work out your own Final Value Fees, you might get an extreme headache — and come up with fractional cents. Know that eBay rounds up fees of $0.005 and more, and rounds down fees of $0.005. This rounding is done on a per transaction basis and generally evens out over time.

If you're starting to get dizzy just reading these examples, perhaps doing your own calculations isn't for you. It's certainly not for me — this stuff makes my eyes glaze over! There's a very cool software program that can handle all these calculations for you. Visit www.hammertap.com/coolebaytools for a free trial and discount.

Optional fees

You don't have to pay a license fee and destination charge, but setting up your auction can be like buying a car. eBay has all sorts of options to jazz up your auction. (Sorry, eBay is fresh out of two-tone metallic paint — but how about a nice pair of fuzzy dice for your mirror?) I explain how all these bells, whistles, and white sidewalls dress up your auction in Book IV, Chapter 13.

As a hint of things to come, Table 12-3 lists the eBay auction options and what they cost you.

Table 12-3	eBay Optional Feature Fees	
Option	**Fee**	**Reserve Price Auction Fee**
Boldface Title	$1.00, $4.00 for vehicles in Motors	
Home Page Featured	$99.95, $199.95 for multiple items	
Featured Plus! (formerly Featured in Category)	$19.95	
List in two categories	Double listing and upgrade fees	
10-Day auction	$0.10	
Highlight	$5.00	
Listing Designer	$0.10	
Scheduled Listings	$0.10	
Gift Services	$0.25	
Subtitle	$0.50	
Picture Services	First picture free, each additional $0.15	
The Gallery	$0.25 and $19.95 (Featured Auction in Gallery), free Gallery for vehicles in Motors	
Auction BIN (Buy It Now) fee	$0.05	
eBay Motors vehicle BIN fee	$1.00 for Vehicles, $0.50 for Motorcycles	
Vehicle Reserve Fee	$0.01 – $24.99	$0.50
	$25.00 – $199.99	$1.00
	$200.00 and up	$2.00

Uncle Sam Wants You — to Pay Your Taxes

What would a chapter about money be without taxes? As Ben Franklin knew (and we've all found out since his time), you can't escape death and taxes. Whether in cyberspace or face-to-face life, never forget that Uncle Sam is always your business partner. If you live outside the United States, check the tax laws in that country so that you don't end up with a real headache down the road.

Two wild rumors about federal taxes

I've heard some rumors about not having to pay taxes on eBay profits. If you hear any variation on this theme, smile politely and don't believe a word of it. I discuss two of the more popular (and seriously mistaken) tax notions running around the eBay community these days.

The U.S. government uses two laws on the books to go after eBay outlaws. One is the Federal Trade Commission (FTC) Act, which prohibits deceptive or misleading transactions in commerce. The other is the Mail or Telephone Order Merchandise Rule, which requires sellers to ship merchandise in a timely manner or offer to refund a consumer's money. The FTC is in charge of pursuing these violations. If you have a question about federal laws, you can find a lot of information online. For example, I found these three Web sites that keep fairly current lists of U.S. law and federal codes:

```
www4.law.cornell.edu/uscode
www.ftc.gov
www.fourmilab.ch/ustax/ustax.html
```

Rumor 1: E-commerce isn't taxed

One story claims that "there will be no taxes on e-commerce sales (sales conducted online) for three years." No one ever seems to know when those three years start or end.

Congress's Internet Tax Freedom Act stated that until October 2001, Congress and state legislatures couldn't institute *new* taxes on Internet transactions. President Bush signed a unanimously approved law that extended a ban on multiple and discriminatory Internet taxes and Internet access taxes through November 1, 2003. (The moratorium didn't apply to sales taxes or federal taxes.) The legislation also lengthened the "Sense of the Congress" resolution that there should be no federal taxes on Internet access or electronic commerce, and that the United States should work aggressively through the EU (European Union) and WTO (World Trade Organization) to keep electronic commerce free from tariffs and discriminatory taxes.

Even though November 1, 2003, has passed, there's still discussion about the law. Some people want to exempt online merchants if they bring in less than $25,000 per year. Others say no taxes should be imposed unless the merchant has sales of $5 million a year. As of this writing, the rules are up in the air. Check Marsha Collier's Web site, www.coolebaytools.com, for news on Internet sales tax.

Rumor 2: Profits from garage sales are tax-exempt

"eBay is like a garage sale, and you don't have to pay taxes on garage sales." Uh-huh. And the calories in ice cream don't count if you eat it out of the carton. Who comes up with this stuff anyway?

This notion is just an urban (or shall I say *suburban*) legend — somebody's wishful thinking that's become folklore. If you make money on a garage sale, you have to declare it as income — just like anything else you make money on. Most people never really make any money on garage sales because they usually sell things for far less than they bought them for. However, the exact opposite is often true of an eBay transaction.

Even if you lose money, you might have to prove it to the government, especially if you're running a small business. You most definitely should have a heart-to-heart talk with your accountant or tax professional as to how to file your taxes. Remember that if something might look bad in an audit if you *don't* declare it, consider that a big hint.

To get the reliable word, I checked with the IRS's e-commerce office. The good folks there told me that even if you make as little as a buck on any eBay sale after all your expenses (the cost of the item, eBay fees, shipping charges), you still have to declare it as income on your federal tax return.

State sales tax

If your state has sales tax, a *sales tax number* is required before you *officially* sell something. If sales tax applies, you may have to collect the appropriate sales tax for every sale that falls within the state that your business is in. A 1992 U.S. Supreme Court decision said that states can only require sellers that have a physical presence in the same state as the consumer to collect so-called use taxes.

To find the regulations for your state, visit one of the following sites, which supply links to every state's tax board. The tax board should have the answers to your questions.

www.taxsites.com/agencies.html
www.aicpa.org/yellow/yptstax.htm

State income taxes

Yes, it's true. Not only is Uncle Sam in Washington, D.C., looking for his slice of your eBay profits, but your state government might be hankering to join the feast.

If you have a good accountant, give that esteemed individual a call. If you don't have one, find a tax professional in your area. Tax professionals actually do more than just process your income tax returns once a year; they can help you avoid major pitfalls even before April 15.

Here's how to find out what your responsibilities are in your home state:

✦ You might need to collect and pay state sales taxes, but only if you sell to someone in your state.

✦ You can get tax information online at this Web site. It offers links to tax information for all 50 states.

www.taxadmin.org/fta/rate/tax_stru.html

✦ You can also call your state tax office and let the good folks there explain what the requirements are. The state tax office should be listed in the government section of your phone book.

Chapter 13: Time to Sell: Completing the Cyber Paperwork

In This Chapter

✓ Getting ready to set up your auction

✓ Selecting your item category

✓ Writing your item description

✓ Setting up your options

✓ Making changes after your auction has started

Are you ready to make some money? Yes? (Call it an inspired guess.) You're on the threshold of adding your items to the hundreds of thousands that go up for auction at eBay every day. Some auctions are so hot that the sellers quadruple their investments. Other items, unfortunately, are so stone cold that they might not even register a single bid.

In this chapter, I explain all the facets of the Sell Your Item page — the page that you fill out to get your auction going at eBay. Here you get some advice that can increase your odds of making money, and you find out the best way to position your item so that buyers can see it and bid on it. I also show you how to modify, relist, or end your auction whenever you need to.

Getting Ready to List Your Item

After you decide what you want to sell, find out as much as you can about it and conduct a little market research. Then you should have a good idea of the item's popularity and value. To get this info, check out Book IV, Chapter 12.

Before you list your item, make sure that you have these bases covered:

✦ **The specific category under which you want the item listed:** Ask your friends or family where they'd look for such an item and remember the categories that you saw most frequently when you conducted your market research with the eBay search function.

✦ **What you want to say in your auction item description:** Jot down your ideas. Take a good look at your item and make a list of keywords that describe your item. Keywords are single descriptive words that can include

  • Brand names

  • Size of the item (citing measurements if appropriate)

  • Age or date of manufacture

- Condition
- Rarity
- Color
- Size
- Material
- . . . and more

I know all about writer's block. If you're daunted by the Sell Your Item page, struggle through it anyway. This way, you've already done the hard work before you even begin.

✦ **Whether you want to attach a picture (or pictures) to your description via a Uniform Resource Locator (URL):** Pictures help sell items, but you don't have to use them.

✦ **The price at which you think you can sell the item:** Be as realistic as you can. (That's where the market research comes in.)

Examining the Sell Your Item Page

The Sell Your Item form is where your auction is born. Filling out your auction paperwork requires a couple minutes of clicking, typing, and answering all kinds of questions. The good news is that when you're done, your auction is up and running and (hopefully) starting to earn you money.

Just like the dizzying menu in a Chinese restaurant, you have four ways to sell an item on eBay, as shown in Figure 13-1. Only four ways might not seem to be very dizzying, but when you're trying to decide just which format is the best for you, believe me, you can get dizzy. Here's what you need to know about each type:

✦ **Sell Item at Online Auction:** This is the tried-and-true traditional sale format on eBay. This is what the newbies look for, and you can combine this with the Buy It Now feature for those who want the item immediately. Often, if you're selling a collectible item, letting it go to auction might net you a much higher profit — remember to do your research before listing.

✦ **Sell at a Fixed Price:** Just like shopping at the corner store, a fixed-price sale is easy for the buyer to complete. The only problem is that many potential buyers might lean toward an auction because of the perception that they *might* get a better deal.

✦ **Sell in Your eBay Store:** Book IV, Chapter 14 covers eBay Stores — a convenient place to sell related items to your auctions or fixed-price sales.

✦ **Advertise Your Real Estate:** If you don't want to put your property up for auction and you'd like to correspond with the prospective buyers, this is the option for you.

Figure 13-1:
Select your selling format before you list your item.

Say, for example, that you want to list a good, old-fashioned eBay auction. You want to sell your item for a fixed price but are willing to let it go to auction. To find eBay's Sell Your Item page from the eBay home page, you can use either of these methods:

✦ Click the Sell link on the navigation bar at the top of the page, and you're whisked there immediately. eBay allows you to select your category and download the Sell Your Item page in seconds.

✦ You can also start your auction from your My eBay page. Just click the Selling link and scroll down the page to the Related Links area. Click the Sell Your Item link, and the Sell Your Item page magically appears.

When listing your item, here's the info that eBay asks you to fill out. Each of the following items is discussed in detail later in this chapter:

✦ **User ID and Password:** If you're not signed in, you need to sign in before you list an item for sale.

✦ **Category:** The category where you've decided to list your item (required).

✦ **Title:** The name of your item (required).

✦ **Description:** What you want to tell eBay buyers about your item (required).

✦ **eBay Picture Services or Image URL:** The Web address of any pictures that you want to add (optional). Note that you get a free Preview picture at the top of your auction.

- **The Gallery:** You can add your item's picture to eBay's photo gallery (optional).

- **Gallery Image URL:** The Web address of the JPG image that you want to place in the Gallery (optional).

- **Item Location:** The region, city, and country from which the item will be shipped (required).

- **Quantity:** The number of items that you're offering in this auction is always one unless you plan to run a Multiple Item auction (required).

- **Minimum Bid:** The starting price that you set (required).

- **Duration:** The number of days that you want the auction to run (required).

- **Reserve Price:** The hidden target price that you set. This is the price that must be met before this item can be sold (optional). eBay charges you a fee for this feature.

- **Private Auction:** You can keep the identity of all bidders secret with this option (optional). This type of auction is used only in rare circumstances.

- **Buy It Now:** You can sell your item directly to the first buyer who meets this price (optional).

- **List Item in Two Categories:** If you want to double your exposure, you can list your item in two different categories. Note that double exposure equals double listing fees (optional).

- **Home Page Featured:** You can place your auction in a premium viewing section and have the possibility that your listing will cycle through the direct links from the front page (optional). eBay charges $99.95 extra for this feature.

- **Featured Plus!:** You can have your auction appear at the top of the category in which you list it (optional). eBay charges $19.95 extra for this feature.

- **Highlight:** Your item title is highlighted in the auction listings and search listings with a lilac-colored band, which might draw eBay members' eyes right to your auction (optional). eBay charges $5 extra for this feature.

- **Boldface Title:** A selling option to make your item listing stand out. eBay charges $1 extra for this feature (optional).

- **Free Counter:** If you wish to avail yourself of page hit counters from Andale, indicate so here (optional).

- **Ship-to-Locations:** Here's where you can indicate where you're willing to ship an item. If you don't want the hassle of shipping out of the United States, select only that option. You can individually select different countries as well (optional).

- **Who Pays for Shipping:** Select the options that apply as to who pays the shipping and handling charges in your auction.

- **Shipping and Handling Charges:** When prospective buyers know the shipping cost in advance (assuming it's a realistic price), they're more likely to bid right then and there. If they have to e-mail you with questions, they might find another auction for the same item — with reasonable shipping — and bid on that one. Also, if you list the shipping charges on the page, winning bidders can pay you instantly through PayPal.

✦ **Payment Instructions:** Here's the place where you put any after-sale information. If you don't want buyers to use Checkout, state that here. If you want them to pay with a different payment service, mention that as well. This information appears at the top of your sale when the sale is completed, at the bottom of the auction while it's active, and in the End of Auction e-mail (optional).

✦ **PayPal and Immediate Payment:** Fill out this area if you want to require the high bidder to pay through PayPal immediately when using Buy It Now. Add the Immediate Payment option if you know the shipping amount and would like the winner to pay with a click of the mouse (optional).

✦ **Escrow:** If using escrow is an option that you'd like to offer the high bidder (a good idea for expensive items), select the option as to who will pay the fees (optional).

Filling In the Required Blanks

Yes, the Sell Your Item form page looks daunting, but filling out its many sections doesn't take as long as you might think. Some of the questions that you're asked aren't things that you even have to think about; just click an answer and off you go — unless you forget your password. Other questions ask you to type in information. Don't sweat a thing; all the answers that you need are right here. You can find info on all the required stuff, and later in this chapter, I talk about optional stuff. After you click your main category, you land on the official Sell Your Item page.

Selecting a category

On the first page of the Sell Your Item form, you need to select the main category for your item. Many eBay sellers say that selecting the exact category isn't crucial to achieving the highest price for your item — and they're right. The bulk of buyers (who know what they're looking for) just input search keywords into eBay's search box and look for their items. Potential buyers, though, will select a category and, just like at the mall, peruse the items and see whether any strike their fancies.

Here's where your creativity can come into play. Who says that a box of note cards featuring *Blue Dog* (the famous doggie icon painted by Cajun artist George Rodrigue) belongs in *Everything Else: Gifts & Occasions: Greeting Cards: Other Cards.* If you use the Find Suggested Categories tool (in a yellow shaded box) in the upper-right corner of the Select Category area, you might find some other creative places to list your item. Check to see whether anyone else is selling the item (and in which category) or just let this tool help you pick a good category. Figure 13-2 shows you how easy it is to select a main category.

Select a Suggested Main Category

Top 10 categories found for **note cards**

You can select a suggested main category below and click **Save**, or use different keywords to refine your search.

Find Suggested Categories

Enter descriptive **item keywords** to see categories sellers have chosen for similar items.

| note cards | Find | Tips |

Category suggestions are based on the keywords you specified. **% Items Found** is an estimate of all items listed by sellers in select eBay categories containing your keywords.

Category	% Items Found
⦿ Everything Else : Gifts & Occasions : Greeting Cards : Other Cards	(9%)
○ Everything Else : Gifts & Occasions : Greeting Cards : Assortments	(7%)
○ Collectibles : Animals : Dog : Other Dogs	(6%)
○ Collectibles : Postcards & Paper : Greeting Cards : Other	(4%)
○ Home : Pet Supplies : Dogs : Other	(4%)
○ Specialty Services : Printing & Personalization : Stationery	(4%)
○ Collectibles : Animals : Bird : Parrot	(3%)
○ Art : Other Art	(2%)
○ Collectibles : Animals : Dog : Scottish Terrier	(2%)
○ Collectibles : Decorative Collectibles : Mary Engelbreit : Other Items	(2%)

Figure 13-2: Let eBay do some of the work to find the proper category for your item.

After you select your main category, you need to select from the thousands of subcategories. eBay offers you this wealth of choices in a handy point-and-click way. If you're unfamiliar with the types of items you can actually *find* in those categories, you might want to pore over Book IV, Chapter 3 before you choose a category to describe *your* item. Figure 13-3 shows you how to narrow down the subcategory listings on the Sell Your Item page. To select a category, here's the drill:

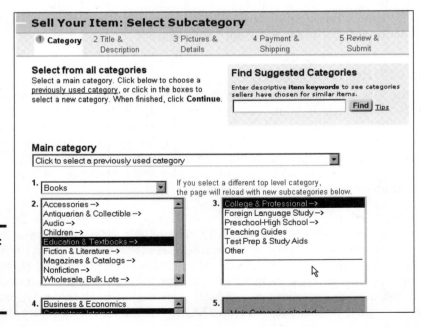

Figure 13-3: Narrowing down your sub-categories.

1. **Click one of the main categories.**

On the next page, you see a list of subcategories.

2. **Select the most appropriate subcategory.**

3. **Continue selecting subcategories until you've narrowed down your item listing as much as possible.**

You know that you've come to the last subcategory when you don't see any more right-pointing arrows in the category list.

Creating the perfect item title

After you figure out what category you want to list in, eBay wants to get down to the nitty-gritty — what the heck to call that thing you're trying to sell. Think of your item title as a great newspaper headline. The most valuable real estate on eBay is the 45-character title of your item. The majority of buyers do title searches, and that's where your item must come up to be sold! Give the most essential information right away to grab the eye of the reader who's just browsing. Be clear and informative enough to get noticed by eBay's search engine. Figure 13-4 shows examples of good titles.

Figure 13-4:
These item titles are clear, concise, and easy on the eyes.

NEW womens ADIDAS Tennis Shirt Skirt sz M $80
1971 ROLLS ROYCE Corniche Sales BROCHURE
Pink 3 Plumerias Sterling Silver Pendant NEW
DICK TRACY RECALLED ADVANCE MOVIE POSTER + B
Alexander McQUEEN Kingdom 30ml Eau De Parfum
EASY French Normandy Original Classic Recipes
2 Photography Photo Light NIB Lighting Kit

Here are some ideas to help you write your item title:

✦ Use the most common name for the item.

✦ If the item is rare or hard to find, mention that.

✦ Mention the item's condition and whether it's new or old.

✦ Mention the item's special qualities, like its style, model, or edition.

✦ Avoid fancy punctuation or unusual characters, such as $, hyphens, and L@@K — they just clutter up the title, and buyers rarely search for them.

Don't put any HTML tags in your title. (HTML stands for *HyperText Markup Language,* which in plain English means that it's the special code you use to create Web pages.) As a matter of fact, despite what you might have been told, you don't need an extensive knowledge of HTML to have successful, good-looking auctions at eBay. In Table 13-2 (which appears in "Writing your description," later in this chapter), I list a few HTML codes to use in your description.

Look for a phrase that pays

Here's a crash course in eBay lingo that can help bring you up to speed on attracting buyers to your auction. Sellers use the following words frequently in eBay auctions, and they can do wonders to jump-start your title:

✦ Mint

✦ One of a kind (or OOAK — see abbreviation list in Table 13-1)

✦ Vintage

✦ Collectible

✦ Rare

✦ Unique

✦ Primitive

✦ Well loved

There's a whole science (called *grading*) to figuring out the value of a collectible. Do your homework before you assign a grade to your item. If you need more information on what these grades actually mean, Book IV, Chapter 5 provides a translation.

eBay lingo at a glance

Common grading terms and the phrases in the preceding section aren't the only marketing standards you have at your eBay disposal. As eBay has grown, so has the lingo that members use as shortcuts to describe their merchandise.

Table 13-1 gives you a handy list of common abbreviations and phrases used to describe items. (**Hint:** Mint means "might as well be brand new," not "cool chocolate treat attached.")

Table 13-1	A Quick List of eBay Abbreviations	
eBay Code	*What It Abbreviates*	*What It Means*
MIB	Mint in Box	The item is in the original box, in great shape, and just the way that you'd expect to find it in a store.
MIMB	Mint in Mint Box	The box has never been opened and looks like it just left the factory.
MOC	Mint on Card	The item is mounted on its original display card, attached with the original fastenings, in store-new condition.
NRFB	Never Removed from Box	Just what it says, as in "bought but never opened."
COA	Certificate of Authenticity	Documentation that vouches for the genuineness of an item, such as an autograph or painting.
MWBMT	Mint with Both Mint Tags	Refers to stuffed animals, which have a hang tag (usually paper or card) and a tush tag (that's what they call the sewn-on tag — really) in perfect condition with no bends or tears.

eBay Code	What It Abbreviates	What It Means
OEM	Original Equipment Manufacture	You're selling the item and all the equipment that originally came with it, but you don't have the original box, owner's manual, or instructions.
OOAK	One of a Kind	You are selling the only one in existence!
NR	No Reserve Price	A reserve price is the price that you can set when you begin your auction. If bids don't meet the reserve, you don't have to sell. Many buyers don't like reserve prices because they don't think that they can get a bargain. (For tips on how to allay these fears and get those bids in reserve price auctions, see "Writing your description," later in this chapter.) If you're not listing a reserve for your item, let bidders know.
NWT	New with Tags	An item, possibly apparel, is in new condition with the tags from the manufacturer still affixed.
HTF, OOP	Hard to Find, Out of Print	Out of print, only a few ever made, or people grabbed up all there were. (HTF doesn't mean you spent a week looking for it in the attic.)

Giving the title punch with a subtitle

A new feature at eBay is the availability of subtitles. eBay allows you to buy an additional 45 characters, which appear under your item title in a search. The fee for this extra promotion is $0.50, and in a few circumstances, it is definitely worth your while. Any text that you input will really make your item stand out in the crowd — but (you knew there would be a *but,* didn't you?) these additional 45 characters won't come up in a title search. So if you have all those words in your description, the words will be found either way with a title and description search. Keep in mind that using a subtitle essentially *doubles* your listing fee.

Writing your description

After you hook potential bidders with your title, reel 'em in with a fabulous description. Don't think Hemingway here; think infomercial (the classier the better). Figure 13-5 shows a great description of some silver dollars. You can write a magnificent description, as well — all you have to do is click in the box and start typing.

Here's a list of suggestions for writing an item description:

✦ **Accentuate the positive.** Give the buyer a reason to buy your item and be enthusiastic when you list all the reasons that everyone should bid on it. Unlike the title, you can use as much space as you want. Even if you use a photo, be precise in your description — how big it is, what color, what kind of fabric, what design, and so on.

UNCIRCULATED MS63+ 1896 Morgan Silver Dollar

I recently purchased a group of MS63+ Morgan Silver Dollars from a long time collector to sell on ebay. The ones I've already sold have been very well received *(please look at my feedback)*. This is your chance to own a beautiful 1896 Morgan Silver Dollar in Premium Quality Brillliant Uncirculated Condition. Bright and well struck, it has very clean surfaces with very sharp features and details. The picture below doesn't do justice to this striking coin. It will make a lovely addition to any coin collection or a great start towards a new one.

Bid with confidence and bid whatever you feel this coin is worth to you as it is selling with NO RESERVE! Winning bidder to pay shipping & handling of $2.50, and must submit payment within a week of winning the auction. Credit cards are accepted through Paypal.com. Good luck!
Click below to...
Win another of my auctions and Save on shipping!

Figure 13-5: Writing a good description can mean the difference between success and failure.

✦ **Include the negative.** Don't hide the truth of your item's condition. Trying to conceal flaws costs you in the long run: You'll get tagged with bad feedback. If the item has a scratch, a nick, a dent, a crack, a ding, a tear, a rip, missing pieces, replacement parts, faded color, dirty smudges, or a bad smell (especially if cleaning might damage the item), mention it in the description.

✦ **Be precise about all the logistical details of the post-auction transaction.** Even though you're not required to list any special S&H (shipping and handling) or payment requirements in your item description, the majority of eBay users do. Try to figure out the cost of shipping the item in the United States and add that to your description. If you offer shipping insurance, add it to your item description.

✦ **While you're at it, promote yourself too.** As you accumulate positive feedback, tell potential bidders about your terrific track record. Add statements like "I'm great to deal with. Check out my feedback section."

✦ **Wish your potential bidders well.** Communication is the key to a good transaction, and you can set the tone for your auction and post-auction exchanges by including some simple phrases that show your friendly side. Always end your description by wishing bidders good luck, inviting potential bidders to e-mail you with questions, and offering the option of providing additional photos of the item if you have them.

When you input your description, you have the option of jazzing things up with a bit of HTML coding, or you can use eBay's new HTML text editor, shown in Figure 13-6. If you know how to use a word processor, you'll have no trouble touching up your text with this tool. Table 13-2 shows you a few additional codes to help you pretty things up.

Figure 13-6:
The HTML
text editor
shows
you the
description
area with
HTML-
coded text.

Table 13-2	A Short List of HTML Codes	
HTML Code	*How to Use It*	*What It Does*
`<b></b>`	`<b>cool collectible</b>`	**cool collectible** (bold type)
`<I></I>`	`<I>cool collectible</I>`	*cool collectible* (italic type)
`<b><I></I></b>`	`<b><i>cool collectible</b></i>`	***cool collectible*** (bold and italic type)
`<font color=red></font>`	`<font color=red>cool collectible</font>`	Selected text appears in red. (This book is in black and white, so you can't see it.)
`<font size=+1></font>`	`<font size=+3>cool</font> collectible`	COO**l** collectible (font size normal+1 through 4, increases size *x* times)
` `	`cool collectible`	cool collectible (inserts line break)
`<p>`	`cool<p>collectible`	cool collectible (inserts paragraph space)
`<hr>`	`cool collectible<hr>cheap`	cool collectible ——— cheap (inserts horizontal rule)
`<h1><h1>`	`<h1>cool collectible</h1>`	**cool collectible** (converts text to headline size)

Listing the number of items for sale

Unless you're planning on holding a Multiple Item (Dutch) auction, the number of items is always 1, which means you're holding a traditional auction. If you need to change the quantity number from 1, just type the number in the text box.

A matching set of cuff links is considered one item, as is the complete 37-volume set of *The Smith Family Ancestry and Genealogical History since 1270.* If you have more than one of the same item, I suggest that you sell the items one at a time because you will more than likely get higher final bids for your items when you sell them individually.

Setting a minimum bid — how low can you go?

What do a baseball autographed by JFK, a used walkie-talkie, and a Jaguar sports car all have in common? They all started with a $1 minimum bid. eBay requires you to set a *minimum bid,* the lowest bid allowed in an auction. You might be surprised to see stuff worth tens of thousands of dollars starting at just a buck. These sellers haven't lost their minds. Neither are they worried that someone could be tooling down the highway in a $100,000 sports car that they bought for the price of a burger.

Setting an incredibly low minimum (just type it in the text box *without* the dollar sign but *with* the decimal point) is a subtle strategy that gives you more bang for your buck. You can use a low minimum bid to attract more bidders who will, in turn, drive up the price to the item's real value — especially if, after doing your research, you know that the item is particularly hot. If you're worried about the outcome of the final bid, you can protect your item by using a reserve price. (I explain reserve prices in "Examining the Sell Your Item Page," earlier in this chapter.) You won't have to sell your item for a bargain-basement price because your reserve price protects your investment. The best advice is to set a reserve price that is the lowest amount you'll take for your item and then set a minimum bid that is ridiculously low. Use a reserve only when absolutely necessary because some bidders pass up reserve auctions.

Starting with a low minimum is also good for your pocketbook. eBay charges the seller an Insertion, or Placement, Fee — based on your opening bid. If you keep your opening bid low and set no reserve, you get to keep more of your money.

Before you set any minimum bid, do your homework and make some savvy marketing decisions. If your auction isn't going as you hoped, you *could* end up selling Grandma Ethel's Ming vase for a dollar. Think about your strategy. See "Mid-Course Corrections: Fixing Current Auctions," later in this chapter, for info on how you can make changes in your listing if you've made some egregious error.

Buy It Now

eBay's Buy It Now (BIN in eBay-speak) is available for single-item auctions. This feature allows buyers who want to purchase an item *now* to do so. Have you ever wanted an item really badly and didn't want to wait until the end of an auction? If the seller offers Buy It Now, you can purchase that item immediately. Just specify the amount that the item can sell for in the Buy It Now price area — the amount can be whatever you wish.

When your item receives a bid, the BIN option disappears, and the item goes through the normal auction process. If you have a reserve price on your item, the BIN feature doesn't disappear until a bidder meets your reserve price through the normal bidding process. To list an item with Buy It Now, you must have a feedback of 10 or be ID Verified.

Setting your auction time

How long do you want to run your auction? eBay gives you a choice — 1, 3, 5, 7, or 10 days. Just select the number that you want. If you choose a 10-day auction, you add $0.10 to your listing fee.

My auction-length strategy depends on the time of year and the item that I'm selling, and I generally have great success. If you have an item that you think will sell pretty well, run a 7-day auction (be sure to cover a full weekend) so that bidders have time to check it out before they decide to bid. However, if you know that you've got a red-hot item that's going to fly off the shelves — like a rare toy or a hard-to-get video game — select a 3-day auction. Eager bidders tend to bid higher and more often to beat out their competition if the item is hot and going fast. Three days is long enough to give trendy items exposure and ring up bids.

Don't start or end your auction on a Saturday or Sunday — *unless* your completed auction research indicates that you should. Certain types of bidders love sitting at their computers waiting for auctions to end on the weekends, but many bidders are busy having lives, and their schedules are unpredictable. Some eager bidders might sign in and place a maximum bid on your auction, but you can bet they won't be sitting at a computer making a last-minute flurry of competitive bids if they have something better to do on a Saturday or Sunday.

Unless you're an insomniac or a vampire and want to sell to werewolves, don't let your auctions close in the middle of the night. Not enough bidders are around to cause any last-minute bidding that would bump up the price.

Your secret safety net — reserve price

Here's a little secret: The reason that sellers list big-ticket items like Ferraris, grand pianos, and high-tech computer equipment with a starting bid of $1 is because they're protected from losing money with a reserve price. It's not required by eBay, but setting one can protect you. eBay charges an additional fee for this feature that varies depending on how high your reserve is.

As with everything in life, using a reserve price for your auctions has an upside and a downside. Many choosy bidders and bargain hunters blast past reserve-price auctions because they see a reserve price as a sign that proclaims "No bargains here!" Many bidders figure they can get a better deal on the same item with an auction that proudly declares NR (for *no reserve*) in its description. As an enticement to those bidders, you see lots of NR listings in auction titles.

On lower-priced items, I suggest that you set a higher minimum bid and set no reserve. Otherwise, if you're not sure about the market, set a low minimum bid but set a high reserve to protect yourself.

If bids don't reach a set reserve price, some sellers e-mail the highest bidder and offer the item at what the seller thinks is a fair price. Two caveats:

✦ eBay can suspend the seller *and* the buyer if the side deal is reported to SafeHarbor. This activity is strictly prohibited.

✦ eBay won't protect buyers or sellers if a side deal goes bad.

I want to be alone: The private auction

In a private auction, bidders' User IDs are kept under wraps. Sellers typically use this option to protect the identities of bidders during auctions for high-priced items. Wealthy eBay users might not want the world to know that they have the resources to buy expensive items. Private auctions are also held for items from the Adult/Erotica category. (Gee, there's a shocker.)

Put me in the Gallery

The Gallery is a visually graphic auction area that lets you post pictures to a special photo gallery that's accessible from the listings. It also causes a postage-stamp-size version of your image to appear next to your listing in the category or search. Many buyers enjoy browsing the Gallery catalog-style, and it's open to all categories. If you choose to go this route, your item is listed in both the Gallery and in the regular text listings.

The best thing about using a Gallery picture in your listings is that it increases the space your listing takes up on a search or category page. If you don't use a Gallery picture and just have an image in your auction, the only thing that will be next to your listing is a teeny, tiny camera icon.

Filling out the item location

eBay wants you to list the general area and the country in which you live. The idea behind telling the bidder where you live is to give him or her a heads-up on what kind of shipping charges to expect. Don't be esoteric (listing where you live as *The Here and Now* isn't a whole lot of help), but don't go crazy with cross-streets, landmarks, or degrees of latitude. Listing the city and state that you live in is enough.

eBay also wants you to indicate in which of its local regions you reside. Doing so allows your auction to be listed under the Regional eBay pages. You also have the option not to be listed. I recommend that, if you live in one of the listed metropolitan areas, you use the benefits of local trading and select your area.

A picture is worth a thousand words

An item on eBay without a picture is almost a waste of time. If you haven't set up photo hosting elsewhere, you can list one picture with eBay's Pictures Service for free. Additional ones cost you $0.15 each. Alternatively, you can put all the pictures that you want in your auction description for free.

Listing Designer

How many times have you seen an item on eBay laid out on the page all pretty-like with a fancy border around the description? If that sort of thing appeals to you, eBay's Listing Designer will supply you with pretty borders for almost any type of item for $0.10. Will the pretty borders increase the amount of bids your auction will get? It's doubtful. A clean item description with a couple of good clear pictures of your item is really all that you need.

Listing the payment methods you'll accept

Yeah, sure, eBay is loads of fun, but the bottom line to selling is the phrase "Show me the money!" You make the call on what you're willing to take as money from the high bidder of your auction. eBay offers the following payment options — just select the ones that you like:

- ✦ **Money Order/Cashier's Check:** From a seller's point of view, this is the safest method of payment. It's the closest thing you can get to cash. As a seller, you want to get paid with as little risk as possible. The only drawback? You have to wait for the buyer to mail it.

- ✦ **Credit Cards:** If you accept credit cards, using PayPal is the cheapest and most convenient way to go. If you have a merchant account through a retail store, be sure to select the little check boxes next to the credit cards that you accept. Offering a credit card payment option often attracts higher bids to your auctions. These higher bids usually more than cover the small percentage that credit card payment services charge you to use their services. See Book IV, Chapter 8 for a more complete description on how to use these services.

  Some sellers who use credit card services try attaching an additional fee (to cover their credit card processing fees) to the final payment. However, that's against the law in California, home of eBay, and therefore against eBay's rules. So forget about it. eBay can end your auction if it catches you.

- ✦ **C.O.D. (Cash on Delivery):** This option is the least attractive for both buyers and sellers. The buyer has to be home with the cash ready to go on the day that the package arrives. Odds are that on the day that the item is delivered, your buyer is taking his or her sick goldfish to the vet for a gill-cleaning. Then the item ends up back at your door, and you have no sale. It also often takes up to 30 days for you to get the money back in your hands.

- ✦ **Personal Check:** This is an extremely popular option, but it comes with a risk: The check could bounce higher than a lob at Wimbledon. If you accept personal checks, explain in your item description how long you plan to wait for the check to clear before sending the merchandise. The average hold is about ten business days. Some sellers wait as long as two weeks. Accepting eChecks through PayPal leaves all the bookkeeping and waiting to PayPal; you don't have to call the bank for confirmation.

Cut down on the risk of bad checks by reading the bidder's feedback when the auction is underway. Be wary of accepting checks from people with negative comments. Never ship an item until you're certain that the check has cleared the buyer's bank.

✦ **Online Escrow:** An escrow service acts as a referee, a neutral third party, as Chapter 8 of Book IV explains. Unless you're selling an expensive item, however, offering escrow is overkill. Usually, the buyer pays for this service. Escrow companies typically charge 5 percent of the sale price. On big-ticket items, it might make the difference between a sale and a pass. Escrow gives bidders an added sense of security. If you do offer escrow, the winning bidder should inform you right after the auction if he or she intends to use it.

✦ **Other:** If you're offering payment options that aren't listed here, select this option. Some buyers (mostly international) like to pay in cash, but I think this is *way* too risky and recommend that you *never*, ever deal in cash. If a problem arises — for either buyer or seller — no one has evidence that payment was made or received. Avoid it.

Most sellers offer buyers several ways to pay. You can select as many as you want. When the auction page appears, your choices are noted at the top of the listing. Listing several payment options makes you look like a flexible, easygoing professional.

Setting shipping terms

Here are your choices when it comes to shipping options:

✦ **Ship to the United States Only:** This option is selected by default; it means you only ship domestically.

✦ **Will Ship Worldwide:** The world is your oyster. But make sure that you can afford it.

✦ **Will Ship to United States and the Following Regions:** If you're comfortable shipping to certain countries but not to others, make your selections here, and they show up on your auction page.

When you indicate that you will ship internationally, your auction shows up on the international eBay sites, which is a fantastic way to attract new buyers! eBay has lots of good international users, so you might want to consider selling your items around the world. If you do, be sure to clearly state in the description all extra shipping costs and customs charges.

Traditionally, the buyer pays for shipping, and this is the point at which you must decide how much to charge. You also have to calculate how much this item will cost you to ship. If it's a small item (weighing under a pound or so), you might decide to charge a flat rate to all buyers. To charge a flat rate, click the Flat Shipping Rates tab and fill in the shipping amount. Before you fill in the amount, be sure to include your charges for packing (see Book IV, Chapter 15 for more info on how much to add for this task) and how much the insurance charges will be. When your item weighs two pounds or more, you might want to use eBay's versatile shipping calculator. Because UPS and the U.S. Postal Service now charge variable rates for packages of the same weight, based on distance, using the calculator simplifies things for your customers (and you). Be sure that you've weighed the item and know how much your handling charge will be. The calculator allows you to input a handling amount and adds it to the overall shipping total, but doesn't break out the amount separately so that the customer can see precisely how much the shipping costs are. The calculator also conveniently calculates the proper insurance amount for the item. Figure 13-7 shows how simple the form is.

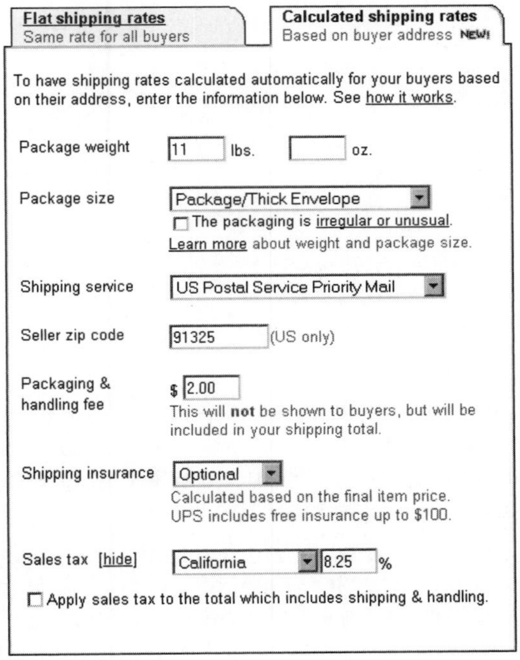

Figure 13-7:
Input
your item
shipping
information
in the
calculator.

The calculator appears on the item page so that prospective buyers can type in their ZIP Codes and immediately know how much shipping to their locations will be.

eBay Options: Ballyhoo on the Cheap

Although eBay's display options aren't quite as effective as a three-story neon sign in Times Square, they do bring greater attention to your auction. Here are your options:

+ **Bold:** eBay fee: $1. Bold type does catch your attention, but don't bother using it on items that'll bring in less than $25. Do use it if you're in hot competition with similar items and you want yours to stand out.

✦ **Highlight:** eBay fee: $5. A yellow highlighter is what I use to point out the high points in books I read. (You're using one now, aren't you?) The eBay highlight feature is lilac, but it can really make your item shine. Check out the category in which you choose to list before selecting this feature. Some categories are overwhelmed with sellers using the highlight option, and the pages look completely shaded in lilac. In these categories, *not* using highlight (and perhaps using a bold title instead) makes your auction stand out more.

✦ **Home Page Featured:** eBay fee: $99.95 ($199.95 for Multiple Item listings). As with expensive real estate, you pay a premium for location, location, location. The $99.95 gives you the highest level of visibility at eBay, and it occasionally appears smack dab in the middle of the eBay home page (although there's no guarantee that it will). Figure 13-8 shows the featured auctions on eBay's home page.

Figure 13-8: If you're lucky, your featured auction will rotate through the home page at a busy time of day.

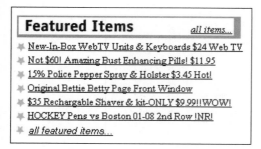

Bidders do browse the Featured Items section to see what's there, just as you might head directly to the New Releases section of your video store. But, because the vast majority of auctions found at eBay are under $25, the average seller doesn't use the Featured Items option.

✦ **Featured Plus!:** eBay fee: $19.95. You want top billing? You can buy it here. This option puts you on the first page of your item category and on search results pages. This is a good option for moving special merchandise. Often, bidders just scan the top items; if you want to be seen, you gotta be there. eBay's statistics say that items listed as Featured Plus! are 58 percent more likely to sell — but it really depends on what you're selling and when. Ask yourself this: Is it worth $20 to have more people see my item? If yes, go for it. Figure 13-9 shows how items are listed in the Featured Plus! listings. You need a feedback rating of at least 10 to make it to the Featured Items and Featured Plus! auctions.

Figure 13-9:
Featured
items
appear at
the top of a
search page
or at the top
of the
category
listings, as
shown here.

Checking Your Work and Starting the Auction

After you've filled in all the blanks on the Sell Your Item page and you think
that you're ready to join the world of e-commerce, follow these steps:

1. Click the Review button at the bottom of the Sell Your Item page.

You waft to the Verification page (shown in Figure 13-10), the place where
you can catch mistakes before your item is listed. The Verification page
shows you a condensed version of all your information and tallies up how
much eBay is charging you in fees and options to run this auction. You
also see a preview of how your auction description and pictures will look
on the site.

You also might find the Verification page helpful as a last-minute chance
to get your bearings. If you've chosen a very general category, eBay
asks you whether you're certain there isn't a more appropriate category. You can go back to any of the pages that need correcting by clicking the appropriate tab on the top of the Verification page. Make
category changes or any other changes and additions, and then head
for the Verification page again.

2. Check for mistakes.

Nitpick for common, careless errors; you won't be sorry. eBay members
often make goofs such as putting an item in the wrong category listing,
including spelling and grammatical errors in the description and omit-
ting information about shipping, handling, insurance, and payment
methods.

Figure 13-10: The Verification page is the last place you can double-check for errors before the listing begins.

3. **When you're sure that everything's accurate and you're happy with your item listing, click the Submit My Listing button.**

An Auction Confirmation page pops up from eBay. At that precise moment, your auction begins, even though it might be a couple of hours before it appears in eBay's search and listings updates. If you want to see your auction right away and check for bids, your Auction Confirmation page provides a link for that purpose. Click the link, and you're there. You can also keep track of your auctions by using the My eBay page. (To find out how, see Book IV, Chapter 4.)

Mid-Course Corrections: Fixing Current Auctions

Don't worry if you make a mistake filling out the Sell Your Item page. If you notice a mistake after the auction is up and running, all is not lost. Pencils have erasers, and eBay allows revisions. You can make changes at two stages of the game: before the first bid is placed and after the bidding war is under-way. The following sections explain what you can (and can't) correct — and when you have to accept the little imperfections of your auction item page.

Making changes before bidding begins

Here's what you can change about your auction before bids have been placed (and when it does not end within 12 hours):

✦ The title or description of your auction

✦ The item category

✦ The item's minimum bid price

✦ The item's Buy It Now price

✦ The reserve price (you can add, change, or remove it)

✦ The duration of your listing

✦ The URL of the picture that you're including with your auction

✦ A private auction designation (you can add or remove it)

✦ Accepted payment methods, checkout information, item location, and shipping terms

When you revise an auction, eBay puts a little notation on your auction page that reads Description_(revised). (Think of it as automatic common courtesy.)

To revise an auction before bids have been received, follow these steps:

1. **Go to the auction page and click the Revise Your Item link.**

This link appears only if you're signed in to eBay. If the item hasn't received any bids, a message appears on your screen to indicate that you may update the item.

You're taken to a page that outlines the rules for revising your item. At the bottom, the item number will be filled in. Click Revise Item.

2. **You arrive at the Revise Item page, which looks like the Sell Your Item form.**

Click the link that corresponds to the area that you'd like to change.

3. **Make changes to the item information, and then click the Save Changes button at the bottom of the page when you're finished.**

A summary of your newly revised auction page appears on your screen.

4. **If you're happy with your revisions, click the Submit Revisions button.**

If not, click the Back button of your browser and redo the Update Your Information page.

You're taken to your newly revised auction item page where you see a disclaimer from eBay that says you've revised the auction before the first bid.

Making changes after bidding begins

If your auction is up and running and already receiving bids, you can still make some slight modifications to it. Newly added information is clearly separated from the original text and pictures. In addition, eBay puts a time stamp on the additional info in case questions from early bidders crop up later.

After your item receives bids, eBay allows you to add to your item's description. If you feel that you were at a loss for words in writing your item's description or if a lot of potential bidders are asking the same questions, go ahead and make all the additions that you want. But whatever you put there the first time around stays in the description as well.

You've discovered that the Apollo 11 cookie jar you thought was a reproduction is really an original? Better change that description before you sell it. When your item has received bids, you can add to your item's description.

Follow the same procedure for making changes before bidding begins. When you arrive at the Revise Your Item page, you're be given *only* the option to add to your Description, add features, or add additional payment information. Your initial listing isn't changed — only appended.

Alternatively, click the Services link on the navigation bar at the top of the page, scroll down to the Manage Your Active Listings; Add to Item Description link. If you use this route, you'll have to have the item number written down because you must enter it prior to making any changes.

Don't let an oversight grow into a failure to communicate and don't ignore iffy communication until the auction is over. Correct any inaccuracies in your auction information now to avoid problems later on.

Always check your e-mail to see whether bidders have questions about your item. If a bidder wants to know about flaws, be truthful and courteous when returning e-mails. As you get more familiar with eBay and with writing auction descriptions, the number of e-mail questions will decrease. If you enjoy good customer service in your day-to-day shopping, here's your chance to give some back.

Chapter 14: Shopping and Selling with eBay Stores

In This Chapter

✔ Shopping eBay Stores

✔ Searching eBay Stores

✔ Opening your own eBay Store

Sometimes you just don't want to buy in an auction. Sometimes you want to buy your item *now*. No waiting for an auction to end — *now!* The easiest place to go for this type of transaction is the eBay Stores area, where you find fixed-price items that feature an eBay Buy It Now price.

All the fine and funky merchandise that you can find on eBay can also be found in the eBay Stores area. eBay Stores is located in a separate area from the regular auctions, and regular eBay sellers run these stores. eBay Stores is a place where sellers can list as many additional items for sale as they'd like for a reduced Insertion Fee. Buyers are lured to the store by the small red eBay Stores icon that appears next to the seller's User ID.

Whenever you're looking at an item, and you see that the seller has a store, be sure to click the link next to the Stores icon. The seller might have the very same merchandise in his or her eBay Store for a lower price.

If a seller has an eBay Store, he or she can list individual items for different sizes of an article of clothing, different variations of items that he or she sells in regular auctions, or anything that falls within eBay's listing policies. The store items have a listing time of at least 30 days, so sellers can also put up specialty items that might not sell well in a short auction term of only one to ten days.

The requirements to open an eBay Store are pretty basic. I suggest that you transact business on the site for quite a while before you open a store. You need to have a solid understanding of how eBay works and know how to handle all types of transactions. These are eBay's requirements:

✦ You must be registered as an eBay seller with a credit card on file.

✦ You must have a feedback rating or 20 or more (or be ID Verified).

✦ You must accept credit card payments, either through PayPal or through a merchant account.

The eBay search engine doesn't directly search the eBay Stores area. If you're looking for a particular item, search eBay, and then on the results page, look at the column of links on the left. Scroll down, and if a store has your item in stock, the store is listed with a clickable link in a box entitled More on eBay, Shop eBay Stores. This box appears under the Display option box.

To get to the eBay Stores main area, visit the eBay home page, look for the Specialty Sites link in the upper-left corner (see Figure 14-1), and click the eBay Stores link. Alternatively, type **www.ebaystores.com** in the Address box of your Web browser.

Figure 14-1: A quick click in the Specialty Sites box on the eBay home page takes you to the eBay Stores hub.

Unlimited Shopping from the Stores Page

Okay, you've arrived! You've come to the hub of power shopping online, the eBay Stores home page (see Figure 14-2). Just like the eBay home page, this is your gateway to many incredible bargains. This section takes a look at what you find there, how to navigate the stores, and how to find the deals.

eBay Stores search

In the top-left corner of the eBay Stores home page is the search engine for eBay Stores. You can perform your search in eBay Stores on different levels. You can search for Buy It Now items. (Being able to buy it now seems a tad redundant to me, but that's how it is.) Anyway, if you type your keyword in the box and stay with the default search, you'll find all the Buy It Now items in the stores that match your keyword.

eBay Stores don't just list the Buy It Now items. If sellers have current auctions on eBay, those auctions are listed in their stores as well — only regular auctions won't come up in an eBay Stores item search. So if you find an auction that interests you at eBay, click the item to read the description and the condition of the item. If you want to buy the item, click the Visit My eBay Store link next to the store name on the top of the item page to go to the seller's eBay store. You just might find some related items that you want. And the seller probably combines shipping so that you save some money!

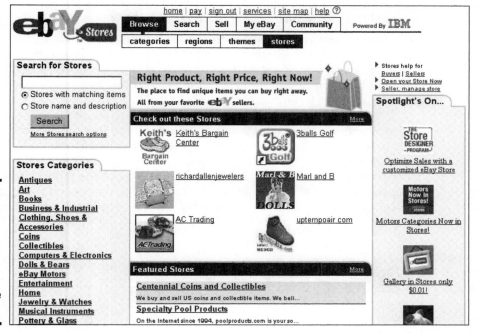

Figure 14-2:
The eBay Stores home page, where you can search stores by item or store name.

By the way, before you click Buy It Now, you should — all together now! — double-check the seller's feedback.

When you get the results of an eBay Stores search, you can click the Find Related Auction Items in All eBay link at the bottom of the page to search for similar items on eBay auctions (see Figure 14-3). By clicking this link, you go to eBay (the auctions) to find auction items that match your search. I highly recommend clicking the link before you decide to buy — you might find your item on auction at a considerably lower price. Time is money, and if you have the time, you can save some money.

Figure 14-3:
Here's a link to more items when performing an eBay Stores search.

Browsing the store categories

Browsing store categories is a great idea when you're looking for a specialist — you know, someone who carries a particular type of item that appeals to you. Perhaps you have an affinity for jewelry, art, limited edition books, or needlepoint. Whatever your interest, you'll probably find a store here to suit your needs.

To browse eBay Stores, just click the eBay Stores link under the Specialty Sites area on the eBay home page. Then, in the eBay Stores hub, look for a list of store categories on the left side of the page and click a category that suits your fancy. When you do that, the left side of the page (surprise!) lists subcategories within that category. I clicked the category Coins and then the subcategory Coins: US, and got the subcategory hub page shown in Figure 14-4.

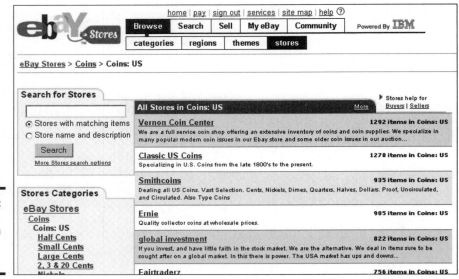

Figure 14-4:
Category browsing in Coins: US stores.

Browsing eBay Stores categories is like strolling down a mall filled with your favorite items. Note that stores with the highest inventories in the category are listed towards the top.

Selling from Your Own Virtual Storefront

After you've shopped the eBay Stores, you might be thinking that this is a good place to open your own store. There's great news on that end because eBay Stores have the most reasonable rent on the Internet. At an eBay Store, you're not constrained by the auction format of a one-to-ten day maximum. You can list your fixed-price items in your eBay Store on a "good till cancelled" basis.

Paying the landlord

Monthly rent for an eBay Store is as low as $9.95 per month. Featured stores have a rent of $49.95, and anchor stores (just like your local department store) pay $499.95 a month. Featured stores' listings are guaranteed to rotate through the special featured section on the eBay Stores home page. These listings also appear on the top level of their category directory page. Anchor stores get extra promotion, and their logos are showcased in the stores' directory pages.

The reasonable pricing behind eBay Stores is a remarkable bargain. For as little as $9.95 a month, you have the opportunity to sell your merchandise to over 73 million registered users! See Table 14-1 for eBay Store item listing fees.

Table 14-1	eBay Store Item Listing Fees		
Listing Period	*Basic Fee*	*Surcharge*	*Total*
30 days	$0.05	$0.00	$0.05
60 days	0.05	0.05	0.10
90 days	0.05	0.10	0.15
120 days	0.05	0.15	0.20
Good Till Cancelled	0.05	0.05 for every additional 30 days	Depends on length of listing

Listing fees and monthly rent can be just the tip of the iceberg if you choose to get fancy by using all kinds of options. My recommendation? Don't spend too much on them until you're fully entrenched in an eBay business — by that time, you'll have the experience to know what to add and when. Stick with the basics. All the same Final Value Fees and listing option costs apply as in regular eBay auctions. (See Book IV, Chapter 12 for the actual figures.)

The Gallery option fee is reduced for use in store listings only. For example, the very valuable option of a Gallery picture adds only $0.01 to your listing cost! That makes the minimum total cost of your individual listing, with a Gallery picture, only $0.06!

Opening your eBay Store

Because this minibook is your introduction to eBay, I'll just give you some ideas about opening an eBay Store. In the more advanced book, *Starting an eBay Business For Dummies* (Wiley Publishing, Inc.), Marsha Collier takes you step-by-step through the basics of opening your store.

The easiest way for a beginner to open an eBay Store is to get a large quantity of a single item, such as six dozen umbrellas, and then list these items separately. Keep in mind the costs of your items before pricing them. List an auction for one of the items and, within your description, mention that you have more in your eBay Store. Also offer to combine shipping costs on multiple purchases.

Naming your store is your first challenge. Pick out a name that describes the type of items that your store will carry or one that includes your User ID. Don't pick a name that is so esoteric or overly creative that it doesn't give possible shoppers a clue as to what you carry. A creative store name and graphic logo are pictured in Figure 14-5.

Figure 14-5:
An eBay
Stores page.

As you can see from the store page, each store can have its own categories. You get to make them up yourself so that your customers can find items within your store in an organized manner. You can define up to 19 custom categories (a maximum of 29 characters for each name) in your store.

Spend some serious time on eBay before you open the store. Study some of the very successful stores. You want to have enough know-how to make your store a success!

Chapter 15: Closing the Deal and Shipping the Merchandise

In This Chapter

✔ Staying organized

✔ Communicating with the buyer

✔ Packing and sending the item

The auction's over, and you have a winning bidder, who (you hope) is eager to send you money. Sounds perfect, doesn't it? It is if you watch your step, keep on top of things, and communicate like a professional.

In this chapter, I help you figure out how to stay organized by showing you what documents you need to keep and for how long. I also include tips and etiquette on communicating with the buyer so that you're most likely to come out with positive feedback. In addition, you find out how to pack your item, assess costs, and make sure that the item reaches the buyer when you say it will (oh, yeah . . . and in one piece).

Bookkeeping and Staying Organized

Although I don't recommend lining your nest with every scrap from every auction that you run, you can safely keep some documents without mutating into a giant pack rat. Until you become an eBay expert and have other ways to electronically store your information, you should print and file these essentials:

✦ **The auction page as it appeared when the auction closed:** This page gives you a record of the item name and number, the bidding history, every bidder's User ID, and a lot of other useful information. The page also includes the auction item description (and any revisions that you've made to it), which is handy if the buyer argues that an item is disintegrating before his eyes, and you honestly believe it's just well loved.

You might think that you don't need this information because you can always look it up, but here practicality rears its head: eBay makes completed auctions seem to disappear after 30 days. However, if you use the custom link that appears in your End of Auction e-mail (see the next bullet), you can access the auction online for up to 90 days. Print your auction page *before* you forget about it, file it where you know you can find it, and *then* forget about it.

✦ **The End of Auction (EOA) e-mail that you receive from eBay that notifies you that the auction is over:** If you lose this e-mail, you can't get it back because eBay doesn't keep it. I set up a separate folder in my Microsoft Outlook e-mail program for End of Auction e-mails. When one comes in, I read it and then drag it over to its special folder. That way, I can always check this folder for the information that I need.

✦ **E-mail between you and the buyer:** In the virtual world, e-mail is as close to having a face-to-face conversation as most people get. Your e-mail correspondence is a living record of all the things that you discuss with the buyer to complete the transaction. Even if you sell just a few items a month at eBay, keep track of who's paid up and who owes you money. And more importantly, if the buyer says, "I told you I'd be out of town," you can look through your e-mail and say, "Nope, it doesn't show up here," or "You're right! How was Timbuktu? Is the payment on the way?" Or something more polite. Be sure to keep that e-mail with the headers and date on it so that you can't be accused of (ahem) creative writing.

✦ **PayPal payment notices:** You get a notice from PayPal when the buyer pays for the item. The notice has the auction information and the buyer's shipping information. (When that e-mail arrives, the clock begins to tick on sending out the item.)

✦ **Any bank statements you receive that reflect a payment that doesn't clear:** Keep anything related to payments, especially payments that didn't go through. That way, if a buyer says he's sure he sent you a check, you can say, "Yes sir, Mr. X, you did send me a check, and it was made of the finest rubber." Or something kinder, especially if you want that payment.

✦ **Any insurance or escrow forms that you have:** Until the item has arrived, and you're sure the customer is satisfied, be sure to keep those shipping and insurance receipts, as well as any documentation that goes along with an escrow sale.

✦ **Refund requests that you make:** If you make a request to eBay for a refund from an auction that doesn't go through, hold on to it until the process is completed.

✦ **Receipts for items that you buy for the sole purpose of selling them on eBay:** This comes in handy as a reference so that you can see whether you're making a profit. It can also be helpful at tax time.

Someday, the Internal Revenue Service (or government agency in your area) might knock on your door. Scary, but true. Like hurricanes and asteroid strikes, audits happen. Any accountant worth his or her salt will tell you that the best way to handle the possibility of an audit is to be prepared for the worst — even if every eBay transaction that you conduct runs smooth as silk and you've kept your nose sparkling clean. See Chapter 12 of Book IV for more tax information.

If you accept online payments by PayPal (PayPal Premier or Business members only), you can download your transaction history for use in QuickBooks, Quicken, or Excel. Additionally, these programs are excellent sources for your documentation.

Once a month, conduct a By Seller search on yourself so that you can print out all the information on the bid histories of your most recent auctions. I do this independently of my auction software. Having the listings neatly printed out easily helps you see what sold for how much and when. Book IV, Chapter 5 gives you the lowdown on how to perform this search.

When it comes to printouts of e-mails and documents about transactions, as soon as the item arrives at the destination and you get your positive feedback, you can dump them. If you get negative feedback, hang on to your documentation a little longer (say, until you're sure the issues it raises are resolved and everyone's satisfied). If selling at eBay becomes a fairly regular source of income, save all receipts for items that you've purchased to sell; for tax purposes, that's inventory.

If you sell specialized items, you can keep track of trends and who your frequent buyers are by saving your paperwork. This prudent habit becomes an excellent marketing strategy when you discover that a segment of eBay users faithfully bids on your auctions. An *audience.* Imagine that.

Talking to Buyers: The ABCs of Good Communication

You've heard it countless times — talk is cheap. Compared to what? Granted, empty promises are a dime a dozen, but honest-to-goodness talk and efficient e-mail are worth their weight in gold and good feedback — especially at eBay. Sometimes, *not* talking is costly.

A smooth exchange of money and merchandise really starts with you (the seller) and your attitude towards the transaction. Your auction description and then your first e-mail — soon after the auction is over — set the entire transaction in motion and set the tone for that transaction. If all goes well, *no more than* a week should elapse between getting paid and sending the item.

Take a proactive approach and start the ball rolling yourself. I suggest contacting the buyer even *before* you get eBay's EOA e-mail. Here's how to get the buyer's e-mail address:

1. **Start on the page of the item that you sold.**

Click the Contact the Buyer link next to the winner's name. If you're signed in to eBay, you're taken to the User ID History page.

2. **Click the winner's e-mail address.**

An e-mail window opens, showing the user's User ID history and e-mail information. This page tells you some needed information:

- The person's e-mail address
- The person's User ID (or multiple User IDs if the person did any name changes in the past)
- The date the User ID became effective
- The end date of the User ID (if this person had others in the past)

Signing in first puts a temporary *cookie* (a computer file that makes it easier to get around a Web site) in your computer so that you automatically get the e-mail addresses of eBay users (and other actions that you've specified on your My eBay, eBay Preferences page) without going through this process again. You have to set your preferences to do this on your eBay Preferences page. If you selected the Keep Me Signed In check box when you signed in to eBay, your password is saved even if you cut off your Internet connection.

Another way to access the buyer's information is to go to your My eBay page, click the Items I've Sold link, and click the buyer's name in the row of the auction in question.

Thank you — I mean it

What do all the successful big-name department stores have in common? Yes, great prices, good merchandise, and nice displays. But with all things being equal, customer service always wins hands-down. One department store in the United States, Nordstrom, has such a great reputation that the store happily took back a set of snow tires because a customer wasn't happy with them. No big deal, maybe — until you notice that Nordstrom doesn't even *sell* snow tires!

A friend of mine who owns restaurants calls this level of customer satisfaction the *Wow!* effect. If customers (no matter what they're buying) say, "Wow!" during or after the transaction — admiringly or happily — you've satisfied the customer. A good rule to go by: Give people the same level of service that you expect when you're on the buying end.

The best way to start satisfying the buyer is with an introductory e-mail. Congratulate the person on winning the auction — making him or her feel good about the purchase — and thank the buyer for bidding on your item. Then provide these important details:

✦ Item name and auction number.

✦ Winning bid amount.

✦ Cost of shipping and packing and any shipping or insurance restrictions. (I give pointers on determining shipping and packaging costs later in this chapter.)

✦ Payment options (check, money order, credit cards, or PayPal).

✦ How long you will hold the item waiting for a check to clear (usually 7 to 14 days).

✦ The shipping timetable.

You should also mind a few vital details in the first e-mail:

✦ Confirm the address (and daytime phone number if you think that you need to call); ask whether this is where you should ship the item. If not, ask for the correct shipping address.

✦ Include your name and the address to which you want the payment sent.

- ✦ Remind buyers to write the item name, auction number, and shipping address on whatever form of payment they send. You'd be surprised how many buyers forget to give you the item number. Also ask buyers to print out and send a copy of your e-mail with the payment.

- ✦ If you're using an online payment service, such as PayPal, be sure to give buyers instructions on how they can pay for the auction online.

- ✦ Include your phone number if you think it will speed up the process.

- ✦ Suggest that if all goes well, you'll be happy to leave positive feedback for the buyer.

You can also send an invoice from your My eBay page, Items I've Sold area. Just click the gray Send Invoice bar, verify all the information, and click Send Invoice. If you select the Copy Me check box on this invoice, you receive a copy. The buyer's copy has a link in the invoice, enabling the buyer to pay directly to PayPal (if you accept it for payment). Figure 15-1 shows what the invoice e-mail looks like.

Figure 15-1:
An eBay invoice, as sent to a buyer.

**Book IV
Chapter 15**

**Closing the Deal and
Shipping the
Merchandise**

Keep e-mailing

If you've got a good transaction going (and the majority of them are), the buyer will reply to your e-mail within three business days. Customarily, most replies come the next day. If your buyer has questions regarding anything that you asked in your e-mail, you get those inquiries in the response. Most of the time, all you get back is, "Thanks. Payment on the way." Hey, that's good enough for me.

If any last-minute details need to be worked out, usually the buyer asks to set up a time to call or request further instructions about the transaction. Respond to this communication as soon as possible. If you can't deal with it at the moment, let the buyer know that you're working on it and will shoot those answers back ASAP. *Never* let an e-mail go unanswered.

As soon as you get the hang of sending e-mail, you can add an eBay link that takes the buyer right to the Feedback Forum with just a click of the mouse. Buyers and sellers can also link to the Feedback Forum from the final auction page by clicking the Leave Feedback link.

Shipping without Going Postal

Shipping can be the most time-consuming (and most dreaded) task for eBay sellers. Even if the selling portion of your transaction goes flawlessly, the item has to get to the buyer in one piece. If it doesn't, the deal could be ruined — and so could your reputation. This section briefs you on shipping etiquette, gives you details about the three most popular shipping options (the U.S. Postal Service, UPS, and FedEx Ground), and offers tips on how to make sure that your package is ready to ride.

The best way to avoid shipping problems is to do your homework beforehand, determine which method is likely to work best, and spell out in your item description exactly how you intend to ship the item. I always say that the "buyer pays actual shipping, handling, and insurance" in my item description, and that's what I charge, although I can make allowances if the buyer wants a specific method of shipment within reason. Here's how I handle the whole process:

1. **After the auction, get the package ready to ship.**

   You don't have to seal the package right away, but you should have it ready to seal because the two critical factors in shipping are weight and time. The more a package weighs and the faster it has to be delivered, the higher the charge. (I cover packing materials and tips later in this section.) The time to think about packing and shipping is *before* you put the item up for auction — that way, last-minute surprises are less likely to arise while your buyer waits impatiently for the item!

2. **Know your carrier options.**

   In the United States, the three main shipping options for most eBay transactions are the U.S. Postal Service, FedEx, and UPS. See the section "Shopping for a shipper" (try saying *that* five times fast) for how you can get rate options from each service, painlessly and online. Compare costs and services.

3. **Before quoting the shipping fees, make sure that you include all appropriate costs.**

   I recommend that you charge a nominal handling fee (up to $1.50 isn't out of line) to cover your packing materials, which can add up quickly as you start making multiple transactions. Also include any insurance costs and any delivery-confirmation costs.

   Some eBay scam artists inflate shipping and handling costs to make added profit. *Shame, shame, shame on them.* Purposely overcharging is tacky, ugly, and immature. And the buyer often figures it out after one look at the postage on the box.

It's best to post the shipping amount to give buyers an idea of how much shipping will be. This way, buyers can include this cost when they consider their bidding strategies. Figure out what the packed item will weigh and then give a good guess; the online calculators can help. If the item is particularly heavy, and you need to use a shipping service that charges by weight and distance, be sure to say in your auction description that you're just giving an estimate and that the final cost will be determined after the auction is over. Optionally, you can tell the bidder how much the item weighs, where you're shipping from, and what your handling charges are. (A few bidders don't mind doing the math.)

Occasionally, shipping calculations can be off-target, and you might not know that until after you take the buyer's money. If the mistake is in your favor and is a biggie, notify the buyer and offer a refund. But if shipping ends up costing you a bit more, take your lumps and pay it. You can always let the buyer know what happened and that you paid the extra cost. Who knows, it might show up on your feedback from the buyer! (Even if it doesn't, spreading goodwill never hurts.)

4. **E-mail the buyer and congratulate him or her on winning; reiterate what your shipping choice is and how long you expect it'll take.**

Make sure that you're both talking about the same timetable. If the buyer balks at either the price or the shipping time, try working out an option that will make the buyer happy.

5. **Send the package.**

When should you ship the package? Common courtesy says it should go out as soon as the item and shipping charges are paid. If the buyer has followed through with his or her side of the bargain, you should do the same. Ship that package no more than a week after payment (or after the check clears). If you can't, immediately e-mail the buyer and explain the delay. You should e-mail the buyer as soon as you send the package and ask for an e-mail to confirm arrival after the item gets there. (Don't forget to put in a plug for positive feedback.)

Send a prompt follow-up e-mail to let the buyer know that the item is on the way. In this e-mail, be sure to include when the item was sent, how long it should take to arrive, any special tracking number (if you have one), and a request for a return e-mail confirming arrival after the item gets there. I also include a thank-you note (a receipt would be a business-like addition) in each package that I send out. I appreciate getting a thank-you note in eBay packages, and it always brings a smile to the recipient's face. It never hurts to take every opportunity to promote goodwill (and future business and positive feedback).

More often than not, you do get an e-mail back from the buyer to let you know the item arrived safely. If you don't, it doesn't hurt to send another e-mail (in about a week) to ask whether the item arrived in good condition. It jogs the buyer's memory and demonstrates your professionalism as a seller. Use this opportunity to gently remind buyers that you'll be leaving positive feedback for them. Ask whether they're satisfied and don't be bashful about suggesting they do the same for you. Leave positive feedback right away so that you don't forget.

Insuring your peace of mind (and your shipment)

Sure, "lost in the mail" is an excuse that everyone has heard hundreds of times, but despite everyone's best efforts, sometimes things do get damaged or misplaced during shipment. The universe is a dangerous place; that's what insurance is for. I usually offer to get insurance from the shipper if the buyer wants to pay for it, and always get it on expensive items, one-of-a-kind items, or very fragile items. I spell out in my item description that the buyer pays for the insurance.

The major shippers all offer insurance that's fairly reasonably priced, so check out their rates at their Web sites. But don't forget to read the details. For example, many items at eBay are sold MIMB (Mint in Mint Box). The condition of the original box often has a bearing on the final value of the item inside, but the U.S. Postal Service insures only what is *in* the box. So, if you sold a Malibu Barbie mint in a mint box, USPS insures only the doll and not the original box. Pack carefully so that your buyer gets what's been paid for. Be mindful that shippers won't make good on insurance claims if they suspect you of causing the damage by doing a lousy job of packing.

Alternatively, when you're selling on eBay in earnest, you can purchase your own parcel protection policy from a private insurer. When you use this type of insurance, combined with preprinted electronic postage, you no longer have to stand in line at the post office to have your insured packaged logged in by the clerk at the counter.

Some sellers also offer their own type of *self-insurance*. No, they're not pretending they're State Farm or Allstate (though their hands *are* pretty good). Here's what I offer my buyers at no cost to them:

✔ On lower-priced items, I'm willing to refund the buyer's money if the item is lost or damaged.

✔ On some items I sell, I have a *risk reserve*. That means I have more than one of the item that I sold. If the item is lost or destroyed, I can send the backup item as a replacement.

Shopping for a shipper

If only you could transport your item the way they do on *Star Trek* — "Beam up that Beanie, Scotty!" Alas, it's not so. Priority Mail via the U.S. Postal Service is pretty much the eBay standard if you're shipping within the United States and Canada. Many Americans also rely on it to ship internationally. FedEx and UPS are global alternatives that work well, too.

U.S. Postal Service

The U.S. Postal Service (USPS) is the butt of many unfair jokes and cheap shots, but when it comes right down to it, I think USPS is still the most efficient and inexpensive way to ship items — eBay or otherwise. It also supplies free boxes, labels, and tape for Priority and Express Mail packages. Here are some ways that eBay members get their items from here to there via USPS:

✦ **Priority Mail:** As mentioned earlier, this is the *de facto* standard method of shipping for eBay users. I love the free boxes, and I like the rates. The promised delivery time is two to three days, although I've experienced rare delays of up to a week during peak holiday periods. Cost? As of this writing (rates are always subject to change), Priority Mail costs $3.85 for a one-pound package. Over a pound, the charge is calculated according to weight and distance.

A $3.85 flat-rate Priority envelope is also available. You can ship as much stuff as you want — as long as you can fit it into the supplied 9½-x-12½ envelope. You can reinforce the envelope with Priority Mail packing tape.

✦ **Express Mail:** If the item needs to be delivered the next day, use Express Mail. The Postal Service promises delivery no later than noon the following afternoon (even on weekends or holidays). And you can get free boxes. Cost? Express Mail runs $13.65 for packages 8 ounces and under, $17.85 for packages 8 ounces to 2 pounds, and about $3 additional for every pound over 2 (up to 10 pounds). Express Mail also has a flat-rate envelope, which is the same size as the Priority flat-rate envelope and ships for $13.85.

The Postal Service makes a special pickup for Priority Mail and Express Mail. It's a flat rate for no matter how many separate packages are included. If you have several packages, this is an excellent option to consider, and the extra cost can be covered in your handling charge.

✦ **First-Class Mail:** If your item weighs 13 ounces or less, you can use First-Class Mail. First-Class Mail is slightly cheaper than Priority Mail — the first ounce is $0.37, and every additional ounce is $0.23.

✦ **Media Mail:** This is a popular option among those who sell books on eBay. It's the *new* name for two older products, Book Rate and Special Standard Mail. Media Mail rates start at $1.42 for the first pound and increase by $0.42 cents for each additional pound.

✦ **Other options:** The Postal Service offers all sorts of add-ons. I always get the Delivery Confirmation service that you can add to Priority Mail, as well as other mailing services. A mere $0.45 cents ($0.55 on First-Class Mail, Parcel Post, or Media Mail) buys you the knowledge of when and where your item was delivered. With the parcel's tracking number, you can check on whether the package was delivered (or whether an attempt was made to deliver it) by calling 800-222-1811 in the United States. If you go online at www.usps.com/shipping/trackandconfirm. htm, you can get a more complete report.

Free delivery confirmations? Yes! If you send out more than 18 packages a month with delivery confirmations, you can save yourself some serious cash if you go to www.shippertools.com. Get unlimited delivery confirmations for just $6.95 a month! The site gives small shippers a gateway to the same USPS electronic Delivery Confirmation system that the big-time shippers use. You can print out prenumbered delivery confirmations on plain paper (no weird labels to buy!) right from your computer, plus use its system to track the package and send customer follow-up messages after shipping. This is a convenient and handy service for eBay sellers!

If you're an occasional shipper (you *buy* more than you sell on eBay), you can print out bar-coded shipping labels with free delivery confirmation (for Priority Mail only) at the USPS site. No online e-mail functions are available, so you have to do all the e-mailing and record keeping yourself. But hey, the service is free. Just go to www.usps.com/cgi-bin/api/shipping_label.htm.

**Book IV
Chapter 15**

Closing the Deal and
Shipping the
Merchandise

Delivery confirmation also comes in handy if you try to collect insurance for an item that was never delivered or if the buyer says the item was never delivered. It gives you proof from the Postal Service that the item was sent. (I explain insuring shipments later in this chapter.) But understand that you cannot accurately track your package. Delivery confirmation is merely proof that the package was mailed and delivered. If your package gets lost in the mail for a few weeks, this number won't act as a tracking number and won't reveal the location of your package until it's delivered.

The USPS Web site (www.usps.com) gives you an overview of the U.S. Postal Service rates so that you can see all your options. It sure beats standing in that endless line! For a complete explanation of domestic rates, check out www.usps.com/consumers/domestic.htm.

Even better, USPS has a page that can help you determine exactly what your item costs to mail (after you've packaged it and weighed it, of course). Start at the Domestic Rate Calculator page at http://postcalc.usps.gov and follow the instructions. To find rates for sending packages from the United States to foreign countries, go to the International Rate Calculator at http://ircalc.usps.gov.

UPS

The folks in the brown UPS trucks love eBay. The options they offer vary, with everything from overnight service to the UPS Ground service. I use UPS for items that are heavy (say, antique barbells) or extremely large (such as a 1920s steamer trunk), because UPS ships anything up to 150 pounds in a single box — 80 more pounds than the U.S. Postal Service takes. UPS also takes many of the odd-shaped large boxes, such as those for computer equipment, that the U.S. Postal Service won't.

UPS makes pickups, but you have to know the exact weight of your package so that you can pay when the UPS driver shows up. But the pickup service is free (my favorite price).

The rates for the same UPS shipment can vary based on whether you have a business account with UPS, whether the package goes to or is picked up at a residence, and whether you use the right kind of form. If you're going to use UPS regularly, be sure to set up an account directly with UPS.

You can find the UPS home page at www.ups.com. For rates, click the Shipping tab and then click the Calculate Time and Cost link on the left side of the page, which gives you prices based on ZIP Codes and package weights. (Note the ominous estimate rates.)

The UPS.com Quick Cost Calculator prices are based on what UPS charges regular and high-volume users. When you get to the counter, the price might be higher than what you find on the Web.

My favorite link on the UPS site is the transit map that shows the United States and how long it takes to reach any place in the country (based on the originating ZIP Code). If you're thinking of shipping that compact refrigerator to Maine, you can check out this fun and informative page at www.ups.com/using/services/servicemaps/servicemaps.html.

Sí, oui, ja, yes! Shipping internationally

Money's good no matter what country it comes from. I don't know why, but lots of people seem to be afraid to ship internationally, and they list "I don't ship overseas" on the auction page. Of course, sending an item that far away might be a burden if you're selling a car or a street-sweeper (they don't fit in boxes too well), but I've found that sending a package across the Atlantic can be just as easy as shipping across state lines. The only downside: My shipper of choice, the U.S. Postal Service, doesn't insure packages going to certain countries (check with your post office to find out which ones; they seem to change with the headlines), so I mail only to insured nations.

Here are a couple of other timely notes about shipping internationally:

✔ You need to tell what's inside the package. Be truthful when declaring value on customs forms. Be sure to use descriptions that customs agents can figure out without knowing eBay shorthand terms. For example, instead of declaring the contents as "MIB Furby," call it a "small stuffed animal toy that talks." Some countries require buyers to pay special duties and taxes, depending on the item and the value. But that's the buyer's headache.

✔ Wherever you send your package (especially if it's going to a country where English is not the native language), be sure to write legibly. (Imagine getting a package from Russia and having to decipher a label written in the Cyrillic alphabet. *'Nuff said.*)

If you have a UPS account, it's useful to buy the delivery confirmation option for $1.00. As soon as the package gets to its destination and is signed for, UPS sends you back a confirmation so that you have evidence that it has been delivered. But what's really cool is the free UPS online tracking. Every package is bar-coded and that code is read everywhere that your package stops along its shipping route. You can follow its progress by entering the package number at www.ups.com/tracking/tracking.html.

FedEx

I use FedEx Express air all the time for rush business, but Express seems rather expensive for my eBay shipping. However, if the buyer wants it fast and is willing to pay, I'll send it by FedEx overnight, you bet. The new FedEx Ground Home Delivery service has competitive prices and carries all the best features of FedEx. I like the online tracking option for all packages, and FedEx Express takes packages greater than 150 pounds. For account holders, FedEx will pick up your package for a $3 charge.

I also like the FedEx boxes. Like one of my favorite actors, Joe Pesci, from *My Cousin Vinny,* these boxes are small but tough. But if you're thinking of reusing these boxes to ship with another service, forget it. The FedEx logo is plastered all over every inch of the freebies, and the company might get seriously peeved about it. You can't use those fancy boxes for the Home Delivery service.

The FedEx Ground Home Delivery service is a major competitor for UPS. The rates are competitive, and FedEx offers a money-back guarantee (if it misses the delivery window) for residential ground delivery. A two-pound package going from Los Angeles to a residence in New York City takes five days and costs $6.09. FedEx includes online package tracking and insurance up to $100 in this price. You have to be a business to avail yourself of home delivery — but plenty of home businesses exist.

The same two-pound U.S. Postal Service Priority Mail package with $100 insurance and a delivery confirmation costs you $6.20. (But remember, you know how to get free Delivery Confirmation forms!) Granted, the package will arrive within two to three days, but FedEx Ground guarantees a five-day delivery, and I've had a few Priority Mail packages take up to two weeks. FedEx Ground won't supply boxes for you, so you're on your own there. When you drop off your box at UPS, you can get five-day service for $8.05.

You can find the FedEx home page at `www.fedex.com/us`. The link for rates is conveniently located at the top of the page.

Getting the right (packing) stuff

You can never think about packing materials too early. You might think that you're jumping the gun, but by the law of averages, if you wait until the last minute, you won't find the right-size box, approved tape, or the labels that you need. Start thinking about shipping even before you sell your first item.

Before you pack, give your item the once-over. Here's a checklist of what to consider about your item before you call it a wrap (love that Hollywood lingo):

✦ **Is your item as you described it?** If the item has been dented or torn somehow, e-mail the winning bidder immediately and come clean. And if you sell an item with its original box or container, don't check just the item; make sure that the box is in the same good condition as the item inside. Collectors place a high value on original boxes, so make sure the box lives up to what you described in your auction. Pack to protect it as well.

✦ **Is the item dirty or dusty? Does it smell of smoke?** Some buyers might complain if the item they receive is dirty or smelly, especially from cigarette smoke. Make sure that the item is fresh and clean, even if it's used or vintage. If something's dirty, check to make sure that you know how to clean it properly (you want to take the dirt off, not the paint), and then give it a spritz with an appropriate cleaner or just soap and water. If you can't get rid of the smell or the dirt, say so in your item description. Let the buyer decide whether the item is desirable with aromas and all.

If the item has a faint smell of smoke or is a bit musty, a deodorizing spray called Febreze might help. Just get a plastic bag, give your item a spritz, and store it in the bag for a short while. *Note:* This is not recommended for cardboard. And, as with any solvent or cleaning agent, read the label before you spray. Or if you're in a rush to mail the package, cut a 1-x-1-inch piece of sheet fabric softener and place it in a plastic bag with the product.

When the item's ready to go, you're ready to pack it up. The following sections give you suggestions on what you should consider using and where to find the right stuff.

Packing material: What to use

This might sound obvious, but you'd be surprised: Any list of packing material should start with a box. But you don't want just any box — you want a heavy cardboard type that's larger than the item. If the item is extremely fragile, I suggest that you use two boxes, with the outer box about 3 inches larger on each side than the inner box that holds the item, to allow for extra padding. And if you still have the original shipping container for such things as electronic equipment, consider using the original, especially if it still has the original foam inserts. (They were designed for the purpose, and this way they stay out of the environment awhile longer.)

As for padding, Table 15-1 compares the most popular types of box-filler material.

Table 15-1	Box-Filler Materials	
Type	**Pros and Cons**	**Suggestions**
Air-popped popcorn	**Pros:** Lightweight, environmentally friendly, absorbs shock well, clean (as long as you don't use salt and butter, but you knew that), low in calories. **Cons:** Cost, time to pop.	You don't want to send it anywhere that there might be varmints who like it. The U.S. Postal Service suggests popcorn. Hey, at least you can eat the leftovers!
Bubble wrap	**Pros:** Lightweight, clean, cushions well. **Cons:** Cost.	Don't go overboard taping the bubble wrap. If the buyer has to battle to get the tape off, the item might go flying and end up damaged. And for crying out loud, don't pop all the little bubbles, okay?
Cut-up cardboard	**Pros:** Handy, cheap. **Cons:** Transmits some shocks to item, hard to cut up.	If you have some old boxes that aren't sturdy enough to pack in, this is a pretty good use for them.
Newspaper	**Pros:** Cheap, cushions. **Cons:** Messy.	Seal fairly well. Put your item in a plastic bag to protect it from the ink. I like shredding the newspaper first. It's more manageable and doesn't seem to stain as much as wadded-up paper. I spent about $30 at an office-supply store for a shredder. (However, you might find one at eBay for much less.)
Styrofoam peanuts	**Pros:** Lightweight, absorb shock well, clean. **Cons:** Environmentally unfriendly, annoying.	Your item might shift if you don't put enough peanuts in the box, so make sure to fill the box. Also, don't buy these — instead, recycle them from stuff that was shipped to you (plastic trash bags are great for storing them). *Warning:* Never use plastic peanuts when packing electronic equipment, because they can create static electricity. Even a little spark can trash a computer chip.

Whatever materials you use, make sure that you pack the item well and that you secure the box. Many shippers contest insurance claims if they feel that you did a lousy job of packing. Do all the little things that you'd want done if you were the buyer — using double boxes for really fragile items, wrapping lids separately from containers, and filling hollow breakables with some kind of padding. Here are a few other items that you need:

✦ **Plastic bags:** Plastic bags protect your item from moisture. I once sent a MIB doll to the Northeast, and the package got caught in a snowstorm. The buyer e-mailed me with words of thanks for the extra plastic bag, which saved the item from being soaked along with the outer box. (Speaking of boxes, if you send an item in an original box, bag it.)

For small items, such as stuffed animals, always protect them in a lunch baggie. For slightly larger items, go to the one-quart or one-gallon size. Be sure to wrap any paper or cloth products, such as clothing and linens, in plastic before you ship.

✦ **Bubble-padded mailers:** The shipping cost for a package that weighs less than 13 ounces (First-Class Mail) is usually considerably cheaper than Priority. Many small items, such as clothing, books, and so on, fit comfortably into the many available sizes of padded envelopes. You can find them made of kraft paper or extra sturdy vinyl. A big plus is that they weigh considerably less than boxes — even when using extra padding. See Table 15-2 for standard sizes.

Table 15-2		Standard Bubble-Padded Mailer Sizes
Size	*Measurements*	*Suggested items*
#000	4" x 8"	Collector trading cards, jewelry, computer diskettes, coins
#00	5" x 10"	Postcards, paper ephemera
#0	6" x 10"	CDs, DVDs, Xbox or PS2 games
#1	7¼" x 12"	Cardboard sleeve VHS tapes, jewel-cased CDs and DVDs
#2	8½" x 12"	Clamshell VHS tapes
#3	8½" x 14½"	Toys, clothing, stuffed animals
#4	9½" x 14½"	Small books, trade paperbacks
#5	10½" x 16"	Hardcover books
#6	12½" x 19"	Clothing, soft boxed items
#7	14¼" x 20"	Much larger packaged items, framed items and plaques

✦ **Address labels:** You need extras because it's always a good idea to toss a duplicate address label inside the box, with the destination address and a return address, in case the outside label falls off or becomes illegible.

✦ **Two- or 3-inch shipping tape:** Make sure that you use a strong shipping tape for the outside of the box. Use nylon-reinforced tape or pressure-sensitive package tape. Remember not to plaster every inch of the box with tape; leave space for those *Fragile* and *Insured* rubber stamps.

✦ **Hand-held shipping tape dispensers:** It's quite a bit easier to zzzzzip! tape from a tape dispenser than unwind it and bite it off with your teeth. Have one dispenser for your shipping tape and one for your clear tape.

✦ **Two-inch clear tape:** For taping the padding around the inside items. I also use a clear strip of tape over the address on the outside of the box so that it won't disappear in the rain.

✦ **Scissors:** A pair of large, sharp scissors. Having a hobby knife to trim boxes or shred newspaper is also a good idea.

✦ **Handy liquids:** Three that I like are GOO GONE (which is available in the household supply section of most retail stores and is a wonder at removing unwanted stickers and price tags); WD-40 (the unstick-every-thing standby that works great for getting stickers off plastic); and un-du (the best liquid I've found to take labels off cardboard). If you can't find un-du in stores, visit Marsha Collier's Web site, `www.coolebay tools.com`, for locations that carry it. Lighter fluid also does the trick, but be careful handling it and be sure to clean up thoroughly to remove any residue.

✦ **Rubber stamps:** Using custom rubber stamps can save you a bunch of time when preparing your packages. I purchased some return address self-inking rubber stamps (at an unbelievably low price) on eBay from the Melrose Stamp Company (eBay User ID melrose_stamp). I use these stamps to stamp all kinds of things that require my identification.

✦ **Thermal label printer:** Once I thought this was a flagrant waste of money, but now I wouldn't be without one. When you begin shipping several packages a week, you'll find it far more convenient to use a separate label printer for addressing and delivery confirmations. Dymo offers one of the best deals on a quality printer. Its new 330 model is one of the fastest that you can get and available on eBay for about $100. If you want to get industrial, try one of the Zebra (I use the LP2844) thermal printers. These printers can print labels for FedEx and UPS as well as USPS.

✦ **Black permanent marker:** These are handy for writing information ("Please leave on porch behind the planter") and the all-important "Fragile" all over the box or "Do Not Bend" on envelopes. I like the big, fat Sharpie markers.

Not sure how to pack your item? No problem — just call a store in your area that deals in that kind of item and ask the folks there how they pack for shipment. They'll probably be glad to offer you a few pointers.

If you plan to sell on eBay in earnest, consider adding a 10-pound weight scale (for weighing packages) to your shipping department. I use a super small, 13-pound maximum scale manufactured by Escali, which I bought on eBay for only $29.95.

When it comes to fragile items such as dishes, pottery, porcelain, and china — anything that can chip, crack, or smash into a thousand pieces — *double box*. The boxes should be about 3 inches different on each side. Make sure that you use enough padding so that the interior box is snug. Just give it a big shake. If nothing rattles, ship away!

CHECK IT OUT

eBay Stores Where You Can Buy Packing Material

Many terrific eBay sellers are out to offer you really good deals on packing material. (You can't beat eBay sellers for quality goods, low prices, and great service.) I recommend the following family-run eBay Stores:

- **GraMur Supply Co,** based in Texas, is where I buy my vinyl padded envelope mailers for my eBay sales. It also has a super selection of multisized Ziploc bags for small items.

- **Gatorpack Shipping Supplies** is based in Tampa, Florida, and has many long-term customers in the eBay seller ranks. It sells everything from tape to peanuts!

- **ShippingSupply.com** (its eBay User ID and Web site address), located in Indiana, serves the selling community with a wide array of packing supplies.

Book V

iTunes

The 5th Wave   By Rich Tennant

"Why can't you just bring your iPod like everyone else?"

Book V: iTunes

Chapter 1: Setting Up iTunes

In This Chapter

✔ **Finding out what you can do with iTunes**

✔ **Configuring iTunes with the Setup Assistant**

✔ **Playing music tracks in iTunes**

✔ **Skipping and repeating tracks in iTunes**

More than half a century ago, jukeboxes were the primary and most convenient way for people to select the music they wanted to hear and share with others, especially newly released music. Juke joints were hopping with the newest hits every night; however, you still had to insert coins every time you played a song. Possibly, you could afford records and a turntable, but you had to throw a party to share the music with others.

Today, using iTunes, you can create a digital jukebox and conveniently click a button to play a song. Connect your computer to the amplifier of your home stereo or connect speakers to your computer, and suddenly your computer is the best jukebox in the neighborhood.

This chapter explains how iTunes changes your music playing and buying habits for the better and how to set up and configure iTunes for your Internet connection. It also describes starting up iTunes for the first time and playing music tracks.

What Is iTunes?

iTunes is a software program that you can acquire at no cost over the Internet. Using the software, you can listen to a new song on the Internet and download it to iTunes immediately. You can also buy music online at 99 cents a song from the iTunes Music Store, which offers some 700,000 songs. iTunes downloads music from the store and puts it in your music library, making it immediately available for playing, burning onto a CD, or transferring to an iPod. You can even listen to Web radio stations and define your favorite stations by using iTunes.

Transferring songs from CD to your computer is called *ripping* a CD (to the chagrin of the music industry old-timers who think people intend to destroy the disc or steal the songs). Ripping an entire CD's worth of songs is quick and easy, and track information including artist name and title arrives automatically over the Internet.

iTunes versus Windows Media Player

As of this writing, the AAC (technically known as MPEG-4 Advanced Audio Coding) files that you download through iTunes cannot be played on Windows Media Player, the Windows application that plays audio and/or video files. It seems that Apple, the manufacturer of iTunes software and the manager of the iTunes Music Store, is having a tiff with Microsoft, the maker of Windows Media Player, and Microsoft doesn't want to support the AAC format.

Having spent some time with both iTunes and Windows Media Player, I believe iTunes is the superior product. iTunes makes storing, finding, arranging, and playing songs easier. If you are a fan of Windows Media Player and you enjoy using it to play songs, however, think twice about buying songs from the iTunes Music Store because you'll have to use iTunes to play those songs.

iTunes gives you the power to organize songs into playlists and burn CDs of any songs in your library, in any order. You can even set up dynamic smart playlists that iTunes updates automatically, based on your preferences and listening habits. iTunes offers an equalizer that includes presets for all kinds of music and listening environments and also enables you to customize and save your own settings with each song.

The iTunes software is available for people with Windows computers as well as Macintosh computers. To be specific, iTunes is available to people who have the Windows XP/2000 or higher operating system or the Mac OS/X or higher operating system. This book gives instructions for using iTunes in both Mac and Windows. If the figures in this book look odd to you as a Mac or Windows user, don't worry about it. Although the Mac and Windows dialog boxes and windows look a little different, instructions for running iTunes are the same in both platforms.

Here are the system requirements for installing and running iTunes on a Windows computer:

✦ Windows XP, Windows 2000, or higher

✦ A 500 MHz Pentium class processor or higher

✦ QuickTime 6.5.1 (don't worry if it's not on your computer; it's included in the iTunes download)

✦ 128MB RAM minimum

✦ Latest Windows service packs (recommended)

✦ A CD-R or CD-RW drive to burn your own CDs

✦ A soundcard to play songs

✦ A high-speed Internet connection such as a DSL, cable modem, or LAN-based connection (recommended)

These are the system requirements for installing and running iTunes on a Mac:

✦ Mac OS X v10.1.5 or higher

✦ A 400 MHz G3 processor or higher

✦ QuickTime 6.2

✦ 128MB RAM minimum

✦ A high-speed Internet connection such as a DSL, cable modem, or LAN-based connection (recommended)

Downloading the Software

To use iTunes, start by downloading the software to your computer from the following address (just follow the on-screen instructions to download iTunes):

`www.apple.com/itunes/download`

The iTunes software is free; however, the download is rather large at 20MB. If you have a dial-up Internet connection, be prepared for a loooong download. Also, make sure that you download the correct software, either for Windows or for the Mac.

The installation procedure asks the usual questions. The only thing that might throw you for a loop is being asked whether you want to make iTunes the default player for audio files and QuickTime the default player for video files. *Default* means that iTunes loads and plays the song automatically when you give instructions for playing an audio file, and QuickTime loads and plays automatically when you give instructions for playing a video file. (If you use Windows, you can always change your mind about default programs by right-clicking an audio or video filename in Windows Explorer or My Computer, choosing Open With, and choosing Choose Program. The Open With dialog box appears. Select the program that you want the file to open in automatically and click OK.)

Using Setup Assistant

iTunes needs to be set up for use with your Internet connection. This happens automatically when you first start iTunes (see Figure 1-1). Follow these steps:

1. **Start iTunes.**

2. **Click Next.**

The next page of the wizard appears with questions for setting up iTunes with the Internet.

3. **Deselect both check boxes.**

   The Setup Assistant asks whether you want iTunes to search your computer for music files. Click the No button because iTunes might find files you don't want to add to your library (such as music for games).

4. **Deselect the Yes option that tells iTunes to reorganize your music files, and then click Next.**

   Reorganizing these files is the subject of Book V, Chapter 7.

5. **Click Yes to go to the iTunes Music Store.**

   Setup Assistant asks if you want to go straight to the iTunes Music Store, which you can read more about in Book V, Chapter 2.

6. **Click Finish.**

   iTunes finishes the setup, quits the Setup Assistant, and launches the iTunes window.

Figure 1-1:
The iTunes Setup Assistant.

Exploring the iTunes Window

When you open iTunes, your music library and other sources of music appear, as shown in Figure 1-2. The iTunes window offers a view of your music library and your sources for music, as well as controls for organizing, importing, and playing music, as follows:

✦ **Source list:** Displays the source of your music — Library (your music library), Radio (access to Web radio), and Music Store (the iTunes Music Store, your iPod, your playlists, and so on).

✦ **Song list/Browse view:** Depending on the source selected in the source list, this view displays the songs in your music library, your playlist, your iPod, or Web radio stations.

✦ **Status window:** Displays the name of the artist and song (if known), and the elapsed time of the track.

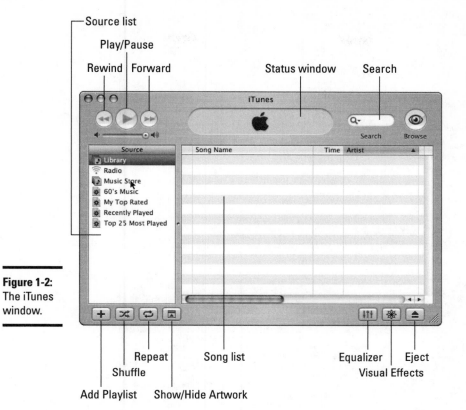

Source list
Play/Pause
Rewind | Forward   Status window   Search

Figure 1-2:
The iTunes
window.

Add Playlist   Show/Hide Artwork
Shuffle
Repeat   Song list   Equalizer   Eject
Visual Effects

✦ **Search text box:** Type characters in this text box to search your music library.

✦ **Player buttons — Forward/Next, Play/Pause, and Previous/Rewind:** Control the playback of songs in iTunes.

✦ **Playlist buttons — Add, Shuffle, Repeat:** Add playlists of your favorite songs and shuffle or repeat playback of playlists.

✦ **Miscellaneous buttons — Show/Hide Artwork, Equalizer, Visual effects, Eject:** Displays or hides song artwork (supplied with purchased songs), the equalizer, and visual effects; ejects a CD or iPod.

Playing Music Tracks in iTunes

iTunes needs music to perform for you. Insert any commercial music CD, and the music tracks appear in the iTunes song list, as shown in Figure 1-3. If your computer is connected to the Internet, iTunes grabs the track information from the Internet for each song automatically after you insert the CD, as shown in Figure 1-4.

Figure 1-3:
The tracks
of an
audio CD.

Figure 1-4:
CD track
info appears
after iTunes
consults
with the
Internet.

When you play a CD in iTunes, it's just like using a CD player. To play a track on the CD, click the track name, and then click the Play button. The Play button turns into a Pause button and the song plays.

When the song finishes, iTunes continues playing the songs in the list in sequence until you click the Pause button (which turns back into the Play button). You can skip to the next or previous song using the arrow keys on your keyboard or by clicking the Forward or Back button.

 The status window above the list of songs tells you the name of the artist and song (if known), and the elapsed time. If you click the Elapsed Time status, the status changes to the remaining time and then, with another click, to the total time (one more click brings you back to the elapsed time).

Eject a CD by clicking the Eject button or by choosing Controls➪Eject Disc.

Rearranging and repeating tracks

You can rearrange the order of the tracks to automatically play them in any sequence you want, similar to programming a CD player. Click the upward-pointing arrow at the top of the first column in the song list, and it changes to a downward-pointing arrow, reversing the order of the tracks.

You can change the order of tracks played in sequence. Just click the track number in the first column for the song and drag the song up or down in the list. By dragging songs, you can set up the tracks to play in a unique sequence.

Skipping tracks

To skip tracks so they don't play in sequence, deselect the check box next to the song name.

To remove a series of check marks simultaneously, Ctrl+click (Windows) or ⌘+click (Mac) the songs you want to skip.

Repeating a song list

You can repeat an entire song list by clicking the Repeat button at the bottom of the Source list on the left side of the iTunes window (or by choosing Controls⇨Repeat All). Click the Repeat button again to repeat the current song (or choose Controls⇨Repeat One). Click it once more to return to normal playback (or choose Controls⇨Repeat Off).

The Shuffle button, to the left of the Repeat button, plays the songs in the list in a random order, which can be fun. You can then press the arrow keys on your keyboard or click the Back and Forward buttons to jump around in random order.

Displaying visuals

The visual effects in iTunes can turn your computer display into a light show synchronized to the currently playing music. You can watch a cool visual display of eye candy while the music plays — or leave it on like a lava lamp.

Click the Visual Effects button on the bottom-right side of the iTunes window to display visual effects. The visual animation appears in the iTunes window and synchronizes with the music.

In addition to the animation replacing the iTunes song list, an Options button replaces the Import button in the upper-right corner of the iTunes window. You can click the Options button to open the Visualizer Options dialog box, as shown in Figure 1-5.

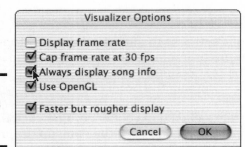

Figure 1-5:
Set options
for visual
effects.

The Visualizer Options dialog box offers the following options that affect
the animation (these settings don't affect the playback of music, however):

✦ **Display Frame Rate:** Displays the frame rate of the animation along with
the animation.

✦ **Cap Frame Rate at 30 fps:** Keeps the frame rate at 30 fps (frames per
second) or lower, which is the speed of normal video.

✦ **Always Display Song Info:** Displays the song name, artist, and album
for the song currently playing, along with the animation.

✦ **Faster but Rougher Display:** The animation plays faster, with rougher
graphics. Choose this option if your animation plays too slowly.

The Visualizer menu in iTunes gives you even more control over visual
effects. You can choose Visualize⇨Small or Visualize⇨Medium to display
the visual effects in a rectangle inside the iTunes window, or you can
choose Visualize⇨Large to fill the iTunes window. Choosing Visualizer⇨
Full Screen sets the visual effects to take over the entire screen. When
displaying the full-screen visual effects, you can click the mouse or press
the Escape key on your keyboard to stop the display and return to iTunes.
Choosing Visualizer⇨Turn Visualizer On is the same as clicking the Visual
Effects button: It displays the visual effects.

While the animated visual effects play, press Shift+slash (the same key combination you would use to type a question mark) to see a list of keyboard
functions. Depending on the visual effect, you might see more choices of
keyboard functions by pressing Shift+slash again.

To turn off the visual effects display, click the Visual Effects button again.
You can leave the effects on (except when in full-screen mode) even
while opening the equalizer because you still have access to the playback controls.

CHECK IT OUT

Supplementing iTunes with Other Programs

Users of Mac OS X are blessed with some wonderful supplementary programs, most of which are free or relatively inexpensive. The fact that OS X is built upon a Unix framework has opened the doors to a wide collection of Unix utilities, and to make things even better, the OS X development tools make putting a Mac interface onto these command-line tools a simple task.

One of the most popular MP3 encoders on many platforms (Mac, Windows, and various implementations of Unix and Linux) is LAME, which stands for LAME Ain't an MP3 Encoder (because, in the beginning, it wasn't). Implemented for iTunes users as an AppleScript around the Unix command-line tool, you install the script, which is a free download from VersionTracker (www.versiontracker.com); in iTunes, you then select the songs you want encoded with LAME and choose Scripts⇨Import with LAME. The iTunes-LAME window appears, and you just click the Import button when you're ready to start the encoding.

Another handy utility, this one shareware ($5), is Josh Aas's iTunes Publisher. iTunes Publisher is the iTunes File⇨Export Song List command on steroids. You can save your playlists as HTML files, which iTunes Publisher links back to your iTunes Library. iTunes Publisher also provides a simple interface to produce QTSS (QuickTime Streaming Server) playlists, as well as to generate the m3u playlists used by many MP3 players (such as Winamp, available at www.winamp.com), or text- or tab-delimited text files.

Though not really an enhancement to iTunes, MacMP3CD (www.mireth.com) is a useful adjunct to iTunes. To switch from burning audio CDs to MP3 CDs in iTunes requires that you change your burning preferences (and then, probably, switch them back when you're done). With MacMP3CD, you can build your MP3 playlist and burn it directly. Additionally, iTunes doesn't recognize MP3 CDs when they're inserted as it does with audio CDs. MacMP3CD also plays back your MP3 CDs.

Chapter 2: Buying Music from Apple

In This Chapter

✔ Signing in to the iTunes Music Store

✔ Previewing and buying songs

✔ Handling authorization

✔ Setting your preferences

*W*hen Apple announced its new music service, Apple chairman Steve Jobs remarked that other services put forward by the music industry tend to treat consumers like criminals. Mr. Jobs had a point. Many of these services charge more than the iTunes Music Store and add a level of copy protection that prevents consumers from burning CDs or using the music they bought on other computers or portable MP3 players.

Apple did the research on how to make a service that worked better and was easier to use, and it forged ahead with the iTunes Music Store. By all accounts, Apple has succeeded in offering the easiest, fastest, and most cost-effective service for buying music for your computer and your iPod. In this chapter, I show you how to sign in and take advantage of what the iTunes Music Store has to offer.

Visiting the iTunes Music Store

As of this writing, the iTunes Music Store offers more than 700,000 songs, with most songs costing only $0.99 each and entire albums available at far less than the price you pay for the CD. You can play the songs on up to three different computers, burn your own CDs, and use them on players such as the iPod.

You can preview any song for up to 30 seconds, and if you already established your account, you can buy and download the song immediately. I don't know of a faster way to get a song.

To open the iTunes Music Store, follow these steps:

1. **From within iTunes, click the Music Store option in the Source list.**

The Music Store's front page appears (see Figure 2-1), replacing the iTunes song list. You can check out artists and songs to your heart's content, although you can't buy songs until you sign in to a Music Store account. You can use the Choose Genre drop-down list to specify music genres, or click links for new releases, exclusive tracks, and so on — just like any music service on the Web.

Figure 2-1:
The iTunes
Music Store
front page.

2. Click the Sign In button on the right to create an account or sign in to an existing account.

You need an account (with a credit card) to buy music. iTunes displays the account sign-in dialog box, as shown in Figure 2-2.

If you already set up an account in the iTunes Store in the .Mac service, you just need to type in your Apple ID and password. Apple remembers the personal information you put in previously, so you don't have to re-enter it. If you forgot your password, click the Forgot Password? button, and iTunes provides a dialog box to answer your test question. If you answer correctly, your password is then e-mailed to you.

Figure 2-2:
Sign in to
the iTunes
Music
Store.

3. To create an account, click the Create Account button.

iTunes displays a new page, replacing the iTunes front page, with an explanation of steps to create an account and the Terms of Use documentation.

4. **Click the Agree button and fill in your personal account information.**

   iTunes displays the next page of the setup procedure, which requires you to type your e-mail address, password, test question and answer (in case you forget your password), birth date, and privacy options.

5. **Click the Continue button to go to the next page of the account setup procedure and enter your credit card information.**

   The entire procedure is secure, so you don't have to worry. The Music Store keeps your personal information, including your credit card information, on file so that you don't have to type it again.

6. **Click the Done button to finish the procedure.**

Previewing a Song

You might want to listen to a song before you buy it, or you might just want to browse the store listening to song previews. When you select an artist or a special offering, or enter an artist's name in the Search Music Store text box and press Enter, the browser window divides and gives you a list of songs you can select to preview, as shown in Figure 2-3. Select a song and click the Play button or double-click a song to play a preview.

The previews play on your computer off the Internet in a stream, so a few hiccups might be in the playback. Each preview lasts about 30 seconds.

Figure 2-3:
Preview songs online in the iTunes Music Store.

Buying and Playing Songs

With an account set up, you can purchase songs from the iTunes Music Store and download them to your computer. Select a song and click the Buy Song button at the far right of the song (you might have to scroll your iTunes window horizontally). The store displays a warning to make sure you want to buy the song, and you can either go through with it or cancel.

The song downloads automatically and shows up in your iTunes song list. Purchased songs also appear in a special Purchased Music playlist under the Music Store heading, as well as in the iTunes Library song list.

If for some reason your computer crashes or you quit before the download finishes, iTunes remembers to continue the download when you return to iTunes. If the download doesn't continue, choose Advanced➪Check for Purchased Music to finish the download.

If you prefer, you can add songs to a shopping cart in the store, rather than using the 1-Click technology, to delay purchasing and downloading until you're ready. If you decide on the shopping cart method, the Buy Song button for each song changes to an Add Song button. When you're ready to purchase everything in your cart, click the Buy Now button to close the sale and download all the songs at once. To switch from 1-Click to a shopping cart, check out the section, "Setting the Music Store Preferences."

All sales are final. If your hard drive dies and you lose your data, you also lose your songs — you have to purchase and download them again. But you can mitigate this kind of disaster by backing up your music library. You can also burn your purchased songs onto an audio CD (an easy backup method), as I describe in Book V, Chapter 10.

For Windows users, music files you buy are stored in `C:\Documents and Settings\`*Your Name*`\My Documents\My Music\iTunes\iTunes Music`. iTunes creates subfolders for artists and albums in the iTunes Music folder.

Handling Authorization

The computer you use to set up your account is automatically authorized by Apple to play the songs you buy. Fortunately, the songs aren't locked to that computer — you can copy them to another computer and play them from within the other computer's iTunes program. When you first play them, iTunes asks for your iTunes Music Store ID and password in order to authorize that computer. You can authorize up to three computers at a time.

If you want to add a fourth computer, you first have to remove the authorization from one of the other computers by choosing Advanced➪Deauthorize Computer.

After you set up an account, you can sign in to the Music Store at any time to buy music, view or change the information in your account, and see your purchase history. To see your account information and purchase history, click the View Account link in the store after signing in with your ID and password. Every time you buy music, you get an e-mail from the iTunes Music Store with the purchase information. If you use the 1-Click option, the Music Store keeps track of your purchases over a 24-hour period so that you are charged a total sum rather than for each individual purchase.

Setting the Music Store Preferences

Your decision to download each song immediately or add songs to a shopping cart and download them as a group later is likely based on how your computer connects to the Internet. If you have a slow connection, you probably want to use the shopping cart method.

You can change your preferences with the iTunes Music Store by choosing Edit➪Preferences. In the Preferences dialog box, click the Store tab. The Store Preferences tab appears, as shown in Figure 2-4. You can enable the following options:

✦ Change from 1-Click to Shopping Cart or vice versa by selecting either the Buy and Download Using 1-Click option (the default) or the Buy Using a Shopping Cart option.

✦ Select the Play Songs after Downloading option to have iTunes automatically play a song when the download is finished.

✦ Choose whether to use a streaming preview or to load the complete preview before playing it. I recommend selecting the Load Complete Preview before Playing check box because this option provides better playing performance (fewer hiccups) with previews over slow Internet connections.

If you use more than one computer with your account, you can set the preferences for each computer differently while still using the same account. For example, your store-authorized home computer might have a faster connection than your authorized PowerBook on the road, and you can set your iTunes preferences accordingly.

Figure 2-4:
Set your
preferences
for the
iTunes
Music
Store.

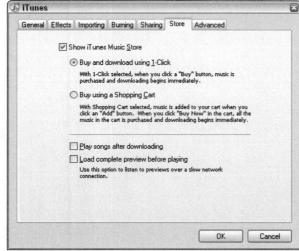

Chapter 3: Importing Music into iTunes

In This Chapter

✔ Importing music from CDs

✔ Importing music files from the Internet and other computers

✔ Importing sound files

To immortalize your music, you need to import it into iTunes from your audio CDs and other sources. After the music is in your iTunes library, you can preserve it forever. You can make backup copies with perfect quality.

Importing music from a CD and changing the music tracks to a different format is called *ripping a CD*. I'm not sure why it's called that, but Apple certainly took the term to a new level with an ad campaign a while back that featured the slogan "Rip, Mix, Burn." That was the hip thing to do a few years ago. Now, it's simply ripping and mixing — with an iPod, you no longer need to burn CDs to play your music wherever you go.

The ripping process is straightforward, but the settings you choose for importing affect sound quality, hard drive space (and iPod space), and compatibility with other types of players and computers. In this chapter, I show you how to rip CDs, import music from the Internet, and provide suggestions for settings.

Setting the Importing Preferences

Before you actually rip a CD, pay a visit to the Importing tab of the Preferences dialog box, as shown in Figure 3-1. To get there, choose Edit➪Preferences, and then click the Importing tab.

Ripping is the process of compressing the song's digital information and encoding it in a particular sound file format. The Import Using drop-down list allows you to set the type of encoding, that is, to select which type of file you want to convert the music into. This is perhaps the most important choice. The Setting drop-down list offers different options, depending on your choice of encoder.

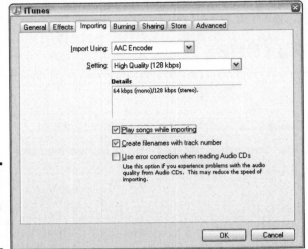

Figure 3-1:
Set your
preferences
for ripping
CDs.

Encoding is a complicated subject and requires a whole chapter of its own (in fact, Book V, Chapter 8 provides a more in-depth look if you want to know more). But for a quick and pain-free ripping session, choose the following encoders from the Import Using drop-down list:

✦ **AAC Encoder:** The iTunes Music Store uses this format, and I recommend it for all uses except when ripping your own CDs in order to burn new audio CDs. Choose the High Quality option from the Setting drop-down list.

✦ **AIFF Encoder:** Use AIFF if you plan on burning the song to an audio CD because it offers the highest possible quality; the downside is that this format also takes up lots of space. Choose the Automatic option from the Setting drop-down list.

✦ **Apple Lossless Encoder:** Select this option if you want very high-quality music files and you are willing to sacrifice hard drive space. Lossless files are not compressed.

✦ **MP3 Encoder:** Use the MP3 format for songs you intend to send to others or use with MP3 players — it's universally supported. Choose the Higher Quality option from the Setting drop-down list.

✦ **WAV Encoder:** WAV is the high-quality sound format used on PCs (like AIFF), and also takes up a lot of space. Use WAV if you plan on burning the song to an audio CD or using it with PCs. Choose the Automatic option from the Setting drop-down list.

You can import a CD using one encoder, and then import it again using a different encoder. For example, you may import *Sgt. Pepper* with the AAC encoder for use on your computer and iPod, and import it again with the AIFF encoder, calling it *Sgt. Pepper-2* or something, in order to burn some songs on a CD. After burning the CD, you can then delete *Sgt. Pepper-2* to reclaim the hard drive space.

Ripping Music from CDs

Importing music from an audio CD takes a lot less time than playing the CD. You want to do it right the first time, with the proper importing settings — not because you can't do it again (because you certainly *can*), but because it takes time.

To rip a CD correctly the first time, follow these steps:

1. **Insert an audio CD.**

The songs appear in your song list as generic unnamed tracks at first. If your computer is connected to the Internet, iTunes retrieves the track information. If you connect first by modem, go ahead and establish your connection, and then choose Advanced⇨Get CD Track Names.

2. **Optional: Deselect the check boxes next to any songs on the CD that you don't want to import.**

iTunes imports the songs that have check marks next to them; when you remove the check mark next to a song, iTunes skips that song.

3. **Optional: To remove the gap of silence between songs that segue together, select those songs and choose Advanced⇨Join CD Tracks.**

This happens often with music CDs — the tracks are separate but the end of one song merges into the beginning of the next song. You don't want an annoying half-second gap between the songs. For example, in Figure 3-2, I joined the first two songs of *Sgt. Pepper* because they're supposed to run together. I also joined the last three songs of the CD for the same reason.

Figure 3-2:
Join songs to avoid the audible gap between them.

To select multiple songs, click the first one, and then ⌘+click (Mac) or Ctrl+click (Windows) each subsequent song. To select several consecutive songs in a row, click the first one and Shift+click the last one.

Be sure to check the importing preferences before actually ripping the CD.

4. Click the Import button.

The Import button is at the top right edge of the iTunes window. The status display shows the progress of the operation. To cancel, click the small x next to the progress bar in the status display.

In Windows, the music files you rip are stored in subfolders of the `C:\ Documents and Settings\`*Your Name*`\My Documents\My Music\iTunes\ iTunes Music` folder. iTunes creates subfolders for the artist and album whose songs you rip. On a Mac, files are kept in your personal folder under the iTunes Music folder.

iTunes plays the songs as it imports them. You can click the Pause button to stop playback (but not the importing). If you don't want to listen to the songs as they import, choose Edit➪Preferences, click the Importing tab, deselect the Play Songs While Importing option, and click OK.

iTunes displays an orange animated waveform icon next to the song it is importing. As iTunes finishes importing each song, it displays a green check mark next to the song, as shown in Figure 3-3. When all the songs are imported, you can eject the CD by clicking the Eject button at the far right bottom edge of the iTunes window or by choosing Controls➪Eject Disc.

Figure 3-3:
When importing is done, eject the CD.

Songs are imported.

Eject button

Importing Music Files

The quality of the music you hear depends on the quality of the source. Web sites and services offering music files vary widely. Some sites provide high-quality, legally derived songs you can download, and some provide only streaming audio, which you can play but not save on your hard drive (such as a Web radio station). The allegedly illegal file-sharing services offering MP3 files can vary widely in quality. Anyone can create MP3 files, so beware of less-than-high-quality knockoffs.

You can download the music file or copy it from another computer to your hard drive. After you save or copy an MP3 file — or for that matter an AIFF or WAV file — on your hard drive, you can drag it into the iTunes window to import it to your library if you have a Mac. If you drag a folder or disk icon, all the audio files it contains are added to your iTunes Library. To import a file on a Windows computer (and a Mac as well), choose File⇨Add File to Library or File⇨Add Folder to Library as an alternative to dragging.

When you add a song to your iTunes library, a copy, not the original, is placed inside the iTunes Music folder. The original file is not changed or moved. You can then convert the song to another format — for example, you can convert an AIFF file to an MP3 file — while leaving the original file intact.

Adding Your Own Pet Sounds

You can import any sound into iTunes, even music from scratchy old vinyl records, or sound effects recorded through a microphone. The *Pet Sounds Sessions* box set by the Beach Boys included just about every spoken word and sneeze in the studio during the recording, and you might have equally unusual sounds or rare music that can't be found anywhere else. How do you get stuff like that into iTunes?

You can import high-quality AIFF-format or WAV-format files from music editing programs. These programs typically record from any analog source device, such as a tape player or even a turntable for playing vinyl records.

After you save the digital music file using a sound-editing program, you can drag it into the iTunes window to import it to your library if you have a Mac. Mac and Windows users can both choose File⇨Add to Library as an alternative to dragging.

AIFF or WAV encoded sound files occupy lots of space in your music library or iPod. Voice recordings and sound effects tend to be low-fidelity and typically do not sound any better in AIFF or WAV format than they do in compressed formats (such as MP3) that save hard drive space. Also, sound effects and voice recordings are typically mono rather than stereo. You can save hard drive and iPod space and still have quality recordings by converting these files to MP3 or AAC formats, changing the sound files from stereo to mono in the process, while leaving the original versions intact.

Importing Audio Books

Do you like to listen to audio books and spoken magazine and newspaper articles? Not only can you bring these sounds into iTunes, but you can also transfer them to an iPod and take them on the road, which is much more convenient than taking cassettes or CDs.

Audible is a leading provider of downloadable spoken audio files. Audible lets you enable up to three computers to play the audio files you purchase, just like the iTunes Music Store.

To purchase and download Audible files and then import them into iTunes, follow these steps:

1. Go to `www.audible.com` **and set up an account if you don't already have one.**

2. Choose and download an Audible audio file.

   Files that end with `.aa` are Audible files.

3. Import the Audible file into your iTunes Music folder.

   If this is the first time you've added an Audible file, iTunes asks for your account information. You need only to enter this information once for each computer you use with your Audible account.

To disable an Audible account, open iTunes on the computer that will no longer be used with the account, and choose Advanced⇨Deauthorize Computer. In the Deauthorize Computer dialog box, select the Deauthorize Computer for Audible Account option and click OK. Remember that you need to be online to authorize a computer or to remove authorization from that computer.

 **CHECK IT OUT**

Listening to the Radio with iTunes

Although you can't transfer radio links to your iPod, you can listen to online Web casts with iTunes. Check out the local news and sports from your hometown no matter where you are. Listen to talk radio and music shows from all over the country and the world.

Apple conveniently provides radio stations within iTunes. Click the Radio option in the Source list, choose your station, and click the Play button.

Remember: If you use a modem connection to the Internet, you might want to choose a stream with a bit rate of less than 56 Kbps for best results.

The Bit Rate column shows the bit rate for each stream.

To find stations not supplied by Apple, all you need to know is the Web address. Choose Advanced⇨Open Stream. Enter the URL (don't forget the `http://`) and iTunes places it at the end of your song list, ready for you to play. *Note:* As of this writing, iTunes supports only MP3 broadcasts. You can find lots of MP3 broadcasts at `www.shoutcast.com`.

When you find the Source list filling up with stations, create a playlist by choosing File⇨New Playlist from Selection.

Chapter 4: Sharing Music (Legally)

In This Chapter

✔ Sharing music purchased from the iTunes Music Store

✔ Copying music files and folders to other hard drives

✔ Sharing music on a network

You want to protect your investments in music. If you buy music online, you want to be able to play the music anywhere and even share the music with your friends.

You can easily share the music you rip yourself from CDs. After the music becomes digital, you can copy it endlessly with no loss in quality. Of course, if the songs are in a protected format (such as music bought from an online music store), some restrictions do apply. In this chapter, I show you how to share music with others. (After all, your parents taught you to share, didn't they?)

Sharing Music from the iTunes Music Store

You can share, to a limited extent, the music you buy online from the iTunes Music Store. Apple uses a protected form of the AAC encoder for the songs. The rights of artists are protected while also giving you more leeway in how to use the music more than most other services (though by the time you read this, other services might have adopted this format with similar privileges).

Some of the features Apple offers through the iTunes Music Store are the following:

✦ **Creating backups:** Easily create backups by copying music several times.

✦ **Copying music:** Play songs on up to three separate computers. See Book V, Chapter 2 to find out how to authorize your computers.

✦ **Sharing music over a network:** Everyone on a network can play the music.

Whether or not you manage files on your hard drive on a regular basis, you might want to know where these songs are stored so that you can copy music to other computers or make a backup of your entire music library. You might also want to move the library to another computer, say if you bought a new computer and you don't plan to keep the old one.

You can play your purchased music on any authorized computer. You can authorize up to three computers at one time, and you can remove the authorization from the computers you don't use.

I fought the law and the law won: Sharing and piracy

Apple CEO Steve Jobs gave personal demonstrations of the iTunes Music Store, iTunes, and the iPod to Paul McCartney and Mick Jagger. According to Steven Levy at *Newsweek* (May 12, 2003), Jobs said, "They both totally get it." The former Beatle and the Stones frontman both conduct music-business affairs personally and both have extensive back catalogs of music. They also know all about the file-sharing services on the Internet, but they agree with Jobs that most people would be willing to pay for high-quality music rather than downloading free copies of questionable quality.

I agree with the idea, also promoted by Jobs, that treating technology as the culprit with regard to violations of copyright law is wrong. The solution to piracy is not technology, because determined hackers will quickly find ways to circumvent copy protection, and only consumers are inconvenienced.

I'm not a lawyer, but I think the law already covers the type of piracy that involves counterfeiting CDs. The fact that you are not allowed to copy a commercial CD and sell the copy to someone else makes sense. You also can't sell the individual songs of a commercial CD.

Giving music away for free is, of course, the subject of much controversy, with some free file-sharing services closed by court order while others continue to flourish. The songs I've heard from file-sharing services such as Kazaa have, for the most part, been low in quality. Nice for listening to new songs to decide if you like them, but not useful for acquiring as part of a real music collection. I believe that music purchased from the iTunes Music Store is clearly superior in quality and convenience. I prefer the original, authorized version of a song, not some knockoff that might have been copied from a radio broadcast.

Copying Songs to Other Computers

You can copy songs freely from your iTunes Music folder to other folders, other hard drives, and other computers using the Finder. The files are organized in folders by artist name and by album within the iTunes Music folder at `C:\Documents and Settings\`*Your Name*`\My Documents\My Music\iTunes\ iTunes Music` on a Windows computer. On a Mac, the files are kept in your personal folder under the iTunes Music folder. Copying an entire album, or every song by a specific artist, is easy — just drag the folder to the other hard drive.

You can find out the location of any song by selecting the song in iTunes and choosing File⇨Get Info. Click the Summary tab in the Get Info dialog box to see the Summary pane.

Sharing Music on a Network

If you live like the Jetsons, with a computer in every room, connected by wireless or wired network, then iTunes is made for you. You can share the music in your library with up to five other computers in the same network.

When you share songs on a network, the song is *streamed* from the library computer to your computer over the network; the song is not copied to your music library. From your computer, you can't burn shared songs onto a CD or copy the shared songs to your iPod. You can, of course, do those things on the library computer. You can share radio links, MP3, AIFF, WAV, AAC files, and music purchased from the iTunes Music Store, but you can't share Audible spoken word files or QuickTime sound files.

If you have a large network (such as an office network), check to make sure the computers share the same subnet. The computers need to be within the same subnet to share music.

To share your music library, turning your computer into the library computer, follow these steps:

1. **Choose Edit⇨Preferences and click the Sharing tab.**

The Sharing tab of the Preferences dialog box appears, as shown in Figure 4-1, with options for sharing music.

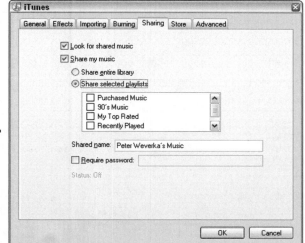

Figure 4-1:
Share your music library with other Macs on the same network.

2. **Select the Share My Music option.**

3. **Select either the Share Entire Library option or the Share Selected Playlists option and choose the playlists to share.**

4. **Enter a name for the shared library and add a password if you want.**

The name you choose appears in the Source list for other computers that share the library. The password restricts access to those who know it.

Pick a password you don't mind sharing with others; for example, your name is a good password, but your ATM PIN isn't.

iTunes displays a `Reminder: Sharing music is for personal use only` message.

5. **Click OK.**

You can access the music from the other computers on the network by following these steps:

1. **Choose iTunes⇨Preferences and click the Sharing tab.**

The Sharing tab of the Preferences dialog box appears, with options for sharing music (refer to Figure 4-1).

2. **Select the Look for Shared Music option and click OK.**

The shared libraries or playlists appear in the Source list in the iTunes window, as shown in Figure 4-2.

3. **Click the shared library or playlist to play it.**

This can be incredibly useful for playing music on laptops, such as PowerBooks, that support the wireless AirPort network.

Shared music library

Figure 4-2: You can access the shared music library in iTunes.

Chapter 5: Searching, Browsing, and Sorting

In This Chapter

✔ Browsing your music library

✔ Changing viewing options

✔ Sorting the song list

✔ Searching for songs or artists

You rip a few CDs, buy some songs from the iTunes Music Store, and watch as your music library fills up with songs. That song list is getting longer and longer, and as a result, your library is harder to navigate.

The iTunes library is awesome even by jukebox standards — it can hold up to 32,000 songs, depending on your disk space. Finding Chuck Berry's "Maybelline" is a challenge using a rotating dial of 32,000 songs. The 40GB iPod holds about 9,000 songs — enough music to last two weeks if played 24 hours a day! But even if you keep your iTunes library down to the size of what you can fit on your iPod, you still have a formidable collection at your fingertips. If you're a music lover, you'll want to organize this collection to make finding songs easier.

This chapter shows you how to search, browse, and sort your music library in iTunes. You can find any song in seconds and display songs sorted by artist, album, genre of music, or other attributes. You can change the viewing options to make your library's display more useful.

Browsing by Artist and Album

You can switch to Browse view to find songs more easily. The Browse view is useful as long as you track information for the songs. You aren't overwhelmed by a long list of songs — when you select an album, iTunes displays only the songs for that album.

To view albums in Browse view, click the Browse button in the upper-right corner of the iTunes window. iTunes organizes your music library by artist and album, which makes finding just the right tune easier, as shown in Figure 5-1. Click the Browse button again to return to the default view — the Browse button toggles between Browse view and the default song list view.

The Browse view sorts by genre, by artist within each genre, and within each artist, by album. It displays the songs in a list underneath a set of columns. This type of column arrangement is a tree structure, although it looks more like a fallen tree.

Figure 5-1:
Click the
Browse
button to
browse the
iTunes
library.

When you click an artist in the Artist column (as shown in Figure 5-2), the
album titles appear in the Album column. At the top of the Album column, the
All selection is highlighted, and the songs from every album by that artist
appear in the Song Name column below the Artist and Album columns.

Figure 5-2:
Select an
artist to see
the list of
albums for
that artist.

To see more than one album from an artist at a time, hold down the ⌘ key and click each artist's name. On a PC, hold down the Ctrl key. iTunes displays the selected albums.

As you click different albums in the Album column, the Song Name column displays the songs from that album. The songs are listed in proper track order, just as the artist intended them.

This is great for selecting songs from albums, but what if you want to look at *all* the songs by *all* the artists in the library at once? You can see all the songs in the library in Browse view by selecting All at the top of the Artist column.

 If you prefer not to see the Genre column in Browse view, choose Edit⇨ Preferences, select the General tab in the Preferences window, and deselect the Show Genre When Browsing option.

Understanding the Song Indicators

As you make choices in iTunes, it displays an action indicator next to each song to show you what iTunes is doing. Here's a list of indicators and what they mean:

✦ **Orange waveform:** iTunes is importing the song.

✦ **Green check mark:** iTunes finished importing the song.

✦ **Exclamation point:** iTunes can't find the song. You might have moved or deleted the song accidentally. You can move the song back to iTunes by dragging it from the Finder to the iTunes window.

✦ **Broadcast icon:** The song is on the Internet and plays as a music stream.

✦ **Black check mark:** Songs marked for the next operation, such as importing from an audio CD or playing in sequence. Click to remove the check mark.

✦ **Speaker:** The song is currently playing.

✦ **Chasing arrows:** iTunes is copying the song from another location or downloading the song from the Internet.

Changing Viewing Options

iTunes gives you the ability to customize the song list. The list starts out with the Song Name, Time, Artist, Album, Genre, My Rating, Play Count, and Last Played categories — you might have to drag the horizontal scroll bar along the bottom of the song list to see all these columns. You can change your display from the default view to show more, less, or different information about your song list; you can also display columns in a different order from left to right or with wider or narrower column widths.

You can make a column fatter or thinner by dragging the dividing line between the column and the next column. As you move your cursor over the divider, it changes to a double-ended arrow; you can click and drag the divider to change the column's width.

You can also change the order of columns from left to right by clicking a column heading and dragging the entire column to the left or right. In addition, you can right-click any of the column headings to display a shortcut menu offering the same options as the View Options window, the Auto Size Column option, and the Auto Size All Columns option.

Maybe you don't like certain columns — they take up valuable screen space. Or perhaps you want to display some other information about the song. You can add or remove columns such as Size (for file size), Date and Year (for the date that the album was released or any other date you choose for each song), Bit Rate, Sample Rate, Track Number, and Comment. To add or delete columns, choose Edit➪View Options.

The View Options window appears, as shown in Figure 5-3, and you can select the columns that you want to appear in the song list. To pick a column, select the check box next to the column heading. Any deselected column headings don't appear. Note that the Song Name column always appears in the listing and can't be removed.

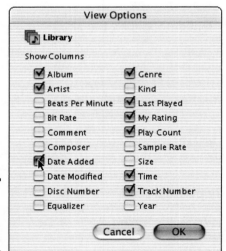

Figure 5-3:
The viewing options for the song list.

The viewing options that you choose depend on your music playing habits. You might want to display the Time column to know at a glance the duration of any song. You might want the Date or Year columns to differentiate songs from different eras, or the Genre column to differentiate songs from different musical genres.

Sorting Songs by Viewing Options

Knowing how to set viewing options is a good idea because you can then sort the listing of songs by them. Whether you're in Browse view or viewing the song list in its entirety, the column headings double as sorting options.

For example, if you click the Time heading, the songs reorder by their duration in ascending order — starting with the shortest song. If you click the Time heading again, the sort reverses, starting with the longest song. This can be useful if you're looking for songs of a certain length — for example, looking for a song to match the length of a slideshow or a movie clip.

You can tell which way the sort is sorting — ascending or descending order — by the little arrow indicator in the heading. When the arrow is pointing up, the sort is in ascending order; when down, it is in descending order.

You can sort the song list in alphabetical order. Click the Artist heading to sort all the songs in the list by the artist name, in alphabetical order (so that the arrow points up). Click it again to sort the list in reverse alphabetical order (so that the arrow points down).

Searching for Songs

As your music library grows, you might find locating a particular song by the usual browsing and scrolling methods (which I describe earlier in this chapter) time consuming. So . . . let iTunes find your songs for you!

Locate the Search text box — the oval text box in the top-right corner, to the left of the Browse button. Click in the Search text box and type the first characters of your search term. Follow these tips for best searching:

✦ Open the drop-down list and make a selection to search by artist, album title, composer, or song title.

✦ Typing very few characters results in a long list of possible songs, but the search narrows as you type more characters.

✦ The Search feature ignores case as well as whole words — when I type *miles,* it finds "Eight Miles High" as well as "She Smiles Like a River."

✦ If you're in Browse view and have an artist and a particular album selected, you can't search for another artist or song. Why not? Browsing with searching narrows your search further. The song that you're looking for isn't on the selected album that you're browsing.

If you want to search the entire library in Browse view, first click the All selection at the top of the Genre or Artist column to browse the entire library before typing a term in the Search text box. Or, if you prefer, click the Browse button again to return to the default song list view, and type a term in the Search text box with the library's song list.

The search operation works immediately, searching for matches in the Song Name, Artist, and Album columns of the listing.

To back out of a search so that the full list appears again, you can either click the circled X in the Search text box (which appears only after you start typing characters) or delete the characters in the Search text box. You then see the entire list of songs in the library's song list, just as before. All the songs are still there and remain there unless you explicitly remove them. Searching manipulates only your view of them.

Chapter 6: Adding and Editing Song Information

In This Chapter

✔ Retrieving information from the Internet

✔ Typing song information

✔ Editing the information for a selected song

✔ Editing multiple songs at once to save time

✔ Adding liner notes, artwork, comments, and ratings

Organization depends on information. You expect the computer to do a lot more than just store this music with "Untitled Disc" and "Track 1" as the only identifiers. Adding all the song information seems like a lot of trouble, but that ol' magic comes through for you. You can get most of the information automatically, without typing.

This chapter shows you how to add song information to your music library in iTunes. Then I show you how to edit it for better viewing.

Retrieving Information from the Internet

Why type song information if someone else has typed it? You can get information about most commercial CDs from the Internet. However, you need to check your Internet connection first. You can retrieve information automatically or manually. Put an audio CD in your computer and follow the techniques in this section to retrieve information about its songs.

Retrieving information automatically

During the setup process, you specify whether iTunes connects automatically or manually to the Internet. But you can also use the following steps to change the setup of your Internet connection so that it connects automatically at any time:

1. **Choose Edit⇨Preferences.**

The Preferences window appears.

2. **Click the General tab.**

The General Preferences window appears.

3. **Select the Connect to Internet When Needed option.**

iTunes triggers your modem automatically (like a Web browser), calls your service provider, and completes the connection process so that it can retrieve the track information.

You can stop an automatic modem connection quickly — a good idea if your service provider or phone service charges extra fees based on timed usage. When iTunes finishes importing, switch to your remote connection program without quitting iTunes, terminate the Internet connection, and then switch back to iTunes.

Retrieving information manually

You can connect to the Internet at any time and get the song information when you need it. After you connect, choose Advanced⇨Get CD Track Names from the iTunes menu.

Even if you automatically connect to the Internet, the song information database on the Internet (known as CDDB, the *CD Database*) might be momentarily unavailable, or you can have a delayed response. If at first you don't succeed, choose Advanced⇨Get CD Track Names again.

After connecting and retrieving track information by using a modem, your Internet service might still be connected until the service hangs up on you. You might want to switch to a browser without quitting iTunes and surf the Web to make use of the connection — iTunes continues to import or play the music while you surf.

Long distance information: Using the CDDB

The first time that I popped an audio CD into my computer was like magic. iTunes, after thinking for less than a minute, displayed the song names, album title, and artist names automatically. How did it know? This information isn't stored on a standard music CD — you have to either recognize the disc somehow or read the liner notes.

The magic is that the software knows how to reach out and find the information on the Internet — in the Gracenote CDDB service. (CDDB stands for, you guessed it, *CD Database*.) The site (www. gracenote.com) hosts CDDB on the Web and offers the ability to search for music CDs by artist, song title, and other methods. The iTunes software already knows how to use this database, so you don't have to!

iTunes finds the track information by first looking up a *key identifying number* on the audio CD — a secret number stored on every publicly released music CD, not for spying on listeners but simply to identify the CD and manufacturer. iTunes uses this number to find the information within the CDDB. The CDDB keeps track information for most of the music CDs you find on the market.

Although the database doesn't contain any information about personal or custom CDs, people can submit information to the database about CDs that the database doesn't know about. You can even do this from within iTunes — type the information for each track while the audio CD is in your computer, and then choose Advanced⇨Submit CD Track Names. The information that you typed is sent to the CDDB site, where the good people who work tirelessly on the database check out your information before including it. In fact, if you spot a typo or something erroneous in the information that you receive from CDDB, you can correct it, and then use the Advanced⇨Submit CD Track Names command to send the corrected version back to the CDDB site. The good folks at Gracenote appreciate the effort.

Typing the Song Information

Because songs come from unofficial sources, artists' names and song titles might be misspelled. Editing song information can make songs easier to find in your song library. This section explains how to edit song information for the songs that you've downloaded.

Editing artist and band names

Just like when typing the song information into iTunes, you can edit a song's information in the Browse view or the song list view. Edit a song's track information by clicking directly in the field and clicking again so that the mouse pointer turns into an editing cursor. You can then select the text and type over it or move tiny bits of text around within the field by using the Copy and Paste commands. As you can see in Figure 6-1, I changed the Artist field to "Beck, Jeff."

Figure 6-1: Click inside the Artist field to edit the information.

You can edit the Song Name, Artist, Album, Genre, and My Ratings fields right in the song list. Editing this information with the File⇨Get Info command is easier. Keep reading to find out.

Speed editing multiple songs

Editing in the song list is fine if you're editing the information for one song, but typically you need to change all the tracks of an audio CD. For example, if a CD of songs by Bob Dylan is listed with the artist as "Bob Dylan," you might want to change all the songs at once to "Dylan, Bob." Changing all the song information in one fell swoop is fast and clean, but like most powerful shortcuts, you need to be careful because it can be dangerous.

You can change a group of songs in the Browse view or the song list view. Follow these steps to change a group of songs at once:

1. **Select a group of songs by clicking the first song and holding down the Shift key while you click the last song.**

The last song, and all the songs between the first and last, highlight at once. (Or you can hold down the Ctrl key for Windows or ⌘ for Macs while selecting songs that aren't grouped together.)

2. **Choose File➪Get Info.**

A warning message displays: `Are you sure you want to edit information for multiple items?`

On a highway, speed can kill. Speed editing in iTunes can also be dangerous for your song information. If, for example, you change the song name, the entire selection then has that song name. You must be careful about what you edit when doing this. I recommend leaving the Do Not Ask Me Again check box deselected so that the warning appears whenever you try this.

3. **Click Yes.**

The Multiple Song Information window appears, as shown in Figure 6-2.

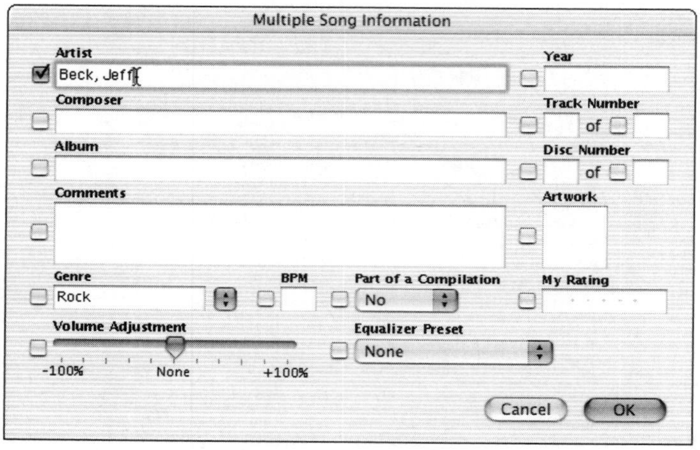

Figure 6-2: Change the artist name for multiple songs at once.

[Figure 6-2: Multiple Song Information window with fields for Artist (Beck, Jeff), Composer, Album, Comments, Genre (Rock), BPM, Part of a Compilation (No), Volume Adjustment, Year, Track Number, Disc Number, Artwork, My Rating, Equalizer Preset (None), and Cancel/OK buttons.]

4. **Edit the field that you want to change (typically the Artist field) for multiple songs.**

When you edit a text box, a check mark appears automatically in the box next to the text box. iTunes assumes that you want that field to be changed throughout the song selection. Make sure that no other check box is selected except the one(s) next to the field(s) that you want to change, which is typically the Artist field (or perhaps the Genre field).

5. **Click OK to make the change.**

iTunes changes the field for the entire selection of songs.

You can edit the song information *before* importing the audio tracks from a CD. The edited track information for the CD imports with the music. (What's interesting is that when you access the library without the audio CD, the edited version of the track information is still there — iTunes remembers CD information from the CDs that you inserted before. Even if you don't import the CD tracks, iTunes remembers the edited song information until the next time you insert that audio CD.)

Adding Liner Notes and Ratings for Individual Songs

Although the track information grabbed from the Internet is enough for identifying songs in your iTunes library, some facts might be incorrect, and you might want to write your own comments about a particular song.

After your songs import into the music library, locate a single song and choose File⇨Get Info. You see the Song Information window, as shown in Figure 6-3.

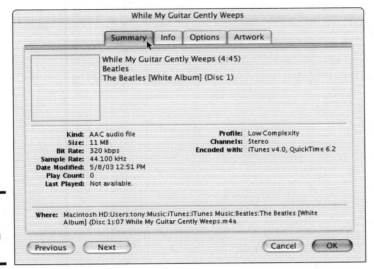

While My Guitar Gently Weeps

| Summary | Info | Options | Artwork |

While My Guitar Gently Weeps (4:45)
Beatles
The Beatles [White Album] (Disc 1)

Kind: AAC audio file
Size: 11 MB
Bit Rate: 320 kbps
Sample Rate: 44.100 kHz
Date Modified: 5/8/03 12:51 PM
Play Count: 0
Last Played: Not available.

Profile: Low Complexity
Channels: Stereo
Encoded with: iTunes v4.0, QuickTime 6.2

Where: Macintosh HD:Users:tony:Music:iTunes:iTunes Music:Beatles:The Beatles [White Album] (Disc 1):07 While My Guitar Gently Weeps.m4a

Previous   Next   Cancel   OK

Figure 6-3:
The Song
Information
window.

When you select one song, the Song Information window appears; when you select multiple songs, the Multiple Song Information window appears (refer to Figure 6-2). Be careful when selecting multiple songs and using the Get Info command.

The Song Information window offers the following tabs to click for different panes:

✦ **Summary:** The Summary tab (shown in Figure 6-3) offers useful information about the music file's format and location on your hard drive, and its file size, as well as information about the digital compression method (bit rate, sample rate, and so on).

✦ **Info:** The Info tab allows you to change the song name, artist, composer, album, genre, year, and comments, as shown in Figure 6-4.

✦ **Options:** The Options tab offers volume adjustment, choice of equalizer preset, ratings, and start and stop times for each song. You can assign up to five stars to a song (your own rating system, equivalent to the Top 40 charts).

✦ **Artwork:** The Artwork tab allows you to add or delete artwork for the song. (The iTunes Music Store supplies artwork with most songs.)

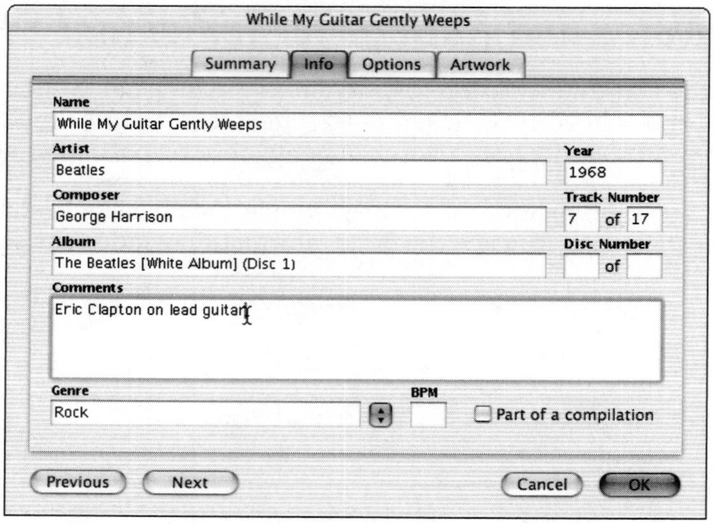

Figure 6-4: View and edit the song information on the Info tab.

Chapter 7: Organizing Music with Playlists

In This Chapter

✔ **Creating a playlist of multiple songs**

✔ **Creating a playlist of albums**

✔ **Creating a smart playlist**

✔ **Viewing and changing a smart playlist**

To organize your music for different operations, such as copying to an iPod or burning a CD, you make a *playlist* — a list of the songs.

You can use playlists to organize your music and pretend that you're a DJ. Select love songs from different albums to play the next time you need a romantic mood. Compile a list of surf songs for a trip to the beach. I create playlists specifically for use with an iPod on road trips. For other playlists, I combine songs from different albums based on themes or similarities.

You can create as many playlists, in any order, as you want. The files don't change, nor are they copied — the music files stay right where they are, and only their names are stored in the playlists. You can even create a smart playlist that automatically adds songs to itself based on the criteria that you set up.

Creating Playlists

The computer was made for dragging items visually to arrange a sequence. Save yourself a lot of browsing time by creating playlists — which, by the way, can really improve the way that you use music with an iPod. You can create playlists of individual songs or whole albums.

Playlists of songs

You can drag individual songs into a playlist and rearrange the songs quickly and easily. To create such a playlist, follow these steps:

1. **Click the + button (in the lower-left corner of the iTunes window) or choose File⇨New Playlist.**

   After you click the + button or choose the New Playlist command, a playlist called "untitled playlist" appears in the Source list.

2. **Type a name for the playlist.**

The playlist appears in the Source list, as shown in Figure 7-1. After you type a new name, iTunes automatically sorts it into alphabetical order in the Source list, underneath the preset smart playlists and other sources.

3. Select the library in the Source list and drag songs from the library to the playlist.

Figure 7-1: Create a playlist and add songs.

4. Drag song titles onto the new playlist.

The order of songs in the playlist is based on the order in which you dragged them to the list. To move a song up or down the list, drag it. You can move a group of songs at once by selecting them before you start dragging.

You can drag songs from one playlist to another. ***Remember:*** Only links are copied, not the actual files. Besides dragging songs, you can also rearrange a playlist by sorting the list — click the column heading for Song Name, Time, Artist, and so on. And when you double-click a playlist, it opens in its own window, displaying the song list.

To create a playlist quickly, select multiple songs at once, and then choose File➪New Playlist from Selection. You can then type a name for the playlist in the Source panel.

To delete a playlist, right-click its name in the Source list and choose Clear from the shortcut menu.

Playlists of albums

You might want to play entire albums of songs without having to select each album. To create a playlist of entire albums in a particular order, follow these steps:

1. Create a new playlist.

Create a playlist by clicking the + button under the Source list or choosing File➪New Playlist. Type a name for the new playlist in the Source panel.

2. **Select the library in the Source list and click the Browse button to find the artist.**

   The Album list appears in the right panel.

3. **Drag the album name over the playlist name.**

4. **Select and drag each subsequent album name over the playlist name.**

   Each time you drag an album, iTunes automatically lists the songs in the proper track sequence.

You can rename a playlist at any time by clicking its name and typing a new one, just like any filename in the Finder.

Viewing a Smart Playlist

Near the top of the Source list, indicated by a gear icon, you can find what Apple (and everyone else) calls a *smart* playlist. iTunes comes with a few sample smart playlists, such as the My Top Rated playlist, and you can create your own. Smart playlists add songs to themselves based on prearranged criteria. For example, as you rate your songs, the My Top Rated playlist changes to reflect your new ratings. You don't have to set anything up — the My Top Rated playlist is already defined for you.

The smart playlists are actually ignorant of your taste in music. You can create one that grabs all the songs from 1966, only to find that the list includes "Eleanor Rigby," "Strangers in the Night," "Over Under Sideways Down," and "River Deep, Mountain High" (in no particular order) — which you might not want to hear at the same time. You might want to fine-tune your criteria.

Creating a smart playlist

To create a new smart playlist, choose File⇨New Smart Playlist. The Smart Playlist window appears (shown in Figure 7-2), giving you the following choices for setting criteria:

Figure 7-2:
Set criteria
for your own
smart
playlist.

✦ **Match the Following Condition:** You can select any of the song information categories from the first drop-down list and select an operator, such as the greater-than or less-than operators, from the second drop-down list. Combined, the two criteria express a condition: `Year is greater than 1966` or something like that. You can also add multiple conditions by clicking the + button and deciding whether to match all or any of the conditions that you entered.

✦ **Limit To:** You can make the smart playlist a specific duration, measured by the number of songs, time, or size in megabytes or gigabytes. The songs can be selected by various methods, such as random, most recently played, and so on.

Limiting a smart playlist can be useful. You can limit it to what can fit on a CD or to the length of a drive or jogging exercise with an iPod.

✦ **Match Only Checked Songs:** This option selects only songs that have a black check mark beside them, along with the rest of the criteria. Selecting and deselecting songs is an easy way to fine-tune your selection for a smart playlist.

✦ **Live Updating:** This allows iTunes to automatically update the playlist continually as you add or remove songs from the library.

After setting up the criteria, click OK to create the smart playlist. iTunes creates the playlist with a gear icon and the name *untitled playlist*. You can click in the playlist in the Source panel and type a new name for it.

Editing a smart playlist

To edit a smart playlist supplied by Apple, select the playlist and choose File⇨Edit Smart Playlist. The Smart Playlist window appears with the criteria for the smart playlist.

You might want to modify the smart playlist so that songs with a higher rating are picked — simply add another star or two to the My Rating criteria.

You can also choose to limit the playlist to a certain number of songs that are selected by various methods, such as random, most recently played, and so on.

A smart playlist for recent additions

Setting up multiple criteria gives you the opportunity to create playlists that are way smarter than the ones supplied with iTunes. For example, I created a smart playlist with criteria shown in Figure 7-2 that does the following:

✔ Adds any song added to the library in the past week that *also* has a rating greater than three stars.

✔ Limits the playlist to 72 minutes of music to fit on an audio CD and refines the selection to the most recently added if the entire selection becomes greater than 72 minutes.

✔ Matches only selected songs and performs live updating.

CHECK IT OUT

Organizing Music
with Playlists

Selecting a Playlist on an iPod

When you update an iPod, the playlist is copied to the iPod. Playlists make playing a selection of songs or albums in a specific order easy. The playlist plays from the first song selected to the end. Follow these steps to play a playlist on an iPod:

1. **Select the Playlists item from the iPod main menu.**

The Playlists item is at the top of the main menu and might already be highlighted. If not, scroll the main menu until Playlists is highlighted, and then press the Select button. The Playlists menu appears.

2. **Select a playlist.**

The playlists are listed in alphabetical order. Scroll the Playlists menu until the playlist name is highlighted, and then press the Select button. A list of songs in the playlist appears.

3. **Select a song from the list to start playing.**

The songs in the playlist are in playlist order (the order defined for the playlist in iTunes). Scroll the list until the song name is highlighted, and then press the Select button. The artist and song name appear. Highlight the first song to play and press the Select button to start playing.

Chapter 8: Choosing an Encoding Format

In This Chapter

✔ Finding out the quality and space tradeoffs with sound encoders

✔ Understanding how encoders use compression

✔ Choosing the appropriate encoder and importing settings

✔ Changing your importing preferences

✔ Customizing the AAC, MP3, ALE, AIFF, and WAV encoders

✔ Converting songs to another encoding format

*Y*ou can specify quality settings to your liking, but as you discover more about digital audio technology, you'll find that you have decisions to make about your music library. This chapter helps you make them. You might be tempted to trade quality for space — that is, importing music at average- or low-quality settings and small file sizes (which allows you to put more songs on your hard drive and iPod). This might make you happy today, but what about tomorrow, when iPods and hard drives double or triple in capacity?

On the other hand, you might be very picky about the sound quality of your music, and with an eye toward future generations of iPods and cheap hard drives, you might decide to import music at the highest possible quality settings and large file sizes. (You could then later convert those large, high-quality songs to make lower-quality, space-saving copies for iPods and other uses.)

This chapter explains which music encoding and compression formats to use for higher quality and which to use for cramming more songs into the same space. It also provides the nuts-and-bolts details on changing your importing settings to customize each type of encoder, importing sounds other than music, and converting songs from one format to another. With the variety of settings for music encoders that iTunes offers, you can import a music collection that is sure to impress your audiophile friends.

Trading Quality for Space

The encoding format and settings you choose for importing music when ripping a CD affect sound quality and hard drive space on your computer. The format and settings might also affect the ability to play the music files on other types of players and computers.

Some encoding formats compress the music; others do not. Compression reduces the sound quality because it throws away information to make the file smaller. The amount of compression depends on the bit rate you choose, as well as the encoding format and other options.

More compression means the files are smaller but music quality is poorer. Less compression means better quality, but the files are larger. The size of files is also an issue with the iPod: Playing larger files takes more power because the hard drive inside the iPod has to refresh its memory buffers more quickly to process more information as the song plays.

I prefer a higher-quality sound overall, and I typically don't use the lower-quality settings for encoders except for voice recordings. I can hear differences in music quality at the higher compression levels and I'd rather go out and buy an additional hard drive to store my music collection if necessary.

Choosing an Encoder

I spare you the techno-speak about digital music file formats and get right to the ones you need to know about. iTunes offers five encoders that you can use to convert your music to a digital file:

✦ **AAC Encoder:** All your purchased music from the iTunes Music Store comes in the AAC format. I recommend it for all uses except when ripping your own CDs in order to burn new audio CDs. Technically known as MPEG-4 Advanced Audio Coding, AAC is a higher-quality format than MP3, comparable to CD quality. (*MPEG* stands for Moving Picture Experts Group, a body that recognizes compression standards for video and audio.) I think AAC offers the best tradeoff of space and quality. It is suitable (though not as good as AIFF) for burning to an audio CD and excellent for playing in an iPod or from a hard drive. However, as of this writing, only Apple products support it — you can play AAC files on an iPod, but you can't play them on other portable MP3 players.

✦ **AIFF Encoder:** The Audio Interchange File Format (AIFF) is the standard digital format for uncompressed sound on a Mac, and it provides the highest-quality representation of the sound. Use AIFF if you plan to burn songs to an audio CD. Mac-based digital sound-editing programs import and export AIFF files, and you can edit and save in AIFF format with absolutely no loss in quality. AIFF files take up enormous amounts of hard drive and iPod space because they're uncompressed.

✦ **Apple Lossless Encoder:** The ALE format offers as high a quality of sound as AIFF and uses less space. The drawback of this format, however, is that files encoded with ALE can only be played on iTunes software, Quick-Time, and iPods with a dock connector.

✦ **MP3 Encoder:** The MPEG-1, Layer 3 format, also known as MP3, is supported almost everywhere. Use the MP3 format for songs you intend to send to others or to listen to on a portable MP3 player or an iPod. The MP3 format offers quite a lot of different compression and quality settings, so you can fine-tune the format to get better quality, sacrificing hard drive space as you dial up the quality. Use the MP3 format for a song you intend to burn on an MP3 CD.

✦ **WAV Encoder:** Waveform Audio File Format (WAV) is a digital audio standard that Windows-based PCs can understand and manipulate. Like AIFF, WAV is uncompressed and provides the highest-quality representation of the sound. Use WAV if you plan on burning the song to an audio CD or using it with PC-based digital sound-editing programs that can import and export WAV files. WAV files take up enormous amounts of hard drive space because they're uncompressed.

If you want to share your music with someone who uses a portable MP3 player other than an iPod, you can import or convert songs with the MP3 Encoder. As an iPod user, you can use the higher-quality AAC Encoder to produce files that are either the same size as their MP3 counterparts but higher in quality, or the same quality but smaller in size.

To have the best possible quality you can have for future growth, you might want to consider importing music at the highest possible quality, using the uncompressed AIFF or WAV Encoders, and then converting the music files to a lesser-quality format for use in the iPod or other devices. I describe how to convert music later in this chapter.

Manic Compression Has Captured Your Song

Everyone hears the effects of compression differently. You might not hear any problem with compressed audio that someone else says is tinny or lacking in depth. This is because the audio compression methods that are good at reducing space have to throw away information. In techno-speak, these methods are known as *lossy* (as opposed to *lossless*) compression algorithms. Further compressing an already compressed music file by converting a song reduces the quality significantly. Not only that, but after the song is compressed, you can't uncompress the song back to its original quality — the song is essentially locked into that format.

MP3 and its new, advanced Apple-sponsored cousin AAC, use two basic lossy methods to compress audio: removing non-audible frequencies and the less important signals. For non-audible frequencies, the compression removes what you supposedly can't hear (although this is a subject for eternal debate). For example, if a background singer's warble is drowned out by a rhythm guitar playing a chord, the compression algorithm loses the singer's sound while maintaining the guitar's sound.

Within the sound spectrum of frequencies that can be heard by humans, some frequencies are considered to be less important in terms of rendering fidelity. Removing specific frequencies is likely to be less damaging to your music than other types of compression, depending on how you hear things. In fact, your dog might stop getting agitated at songs that contain ultra-high frequencies that you can't hear (such as the ending of "Day in the Life" by the Beatles).

Deciding Importing Settings

The AAC and MP3 formats compress music at different quality settings. iTunes enables you to set the bit rate for importing, which determines how many bits (of digital music information) can travel during playback in a given second. Measured in kilobits per second (Kbps), you need to use a higher bit rate (such as 192 or 320 Kbps) for higher quality, which of course increases the file size.

Variable Bit Rate encoding (VBR) is a technique that varies the number of bits used to store the music, depending on the complexity of the sound. While the quality of VBR is endlessly debated, it's useful when set to the Highest setting because VBR can encode at up to the maximum bit rate of 320 Kbps in those rare cases where the sound requires it, while keeping the rest at a lower bit rate.

iTunes also enables you to control the sample rate during importing, which is the number of times per second the sound waveform is captured digitally (or *sampled*). Higher sample rates yield higher-quality sound and large file sizes. However, never use a higher sample rate than the rate used for the source. CDs use a 44.100 kHz rate, so choosing a higher rate is unnecessary unless you convert a song that was recorded from digital audiotape (DAT) or directly into the computer at a high sample rate, and you want to keep that sample rate.

Another setting to consider during importing is the Channel choice. Stereo, which offers two channels of music for left and right speakers, is the norm for music. However, mono — monaural or single-channel — was the norm for pop records before the mid-1960s. (Phil Spector was known for his high-quality monaural recordings, and the early Rolling Stones records are in mono.) Monaural recordings take up half the space of stereo recordings when digitized. Choose the Auto setting to have iTunes use the appropriate setting for the music.

Most likely you want to keep stereo recordings in stereo, and mono recordings in mono, and the Auto setting guarantees that. But you can also use the Joint Stereo mode of the MP3 Encoder to reduce the amount of information per channel. Joint Stereo mode removes information that is identical in both channels of a stereo recording, using only one channel for that information, while the other channel carries unique information. At bit rates of 128 Kbps and below, this mode can improve the sound quality. On the other hand, I rarely (if ever) import music at such a low bit rate, which is useful mostly for voice recordings.

You might want to change your import settings before ripping CDs, depending on the type of music, the source of the recording, or other factors, such as whether you plan to copy the songs to an iPod or burn an audio or MP3 CD. The music encoders offer general quality settings, but you can also customize the encoders and change those settings to your liking. iTunes remembers your custom settings until you change them again.

Customizing the Encoder Settings

To change your encoder and quality settings and other importing preferences before ripping an audio CD or converting a file, follow these steps:

1. **Choose Edit⇨Preferences; in the Preferences dialog box that appears, click the Importing tab.**

2. **Choose the encoding format you want to convert the song into and the settings for that format.**

The drop-down lists help you make your changes. The Setting drop-down list offers different settings depending on your choice of encoder in the Import Using drop-down list. See the sections on each encoding format later in this chapter for details on settings.

3. **Click OK to accept changes.**

   After changing your importing preferences, and until you change them again, iTunes uses these preferences whenever it imports or converts songs.

Changing AAC Encoder settings

I recommend using the AAC Encoder for everything except music you intend to burn on a CD. AAC offers the best trade-off of space and quality for hard drives and iPods.

The AAC Encoder offers only two choices: High Quality and Custom, as shown in Figure 8-1. You might want to use the High Quality setting for most music, but for very complex music (such as jazz and classical), you might want to fine-tune the AAC Encoder settings. To customize your AAC Encoder settings, choose Custom from the Setting drop-down list.

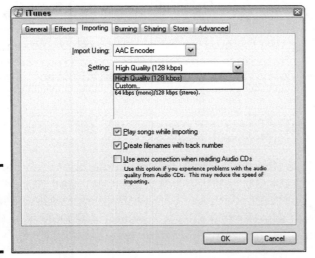

Figure 8-1:
Customize
the settings
for the AAC
Encoder.

The custom settings for AAC, as shown in Figure 8-2, allow you to change the following:

✦ **Stereo Bit Rate:** This drop-down list enables you to select the bit rate at which you want the song encoded. Select a higher bit rate for higher quality, which also increases the file size. 320 Kbps is the highest-quality setting for this format; 128 Kbps is considered high quality.

✦ **Sample Rate:** Use this drop-down list to set the sample rate. Higher sample rates yield higher-quality sound and large file sizes.

If you're converting songs to AAC format from a CD, select the 44.100 kHz option from the Sample Rate drop-down list.

✦ **Channels:** This drop-down list enables you to choose whether you want the song to be encoded as stereo or mono. Stereo offers two channels of music for left and right speakers, whereas mono offers only one channel but takes up half the space of stereo recordings when digitized. Select the Auto option to have iTunes use the appropriate setting for the music.

Figure 8-2:
Set the AAC Encoder to import with the highest bit rate and with automatic detection of sample rate and channels.

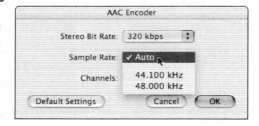

Changing MP3 Encoder settings

Although I prefer using the AAC Encoder for music I play on my iPod, other portable MP3 players as of this writing don't support the AAC format. You might want to use the MP3 Encoder for other reasons than compatibility with a portable MP3 player, such as having more control over the compression parameters and compatibility with other applications and players that support MP3.

The MP3 Encoder offers four choices for the Setting drop-down list on the Importing tab of the Preferences dialog box:

✦ **Good Quality (128 Kbps):** Certainly fine for audio books, comedy records, and old scratchy records. You might even want to go lower in bit rate (Kbps stands for kilobits per second) for voice recordings.

✦ **High Quality (160 Kbps):** Most people consider this high enough for most popular music, but I go higher with my music.

✦ **Highest Quality (192 Kbps):** High enough for just about all types of music.

✦ **Custom:** To fine-tune the MP3 Encoder settings, select the Custom setting. You can customize the MP3 settings to increase the quality of the sound while also keeping the file size low.

The MP3 Encoder offers a boatload of choices in its custom settings dialog box (see Figure 8-3):

✦ **Stereo Bit Rate:** Select a higher bit rate for higher quality (which increases the file size) from this drop-down list. The most common bit rate for MP3 files you find on the Web is 128 Kbps. Lower bit rates are more appropriate for voice recordings or sound effects.

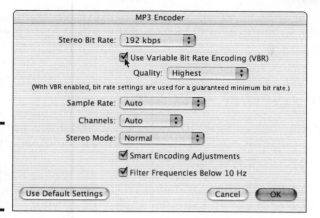

Figure 8-3:
Customize
the settings
for the MP3
Encoder.

I recommend at least 192 Kbps for most music, and I use 320 Kbps, the maximum setting, for songs I play on my iPod.

✦ **Use Variable Bit Rate Encoding (VBR):** This option helps keep file size down, but quality might be affected. VBR varies the number of bits used to store the music depending on the complexity of the sound. If you use the Highest setting for VBR, iTunes encodes at up to the maximum bit rate of 320 Kbps in sections of songs where the sound is complex enough to require a high bit rate, while keeping the rest of the song at a lower bit rate to save file space. The lower limit is set by the rate you choose in the Stereo Bit Rate drop-down list.

Some audiophiles swear by VBR; others never use it because they believe it affects sound quality. I use it only when importing at low bit rates, and I set VBR to its highest-quality setting.

The iPod can play VBR-encoded MP3 music; however, other MP3 players might not support VBR.

✦ **Sample Rate:** Select a higher sample rate from this drop-down list to get higher-quality sound (and larger file sizes). However, never use a higher sample rate than the rate used for the source — CDs use a 44.100 kHz rate, so choosing a higher rate is unnecessary.

✦ **Channels:** Select Stereo, Mono, or Auto from this drop-down list.

✦ **Stereo Mode:** This drop-down list offers additional options for encoding stereo files. The Normal option is just what you think it is — normal stereo. Choose the Joint Stereo option to make the file smaller by removing information that is identical in both channels of a stereo recording, using only one channel for that information while the other channel carries unique information. At bit rates of 128 Kbps and below, this mode can actually improve the sound quality. However, I typically don't use the Joint Stereo mode when using a high-quality bit rate.

✦ **Smart Encoding Adjustments:** Select this option to have iTunes analyze your MP3 encoding settings and music source and change your settings as needed to maximize the quality of the encoded files.

✦ **Filter Frequencies Below 10 Hz:** Select this option to remove the low frequencies (those below 10 Hz). Most people don't notice when these low tones are missing. Filtering inaudible frequencies helps reduce the file size with little or no perceived loss in quality. However, I think removal detracts from the overall feeling of the music, and I prefer not to filter frequencies.

Converting Songs to Another Encoder

Converting a song from one encoder to another is useful if you want to use one encoder for one purpose, such as burning a CD, and another encoder for another purpose, such as playing on your iPod.

You want to use different encoding formats if you have a discerning ear and you want to burn a CD of songs and also use the songs on your iPod. You can first import and then burn AIFF-encoded songs to a CD, and then convert the songs to AAC or MP3 format, which are compressed formats. You can then save space by deleting the original AIFF versions.

 You can tell what format a song is in by selecting it and choosing File⇨Get Info. The Summary tab displays what kind of music file the song is and the format it's in. You might want to keep track of formats by creating CD-AIFF version and iPod-MP3 version playlists for different formats.

To convert a song to another format, follow these steps:

1. **Choose Edit⇨Preferences; in the Preferences dialog box that appears, click the Importing tab.**

2. **Choose the encoding format you want to convert the song into and the settings for that format.**

For example, if you're converting songs in the AIFF format to the MP3 format, you choose the MP3 format and its settings.

3. **Select the song(s) that you want to convert and choose Advanced⇨Convert Selection.**

The encoding format you chose in Step 2 appears in the menu: Convert Selection to MP3, Convert Selection to AAC, Convert Selection to AIFF, Convert Selection to Apple Lossless, or Convert Selection to WAV. Choose the appropriate menu operation to perform the conversion.

iTunes creates a copy of each song and converts the copy to the new format. Both the original and the copy are stored in your music library.

If you convert songs obtained from the Internet, you'll find that the most common bit rate for MP3 files is 128 Kbps, and choosing a higher stereo bit rate won't improve the quality — it only wastes space.

 This automatic copy-and-convert operation can be useful for converting an entire music library to another format. If you have a library of AIFF tunes, you can quickly copy and convert them to AAC or MP3 in one step, and then assign the AIFF songs to the AIFF-associated playlists for burning CDs, and assign MP3 or AAC songs to MP3 or AAC playlists that you intend to copy to your iPod.

Chapter 9: Equalizing the Sound in iTunes

In This Chapter

✓ Controlling the volume in iTunes

✓ Fine-tuning music playback

✓ Adjusting the preamp volume

✓ Creating and assigning equalizer presets to songs

✓ Cross-fading song playback

The Beach Boys were right when they sang "Good Vibrations" because that's what music is — vibrations conveyed to the ear through a medium such as air. The frequency of vibrations (or sound waves) per second is how the pitch of a particular sound is measured.

When you turn up the bass or treble on a home stereo system, you are actually increasing the volume, or intensity, of certain frequencies while the music is playing. You are not actually changing the music itself, just the way it's amplified and produced through speakers. On more sophisticated stereo systems, an equalizer with a bar-graph display replaces the bass and treble controls. An equalizer (EQ in audio-speak) enables you to fine-tune the volume of specific sound-spectrum frequencies. An equalizer gives you far greater control than merely adjusting the bass or treble controls.

If you are a discerning listener, you might fiddle with the equalizer settings a lot — perhaps even for each song. With iTunes, you only have to change those settings once, and you can then save those settings for that particular song. This chapter shows you how to make and save presets for the songs in your library.

Leveling the Volume for Songs

Some songs play more loudly than others, and occasionally, individual tracks within a CD are louder than others. Music CDs are all mastered differently, with large discrepancies in volume between songs on different albums. You can change the volume level at any time by sliding the volume slider in the upper-left section of the iTunes window. The maximum volume of the iTunes volume slider is the maximum set for the computer's sound.

To adjust the overall volume of a particular song, click a song to select it, and then choose File➪Get Info. In the Get Info dialog box, click the Options tab, and then drag the Volume Adjustment slider left or right to adjust the volume.

You can standardize the volume level of all the songs in your iTunes music library with the Sound Check option. To ensure that all the songs in your library that are ripped from CDs play at the same volume level, follow these steps:

1. **Choose Edit⇨Preferences.**

The Preferences dialog box appears.

2. **Click the Effects tab.**

3. **Select the Sound Check check box.**

iTunes sets the volume level for all songs according to the level of the slider.

4. **Click OK.**

Fine-Tuning Playback in iTunes

The iTunes equalizer allows you to fine-tune the specific sound spectrum frequencies in a more precise way than with bass and treble controls. You can use the equalizer to improve or enhance the sound coming through a particular stereo system and speakers. You might pick entirely different equalizer settings for car speakers, home speakers, and headphones.

With the equalizer settings, you can customize playback for different musical genres, listening environments, or speakers. To see the iTunes equalizer, click the Equalizer button, which is on the bottom-right side of the iTunes window.

Adjusting the preamp volume

The preamp in your stereo is the component that offers a volume control that applies to all frequencies equally. Volume knobs generally go up to 10 (except of course for Spinal Tap's preamps, which go to 11).

The iTunes equalizer, shown in Figure 9-1, offers a Preamp slider on the far left side. You can increase or decrease the volume in 3-decibel increments up to +/-12 dB. Decibels are units that measure the intensity (or volume) of the frequencies. You can adjust the volume while playing the music to hear the result right away.

Figure 9-1: The equalizer's Preamp slider adjusts the volume across all frequencies.

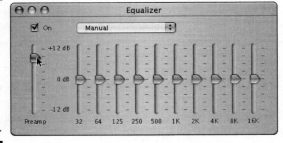

You might want to increase the preamp volume for songs recorded too softly, or decrease it for songs playing so loudly that you can hear distortion. If you want to make any adjustments to frequencies, you might need to adjust the preamp volume first if volume adjustment is needed, and then move on to the specific frequencies.

Adjusting frequencies

You can adjust frequencies in the iTunes equalizer by dragging sliders that look like mixing-board faders. The horizontal values across the equalizer represent the spectrum of human hearing. The deepest frequency ("Daddy sang bass") is 32 Hz (hertz); the mid-range frequencies are 250 Hz and 500 Hz, and the higher frequencies go from 1 kHz (kilohertz) to 16 kHz.

The vertical values on each bar represent decibels (dB), which measure the intensity of each frequency. Increase or decrease the frequencies at 3-decibel increments by dragging the sliders up and down. You can drag the sliders to adjust the frequencies while the music is playing and hear the effect immediately.

Utilizing an Equalizer Preset

iTunes offers *presets,* which are equalizer settings made in advance and saved by name. You can quickly switch settings without having to make changes to each frequency slider. iTunes comes with more than 20 presets of the most commonly used equalizer settings, including presets for musical genres from classical to rock. You can then assign the equalizer settings to a specific song or set of songs in your iTunes library. These settings copy to your iPod along with the songs when you update your iPod.

Select an equalizer preset, shown in Figure 9-2, from the drop-down list at the top of the Equalizer window. If a song is playing, you hear the effect in the sound immediately after choosing the preset.

Saving your own presets

You can create your own equalizer presets. Select the Manual option in the drop-down list at the top of the Equalizer window and make any changes you want to the frequencies. Then select the Make Preset option from the same drop-down list to save your changes. The Make Preset dialog box appears, as shown in Figure 9-3. Give your new preset a descriptive name and click OK. The name appears in the drop-down list from that point on — your very own preset.

You can rename or delete the presets by selecting the Edit List option from the drop-down list, which displays the Edit Presets dialog box for renaming or deleting presets, as shown in Figure 9-4. You can rename or delete any preset, including the ones supplied with iTunes.

Figure 9-2:
Choose one of the built-in equalizer presets.

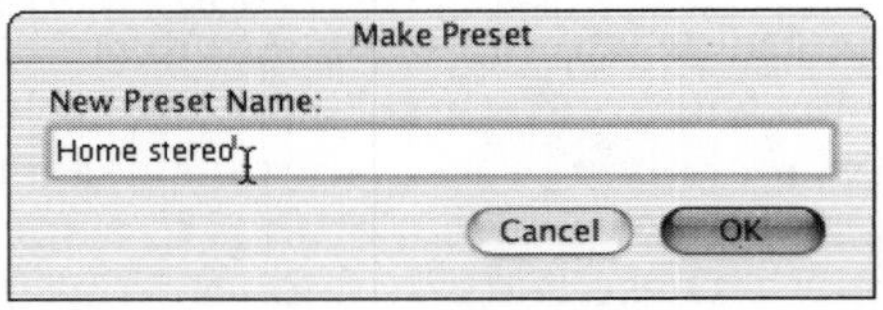

Figure 9-3:
Save your adjustments as your own preset.

Figure 9-4:
Edit the preset list.

Assigning equalizer presets to songs

One reason why you would want to bother creating equalizer presets is to assign the presets to songs. Then when you play the songs, the equalizer preset for each song takes effect. Assign an equalizer preset to a song or set of songs by following these steps:

1. **Choose Edit⇨View Options.**

The View Options dialog box appears, as shown in Figure 9-5.

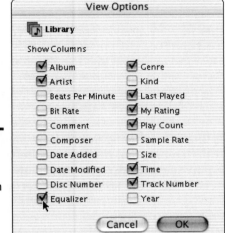

Figure 9-5:
View the
Equalizer
column with
the View
Options
dialog box.

2. **Select the Equalizer check box and click OK.**

The Equalizer column appears in the song list in the iTunes window.

3. **Locate a song in the song list and scroll the song list horizontally to see the Equalizer column.**

You can also open a playlist or locate a song in Browse view.

4. **Select a preset from the drop-down list in the Equalizer column.**

The Equalizer column has a tiny drop-down list that allows you to assign any preset to a song, as shown in Figure 9-6.

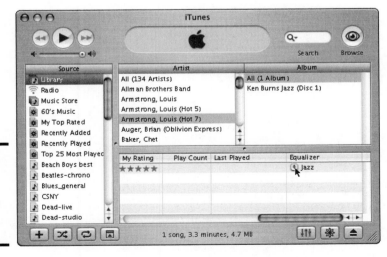

Figure 9-6:
Assign an
equalizer
preset to a
song in
iTunes.

When you transfer songs with presets to an iPod, the presets are used for playback.

Cross-Fading Songs

When playing songs in iTunes (either in your music library or on your iPod playing through your computer), you can fade the ending of one song into the beginning of the next one to slightly overlap songs, just like you hear on the radio. Ordinarily, iTunes is set to have a short *cross-fade* — a short amount of time between the end of the fade out from the first song and the start of the fade in to the second song.

You can change this cross-fade setting by choosing Edit⇨Preferences and then clicking the Effects tab. On the Effects tab of the Preferences dialog box, you can select the Crossfade Playback option, and then increase or decrease the amount of the cross-fade. Click OK to save your settings.

Chapter 10: Burning CDs

In This Chapter

- ✔ Choosing the right discs to burn
- ✔ Creating a burn playlist
- ✔ Setting the burn preferences
- ✔ Burning a disc
- ✔ Exporting song information
- ✔ Troubleshooting tips

*W*hen vinyl records were popular, rock radio disk jockeys who didn't like disco held disco meltdown parties. People were encouraged to throw their records into a pile to be burned or steamrolled into a vinyl glob. Despite it's title, this chapter isn't about that, nor is it about anything involving fire or heat.

Burning a compact disc (CD) actually refers to the process in which the recorder's laser meets the surface of the disc and creates a new impression loaded with digital information. People burn CDs for a lot of reasons — reason *numero uno* is to make a backup of songs on your computer. Perhaps having your 12 favorite love songs on one CD for your next special occasion with your sweetie is convenient. Or perhaps you want to burn a few CDs of obscure songs to impress your friends on your next big road trip. Blank discs are cheap — pennies to the dollar compared with the older technology of cassette tapes for taking music on the road.

This chapter boils everything down for you by telling you what kind of discs to use, where the discs play, how to get your playlist ready for burning, and what settings to use for burning. You find out what you need to know to make sure that your burns are not meltdowns.

Selecting Recordable CDs

After importing music into your iTunes library, you can arrange any songs in your library into a playlist and burn a CD by using that playlist (see Chapter 7). If you have a CD-R, CD-RW, or DVD-R drive (such as the Apple Super-Drive), and a blank CD-R (R is for *recordable*), you can create your own music CDs that play in most CD players. Blank CD-Rs are available in most electronics and computer stores, and you can also get them online from the Apple Store. Choose Help⇨Shop for iTunes Products to reach the Apple Store online.

The discs are called CD-Rs because they use a recordable format related to commercial CDs (which are not recordable, of course). CD-Rs play just like commercial CDs in most CD players, including cars and portables. The CD-R format is the most universal and is compatible with older players. I recommend that you stick with CD-Rs when burning CDs.

As for CD-RWs (rewriteable) that you can erase and reuse, CD players don't recognize them as music CDs. Apple's SuperDrive can also create data DVD-Rs and DVD-RWs, which are useful for holding data files, but you can only use these discs with computers — most commercial DVD players won't read data DVD-R or DVD-RW.

CDs encoded in the MP3 format can play on the new consumer MP3 disc players and combination CD/MP3 players, as well as on computers that recognize MP3 CDs.

What You Can Fit on a CD-R

You can fit up to 74 minutes of music on high-quality CD-Rs (some can go as high as 80 minutes). You measure the amount of music in minutes and seconds because the Red Book encoding format for audio CDs and CD-Rs compresses the music information. Although CD-Rs (and CD-RWs) hold about 650MB of data, the actual storage of music information varies. The sound files on your hard drive might take up more space but still fit within the 650MB confines of the CD.

MP3 discs can hold more than 12 hours' worth of music. You read that right — 12 hours on one disc. Now you know why MP3 discs are popular. MP3 discs are essentially CD-Rs with MP3 files stored on them.

The little Red Book that launched an industry

The typical audio CD and CD-R uses the CD-DA (compact disc, digital audio) format, which is known as *Red Book* — not something from Chairman Mao, but a document, published in 1980, that provides the specifications for the CD standard that was developed by Sony and Philips. According to legend, this document was in a binder with red covers.

Also according to legend, in 1979, Norio Ohga, honorary chairman and former CEO of Sony (who also happens to be a maestro conductor), insisted that the CD format be able to hold Beethoven's *Ninth Symphony* (which is a whopping 74 minutes and 42 seconds).

CD-DA defines audio data digitized at 44,100 samples per second (44.1 kHz) and in a range of 65,536 possible values (16 bits). Each second of hi-fi stereo sound requires almost 1.5 million bits of storage space. Data on a CD-DA is organized into sectors (the smallest possible separately addressable block) of information. CD data isn't arranged in distinct physical units; data is organized into frames that are each 1/75 of a second. These frames are intricately interleaved so that damage to the disc doesn't destroy any single frame, but only small parts of many frames.

To import music into the computer from an audio CD, you have to convert the music to digital sound files by using a program such as iTunes. When you burn an audio CD, iTunes converts the sound files into the CD-DA format as it burns the disc.

If you have a DVD (digital versatile disc) burner, such as the Apple Super-Drive, you can burn data DVD-Rs or DVD-RWs to use with other computers. This approach is suitable for making backup copies of music files or even any data files. DVD-Rs can hold about 4.7GB, which is enough to hold part of a music library.

To burn a CD-RW or DVD-RW that already has data on it, you must first erase it by reformatting it with the application supplied with the drive. CD-RWs and DVD-RWs work with computers but don't work with consumer players.

Creating a Burn Playlist

To burn a CD, you must first define a playlist for the CD. See Book V, Chapter 7 to find out how to create a playlist. You can use songs encoded in any format that iTunes supports. However, you get higher-quality music with the uncompressed formats AIFF and WAV.

If your playlist includes music purchased from the iTunes Music Store or other online stores in the protected AAC encoding format, some rules might apply. For example, the iTunes Music Store allows you to burn ten copies of the same playlist containing protected songs to an audio CD, but no more. You can, however, create a new playlist and copy the protected songs to the new playlist, and then burn more CDs with the songs.

Calculating how much music to use

When you create a playlist, you find out how many songs can fit on the CD by totaling the durations of the songs, using time as your measure. You can see the size of a playlist by selecting the playlist. The number of songs, the amount in time, and the amount in megabytes all appear at the bottom of the iTunes window, as shown in Figure 10-1.

Figure 10-1:
Check the duration of the playlist below the song list.

Size of playlist

In Figure 10-1, the selected playlist has 23 songs that total 1.1 hours and 724.1MB. You might notice the discrepancy between the megabytes (724.1MB) and what you can fit on an audio CD (650MB). Although a CD holds only 650MB, the music is compressed and stored in a special format known as CD-DA (known as *Red Book*). Thus, you can fit a bit more than 650MB of AIFF-encoded sound because AIFF is uncompressed. I can fit 1.1 hours (66 minutes) of music on a 74-minute or 80-minute CD-R with many minutes to spare.

Always use the actual duration in hours, minutes, and seconds to calculate how much music you can fit on an audio CD — either 74 or 80 minutes for blank CD-Rs. Leave at least an extra minute for gaps between songs.

You do the *opposite* for an MP3 CD — use the actual megabytes to calculate how many songs to fit — up to 650MB for a blank CD-R. You can fit lots more music on an MP3 CD-R because you use MP3-encoded songs rather than uncompressed AIFF songs.

Switching import encoders for audio CD-R

Before you rip an audio CD of songs that you want to burn to an audio CD-R, you might want to change the import settings. Check out Book V, Chapter 8 if you need to do so. With the exception of iTunes Music Store songs provided in the protected AAC format (which you can't convert anyway), use AIFF or WAV for songs from audio CDs if you want to burn your own audio CDs with music.

AIFF is the standard digital format for uncompressed sound on a Mac, and you can't go wrong with it. WAV is basically the same thing for Windows. Both the AIFF Encoder and the WAV Encoder offer the same custom settings window, with settings for sample rate, sample size, and channels. You can choose the automatic settings, and iTunes automatically detects the proper sample rate, size, and channels from the source.

The Apple AAC music file format is a higher-quality format than MP3, comparable to CD quality. I think it offers the best trade-off of space and quality. All your purchased music from the iTunes Music Store comes in this format. It is suitable (though not as good as AIFF) for burning to an audio CD.

Switching import encoders for MP3 CD-R

MP3 discs are essentially CD-Rs with MP3 files stored on them. Consumer MP3 CD players are now on the market, including hybrid models that play both audio CDs and MP3 CDs. You can fit up to 12 hours of music on a CD by using the MP3 format. The amount of music varies with the encoding options and settings that you choose, as does the quality of the music. If you rip an audio CD, you can set the importing options to precisely the type of MP3 file that you want (see Chapter 9 of Book V).

You can use only MP3-encoded songs to burn an MP3 CD-R. Any songs not encoded in MP3 are skipped. Audible books and Spoken-Word titles are provided in an audio format that uses security technologies, including encryption, to protect purchased content. You can't burn an MP3 CD-R with Audible files — any Audible files in a burn playlist are skipped when you burn an MP3 CD-R.

Setting the Burning Preferences

Burning a CD is a simple process, and getting it right the first time is a good idea — when you burn a CD-R, it's *done,* right or wrong. You can't erase content as you can with a CD-RW. But you can't play a CD-RW in most CD players. Fortunately, CD-Rs are cheap.

Setting the sound check and gaps

Musicians do a sound check before every performance to check the volume of microphones and instruments and its effect on the listening environment. The aptly named Sound Check option in iTunes allows you to do a sound check on your tunes to bring them all in line, volume-wise.

To have all the songs in your library play at the same volume level all the time, choose Edit➪Preferences and click the Effects tab to see the Effects Preferences window. Select the Sound Check check box, which sets all the songs to the current volume controlled by the iTunes volume slider.

After turning on Sound Check, you can burn your audio CD-R so that all the songs play back at the same volume, just like they do in iTunes in your computer. Choose Edit➪Preferences, and then click the Burning tab. Select the Use Sound Check check box, which you can see in Figure 10-2. This option is active only if you're already using the Sound Check option in the Effects preferences.

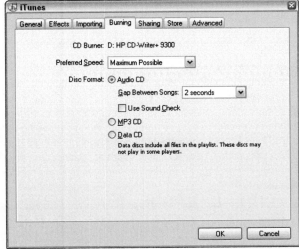

Figure 10-2:
Select the Use Sound Check check box for the CD-R burn.

Consistent volume for all tracks makes the CD-R sound professional. Another professional touch is an appropriate gap between songs, just like commercial CDs. Follow these steps to control the amount of the gap between the songs on your audio CD-Rs (not MP3 CD-Rs):

1. **Choose iTunes⇨Preferences, and then click the Burning tab in the Preferences window.**

   The Burning Preferences window displays, as shown in Figure 10-3.

2. **Select an amount from the Gap Between Songs drop-down list.**

   You can select from a gap of none to five seconds.

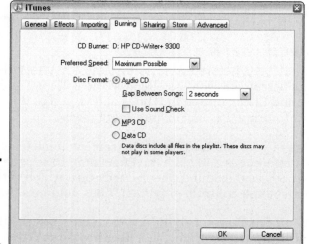

Figure 10-3:
Set the gap between songs for an audio CD.

Setting the format and recording speed

Before burning a CD-R, you have to set the disc format and the recording speed. Choose iTunes⇨Preferences and then click the Burning button in the Preferences window.

Abiding by the copyright laws

The coming years will see an epic battle between the people who own the copyrights to music and video files and the people who download the files from the Internet and copy them to and from CDs and DVDs. Some argue that you shouldn't be able to legally burn songs to a CD. Whatever the argument, one thing is certain: Burning songs to a CD and then reselling the CD is a clear violation of the copyright laws. Also remember that many people make a living by earning income or collecting royalties from the sale of songs and videos that are now being copied freely over the Internet. The artists deserve your respect and consideration.

The Disc Format setting in the Burning Preferences window (refer to Figure 10-2) offers three choices:

✦ **Audio CD:** You can burn a normal audio CD of up to 74 or 80 minutes (depending on the type of blank CD-R) by using any iTunes-supported music files, including songs bought from the iTunes Music Store. Although connoisseurs of music might use AIFF-encoded or WAV-encoded music to burn an audio CD, you can also use songs in the AAC and MP3 formats.

✦ **MP3 CD:** You can burn an MP3 CD with songs encoded in the MP3 format, but no other formats are supported.

✦ **Data CD or DVD:** You can burn a data CD-R, CD-RW, DVD-R, or DVD-RW with the music files. You can use any encoding formats for the songs. Data discs don't play on most consumer CD players — they're meant for use with computers.

Blank CD-Rs are rated for recording at certain speeds. Normally iTunes detects the rating of a blank CD-R and adjusts the recording speed to fit. But if your blank CD-Rs are rated for a slower speed than your burner, or you're having problems creating CD-Rs, you can change the recording speed setting to match the CD's rating. Choose Edit⇨Preferences, and then click the Burning tab in the Preferences window. From the Preferred Speed drop-down list in the Burning Preferences window (refer to Figure 10-3), select a specific recording speed or the Maximum Possible option to set the recording speed to your burner's maximum speed.

Burning a Disc

After you set the burning preferences, you're ready to start burning. Follow these steps to burn a CD:

1. **Select the playlist that you want to burn and click the Burn Disc button or choose File⇨Burn Playlist to Disc.**

   A message appears telling you to insert a blank disc.

2. **Insert a blank disc.**

   iTunes immediately checks the media and displays a message in the status window that the disc is ready to burn.

3. **Click the Burn Disc button *again*.**

   This time, the button displays a radioactive symbol. The burn process begins. The radioactive button rotates while the burning takes place, and a progress bar appears with the names of the songs displayed as they burn to the disc.

Burning takes several minutes. You can cancel the operation at any time by clicking the X next to the progress bar. But canceling the operation isn't like undoing the burn. After the burn starts, you can't use the CD-R again.

If the playlist has more music than fits on the disc with the chosen format, iTunes burns as much as possible from the beginning of the playlist, cutting off the end. If you didn't calculate the amount of music right the first time, turn to "Calculating how much music to use," earlier in this chapter.

If you choose the MP3 CD format, iTunes skips over any songs in the playlist that aren't in the MP3 format.

Exporting Song Information for Liner Notes

Don't delete the playlist yet! You can export the song information for all the songs in the playlist to a text file, and then edit liner notes for the CD.

iTunes exports all the song information that you could possibly want into a text file. Select the songs or playlist and choose File⇨Export Song List to create a text file with song information. You can open this text file in a word-processing program, such as Microsoft Word. iTunes formats the information in a text (.txt) file so that you can easily import it into a database or spreadsheet program. You can change the formatting by manipulating the tab settings. (Tab stops are inserted between pieces of information.)

iTunes exports all the song information, which might be too much for your liner notes. Edit the liner notes by following these steps:

1. **Open the word-processing program while you're using iTunes.**

2. **Switch to iTunes, select the playlist, and choose Edit⇨View Options.**

   The View Options window opens.

3. **Select the columns that you want to appear in the song list.**

   To pick a column, select the check box next to the column heading. Any deselected column headings don't appear. *Note:* The Song Name column always appears in the listing and can't be removed.

4. **Select all the songs in the playlist and choose Edit⇨Copy.**

   To select all the songs in the playlist, click the first song and hold down Shift while clicking the last song to highlight all the songs.

5. **Switch to your word-processing program and choose Edit⇨Paste.**

   The liner notes appear in your word-processing program, as shown in Figure 10-4.

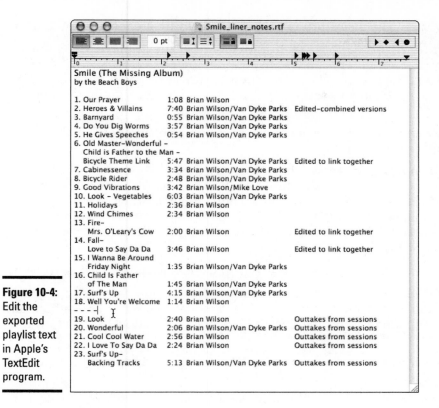

Figure 10-4:
Edit the
exported
playlist text
in Apple's
TextEdit
program.

Troubleshooting

Murphy's Law applies to everything, even something as simple as burning a CD-R. Don't think for a moment that you're immune to the whims and treacheries of Murphy, who in all his infinite wisdom pronounced that if anything *could* go wrong, it would go wrong. I cover some of the most common problems with burning discs in this section.

The best way to test your newly burned disc is to pop it right back into your SuperDrive or any CD-ROM drive, or try it on a consumer CD player. Audio CD-Rs play just like any commercial audio CD. MP3 CDs play fine on consumer MP3 CD players and also work in computers with CD-ROM and DVD drives.

If the CD works on your computer but not on a commercial CD player, you might have a compatibility problem with the commercial player and CD-Rs. I have a five-year-old CD player that doesn't play CD-Rs very well, and car players sometimes have trouble with them. If you have the following problems, try the appropriate solution:

✦ ***Problem:*** The disc won't burn.

   Solution: Perhaps you have a bum disc (which happens). Try another one.

✦ *Problem:* The disc stutters or doesn't play with a consumer CD player.

Solution: This happens often with older consumer players that don't play CD-Rs well. Try the disc in your computer's CD-ROM or DVD-ROM drive or SuperDrive. If it works there, and you set the format to Audio CD, you probably have a compatibility problem with your consumer player.

✦ *Problem:* The disc doesn't show tracks on a consumer CD player, or it ejects immediately.

Solution: Be sure to use the proper disc format — choose Edit⇨ Preferences and click the Burning tab to see the Disc Format setting in the Burning Preferences window. The Audio CD format works in just about all consumer CD players that play CD-Rs. MP3 CDs work in consumer MP3 CD players and computer CD-ROM and DVD drives. Data CDs or DVDs work only in computer drives.

✦ *Problem:* My computer went to sleep while burning and never woke up.

Solution: You've found a strange glitch that fortunately only applies to computers that are set to go into sleep mode. As a safety precaution, turn off sleep mode in the Energy Saver preferences window before starting a burn.

✦ *Problem:* Some songs in my playlist were skipped and not burned onto the disc.

Solution: Audio CD-Rs burn with songs that are encoded in any format, but you can use only MP3-encoded songs to burn an MP3 CD-R — any songs not encoded in MP3 are skipped. (Any Audible files are also skipped because they can't be put onto an MP3 CD.) If your playlist for an audio CD-R includes music purchased from the iTunes Music Store or other online stores in the protected AAC encoding format, some rules might apply — see "Creating a Burn Playlist," earlier in this chapter.

Burning CDs is a personal matter. Piracy isn't a technology issue — it's a behavior issue. Don't violate copyright law.

Chapter 11: Updating Your iPod with iTunes

In This Chapter

✔ Copying your entire iTunes music library

✔ Copying only certain playlists

✔ Copying only selected songs

✔ Setting up your iPod to update manually

✔ Copying music directly to your iPod

✔ Deleting music from your iPod

*i*Tunes is the software that puts music on your iPod (or more than just music — you can include audio books or anything stored as a sound file in iTunes). iTunes can fill your iPod very quickly with the tunes in your library.

If you're too busy to copy specific songs to your iPod, and your entire iTunes music library fits on your iPod anyway, why not just copy everything? Copying your library is just as fast as copying individual songs, if not faster, and you don't have to do anything except connect the iPod to the Mac. This chapter shows you how to set up iTunes to automatically update your iPod.

This chapter also shows how you can update your iPod manually, choosing which songs to copy. iTunes is flexible — you can use either option or *both* options to update your iPod. You can, for example, update automatically with all the songs in playlists, and then go into iTunes and copy other music not in playlists directly to your iPod, and delete songs from your iPod if you need to make room. This chapter explains how to set your preferences for updating and change them when you need to.

Changing Your Update Preferences

If you at some point changed your iPod preferences to update manually, you can change them back to update automatically any time, and vice versa. Change your iPod preferences by following these steps:

1. **Connect the iPod to your Mac through the Mac's FireWire connection.**

Your iPod must be connected for you to change the update preferences.

2. **Select the iPod name in the iTunes Source list.**

3. **Click the iPod options button on the bottom-right side of the iTunes window.**

The iPod Preferences window appears, as shown in Figure 11-1.

Figure 11-1:
Set your
preferences
with the
iPod
Preferences
window.

4. Select the update preferences that you want.

Set the update preferences by clicking OK on the iPod Preferences window, and then click OK to the warning message that appears. For example, if you select the Automatically Update All Songs and Playlists option, iTunes displays a confirmation message (see Figure 11-2).

Figure 11-2:
Confirm that
you want
to update
your music
library auto-
matically.

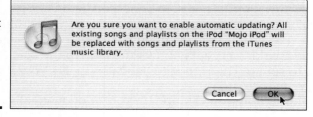

Updating Your iPod Automatically

Out of the box, the iPod updates itself automatically, *synchronizing* itself — the iPod matches your library exactly, song for song, playlist for playlist — with your music library. If you made changes in iTunes after the last time you synchronized, those changes are automatically made in the iPod when you synchronize again.

If you share an iPod and a large iTunes library with someone and you can't fit the entire library on your iPod, you can update automatically by playlist rather than the entire library. That way, when it's your turn to use the iPod, you can automatically erase all the music on the iPod associated with the other person's playlists and copy your playlists. The other person can do the same when you switch. You can update the iPod with different songs as often as you like.

Of course, because the music for your iPod is on your computer, someone erasing your music from the iPod isn't a big deal — you can update the iPod quickly with your music when it's your turn. Make backups of your music library regularly.

Before you actually connect your iPod to a Mac to automatically update, keep these things in mind:

✦ iTunes remembers your updating preferences from the last time that you updated your iPod. If you already set your preferences to update automatically, iTunes remembers and starts to automatically update your iPod. If you already set your preferences to update manually, iTunes remembers and makes your iPod active in the iTunes Source list.

✦ You can prevent your iPod from automatically updating by holding down the ⌘ and Option keys as you connect the iPod and keeping them held down until the iPod name appears in the iTunes Source list. This works even if you choose to automatically update the iPod in the Setup Assistant.

✦ If you connect your iPod to another Mac, you might be in for a surprise. When you connect an iPod that was previously linked to another Mac, iTunes displays this message: `This iPod is linked to another iTunes music library. Do you want to change the link to this iTunes music library and replace all existing songs and playlists on this iPod with those from this library?` If you don't want to change your iPod to have this other music library, click No. Otherwise, iTunes erases your iPod and updates your iPod with the other Mac's library. By clicking No, you change that computer's iTunes preferences to manually update, thereby avoiding automatic updating.

✦ Songs stored remotely (such as songs shared from other iTunes libraries on a network) aren't synchronized because they aren't physically on your computer. See Book V, Chapter 4 for more info on how to share music over a network with iTunes.

Updating the entire library

Your iPod is set up by default to automatically update itself from your iTunes library. Just follow these simple steps to set the updating process in motion:

1. **Connect the iPod to your Mac through the Mac's FireWire connection.**

When you connect the iPod to the Mac, your iPod automatically synchronizes with your iTunes music library.

2. **When the updating finishes, the iTunes status view says** `iPod update is complete` **(shown in Figure 11-3) and you can then click the iPod eject button, which appears in the lower-right corner of the iTunes window.**

You can also eject (or *unmount*) the iPod by dragging the iPod icon on the desktop to the Trash. After you drag it to the Trash, the iPod displays an `OK to disconnect` message. You can then disconnect the iPod from its dock or disconnect the dock from the computer.

While the updating is in progress, don't disconnect your iPod. The iPod displays a `Do not disconnect` warning. The iPod is a hard drive, after all, and hard drives need to be closed down properly so that you don't lose any critical data.

The update is finished.

iTunes

iPod update is complete.

Search   Browse

Source		Song Name	Time	Artist	Albu
Library		Don't Want You No More	2:25	Allman Brothers Band	Begi
Radio		It's Not My Cross To Bear	4:56	Allman Brothers Band	Begi
Music Store		Black Hearted Woman	5:18	Allman Brothers Band	Begi
Mojo iPod		Trouble No More	3:48	Allman Brothers Band	Begi
60's Music		Every Hungry Woman	4:17	Allman Brothers Band	Begi
My Top Rated		Dreams	7:17	Allman Brothers Band	Begi
Recently Added		Whipping Post	5:22	Allman Brothers Band	Begi
Recently Played		Revival	4:06	Allman Brothers Band	Begi
Top 25 Most Played		Don't Keep Me Wonderin'	3:31	Allman Brothers Band	Begi
Beach Boys best		Midnight Rider	2:58	Allman Brothers Band	Begi
Beatles-chrono		In Memory Of Elizabeth Reed	6:56	Allman Brothers Band	Begi
Blues_general		Hoochie Coochie Man	4:57	Allman Brothers Band	Begi
CSNY		Please Call Home	4:01	Allman Brothers Band	Begi
Dead-live					

Used: 12.49 GB   Free: 15.43 GB

2011 songs, 5.5 days, 12.45 GB

Figure 11-3: iTunes lets you know when the iPod finishes updating.

Eject button

Updating playlists

If you share an iPod with someone else, you can keep track of the music that you use in the iPod by including those songs or albums in playlists in your iTunes library, and then updating the iPod automatically with your playlists, deleting whatever was in the iPod before. To do this, set up the iPod to update only selected playlists automatically.

Before using this update option, create the playlists in iTunes (see Book V, Chapter 7) so that you can copy them to the iPod. Then follow these steps:

1. **Connect the iPod to your Mac through the Mac's FireWire connection.**

2. **Select the iPod name in the iTunes Source list.**

3. **Click the iPod options button.**

The iPod Preferences window appears (see Figure 11-4).

iPod Preferences

○ Automatically update all songs and playlists
● Automatically update selected playlists only:

☐ Recently Played
☐ Top 25 Most Played
☑ Beach Boys best
☑ Beatles-chrono
☑ Blues_general

○ Manually manage songs and playlists

☑ Open iTunes when attached
☑ Enable FireWire disk use
☐ Only update checked songs

Cancel   OK

Figure 11-4: Set up the iPod to automatically update with only the selected playlists.

4. **Select the Automatically Update Selected Playlists Only option.**

5. **In the list box, select the check box next to each playlist that you want to copy in the update.**

6. **Click OK.**

   iTunes automatically updates the iPod by erasing its contents and copying only the playlists that you selected in Step 5.

7. **When updating finishes, the iTunes status view says** `iPod update is complete`. **You can then click the iPod eject button, which appears in the lower-right corner of the iTunes window.**

Updating selected songs

You might want to update the iPod automatically, but only with selected songs — songs that have a black check mark. To use this method, you must first deselect the songs that you don't want to transfer. To deselect a song, click the black check mark so that it disappears. (Clicking it again makes it reappear, reselecting the song.)

You can quickly select or deselect an entire album by selecting an album in Browse view and holding down the ⌘ key.

After making your selections, follow these steps:

1. **Connect the iPod to your Mac through the Mac's FireWire connection.**

2. **Select the iPod name in the iTunes Source list.**

   You can select the iPod name even when it is grayed out.

3. **Click the iPod options button.**

   The iPod Preferences window appears (refer to Figure 11-1).

4. **Select the Automatically Update All Songs and Playlists option, and when the** `Are you sure you want to enable automatic updating?` **message appears, click OK.**

5. **Select the Only Update Checked Songs check box and click OK.**

   iTunes automatically updates the iPod by erasing its contents and copying only the songs in the iTunes library that are selected.

6. **When the updating finishes, the iTunes status view says** `iPod update is complete`. **You can then click the iPod eject button, which appears in the lower-right corner of the iTunes window.**

Updating Your iPod Manually

With manual updating, you can add music to your iPod directly by using iTunes, and you can delete music from your iPod as well. The iPod name appears in the iTunes Source list, and you can double-click it to open it, displaying the iPod playlists.

You might have one or more reasons for updating manually, but some obvious ones are the following:

✦ Your entire music library might be too big for your iPod, and therefore, you want to copy individual albums, songs, or playlists to the iPod directly.

✦ You want to share a single music library with several iPods, and you have different playlists that you want to copy to each iPod directly.

✦ You want to copy some music from another computer's music library, without deleting any music from your iPod.

✦ You want to edit the playlists and song information directly on your iPod without changing anything in your computer's library. See Book V, Chapter 7 to discover how to edit playlists and song information on your iPod.

✦ You want to play the songs on your iPod by using iTunes on the Mac, playing through the Mac's speakers.

When you set your iPod to update manually, the entire contents of the iPod are active and available in iTunes. You can copy music directly to your iPod, delete songs on the iPod, and edit the iPod playlists directly.

To set your iPod to update manually, follow these steps:

1. **Connect the iPod to your Mac, holding down the ⌘ and Option keys to prevent automatic updating.**

Continue holding the keys down until the iPod name appears in the iTunes Source list.

2. **Select the iPod name in the iTunes Source list.**

3. **Click the iPod Options button.**

The iPod Preferences window appears (refer to Figure 11-1).

4. **Check the Manually Manage Songs and Playlists option.**

iTunes displays the `Disabling automatic update requires manually unmounting the iPod before each disconnect` **message.**

5. **Click OK to accept the new iPod preferences.**

The iPod contents now appear active in iTunes and aren't grayed out.

Copying music directly

To copy music to your iPod directly, follow these steps (with your iPod connected to your Mac):

1. **Select the iTunes music library in the Source list.**

The library's songs appear in a list view or in Browse view.

2. **Drag items directly from your iTunes music library over the iPod name in the Source list, as shown in Figure 11-5.**

Figure 11-5:
Copy an album of songs directly from the iTunes library to the iPod.

When you copy a playlist, all the songs that are associated with the playlist copy along with the playlist itself. When you copy an album, all the songs in the album are copied.

3. **When the updating finishes, the iTunes status view says** `iPod update is complete`, **and you can then click the iPod eject button, which appears in the lower-right corner of the iTunes window.**

Deleting music on your iPod

With manual updating, you can delete songs from the iPod directly. An automatic update adds and deletes songs, but manual deletion is a nice option if you just want to go in and delete a certain song or an album to make room for more music.

To delete any song in the song list with your iPod set to manual updating, follow these steps:

1. **Select the iPod in the iTunes Source list.**

2. **Open the iPod's contents in iTunes.**

3. **Select a song or album on the iPod in iTunes, and then press Delete or choose Edit⇨Clear.**

   iTunes displays a warning to make sure that you want to do this; click OK to go ahead or Cancel to stop. If you want to delete a playlist, select the playlist and press Delete or choose Edit⇨Clear.

As in the iTunes library, if you delete a playlist, the songs themselves aren't deleted — they're still on your iPod unless you delete them from the iPod song list or update the iPod automatically with other songs or playlists.

Chapter 12: Editing on Your iPod

In This Chapter

✔ Creating playlists

✔ Editing and rearranging playlists

✔ Editing song information

The song information and playlists for your iPod are automatically copied to your iPod when you update the iPod. However, you might want to edit your iPod's music library separately, perhaps creating new playlists or changing the song information. This chapter describes how you can edit playlists and song information manually just on your iPod.

First you must connect your iPod to your Mac, open iTunes, and set your iPod to update manually, as I describe in Book V, Chapter 11.

Creating Playlists

You can create a playlist just on the iPod itself by using songs that are on the iPod. The songs must already be on the iPod. To create a new playlist, follow these steps:

1. **Select the iPod in the iTunes Source list and open the iPod contents.**

2. **Create a new playlist by clicking the + button in the lower-left corner of iTunes under the Source list or choosing File⇨New Playlist.**

    An untitled playlist appears in the Source list.

3. **Type a name for the untitled playlist.**

    The new playlist appears in the Source list under the iPod, as shown in Figure 12-1. After you type a new name, iTunes automatically sorts it into alphabetical order in the list.

4. **Click the name of the iPod in the Source list and drag songs from the iPod song list to the playlist.**

    You can also click the Browse button to find songs on the iPod more easily, as shown in Figure 12-2.

The order of songs in the playlist is based on the order in which you drag them to the list. You can rearrange the list by dragging songs within the playlist.

You can create smart playlists in exactly the same way as in the iTunes music library — read all about it in Book V, Chapter 7.

Figure 12-1:
Type a name for a new playlist created directly on the iPod.

Figure 12-2:
Add a song on the iPod to the iPod's new playlist.

Editing Playlists

To edit an existing playlist on your iPod, do the following:

1. **Select the iPod in the iTunes Source list and open the iPod contents.**

2. **Scroll the Source list to locate the playlist.**

   The iPod's playlists appear in the Source list under the iPod itself.

3. **Select the playlist to rearrange songs.**

4. **Click the name of the iPod in the Source list and drag more songs from the iPod song list to the playlist.**

   You can also click the Browse button to find songs more easily.

   The songs and albums that you drag to an iPod playlist must already be on the iPod — if you want to copy songs from your iTunes library, see Book V, Chapter 11.

Editing Song Information

With the iPod contents open in iTunes, you can edit song information just like you do in the iTunes library by scrolling down the song list and selecting songs.

After selecting the iPod in the Source list and opening its contents, click the Browse button. In Browse view, you can browse the iPod contents and find the songs by artist and album.

You can edit the Song Name, Artist, Album, Genre, and My Ratings information for the iPod songs directly in the columns in the song list. To edit song information, locate the song and click inside the text field of a column to type new text.

You might find it easier to edit this information by choosing File⇨Get Info and typing the text into the Song Info window, as shown in Figure 12-3.

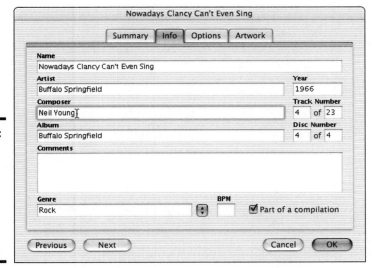

Figure 12-3:
Type the composer credits for a song on the iPod in the Song Info window.

Chapter 13: Locating and Playing Songs

In This Chapter

⌐ **Locating songs by artist, album, or playlist**

⌐ **Repeating and shuffling a song list**

⌐ **Creating on-the-go playlists**

⌐ **Changing the volume level**

⌐ **Bookmarking Audible books**

*A*fter you add music to your iPod, you can locate and play that music easily, browsing by artist, album, or even composer. Selecting a playlist is simplicity itself. And if you don't have playlists from iTunes (or you don't want to hear those playlists), you can create a temporary on-the-go playlist. This chapter shows you how.

Locating Songs

With so many songs on your iPod, finding a particular one can be hard (like trying to find "Needle in a Haystack" by the Velvelettes in the Motown catalog). In this section, I show you how to search for songs by artist, album, or playlist.

By artist

Your iPod organizes music by artist and within each artist by album. Follow these steps to locate a song by artist and then album:

1. Select the Browse item from the iPod main menu.

Scroll down the main menu until Browse is highlighted, and then press the Select button to select it. The Browse menu appears.

2. Select the Artists item.

The Artists item is at the top of the Browse menu and should already be highlighted; if not, scroll down the menu until Artists is highlighted, and then press the Select button. The Artists menu appears.

To browse by genre, select the Genres item, and then select a genre from the Genres menu to get a reduced list of artists that have songs in that genre (in alphabetical order).

3. Select an artist from the Artists menu.

The artists are listed in alphabetical order. Scroll down the Artists menu until the artist name is highlighted, and then press the Select button. The artist name menu appears.

4. Select the All item or the name of an album from the artist name's menu.

The All item is at the top of the menu and is already highlighted; you can press the Select button or scroll until an album name is highlighted and then press the Select button. A song list appears.

5. Highlight the song from the list.

The songs in the album list are in album order (the order that they appear on the album); in the All list, they are in album order for each album. Scroll up or down the list to highlight the song.

By album

Follow these steps to locate a song by album directly:

1. Select the Browse item from the iPod main menu.

Scroll down the main menu until Browse is highlighted, and then press the Select button. The Browse menu appears.

2. Select the Albums item.

Scroll down the Browse menu until Albums is highlighted, and then press the Select button. The Albums menu appears.

To search by composer, select the Composers item and make a selection from the Composers menu to get a list of songs for that composer.

3. Select an album from the Albums menu.

The albums are listed in alphabetical order (without any reference to artist, which might make identification difficult). Scroll down the Albums menu until the album name is highlighted, and then press the Select button to select it. A song list appears.

4. Highlight the song from the list.

The songs in the album list are in album order (the order that they appear on the album). Scroll down the list until the song name is highlighted.

By playlist

Follow these steps to locate a song by playlist:

1. Select the Playlists item from the iPod main menu.

The Playlists item is at the top of the main menu and might already be highlighted. If it isn't, scroll down the main menu until Playlists is highlighted, and then press the Select button. The Playlists menu appears.

2. Select a playlist.

The playlists are listed in alphabetical order. Scroll down the Playlists menu until the playlist name is highlighted, and then press the Select button. A list of songs in the playlist appears.

3. **Highlight the song from the list.**

The songs in the playlist are in playlist order (the order defined for the playlist in iTunes). Scroll up or down the list to highlight the song you want.

Playing a Song

After scrolling through the song list until the song name is highlighted, press the Select button to play the selected song or press the Play/Pause button — either button starts the song playing. When the song finishes, the iPod starts playing the next song in the song list.

While a song is playing, the artist name and song name appear, and you can use the scroll pad to adjust the volume. See "Adjusting the Volume," later in this chapter.

Press the Play/Pause button when a song is playing to pause the playback — because the iPod is a hard drive, pause is the same as stop, and you don't find any delay in resuming playback.

Repeating Songs

If you want to drive yourself crazy repeating the same song over and over, the iPod is happy to oblige. More likely, you want to repeat a sequence of songs, and you can easily do that too.

You can set the iPod to repeat a single song automatically by following these steps:

1. **Locate and play a song.**

2. **As the song plays, press the Menu button repeatedly to return to the main menu, and then select the Settings item.**

The Settings menu appears.

3. **Scroll the Settings menu until Repeat is highlighted.**

The Repeat setting displays Off next to it.

4. **Press the Select button once (Off changes to One) to repeat one song.**

If you press the Select button more than once, keep pressing until One appears.

You can also press the Previous/Rewind button to repeat a song.

Follow these steps to repeat all the songs in the selected album or playlist:

1. **Locate and play a song in the album or playlist.**

2. **As the song plays, press the Menu button repeatedly to return to the main menu, and then select the Settings item.**

The Settings menu appears.

3. **Scroll down the Settings menu until the Repeat item is highlighted.**

   The Repeat setting displays Off next to it.

4. **Press the Select button twice (Off changes to All) to repeat all the songs in the album or playlist.**

Shuffling the Song Order

You can *shuffle* (play in random order) songs within an album, playlist, or the entire library.

To shuffle songs in an album or playlist:

1. **Locate and play a song in the album or playlist.**

2. **As the song plays, press the Menu button repeatedly to return to the main menu, and then select the Settings item.**

   The Settings menu appears.

3. **Scroll the Settings menu until the Shuffle item is highlighted.**

   The Shuffle setting displays Off next to it.

4. **Press the Select button once (Off changes to Songs) to shuffle the songs in the selected album or playlist.**

You can always set your iPod to repeat an album or playlist but still shuffle the playing order.

To shuffle all the albums in your iPod while still playing the songs in each album in normal album order:

1. **Press the Menu button repeatedly to return to the main menu, and then select the Settings item.**

   The Settings menu appears.

2. **Scroll down the Settings menu until the Shuffle item is highlighted.**

   The Shuffle setting displays Off next to it.

3. **Press the Select button twice (Off changes to Albums) to shuffle the albums without shuffling the songs within each album.**

When the iPod is set to shuffle, it doesn't repeat a song until it has played through the entire album, playlist, or library.

Creating On-the-Go Playlists

If you don't have playlists from iTunes (or you don't want to hear those playlists), you can create a temporary on-the-go playlist. (This feature isn't available in older iPod models.) You can select a list of songs or entire albums to play in a certain order, queuing up the songs or albums on the iPod. Queued songs appear automatically in an on-the-go playlist in the Playlists menu, which you select from the main menu.

To select songs or entire albums for the on-the-go playlist:

1. **Locate and highlight a song or album title.**
2. **Press and hold the Select button until the title flashes.**
3. **Repeat Steps 1 and 2 in the order that you want the songs or albums played.**

To play the on-the-go playlist, scroll down the main menu until Playlists is highlighted, and then press the Select button. The Playlists menu appears. Scroll to the On-The-Go item, which is always at the very end of the list in the Playlists menu.

You can continue to add songs to the list of queued songs in an on-the-go playlist at any time. Your iPod saves the on-the-go playlist until you clear it. To clear the list of queued songs:

1. **Press the Menu button repeatedly to return to the main menu, and then select the Playlists item.**

   The Playlists menu appears.

2. **Select the On-The-Go item.**

   The song list in the on-the-go playlist appears.

3. **Scroll down to the very end of the song list and select the Clear Playlist item.**

   The Clear menu appears.

4. **Select the Clear Playlist item.**

   The songs disappear from the playlist.

Adjusting the Volume

The iPod is quite loud when set to its highest volume. To adjust the volume:

1. **Select and play a song on the iPod.**
2. **Change the volume with the scroll pad.**

   A volume bar appears in the iPod display to guide you. Scroll with your thumb or finger clockwise to increase the volume, and counterclockwise to decrease the volume.

If you have the Apple iPod Remote — a handy controller that attaches by cable to the iPod headphone connection — you can control the volume by using the volume button on the remote. With the remote, you can also play or pause a song, fast-forward or rewind, and skip to the next or previous song. You can disable the buttons on the remote by setting the controller's Hold switch (similar to the iPod Hold switch).

Bookmarking Audible Audio Books

Audible books, articles, and Spoken-Word titles are stored and played just like songs in iTunes and your iPod. (You can download titles from www.audible. com.) When you play an Audible title, you can automatically bookmark your place in the text with the iPod. Bookmarks work only with Audible files. If you have an audio book or spoken-word file in any other format, such as MP3, bookmarks aren't available.

To find out how to download Audible audio files into iTunes, see Book V, Chapter 3.

When you use the Pause/Play button to pause an Audible file, the iPod automatically bookmarks that spot. When you hit the Play button again, the Audible file starts playing from that spot.

Bookmarks synchronize when you copy an Audible title to your iPod — whichever bookmark is farther along in iPod or iTunes becomes the effective bookmark.

Book VI

Creating Web Pages

The 5th Wave   By Rich Tennant

"You'd better come out here — I've got someone who wants to run a banner ad on our Web site."

Book VI: Creating Web Pages

Chapter 1: Creating a Successful Web Site

In This Chapter

✔ Understanding the different kinds of Web sites

✔ Creating a Web site step by step

✔ Finding space for your Web site

✔ Determining what to include on your Web site

Web sites are many things to many people. To some, a Web site is an electronic business card; to others, an online storefront; to still others, a classified advertisement or a family photo album. The trick to creating a successful Web site is to figure out what a Web site is to *you* — and then to build your site and make it available on the Web by following a few simple steps.

Web Site Basics

Although the steps that you take to create and *publish* (make it available on the Web) a Web site are pretty straightforward, the geeky terminology surrounding the Web can make the whole process seem downright confusing. The following sections give you an overview of the different kinds of sites you can create, followed by a description of the big picture — in other words, a description of what you need to do to turn your great idea into a live Web site that people all over the world can view and enjoy.

Different kinds of Web sites

The following sections describe three very broad categories of Web sites. The Web site that you intend to publish probably falls into one of these three categories.

Personal home pages

Just about anyone with access to the Internet can create a personal home page. The simplest personal home pages contain basic information, such as your name, information about your family, your occupation, your hobbies, and any special interests that you have. You can also throw in pictures. Oh, and many personal home pages also include links to favorite pages on the Web.

More elaborate personal home pages can include pictures from your last family vacation, the first chapter of your soon-to-be-published novel, or anything else that you think others might be interested in.

Company Web sites

More and more companies are joining the Web bandwagon. Even mom-and-pop pizza parlors are putting up Web pages. The simplest corporate Web pages provide basic information about a company, such as a description of the company's products or services, phone numbers, and so on.

A more elaborate corporate Web site can include any or all of the following:

✦ An online catalog that enables Internet users to see detailed information about products and services. The catalog might include pictures and, if you want, prices.

✦ Online ordering, which enables Internet users to actually place orders over the Internet.

✦ A customer survey.

✦ Lists of frequently asked questions (FAQs) about the company's products or services.

✦ Online support, where a customer can leave a question about a problem that he or she is having with a product and receive an answer within a day or two.

✦ Articles and reviews of the company's products.

✦ Press releases.

✦ Biographies of company employees.

Special-interest Web sites

Many of the most interesting Web sites are devoted to special interests. For example, if you're involved with a youth soccer league, you might want to create a Web page that includes team rosters, schedules, and standings. Or, if you're one of those festive neighbors who decorates your house with 100,000 lights at Christmas, create a Web page that focuses on Christmas decorating. The list of possible topics for a special-interest Web site is limitless.

Creating a Web site: An overview

Although you don't have to be obsessively methodical about creating a Web site, following these three basic steps helps ensure that you end up with a site that you're proud to call your own (in the least possible amount of time):

1. **Plan your Web site.**

   Taking a bit of time up front to decide exactly how you want your site to look and behave can save you loads of time, as you see in the following section, "Planning Your Web Site."

2. **Create your Web pages.**

   A Web site is a collection of Web pages. And although all Web pages must be created in a special language called HTML (which stands for Hyper-Text Markup Language), you have several options besides becoming an

HTML guru and typing all your HTML code into a text editor by hand. The section "Creating Your Web Pages," later in this chapter, describes some of those options.

3. Publish your Web pages.

Before anyone can view your Web site, you must first *publish* it — that is, you must first copy your Web pages to a Web server so that other computers on the Internet can access them. In the section "Publishing Your Web Pages," later in this chapter, you find out how to do that.

Planning Your Web Site

Start by making a plan for your Web site. If all you want to do is create a simple, one-page "Here I Am" type of personal Web site, you might not need a plan. However, if this Web site is your first one, a little planning can help you avoid some frustration as you figure out the nuts and bolts of creating a Web page. Your plan might be a simple sketch (you can even do it on a napkin) of what information your site will contain and how that info will look. For a more elaborate Web site, the planning is more complicated and even more necessary, but the principle remains the same.

One good way to plan a more complex Web site is to sketch a simple diagram on paper, showing the various pages that you want to create, complete with pictures and arrows showing the links between the pages. Or you can create an outline that represents your entire site. You can be as detailed or as vague as you want, but in general, the more detailed your plan, the less time you spend later when you actually begin building your site.

Creating Your Web Pages

You can take a couple different approaches to creating the pages that will make up your Web site: You can hand-code the site from scratch by using a text editor, or you can use a point-and-click graphical editor that generates HTML code for you. Either approach works just fine. You can always choose one approach, work with it awhile, and then switch to the other approach later if you change your mind.

From scratch, using a text editor

If you dream in Boolean, feel free to fire up Notepad and start banging away HTML code from scratch. You have to figure out the intricacies of using HTML code to format your Web pages, but you gain satisfaction from knowing you did it the hard way! (You also have complete control over every aspect of your Web pages — something that you don't always have when you use a graphical Web page editor.) Chapters 7 through 13 of Book VI introduce you to the HTML basics that you need to get started creating HTML code from scratch.

Using a graphical Web page editor

If the mere thought of programming gives you hives, you can use a simple Web page editor to create your Web pages. (Book VI, Chapter 2 shows you a free Web page creation tool in action.) Or, you can purchase inexpensive programs for creating complete Web sites. Two of the best known Web site development programs are Microsoft FrontPage 2003 (which I cover in Book VI, Chapters 14 through 18) and Dreamweaver (which I cover in Book VI, Chapters 19 through 27).

Beyond HTML: Adding nifty features

After you have your basic site up and running, you might want to get fancy and add some cool extras — features such as

 ✦ Images, sound, animations, and Java applets
 ✦ Interactive images and forms that automatically check user input for errors
 ✦ Movie clips
 ✦ Credit card handling

If you're serious about sprucing up your site, XML is the way to go. XML is one of the latest Web-related meta-languages. You can use it to create your very own specialized markup language, complete with semantic definitions called *vocabularies*. Using a combination of XML and a few other tools, you can create your own HTML-like markup tags and your own language processor — in effect, creating a means for extending HTML or exchanging non-HTML data over the Web in a standard, civilized way. For example, some folks in the automobile industry are using XML to enable automobile parts producers and buyers to exchange automobile-related data quickly and easily over the Web. For more about XML, check out *XML For Dummies*, 3rd Edition, written by Ed Tittel, Natanya Pitts, and Frank Boumphrey (Wiley Publishing, Inc.).

Publishing Your Web Pages

After your Web pages are complete, it's time to publish them on the Internet. First, you have to find a Web server to host your Web pages. The next section gives you ideas for finding a Web server. Next, you copy your Web pages to the Web server. Finally, you can publicize your Web site by cataloging it in the major search services.

Finding space for your Web site

Before Web surfers can see your Web pages, you must transfer the pages to a *Web server*. A Web server is a computer that's hooked up to the Internet, running special Web server software. The following sections give you some ideas about where to find a Web server to host your Web pages.

Internet service providers

If you access the Internet through an Internet service provider (ISP), you probably already have space set aside on its server to set up a home page. Most ISPs include a small amount of disk space for Web pages with their monthly service. The space might be limited to a few megabytes (for example, AOL offers up to 20MB), but that should be enough to set up several pages. If you need to, you can probably get additional disk space for a modest charge.

Your ISP should be able to give you step-by-step instructions for copying your Web pages to the ISP's Web server.

If you're interested in creating a business Web site, you might want to go shopping for an ISP. Some places to start: http://reviews.cnet.com (click the Web Hosting link), http://webhostinginspector.com, and www.webhostingratings.com. As you research ISPs, keep these criteria in mind:

✦ **Price:** Some ISPs charge by the month; others give you discounts for paying a year or more in advance.

✦ **Downtime:** You might not care if your personal home page is inaccessible for a couple hours a day, but if you're doing business over the Web, you might care very much indeed. Downtime can occur due to power outages, scheduled equipment maintenance, and so on. Because some ISPs have backup servers that minimize (or even eliminate) downtime, and others don't, be sure to ask any ISP that you're considering what you can expect in terms of average site downtime.

✦ **Services:** Knowing up front which additional services (in addition to plain vanilla Web hosting) you want makes deciding on an ISP easier. Some common services an ISP might offer include

 • The ability to assign a unique URL of your own choosing (for example, www.ralphswidgets.com) to your Web site

 • The ability to stream special multimedia formats, such as RealPlayer files

 • Built-in management and e-commerce tools, such as shopping carts and usage monitors

 • The ability to create and run server-side applications (such as server-side JavaScript)

Free Web hosts

If you can't find a home for your Web page at your Internet service provider, consider using a free Web host to host your Web site. The best known free home page service is Yahoo! GeoCities, which hosts well over 1.2 million home pages. (Book III, Chapter 9 describes GeoCities.) Each free Web site can use up to 15MB of disk space. The only limitation is that you must include a banner advertisement at the top of your Web page and a link to the GeoCities home page at the bottom of your page. You can find Yahoo! GeoCities at http://geocities.yahoo.com.

Many other free home page services are available, although most cater to specific types of home pages, such as artist pages, churches, chambers of commerce, and so on. You can find a good directory of free home page services by going to Yahoo! (www.yahoo.com) and searching for *free Web pages*.

If your idea of the perfect Web site is a simple online diary, or Web log (*blog* for short), check out Blogger (www.blogger.com) for free hosting.

Publicizing your Web site

Just publishing a Web site doesn't ensure that any visitors will find it. To make your presence on the Web known, you must publicize your site. Depending on the type of site you're creating, your online publicity plan might include registering your site with search engines, advertising your site (both on- and offline), and getting other people to link to your site from theirs.

Elements of a Successful Web Site

A successful Web site doesn't just happen by accident. To create a Web site that people will visit over and over again, keep the following time-tested guidelines in mind:

✦ **Offer something useful on every page.** Too many Web sites are filled with fluff — pages that don't have any useful content. Avoid creating pages that are just steps along the way to truly useful information. Instead, strive to include something useful on every page of your Web site.

✦ **Check the competition.** Find out what other Web sites similar to yours have to offer. Don't create a "me, too" Web site that offers nothing but information that's already available elsewhere. Instead, strive for unique information that people can find only on your Web site.

✦ **Make it look good.** No matter how good the information at your Web site is, people will stay away if the layout is disorganized or the design is too busy or looks thrown together. Yes, substance is more important than style. However, an ugly Web site turns people away, and an attractive Web site draws people in.

✦ **Proofread it carefully.** Misspelled words and typos make visitors think that the information on your Web site is unreliable. If your HTML editor has a spell-check feature, use it — and always proof your work carefully before you post it to the Web.

✦ **Provide links to other sites.** Some of the best pages on the Internet are links to other Web sites that have information about a particular topic. In fact, many of the pages that I have bookmarked for my own use are pages of links to topics as diverse as hobby electronics, softball, and backpacking. The time that you spend creating a directory of links to other sites with information similar or complementary to your own is time well spent.

✦ **Keep it current.** Out-of-date information turns away visitors. Make sure that you frequently update your Web pages with current information. Obviously, some Web pages need to be changed more than others. For example, if you maintain a Web page that lists the team standings for a soccer league, you have to update the page after every game. On the other hand, a page that features medieval verse romances doesn't need to be updated very often, unless someone discovers a previously unpublished Chaucer text hidden in a trunk.

✦ **Don't make hardware assumptions.** Remember that not everyone has a 21-inch monitor and a high-speed cable-modem connection to the Internet. Design your Web site so that people who are stuck with a 14-inch monitor and — gasp — a 28.8 Kbps modem connection to the Internet can use it.

✦ **Publicize it.** Few people will stumble across your Web site by accident. If you want people to visit your Web site, you have to publicize it. Make sure that your site is listed in the major search engines, such as Yahoo! and Google. Also, you can promote your site by putting its address on all your advertisements, correspondence, business cards, e-mails, and so on.

Organizing Site Content

Organizing your site's content can mean the difference between creating a great site and a site that visitors click away from screaming in frustration. The following sections describe several popular ways to organize the information on your Web site.

Sequential organization

In *sequential organization,* you simply organize your pages so that they follow one after another, like the pages in a book, as shown in Figure 1-1.

Figure 1-1:
Sequential
organization.

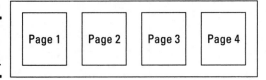

On each page, provide navigation links that enable the user to go to the next page, go to the previous page, or return directly to the first page. You implement navigation links by using HTML links and anchors (both of which I describe in Chapter 3 of Book VI), but you can also make them more descriptive than a plain underlined text link. For example, you can create navigation links that look like right and left arrows (for next and previous pages, respectively).

TIP

One of the most popular ways to arrange navigation links is the *navigation bar*. A navigation bar is a strip of navigation links that runs vertically (along the left or, more rarely, the right side) or horizontally (across the top or bottom) on a page. You find more information about navigation bars in Book VI, Chapter 3.

Hierarchical organization

In hierarchical organization, you organize your Web pages into a hierarchy, categorizing the pages according to subject matter. The topmost page serves as a menu that enables users to access other pages directly (see Figure 1-2). On each page, provide a navigation link that returns the user to the menu. If you want, you can include more than one level of menu pages, as shown in Figure 1-3.

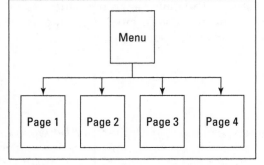

Figure 1-2:
Hierarchical organization with one menu level.

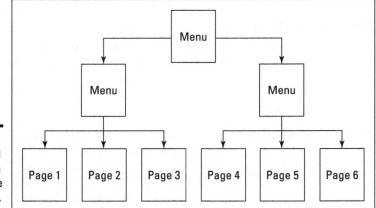

Figure 1-3:
Hierarchical organization with multiple menu levels.

However, don't overdo the menus. Most users are frustrated by Web sites that have unnecessary menus, each containing only two or three choices. When a menu has more than a dozen choices, however, consider splitting the menu into two or more separate menus.

Combination sequential and hierarchical organization

Many Web sites use a combination of sequential and hierarchical organization, in which a menu enables users to access content pages that contain sequential links to one another, as shown in Figure 1-4.

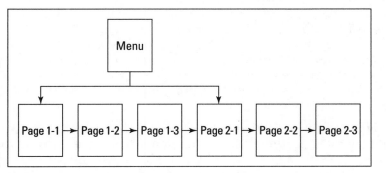

Figure 1-4:
Combination
sequential
and hier-
archical
organization.

In a combination style of organization, each content page includes a link to the next page in sequence in addition to a link back to the menu. The menu page contains links to the pages that mark the start of each section of content pages.

Web organization

Some Web sites have pages that are connected with links that defy a strict sequential or hierarchical pattern. In extreme cases, every page in the site is linked to every other page, creating a structure that resembles a web, as shown in Figure 1-5. Web organization — where every Web page links to every other page in a Web site — is a good style of organization if the total number of pages in the web is limited and you can't predict the sequence in which a user might want to view the pages.

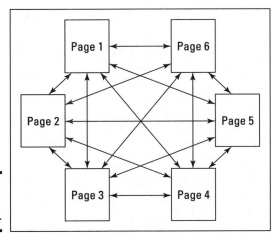

Figure 1-5:
Web
organization.

What to Include on Every Page

Although every Web page should contain unique and useful information, all Web pages ought to contain the following three elements:

✦ **Title:** At the top of every page, place a descriptive title that identifies the specific contents of the page and the Web site itself. A descriptive title is important because some users might not enter your site through your home page. Instead, they might go directly to one of the content pages on your site. In addition, many users *bookmark* pages for quick access at a later date, and a good title, such as, "Sarah Bellum's Definitive Guide to Lemurs," helps users remember why they bookmarked your page in the first place.

✦ **Navigation links:** All the pages of your Web site should have a consistent set of navigation links. At a minimum, provide a link to your home page on every page in your site. In addition, you might want to include links to the next and previous pages if your pages have a logical sequential organization. Figure 1-6 shows examples of navigational links at `www.dummies.com`.

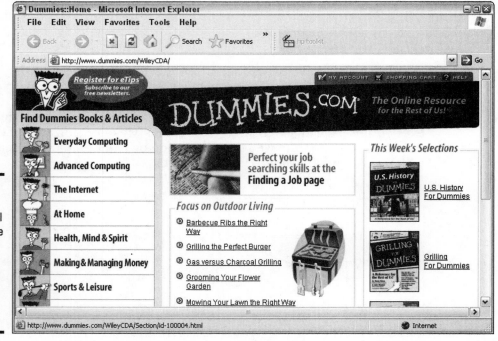

Figure 1-6: Here the navigational links include Everyday Computing, Advanced Computing, and The Internet.

✦ **Author and copyright information:** Every page should also include author credits and a copyright notice. Because users can enter your site by going directly to any page, placing the authorship and copyright notices on only the home page isn't sufficient.

What to Include on Every Web Site

Although every Web site is different, you can find certain common elements on most Web sites. The following sections describe the items that you should consider including on your Web site.

Home page

Every Web site should include a home page that serves as an entry point into the site. The home page is the first page that most users see when they visit your site (unless you include a cover page, as I describe in the next section). To encourage your visitors to browse and maybe even come back, devote considerable time and energy to making sure that your home page makes a good first impression.

Place an attractive title element at the top of the page. Remember that most users have to scroll down to see all of your home page. They see just the top of the page first, so you want to make sure that the title is immediately visible.

After the title, include a site menu that enables users to access the content available on your Web site. You can create a simple text menu, or you can opt for a fancy graphics-based menu in which the user can click different parts of the image to go to different pages. However, if you use the graphics-based menu, called an *image map,* be sure to provide a text menu as an alternative for users who don't want to wait for the image map to download or who have turned off graphic downloads altogether. For more information about image maps, see Book VI, Chapter 4.

Here are a few other goodies you might want to include on your home page:

✦ **An indication of new content that's available on your Web site:** Users who return to your site often want to know right away when new information is available.

✦ **The date your site was last updated:** Adding a so-called freshness date lets visitors know that you're actively maintaining your site, which inspires confidence in your content and encourages users to return.

✦ **A copyright notice:** You can include a link to a separate copyright page where you spell out whether others can copy information from your site. In addition, you might want to add a sentence or two at the bottom of each page informing visitors that your site content is copyrighted and that you're the copyright owner: for example, Copyright 2004–2005, Sue Smith. (This is true if you create the content yourself.)

✦ **A reminder to bookmark the page so that users can get back to the page easily:** Reminding your visitors to bookmark your page is a win-win situation: They find your site the next time more easily, and you get their repeat business without having to do a lot of extra work.

✦ **A hit counter:** If users see that 4 million people have visited your site since last Tuesday, users automatically assume that yours must be a hot site. On the other hand, if they see that only three people have visited

Book VI
Chapter 1

Creating a Successful
Web Site

since Truman was president, they'll yawn and leave quickly. If your site isn't very popular, or if you're going for a strictly professional look, you might want to skip the hit counter.

 Avoid placing a huge amount of graphics on your home page. Your home page is the first page on your Web site that most users are likely to see. If it takes more than 15 seconds for your page to load, users might lose patience and skip your page altogether. As a simple test, try holding your breath while your home page downloads. If you turn blue before the page finishes downloading, the page is too big.

Cover page

A *cover page* (sometimes called a *splash* page) is a page that displays temporarily before your home page displays. Cover pages usually feature a flashy graphic logo or an animation. On most cover pages, the user must click the logo or some other element on the page to enter the site's home page. Alternatively, the page can be programmed so that it automatically jumps to the home page after a certain amount of time — say 10 or 15 seconds — elapses.

 Many users are annoyed by cover pages, especially cover pages that take more than a few seconds to download and display. Think carefully about whether the splashy cover page actually enhances your site or is more of an annoyance.

Site map

If your site has a lot of pages, you might want to include a site map. A *site map* is a detailed menu that provides links to every page on the site. By using the site map, a user can bypass intermediate menus and go directly to the pages that interest him or her.

Contact information

Be sure that your site includes information about how to contact you or your company. You can easily include your e-mail address as a link right on the home page. When the user clicks this link, most Web browsers fire up the user's e-mail program, ready to compose a message with your e-mail address already filled in.

 This should go without saying, but just in case, if you decide to include contact information, make sure that you're diligent in reading and responding to the comments that your visitors e-mail you. (This advice goes double for those of you contemplating a commercial Web site.)

 If you want to include complete contact information, such as your address and phone number, or if you want to list contact information for several individuals, you might want to place the contact information on a separate page that can be accessed from the home page.

Help page

If your Web site contains more than just a few pages, consider providing a help page that provides information about how to use the site. The help page can include information about how to navigate the site, how you obtained your site content, how often you update the site, how someone would go about contributing to the site, and so on.

FAQ

FAQ pages are among the most popular sources of information on the Internet. You can organize your own FAQ page on any topic you want. Just come up with a list of questions and provide the answers. Or solicit answers from readers of your page.

Related links

At some sites, the most popular page is the links page, which provides a list of links to related sites. As the compiler of your own links page, you can do something that search engines such as Yahoo! can't: You can pick and choose the links that you want to include, and you can provide your own commentary about the information contained on each site.

Discussion group

A discussion group adds interactivity to your Web site. Visitors can post articles that other visitors can read and respond to.

Troubleshooting Web publishing

The following points summarize the most troublesome aspects of creating high-quality Web pages.

✔ **Too many Web browsers:** Different Web browsers display Web pages differently. Each new version of the two most popular Web browsers — Netscape Navigator and Microsoft Internet Explorer — adds new HTML features. Unfortunately, in their efforts to get ahead of one another, both Netscape and Microsoft put the notion of *compatibility* in the back seat. Whenever you use a new HTML feature, you have to make sure that your page looks good no matter which browser the user views your page with.

✔ **Different screen sizes and resolutions:** Some users have computers with puny 14-inch monitors that are set to 640 x 480 resolution. Others have giant 19-inch monitors that run at a 1,280 x 1,024 resolution. Your pages look different depending on the display resolution of the user's computer. A good middle-of-the-road approach is to design your pages for a 800 x 600 resolution.

✔ **Different connection speeds:** Some users are connected to the Internet over high-speed T3 lines or cable modems, which can send megabytes of data in seconds. Others are connected over a phone line at 56 Kbps (common in the United States) or even 28.8 Kbps (still common in other countries), both of which download large graphic files at a snail's pace. To compensate for lack of speed, some users set up their browsers so that graphics don't automatically download. That means that if you want to reach the widest possible audience, your pages shouldn't be overly dependent on graphics.

Chapter 2: Building Your First Web Site

In This Chapter

✔ **Registering with a free Web host**

✔ **Using a free Web site creation tool**

✔ **Viewing your first Web page**

Nothing helps give you a feel for how a process works better than walking through each of the steps yourself. In this chapter, you see how to create, publish, and view your first Web page by using the free graphical Web editor available from Yahoo! GeoCities, a free Web host.

Registering with a Free Web Host

You have many options when it comes to finding space for your Web site. In this chapter, I show you how to register and create a site with Yahoo! Geo-Cities, one of the most popular free Web hosting services (if this chapter whets your appetite for GeoCities, be sure to visit Book III, Chapter 9, which offers more information about this free Web hosting service). Other free Web hosting services at the time of this writing are Angelfire (`http://angelfire.lycos.com`) and Tripod (`www.tripod.lycos.com`).

If you already have a Yahoo! GeoCities account, go ahead and skip to "Using a Free Web Site Creation Tool," later in this chapter. Otherwise, to register with Yahoo! GeoCities, follow these steps:

1. **Type** http://geocities.yahoo.com/home/ **into your browser's Address box and press Enter.**

   The Yahoo! GeoCities home page appears, as shown in Figure 2-1.

2. **Click the Free link on the Yahoo! GeoCities home page, as shown in the lower-left corner of Figure 2-1.**

   The Free: Highlights window appears.

3. **Click the Sign Up link, which you see on the Free: Highlights window. When the Welcome to Yahoo! GeoCities page appears, click the Sign Up Now link.**

   A Sign Up for Your Yahoo! ID window similar to the one you see in Figure 2-2 appears.

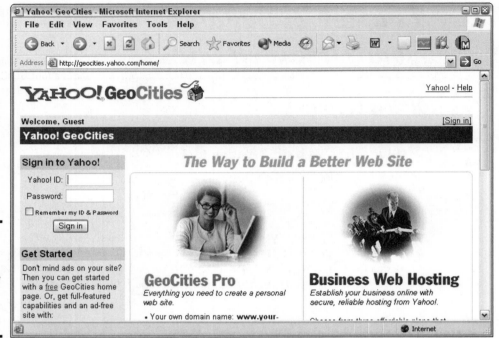

Figure 2-1:
Yahoo!
GeoCities is
one of many
free Web
hosting
services.

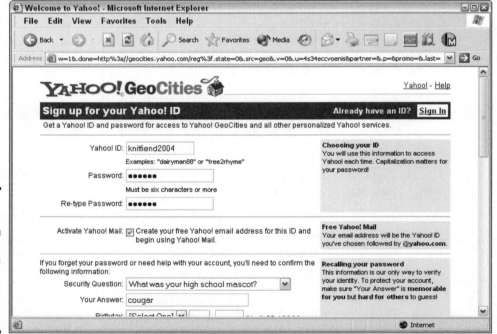

Figure 2-2:
You use this
sign-up form
to register
for free Web
hosting
services
with Yahoo!
GeoCities.

No such thing as a free lunch?

As you might suspect, free Web services aren't *completely* free. Most free Web services don't charge you setup or hosting fees, but they do require you to display advertising messages on your site. Although you might be able to restrict the types of advertising that the Web services display on your site (for example, you may request family- or environmentally friendly messages), the Web service always has the last word.

One more thing to consider when choosing a service: Free providers such as Yahoo! GeoCities typically reserve the right to pull the plug at any time. In other words, you might wake up one morning to find out that the free provider you were relying on has decided to stop offering its services. For that reason, you might want to choose a for-pay provider if you're creating a business-related or some other gotta-be-available-24/7 Web site. (Hey, you get what you pay for, right?)

4. Fill out each field following the instructions provided on the form and then click the Submit This Form button.

If you forget the ID or password that you choose, you can't access your account (or the Web page creation tools). Chances are that your memory, like mine, isn't infallible — so make sure that you write this information on a slip of paper and tuck it in a safe place next to your computer. The Registration Completed window appears (see Figure 2-3).

5. Click the Continue to Yahoo! button.

You're done!

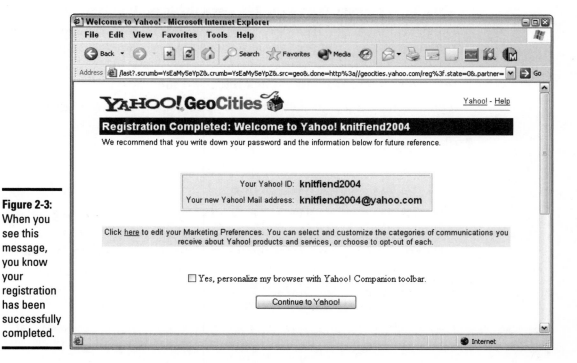

Figure 2-3: When you see this message, you know your registration has been successfully completed.

Using a Free Web Site Creation Tool

Most free Web services provide their own graphical Web site creation tools to make creating your first Web pages quick and easy. However, most free Web services don't restrict you to using their Web site creation tools; instead, they allow you to create Web pages by using any tool you like. If you choose not to use their built-in tools, however, you need to take an extra step to transfer your Web pages to your free site host — typically by using a transfer utility based on *File Transfer Protocol* (FTP).

In the following steps, you see how to use the Yahoo! PageWizards Web tool (available free when you register with Yahoo! GeoCities) to create a simple Web page. First, I show you how to choose a look, or *theme,* for your Web page; then I show you how to add content, such as text, links, and a picture.

To use Yahoo! PageWizards to create a simple Web page, follow these steps:

1. **Type** http://geocities.yahoo.com/home/ **into your browser's Address box and press Enter.**

   A Welcome page appears (refer to Figure 2-1).

2. **Click the Free link on the Yahoo! GeoCities home page, as shown in the lower-left corner of Figure 2-1.**

   The Free: Highlights page appears.

3. **Click the Sign Up link. When the Welcome to Yahoo! GeoCities page appears, type your ID and password into the Yahoo! ID and Password text boxes, respectively, and then click the Sign In button.**

   The previous section describes how to register an ID and password with Yahoo! GeoCities. You see the GeoCities Free page, similar to the one you see in Figure 2-4.

4. **Select an ad topic and then click the Continue button.**

   A page containing your Web site URL appears. Be sure to write down your Web site URL so that you don't forget it.

5. **Click the Build Your Web Site Now! link.**

   A page similar to the one you see in Figure 2-5 appears.

6. **Click the Yahoo! PageWizards link.**

   A Yahoo! PageWizards page appears, offering a selection of page themes (see Figure 2-6).

7. **Click any of the theme links shown in Figure 2-6 (for example, you can click the Fun D'Mental link).**

   A *theme* is a named set of characteristics — color, layout, and so on. The Yahoo! Quick Start Page Wizard window appears (see Figure 2-7).

   Themes are sometimes referred to as styles or templates. To see what your Web page looks like at any stage of the building process, click the Preview button located near the bottom of the Yahoo! Quick Start Page Wizard window.

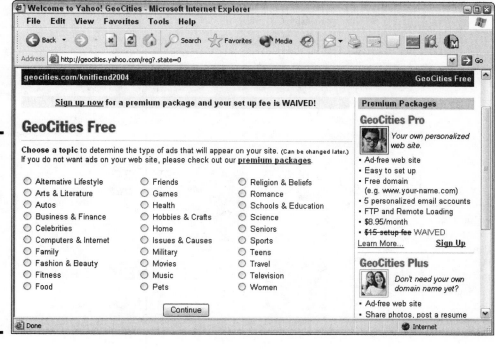

Figure 2-4: The first step in creating a free Yahoo! GeoCities site is selecting which type of ad you want to display on your site.

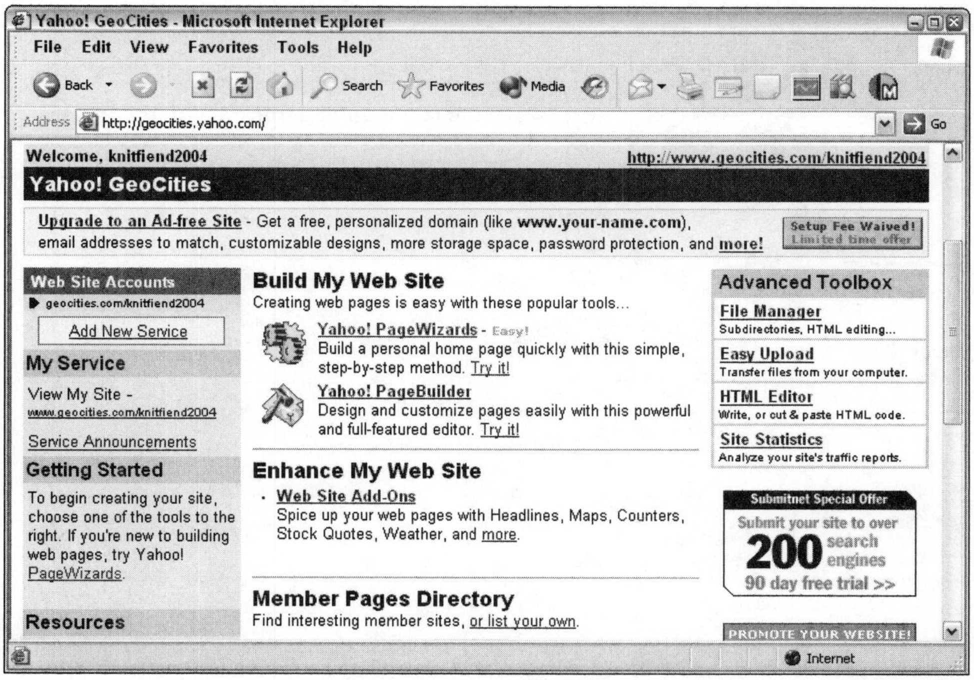

Figure 2-5: The easiest way to begin creating your Web site is to click the Yahoo! Page-Wizards link.

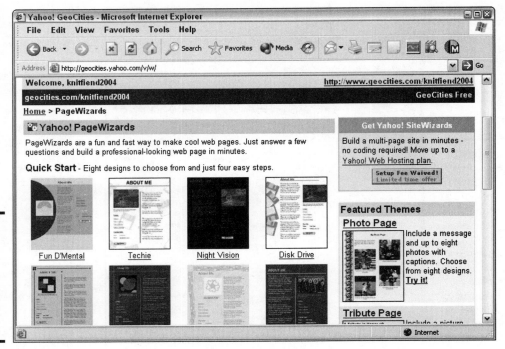

Figure 2-6:
The Yahoo!
Page-
Wizards
tool offers
a selection
of page
themes.

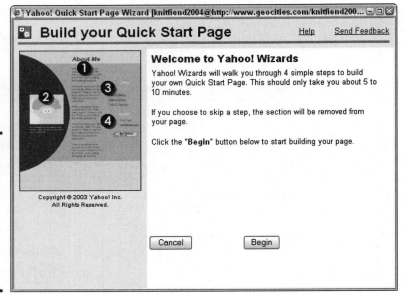

Figure 2-7:
The Yahoo!
Quick Start
Page
Wizard is
ready for
you to begin
building
your Web
page.

8. Click Begin.

The page shown in Figure 2-8 appears.

9. Select a theme (style) and click Next.

For example, you can select Fun D'Mental, Techie, or Night Vision. (If you wait a few seconds after clicking a style button, a preview of that style appears on the left side of the screen.)

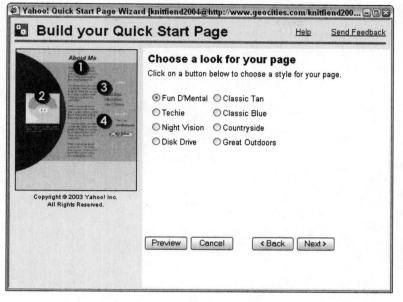

Figure 2-8:
Choosing a
look for your
Web page is
as easy as
clicking a
button.

Does this step sound familiar? It should. You selected a theme, or style,
for your Web page in Step 7. However, the Yahoo! Quick Start Page
Wizard requires you to specify the style that you want for your Web
page again! If you want, you can use this opportunity to change your
mind and select a different style.

10. **Enter a page title and any text that you want on the page, and then
click Next.**

Figure 2-9 shows how to do it. This is your only chance to write some
text, so write well and carefully.

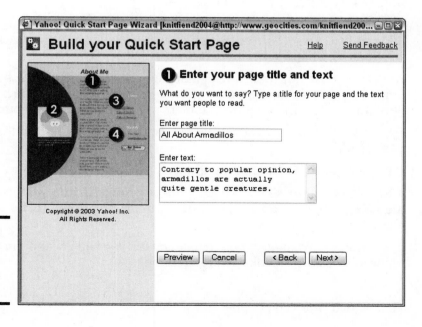

Figure 2-9:
Adding a
page title
and text
content.

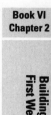

11. **Select a picture for your page, type a caption, and click Next.**

You may place only one picture on the page. You can use the default picture that comes with the style or upload a photo from your hard drive (see Figure 2-10).

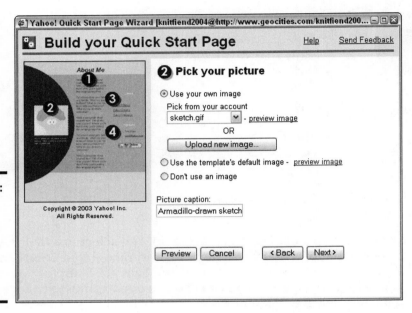

Figure 2-10: Adding a picture to your Web site, complete with a caption.

By the way, the *fully qualified filename* that you're asked to produce includes both the filename and the directory in which that file resides on your computer: for example, `c:\photos\ralph.gif` is the fully qualified filename of a file (`ralph.gif`) that's located in the `photos` directory, which is located in turn on the `c:` drive.

The kinds of image file formats that work best on Web pages are JPEG, GIF, and PNG files. (For the skinny on using images in Web pages, check out Book VI, Chapter 4.)

You can choose not to include a picture on your page by selecting the Don't Use an Image radio button. To use a picture ready-made by GeoCities, select the Use the Template's Default Image radio button.

12. **Type a few words of descriptive text in the Picture Caption text box and click Next.**

The page shown in Figure 2-11 appears.

13. **Add links to other sites by typing the appropriate information in the Link Name text boxes and Web Address text boxes (refer to Figure 2-11).**

If you want, you can also type a heading for your link section in the Name Your Favorite Links Section text box.

14. **Click Next.**

The page in Figure 2-12 appears.

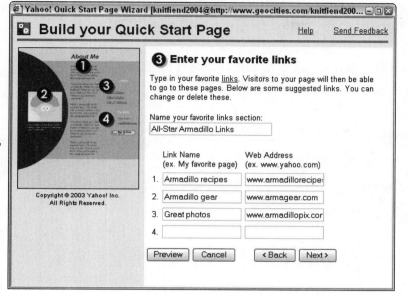

Figure 2-11:
Adding links from your Web page to other Web pages makes the Web go 'round.

**Book VI
Chapter 2**

**Building Your
First Web Site**

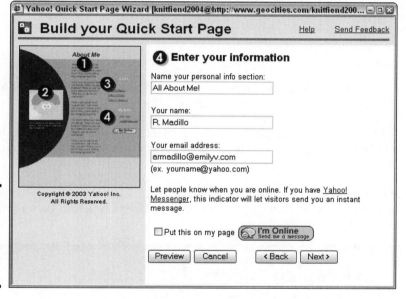

Figure 2-12:
Adding contact information to your Web site.

15. **Add contact information to your site by typing your name and e-mail address into the Your Name and Your Email Address text boxes. Click Next.**

Adding contact information to your Web site is a good idea, especially if you're creating a business or community-oriented site. Even if you're setting up a personal Web site, you'll want to create a special e-mail address just for your e-mail from your Web site. If you put your personal e-mail address on the Web for all to see, you'll be deluged with junk e-mail.

16. On the next page, name your page by typing a short, descriptive name into the Page Name text box (see Figure 2-13).

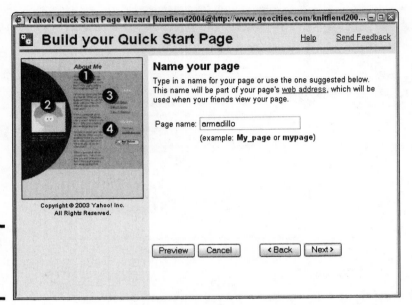

Figure 2-13: Naming your Web page.

17. **Click Next.**

Don't bother adding an `.htm` or `.html` suffix; the Yahoo! Quick Start Page Wizard adds the appropriate extension for you.

The congratulations page appears, complete with the URL of your brand-spanking-new Web page. As the wizard suggests, take a second to jot down the URL on a piece of scratch paper.

To view your newly created Web page, type the URL (Uniform Resource Locator) of your Web page into your browser's Address box and press Enter.

Keeping copies of your files

Online Web creation tools like the one that I demonstrate in this chapter save your Web page files directly to their Web servers. What this means is that your Web page is available on the Web as soon as you create it. But this also means that you don't have a copy of the file saved on your own computer, which, depending on how paranoid you are, may be a problem — or maybe not.

Web creation tools that you install on your own machine work differently. In the case of a Web editor (such as FrontPage), you save your Web page files to your own computer and then transfer, or upload, those files to a Web server in a separate step. Although this approach requires a bit more work on your part, you can be sure you have a copy of your file saved on your own machine in case you need it.

Chapter 3: Exploring the Essential Elements of Web Page Design

In This Chapter

✔ Starting an HTML page

✔ Adding headings and titles

✔ Formatting text

✔ Specifying page and background settings

✔ Creating lists and tables

✔ Adding navigation tools and links

You can think of HTML as a kind of primitive word-processing language for Web pages. HTML defines a bunch of directives, or *tags,* that you use to surround individual Web page elements to tell the browser how to display those elements. For example, if you want to display a paragraph in italics, you surround that paragraph with the beginning and ending HTML italic tags <I> and </I>. Chapters 7 through 13 of Book VI describe what you can do with HTML in detail. This chapter gives you a quick overview of the most essential, most popular features to get you up and running in record time.

HTML Basics

HTML defines two types of tags:

✦ **Beginning tags,** as you might guess, tell a Web browser to begin some kind of formatting process. For example, <B> tells a Web browser to begin displaying text in bold font.

✦ **Ending tags** tell a Web browser to stop a particular formatting process. Ending tags are identical to beginning tags except for one tiny detail: Ending tags sport a backslash just after the opening angle bracket, like this: </B>.

The following HTML code snippet shows you how the beginning and ending tags look in a typical HTML file:

```
This text will appear in regular font.
<B>This text will appear in bold font.</B>
This text will appear in regular font.
```

Most HTML tags come in the beginning-ending pair, but not all.

Now that you're familiar with beginning and ending tags, you're ready to take a look at the bare-bones tags that virtually all HTML documents contain.

```
<HTML>
<HEAD>
<TITLE>Your title goes here</TITLE>
</HEAD>
<BODY>
The body of your document goes here.
</BODY>
</HTML>
```

Here's an explanation of each of these tags:

✦ The `<HTML>` tag always appears as the very first thing in an HTML document. It tells the browser that the file is an HTML file.

✦ The `<HEAD>` and `</HEAD>` tags mark the section of the document called the *header,* which contains information that applies to the entire document.

✦ The `<TITLE>` and `</TITLE>` tags mark the document title. Any text that appears between the `<TITLE>` and `</TITLE>` tags is used as the title for your HTML document.

✦ The `<BODY>` and `</BODY>` tags mark the beginning and ending portions of your document that is displayed by the browser when the page is viewed. In most HTML documents, a lot of stuff falls between the `<BODY>` and `</BODY>` tags.

✦ The `</HTML>` ending tag is always the last tag in your document.

Adding Text

To add text to an HTML document, you place the text that you want to add between the beginning `<BODY>` and ending `</BODY>` tags:

```
<BODY>
All the text for this Web page goes right here. You can
    surround this text with many different HTML tags to
    format it attractively.
</BODY>
```

You typically include many HTML tags on a Web page — not just the required tags, which I describe in "HTML Basics," but also a handful of formatting tags to make your Web page look attractive. With all those angle brackets (`<. . .>`) lying around, you might find yourself accidentally slipping text inside an HTML tag. If that happens, you might be surprised when you try to load your Web page and the text doesn't display! So, for example, the following text does *not* appear on-screen when the HTML snippet loads:

```
<BODY Text inside tag declarations is NOT displayed on-
    screen.></BODY>
```

Instead, make sure that text falls between tags:

```
<BODY>Text placed properly between tag pairs IS displayed
    on-screen.</BODY>
```

Aligning text

HTML doesn't give you many options for aligning text. By default, text is left-aligned on the page. But you can use the `<CENTER>` tag to specify text to be centered, as in the following example:

```
<CENTER>This text is centered.</CENTER>
```

For more precise control of text alignment, use the text-align style property. It gives you four text-alignment options: left, right, center, and justify. The following example creates a right-aligned heading using the `<H1>` tag:

```
<H1 STYLE="text-align: right">This heading is right
    aligned.</H1>
```

Specifying headings

Don't fill your Web pages with a constant stream of uninterrupted text. Instead, use headings and paragraphs to organize the content on each page. The HTML heading tags make creating headings that break your text into manageable chunks easy.

You can include up to six levels of headings on your Web pages by using the HTML tags `<H1>`, `<H2>`, and so on through `<H6>`. The following snippet of HTML shows all six heading styles in use. It also shows the basic paragraph tag, `<P>`. Adding a paragraph causes a browser to display a vertical double-space directly after the text, as you see in Figure 3-1, which shows how this HTML appears when displayed in Internet Explorer 6.

```
<H1>This is a heading 1</H1>
<H2>This is a heading 2</H2>
<H3>This is a heading 3</H3>
<H4>This is a heading 4</H4>
<H5>This is a heading 5</H5>
<H6>This is a heading 6</H6>
<P>This is a normal text paragraph.</P>
```

Each Web browser uses its own point sizes for displaying the various heading levels, and most browsers use huge type for the highest heading levels — `<H1>` and `<H2>`. Fortunately, you can override the browser's type size by using styles as described in *Creating Web Pages For Dummies,* 6th Edition, by Bud Smith and Arthur Bebak (Wiley Publishing, Inc.).

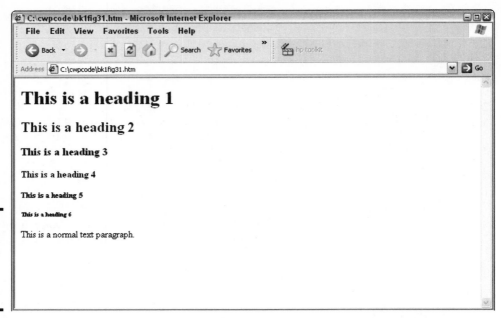

Figure 3-1:
Six levels
of headings
plus one
normal text
paragraph.

Changing text appearance

In addition to changing font face, size, and color (see "Changing fonts" for details), you can make text appear bold or italicized.

✦ **Bold:** You can use the `<B>` tag to format your text in boldface type. Add a `<B>` tag immediately before the text that you want to appear in boldface. Then, turn the boldface off by adding a `</B>` ending tag. For example:

```
This is <B>bold</B>.
```

✦ *Italic:* You can use the `<I>` tag to format your text in italic type. Add an `<I>` tag immediately before the text that you want to appear in italic. Then, turn the italic typeface off by adding an `</I>` ending tag. For example:

```
This is <I>italic</I>.
```

Changing fonts

HTML has two tags that let you control font settings: `<FONT>` and `<BASEFONT>`. The `<FONT>` tag lets you control font settings for an individual block of text, and the `<BASEFONT>` tag sets the default font used for a document. You can use attributes to fine-tune HTML tags. *Attributes* are description-value pairs joined by an equal sign (for example, `FACE="Arial"`). The following list explains the most important attributes of the `<FONT>` and `<BASEFONT>` tags:

✦ `FACE`: Sets the typeface.

✦ `SIZE`: Gives the type size on a scale of 1 to 7, where 7 is the largest and 1 is the smallest. The default size is 3.

✦ COLOR: Sets the color of the text. (For more information about using this attribute, see the section "Adding Color," later in this chapter.)

Many HTML tags come in pairs, but not all. <BASEFONT>, for example, contains only the beginning tag; no corresponding </BASEFONT> tag exists.

Here is a snippet of HTML that sets the typeface used for text on a Web page:

```
<BODY>
<BASEFONT SIZE=4 COLOR=BLACK FACE="Times New Roman">
<P>This is normal body text using the font set by the
    BASEFONT tag.</P>
<H1><FONT FACE="Arial">This is a heading</FONT></H1>
<P>After the heading, the text reverts to the BASEFONT
    setting.
</P>
</BODY>
```

Figure 3-2 shows how this HTML appears when displayed in a Web browser.

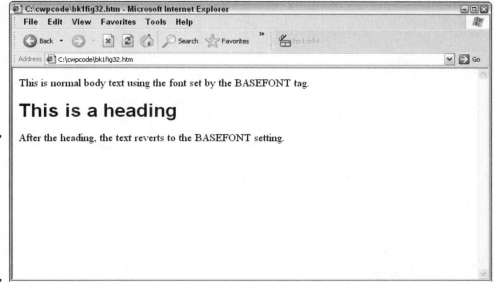

Figure 3-2:
Using the
<FONT>
and <BASE-
FONT>
tags to
modify the
appearance
of text.

Because the stock fonts that ship with operating systems vary, good programming practice dictates that you include at least a couple of font choices every time you specify a font face. For example, the following HTML snippet tells a Web browser to look first for the Helvetica typeface (which comes installed with Macintosh computers) and, if Helvetica can't be found, to look for the Arial typeface (which comes installed with Windows computers). Make sure that you separate typefaces with commas, as shown in the following line of code. You can specify as many typefaces as you like.

```
<FONT SIZE="2" FACE="helvetica, arial, sans-serif">
```

Both the `<FONT>` and `<BASEFONT>` tags are superseded by an even better method of setting fonts and other typographical options: style sheets. For more information about how to use styles, check out Book VI, Chapter 13.

Creating line breaks

HTML ignores line endings in an HTML document. As a result, you can't insert line breaks just by pressing the Enter key when you create an HTML document. For example, the following lines of text in an HTML document produce just one line of text rather than two:

```
HTML ignores
line endings.
```

To force a line break, use a `<BR>` tag where you want the line break to occur, as in this example:

```
HTML pays attention<BR>
to the line break tag.
```

The `<BR>` tag contains only the beginning tag; no corresponding `</BR>` tag exists.

Adding Color

You can specify colors in various HTML tags. For example, `<BODY>` has a `BGCOLOR` attribute that lets you specify the background color for your page. You can also use the `COLOR` attribute in a `<FONT>` tag to set the text color. Standard HTML defines 14 color names that you can use to set a predefined color. The easiest way to set color is to use one of these color names. For example, to create yellow text, you can use a `<FONT>` tag this way:

```
<FONT COLOR=YELLOW>This text is yellow.</FONT>
```

For more precise color control, you can specify a color by using a six-digit hexadecimal number to indicate the exact mixture of red, green, and blue that you want to use — kind of like mixing paint from a palette containing globs of red, green, and blue. The first two hexadecimal digits represent the amount of red, the next two represent the amount of green, and the last two are for blue. A value of 00 means that the color is completely absent, and FF means the color is completely saturated. A pound sign (#) must precede the entire six-digit color string. For example, you can replace the HTML tag `<FONT COLOR=YELLOW>` shown in the previous example with `<FONT COLOR="#FFFF00">`. The result is the same: nice, bright, yellow text.

Hexadecimal numbers are made up of the digits 0 through 9 and the letters A through F. For example, 14, 3F, B9, and AC are valid hexadecimal numbers.

Here are the 14 standard HTML color names along with their corresponding hexadecimal color strings:

Black	#000000	Green	#008000
Silver	#C0C0C0	Lime	#00FF00
Gray	#808080	Olive	#808000
White	#FFFFFF	Yellow	#FFFF00
Maroon	#800000	Navy	#000080
Purple	#800080	Teal	#008080
Fuchsia	#FF00FF	Aqua	#00FFFF

These standard colors, sometimes referred to as *Web-safe* colors, appear the same in all browsers. (Thanks to hardware and software differences, other non-Web-safe colors don't always appear the same when loaded in two different browsers.) So to be compatible with as many browser versions as possible, stick to these 14 standard Web-safe colors. (Both Internet Explorer 6 and Navigator 6 support additional color names.)

Watch out for color combinations that result in illegible text. For example, avoid maroon text on a purple background or green text on an olive background.

Book VI
Chapter 3

Exploring the Essential
Elements of Web
Page Design

Changing the Background

When creating Web pages, you don't have to settle for white; you can use colors and images to create an interesting, attractive background. One caveat, though: Keep readability in mind when you choose a background. If you use a background image for your pages, choose an image that doesn't interfere with the text and other elements on the page. By the same token, if you'd rather use a background color, select a neutral color, such as white, light gray, or one of those infamous earth tones. Neutral colors help your visitors read your text without eye strain.

Setting the background color

To set the background color of your Web page, follow these steps:

1. **Create the following** <BODY> **tag at the start of your document:**

```
<BODY BGCOLOR=>
```

2. **Type a color name or a hexadecimal color value for the** BGCOLOR **attribute into the tag that you created, insert the text for your Web page, and then add a closing** </BODY> **tag.**

For example:

```
<BODY BGCOLOR="white">
The body of your Web page goes here
</BODY>
```

This tag sets the background color to white.

For more information about using color, see "Adding Color," earlier in this chapter.

Using a background image

To use a background image for your Web page, follow these steps:

1. **Create the following `<BODY>` tag at the start of your document:**

```
<BODY BACKGROUND=>
```

2. **Type the name of the image file that you want to use for the background as the `BACKGROUND` attribute value:**

```
<BODY BACKGROUND="bgpic.gif">
```

This tag uses the file `bgpic.gif` as a background picture. Note that GIF images are the preferred type for background images because they keep the file size small, which in turn helps pages load faster.

The background image repeats as many times as necessary to completely fill the page. Avoid background images that use loud colors or bold designs; such images can overpower the text on your page, rendering your page next to unreadable. For more information about creating and using images, check out Book VI, Chapter 4.

Creating Visual Interest with Horizontal Rules

Horizontal rules are horizontal lines that you can add to create visual breaks on your Web pages. To add a rule to a page, you use the `<HR>` tag. You can control the height, width, and alignment of the rule by using the `SIZE`, `WIDTH`, and `ALIGN` attributes. For example:

```
<HR WIDTH="50%" SIZE=6 ALIGN=CENTER>
```

The `<HR>` tag contains only the beginning tag; no corresponding `</HR>` tag exists. In this example, the rule is half the width of the page, six pixels in height, and is centered on the page.

Many Web designers prefer to use graphic images rather than the `<HR>` tag to create horizontal rules. Because different Web browsers display the `<HR>` tag differently, using an image for a rule enables you to precisely control how your rule appears on-screen. To use an image rule, follow these steps:

1. **Type an `<IMG>` tag where you would normally use an `<HR>` tag to create a horizontal rule:**

```
<IMG>
```

2. **Type the name of the graphic file that contains the image rule in the `<IMG>` tag's `SRC` (shorthand for *source*) attribute:**

```
<IMG SRC="grule1.gif">
```

3. **Add a `WIDTH` attribute that specifies the number of pixels that you want the rule to span or a percentage of the screen width:**

```
<IMG SRC="grule1.gif" WIDTH="100%">
```

4. Follow up with a
 tag to force a line break:

```
<IMG SRC="grule1.gif" WIDTH="100%"><BR>
```

Organizing Information into Lists

Using HTML, you can create two basic types of lists for your Web page:

✦ **Bulleted lists:** In a bulleted list, each item in the list is marked by a bullet character (typically a dot).

✦ **Numbered lists:** Each item in a numbered list is marked by a number. The Web browser takes care of figuring out which number to use for each item in the list.

HTML also lets you create several other types of lists, known as menu lists, directory lists, and definition lists. Because these types of lists aren't as commonly used as bulleted and numbered lists, I don't describe them here.

Bulleted lists

A bulleted list (more properly called an *unordered list*) requires you to use three tags:

✦ <UL> marks the beginning of the unordered list.

✦ <LI> marks the start of each item in the list. No corresponding </LI> tag is needed.

✦ </UL> marks the end of the entire list.

Here is a snippet of HTML that sets up a bulleted list. Figure 3-3 shows how this list appears when displayed in a browser.

```
<H3>The Inhabitants of Oz</H3>
<UL>
<LI>The Scarecrow
<LI>The Tin Man
<LI>The Cowardly Lion
<LI>Munchkins
<LI>The Wizard
<LI>The Wicked Witch of the West (WWW)
<LI>Glenda
</UL>
```

Numbered lists

A numbered list (more properly called an *ordered list*) requires you to use three tags:

✦ <OL> marks the beginning of the ordered list.

✦ <LI> marks the start of each item in the list. No corresponding </LI> tag is needed.

✦ </OL> marks the end of the entire list.

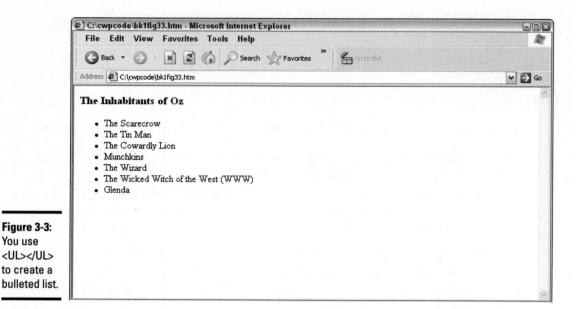

Figure 3-3:
You use
<UL></UL>
to create a
bulleted list.

Here is an HTML snippet that creates a numbered list. Figure 3-4 shows how the numbered list appears when displayed in a browser.

```
<H3>The Inhabitants of Oz</H3>
<OL>
<LI>The Scarecrow
<LI>The Tin Man
<LI>The Cowardly Lion
<LI>Munchkins
<LI>The Wizard
<LI>The Wicked Witch of the West (WWW)
<LI>Glenda
</OL>
```

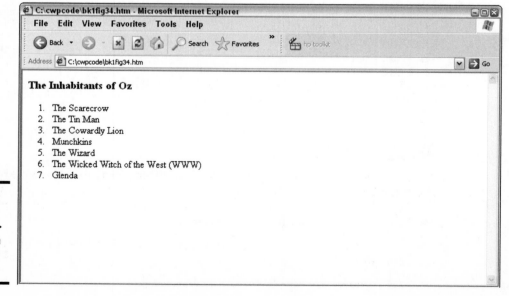

Figure 3-4:
You use
<OL></OL>
to create a
numbered
list.

Creating Links

Links are an integral part of any Web page. Links let your reader travel to a different location, which can be a part of the same HTML document, a different page located on your Web site, or a page from a different Web site located elsewhere on the Internet. All the user has to do to be transported to a different page is click the link.

Using text links

A *text link* is a portion of text that someone viewing your page can click to jump to another location. To create a text link, follow these steps:

1. **Determine the address of the page that you want the link to jump to.**

2. **Type an <A> tag at the point on the page where you want the link to appear.**

   In the <A> tag, use an HREF attribute (it stands for http reference URL) to indicate the address of the page that you want to link to. For example:

   ```
   <A HREF="http://www.dummies.com">
   ```

3. **After the <A> tag, type the text that you want to appear in your document as a link:**

   ```
   <A HREF="http://www.dummies.com">The Official For
   Dummies Web Page
   ```

4. **Add a closing </A> tag:**

   ```
   <A HREF="http://www.dummies.com">The Official For
   Dummies Web Page</A>
   ```

The text that appears between the <A> and </A> links is called the *anchor*. The Web address that appears in the HREF attribute is called the *target*. The anchor text displays on the Web page in a special color (usually blue) and is underlined so that the person viewing the page knows the text is a link.

If the target refers to another page at the same Web site as the page that the link appears on, you can use just the filename as the target. For example:

```
<A HREF="emerald7.html">See the Wizard</A>
```

When a user clicks the See the Wizard link, the emerald7.html file appears on-screen.

Using graphic links

A *graphic link* is a graphic image that a user can click to jump to another page or a different location on the current page. To create a graphic link, follow the procedure that I describe in the previous section. But in Step 3, instead of typing text for the link, type an <IMG> tag that identifies the image file to use for the link in its SRC attribute. For example:

```
<A HREF="emerald7.html"><IMG SRC="emerald.gif"></A>
```

In this example, the `emerald.gif` file appears on-screen. If a user clicks it, the browser displays the `emerald7.html` page.

Linking within the same page

To create a link that simply moves the user to another location on the same page, follow these steps:

1. **Create the following `<A>` tag at the start of your document: `<A NAME="`*`namehere`*`">`. Replace** *namehere* **with the name of the section that you want to link to.**

In this example, the section name is Top.

```
<A NAME="Top">
```

2. **Immediately follow the `<A>` tag with an `</A>` end tag.**

The finished product looks like this:

```
<A NAME="Top"></A>
```

3. **Create a text or graphic link to that section by typing the section name, preceded by the # symbol, in the `HREF` attribute of a link.**

Here is a snippet of HTML that creates a link that jumps to the Top location.

```
<A HREF="#Top">Go back to the top of the page</A>
```

Using Tables

Tables are a basic HTML feature frequently used for two distinct purposes. The first is presenting information in a tabular format, in which it is obvious to the user that a table is being used. The second is controlling a Web document's page layout, in which the user is (or at least should be) unaware that a table is being used.

Creating a table requires you to use some very complicated HTML tags. For that reason, setting up a table by using an HTML editor such as FrontPage or Dreamweaver is often easier. (FrontPage is covered in Part III of Book VI, and Dreamweaver in Part IV of Book VI.)

Creating a basic table

The following steps explain how to set up a basic table in which the first row contains headings and subsequent rows contain data:

1. **Type a set of `<TABLE>` and `</TABLE>` tags in the Web document where you want the table to appear:**

```
<TABLE>
</TABLE>
```

2. **Add a `BORDER` attribute to the `<TABLE>` tag to create a border and establish its width in pixels.**

For example:

```
<TABLE BORDER=6>
</TABLE>
```

3. **Create the first table row by typing a set of** `<TR>` **and** `</TR>` **tags between the** `<TABLE>` **and** `</TABLE>` **tags:**

```
<TABLE BORDER=6>
<TR>
</TR>
</TABLE>
```

This first row holds the headings for the table.

4. **For each column in the table, type a** `<TH>` **tag, followed by the text that you want to display for the heading, followed by a** `</TH>` **tag. Place each of these heading columns between the** `<TR>` **and** `</TR>` **tags:**

```
<TR>
   <TH>Web Feature</TH>
   <TH>Love It</TH>
   <TH>Hate It</TH>
</TR>
```

5. **Create additional rows for the table by typing** `<TR>` **and** `</TR>` **pairs of tags. Between these tags, type a** `<TD>` **tag followed by the text you want to appear in each column in the row and then a** `</TD>` **tag.**

   For example, here are the tags and text that you'd type to add a row to show that 62 percent of Web users love tables and 38 percent hate them:

```
<TR>
   <TD>Tables</TD>
   <TD>62%</TD>
   <TD>38%</TD>
</TR>
```

Putting all this together, here is the HTML for a table with four rows including the heading row:

```
<TABLE BORDER=6>
<TR>
   <TH>Web Feature</TH>
   <TH>Love It</TH>
   <TH>Hate It</TH>
</TR>
<TR>
   <TD>Tables</TD>
   <TD>62%</TD>
   <TD>38%</TD>
</TR>
<TR>
   <TD>Frames</TD>
   <TD>18%</TD>
   <TD>72%</TD>
</TR>
<TR>
   <TD>Style Sheets</TD>
   <TD>55%</TD>
   <TD>45%</TD>
</TR>
</TABLE>
```

Figure 3-5 shows how this table appears when displayed in a Web browser.

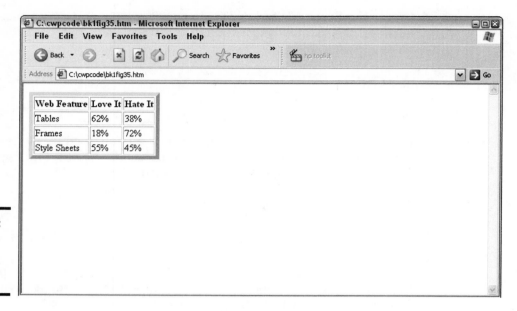

Web Feature	Love It	Hate It
Tables	62%	38%
Frames	18%	72%
Style Sheets	55%	45%

Figure 3-5:
A three-column, four-row table.

Using a table for page layout

You can use tables to set up a neat layout for the text and other elements that appear on your Web pages. The following procedure shows you how to set up a simple layout that provides for a page header area at the top of the page, a sidebar area on the left side of the page, and a main text area in the central portion of the page:

1. **Determine the dimensions of the layout that you want to use.**

Be sure to allow for empty areas (also called *gutter* areas) in your layout. Figure 3-6 shows the layout used for this example.

2. **Type a set of** `<TABLE>` **and** `</TABLE>` **tags to begin the table that will establish your page layout. In the** `<TABLE>` **tag, use the** `WIDTH` **attribute to set the overall width of your page layout in pixels and include the attributes** `BORDER=0`, `CELLSPACING=0`, **and** `CELLPADDING=0`.

You set these attributes to zero so that the table doesn't have borders or extra space between the cells. `CELLSPACING` specifies the width of the border between cells; `CELLPADDING` defines the space between the contents of cells and those cells' borders.

The `<TABLE>` tag should look like this:

```
<TABLE BORDER=0 CELLSPACING=0 CELLPADDING=0 WIDTH=780>
```

3. **Create a row for the page header area by adding the following tags between the** `<TABLE>` **and** `</TABLE>` **tags:**

```
<TR>
<TD BGCOLOR=YELLOW HEIGHT=50 COLSPAN=6>
<H1>Page Header Area</H1>
</TD>
</TR>
```

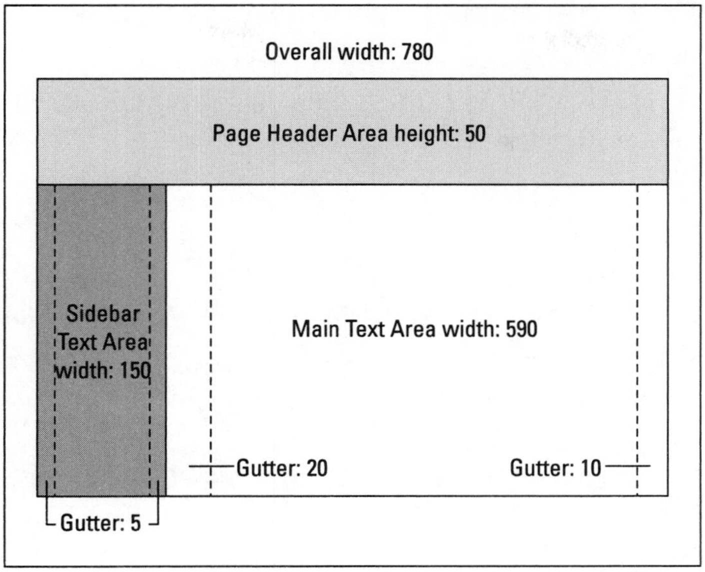

Figure 3-6:
Table layout
including
page
header,
sidebar
area, and
main text
area.

Overall width: 780

Page Header Area height: 50

Sidebar
Text Area
width: 150

Main Text Area width: 590

Gutter: 20

Gutter: 10

Gutter: 5

Use whatever color you want for the background color (BGCOLOR) and set the HEIGHT attribute value to the height of the page header area you want to provide for your layout. COLSPAN, which is short for *columns to span*, specifies how many columns you want the page header to run across.

4. **Add a set of <TR> and </TR> tags to use for the second table row, which will contain the six columns required to set up the gutter and text areas for the sidebar and main text portions of the page layout.**

5. **Between the second set of <TR> and </TR> tags, add a set of <TD> and </TD> tags for each of the three columns used for the sidebar area, similar to these:**

```
<TD BGCOLOR=SILVER WIDTH=5 HEIGHT=600
    VALIGN=TOP> </TD>
<TD BGCOLOR=SILVER WIDTH=150 VALIGN=TOP>Sidebar
    Area</TD>
<TD BGCOLOR=SILVER WIDTH=5 VALIGN=TOP> </TD>
```

Set the background color (BGCOLOR) to the color that you want to use for the sidebar background and set the WIDTH value to the width that your layout calls for. Also, use VALIGN=TOP so that any text that you place in the columns is aligned with the top of the cell rather than the middle. And, for the first column only, use a HEIGHT attribute in the <TD> tag to set the overall height of the page.

The text for the first and third columns uses a   (nonbreaking space) character as a placeholder for the gutters. For the second column, Sidebar Area is used as a placeholder.

6. **Add three more pairs of <TD> and </TR> tags to create the columns for the main text area and its two gutter areas, similar to these:**

```
<TD BGCOLOR=WHITE WIDTH=20 VALIGN=TOP> </TD>
<TD BGCOLOR=WHITE WIDTH=590 VALIGN=TOP>Main Text
    Area</TD>
<TD BGCOLOR=WHITE WIDTH=10 VALIGN=TOP> </TD>
```

The HTML for the entire layout should look something like the following:

```
<TABLE BORDER=0 CELLSPACING=0 CELLPADDING=0 WIDTH=780>
<TR>
<TD BGCOLOR=YELLOW HEIGHT=50 COLSPAN=6>
<H1>Page Header Area</H1>
</TD>
</TR>
<TR>
<TD BGCOLOR=SILVER WIDTH=5 HEIGHT=600
    VALIGN=TOP> </TD>
<TD BGCOLOR=SILVER WIDTH=150 VALIGN=TOP>Sidebar
    Area</TD>
<TD BGCOLOR=SILVER WIDTH=5 VALIGN=TOP> </TD>
<TD BGCOLOR=WHITE WIDTH=20 VALIGN=TOP> </TD>
<TD BGCOLOR=WHITE WIDTH=590 VALIGN=TOP>Main Text
    Area</TD>
<TD BGCOLOR=WHITE WIDTH=10 VALIGN=TOP> </TD>
</TR>
</TABLE>
```

7. **Save the file and test the layout that it creates by using your Web browser. Adjust the settings if necessary until the layout looks just the way you want it to.**

Figure 3-7 shows how the layout appears in Internet Explorer 6.

8. **To create a document based on the layout, open the file and save it under a new name. Then replace the Page Header Area, Sidebar Area, and Main Text Area placeholders with the text and other page elements that you want to appear in these areas.**

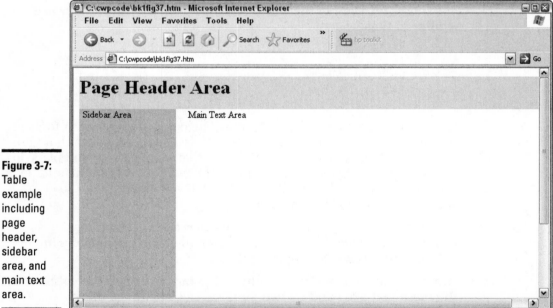

Figure 3-7:
Table example including page header, sidebar area, and main text area.

Creating Navigation Bars

A *navigation bar* is a collection of text or graphic links that enables users to work their way through a series of pages on your Web site easily. The navigation bar appears in the same place on every page in the site so that the user can easily find it.

You can create a navigation bar in several ways. The most common is to create a table, placing a link in each cell of the table. An alternative is to create a single GIF image for the entire navigation bar and use that image in an image map. For more information about how to do this, take a peek at Chapter 4 of Book VI.

Deciding what to include in a navigation bar

Depending on the site, a navigation bar can include some or all of the following links:

✦ **Home:** Takes the user to the site's home page.

✦ **Next:** Takes the user to the next page in sequence when viewing a series of Web pages.

✦ **Previous:** Takes the user to the page that precedes the current page when viewing a series of pages.

✦ **Up:** Takes the user to the page at the next level up in the hierarchy of pages.

✦ **Help:** Takes the user to a help page.

✦ **Site map:** Takes the user to a page that includes links to all the pages on the site.

A navigation bar can also contain links to major sections of your Web site, such as a Product Information section or an Online Catalog section.

Creating a text-based navigation bar

The easiest way to create a navigation bar is to use text links in a table. Each cell in the table contains a link. The following bit of HTML shows how to create a navigation bar with links to four pages (Home, Help, Next, and Previous). (For more information about the <TABLE>, <TR>, and <TD> tags, see "Using Tables," earlier in this chapter.)

```
<TABLE BORDER="0" CELLSPACING="0" CELLPADDING="0" WIDTH=800>
<TR>

<TD BGCOLOR="SILVER" HEIGHT="25" WIDTH="160" VALIGN="TOP">
<IMG SRC="blank.gif">
</TD>

<TD BGCOLOR="SILVER" HEIGHT="25" WIDTH="100" VALIGN="TOP">
<A HREF="home.html">Home</A>
</TD>
```

```
<TD BGCOLOR="SILVER" HEIGHT="25" WIDTH="100" VALIGN="TOP">
<A HREF="help.html">Help</A>
</TD>

<TD BGCOLOR="SILVER" HEIGHT="25" WIDTH="100" VALIGN="TOP">
<A HREF="page3.html">Next</A>
</TD>

<TD BGCOLOR="SILVER" HEIGHT="25" WIDTH="100" VALIGN="TOP">
<A HREF="page1.html">Previous</A>
</TD>

<TD BGCOLOR="SILVER" HEIGHT="""25" WIDTH="240" VALIGN="TOP">
<IMG SRC="blank.gif">
</TD>

</TR>
</TABLE>
```

This HTML table is set up so that the entire table is 800 pixels wide. The table has a single row, which has six cells. The first and last cells contain the image file `blank.gif`, which displays a blank cell; they provide the spacing necessary to precisely position the four middle cells, which contain the text links for the Home, Help, Next, and Previous pages. Figure 3-8 shows how this navigation bar appears when positioned at the top of a blank page.

You have to modify the HREF attributes in the text links used for the Next and Previous links on each page.

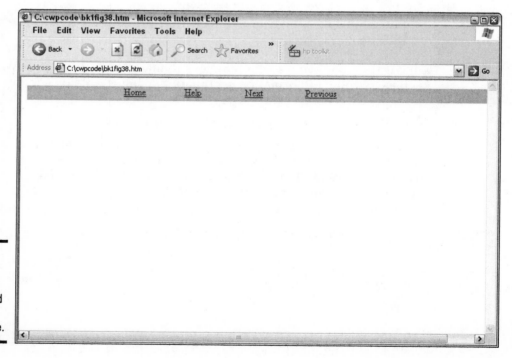

Figure 3-8:
A text navigation bar created using an HTML table.

Using images in a navigation bar

You can create a navigation bar by using images of the buttons that the user clicks to move from page to page. Here is the HTML for a simple navigation bar that uses two images of arrows (one facing left, the other right) to link to the Next and Previous pages. A simple two-cell table positions the buttons side by side. (The images in this navigation bar are created as links within the cells of a table. For more information about the <TABLE>, <TR>, and <TD> tags, see "Using Tables," earlier in this chapter.)

```
<TABLE BORDER="0" CELLSPACING="0" CELLPADDING="0" WIDTH=50>
<TR>

<TD HEIGHT="25" WIDTH="25">
<A HREF="page1.html"><IMG SRC="larrow.gif" BORDER="0"
    HEIGHT="25" WIDTH="25"></A>
</TD>

<TD HEIGHT="25" WIDTH="25">
<A HREF="page3.html"><IMG SRC="rarrow.gif" BORDER="0"
    HEIGHT="25" WIDTH="25"></A>
</TD>

</TR>
</TABLE>
```

In this example, larrow.gif and rarrow.gif are GIF images 25 pixels tall by 25 pixels wide that show a left and right arrow.

Chapter 4: Working with Graphics, Sounds, and Video

In This Chapter

✓ Understanding formats for image, sound, and video files

✓ Working with images

✓ Using image maps

✓ Creating transparent GIF images

✓ Adding sounds and video clips to a Web page

Adding images, sounds, and movie clips to your Web pages can make your pages come alive. If you already have a few multimedia files and want to incorporate them into your pages, this is the chapter for you. Here you find the guidelines and specific steps that you need to add multimedia files to your Web pages like a pro.

Getting Familiar with File Formats for Image, Sound, and Video

You can choose from many different file formats for images, sounds, and videos. Fortunately, you can construct almost all Web pages by using just the formats that I describe in the following sections.

Image file

Although dozens of different image file formats exist, only two are widely used for Web page images: GIF and JPEG.

GIF images

GIF, which stands for Graphic Interchange Format, was originally used on the CompuServe online network and is now widely used throughout the Internet. GIF image files have the following characteristics:

✦ GIF images can have a maximum of 256 different colors.

✦ GIF files are compressed to reduce their sizes. The compression method that GIF uses doesn't reduce the image quality.

✦ A GIF image can include a transparent color, which, when displayed in a Web browser, allows the background of the Web page to show through.

✦ GIF images can be interlaced, which allows the Web browser to quickly display a crude version of the image and then display progressively better versions of the image.

✦ GIF supports a simple animation technique that enables you to store several distinct images in the same file. The Web browser displays the animation by displaying the images one after the other in sequence.

✦ GIF files usually have the .gif filename extension.

The GIF format is the best choice for most Web graphics that are created with drawing or paint programs and that do not contain a large number of different colors. It's ideal for icons, buttons, background textures, bullets, rules, and line art.

A format called PNG (Portable Network Graphic) was developed in 1995 as a successor to the GIF format. PNG (pronounced *ping*) supports all the features of GIF and then some, including support for more colors than GIF. PNG hasn't really caught on, however, so GIF remains the most widely used image format.

JPEG images

JPEG, a format developed by the Joint Photographic Experts Group, is designed for photographic quality images. It has the following characteristics:

✦ JPEG images can have either 16.7 million or 2 billion colors. Most JPEG images use 16.7 million colors, which provides excellent representation of photographic images.

✦ To reduce image size, JPEG uses a special compression technique that slightly reduces the quality of the image while greatly reducing its size. In most cases, you have to carefully compare the original uncompressed image with the compressed image to see the difference.

✦ JPEG supports progressive images that are similar to GIF interlaced images.

✦ JPEG doesn't support transparent background colors as GIF does.

✦ JPEG doesn't support animation.

✦ JPEG files usually have the .jpg filename extension.

Other image file formats

Many other image file formats exist that *don't* work on the Web. (To use a graphic file saved in one of these non-Web-friendly formats, you must convert the file to JPEG or GIF by using a graphics program, such as Jasc Software's Paint Shop Pro.) Here are just a few non-Web-friendly graphics formats:

✦ **BMP:** Windows bitmap

✦ **PCX:** Another bitmap format

✦ **TIF:** Tagged Image File

✦ **PIC:** Macintosh picture file

Sound file formats

The following paragraphs describe the most commonly used sound file formats.

◆ **WAV:** The Windows standard for sound recordings. WAV is short for Wave.

◆ **SND:** The Macintosh standard for sound recordings. SND is short for Sound.

◆ **AU:** The UNIX standard for sound recordings. AU is short for Audio.

◆ **MID:** MIDI files, which are not actually sound recordings but are instead music stored in a form that a sound card's synthesizer can play. MIDI stands for Musical Instrument Digital Interface.

Don't confuse sound files with sound that you can listen to in real time over the Internet, known as *streaming audio.* The most popular format for streaming audio is RealPlayer. RealPlayer enables you to listen to a sound as it is being downloaded to your computer, so you don't have to wait for the entire file to be downloaded before you can listen to it. To listen to RealPlayer sound, you must first install RealPlayer (available at `www.real.com`) in your Web browser.

Video file formats

Three popular formats for video clips are used on the Web:

◆ **AVI:** The Windows video standard. AVI stands for Audio Video Interleaved.

◆ **QuickTime:** The Macintosh video standard. QuickTime files usually have the `.mov` extension.

◆ **MPEG:** An independent standard. MPEG stands for Motion Picture Experts Group.

Although AVI is known as a Windows video format and QuickTime is a Macintosh format, both formats — as well as MPEG — have become cross-platform standards. Both Netscape Navigator and Microsoft Internet Explorer can play AVI, QuickTime, and MPEG videos.

Inserting a Graphic Image

To insert a graphic image on a Web page, follow these steps:

1. **Obtain an image file that you want to include on your page and store the image file in the same directory as the HTML document that displays the image.**

If necessary, use a graphics program to convert the file to the format you want to use (GIF or JPEG).

2. **In the HTML file, add the** `<IMG>` **tag at the point in the document where you want the image to appear and use the** `SRC` **attribute to provide the name of the image file.**

For example:

```
<IMG SRC="image1.gif">
```

Working with Graphic Images

Here are some guidelines for using graphic images wisely on your Web pages:

✦ Don't add so many images or such large images that your page takes too long to download. As a general rule, try holding your breath while your page downloads with a 28.8 Kbps modem. If you turn blue, the download takes too long.

✦ Use the `ALT` attribute with the `<IMG>` tag to provide text for users who view your page with images turned off. For example:

```
<IMG SRC="chicken.gif" ALT="Picture of a chicken">
```

✦ Use the `HEIGHT` and `WIDTH` attributes with the `<IMG>` tag to preformat your pages for the correct image dimensions.

```
<IMG SRC="chicken.gif" HEIGHT=100 WIDTH=50>
```

✦ Use the GIF format for most images created with drawing or painting programs. Use the JPEG format for photographic images.

✦ Use `BORDER=0` in the `<IMG>` tag to eliminate the border that appears around your images (unless you want the borders to appear):

```
<IMG SRC="chicken.gif" BORDER=0>
```

✦ Use transparent GIFs to create images that blend seamlessly with your page background.

For more information about transparent GIFs, skip ahead to "Using Transparent GIF Images," later in this chapter.

✦ If you want to make large image files available for download on your Web site, provide smaller, thumbnail versions of the images that people can preview before deciding whether to download the full-sized image. Many graphics editing programs, including Paint Shop Pro, enable you to create thumbnail versions of graphics files quickly and easily.

Keep in mind that many of the images you see displayed on the Web are copyrighted materials that you cannot simply copy and use on your own Web site without permission from the copyright holder. Similarly, photographs, artwork, and other images that appear in magazines and books are copyrighted. (In other words, if you didn't create the materials yourself or purchase them, someone else owns them.) You cannot legally scan copyrighted images and post them on your Web site without the copyright owner's permission. For the skinny on United States copyright law, check out `www.copyright.gov`. If you're not based in the United States, you might want to check out the Canadian Intellectual Property Office at `http://cipo.gc.ca`, the U.K. Patent Office at `www.patent.gov.uk/copy/index.htm`, or the Australian Copyright Council home page at `www.copyright.org.au`.

Carving Up Graphics with Image Maps

An *image map* is a graphic image in which specific regions of the image serve as links to other Web pages. For example, if you're creating a Web site about *The Wizard of Oz,* you can use an image map showing the Scarecrow, Tin Man, and Cowardly Lion to link to pages about these characters. To create an image map, you must use several HTML tags: `<MAP>` and its companion `</MAP>`, `<AREA>`, and `<IMG>`. Here are the steps to follow to create an image map:

1. **Find or create a graphic image that can serve as an image map.**

   The image should have distinct regions that will serve as the map's links.

   For example, you can use the image that you see in Figure 4-1 as an image map that will provide two links: one for the dog, the other for the woman.

2. **Using your favorite graphics drawing program to display the image, determine the rectangular boundaries of each area of the image that will serve as a link. Write down the pixel coordinates of the top, left, bottom, and right edges of these rectangles.**

   The example in Figure 4-2 shows these coordinates: 32, 367 (width) and 161, 554 (height). Most graphics programs display these coordinates in the program's status bar as you move the mouse around or when you use the selection tool to select an area. For example, Figure 4-2 shows an area selected (using the crop tool) in Paint Shop Pro.

Figure 4-1:
Use an image with at least two distinct regions as an image map.

Figure 4-2:
You use the coordinates a graphics program displays to create an image map.

For the dog-and-woman image in Figure 4-2, the following coordinates define the rectangular areas for the links:

	Top	Left	Bottom	Right
Dog	32	367	161	554
Woman	168	99	350	568

3. Type a set of `<MAP>` and `</MAP>` tags. In the `<MAP>` tag, use the `NAME` attribute to provide a name for the image map:

```
<MAP NAME="IMGMAP1">
</MAP>
```

4. Between the `<MAP>` and `</MAP>` tags, type an `<AREA>` tag for each rectangular area of the image that will serve as a link. In the `<AREA>` tag, include the following attributes:

- `SHAPE=RECT`
- `COORDS="top, left, bottom, right"`
- `HREF="url"`

For example:

```
<MAP NAME=IMGMAP1>
  <AREA SHAPE=RECT COORDS="32, 367, 161, 554"
  HREF="dog.html">
  <AREA SHAPE=RECT COORDS="168, 99, 350, 568"
  HREF="woman.html">
</MAP>
```

5. Type an `<IMG>` **tag. Use the** `SRC` **attribute to name the image file and the** `USEMAP` **attribute to provide the name of the image map listed in the** `<MAP>` **tag:**

```
<IMG SRC="dog_and_woman.jpg" USEMAP="#imgmap1">
```

Be sure to type a pound sign (#) before the image map name in the `<IMG>` tag's `USEMAP` attribute. But don't use the pound sign when you create the name in the `<MAP>` tag's `NAME` attribute.

Putting it all together, here is a complete HTML document to set up an image map:

```
<BODY>
<MAP NAME=IMGMAP1>
<AREA SHAPE=RECT COORDS="32, 367, 161, 554" HREF="dog.html">
   <AREA SHAPE=RECT COORDS="168, 99, 350, 568"
   HREF="woman.html">
</MAP>
<IMG SRC="dog_and_woman.jpg" USEMAP="#imgmap1">
</BODY>
```

Figure 4-3 shows how this page appears when displayed. Clicking the dog in Figure 4-3 loads the file `dog.html`; clicking the woman loads `woman.html`. The in-between parts of the image — for example, the trees over the dog's head — aren't clickable; in other words, clicking the in-between areas of the image doesn't cause a new file to load.

Figure 4-3:
A clickable image map displayed in a browser.

Use the `TITLE` attribute in the `<AREA>` tags to create ToolTips that display when the user pauses the mouse pointer briefly over an image map area. For example:

```
<AREA SHAPE=RECT COORDS="32, 367, 161, 554"
  HREF="dog.html" TITLE="Panda the Wonder Dog">
<AREA SHAPE=RECT COORDS="168, 99, 350, 568"
  HREF="woman.html" TITLE="Panda's Human Companion">
```

Some people configure their settings so that their browsers don't download and display images. Whenever you use an image map, be sure to provide text links as an alternative to the image map. Otherwise, users who visit your page with images turned off can't navigate your site.

Using Transparent GIF Images

Most graphics programs can create transparent GIF images in which one color is designated as transparent. When the image displays on your page, the background color of the page shows through the transparent area. You can also create sophisticated designs by stacking images of different transparency levels on top of each other. (Imagine a stack of plastic overhead transparencies, each containing a different image.) Stackable images — whether transparent or opaque — are referred to as *layers* in most graphics programs.

The procedures for setting the transparent color are similar in most graphics programs. Follow these steps to set transparent color in Paint Shop Pro:

1. **Open the image that you want to make transparent.**

2. **Choose Layers⇨Properties.**

   The Layer Properties dialog box appears, as shown in Figure 4-4.

Figure 4-4: You use the Layer Properties dialog box to set the transparency attribute for an image.

3. Click the Opacity Selector in the Layer Properties dialog box and choose an opacity setting from 0 (fully transparent, or invisible) to 100 (fully opaque).

The preview image changes based on your selection.

4. When you're happy with the transparency of your image, click OK.

5. Choose File⇨Save to save the file with the transparent color information.

To use a transparent background color, make sure that the image's background consists of a single color and that the background color doesn't appear elsewhere in the image. You might need to fiddle with your paint program's painting tools to adjust the background of the image accordingly.

Incorporating Sounds

You can insert a sound file on a Web page in one of two ways: as a link or as an embedded sound. The following sections show you how to use the HTML tags necessary for each method. You can also insert a sound as a part of the page's background so that the sound plays automatically whenever the page displays. Flip to "Creating a background sound," later in this chapter, for more information.

Inserting a link to a sound file

Not everyone likes sound to play automatically. The advantage of linking to a sound file is that it gives your visitors a choice. The sound file isn't downloaded to the user's computer until the user clicks the sound file link. To insert a link to a sound file, follow these steps:

1. Obtain a sound file that you want linked to your Web site.

2. Place the sound file in the same directory as the HTML document that will contain the link.

3. Add an <A> tag, some descriptive text, and an </A> tag to the HTML file as follows:

```
<A HREF="sound.wav">Click here to play the sound.</A>
```

Be sure to type the name of your sound file in the HREF attribute.

Embedding a sound file

Embedding a sound file displays sound controls (stop, play, and start) on a Web page, allowing visitors to control when and how the sound file plays. You can embed a sound file on a Web page by using an <EMBED> tag as follows:

```
<EMBED SRC="sound.wav">
```

The SRC attribute specifies the name of the sound file.

Be sure to specify a fully qualified filename (one that includes the full path to the file) if your sound file is located in a different directory than your HTML file (for example: `SRC="d:\mysite\mysounds\sound.wav"`).

Creating a background sound

A *background sound* plays automatically whenever a user displays your Web page. To add a background sound to a page, follow these steps:

1. Obtain a sound file that you want to use as a background sound.

2. Place the sound file in the same directory as the HTML file.

3. Add a `<BGSOUND>` tag following the document's `<BODY>` tag. Use the `SRC` attribute to name the sound file you want to be played:

```
<BODY>
<BGSOUND SRC="music.mid">
```

4. If you want the sound to repeat several times, add the `LOOP` attribute:

```
<BGSOUND SRC="music.mid" LOOP=3>
```

You can type any number that you want in the `LOOP` attribute to indicate how many times the sound should be repeated. You can use `LOOP=INFINITE` to repeat the sound repeatedly as long as the page is displayed.

Some people would rather listen to fingernails dragged across a chalkboard than annoying background sounds that play over and over again. If you want people like me to visit your site more than once, avoid `LOOP=INFINITE` like the plague.

Incorporating Video Clips

You can insert a video file on a Web page in one of two ways: as a link or as an embedded object. This section describes how.

Inserting a link to a video

Inserting a link to a video clip enables your visitors to decide whether and when to view your visual masterpiece. All your visitors need to do to view a linked video is click the link. (To view an embedded video, on the other hand, visitors need to click the embedded playback controls. Check out the next section, "Embedding a video," for details.)

Follow these steps to insert a link to a video file:

1. Locate a video file that you want to link to from your Web page.

2. Add an `<A>` tag, some descriptive text, and an `</A>` tag to the HTML file as follows:

```
<A HREF="movie.avi">Click here to download a movie.</A>
```

Provide the name of the video file in the `<A>` tag's `HREF` attribute.

When the user clicks the link, the Web browser downloads the file and plays the video.

Embedding a video

Embedding a video differs from inserting a link to a video — which I describe in the preceding section — in one very important respect: Embedding a video automatically displays a video control panel that your visitors can use to stop, start, and pause video playback.

Use the `<EMBED>` tag to embed a video on a Web page. Follow these steps:

1. **Locate a video file that you want to embed on a Web page.**

2. **In the HTML document for the Web page, add an `<EMBED>` tag specifying the name of the video file in the `SRC` attribute:**

   ```
   <EMBED SRC="movie.avi">
   ```

3. **If you want to change the size of the area used to display the video, add the `HEIGHT` and `WIDTH` attributes:**

   ```
   <EMBED SRC="movie.avi" HEIGHT=200 WIDTH=200>
   ```

4. **If you want the video to play automatically as soon as it finishes downloading, add `AUTOSTART=TRUE` to the `<EMBED>` tag:**

   ```
   <EMBED SRC="movie.avi" AUTOSTART=TRUE>
   ```

5. **If you want the video to repeat, add a `LOOP` attribute to the `<EMBED>` tag.**

   You can set the `LOOP` value to a number to cause the video to repeat a specific number of times, or you can specify `LOOP=INFINITE` to cause the video to replay over and over again as long as the page is displayed.

Chapter 5: Building Your Web Workshop

In This Chapter

✔ Examining Web browsers

✔ Choosing a graphics program

✔ Selecting an HTML editor

✔ Perusing Java, JavaScript, and multimedia tools

✔ Opting for office suites

*W*hether you're cooking, building furniture, or creating Web pages, the right tool for the job can be a big help. Fortunately, an enormous selection of Web tools is on the market today, ranging from free to pricey, from general, all-purpose tools to unbelievably specialized wizards. For every Web developer and every project, you can find the perfect tool.

In this chapter, I introduce you to some popular, useful tools that you might want to consider adding to your Web toolbox. Some of these tools are commercial programs that you must buy, and others are programs that you can download for free from the Internet.

Web Browsers

Two Web browsers are in widespread usage on the Internet. If you're a serious Web developer, you should have both of them so that you can make sure that your Web pages work with both browsers.

Netscape 7.1

Netscape 7.1 is the complete package of Internet access tools from Netscape, including the following components:

✦ Navigator, for Web browsing

✦ Mail, for e-mail

✦ Instant Messenger, for instant messaging

✦ Composer, for creating Web pages

You can download Netscape free, or you can purchase one of several Netscape editions that include additional software. You can also order Netscape on CD-ROM for $2.95.

Price: Free

Web site: http://channels.netscape.com/ns/browsers/default.jsp

Internet Explorer 6

Internet Explorer 6 features the latest Web technologies from Microsoft: Dynamic HTML (a combination of HTML, style sheets, and scripting tools that enables you to create Web pages that respond to user interaction), Visual Basic Scripting Edition (VBScript), channels, ActiveX (a language for creating and plugging self-contained programs — similar to Java applets — into Web pages), and more.

The complete Internet Explorer 6 suite includes the following components:

+ Internet Explorer 6, for Web browsing
+ Outlook Express, for e-mail and newsgroups
+ MSN Messenger Service, for instant messaging
+ NetMeeting, for online conferencing

All these components are available to download from the Microsoft Web site. (If you prefer, you can order Internet Explorer on a CD-ROM for $5 shipping and handling.)

Price: Free

Web site: www.microsoft.com/windows/ie/default.htm

Graphics Programs

Graphics programs are an essential part of your Web toolkit. You need a graphics drawing program that can create images in either the GIF or JPEG format, and the program should be able to handle advanced features, such as GIF transparent backgrounds, interlaced images, and animations. The following sections describe several graphics programs you can use for creating Web pages.

Photoshop

Photoshop, from Adobe, is one of the oldest, best known, and most consistently top-rated graphics programs around. As you might guess from the name, Adobe Photoshop originally focused on helping professional photographers (and graphic designers) retouch and manipulate photos. These days, Photoshop offers much more: a full range of professional-strength tools for graphic design and video as well as photography.

Price: $649

Web site: www.adobe.com

CorelDRAW

CorelDRAW 11 Graphics Suite is one of the best suites of graphics programs available. The relatively stiff price makes sense when you realize that the comprehensive CorelDRAW 11 Graphics Suite package includes not just the

CorelDRAW drawing program, but Corel PHOTO-PAINT 2, Corel R.A.V.E. (Real Animated Vector Effects 2), and a bunch of photos, fonts, and graphics utility programs, as well.

Price: $529

Web site: www.corel.com

Paint Shop Pro

Paint Shop Pro 8, from Jasc Software, Inc., is a powerful yet inexpensive painting program that you can download from the Internet to use free for a 30-day evaluation period. If you like it, you can purchase it after the trial period. Paint Shop Pro 8 has just about everything that you could possibly want in an image drawing program. It supports more than 30 graphic image formats, including, of course, GIF and JPEG, and it includes sophisticated features, such as gradient fills, blur effects, and textured brush effects for creating stunning images. Paint Shop Pro 8 also comes with Animation Shop for creating GIF animations.

Price: $99 download or $109 on CD-ROM

Web site: www.jasc.com

Windows Paint

Paint is the free image drawing program that comes with Windows. Beginning with Windows 98, Microsoft has beefed up Paint to make it suitable for working with Web images by supporting the GIF and JPEG file formats. Paint can handle transparent background colors for GIF images, but it can't create interlaced GIF images or GIF animations.

Price: Included with Windows 98, 2000, and XP

Web site: www.microsoft.com

HTML Editors

You can create HTML documents with a simple text editor, such as Notepad, but for serious HTML work, you should invest in a more sophisticated HTML editor, such as one of the programs that I describe in the following sections. Most HTML editors let you work in two modes:

✦ Graphical WYSIWYG (What You See Is What You Get) mode lets you create Web pages by dragging and dropping, like a cross between a word processor and a drawing program.

✦ HTML mode lets you work directly with HTML tags and attributes. In addition, many HTML editors generate not just HTML code, but also simple JavaScript code, Java code, and more.

Dreamweaver

Dreamweaver MX 2004, from Macromedia, Inc., combines a text editor with a visual development environment so that you can choose the Web page creation style you're most comfortable with. A bonus for developers interested in creating animations for their Web sites: Dreamweaver is compatible with Flash (Macromedia's animation creation tool). Chapters 19 through 27 of Book VI explore Dreamweaver.

Price: $399

Web site: www.macromedia.com/software/dreamweaver

Composer

Composer is a free HTML editor that comes bundled with the Netscape Web browser. Nifty toolbar buttons let you quickly add lists, tables, images, links, colors, and font styles to your pages.

Price: Free download or $2.95 on CD-ROM

Web site: http://channels.netscape.com/ns/browsers/default.jsp

FrontPage 2003

FrontPage 2003 is the Microsoft full-featured Web site development tool. The FrontPage 2003 WYSIWYG HTML editor enables you to use advanced HTML features, such as layers and Cascading Style Sheets, and it enables you to edit HTML tags and attributes directly. In addition, FrontPage 2003 includes tools that let you manage and coordinate all the pages that make up your Web site, including a feature that maintains your hyperlinks automatically. Chapters 14 through 18 of Book VI examine FrontPage 2003.

Price: $199

Web site: www.microsoft.com/frontpage

HotDog Professional

HotDog Professional 7.0, made by a company called Sausage Software, is a sophisticated code-based HTML editor that uses wizards to create HTML tags for your documents. Unlike most HTML editors, HotDog Professional 7.0 lets you utilize advanced features such as style sheets, Java, and push channels. (*Push channels* work much like radio and television channels: They push, or *broadcast,* content to users, rather than waiting for users to request content. In contrast, traditional Web sites are considered *pull channels* because users must take a specific action, such as clicking a link, to download content.)

Price: $99.95 download or $129.95 on CD-ROM

Web site: www.sausage.com

Java and Animation Tools

If you're interested in creating Java *applets* (self-contained programs written in the Java programming language) or flashy animations to add to your Web pages, you want to invest in a top-notch development tool such as one of the following.

JBuilder

JBuilder 9, from Borland Software Corporation, is a popular visual Java development environment for creating Java-based Web sites. It is available in three editions: Personal, Developer, and Enterprise. A free trial version of JBuilder is available for download at the Borland Web site.

Price: $9.95 (trial version), $999 (Developer Edition), $3,500 (Enterprise Edition)

Web site: www.borland.com/jbuilder/index.html

Flash

Macromedia Flash MX 2004 has become the standard for any Web designer wanting to produce high-quality, high-impact animations for Web sites. This tool offers advanced drawing tools and interactive support that you can use to create *navigation bars* (cool rows of clickable buttons that enable users to visit other sections of a site) and presentations complete with synchronized sound.

Price: $499

Web site: www.macromedia.com/software/flash

Office Suites

All three of the popular Office suites — Microsoft Office, Corel WordPerfect Suite, and Lotus SmartSuite — include Web authoring features. These features enable you to use a word processor, spreadsheet, or desktop presentation program to create Web pages. One of the useful features is the ability to quickly convert an existing document, spreadsheet, or presentation to a Web page.

Corel WordPerfect Office 11

The Corel basic office suite features these programs:

✦ **Word processing:** Corel WordPerfect 11
✦ **Spreadsheet:** Corel Quattro Pro 11
✦ **Desktop presentations:** Corel Presentations 11

You can use all these programs to create new Web pages by using HTML, PDF, and XML. The Professional Edition also includes the database program Paradox, which can also publish database data to a Web page.

Price: $299.99 (Standard Edition). The Professional Edition is available through a licensing program; total cost depends on a number of criteria. Contact Corel for details.

Web site: www.corel.com

Lotus SmartSuite Millennium Edition

SmartSuite Millennium Edition 9.8 includes the following programs:

✦ **Word processing:** Lotus Word Pro

✦ **Spreadsheet:** Lotus 1-2-3

✦ **Desktop presentations:** Lotus Freelance Graphics

✦ **Database:** Lotus Approach

You can use all the SmartSuite programs for Web publishing. SmartSuite programs can automatically convert documents, presentations, and spreadsheets to HTML format and publish them on the Web. SmartSuite is especially adept at collaborative work by enabling you to electronically distribute documents to other Internet users and automatically consolidate multiple versions of a document to create a final, edited document.

Price: $202

Web site: www.lotus.com/products/smartsuite.nsf

Microsoft Office

Microsoft Office 2003 comes in several versions; the most popular are the Standard Edition and the Professional Edition. Office 2003 Standard Edition includes the following programs:

✦ **Word processing:** Word 2003

✦ **Spreadsheet:** Excel 2003

✦ **Desktop presentations:** PowerPoint 2003

✦ **E-mail/organizer:** Outlook 2003

The Professional Edition also includes the database program Access 2003, as well as Publisher 2003 and FrontPage 2003.

All the Office 2003 programs include features for creating Web pages. You can use Word 2003 as a simple WYSIWYG HTML editor, or you can convert existing documents to HTML pages. You can also use Access 2003 and Excel 2003 to publish database or spreadsheet data to the Web.

Price: $250

Web site: www.microsoft.com/office

Chapter 6: Publishing Your Web Site

In This Chapter

✔ Using FTP to publish your Web pages

✔ Using Microsoft's Web Publishing Wizard to publish your Web pages

✔ Rating your site by using the ICRA rating service

*I*n Web parlance, *publishing* your Web site means taking the steps necessary to move your Web pages from your computer to a Web server — whether that Web server is maintained by an Internet service provider (ISP) or a Web hosting company. After your pages are on a Web server, anyone with a Web browser and a working Internet connection can see them.

Because visitors won't exactly flock to your site just because it exists on a Web server, this chapter shows you not only how to transfer your files to a Web server but also how to rate your site (an optional step that you can take to announce to the world that your Web pages contain, for example, no sexually explicit content).

Always make sure that you test your Web pages — in other words, load them in a Web browser and double-check that they look and behave the way you want them to — before you publish them to the Web for the whole world to see. Many Web page creation tools, such as Dreamweaver and FrontPage, make the testing process easy by including a Preview/Debug in Browser button on the main toolbar. (See Chapter 17 of Book VI for information about testing Web sites in FrontPage 2003. See Chapter 27 of Book VI about testing them in Dreamweaver.)

Publishing Your Web Pages

Before anyone on the Web can see your Web pages, you must first upload, or *transfer,* them from your computer to a Web server. You have a couple options for making this transfer:

✦ **File Transfer Protocol (FTP):** If your computer is running Windows 98, Windows 2000, or Windows XP, you can use the command-line program called `ftp.exe` to upload your pages to any Web server. You can also purchase and use one of the popular graphical FTP programs on the market, such as WS_FTP Pro (`www.ipswitch.com`) for Windows users or Fetch (`www.fetchsoftworks.com`) for Mac users.

✦ **Web Publishing Wizard:** If your computer is running Windows 98, Windows 2000, or Windows XP, or if you have Internet Explorer Version 4 or higher installed, you can use the Web Publishing Wizard to walk you through the process of uploading your files to a Web server on the free Microsoft Web hosting service, MSN Groups.

Most Web page creation tools, such as FrontPage and Dreamweaver, come with their own built-in utilities to help you publish your Web pages.

FTP

FTP, or *File Transfer Protocol,* is a commonly used method of transferring your Web files to a Web server.

What you need to know to use FTP

To use FTP to transfer your Web files to a Web server, you need to obtain the following information from your ISP:

✦ **The host name for the FTP server:** This name usually, but not always, starts with `ftp`, as in `ftp.yourwebserver.com`.

✦ **The user ID and password that you must use to log on to the FTP server:** Your user ID is probably the same user ID and password that you use to log on to your service provider's Web, e-mail, and news servers.

✦ **The name of the directory into which you can copy your Web files:** On the server that I use, the directory is named `PUBLIC_HTML`. (A directory on an FTP server is similar to a folder in Windows 98 or Windows XP.)

The Windows FTP client

If you use Windows 98, Windows 2000, or Windows XP, you already have the software that you need to access an FTP server. The following steps describe how to transfer files to a Web server by using the FTP program that comes with Windows:

1. **Collect all the files required for your Web site in one folder.**

   If you have a lot of files — for example, 50 or more — you might want to consider using several subfolders to organize the files. But if you do, keep the folder structure as simple as possible.

2. **Make sure that you have the information you need to access the FTP server.**

   To find out what you need, refer to the previous section, "What you need to know to use FTP."

3. **Open an MS-DOS command window by choosing Start⇨All Programs⇨Accessories⇨Command Prompt.**

4. **Use the CD (change directory) command to change to the folder that contains the Web files that you want to transfer to the Web server.**

   For example, if your Web files are stored in a folder named \Webfiles, type the following command into the MS-DOS command window:

   ```
   cd \Webfiles
   ```

5. **Type ftp followed by the name of your FTP host:**

   ```
   ftp ftp.yourwebserver.com
   ```

A line similar to *User* (ftp.*yourwebserver*.com) appears in the MS-DOS command window, followed by a colon.

6. Type your user ID.

The Password: prompt appears.

7. Type your password.

After you successfully log in to the FTP server, you see an FTP prompt that looks like this:

```
ftp>
```

This prompt indicates that you're connected to the FTP server, and any commands that you type are processed by the FTP server, not by the DOS command prompt on your own computer.

8. Use the CD command to change to the directory to which you want to copy your files.

For example:

```
cd public_html
```

You can verify your current directory at any time by typing **PWD** (the command for *print working directory*) at the FTP command prompt.

Remember that the FTP server processes this command, so it changes the current directory on the FTP server, not on your own computer. The current directory for your own computer is still set to the directory that you specified in Step 4.

9. Use the ascii or binary command to set the appropriate file transfer mode.

If you plan to upload nontext files such as GIF files, JPG files, or sound files — or a mix of both text and nontext files — type **binary** at the FTP command prompt and press Enter. If, on the other hand, you plan to upload only plain text (HTML) files, type **ascii** (short for ASCII text) at the FTP command prompt and press Enter.

Setting the file transfer mode to ASCII and uploading nontext files causes your nontext files to arrive at the Web server in a horribly mangled form. When in doubt, always set the file transfer mode to binary.

10. Use the following MPUT command to copy all the files from the current directory on your computer (which you set in Step 4) to the current directory on the FTP server (which you set in Step 8):

```
mput *.*
```

You're prompted to copy each file in the directory:

```
mput yourfile.html?
```

11. Type Y and then press Enter to copy the file to the FTP server. Type N and then press Enter if you want to skip the file.

After you copy all the files, the ftp> prompt displays again.

12. Type bye to disconnect from the FTP server.

Windows and Macintosh use the terms *folders* and *subfolders*. FTP uses the terms *directories* and *subdirectories* to refer to the same concept. Throughout the following discussion, keep in mind that the terms *subdirectory* and *subfolder* mean essentially the same thing, except that folders and subfolders exist on Windows or Macintosh computers, and directories and subdirectories exist on the FTP server.

If you have files stored in subfolders on your computer, you must copy those files to the FTP server separately. First, though, you must create the subdirectories on the FTP server. Use the MKDIR command to do that. For example, to create a subdirectory named IMAGES, type a command at the FTP prompt:

```
mkdir images
```

Now you can copy files to the new directory. First, use the CD command to change to the new directory:

```
cd images
```

Then, use the MPUT command to copy the files. You must specify the name of the subfolder that contains the files on your computer in the MPUT command:

```
mput images\*.*
```

You're prompted to copy the files in the IMAGES folder one at a time.

Partial FTP command summary

Table 6-1 lists the FTP commands that you're most likely to use when you store your Web files on an FTP server.

Table 6-1	Common FTP Commands
Command	**Description**
ascii	Sets the transfer mode to ASCII text (for plain text files).
binary	Sets the transfer mode to binary (for nontext files).
bye	Disconnects from the FTP server and exits the FTP program.
cd	Changes the current FTP server directory.
delete	Deletes a file on the FTP server.
dir	Displays the names of the files in the current FTP server directory.
get	Copies a single file from the FTP server to your computer.
help	Displays a list of commands (`help command` displays instructions for `command`).
mget	Copies multiple files from the FTP server to your computer.
mkdir	Creates a new directory on the FTP server.
mput	Copies multiple files from your computer to the FTP server.
put	Copies a single file from your computer to the FTP server.
rename	Renames a file on the FTP server.
rmdir	Removes (deletes) a directory on the FTP server.

Web Publishing Wizard

The Microsoft Web Publishing Wizard simplifies the task of publishing your Web site. The Web Publishing Wizard comes with Internet Explorer versions 4 and higher; it also comes with Windows XP (and Windows 98, if you're still using an older computer).

The Web Publishing Wizard doesn't allow you to upload your Web files to any Web server that you want. Instead, the Web Publishing Wizard allows you to upload your Web files to MSN Groups — Microsoft's own free Web hosting service — and your photos to HP Photo, a free Web hosting service devoted to personal photo albums. If you want to upload your files to another Web host, see the FTP section earlier in this chapter. For more information about MSN Groups, visit `http://groups.msn.com`. For the skinny on HP Photo, point your Web browser to `www.hpphoto.com`.

Follow these steps to set up the Web Publishing Wizard for your Web site and copy the Web files to your Web server for the first time if you're running Windows XP:

1. **Choose Start⇨My Documents and then open the folder that contains the files that you want to upload.**

   The File and Folder Tasks menu appears, as shown in Figure 6-1.

Figure 6-1: You can publish your Web files quickly and easily in Windows XP by using the File and Folder Tasks menu.

2. **If you don't want to upload the entire folder, select the file or files that you want to upload.**

   The publishing options in the File and Folder Tasks menu change to reflect your selections.

3. **Click the Publish This File to the Web link.**

If you didn't select specific files in Step 2, click the Publish This Folder to the Web link; if you selected multiple files, click the Publish Selected Items to the Web link.

The Web Publishing Wizard springs to life.

4. **Click Next.**

A Change Your File Selection dialog box similar to the one shown in Figure 6-2 appears.

Figure 6-2:
You can
change your
upload
selections
by using this
Web
Publishing
Wizard
screen.

5. **Select the check box next to each file icon to deselect any files that you don't want to upload (or, conversely, select any additional files that you do want to upload) and then click Next.**

A Where Do You Want To Publish These Files? dialog box similar to the one shown in Figure 6-3 appears.

The service providers (Web hosts) listed might vary from the ones shown in Figure 6-3, depending on the type of file you select to publish. For example, if you select an image file, HP Photo appears in the Service Providers list.

6. **Select a service provider from the list and click Next.**

A welcome dialog box appears. In the example you see in Figure 6-4, the Connect to www.msnusers.com dialog box appears.

7. **Follow the service provider instructions that appear and click OK when you're finished.**

The Completing the Web Publishing Wizard dialog box appears.

8. **Select the Open This Site When I Click Finish check box and then click Finish.**

Whee! Your successfully uploaded files appear.

Figure 6-3:
Using
the Web
Publishing
Wizard, you
can upload
your Web
files to MSN
Groups.

Figure 6-4:
You need
to create
an MSN
account to
upload your
files to MSN
Groups.

Note: Accessing the wizard works differently in Windows 98 than in Windows XP. If you're working in Windows 98, choose Start⇨Programs⇨ Internet Explorer⇨Web Publishing Wizard.

Rating Your Site

Many Web users activate their Web browser's content filtering features (or purchase third-party filtering software packages, such as Net Nanny or CYBERSitter) to ban access to sites that contain offensive material. For example, Internet Explorer includes a Content Advisor feature that enables users to prevent access to offensive Web sites. Content Advisor (as well as most third-party filtering software) limits the kind of content that it allows based on a system of ratings similar to — but more detailed than — the ratings used for movies.

Here's how Web rating works. Web publishers voluntarily assign ratings to their Web pages for four categories: violence, nudity, sex, and language. The ratings are stored in special HTML tags that appear in the <HEAD> section of Web pages.

If you fail to provide a rating for your Web site, your site might be banned even if it doesn't contain offensive material. So providing ratings for your site is a good idea even if your site is G-rated.

An organization called the Internet Content Rating Association (ICRA) oversees Internet ratings. ICRA has an online service that simplifies the task of rating your site, and best of all, it's free. Just follow these steps to rate your site:

1. **Go to the ICRA home page at** `www.icra.org`.

2. **Follow the link to label your site.**

3. **Type the site information requested by ICRA (your Web page URL, contact name, phone number, and so on).**

   This information is kept private, so you don't have to worry about your address being sold to junk mailers.

4. **Answer the questions about the content level of your Web site for language, sex, nudity, and violence.**

   Answer truthfully so that you can give your site an accurate rating. After you finish, the ICRA Web page displays a snippet of HTML that contains the appropriate tags to add to your Web page.

5. **Use the mouse to highlight these HTML lines, and then press Ctrl+C to copy them onto the clipboard.**

6. **Open your home page in your favorite HTML editor, switch to HTML view so that you can see the actual HTML code, and paste the ICRA tags into the <HEAD> section of your home page.**

If you want to let people know that you rated your site, flip back to the ICRA page that contains the HTML tags that you copied in Step 5. On that page is a "Labeled with ICRA" graphic. Save this graphic to your hard drive and then insert it into your Web page.

Because rating Web sites is a voluntary process, most filtering software uses the ICRA ratings as a first line of defense only and adds extra measures to keep unwanted content from loading into a filter-protected browser.

Chapter 7: Creating an HTML Page

In This Chapter

✔ Figuring out HTML text and tags

✔ Working with structure tags

✔ Recognizing common HTML tags

Whether you choose to create HTML pages by hand or by using one of the many fine HTML editors on the market, you should become familiar with the HTML basics that I present in this chapter. Why? Because understanding the basics — such as which HTML tags are necessary to create a bona fide HTML file, which tags are the most common and why, and how tags work in general — helps you create your pages in record time. Being familiar with the tags that you see in this chapter even helps you catch errors that your HTML editing program might make.

If you haven't already, go ahead and open your favorite text editor and browser so that you can try out the examples in this chapter. The examples help you insert tags and set up your first HTML document.

Understanding HTML Basics: Text and Tags

HTML documents basically contain the following three elements:

✦ Text that you're working with

✦ Tags that determine document elements, such as headings, lists, and paragraphs

✦ Tags that insert effects, such as bold or italics, or that insert other objects, such as images, style sheets, sounds, little programs called applets, and movies (although a description of many of these is outside the scope of this book)

You use most of the HTML tags that I describe in this chapter in pairs — one tag goes before the text, and the other tag goes after the text, as in the following example:

```
<TAG>whatever your text is</TAG>
```

✦ The first tag (the *opening* tag) indicates the beginning of a tag that you're applying to some of the text in your document.

✦ The second tag (the *closing* tag) indicates the end of a tag that you're applying to some text in your document.

Not all HTML tags require a closing tag, although many do. An example of an effect that doesn't require a closing tag is <HR>, which displays on a Web page an attractive separator called a *horizontal rule*. No closing </HR> tag is required in order to display a horizontal rule.

The tags affect everything between the opening and closing tags. Opening and closing tags are generally identical, except that the closing tag has a forward slash (/) in front of the tag name. The tag name is always exactly the same in the opening and closing tags.

Sometimes, opening tags also include an *attribute,* which is just an additional bit of information that further specifies information such as color, alignment, or the text that should appear in order to describe an image. So, in such a case, an attribute appears in the initial tag:

```
<TAG ATTRIBUTE="More Info">whatever your text is</TAG>
```

HTML tags are *case-insensitive,* which means that you can type the tags by using UPPERCASE or lowercase letters, or BoTh. Typing the tags in all caps is a good idea because it helps you differentiate between the tags and text, particularly after your HTML document becomes pages and pages long.

Formatting text

Browsers disregard all formatting that doesn't appear between *tags*. For example, browsers ignore extra spaces in the HTML document or blank lines that you use to move things down the page. As a result, the extra spaces, lines, or tabs that you insert don't affect your document's appearance.

You can type your line this way, for example:

```
<TAG>hill of beans information</TAG>
```

or even like the following example:

```
<TAG>
hill
    of beans information
</TAG>
```

The next generation of HTML: XHTML

Recently released as a recommendation by the World Wide Web Consortium (www.w3.org), XHTML 2.0 is the reformulation of HTML 4 as an XML application. XHTML tags and attributes are almost identical to those in HTML; the difference is that XHTML is a stricter, tidier version of HTML. (In other words, sloppy programming practices that you can get away with in HTML don't fly in XHTML.) When XHTML is fully supported by Web browsers — which could be soon — you will notice the following changes in how you code your Web pages:

- ✔ XHTML tags are all lowercase.
- ✔ All XHTML tags must be closed.

Nesting tags

In many cases, you might want to nest tags inside other tags. *Nesting tags* simply means enclosing tags within tags. By nesting tags, you apply multiple tags to the same bit of text. Suppose that you want to make text both bold and italic. You can't achieve this effect by using only one tag — no BOLD-n-ITALICS HERE tag exists. Instead, you nest one tag inside the other, as the following example shows:

```
<B><I>more hill of beans information</I></B>
```

Notice that the tag that appears first (in this case, the bold tag) also appears last. If a tag starts first, it ends last. If a tag is right beside the text on the front end, it's right beside the text on the back end.

Using HTML Structure Tags

This section introduces you to a group of HTML tags that you use in every HTML document that you create. The first tags in this group are *structure tags* (so named because they define and describe a document's structure). Although most structure tags don't generally affect the appearance of the document or the information contained within it, they do help some browsers and HTML editing programs identify document characteristics.

For most HTML documents, you use the structure tags listed in Table 7-1 and described in the following sections.

Table 7-1	HTML Structure Tags	
HTML Tag	*Purpose*	*Use in Pairs?*
`<!DOCTYPE HTML PUBLIC "-//W3C//DTD HTML4.01 Frameset//EN" "http://www.w3.org/TR/html4/frameset.dtd">`	Identifies a document as an HTML document and specifies the HTML version; mandatory in all HTML documents	No
`<HTML>. . .</HTML>`	Defines a document as an HTML document	Yes
`<HEAD>. . .</HEAD>`	Includes introductory information about the document	Yes
`<TITLE>. . .</TITLE>`	Indicates the document title; mandatory in all HTML documents	Yes
`<META NAME="KEYWORDS" CONTENT=". . .">`	Indicates keywords that describe the document	No
`<META NAME="DESCRIPTION" CONTENT=". . .">`	Provides a short summary or description of a document	No
`<BODY>. . .</BODY>`	Encloses all elements within the main portion of a document	Yes

The <!DOCTYPE> tag

The `<!DOCTYPE>` tag identifies the document as an HTML document. It appears at the top of HTML documents and notes that the document conforms to specific HTML standards — in this example, to the final HTML version 4.01 standards. If you use HTML editing programs, they probably insert the `<!DOCTYPE>` tag automatically. If they don't, however, make sure that you type the `<!DOCTYPE>` tag at the top of all your documents.

Suppose that you want to create an HTML document about making a water balloon. Enter the `<!DOCTYPE` tag:

```
<!DOCTYPE HTML PUBLIC "-//W3C//DTD HTML 4.01
    Frameset//EN"
    "http://www.w3.org/TR/html4/frameset.dtd">
```

The <HTML> tag

The `<HTML>` tag encloses everything except the `<!DOCTYPE>` tag in every document. This tag, as its name suggests, indicates that the document is HTML. If you don't specify HTML, the browser might conceivably not read the tags as tags. Instead, the browser might read the tags as text, in which case the document looks pretty much as it does in the text editor. Yuck!

You enter the `<HTML>` tags at the beginning and end of the document (but after the `<!DOCTYPE>` tag), as shown in the following example:

```
<!DOCTYPE HTML PUBLIC "-//W3C//DTD HTML 4.01
    Frameset//EN"
    "http://www.w3.org/TR/html4/frameset.dtd">
<HTML>
...all the stuff about making water
    balloons will go here eventually...
</HTML>
```

The <HEAD> and <TITLE> tags

The `<HEAD>` tag is part of what many browsers use to identify or reference the document. For many HTML developers, the `<HEAD>` tag seems useless. Keep in mind that although this tag doesn't have a visible application for creating an HTML document, it does have a technical application — it contains information about the document that doesn't appear within the browser window.

The `<TITLE>` tag, one of those about-this-document bits, goes within the `<HEAD>` tags. This tag is required by the HTML specification to apply a title of your choice to the document. Titles appear on the title bar of a browser window. Make your title as descriptive as you can so that people can find or identify your documents more easily on the Internet.

You add the `<HEAD>` and `<TITLE>` tags, as shown in the following example:

```
<!DOCTYPE HTML PUBLIC "-//W3C//DTD HTML 4.01
    Frameset//EN"
```

```
    "http://www.w3.org/TR/html4/frameset.dtd">
<HTML>
<HEAD><TITLE>Making Effective Water Balloons
</TITLE></HEAD>
. . .all the stuff about making water balloons
    will go here eventually. . .
</HTML>
```

Notice that the <HEAD> and <TITLE> tags appear immediately after the initial <HTML> tag.

The <META> tag

The <META> tag appears in dozens of permutations and combinations, only a couple of which have any significant effect on most HTML developers. These tags, cleverly positioned right alongside the <TITLE> tag between the <HEAD> tags, provide more about-this-document information. This meta-information fuels Internet directories (such as Lycos, at www.lycos.com) and search services (such as AltaVista, at www.altavista.com) because providing the information makes categorizing and finding your documents easier. Although you don't have to include these tags, you greatly improve your chances of being found by Web surfers if you do.

You add the <META NAME="KEYWORDS" CONTENT="..."> and <META NAME= "DESCRIPTION" CONTENT="..."> tags, as shown in the following example:

```
<!DOCTYPE HTML PUBLIC "-//W3C//DTD HTML 4.01
    Frameset//EN"
    "http://www.w3.org/TR/html4/frameset.dtd">
<HTML>
<HEAD><TITLE>Making Effective Water Balloons
</TITLE>
<META NAME="KEYWORDS" CONTENT="water balloon
    surprise splash splat cat oops sorry
    ouch cold wet">
<META NAME="DESCRIPTION" CONTENT="This document
    provides basic instructions for developing and
    using water balloons.">
</HEAD>
. . .all the stuff about making water balloons
    will go here eventually. . .
</HTML>
```

The <BODY> tag

The <BODY> tag surrounds all the information that's supposed to be visible to your readers — the real heart of the document. Everything that you want people to see must be contained between the <BODY> and </BODY> tags.

Place the <BODY> tag just before the information that you want to put into your HTML document and then just before the closing </HTML> tag. Technically, all other tags that you use are nested between the <BODY> and </BODY> tags.

You begin the water balloon project by adding the `<BODY>` tags:

```
<!DOCTYPE HTML PUBLIC "-//W3C//DTD HTML 4.01
    Frameset//EN"
      "http://www.w3.org/TR/html4/frameset.dtd">
<HTML>
<HEAD><TITLE>Making Effective Water Balloons
</TITLE>
<META NAME="KEYWORDS" CONTENT="water balloon
    surprise splash splat cat oops sorry
    ouch cold wet">
<META NAME="DESCRIPTION"CONTENT="This document
    provides basic instructions for developing and
    using water balloons.">
</HEAD>
<BODY>
. . .all the stuff about making water balloons. . .
</BODY>
</HTML>
```

Getting Familiar with Basic HTML Tags

Basic HTML tags are the ones that enable you to create simple, functional effects in your HTML documents. This section describes the tags necessary for making headings, paragraphs, and lists, and for emphasizing and setting off text.

Making headings

HTML offers you six choices in headings, labeled `<H1>` through `<H6>`. `<H1>` is the largest and boldest of the headings, and `<H6>` is the smallest and least bold (most timid?). You can use these headings, as shown in Table 7-2, to show a hierarchy of information (such as the headings in this book).

Table 7-2	Your HTML Heading Options	
HTML Tag	*Effect*	*Use in Pairs?*
`<H1>. . .</H1>`	Heading 1	Yes
`<H2>. . .</H2>`	Heading 2	Yes
`<H6>. . .</H6>`	Heading 6	Yes

As with all other paired tags, the text that you want to include goes between the tags (for example: `<H1>Here is my heading</H1>`).

Making paragraphs

By using HTML, you can separate information into paragraphs. The HTML paragraph tag, `<P>`, indicates the beginning and the end of a paragraph of text. Although using the end `</P>` tag is optional, including it is good programming practice. When you add this tag around a paragraph of text, the text appears in a block with a line of space at the end.

Emphasizing text

After you write something, you might want to make some of the words within the text stand out. HTML offers several options for doing this, including emphasizing text and adding bold and italics to text. Table 7-3 describes some of these options.

Table 7-3	Tags to Create Standout Text	
HTML Tag	**Effect**	**Use in Pairs?**
`<EM>. . .</EM>`	Adds emphasis (usually appears as italics)	Yes
`<STRONG>. . . </STRONG>`	Adds strong emphasis (usually appears as bold)	Yes
`<B>. . .</B>`	Adds boldface	Yes
`<I>. . .</I>`	Adds italics	Yes

Making lists

Often, you might want to provide information in lists rather than in paragraphs. Providing information in lists is especially valuable in HTML documents because lists enable the reader to skim through information quickly without needing to wade through paragraphs of text. For you, the writer, making lists is an easy way to help organize your information and provide easy links to other pages.

Making lists is a two-part process. First, you must add a pair of tags to specify that the information appears in a list. You can specify, for example, an ordered (or numbered) list, `<OL>. . .</OL>`; or an unordered (or bulleted) list, `<UL>. . .</UL>`.

Then, you must specify each line of the list, called line items. Just insert the `<LI>` tag at the beginning of each line, where you want the number or bullet to be. No closing tag is required.

Table 7-4 shows the tags that you use to create lists.

Table 7-4	Tags to Create Numbered and Bulleted Lists	
HTML Tag	**Effect**	**Use in Pairs?**
`<LI>`	Identifies each item in a list	No
`<OL>. . .</OL>`	Specifies ordered (numbered) lists	Yes
`<UL>. . .</UL>`	Specifies unordered (bulleted) lists	Yes

To add an unordered (bulleted) list of materials to a page, place the following HTML code between the `<BODY>` and `</BODY>` tags:

```
<BODY>
<UL>
<LI>Water
```

```
<LI>Big, big balloon
<LI>Balloon ties (optional)
<LI>Second-story window
<LI>Target below window
</UL>
</BODY>
```

The bulleted list shown in Figure 7-1 shows the results of adding these tags and text. Notice that the list tags don't have <P> tags around them. If you have a list, you don't need a <P>.

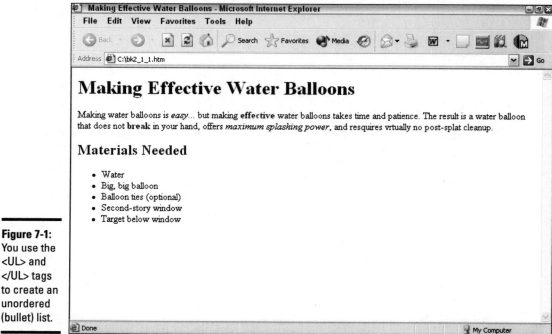

Figure 7-1:
You use the
<UL> and
</UL> tags
to create an
unordered
(bullet) list.

To add an ordered list of instructions, you simply use the <OL> tags:

1. Add opening and closing <OL> tags where the list appears.

For example, if you are creating a page about making effective water balloons, you add the following:

```
<H2>Instructions</H2>
<OL>
</OL>
```

2. Add <LI> tags and text for each item.

```
<H2>Instructions</H2>
<OL>
<LI>Fill balloon with water.
<LI>Tie balloon using a tie or by making a knot.
<LI>Go to second-story window.
```

```
<LI>Aim at spot below window.
<LI>Drop balloon.
</OL>
```

The result is a numbered list containing five items.

 You can add attributes (extra information) to your list tags to control what the bullets look like, what kind of numbers (Roman, capital letters, or regular Arabic numbers, for example) appear, and what the starting number is for sequential lists.

Chapter 8: Setting Background and Text Characteristics

In This Chapter

✔ Spicing up your background with color and images

✔ Adding your perfect image

✔ Working with text colors and text alignment

✔ Specifying the font type

In this chapter, you discover how to set background and text characteristics, which can help you liven up your pages with various color and alignment options. This chapter assumes that you have a basic understanding of how HTML tags work. If you don't, check out Book VI, Chapter 7, and then flip back here to continue. Before beginning to work through the examples in this chapter, make sure that you have your browser and text editor open and ready to create a new document.

Because the formatting attributes and tags in this chapter work with nearly all current browsers but aren't recommended in HTML 4.01, consider using style sheets for all your formatting needs. (For a more in-depth look at style sheets, see Chapter 13 of Book VI.)

Applying a Color Background

To include a background color, all you need to do is insert the BGCOLOR attribute in the opening <BODY> tag. Here's an example of how specifying sky blue as the background color might look:

```
<HEAD><TITLE>Fleabag Kitty</TITLE></HEAD>
<BODY BGCOLOR="#3399CC">With a scratcha scratcha here and a
    scratcha scratcha there...
</BODY>
```

#3399CC is an RGB value that translates to sky blue, but you can substitute any RGB value (which all follow the RRGGBB format). To get a black background, for example, you use #000000. (If you *do* specify a black background, look at the section "Setting Document Text Colors," later in this chapter, to find out how to set the text to a nonblack color.)

Alternatively, you can specify some colors by name. The following colors work in most browsers: aqua, black, blue, fuchsia, gray, green, lime, maroon, navy, olive, purple, red, silver, teal, white, and yellow. The code would look something like BGCOLOR="purple".

RGB stands for red, green, blue. RGB values string together three hexadecimal numbers representing a color's red, green, and blue components, respectively.

So just where do you come up with the RGB values? Try one of the following two ways:

✦ **Find a list of RGB numbers on the Web.** If you browse enough on the Web, you're likely to find general sources of information that provide you with lists of commonly used Web page features, including RGB numbers, complete with samples. One useful reference is the Web Source color chart at `www.web-source.net/216_color_chart.htm`.

✦ **Look for RGB values in your image-editing or paint software.** Many packages offer the option of altering the colors with which you're working and provide the RGB value for the colors that you choose. Look in the color-related screens for RGB values.

Applying an Image Background

In addition to using simple colors for backgrounds, you can use images as backgrounds. To do so, you specify a URL pointing to an image for the BACKGROUND attribute of the <BODY> tag. You can specify a relative URL or an absolute URL:

✦ A **relative** URL points to a file located in or below the same directory as the Web page (for example, `picture.gif`).

✦ An **absolute** URL points to a file located anywhere on your computer (for example, `/mypictures/picture.gif`).

Here's an example of specifying an image for the background (see Book VI, Chapter 7 for more information on the <BODY> tag):

```
<HTML>
<HEAD><TITLE>Adding a background to your Web
    page</TITLE></HEAD>
<BODY BACKGROUND="star.gif">
<H1>Backgrounds can make text hard to read!</H1>
</BODY>
</HTML>
```

Figure 8-1 shows the `star.gif` image (one star) tiled throughout the page.

Background images, such as the `star.gif` image, that don't fill the entire background are tiled to cover all available space — that is, copies of the image are automatically placed together, like a tile floor. The background image in the example is really only one star — the browser makes the copies automatically.

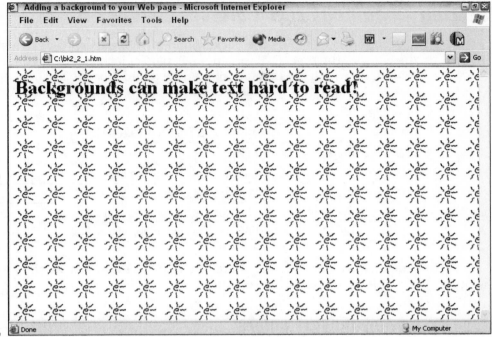

Figure 8-1:
Using the BACK-GROUND attribute of the <BODY> tag to specify a background image.

Finding Images to Use

Coming up with images to use for a background is about as easy as using simple colors. The only difference is that you use an image file rather than just a color number. Here are two ways to find background images:

✦ **Design your own.** You might want to use a background image that's specific to the Web site that you're creating. I strongly suggest doing so if you have *any* graphics talent. (If you do what I do and make fleas that look like roaches, check out the other options.)

✦ **Look for image or background CDs or floppy disks in your local software store.** Many CDs chock-full of cool stock images are available at varying prices. Make sure that the images you choose are, indeed, *stock* images, which are images that you can freely use without obtaining additional copyright permission. Putting nonstock, copyrighted images on your Web site, by contrast, is immoral and illegal and has been proven to cause hair to grow on your palms.

Make sure that you choose simple backgrounds — ones with no more than a few subtle colors or with only a few elements. Busy backgrounds make reading difficult for your users.

Setting Document Text Colors

In addition to changing the background of Web pages, you can also change the color of the text. This technique is particularly handy if you use a background on which the default colors of text and links don't show up well. Table 8-1 shows the attributes used to color text in an HTML document:

Table 8-1	Attributes That Set Text Color
HTML Attribute	*Effect*
TEXT="#RRGGBB"	Changes the color of the body text
LINK="#RRGGBB"	Changes the color of the link
ALINK="#RRGGBB"	Changes the color of the active link
VLINK="#RRGGBB"	Changes the color of the visited link

You fill in a color number where "#RRGGBB" is indicated, as shown in the example in the following section.

Changing text colors

To change text colors on your Web page, you specify an RGB value for the TEXT attribute of the <BODY> tag:

```
<BODY BGCOLOR="#3399CC" TEXT="#FFFFFF">With a scratcha
    scratcha here and a scratcha scratcha there...
</BODY>
```

Changing link colors

To change link colors on your Web page, you specify an RGB color value for the ALINK (active, or normal) attribute of the <BODY> tag and the VLINK (visited) attribute of the <BODY> tag, as the following code shows:

```
<BODY BGCOLOR="#3399CC" TEXT="#FFFFFF"
    LINK="#FF0000" ALINK="#FFFF00"
    VLINK="#8C1717">With a scratcha scratcha here and a
    scratcha scratcha there...
</BODY>
```

Specifying Text Alignment

In addition to recoloring text and links, you can move text around so that it's not all aligned on the left. You can align headings, paragraphs, other text, and images by using the attributes in Table 8-2.

Table 8-2	Text-Alignment Attributes	
HTML Attribute	*Effect*	*Example*
ALIGN="CENTER"	Centers text within the left and right margins	`<H1 ALIGN="CENTER">Text goes here</H1>`
ALIGN="RIGHT"	Aligns text on the right margin	`<P ALIGN="RIGHT">Text goes here</P>`

Keep in mind that although most browsers support these attributes, not all do, so your text might not align correctly in some browsers. Always try designs in more than one browser to make sure that your design works the way that you think it should.

You don't need to add an attribute if you want the element aligned on the left. Browsers align text on the left unless you tell them to do otherwise.

If you want to use center and right alignment for headings, paragraphs, and images, follow these steps:

1. **Start your HTML page, which should look similar to the following example:**

```
<!DOCTYPE HTML PUBLIC "-//W3C//DTD HTML 4.01
   Frameset//EN"
   "http://www.w3.org/TR/html4/frameset.dtd">
   <HTML>
<HEAD><TITLE>Birthday</TITLE></HEAD>
<BODY>
</BODY>
</HTML>
```

2. **Type a heading:**

```
<BODY>
<H1>Happy Birthday, Winchester</H1>
</BODY>
```

3. **Add the** `ALIGN="right"` **attribute to the heading, as shown in the following example:**

```
<H1 ALIGN="right">Happy Birthday,
   Winchester</H1>
```

4. **Insert a graphical image on the left side of the heading:**

```
<H1 ALIGN="right"><IMG SRC="winch.jpg">Happy
   Birthday, Winchester</H1>
```

5. **Type some paragraph information, as shown in this example:**

```
<H1 ALIGN="right"><IMG SRC="winch.jpg">Happy
   Birthday, Winchester</H1>
<P>On March 3rd, Deb and Eric snuck up on their cat,
   Winchester, and surprised him with a water balloon
   for his birthday. It was lucky #13 for
   Winchester.</P>
</BODY>
```

6. Add the `ALIGN="center"` **attribute to the paragraph, as shown here:**

```
<P ALIGN="center">On March 3rd, Deb and Eric
    snuck up on their cat, Winchester, and
    surprised him with a water balloon for his
    birthday. It was lucky #13 for
    Winchester.</P>
```

Figure 8-2 shows the result.

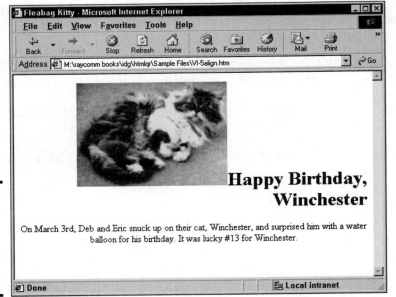

Figure 8-2:
Aligning
headings,
text, and
images with
the ALIGN
attribute.

Using Font Type Specifications

HTML wasn't designed to support specific formatting. HTML was conceived with the idea that authors would specify headings and lists, and readers (or the readers' browsers) would take care of applying fonts and sizes. A generation of designers accustomed to desktop publishing and to being able to control every aspect of document design, however, sought out ways to control HTML design as well. In response, newer browsers and the most widely supported HTML specification provide some tags designed for formatting text precisely.

The combination of so-called pure HTML, without the formatting tags in this section, and style sheets (which I cover in Book VI, Chapter 13) provides the best of both worlds: HTML coding simplicity and complete layout and design control.

If you choose to use the formatting commands in this section, remember that not all browsers support them. In particular, remember that a font you specify isn't necessarily installed on your readers' machines!

Table 8-3 shows the tags and attributes used to format type:

Table 8-3	Formatting Type	
HTML Tag or Attribute	*Effect*	*Example*
`<FONT>. . .</FONT>`	Changes the font	`<FONT COLOR="red">Text goes here</FONT>`
`COLOR="#RRGGBB"`	Colors the text based on the RRGGBB number	`<FONT COLOR="#FFHHAA">Text goes here</FONT>`
`FACE="..."`	Sets the typeface NAME; a list of font names can be specified	`<FONT FACE="Helvetica">Text goes here</FONT>`
`SIZE="n"`	Changes the font size *n* on a scale from 1 to 7	`<FONT SIZE="3">Text goes here</FONT>`

To change the characteristics of a specific block of text, follow these steps:

1. **Start your HTML document, which should look something like the following example:**

```
<!DOCTYPE HTML PUBLIC "-//W3C//DTD HTML 4.01
    Transitional//EN"
    "http://www.w3.org/TR/html4/
    transitional.dtd"> <HTML>
<HEAD><TITLE>Making Effective Water
    Balloons</TITLE>
</HEAD>
<BODY>
<H1>Making Effective Water Balloons</H1>
<P>
Making water balloons is <EM>easy</EM>...
    but making <B>effective</B> water balloons takes
    time and patience. The result is a water balloon
    that does not break in your hand, offers <I>maximum
    splashing power</I>, and requires virtually no post-
    splat clean up.
</P>
</BODY>
</HTML>
```

2. **Add the `<FONT>` tags around the text that you want to change:**

```
<H1>Making Effective Water Balloons</H1>
<P>
<FONT>
Making water balloons is <EM>easy</EM>...
    but making <B>effective</B> water balloons takes
    time and patience. The result is a water balloon
    that does not break in your hand, offers <I>maximum
    splashing power</I>, and requires virtually no post-
    splat clean up.
</FONT>
</P>
```

3. **To change the size, add the appropriate** `SIZE` **attribute to the font tag.**

By default, the size is 4. (The number doesn't represent anything — it just is.) You can specify a size relative to the default (+1 for one size larger or –2 for two sizes smaller) or in absolute numbers, such as 1 or 7:

```
<FONT SIZE=+2>
Making water balloons is <EM>easy</EM>...
    but making <B>effective</B> water balloons takes
    time and patience. The result is a water balloon
    that does not break in your hand, offers <I>maximum
    splashing power</I>, and requires virtually no post-
    splat clean up.
</FONT>
```

4. **To change the typeface, add the** `FACE` **attribute, as the following example shows:**

```
<FONT FACE="Gill Sans, Arial, Courier"
    SIZE=+2>
Making water balloons is <EM>easy</EM>...
    but making <B>effective</B> water balloons takes
    time and patience. The result is a water balloon
    that does not break in your hand, offers <I>maximum
    splashing power</I>, and requires virtually no post-
    splat clean up.
</FONT>
```

You can name any font on your system. (Bear in mind that to appear correctly, the font must be available on the reader's system also.) You can also list fonts in descending order of preference. If the first one isn't available, the reader's browser moves along to the next and then the next.

Figure 8-3 shows the new typeface in a Web browser.

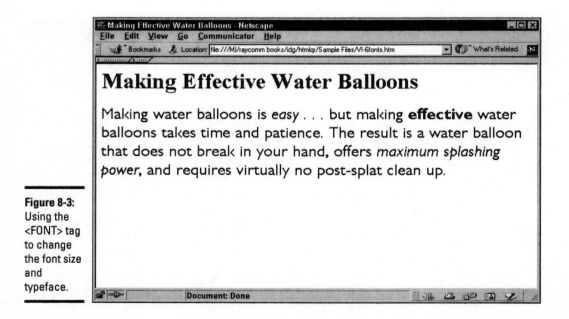

Figure 8-3:
Using the <FONT> tag to change the font size and typeface.

Reliable fonts for Windows include Arial, Times New Roman, and Courier New. Helvetica and Times are similar to Arial and Times New Roman and also are frequently available.

5. **To change the text color, add the** `COLOR` **attribute, as shown in the following example:**

As with other text color settings (which I describe earlier in this chapter), you use a #RRGGBB number to specify the color:

```
<FONT FACE="Gill Sans, Courier, Arial"
    COLOR="#000000" SIZE=+2>
Making water balloons is <EM>easy</EM>...
    but making <B>effective</B> water balloons takes
    time and patience. The result is a water balloon
    that does not break in your hand, offers <I>maximum
    splashing power</I>, and requires virtually no post-
    splat clean up.
</FONT>
```

Chapter 9: Adding Internal and External Links

In This Chapter

↙ **Understanding links and anchors**

↙ **Linking your documents to URLs on the Web**

↙ **Making links between and within documents**

↙ **Taking advantage of a link-checker utility**

In this chapter, you see how to add anchors and links to your HTML documents. Anchors and links enable readers to jump from place to place within your document or to other documents and files. Put another way, anchors and links are the sticky strands that connect your site to the rest of the Web.

You apply lots of tags in this section, so if initial tags, closing tags, and phrases such as "apply markup tags to your document" are unfamiliar, you might want to flip to Book VI, Chapter 7 for more information about HTML basics.

Understanding Links

When you create HTML documents, you create documents that users can read by *linking* from topic to topic — that is, by jumping from page to page and from topic to topic rather than reading linearly, as in a novel. *Links* (or *hyperlinks*) are places that users can select to access other topics, documents, or *Web sites* (collections of HTML documents).

As you build your HTML documents, think about how you want your documents to link. As a rule, you should create several short HTML documents rather than one long document. Short documents are easier for readers to follow and are therefore more likely to be read. You can then link these shorter documents into a single cohesive set of documents (that is, a Web site).

To create a link, you need the following two elements:

✦ **A URL (or Uniform Resource Locator):** This is just an address on the Web.

✦ **An anchor tag:** This marks the link in a Web page. (You read more about anchor tags later in this chapter, in "Understanding Anchors.")

About URLs

A URL (pronounced *you-are-ell*) is a fancy way of saying an address for information on the Internet. If you read "URL," just think "address" or "location." URLs differ based on how specific you need to be.

All HTML documents can use URLs to link to other information. URLs, in turn, can point to many different things, such as HTML documents, other sites on the Internet, or even images and sound files. Depending on what the URL points to, it can be absolute (full) or relative (partial), as I explain in more detail later in this chapter.

URLs are *case-sensitive*. On some computers, typing a filename such as `Kitten.html` is quite different from typing `kitten.html`. If you create a filename that uses special capitalization (rather than, for example, all lowercase characters), you must use this same capitalization the same way every time you link to the document. (Frankly, just using lowercase is easier for you and your readers.)

Anatomy of URLs

If you're not used to them, URLs can be pretty odd-looking. Each part of a URL has a built-in specific meaning, much like each part of your home address. The street address, 12 Fritter Lane, Apartment G, Santa Clara, CA 95051, for example, provides a postal carrier with essential and complete information — the specific apartment in a specific building on a specific street in a specific town in a specific state in a specific ZIP Code. Specifically, URLs work the same way by providing a browser with all the parts that it needs to locate information. A URL consists of the *protocol indicator,* the *hostname,* and the *directory name* or *filename*. The following (fictitious) URL is an example of an absolute URL:

`http://cat.feline.org/fur/fuzzy.html`

Here's a description of each URL part:

✦ **Protocol indicator (the `http://` portion):** Tells the server how to send the information. The `http://` protocol indicator is the standard used by Web servers and browsers that lets them talk to each other. The `http://` protocol indicator often is omitted by publications because of space issues and because most URLs (at least those published in the media) tend to be `http://` URLs.

   Note: Even though you can usually leave the `http://` off the URL in casual usage, you must include it when linking to another Web site.

   Another common protocol indicator that you see on the Web is `https://`. Different from `http://`, `https://` means that the transmission of data between the Web server and the browser occurs using a special transmission protocol called *Secure Sockets Layer* (SSL).

✦ **Hostname (the `cat.feline.org` portion):** Specifies a computer on the Internet. If you publish an HTML document, you're placing it on a computer that serves the document to anyone who knows the correct URL.

The server thus hosts all these documents and makes them accessible to users. To obtain the hostname of the server on which you place your files, check with your system administrator.

✦ **Directory name (the `fur` portion):** You might not need to show a directory name, or you might have several that represent directories inside directories (or folders inside folders).

✦ **The name of the file located on the host computer (the `fuzzy.html` portion):** Sometimes, you don't need to provide a filename — the server simply gives out the default file in the directory. The default filenames are usually one of three: `index.html`, `default.html`, or `homepage.html`, depending on which kind of Web server the files are located. The filename is like many other files; it contains a name (`fuzzy`) and an extension (`.html`).

Sometimes, URLs have a hostname with a *port number* at the end (for example, `cat.feline.org:80`). This number gives the server more precise information about the URL. If you see a URL with a number, just leave the number on the URL. If you don't see a number, don't worry about it.

Try to avoid creating directory names or filenames with spaces or other unusual characters. Stay with letters (lowercase is best), numbers, underscores (_), periods (.), and plus signs (+). Why? Because some servers have problems with odd characters and spaces. (In addition, most humans have trouble remembering odd characters and spaces in URLs. Keeping your filenames simple helps visitors find your site more easily.)

**Book VI
Chapter 9**

Adding Internal and
External Links

Absolute and relative URLs

Links on Web pages use two different types of URLs: absolute URLs and relative URLs. These types of URLs each have a specific purpose and use specific components:

✦ **Absolute URLs:** These URLs give the full address of something on the Internet. They include the protocol indicator, hostname, and directory name or filenames. You use absolute URLs to indicate any location on the Internet.

Keep in mind that pointing people to Internet locations requires as much information as you can provide, just as you would provide detailed information to an out-of-town friend who's driving to your apartment. You would provide, for example, the state, city, building number, and apartment number (unless, of course, you want that friend to get lost). Similarly, you need to provide as complete a URL as possible — including the protocol indicator — so that people around the world can find your Web site.

✦ **Relative URLs:** These URLs don't contain a complete address, but they can still provide all the information that you need for linking to other documents. A relative URL usually contains only the last part of the absolute URL — the directory name (possibly) and the filename. You use relative URLs to link to locations within the same folder or same group of folders.

To go back to the postal address analogy, if you're giving a local friend directions to your apartment, you'd probably provide just the street address, building, and apartment. The city and state are implicit. In the same way, a relative URL implies the missing information based on the location of the file containing the relative URL. The browser infers the missing information from the location of the document containing the link.

Check out Figure 9-1, which shows you how absolute URLs and relative URLs work.

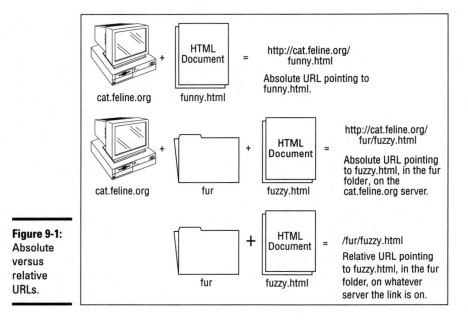

Figure 9-1:
Absolute versus relative URLs.

Understanding Anchors

The linking process begins with *anchors;* this term is just a fancy way of saying links. (Folks call them anchors because the tag is <A>.) Table 9-1 describes some anchor tags and attributes. Anchor tags are generally used with one of the following two attributes:

✦ HREF: Enables users to jump from one bit of information to another — either to material within the same Web site or to other material out on the Internet. These tags create the hyperlinks.

✦ NAME: Labels a spot within a document. That spot can then be part of a URL so that readers can jump directly to it. The NAME anchor is useful in long documents that users must otherwise scroll through. If NAME anchors and links to them are present, users can jump to specific information and don't need to wade through pages of material.

Table 9-1	Common Anchor Tags and Attributes	
HTML Tag or Attribute	*Effect*	*Example*

`<A>...</A>`	Marks anchor	`<A HREF="http://www.`
		`dummies.com">Click to`
		`visit the Dummies site</A>`

`HREF="..."`	Indicates where to jump	`<A HREF="#middle">Click to`
		`jump to the middle of my`
		`Web page</A>`

`NAME="..."`	Identifies an internal label	`<A NAME="middle"></A>`

Making Links

Links are the connections to other material within or among HTML documents. Links are visible as text (often blue) that you select as you're surfing the Web. (After you link to a document, the link often appears in a different color to indicate that you've already been there.) The next three sections show you how to link to other documents within your site, link to HTML documents out there on the Web, and link to other information on the Internet. For now, you work with the `<A>` tag's `HREF` attribute.

Linking to documents within your site

Start with plain text and build your first hyperlink. To make things easy on yourself, work with two (preferably small) HTML documents at first so that you can link from one to the other and back again. Practicing linking is much more difficult if you work with just one document.

Note: Before you begin the example in this section, open your text editor and browser. While you follow these examples, have a basic HTML document available, such as the following:

```
<!DOCTYPE HTML PUBLIC "-//W3C//DTD HTML 4.01
    Frameset//EN"
    "http://www.w3.org/TR/html4/frameset.dtd">
<HTML><HEAD><TITLE>Cats</TITLE></HEAD>
<BODY>
</BODY>
</HTML>
```

Follow these steps to build your first hyperlink:

1. **Enter the text that you want to appear on the page between the
`<BODY>` tags, as the following example shows:**

```
<BODY>
Cats are funny.
</BODY>
```

2. **Apply the anchor tags to the text that you want to be the anchor (the
part that your visitors click to link to something else):**

```
Cats are <A>funny</A>.
```

675

3. **Add an attribute (**HREF**, in this case) to link to another document:**

```
Cats are <A HREF="funny.html">funny</A>.
```

The HREF attribute specifies which document appears after your readers click the anchor. And funny.html is the name of the document to which you're linking. In this case, funny.html is a file in the same directory or folder as the document that you're building.

Linking to pages out on the Web

To create links to other documents on the Internet, follow the same procedure as with other links and include the complete URL in the HREF attribute. To make a link from the word *cats* to a completely different address on the Web, use the following example, starting with the following basic HTML document.

Note: Before you begin, open your text editor and browser.

```
<!DOCTYPE HTML PUBLIC "-//W3C//DTD HTML 4.01
    Frameset//EN"
    "http://www.w3.org/TR/html4/frameset.dtd">
<HTML><HEAD><TITLE>Cats</TITLE></HEAD>
<BODY>
</BODY>
</HTML>
```

Use the following steps to add a link to a document at another location:

1. **Type** Cats are funny. **between the** <BODY> **tags:**

```
<BODY>
Cats are funny.
</BODY>
```

2. **Add the following anchor tags:**

```
<A>Cats</A> are funny.
```

3. **Add the** HREF **attribute to link to a sample (fictitious) Web site about cats:**

```
<A HREF="http://cats.com/home.html">Cats</A>
    are funny.
```

You can also link to non-HTML files from a regular http:// type of address. If, for example, you have a Word document that you want people to be able to download from your Web site, you can add a link such as the following:

```
<A HREF="catjokes.doc">Download original cat
    stories here</A>.
```

Or, you can use an absolute URL, like this one:

```
<A HREF="http://cat.feline.org/furry/catpix.jpg">
    Download a picture of the cutest cat in history</A>.
```

Then all you need to do is upload the `catjokes.doc` and `catpix.jpg` files to the server at the same time as you upload your HTML document to the server.

Linking to other stuff on the Internet

Just as you can link to HTML documents or images or files on the Internet by including the right URL, you can also link to other types of information (such as discussion groups or file archives) on the Internet. All kinds of other protocols (the language that computers use to transfer information) are in use.

For example, if you see or hear of neat material on the Internet that's available through an FTP (File Transfer Protocol) site, you can link that material into your document.

Suppose that your best friend found a collection of cat jokes at an FTP site on the Internet. You can simply copy the URL from your friend. The URL might look something like `ftp://humor.central.org/jokes/animals/cats.zip`. You can put that URL into your document, as shown here:

```
A collection of <A HREF="ftp://humor.central.org/jokes/
   animals/cats.zip">cat jokes</A> is good to have.
```

To create a hyperlink to an e-mail address, type this line:

```
<A HREF="mailto:me@mycompany.com">E-mail me</A>
```

Making Links within Documents

Making links to places within an HTML document requires a little more work than creating links to other documents. On regular links to other documents or to documents on other servers, you just point to a computer and a file. If you're going to point to a place within a document that you're creating, however, you must also identify the targets to which you intend to link.

Making internal links

An internal link points to a specific location within a document. Internal links work well if you have a long HTML document that really doesn't lend itself to being split into different files. If you're dealing with one of these long documents, you can use internal links to point from one place to another within the same document. As a result, readers don't need to scroll through pages of information; they can just link to a place (defined by a special anchor) within the document.

Within the `kitten.html` file, you might have a long list of favorite kitten names along with a description of the names' origins. You can enable readers to jump right to the W names without needing to scroll through the A through V names. The following URL points directly to the `w` anchor within the `kitten.html` file. (I show you how to create the named `w` anchor in the next section.)

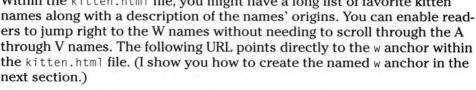

```
kitten.html#w
```

You can also write the relative URL this way:

```
fur/kitten.html#w
```

or

```
/fur/kitten.html#w
```

Or, you can write the address as the following absolute URL:

```
http://cat.feline.org/fur/kitten.html#w
```

Marking internal targets

Developing anchors to permit links to points within a document is quite similar to creating the links themselves. You use the NAME attribute to create internal targets (also called *named anchors*).

In the preceding section's hypothetical example, the author of kitten.html inserted name anchors for all 26 A through Z headings just so that you can link to them. For the following example, imagine that you have within your document the heading Funny Cats I've Known, as shown here:

```
<!DOCTYPE HTML PUBLIC "-//W3C//DTD HTML 4.01
    Frameset//EN"
    "http://www.w3.org/TR/html4/frameset.dtd">
<HTML><HEAD><TITLE>Cats</TITLE></HEAD>
<BODY>
<H2>Funny Cats I've Known</H2>
General information about the cats would be here.
</BODY>
</HTML>
```

Follow these steps to add an anchor to your page:

1. Include an anchor:

```
<H2><A>Funny</A> Cats I've Known</H2>
```

2. Insert the NAME attribute:

```
<H2><A NAME="funny">Funny</A> Cats I've
    Known</H2>
```

This anchor doesn't show up in the browser view of your document, but you know that it's there.

If you want to link directly to the funny cats section of your document from within the same document, you include a link to funny by using the pound sign (#):

```
<A HREF="#funny">Funny cats</A> are here.
```

The #funny anchor to which you want to link, for example, might be in the cats.html file on the server named cat.feline.org. You just create a URL that looks like this:

```
http://cat.feline.org/cats.html#funny
```

Your friends and admirers can then set up links to your funny cats section:

```
Boy, you know, those <A HREF="http://
    cat.feline.org/cats.html#funny">funny cats
    </A> are something else.
```

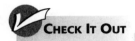

CHECK IT OUT

Using a Link-Checker Utility

As you've no doubt noticed if you spend much time surfing the Web, Web sites come and go with lightning speed. Unfortunately, this volatility means that the links you create to other peoples' Web pages can break at any time. Although broken links might not be a problem if you're creating a personal home page, it reflects poorly on a professional or business-related site.

The only way to prevent broken links is to check them periodically. Checking links yourself — by loading your own Web page into a browser, clicking each link, and noting whether the linked site appears — can be awfully time-consuming, depending on how many links you've created. To automate the process, you can use a *link-checker utility.* A link-checker utility follows all the links in your Web page and then issues a report telling you which ones are broken. You then decide whether to delete or change any links reported as broken.

If you haven't decided on an HTML tool, however, you can still check your links by visiting an online link-checking utility, such as the World Wide Web Consortium's link checker: http://validator.w3.org/checklink.

Chapter 10: Working with Images

In This Chapter

✔ Adding images to your Web page

✔ Making downloads faster

✔ Adjusting image alignment

✔ Maximizing blank space

✔ Creating clickable images

*I*f you're interested in incorporating images into your Web pages (and who isn't?), you're in luck: This chapter shows you everything that you need to know. In it, you find out how to add images, position them on the page attractively, and even make them clickable. (As you might guess, *clickable* images are images that do something — for example, load another Web page — when someone viewing your page clicks them.)

Before working through the examples in this chapter, make sure that your browser and text editor are open and ready to create a new document. You should also have an image available to use in the document.

Adding Images

Adding images to your HTML documents is just as straightforward as the basic link and text tags are. (An image can be a picture, drawing, diagram, or what-have-you.) You can include images with either GIF (usually pronounced *jiff*), JPG (pronounced *jay-peg*), or PNG (pronounced *ping*) file formats. These formats are compressed, so they take up minimal hard drive space and downloading time. You choose which format to use based on the image itself.

✦ **GIF:** Choose GIF images for line drawings, images with only a few colors, images that blend into the background, or animated images. GIF remains a popular file format because all graphical browsers can interpret and display them and because transparent images are far spiffier than the regular kind. (*Transparent images* contain see-through portions, so they can be any shape — unlike regular images, which are always square.)

✦ **JPG:** Choose JPG images for photographic images or images with fancy shading. JPG files are considerably smaller than GIF files in terms of file size and therefore don't take f-o-r-e-v-e-r to download to your readers' browsers.

✦ **PNG:** Choose PNG images if you have photographic or complex images and you know that your readers will be using newer browsers: Microsoft Internet Explorer 6 and Netscape Navigator 7.1 or newer.

Adding images isn't too complicated: Just include an <IMG> tag and the SRC attribute, pointing to a valid URL (either absolute or relative) for your image. Table 10-1 shows some common image-related tags and attributes.

Table 10-1	Common Image Tags and Attributes	
HTML Tag or Attribute	*Effect*	*Example*
`<IMG SRC="...">`	Inserts an image	`<IMG SRC="myPicture.gif">`
`ALT="..."`	Specifies the text to display if the image isn't displayed	`<IMG SRC="myPicture.gif" ALT="Photo of Australian shepherd">`
`BORDER=n`	Controls the thickness of the border around an image in pixels	`<IMG SRC="myPicture.gif" ALT="Photo of Australian shepherd" BORDER=5>`

To include an image in your document, follow these steps:

1. **Start your HTML page:**

   Start with the following sample of HTML code:

```
<!DOCTYPE HTML PUBLIC "-//W3C//DTD HTML 4.01
    Frameset//EN"
    "http://www.w3.org/TR/html4/frameset.dtd">
<HTML>
<HEAD><TITLE>My Family Photo Album</TITLE></HEAD>
<BODY>
<H1>Photos circa 1940</H1>
</BODY>
</HTML>
```

2. **Add the** `<IMG>` **tag wherever you want your image to appear, as shown in the following example:**

```
<H1>Photos circa 1940</H1>
<IMG>
```

3. **Add the** SRC **attribute to provide the address of the image, as the following example shows:**

   The image I'm using is named `uncleNeil.jpg`, and it's in the same folder as my HTML document:

```
<IMG SRC="uncleNeil.jpg">
```

4. **Add the** ALT **attribute to describe the image, just in case viewers can't view (or choose not to view) the image:**

```
<IMG SRC="uncleNeil.jpg" ALT="Photo of Uncle Neil taken
    at Clear Lake">
```

The resulting Web page looks like what you see in Figure 10-1.

Technically, you don't *have to* provide the ALT text (which stands for *alternative* text) with the image; however, doing so is a good idea. Sometimes, people use browsers — including read-aloud browsers for the visually impaired — that can't display images.

Figure 10-1:
Using the
<IMG> tag
to add an
image to
your Web
page.

Section 508 of the U.S. Rehabilitation Act requires all U.S. government (and government vendor) Web sites to include ALT attributes where appropriate. You can find out more about accessibility by checking out the Website Tips Accessibility page (www.websitetips.com/accessibility), the World Wide Web Consortium's Web Content Accessibility Guidelines, (www.w3.org/TR/ WAI-WEBCONTENT), or the U.S. government site devoted to Section 508 (www. section508.gov).

Many people also commonly stop their browsers from showing images so that they don't need to wait for the images to copy to their computers over slow modem connections. By using alternative text, you tell people what they're missing rather than make them guess. As a bonus, many browsers use the alternative text for those cute little pop-up blurbs that appear when you hover your mouse over images. Figure 10-2 shows you an example of how the alternative text might look to readers viewing the same page without the images.

Finding images to use on your Web pages

Unless clearly stated otherwise, all images are copyrighted. Don't even think about copying images from other peoples' Web sites and using the images on your own pages. Instead, check out one of the hundreds of good sites on the Internet that offer clip art or Web art that's free for noncommercial use. Check out Yahoo! (www.yahoo.com) and search for *free clip art*. You can find all that you could ever use.

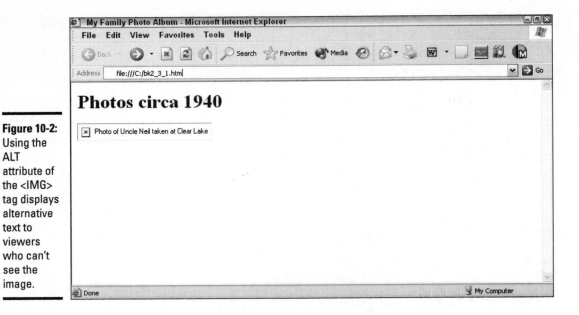

Figure 10-2:
Using the ALT attribute of the <IMG> tag displays alternative text to viewers who can't see the image.

Optimizing Images for Quick Download

Images take quite a while to download (particularly over a slow Internet connection), and readers are likely to give up on your Web site and move on if the images take too long to appear. If you're on a fast Internet connection or if you're testing your HTML documents directly from your hard drive (as most people do), you probably don't notice how long some images take to load; 28.8 Kbps or 56.6 Kbps modems (which are still common) take a long time to transfer images — sometimes up to several minutes.

You can shorten the image download time in either of the following two ways:

✦ Reduce the image's file size. You do this when you create an image.

✦ Indicate image dimensions in the HTML document by using the WIDTH and HEIGHT attributes associated with the <IMG> tag.

Thumbnail images, which I cover later in this chapter in "Making Clickable Images," can also be helpful in managing the World Wide Wait when you want to use large images.

You specify the dimensions of an image (generally displayed on the title bar or status bar of image-editing programs) by including HEIGHT and WIDTH attributes in the <IMG> tag. When you do so, browsers leave space for the image, finish loading the text (at which point your readers can start reading), and then continue loading the images. The images don't really load faster, but specifying the image size can help readers *think* that the images are loading faster, which is almost as good. The numbers that you specify for height and width specify the size in *pixels,* which are those itty-bitty dots on-screen that make up the image.

Table 10-2 shows the attributes used to specify image height and width.

Table 10-2	Image Height and Width Attributes	
HTML Attribute	*Effect*	*Example*
`HEIGHT=n`	Specifies the height of the image in pixels	`<IMG SRC="picture.gif" HEIGHT="200">`
`WIDTH=n`	Specifies the width of the image in pixels	`<IMG SRC="picture.gif" WIDTH="150">`

The code for specifying `HEIGHT` and `WIDTH` attributes looks something like this:

```
<IMG SRC="auntEliza.gif" ALT="Aunt Eliza on her wedding day"
     WIDTH=300 HEIGHT="300">
```

Controlling Image Alignment

By default, browsers align images on the left side of the page. If you want, you can realign the images so that they appear aligned at the right or aligned vertically.

HTML 4.0 (and 4.01) recommends that you use style sheets to control image alignment rather than use the attributes given in this section. However, using the attributes that you find in Table 10-3 can be useful if the folks visiting your site are using old browsers — for example, versions of Internet Explorer before version 6 and versions of Netscape before 7.1. See Book VI, Chapter 13 for the lowdown on style sheets.

Table 10-3 shows the attributes used to control image alignment.

Table 10-3	Image Alignment Attributes
HTML Attribute	*Effect*
`ALIGN="bottom"`	Aligns the bottom of the image with the baseline of the current line
`ALIGN="left"`	Allows an image to float down and over to the left margin (into the next available space); subsequent text wraps to the right of that image
`ALIGN="middle"`	Aligns the baseline of the current line with the middle of the image
`ALIGN="right"`	Aligns the image with the right margin and wraps the text around the left
`ALIGN="top"`	Aligns the text with the top of the tallest item in the line
`HSPACE=n`	Controls the horizontal space (white space) around the image in pixels
`VSPACE=n`	Controls the vertical space (white space) around the image in pixels

All you need to do is include these attributes in the <IMG> tag in your HTML document. The order of the attributes within the <IMG> tag isn't important. You can put them in the order that you find most convenient. The following HTML code shows you how to align an image to appear on the right side of the page:

```
<IMG SRC="auntEliza.jpg" ALT="Aunt Eliza on her wedding day"
    ALIGN="RIGHT">
```

Surrounding Images with Blank Space

You can include these alignment effects by adding vertical and horizontal space around the images.

Just add the HSPACE or VSPACE attribute (or both). The number following the attribute is the number of pixels wide that the space should be on each side of the image; thus, the total width that is added is two times n. Here's an example:

```
<IMG SRC="cousins.jpg" ALT="Girl cousins" ALIGN="left"
    HSPACE=50>
<IMG SRC="cousins2.jpg" ALT="Girl cousins - second take"
    ALIGN="right" HSPACE=50>
```

Figure 10-3 shows you the results of the extra space around the images.

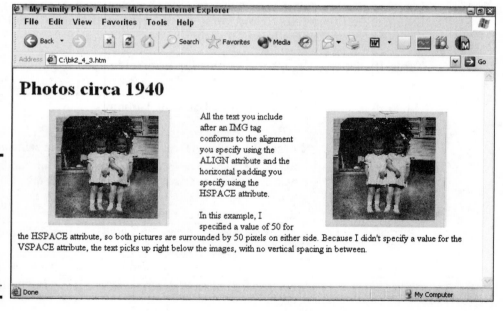

Figure 10-3: Using the HSPACE attribute of the <IMG> tag to surround images with blank space.

Note: If most of your readers will be using browsers compliant with HTML 4.0, such as Internet Explorer 6 (and higher) and Netscape 7 (and higher), consider achieving the same effects with style sheets, which I cover in Book VI, Chapter 13.

Making Clickable Images

You can use images as your anchors for making links. Using images as anchors isn't any more complicated than creating a link and then adding an image. To use an image as the anchor to link to another document, follow these steps:

1. **Start your HTML document:**

   Your document might look similar to the following example:

   ```
   <!DOCTYPE HTML PUBLIC "-//W3C//DTD HTML 4.01
       Frameset//EN"
       "http://www.w3.org/TR/html4/frameset.dtd">
   <HTML>
   <HEAD><TITLE>My Family Photo Album</TITLE></HEAD>
   <BODY>
   <H1>Click a picture for more information</H1>
   </BODY>
   </HTML>
   ```

2. **Add a link, as shown in the following example:**

   ```
   <H1>Click a picture for more information</H1>
   <A HREF="cousinInfo.html"></A>
   ```

   For more information about links, take a look at Book VI, Chapter 9.

3. **Add the `<IMG>` tag between the opening and closing link tags (between `<A>` and `</A>`):**

   ```
   <A HREF="cousinInfo.html"><IMG></A>
   ```

4. **Add the `SRC` attribute to the `<IMG>` tag.**

   The `SRC` attribute tells which graphical image you're including in your HTML document.

   ```
   <A HREF="cousinInfo.html"><IMG SRC="cousins.jpg"></A>
   ```

5. **Add the `ALT` attribute to the `<IMG>` tag.**

   The `ALT` attribute tells what text to display if the image isn't displayed.

   ```
   <A HREF="cousinInfo.html"><IMG SRC="cousins.jpg"
   ALT="Girl cousins"></A>
   ```

The Web page looks something like what you see in Figure 10-4. Notice that the image shown in the figure contains a border. It's the same color as other links in the document, which indicates to readers that the image links to other information or files.

You can remove the border from around the linked image. To do so, just add the `BORDER` attribute to the `<IMG>` tag with the value `BORDER=0`. For example:

```
<A HREF="cousinInfo.html"><IMG SRC="cousins.jpg"
ALT="Girl cousins" BORDER=0></A>
```

TIP

Making an image into a link is useful when you want to link a small *thumbnail* image file to a large, full-sized version. (Using thumbnail images is a good idea if you have many images or very large images on your Web page because visitors get the idea of what the pictures look like but don't need to wait all day for the bigger image files to download.) To link a thumbnail image to a full-sized version, follow the steps that I describe in the preceding example, placing the name of the full-sized image in the link and the name of the thumbnail image in the SRC attribute. For example:

```
<A HREF="big_img.jpg"><IMG SRC="thumb_img.jpg"
   ALT="Thumbnail image"></A>
```

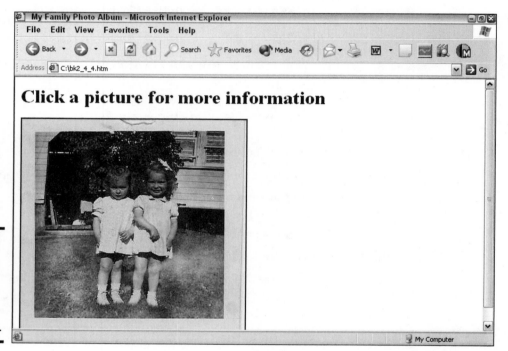

Figure 10-4:
This image is also a link, courtesy of the <A> and <IMG> tags.

Chapter 11: Controlling Page Layout

This chapter introduces you to some nifty things that you can do with HTML to format your pages attractively. You need to be familiar with the basic HTML tags before diving into this chapter. Most examples in this chapter include only the tags and attributes discussed under a particular heading and don't include structure or body tags. I assume that you know where structure and body tags are placed. If you don't, flip to Book VI, Chapter 7.

Although not as widely supported as tables, layers are another way to create slick-looking layouts for your Web site. You can use an HTML editor, such as Dreamweaver, to work with layers easily. Chapters 19 through 27 of Book VI cover Dreamweaver. Layers are also available in FrontPage 2003, which I cover in Chapters 14 through 18 of Book VI.

Developing Tables

Tables aren't just for dinner any more. In the context of HTML, tables are quite handy for the following purposes:

✦ Lining up material vertically and horizontally

✦ Making creative layouts

✦ Placing text next to graphics

Table 11-1 shows the tags and attributes used to create tables.

Table 11-1	Creating Tables	
HTML Tag or Attribute	**Effect**	**Use in Pairs?**
`<TABLE>...</TABLE>`	Indicates table format	Yes
`BORDER=n`	Controls table border width in pixels; 0 specifies no border	No
`<TD>...</TD>`	Indicates table data cells	Yes
`<TH>...</TH>`	Indicates table headings	Yes
`<TR>...</TR>`	Indicates table row items	Yes

These steps describe how to create a table, such as the one that follows, with three rows and two columns. *Note:* Before you begin, make sure that your browser and text editor are open and ready to create a new document. Or, you can apply this information to an existing document.

Culprit	*Water Balloon Skills*
Deborah	Fair
Eric	Excellent

Follow these steps to create a simple table:

1. **Type text, row by row, using a space or two between row elements:**

```
Culprit Water Balloon Skills

Deborah Fair
Eric Excellent
```

2. **Insert <TABLE> tags before and after the text to indicate the <TABLE> information to be inserted into the table:**

```
<TABLE>
Culprit Water Balloon Skills
Deborah Fair
Eric Excellent
</TABLE>
```

3. **Add <TR> tags to show where the table rows should be placed.**

TR stands for table rows, and rows go across the page.

```
<TABLE>
<TR>Culprit Water Balloon Skills</TR>
<TR>Deborah Fair</TR>
<TR>Eric Excellent</TR>
</TABLE>
```

4. **Add pairs of <TH> tags to show where the table heading cells go (in the top row).**

At this point, adding some spacing can help you more easily see what's going on:

```
<TABLE>
<TR><TH>Culprit</TH>
<TH>Water Balloon Skills</TH>
</TR>
<TR>Deborah Fair</TR>
<TR>Eric Excellent</TR>
</TABLE>
```

5. **Add pairs of <TD> tags to indicate the individual data cells of a table:**

```
<TABLE>
<TR><TH>Culprit</TH>
<TH>Water Balloon Skills</TH>
</TR>
```

```
<TR><TD>Deborah</TD> <TD>Fair</TD></TR>
<TR><TD>Eric</TD> <TD>Excellent</TD></TR>
</TABLE>
```

6. Add the `BORDER` **attribute to the** `<TABLE>` **tag to create lines around each table cell:**

```
<TABLE BORDER=1>
<TR><TH>Culprit</TH>
<TH>Water Balloon Skills</TH>
</TR>
<TR><TD>Deborah </TD> <TD>Fair</TD></TR>
<TR><TD>Eric </TD> <TD>Excellent</TD></TR>
</TABLE>
```

Figure 11-1 shows the result of all this work.

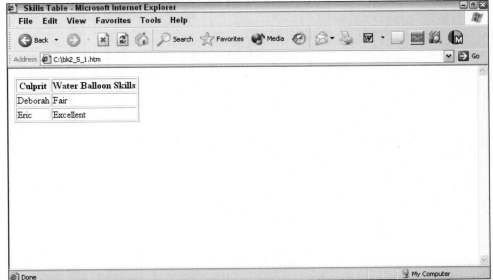

Figure 11-1:
Use the
`<TABLE>`
tag to
create nice,
even rows
and
columns.

Experiment with tables. You can come up with many creative layouts and page designs. Here are some ideas:

✦ Embed images in tables (to align graphics and text the way you want).

✦ Place text in table cells to make columns — like a newspaper.

✦ Place headings to the left (or right) of a paragraph of text.

If you find that your tables have problems — or don't seem to work — make sure that your tags are paired correctly and that you haven't omitted any tags. Printing a copy of your HTML code and marking pairs of tags are sometimes necessary for troubleshooting tables. As you can see from the very small example in this section, getting confused is easy because of all the different tags necessary for tables. Additionally, save yourself some trouble by liberally using white space and blank lines as you create the table. The extra white space can help you see what's going on.

Embedding Horizontal Rules

HTML allows you to break up Web pages by applying a horizontal rule: <HR>. This horizontal rule can serve as not only a visual break for long pages, but also an informational break. Table 11-2 illustrates the tag used to create horizontal rules and the attributes that let you format them.

Table 11-2	Adding Horizontal Rules
HTML Tag or Attribute	*Effect*
<HR>	Applies a horizontal rule.
SIZE="*number*"	Indicates how thick the rule is.
WIDTH="*number*"	Specifies an exact width in pixels or percentage (%) of document width. A percentage value must appear in quotes, like WIDTH="50%".
ALIGN="LEFT"	Specifies the alignment. "LEFT" works only in combination with "CENTER", and "RIGHT" works only with "WIDTH".

To use horizontal rules, apply the following tags and attributes:

```
<P><EM><H1 ALIGN=CENTER>Lost
    Cat!</H1></EM></P>
<HR WIDTH="80%" ALIGN=CENTER>
<HR WIDTH="60%" ALIGN=CENTER>
<HR WIDTH="40%" ALIGN=CENTER>
<P>Fuzzy tortoise shell Persian--lost in Big
    Lake area. Probably looks confused.</P>
<HR>
<P>Answers to:
<UL>
<LI>Winchester
<LI>Hairheimer
<LI>Fritter
<LI>Sound of can opener
</UL></P>
<P>Please call if you find him: 555-9999</P>
<HR WIDTH=200>
<HR WIDTH=400>
<HR WIDTH=200>
```

Getting carried away with horizontal rules is easy. Figure 11-2 shows horizontal rules used to excess. Use these rules only where they help readers find information more easily or help them wade through long passages of information.

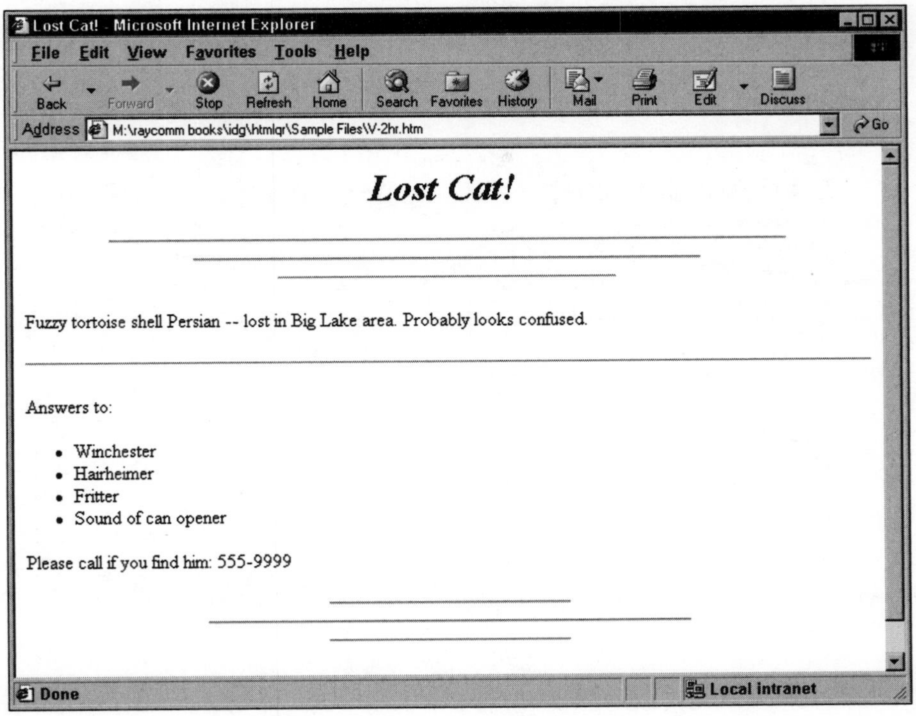

Figure 11-2:
Don't
overuse the
<HR> tag.

Forcing Line Breaks

HTML allows you to break lines of text so that you can determine exactly
(or as much as possible) how they appear on the users' end. Table 11-3
shows the tag used to force line breaks.

Table 11-3	Inserting Line Breaks	
HTML Tag or Attribute	*Effect*	*Use in Pairs?*
 	Breaks line; new line begins after tag	No
CLEAR="..."	Requires that LEFT, RIGHT, NONE, or ALL margins are clear before new line starts	No

To break lines of text so that each line appears the way that you want (for
example, in a poem), use the <BR> tag as in the following block of code:

```
<BODY>
<P>
I'm Hungry, I'm Hungry! I said with a
   sigh,<BR>
I want to cancel dinner and go straight to my
   pie.<BR>
I want cake and ice cream and toast with
   jelly,<BR>
And I don't care if I grow a big belly.<BR>
</P>
</BODY>
```

If you include a line break and want to make sure that the new line starts after an image, for example, add the `CLEAR=ALL` attribute to the `<BR>` tag. That forces the new line below all other objects on the line. Figure 11-3 shows the effects of these line breaks.

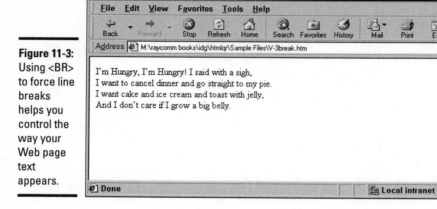

Figure 11-3: Using <BR> to force line breaks helps you control the way your Web page text appears.

Chapter 12: Creating Forms

In This Chapter

✔ Adding a basic form

✔ Working with buttons, check boxes, and radio buttons

✔ Adding pizzazz with drop-down lists, text fields, and more

This chapter introduces forms, which you might think of as online versions of hard-copy forms that have check boxes and blanks to fill in, among other possible features. These online forms can help you get feedback and information from the folks who visit your Web site.

To develop a fully functional form, you need the help of your server administrator. In this chapter, I tell you where you need to ask for help and what information to request.

Creating a Basic Form

In HTML, forms are just what they are in real life — a fairly impersonal and effective means of getting standardized information from other people. Table 12-1 shows you the basic <FORM> tags and attributes that you can use. You can use forms to

✦ Conduct a survey.

✦ Collect addresses or information about visitors to your site.

✦ Enable people to register for something.

Table 12-1	Creating Forms	
HTML Tag or Attribute	*Effect*	*Example*
`<FORM...>` ... `</FORM>`	Encloses the entire form.	`<FORM METHOD ="POST" ACTION="http://www.your Server.yourScript">`*form components* `</FORM>`
`ACTION="..."`	Identifies what should happen to the data after the form is submitted.	`<FORM METHOD ="POST" ACTION="http://www. yourServer.yourScript">` *form components*`</FORM>`
`METHOD="..."`	Identifies methods. Valid options are GET or POST — one is required.	`<FORM `**`METHOD="POST"`**` ACTION="http://www. yourServer.yourScript">` *form components*`</FORM>`

When you create forms, you need to make sure that the information gets back to you after readers fill out the form and click Submit. Although form results can be processed and returned in various ways, your server administrator most likely has the server set up to e-mail form results directly to you.

The basic <FORM> tag is a two-parter, having both an initial tag and a closing tag. You can use the <FORM> tag to have information sent back to you directly or to a program that compiles the information for you. The <FORM> tag has two primary (essential) attributes:

✦ ACTION: Tells the server what to do with the information after the server receives it.

✦ METHOD: Tells the server how to get the processed information back to you.

Exactly what you fill in as values for these two attributes depends on what your server administrator tells you. So, before you get started creating your form, go ahead and contact your server administrator and tell her that you want to create a form that can be e-mailed to your personal address and ask what you should fill in for the ACTION and METHOD attributes.

For example, my administrator told me to use the following elements:

```
ACTION="http://www.raycomm.com/
    cgi-bin/email?raycomm"
Method=POST
```

Notice that the rest of the examples in this chapter are constructed based on this information. Just ask your server administrator exactly what to use (or where to look for instructions).

Before I outline how to create a form, I assume that the following information is true:

✦ You have already contacted your server administrator and have the ACTION and METHOD information.

✦ You have your HTML document open in an editing program.

✦ You have opened the HTML document in your browser so that you can view and test the document.

To include a form in your Web page, follow these basic steps:

1. **Start with a basic HTML document, similar to this one:**

```
<!DOCTYPE HTML PUBLIC "-//W3C//DTD HTML 4.01
    Frameset//EN"
    "http://www.w3.org/TR/html4/frameset.dtd">
<HTML>
<HEAD><TITLE>Survey: How to Get the
    Cats</TITLE></HEAD>
<BODY>
<H1>Survey: How to Get the Cats</H1>
<P>We've decided to take a survey about the best pranks
    to play on the cats. Please complete the survey and
    click the Submit button.</P>
```

```
</BODY>
</HTML>
```

2. Add the `<FORM>` **and** `</FORM>` **tags to show where the form goes:**

```
Please complete the survey and click the Submit
    button.</P>
<FORM>
</FORM>
</BODY>
</HTML>
```

3. Add the information that your server administrator gave you for the `ACTION` **and** `METHOD` **attributes.**

Remember that the information that I show here is what my administrator told me to fill in.

```
<FORM METHOD="POST"
    ACTION="http://www.raycomm.com/
    cgi-bin/email?raycomm">
</FORM>
```

At this point, you can't see anything different about your page. Nor can you test the page to find out whether it works. Just forge ahead, finish up the form, and satisfy your curiosity.

Using Form Components to Collect Information

After you have the basics of the form under control, add some `<INPUT>` fields so that you can start collecting information. The basic form-input tags (see Table 12-2), in many permutations, should carry you through the next several sections.

Table 12-2	Form-Input Tags	
HTML Tag	**Effect**	**Example or Attribute**
`<INPUT...>`	Identifies some type of input field.	`<INPUT TYPE="SUBMIT">`
`CHECKED`	Shows which item is selected by default (used with a check box and radio button).	`<INPUT TYPE="CHECKBOX" CHECKED>`
`MAXLENGTH=n`	Indicates the maximum number of characters in the field width.	`<INPUT TYPE="TEXT" MAXLENGTH=25>`
`NAME="..."`	Indicates the name of the field.	`<INPUT TYPE="TEXT" NAME="HomeAddress">`
`SIZE=n`	Displays field *n* characters wide.	`<INPUT TYPE="SELECT" SIZE=4>`
`TYPE="..."`	Indicates the type of field. Valid types are TEXT, PASSWORD, CHECKBOX, RADIO, SUBMIT, RESET, FILE, IMAGE, BUTTON, and HIDDEN.	`<INPUT TYPE="RADIO">`
`VALUE="..."`	Indicates the value of the button (and the label for Submit and Reset).	`<INPUT TYPE="BUTTON" VALUE="Click this button">`

Including Submit and Reset buttons

After you create a form, you need to add Submit and Reset buttons that readers click to submit the form (or start over again if they goof up). The Submit button sends the information after your readers click it, but the Reset button just clears the input from the form.

Remember: You need a functional form before you start adding Submit and Reset buttons. To include Submit and Reset buttons, enter the following text and tags in your HTML document:

```
<FORM METHOD="POST" ACTION="http://www.raycomm.com/
    cgi-bin/email?raycomm">
<INPUT TYPE="SUBMIT" VALUE="Submit">
<INPUT TYPE="RESET" VALUE="Reset">
</FORM>
```

To change the text that appears on the Submit and Reset buttons, change the values associated with the VALUE attributes of the Submit and Reset buttons, respectively. Here's an example:

```
<INPUT TYPE="RESET" VALUE="Forget it!">
```

Including check boxes, radio buttons, and more

Check boxes and radio buttons are the objects that users can click to select choices from a list. *Check boxes* allow you to select multiple options. *Radio buttons,* also called *option buttons,* are designed so that you can choose only one from a list — just like with pushing buttons on a car radio. Check boxes and radio buttons are variations on the <INPUT> field. You see examples of both in the following sections.

Making check boxes

Making check boxes isn't complicated: You use several tags, but the process is the same as creating anything else with HTML.

Remember: You need to have a functional form, including Submit and Reset buttons, before you add check boxes. Start with the following example — just a section of a complete document — and build on it:

```
<FORM METHOD="POST"
    ACTION="http://www.raycomm.com/
    cgi-bin/email?raycomm">
<INPUT TYPE="SUBMIT" VALUE="Submit">
<INPUT TYPE="RESET" VALUE="Reset">
</FORM>
```

To use check boxes in your document, follow these steps:

1. Enter <INPUT TYPE="CHECKBOX"> **on the blank line after the beginning of the form:**

```
<FORM METHOD="POST"
    ACTION="http://www.raycomm.com/
    cgi-bin/email?raycomm">
<INPUT TYPE="CHECKBOX">
<INPUT TYPE="SUBMIT" VALUE="Submit">
<INPUT TYPE="RESET"VALUE="Reset">
</FORM>
```

2. Insert the text that you want people to see next to that check box.

Until you do so, they see a check box with no description.

```
<FORM METHOD="POST"
    ACTION="http://www.raycomm.com/
    cgi-bin/email?raycomm">
<INPUT TYPE="CHECKBOX">Throw a balloon!
<INPUT TYPE="SUBMIT" VALUE="Submit">
<INPUT TYPE="RESET" VALUE="Reset">
</FORM>
```

3. Identify the name of the <INPUT> **field.**

You see this field as you're reading the input from your form. Make the name something short and logical.

```
<FORM METHOD="POST"
    ACTION="http://www.raycomm.com/
    cgi-bin/email?raycomm">
<INPUT TYPE="CHECKBOX" NAME="Throw">
    Throw a balloon!
<INPUT TYPE="SUBMIT" VALUE="Submit">
<INPUT TYPE="RESET" VALUE="Reset">
</FORM>
```

4. Enter the text that you want to see if someone selects this option, as shown in the following example:

```
<FORM METHOD="POST"
    ACTION="http://www.raycomm.com/
    cgi-bin/email?raycomm">
<INPUT TYPE="CHECKBOX" NAME="Throw"
    VALUE="ThrowBalloon"> Throw a balloon!
<INPUT TYPE="SUBMIT" VALUE="Submit">
<INPUT TYPE="RESET" VALUE="Reset">
</FORM>
```

5. Enter a couple more lines to complete the list because, of course, you don't want a check box list with only one item to select.

```
<INPUT TYPE="CHECKBOX" NAME="Throw"
    VALUE="ThrowBalloon"> Throw a balloon!
<INPUT TYPE="CHECKBOX" NAME="Hurl" VALUE="HurlBalloon">
    Hurl a balloon!
<INPUT TYPE="CHECKBOX" NAME="Lob" VALUE="LobBalloon">
    Lob a balloon!
```

6. Enter a `CHECKED` **attribute in the line for the check box that you want to have selected by default.**

Do so if you want to have a check box selected in advance to give a recommendation or to make sure that something gets checked.

```
<INPUT CHECKED TYPE="CHECKBOX" NAME="Hurl"
    VALUE="HurlBalloon"> Hurl a balloon!
```

Making radio buttons

Making radio buttons is similar to making check boxes — you use several tags, and the process is the same as that for using other HTML tags. *Note:* Before you start making radio buttons, make sure that you have already completed your functional form. To include radio buttons in your form, follow these steps:

1. Enter <INPUT TYPE="RADIO"> **and insert the text that people should see:**

```
<INPUT>Do it--it'll be funny!
<INPUT TYPE="SUBMIT" VALUE="Submit">
<INPUT TYPE="RESET" VALUE="Reset">
</FORM>
```

2. Add the `NAME` **and** `VALUE` **indicators.**

The `NAME` field applies to the whole set of radio buttons, so I've chosen a less-specific name:

```
<INPUT TYPE="RADIO" NAME="Prank" VALUE="Do" >Do it--
    it'll be funny!
```

3. Add the `CHECKED` **attribute because this selection is the recommended choice:**

```
<INPUT TYPE="RADIO" NAME="Prank" VALUE="Do"
CHECKED>Do it--it'll be funny!
```

4. Add as many more radio buttons to this set as you want, along with line breaks (
 or <P>**) between them, just to make them look nice.**

Radio buttons are designed to accept only one selection from the group, so make sure that they all share the same `NAME` field. This way, the computer knows that they belong together:

```
<INPUT TYPE="RADIO" NAME="Prank" VALUE="Do" CHECKED>Do
    it--it'll be funny!<BR>
<INPUT TYPE="RADIO" NAME="Prank" VALUE="DoNot">
    Don't play a prank, meanie!<BR>
<INPUT TYPE="RADIO" NAME="Prank"
    VALUE="DoNotCare">I couldn't care less.
    They're your cats, and you'll have to live with
    yourself.<P>
```

Using other input types

Other input types, such as `TEXT`, can be quite useful. The `TEXT` type allows visitors to insert a small amount of information (such as a name or an address) into your form. Before you start adding other input attributes, make sure that you have already completed your functional form. To include text box input areas in your form, follow these steps:

1. **Insert the** `<INPUT>` **tag and the text that people should see, plus a tag (**`<BR>` **or** `<P>`**) to force a new line:**

```
<INPUT>Your Name<P>
<INPUT TYPE="SUBMIT" VALUE="Submit">
<INPUT TYPE="RESET" VALUE="Reset">
</FORM>
```

2. **Add the** `TYPE` **indicator to show that it's a text box input area:**

```
<INPUT TYPE="TEXT">Your Name<P>
```

3. **Add the** `NAME` **indicator:**

```
<INPUT TYPE="TEXT" NAME="name">Your Name<P>
```

4. **Add the** `SIZE` **indicator to tell the text box how many characters wide it should be:**

```
<INPUT SIZE=35 TYPE="TEXT" NAME="name">Your Name<P>
```

Including drop-down lists

Drop-down lists are lists from which readers can choose one or more items, just like in a dialog box or window. You create a drop-down list by using the `<SELECT>` tag. Table 12-3 shows you the tags and attributes that you use to include drop-down lists in your HTML documents.

Table 12-3	Adding Lists	
HTML Tag or Attribute	**Effect**	**Use in Pairs?**
`<SELECT...> ... </SELECT>`	Provides a drop-down list of items to select	Yes
`MULTIPLE`	Indicates that multiple selections are allowed	No
`NAME="..."`	Indicates the name of the drop-down list field	No
`SIZE=n`	Determines the size of the scrollable list by showing *n* options	No
`<OPTION...>`	Precedes each item in an option list	Yes, optionally
`SELECTED`	Identifies which option is selected	No by default
`VALUE="..."`	Indicates the value of the drop-down list field option	No

The following steps describe how to add a drop-down list to your form. Before you include drop-down lists, make sure that you already have a functional form completed.

1. Insert the `<SELECT>` **tags into your document and a tag (**`<BR>` **or** `<P>`**) to force a new line:**

```
<SELECT>
</SELECT><P>
<INPUT TYPE="SUBMIT" VALUE="Submit">
<INPUT TYPE="RESET" VALUE="Reset">
</FORM>
```

2. Add the `NAME` **attribute to the** `<SELECT>` **tag.**

The `NAME` should be appropriately broad to cover the spectrum of choices:

```
<SELECT NAME="Method">
</SELECT><P>
```

3. Add an `<OPTION>` **tag defining an option that your readers can select:**

```
<SELECT NAME="Method">
<OPTION VALUE="single">Single Balloon
</SELECT><P>
```

4. Complete your `<SELECT>` **section by adding the other possible choices:**

```
<SELECT NAME="Method">
<OPTION VALUE="single">Single Balloon
<OPTION VALUE="multiple">Multiple Balloons
<OPTION VALUE="hose">Just Use the Hose
</SELECT><P>
```

Figure 12-1 demonstrates the addition of the drop-down list to your form.

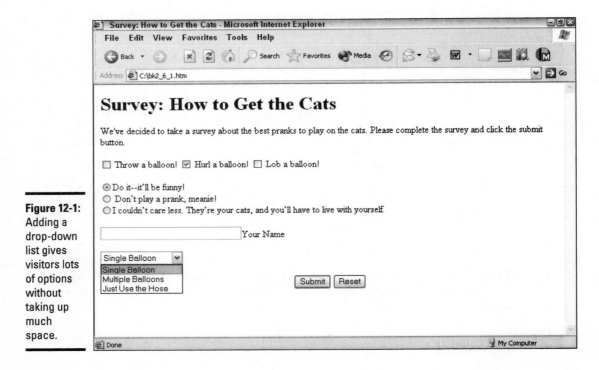

Figure 12-1:
Adding a drop-down list gives visitors lots of options without taking up much space.

Including text areas

Text areas are open spaces in your form in which readers can type comments or enter other information. Table 12-4 lists the tags and attributes used to add text areas to your form.

Table 12-4	Adding Text Areas	
HTML Tag or Attribute	*Effect*	*Use in Pairs?*
`<TEXTAREA ...>` `...</TEXTAREA>`	Encloses a multiline text area. The enclosed text is the value displayed in the field.	Yes
`COLS=n`	Indicates the number of columns in the field.	No
`NAME="..."`	Indicates the name of the field.	No
`ROWS=n`	Indicates the number of rows in the field.	No

Book VI
Chapter 12

Creating Forms

To add a text area to your form, you include the opening and closing `<TEXTAREA>` tags, along with values for the NAME, ROWS, and COLS attributes:

```
<TEXTAREA NAME="comments" ROWS=3 COLS=40>Enter your comments
    here.
</TEXTAREA><P>
<INPUT TYPE="SUBMIT" VALUE="Submit">
<INPUT TYPE="RESET" VALUE="Reset">
</FORM>
```

Check out Figure 12-2 to see the text area that the preceding HTML code produces.

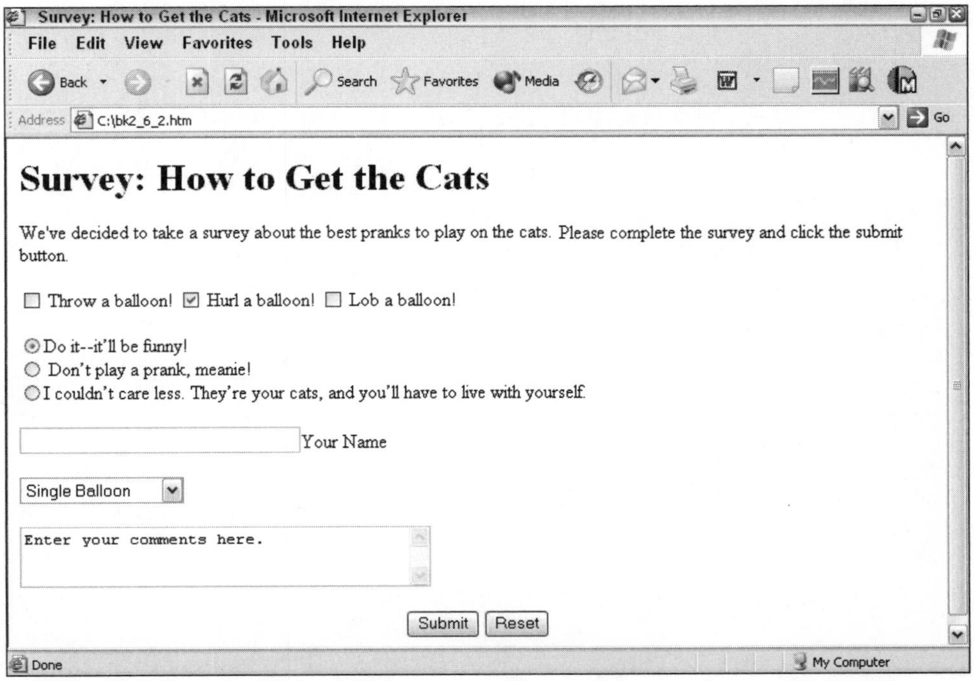

Figure 12-2: Use the <TEXT­AREA> tag to enable visitors to enter free-form comments.

703

Chapter 13: Developing Style Sheets

In This Chapter

✔ Understanding style sheets

✔ Tying style sheets into HTML documents

✔ Creating style sheets from scratch

Style sheets, another standard from the World Wide Web Consortium, provide all the formatting capabilities that you could ever want for your Web pages. The bad news is that even though both Microsoft Internet Explorer and Netscape Navigator support style sheets, that support isn't identical. Each browser displays style sheet code just a bit differently from the other. Readers who aren't using browsers capable of reading HTML 4.0 or higher cannot see the nifty formatting effects that you add by using style sheets.

About Style Sheets

Style sheets provide formatting commands for Web pages in a more convenient and efficient manner than regular HTML offers. By using style sheets, you can format practically any element of your HTML document and have that formatting applied to the same elements throughout your entire Web site. So, rather than manually change all those pesky headings, you can simply change the heading style and change the appearance of all of them in one fell swoop.

Accommodating browser differences

If you know that your readers use style-sheet-capable browsers (which roughly 95 percent of the Internet population does), by all means use style sheets, but with some care. If, as is more likely, some of your readers have style-sheet-capable browsers and some have older browsers, you have three choices:

✦ Use style sheets exclusively and let readers with older browsers see the plain, mostly unformatted text.

✦ Use only regular HTML formatting commands and pretend that style sheets don't exist.

✦ Use both style sheets and regular HTML formatting options. You spend twice as much effort using this approach (and it's redundant and repetitive and formats the same thing over and over again), but it accommodates a larger percentage of your readers more effectively than the other options do.

A good compromise for using style sheets and accommodating browsers that don't reliably handle them is to do the following:

✦ Format the background and basic text colors (as defined in the `<BODY>` tag of regular HTML documents) with HTML commands.

✦ Format the background and basic text colors with style sheets. (If necessary, these style sheet commands override the analogous commands from the regular HTML document.)

✦ Provide any additional formatting commands through style sheets and, optionally, HTML markup tags.

Understanding inheritance

Inheritance means that a document takes on global basic characteristics, and each more specific formatting command that you define overrides the last (for most elements). For example, if you define the background of the whole page as red, the background of a table as blue, and the background of a table cell as green, the most specific formatting (green for the cell) takes precedence.

Here's the general order of precedence:

✦ Document-wide formatting from an HTML document (as defined in the `<BODY>` tag) is the most basic level of formatting.

✦ Document-wide formatting from a style sheet overrides document-wide formatting from an HTML document.

✦ Specific formatting in HTML overrides document-wide formatting.

✦ Specific formatting from a style sheet overrides specific formatting in HTML.

✦ Specific formatting from a style sheet overrides general formatting.

If specific formatting is defined in the HTML document and the format for the same element is also defined in a style sheet, the style sheet formatting generally wins. If a more specific element (such as a table cell rather than the whole table) is specified in either the style sheet or HTML document, the specific element wins.

Before you get started using style sheets, remember that the style sheet isn't necessarily part of the HTML document. In fact, depending on how you do it (see the options in the next section), the style sheet can be a completely different document. So, your first step is to decide how you want to connect the style sheet to the HTML document. Then you can develop the style sheet, which specifies all the bells and whistles that you want to include.

Connecting Style Sheets to HTML Documents

The first step in using style sheets is to decide how you want to connect them to your HTML documents. After you get the hang of using style sheets and know how you want to connect them, you can just dive in and start creating them. (You find the exact process later in this chapter, in the section "Understanding Style Rules.") However, first I share with you the idea of how style sheets and HTML documents can relate.

Basically, style sheets can connect to HTML documents in four ways. You can do any one of the following:

✦ Embed the style sheet in the HTML document.

✦ Link the style sheet to the HTML document.

✦ Import the style sheet into the HTML document.

✦ Add style sheet rules as attributes to regular HTML tags.

This chapter covers only the first two options because they are the most widely supported and the most practical to use. (The latter two are somewhat more complicated and convoluted, and describing them is beyond the scope of this book.) If you're interested in knowing how to use the latter two options, check out *HTML 4 For Dummies,* 4th Edition, written by Ed Tittel and Natanya Pitts (Wiley Publishing, Inc).

Embedding style sheets

The easiest way to handle style sheets is to embed them within the `<HEAD>` tag (technically, within `<STYLE>` tags within the `<HEAD>` tag) of the HTML document. Embedding them is easy because you don't have to create a completely different document for the style sheet. You can simply work with an HTML document that you already have. To embed a style sheet, use the tags and attributes listed in Table 13-1.

Table 13-1	Embedding a Style Sheet	
HTML Tag or Attribute	*Description*	*Example*
`<STYLE>...</STYLE>`	Specifies the style block	`<STYLE TYPE="text/css"></STYLE>`
`TYPE="text/css"`	Specifies the type of style sheet	`<STYLE TYPE="text/css"></STYLE>`
`<!- ->`	Hides style sheet commands from older browsers	`<STYLE TYPE="text/css"><!- -></STYLE>`

The following steps show you how to add the `<STYLE>` tag and its attributes:

1. **Start with a functional HTML document.**

The top of the document should look something like the following block of code:

```
<!DOCTYPE HTML PUBLIC "-//W3C//DTD HTML 4.01
    Frameset//EN"
    "http://www.w3.org/TR/html4/frameset.dtd">
<HTML>
<HEAD>
<TITLE>Cats Galore</TITLE>
</HEAD>
<BODY>
</BODY>
</HTML>
```

2. **Add** `<STYLE>` **tags:**

```
<TITLE>Cats Galore</TITLE>
<STYLE>
</STYLE>
</HEAD>
```

3. **Add comment tags within the** `<STYLE>` **tags to hide the styles from older browsers:**

```
<STYLE>
<!--
-->
</STYLE>
```

4. **Add the** `TYPE="text/css"` **attribute to specify that you're using a Cascading Style Sheet:**

```
<STYLE TYPE="text/css">
<!--
-->
</STYLE>
```

Other style sheet formats exist (most notably, JavaScript Style Sheets) but they're less common and nonstandard, so this chapter doesn't address them.

That's it! You don't see anything different in the document, but you have found a home for your styles. When you develop the style sheet and specify cool formatting, you add it between the `<STYLE>` tags, as shown in "Understanding Style Rules," later in this chapter.

Linking style sheets

Linking style sheets can be a little more confusing than embedding them, mostly because the formatting information is in one location and the HTML code is in a completely separate document. That arrangement, however, also provides the biggest advantage of style sheets. Here's why. Suppose that you have 17 documents on your Web site. You decide that you want to add a background image to them all. If you're using embedded style sheets or traditional HTML coding, you have to open and edit every one of those 17 documents to add the appropriate code. If, however, you have linked a single style sheet to each of those 17 documents, you need to make only a single change in that style sheet, and — voilà! — the change happens in each linked document.

You can use the tags and attributes in Table 13-2 to link your style sheets.

Table 13-2	Linking Style Sheets	
HTML Tag or Attribute	*Description*	*Use in Pairs?*
`<LINK>`	Connects a document to other information	No
`REL="StyleSheet"`	Specifies that the link is to a style sheet	No
`TYPE="text/css"`	Specifies the type of style sheet	No
`HREF="..."`	Indicates the URL of the linked style sheet	No

In linking style sheets, you need to create the style sheet file (so that you have a filename to link *to*). Only then can you include a link to the style sheet file within your HTML document.

Creating the style sheet file

If you choose to link to a style sheet, you need to create a file that contains the style sheet. The file must be a plain-text file, just like regular HTML documents, and have the extension `.css` (rather than `.htm` or `.html`). The file contains the same style sheet rules that you use in an embedded style sheet. Check out "Understanding Style Rules," later in this chapter, for help with creating a style sheet file.

Putting in the link

To link a style sheet to an HTML document, you use the `<LINK>` tag, including the `REL`, `TYPE`, and `HREF` attributes, as shown in the following block of code:

```
<LINK REL="StyleSheet" TYPE="text/css"
   HREF="newstyle.css">
```

You must specify the values for the `REL` and `TYPE` attributes as shown; for the `HREF` attribute, simply fill in the name (or address) of the style sheet file to which you want to link.

You can link and embed a style sheet in the same document. For example, you might have a generic style sheet that applies to most of your HTML documents — that style sheet, you would link. Then, just below the `<LINK>` tag, you could embed another style sheet with exceptions or additions to the generic style sheet. Both style sheets affect your document, and the style definitions embedded in the document override the linked ones.

This capability of using multiple style sheets is the *cascading* part of the term Cascading Style Sheet. You could use a generic style sheet that applies to all your documents and then a second (or third or fourth) style sheet with formatting specific to the particular document.

Understanding Style Rules

Style sheets are made up of rules that tell browsers how to format HTML elements. Just as HTML tags identify parts of a document — such as a paragraph, heading, table, or list — style rules specify formatting for those elements. Style rules look a bit different from HTML. For example, rather than use angle brackets as you do with HTML code, you use curly braces ({ }). And, rather than use HTML-like abbreviations, you get to use some spelled-out words and descriptions. After you get familiar with the differences, you might even find style sheets easier to read and work with than HTML code.

Style rules have two basic parts:

✦ **Selector:** The part that identifies which element the style applies to.

✦ **Declaration:** The part that tells browsers how to display that element.

709

Take a look at the following:

```
P { color: blue }
```

In this example, the P (the selector) identifies which HTML element the style applies to, and the information within the curly braces (the *property* and the *value,* respectively) tells browsers how to display the element. In this case, the style rule specifies that all paragraphs (P) in the document should be blue.

Also, note that you can string together style rules if you want to. For example, rather than have two separate rules on two lines, like this:

```
P { color: red }
P { background-color: white }
```

you can put the rules together within the same set of braces by using a semicolon (;), like this:

```
P { color: red ; background-color: white }
```

And, just as you can add multiple declarations and values within the braces, you can specify multiple elements, like this:

```
H1, H2, H3, H4, H5, H6 { color: green }
```

Notice that when you string together elements, you separate them with commas (not semicolons, as you do between multiple declarations).

With these basic concepts of style rule construction in mind, find out in the following sections how to bring them all together.

Applying style rules

Table 13-3 summarizes the various declarations and values that you see in the next several sections.

Table 13-3	Declarations and Their Values
Property	*Selected Possible Values*
font-family	Font names from readers' systems, plus generic choices of serif, sans-serif, or monospace
font-size	xx-small, x-small, small, medium, large, x-large, xx-large, smaller, larger
font-style	normal, italic, oblique
font-variant	normal, small-caps
font-weight	normal, bold, bolder, lighter
color	#RRGGBB hexadecimal number
background-color	#RRGGBB hexadecimal number or color name
background-image	url(. . .)
background-attachment	fixed, scroll

Property	Selected Possible Values
background-repeat	repeat, repeat-x, repeat-y, no-repeat
background-position	%, %
float	left, right

As you can see from this limited sample of declarations and values, the number of style combinations is endless.

Setting a font for an entire document

With just a few commands, you can apply formatting to an entire document. To set the font for the entire body (everything within the `<BODY>` and `</BODY>` parts of the HTML document), follow these steps:

**Book VI
Chapter 13**

Developing Style Sheets

1. **In the style sheet, add the `BODY` element to specify what the style rule applies to:**

```
<STYLE>
<!--
BODY
-->
</STYLE>
```

2. **Add { and } to contain the style declaration:**

```
<STYLE>
<!--
BODY { }
-->
</STYLE>
```

3. **Add the `font-size` property, followed by a colon (:), a font size, and a semicolon (;):**

```
BODY { font-size: 32pt; }
```

4. **Add the `font-family` property, followed by a colon:**

```
BODY { font-size: 32pt;
       font-family: }
```

5. **Add your first-choice font:**

```
BODY { font-size: 32pt;
       font-family: Arial }
```

6. **Add other font choices if you want, separated by commas:**

```
BODY { font-family: Arial, Helvetica,
     Swiss }
```

7. **Add the closest generic choice from the preceding table:**

```
BODY { font-family: Arial, Helvetica,
     Swiss, sans-serif }
```

When this style sheet is applied to the document shown in Figure 13-1, the result is the niftily styled page that you see in Figure 13-2.

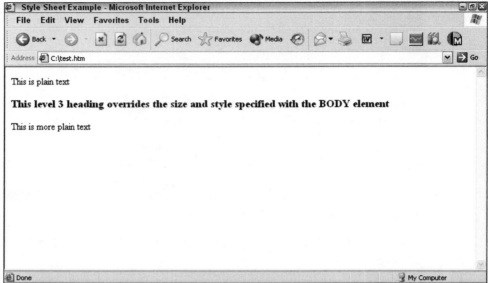

Figure 13-1:
This is how the example Web page looks before any styles are added.

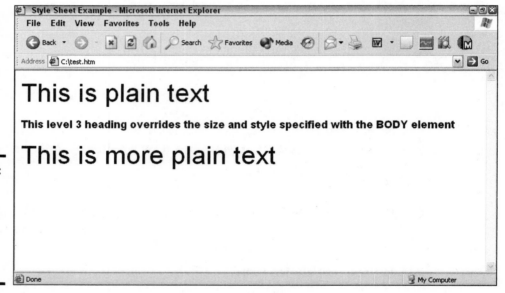

Figure 13-2:
Setting the font for an entire document using the BODY selector.

Specifying text and background colors

Another popular use of style sheets is to specify text and background colors. The following steps describe how to do both within the same rule:

1. **Add a** `color` **style declaration to color the text in the body of the document dark blue:**

```
BODY { font-family: Arial, Helvetica,
        Swiss, sans-serif ;
      color: #000066 }
```

2. Add a `background-color` **style declaration to set the entire document background to pale yellow:**

```
BODY { font-family: Arial, Helvetica,
       Swiss, sans-serif ;
       color: #000066 ;
       background-color: #ffffcc }
```

Note that you can more easily read the styles if each one is on a separate line, as shown in the preceding code. You're welcome to use spaces or tabs because you need to make the style rule easy to read by humans as well as by computers.

To add other style rules, you need only put more rules on additional lines. Follow these steps:

1. **To color first-level headings, you can add an H1 element:**

```
BODY { font-family: Arial, Helvetica,
       Swiss, sans-serif ;
       color: 000066 ;
       background-color: ffffcc }
H1 { color: #ff0000 }
```

2. If you want the background of (only) the first-level headings to be white, you can set that, too:

```
BODY { font-family: Arial, Helvetica,
       Swiss, sans-serif ;
       color: #000066 ;
       background-color: #ffffcc }
H1 { color: #ff0000 ;
     background-color: #ffffff }
```

Specifying background images

You can specify background images for the document as a whole, as you do in HTML, and for individual elements (which you cannot do in HTML). You can also control many aspects of the background image's appearance. Here's how:

1. **Add a style declaration to set a background image:**

```
BODY { font-family: Arial, Helvetica,
       Swiss, sans-serif ;
       color: #000066 ;
       background-color: #ffffcc ;
       background-image:
       url(winchesterback.jpg) }
```

2. Add another style declaration to keep the image from scrolling so that it looks like a watermark on the screen:

```
BODY { font-family: Arial, Helvetica,
       Swiss, sans-serif ;
       color: #000066 ;
       background-color: #ffffcc ;
       background-image:
```

```
                    url(winchesterback.jpg) ;
                    background-attachment: fixed }
```

3. Specify the location of the image on the background:

The following code specifies background-position values of 50% and 0% to move the image horizontally halfway across the screen and position it at the top, respectively:

```
BODY { font-family: Arial, Helvetica,
        Swiss, sans-serif ;
    color: #000066 ;
    background-color: #ffffcc ;
    background-image:
    url(winchesterback.jpg) ;
    background-attachment: fixed ;
    background-position: 50% 0% }
```

4. Set background images to repeat only horizontally, only vertically, both, or not at all.

To preserve the watermark effect, this case specifies "not at all":

```
BODY { font-family: Arial, Helvetica,
        Swiss, sans-serif ;
    color: #000066 ;
    background-color: #ffffcc ;
    background-image:
    url(winchesterback.jpg) ;
    background-attachment: fixed ;
    background-position: 50% 0% ;
    background-repeat: no-repeat}
```

The result of the code in Steps 1 through 4 is a background image that remains in a specific location on a Web page — even when users scroll that Web page. I encourage you to experiment with specifying different values for the background-attachment, background-position, and background-repeat attributes until you create the perfect background effect for your site.

Using style sheets effectively

Although no right way to develop and format style sheets exists, some techniques prove more effective than others. Here are a few tips to get you started:

✔ Take care of document-wide formatting first — that is, specify the background image, background color, and font before you start specifying the nitpicky individual formatting.

✔ Add one or two styles at a time and test them. Troubleshooting just a few new styles is easier than troubleshooting a whole blob of new ones.

✔ Stay as simple as possible and expand gradually as needed. Adding new styles one at a time is easier than backtracking and removing styles.

✔ Remember not to get caught up in the apparent WYSIWYG-ness of style sheets. You still don't have absolute control of the final appearance of the document because your readers might not have style-sheet-capable browsers, might have their browsers set not to use style sheets, or might override your formatting with their own, preferred formatting.

Chapter 14: Introducing FrontPage

In This Chapter

- Getting acquainted with FrontPage
- Understanding the FrontPage Server Extensions
- Tips for designing Web pages and Web sites
- Creating Web sites and Web pages
- Switching views
- Managing a Tasks List

This chapter takes the proverbial bull by the horns and shows you how to create a Web site and populate your Web site with Web pages. Along the way, you get a brief lesson in how to design Web pages and Web sites, discover how to switch views, and find out how to manage a Task List.

What Is FrontPage, Anyway?

FrontPage is a computer program used for creating Web sites and the Web pages of which a Web site is composed. As Figure 14-1 shows, the FrontPage screen looks a little like Microsoft Word. Many of the same buttons and commands for formatting text and pages are found on the main menu and toolbars. The commands for inserting text and graphics are the same as well.

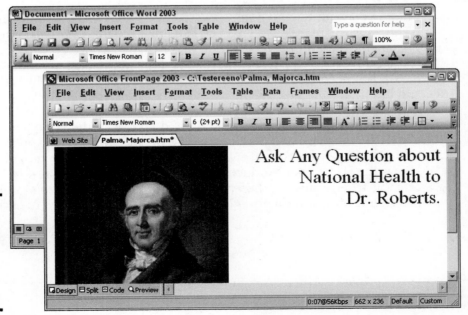

Figure 14-1:
The Word screen (top) and FrontPage screen (bottom).

FrontPage offers windows for entering text and laying out Web pages, windows for viewing HTML codes, windows for examining hyperlinks, and other windows. The program makes it possible to create full-fledged Web sites without having to be an expert in coding or programming.

What You Should Know Before You Begin

With the idea that you should look before you leap, the following pages explain a few things worth knowing before you start constructing a Web site. Read on to find out what HTML is, how easy creating a Web site can be, how to keep organized, what the FrontPage Server Extensions are, and how to choose a Web server provider.

This is easier than you think

Creating a Web site is not as hard as people make it out to be. True, if you want to make a fancy Web site with all kinds of interactive gizmos, you need to know FrontPage well (or you might prefer to use Dreamweaver to create advanced Web pages — Dreamweaver is covered in Book VI, Chapters 19 through 27). You need to know how to write scripts and code in HTML (HyperText Markup Language). But if your aim is to create a simple Web site with a handful of Web pages, a few graphics, and buttons for getting from place to place, you can do it very easily with FrontPage.

All in all, FrontPage works like a word processing program. You lay out the page, write the words, and stick the images on the page, and what you see is pretty much what others will see when they view your Web pages over the Internet. If you know your way around Microsoft Word, you will soon make yourself at home in FrontPage.

You don't have to deal with HTML

Unless you want to, you don't have to concern yourself with the dreaded HTML tags to create a Web page. HTML, or *HyperText Markup Language,* is the language that browsers read in order to display Web pages on computer screens. In FrontPage, HTML markup is done in the background. All you have to do is enter the text, graphics, and other items on your Web pages, and FrontPage creates the proper HTML tags for you.

However, FrontPage *does* permit you to do HTML coding on your own. To see HTML in action and perhaps enter a tag or two, click the Split or Code button in Page view (choose View⇨Page to switch to Page view). Figure 14-2 shows the HTML that produces the Web page shown in Figure 14-1. Not so scary, is it? Fortunately, these tags are entered for you as you format text, insert graphics, and do other layout chores. You don't have to enter HTML unless you want to.

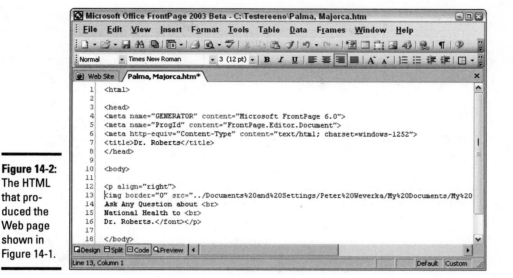

Figure 14-2: The HTML that produced the Web page shown in Figure 14-1.

Staying organized

The difference between a Web page and a Word document or a Publisher publication is that a Web page is actually composed of several different files. The Web page you see on-screen with four photographs of a camping trip is actually composed of five files: one for the page itself (the `.htm` file) and four for the photographs (most likely `.jpg` files). HTML codes tell the browser where to fit the photographs on the page when it is displayed. When you send your Web page or pages to a Web server provider so that your pages can be displayed on the Internet, you send all the files that are needed to display the Web pages.

Because a Web page is composed of different files, misplacing a file or two can render a Web page unintelligible. If you accidentally move or delete a graphic that is part of a Web page, you end up with an empty hole where that image is supposed to be. To prevent that from happening, organizing files into folders is more important than ever.

Choosing where to publish a Web site

For others to see your Web site, it must be uploaded to a *Web server,* a powerful computer that holds all the Web site's files. In Web-site lingo, *publish* means to upload your Web site to a Web server (Book VI, Chapter 17 explains how) so that others can view the pages that make up the site. Obviously, creating a bunch of nifty Web pages doesn't do much good unless you publish them. Table 14-1 summarizes the advantages and disadvantages of the different Web server providers.

Table 14-1	Different Kinds of Web Server Providers	
Provider	*Advantages*	*Disadvantages*
Free Web site (ad-supported)	Free	Limited storage space (usually 3MB to10MB); annoying ads; might not support FrontPage Server Extensions; might not be able to use your own domain name
Free Web site (ISP provided)	Free, no ads	Limited storage space; might not support FrontPage Server Extensions; might not be able to use your own domain name
Professional Web hosting	FrontPage Server Extensions; can use your own domain name; extra e-mail accounts, lots of storage space	Monthly fee

Your needs and budget will determine which is the best Web server for you. As part of the monthly subscription fee, most Internet service providers (ISPs) — the companies that connect computers to the Internet — offer their subscribers space on a Web server for hosting a Web site. If yours is one such ISP, by all means take advantage of the free server space that is provided for you. However, if your ISP doesn't give you space on a Web server, your options for publishing your Web site are

✦ Use a free Web hosting service, such as www.tripod.com or www.geo cities.com, and make visitors to your Web site suffer the annoying pop-up or banner advertisements.

✦ Pay for a professional Web server provider. Go this route if you're serious about creating a Web site or your Web site pertains to a business or other important organization.

A Word about FrontPage Server Extensions

Microsoft makes a set of programs called *FrontPage Server Extensions*. These programs run on Web servers, the computers where Web sites are hosted so that they can be viewed on the Internet. The Server Extensions are designed to make certain FrontPage features work. For example, FrontPage Server Extensions make it possible to create Web forms and hit counters.

However, FrontPage Server Extensions are not installed on every Web server. For various reasons, some technicians who run Web servers choose not to install FrontPage Server Extensions. This is an important issue for someone building a Web site with FrontPage because certain things can't be done in FrontPage unless the Server Extensions are installed on the Web server where you publish your Web site.

The first thing to do before you start creating a Web site is to find out from your Web server provider whether FrontPage Server Extensions are installed on the Web server where your Web site will go. Call your provider to find out. You don't need FrontPage Server Extensions to create and publish basic Web sites — FrontPage works just fine with Web servers that use *File Transfer Protocol,* or FTP, the basic protocol for uploading files to a Web server. But if you want to create Web forms to gather information from visitors, for example, make sure that your Web server provider has installed FrontPage Server Extensions. You also need FrontPage Server Extensions if you want to include a hit counter on a Web page or view Web site usage data from within FrontPage. Table 14-2 lists FrontPage features that require FrontPage Server Extensions as well as SharePoint Services, the software needed to collaborate with others over an intranet.

Table 14-2	FrontPage Features that Require Server Extensions or SharePoint Services
FrontPage Feature	*Required Service*
Discussion board	SharePoint Services
Document check in and check out	FrontPage 2000 Server Extensions or later; or (Web) DAV support
File uploading for visitors	FrontPage 2002 Server Extensions
Forms (user input forms, search forms, discussion forums)	FrontPage 98 Server Extensions or later
Hit counter	FrontPage 98 Server Extensions or later
List and document library views	SharePoint Services
Nested subwebs (Web sites stored within Web sites)	FrontPage 2000 Server Extensions or later
SharePoint team Web site wizard	SharePoint Services
Surveys	SharePoint Services
Top Ten List Web component	FrontPage 2002 Server Extensions
Web site usage analysis reports	FrontPage 2002 Server Extensions

Designing Web Pages and Web Sites

Before you create your Web site, take a moment to consider what it will look like. The following pages are devoted to that very topic. They explain how to make professional-looking Web pages that others will admire. By heeding this advice, you can create Web pages that are useful, pleasant to look at, and easy to read.

Consider the audience

The cardinal rule for developing Web sites is to always remember who your audience is. Obviously, a Web site whose purpose is to publicize an amusement park needs to be livelier than a Web site whose purpose is to compare car insurance rates. Likewise, a Web site that posts pictures of a newborn baby should be brighter and more colorful than one that promotes a small business.

A corollary to the "Who's my audience?" question, and one that's good to ask yourself as well, is "Why exactly am I developing this Web site?" You're doing the hard work of creating a Web site for a good reason. Ask yourself what that reason is so that you can think of how to present the topic in a way that will encourage others to become as passionate about it as you are.

Remember to be consistent

If you opened a magazine at a newsstand and discovered that the text on each page had a different font, each page was laid out differently, and each page was a different size, you probably would get a headache from reading it and you wouldn't buy it. The same goes for Web sites. A Web site that is wildly inconsistent from page to page gives a bad impression. Visitors will conclude that little thought was put into the design of the site or the organization and validity of the content, and they won't stick around.

To be consistent, lay out all your Web pages in a similar manner. Make sure that headings are the same size. Use similar dividers on each page. Pages don't have to have the exact same background, but backgrounds should be similar. For example, you can use the same pattern but a different hue. Or you can use different shades of the same color. The point is to give visitors the impression that a lot of thought was put into your Web site and that you care very much about its presentation.

The home page as an introduction

The *home page* is the first page, or introductory page, of a Web site. Usually a home page offers hyperlinks that you can click to go to other pages on the Web site. Because most visitors go to the home page first, be sure that the home page makes a fine introduction to your Web site. The home page should include lots of hyperlinks to the other pages on the site. It should be enticing. It should be alluring. It should make people want to stay and explore your Web site in its entirety.

However, to make the home page serve as an introduction, you have to do a little planning. You might sketch a diagram showing how the introductory stuff you plan to place on the home page will link to the other pages on the Web site.

Divide your Web site into distinct topics, one to a page

An unwritten rule of Web site developers is to never create such a long Web page that visitors have to scroll far to reach the bottom. Topics on Web pages should be presented in small, bite-sized chunks. Rather than dwell upon a topic at length, divide the topic across several pages.

What's more, a Web site isn't like a book or article. No one reads Web sites from start to finish. A Web site is like a garden of forking paths in that visitors can click hyperlinks and take different routes through a Web site. (Visitors don't hesitate to try different routes because they know they can always click the Back button or a navigation button to return to where they came from.)

When you build your Web pages, be sure to include hyperlinks and buttons like the ones shown in Figure 14-3. Hyperlinks and buttons give visitors the chance to go to different pages of the Web site or other Web sites altogether. Instead of presenting long pages that visitors have to scroll to read, let visitors choose what to read next. Navigation buttons and hyperlinks are explained in Book VI, Chapter 15.

Figure 14-3:
Navigation buttons and hyperlinks let visitors choose where to go next.

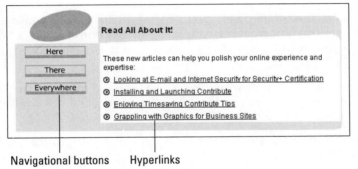

Navigational buttons Hyperlinks

Write the text and assemble the graphics beforehand

Before you start constructing your Web site, write the text. Rewriting and editing text after it has been placed on a Web page isn't easy. Open your word processor, start typing, say exactly what you want to say on your Web pages, correct all misspellings and grammatical errors, and save the file. Later, you can copy and paste the text from the word-processed file to the Web page.

If you intend to use graphics or pictures on your Web site, set them aside in a folder where you can find them easily. You might also find it helpful to use a naming scheme so that you can tell by the filename what Web page an image goes with — for example, the pictures that go on the home page could be named `homepic1.jpg`, `homepic2.jpg`, and so on. While you're at it, take a good look at your images. Which graphics you use will influence the design decisions you make as you construct your Web page. Make sure that you intimately know the graphics you intend to use so that you can use them wisely and well. Book VI, Chapter 16 explores the issue of choosing art for a Web site.

Keep it clean

Maybe it's just me, but I prefer clean, easy-to-read Web pages to pages that are crowded with gizmos and fancy graphics. In the early days of the World Wide Web, Web site designers tended to load their Web sites with fancy stuff, but today's designers take their cue from the people who design magazines and newspapers. They keep it simple. The idea is to communicate, not to show off or demonstrate your technical skill. Make it easy for visitors to stick around and find out what you have to say. You can do that by making liberal use of empty space, balancing the elements on Web pages, and not overloading Web pages with too much stuff.

Creating and Opening a Web Site

Creating a Web site entails creating a *Web,* the FrontPage word for a Web site. To begin with, a Web is actually a shell for holding Web pages. When you create a new Web, FrontPage creates a Web-page file called index.htm and two subfolders for you — _private and images.

✦ **index.htm:** The home page, the one that most visitors come to first. Do not change the name of this Web page file. By convention, a Web site's home page is always called index.htm. You will create your home page in the index.htm file.

✦ **_private:** A folder for storing files that you need for your Web site but you don't want visitors to see. Visitors cannot view the contents of this folder.

✦ **images:** A folder for storing the pictures and photographs you will place on your Web pages.

You can change the name of the subfolders and create subfolders of your own for storing text files or graphics (which I explain shortly). But allow me to repeat myself: Do not change the name or location of the index.htm file, and use this file as your home page. If somewhere down the road you want to make a different Web page the home page for your Web site, right-click it in Folders view and choose Set As Home Page. FrontPage renames the file index.htm and gives your old home page file the name index-old.htm.

Creating a so-called Web

Before you create a Web (site), create a new folder on your computer for storing it. Then follow these steps to create a Web in the folder you created:

1. **Open the Web Site Templates dialog box, shown in Figure 14-4.**

How you do that is up to you. Try one of these techniques:

- Click the down arrow beside the Create a Normal Page button and select Web Site from the drop-down list.

- Choose File⇨New and, on the New task pane, click the One Page Web Site hyperlink.

2. **In the Web Site Templates dialog box, click the Browse button and, in the New Web Site Location dialog box, find and select the folder you created; then click the Open button.**

In the Web Site Templates dialog box, the folder you selected appears in the Specify the Location of the New Web Site text box.

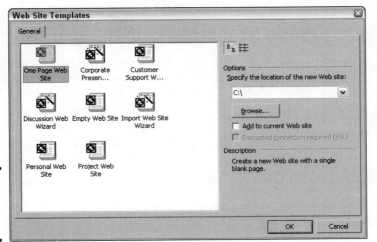

Figure 14-4:
Creating a
new Web
site.

3. **Make sure that One Page Web Site is selected in the Web Site Templates dialog box, and then click OK.**

You see the new Web site in Folders view (views are explained later in this chapter). Notice the `index.htm` file and the two subfolders.

Click the Save button, press Ctrl+S, or choose File➪Save to save a Web site and all its pages. To close a Web site, choose File➪Close Site or click the Close button in the upper-right corner of the window.

Folders that store Web sites are marked with the Web Site icon, the standard manila folder with a blue globe on it. If you open Windows Explorer or My Computer and look at the folder you created for your new Web site, you will see the blue globe.

Opening a Web site so that you can work on it

Here are the ways to open a Web site:

✦ Choose File➪Recent Sites and select the Web site's name on the submenu.

✦ Click the down arrow beside the Open button and select Open Site from the drop-down list. You see the Open Site dialog box. Find and select the folder that holds the site you want to open (it is marked with a Web Site icon) and click the Open button.

The last Web site you worked on appears on-screen when you start FrontPage, but if you prefer to see a blank Web page instead, choose Tools➪Options and, on the General tab of the Options dialog box, deselect the Open Last Web Site Automatically When FrontPage Starts check box.

Creating Webs from a template or wizard

You might have noticed several templates and wizards in the Web Site Templates dialog box (refer to Figure 14-4). Yes, you can create a Web site from a template or wizard, but I don't recommend it. You end up with a full-fledged Web site that needs all kinds of tweaking. Boilerplate text needs replacing. Headings have to be rewritten. Worst of all, you end up tailoring your text and graphics to work with a design, when ideally it should work the other way — the ideas you want to communicate should determine what kind of design you create.

Still, if templates and wizards are your cup of tea, simply double-click the template or wizard that interests you in the Web Site Templates dialog box and take it from there.

Handling the subfolders in a Web

Although FrontPage creates the images and _private subfolders for you, most people require more subfolders than that. Here are instructions for creating, deleting, and changing the names of subfolders:

✦ **Creating a new subfolder:** Choose View➪Folders to switch to Folders view and display the folders in the Web site. Then click the New Folder button or right-click and choose New➪Folder, and enter a folder name beside the folder icon that appears.

✦ **Deleting a subfolder:** In Folders view, right-click the folder and choose Delete. Then click the Yes button in the confirmation dialog box. Items stored in the folder are deleted as well.

✦ **Moving from subfolder to subfolder:** Double-click a folder to display its contents. To close a folder and move up the folder hierarchy, click the Up One Level button. You will find this button on the right side of the Folders window.

✦ **Changing the name of a subfolder:** In Folders view, right-click the folder, choose Rename, and enter a new name.

Importing files and folders to a Web

To import files and folders into the Web site you're working on, start in Folders view by selecting the folder where you want to store the files or folders and then choose File➪Import. You see the Import dialog box. Take it from there, compadre:

✦ **Importing a file:** Click the Add File button and, in the Add File to Import List dialog box, select the file you want to import and click the Open button. You can Ctrl+click to select more than one file.

✦ **Importing a folder and its contents:** Click the Add Folder button and, in the File Open dialog box, locate and select the folder and click the Open button. The files in the folder appear in the Import dialog box.

In the Import dialog box, you can remove files from the batch that you're going to import by selecting them and clicking the Remove button. Click the OK button to import the files or folders.

Deleting and renaming Web sites

Before you delete a Web site, make sure that you can really do without it. A deleted Web site is gone for good and can't be recovered. Here are instructions for deleting and renaming Web sites:

✦ **Deleting:** Choose View⇨Folders or click the Toggle Pane button to display the folders in your Web site. Then right-click the topmost folder and choose Delete. You see the Confirm Delete dialog box. Choosing the second option button, Delete This Web Site Entirely, is tantamount to deleting a folder and all its contents in Windows Explorer. Choosing the first option button, Remove Front Page Information from This Web Site Only, retains all files but removes hyperlinks and all else that pertains to Web sites and Web pages.

✦ **Renaming:** Choose Tools⇨Site Settings and, on the General tab of the Site Settings dialog box, enter a new name in the Web Name text box and click OK.

All about Web Pages

Now you're getting somewhere. After you create a Web site — or *Web*, as the tight-lipped engineers at Microsoft call it — you can create the Web pages. Herewith are instructions for (take a deep breath) creating, naming, titling, saving, opening, closing, deleting, moving, and renaming Web pages.

Creating and naming Web pages

A *Web page* is simply a hypertext markup (.htm or .html) file that can be viewed through a Web browser. A Web site can include one page or many pages. Creating a Web page is a two-step business: First you create the page and then you save, name, and title it. Better read on.

To create one Web page from another — in other words, to create a new Web page from a prototype — choose View⇨Folders to switch to Folders view, right-click the page you want to copy, and choose New From Existing Web Page.

Creating a Web page

In Folders view (choose View⇨Folders to get there), select the folder or subfolder where you want to keep the new Web page and then use one of these techniques to create it:

✦ **A blank Web page:** Click the New Page button. Figure 14-5 shows where the New Page button is located.

✦ **A predesigned Web page from a template:** Click the down arrow beside the Create a Normal Page button and select Page from the drop-down list, or choose File⇨New and click the More Page Templates hyperlink in the New task pane. You see the Page Templates dialog box, also shown in Figure 14-5. Select a template and click OK.

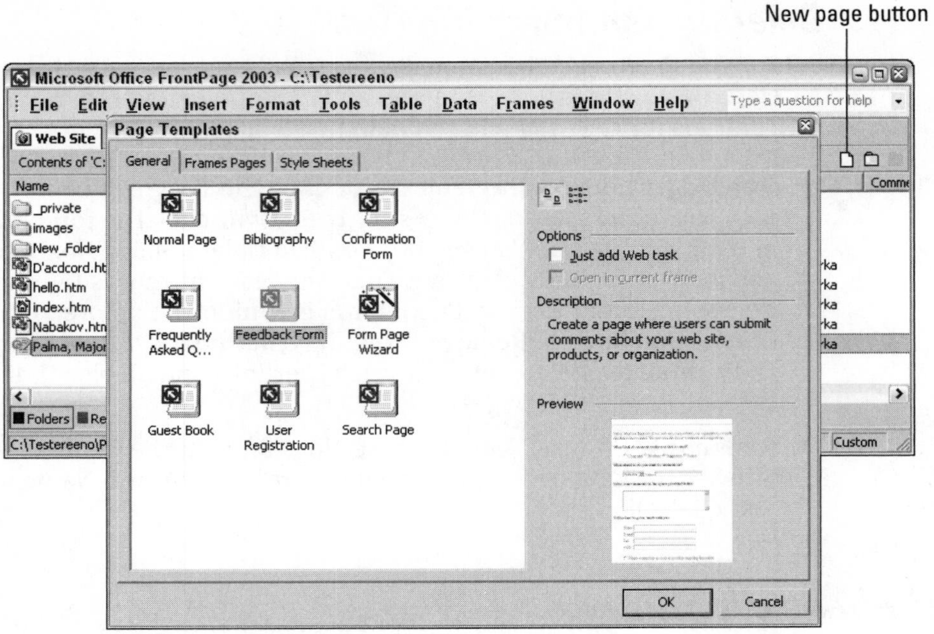

New page button

Figure 14-5:
Creating a
Web page.

Saving, naming, and titling a Web page

The next step is to save, name, and title your new Web page:

1. **Click the Save button or right-click the tab of the Web page you just created and choose Save.**

   You see the Save As dialog box.

2. **In the File Name text box, enter a descriptive name for the Web page file you created.**

   Names can't include these characters: / \ * : ? # > < |.

3. **Click the Change Title button, enter a name in the Set Page Title dialog box, and click OK.**

   A visitor who comes to your Web page will see the title you entered on the title bar at the top of his or her browser.

4. **Click the Save button.**

   Instead of `new_page_1.htm` or some such, the page tab now bears the filename you entered.

To rename a Web page file, right-click its name in Folders view, choose Rename, and enter a new name.

Handling and managing Web pages

Following are instructions for doing this, that, and the other thing with Web pages. To handle and manage Web pages, start by choosing View➪Folders to switch to Folders view:

✦ **Opening a Web page:** Double-click the page's name or right-click it and choose Open. You can also choose File➪Recent Files and then click the name of a Web page on the submenu. The submenu lists the last eight files you worked on.

✦ **Closing a Web page:** Right-click the page tab and choose Close or choose File➪Close while the page is displayed.

✦ **Deleting a Web page:** Select the page in Folders view and press the Delete key, choose Edit➪Delete, or right-click and choose Delete.

✦ **Moving a Web page to another folder:** Drag the file to another folder.

✦ **Renaming a Web page:** Right-click the file and choose Rename. Then enter a new name.

To open a Web page in its own window far from the distractions of the other pages in the Web site, right-click it and choose Open in New Window.

Exploring the Different Views

The seven views and when to employ them are explained throughout Chapters 14-18 of Book VI. Rather than me boring you with a detailed description of each view, Table 14-3 shows you the seven views in a nutshell.

Table 14-3	**The Severn Views of FrontPage**
View	*What It Does*
Page	For laying out Web pages, entering text, and entering graphics. You can also enter HTML tags in this view and see what a Web page looks like in a browser window.
Folders	For handling and managing folders and Web page files.
Remote Web Site	For managing Web sites that aren't kept on your computer.
Reports	For generating different reports about the health and well-being of your Web site. Book VI, Chapter 17 explains the different reports.
Navigation	For seeing how Web pages fit together in the hierarchy of folders and files. You can drag pages to new folders in this view.
Hyperlinks	For seeing how hyperlinks connect the Web pages in your site to one another, as shown in Figure 14-6.
Tasks	For viewing the list of tasks that need completing. The next section in this chapter explains tasks.

To change views, choose an option from the View menu. In all views except Page view, you can also change views by clicking a View button — Folders, Remote Web Site, Reports, Navigation, Hyperlinks, or Tasks — along the bottom of the window, as shown in Figure 14-6.

Choose a view option.

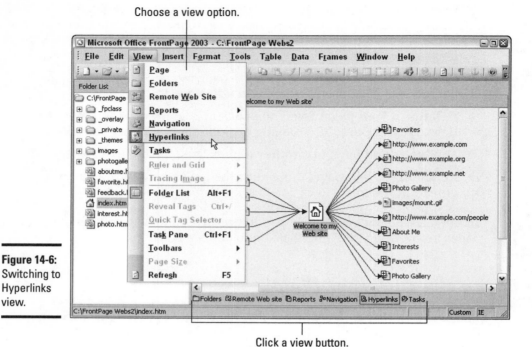

Figure 14-6:
Switching to Hyperlinks view.

Click a view button.

In Page view, click one of these buttons along the bottom of the window to undertake your work in different ways:

✦ **Design:** For laying out Web pages, entering the text, and entering graphics.

✦ **Split:** For seeing layouts and HTML code. The HTML appears in the top of the window and the Web page appears in the bottom. Select an item in either half of the window, and the other half scrolls to the item you selected.

✦ **Code:** For viewing the HTML tags on which a Web page is based.

✦ **Preview:** For seeing roughly what the Web page will look like on a Web browser.

You can see the Folder List on the left side of the window at any time by pressing Alt+F1, choosing View➪Folder List, or clicking the Toggle Pane button.

Tracking and Prioritizing Tasks

Especially if more than one person is working on the creation of a Web site, the Tasks List can be a convenient way of determining what needs to be done, dividing tasks, prioritizing tasks, and tracking progress. Figure 14-7 shows the Tasks List along with the New Task dialog box, where you describe a task that needs doing. Choose View➪Tasks or click the Tasks button to see the list. If a task is associated with a Web page, you can right-click the task, choose Start Task, and go immediately to the Web page that pertains to the task.

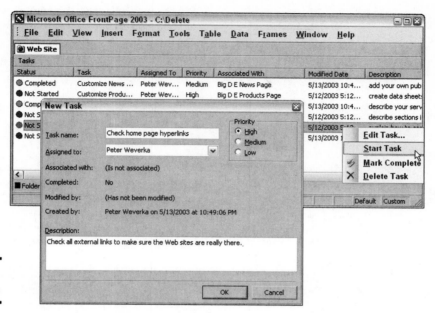

Figure 14-7:
A Tasks List.

Here is everything a mere mortal needs to know about tasks:

✦ **Assigning a new task:** Click the down arrow beside the Create a New
Normal Page button and choose Task, or choose Edit⇨Tasks⇨Add Task.
You see the New Task dialog box (refer to Figure 14-7). Name the task,
assign it to a person, describe it, prioritize it, and click OK.

✦ **Associating a task with a Web page:** To associate a task with a Web
page and be able to open the Web page from the Tasks List, select a Web
page in Folders view before assigning the task. To go to a Web page from
the Tasks List, right-click a task and choose Start Task.

✦ **Marking a task as complete:** Right-click the task in the Tasks window
and choose Mark Complete.

✦ **Deleting tasks:** Right-click the task in the Tasks window and choose
Delete Task.

CHECK IT OUT

Giving your Web page a title

Choose a descriptive title for your Web pages.
Lycos, Yahoo!, and other search engines keep
careful track of the words on Web pages, and the
word or words in the title bar are given extra
weight. If "Welcome to Madagascar" is the title
of your Web page, for example, a Web surfer who
enters the keyword *Madagascar* in order to conduct a Web search is more likely to find your
page than he or she is if you make "Welcome to
Greenland" the title. Including the word

Madagascar in the title red flags the page for
people searching about information pertaining to
Madagascar.

To change the title of a Web page, right-click it in
Folders view and choose Properties, or right-
click it in Page view and choose Page Properties.
Then, on the General tab of the Properties or
Page Properties dialog box, enter a new title in
the Title text box.

Chapter 15: Laying Out a Web Page

In This Chapter

✔ **Using tables, shared borders, layers, and dynamic Web templates to lay out pages**

✔ **Testing your Web site in different browsers**

✔ **Choosing a theme for a Web page**

✔ **Giving a background color or image to a Web page**

✔ **Inserting hyperlinks in Web pages**

✔ **Creating a mail-to hyperlink so that others can get in touch with you**

*I*n this chapter, your Web site starts to take shape. You discover how to lay out a Web page so that headings, text, graphics, and other elements appear on the page precisely where you want them. You find out how to peer into your Web site through different Web browsers. You get to play interior decorator by splashing color on a Web page or by giving it a theme. This chapter also explains how to hyperlink the pages of your Web site with one another and with pages on the Internet at large.

Techniques for Laying Out Web Pages

Laying out a Web page means to set up the page so that you can put items — headlines, text, and graphics — in the right places. The easiest way to lay out a Web page is to treat the page as though it were a page in a word-processing document and, as they say in New York City and parts of New Jersey, *fuhgeddaboudit*. Under this scheme, visitors to your Web site scroll down the page and read it in much the same way they read a page in a book.

If your Web page calls for a simple layout like that, more power to you, but if you want something more sophisticated, you have to look into layout tables, shared borders, layers, and dynamic Web templates. With these techniques, you can place items in different parts of a Web page and rest assured that they will stay there. For example, you can place navigation buttons on the side, a copyright notice along the bottom, and graphics with captions. The following pages examine and compare the different ways to lay out Web pages. I suggest reading these pages carefully to choose the layout technique that works best for you.

Using layout tables for block layouts

One way to arrange items on a Web page is to create a *layout table* like the one shown in Figure 15-1 and place text, graphics, and whatnot in the table cells. Layout tables make putting text and items in the right place easier.

People who visit your Web site need not know that you created a table for layout purposes. They can't see the table because the table borders — they appear as dotted lines in the figure and the FrontPage window — are invisible. What's more, the layout table changes shape to accommodate different browsers and screen resolutions, but as it changes shape, the items in the table cells remain in the same positions relative to one another. (By the way, don't confuse a layout table with a standard table like the kind for presenting data. You can create those as well in FrontPage with the Insert Table button and commands on the Table menu.)

Creating a layout table

Follow these steps to create a layout table for arranging items on a Web page:

1. **Choose Table⇨Layout Tables and Cells.**

   The Layout Tables and Cells task pane opens.

2. **Choose a predefined table layout from the bottom of the task pane or click the Insert Layout Table hyperlink and create your own table.**

   You can save a lot of time by choosing a predefined table layout. If that doesn't work for you, you can draw the layout table, but it requires work, as the next section in this chapter explains.

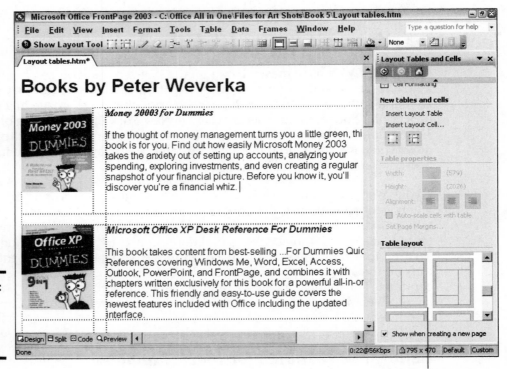

Figure 15-1: Using a table to lay out a Web page.

Choose a table layout.

After you create a table in the Layout Tables and Cells task pane, the so-called Layout Tools appear on-screen. These blue and green lines are meant to help you lay out the table, but they are very, very unwieldy. To turn them off and construct your table using commands on the Tables toolbar, click the Show Layout Tool button on the Tables toolbar.

Drawing and rearranging layout tables

Unlike the standard tables you use for presenting data, layout tables are *dynamic,* meaning that they are designed to change shape and size to accommodate different browsers and screen resolutions. Dynamic tables are great, of course, but changing the size of and inserting columns and rows in these tables is a bit difficult. Layout tables are slippery and hard to wrestle with, unless you use the following techniques for handling them:

✦ **Inserting a column or row:** Click in the column to the left of where the new column will be or the row below where the new row will be and then click the Insert Rows or Insert Columns button.

✦ **Merging and splitting rows and columns:** To join cells in the table or split a single cell into more than one cell, click the Merge Cells or Split Cells button. If you split cells, you see the Split Cells dialog box, where you enter the number of columns or rows you want to split the cell into.

✦ **Aligning text items in table cells:** To align items horizontally, click an Align or a Center button on the Formatting toolbar. To align items vertically, click the Align Top, Center Vertically, or Align Bottom button on the Table toolbar.

✦ **Changing the size of columns and rows:** Drag borders between columns and rows to change column and row size.

✦ **Making space between borders and text:** If text is too close to a border, it can crash into another item on the page and be hard to read. To put extra space between text and table borders, choose Table➪Table Properties➪Table and, in the Table Properties dialog box, enter a pixel measurement in the Cell Spacing text box to put extra space between table cells. Enter a pixel measurement in the Cell Padding text box to put space between items in the table and the interior border of cells.

Using shared borders for consistent layouts

Another way to handle a table layout is to use *shared borders.* With this technique, space on the border of some Web pages in your Web site or all the pages in your Web site hold the same elements — a navigation bar, a company name, or a company logo, for example. Shared borders save you layout work. Instead of laboriously putting the same navigation bar on several Web pages, you can create shared borders for the Web pages and place the navigation bar in the shared border. The navigation bar will appear on all the pages. Microsoft uses the word *shared* to describe this layout technique because different Web pages share the same items. Shared borders are a bit like headers and footers in word-processed documents in that the same items appear along the borders — the top, left, right, or bottom — of several pages.

Setting up shared borders

Choose Tools➪Page Options and, on the Authoring tab, select the Shared
Borders check box (unless it's already selected) to activate shared borders.
Then, if you want a handful, not all, of the pages in your Web site to have
shared borders, switch to Folders view and select the Web pages. Follow
these steps to place a shared border on more than one page in a Web site:

1. **Choose Format➪Shared Borders.**

   FrontPage displays the Shared Borders dialog box. If you're giving borders to a handful of pages, select the Selected Page(s) option button.

2. **Select a check box or check boxes that describe where you want the
   border to appear on the Web pages.**

3. **Click OK.**

   FrontPage creates a new folder called borders for holding the .htm files
   on which the elements on the shared border are kept. To remove shared
   borders from Web pages, select the pages with shared borders in
   Folders view, choose Format➪Shared Borders, and deselect check
   boxes in the Shared Borders dialog box.

Putting stuff in a shared border

After you've created a shared border, it's time to stuff it like a Thanksgiving
turkey:

✦ **Inserting a column or row:** Open any Web page for which you've created a shared border and enter the element — a navigation bar, a company name — that you want. Insert text and images as though the
  shared borders were table cells. The shared borders expand to make
  room for the content you place in them (this is the only way to resize
  shared borders).

✦ **Choosing a background color or picture:** Choose Format➪Shared
  Borders and click the Border Properties button in the Shared Borders
  dialog box. Then use the Border Properties dialog box to select a background color or picture.

Unless your Web server supports FrontPage 2002 (or newer) Server
Extensions, changes you make to the background of a shared border are
lost when you publish your Web site. To work around this problem, insert a
one-cell table with no borders (so that it's invisible) into a shared border
and then change the background properties of the table. Or use dynamic
Web templates instead of shared borders.

Using layers to place elements on-screen

With layers, you can place screen elements such as graphics, headings, and
text anywhere you choose on a Web page. Each element appears in a layer
box, and you can move the boxes at will. You can even overlap different
screen elements, as shown in Figure 15-2. Layers permit you to create very
elegant and sophisticated Web pages. However, not all browsers are capable of handling layers, and browsers that can handle layers sometimes get it

wrong and display the pages incorrectly. Layers aren't very good about handling different screen resolutions, either. Depending on screen resolution, a visitor to your Web page might have to scroll here and there to view the page or gaze at a lot of empty screen space.

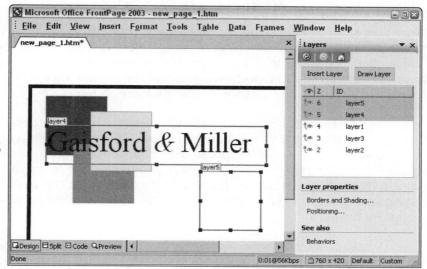

Figure 15-2: Layers are actually boxes for placing elements on Web pages.

In deciding whether to use layers or tables, consider the all-important target audience. Is the audience likely to have up-to-date browsers that are capable of handling layers? If not, use tables for laying out Web pages. On the other hand, if you want a sophisticated layout, you don't care to muck around with tables, or you don't mind designing the Web page for a single screen resolution, go with layers.

Follow these instructions to work with layers:

✦ **Creating a layer:** Choose Insert⇨Layer. A blue layer box appears. Drag a corner or side handle to adjust the size of a layer box. Start typing in the box to insert text. To insert an object such as a clipart image or picture, insert it using the standard commands.

✦ **Adjusting the position of layers:** Click the layer and move the pointer over its perimeter. When you see the four-headed arrow, click and start dragging.

✦ **Displaying the Layers task pane:** Right-click a layer's ID number — layer1, layer2, and so on — and choose Layer Properties.

✦ **Making layers overlap:** Double-click a Z number in the Layers task pane. Numbers in the Z column determine the order in which layers appear. Layers with high numbers overlap those with lower numbers. After you double-click, you can enter a number in the Z column. The higher the number, the higher it appears in the stack.

✦ **Borders and shading for layer boxes:** Click the Borders and Shading link in the Layers task pane to open the Borders and Shading dialog box and make selections there.

You can group layers together so that they can be treated as a single unit. To group two layers, go to the Layers task pane and drag a layer onto the ID of another layer. When you move or change the visibility of a "parent" layer, all "child" layers are affected as well.

Using dynamic Web templates

Most Web sites include elements that appear on all or most of the Web pages. A navigation bar with hyperlinks to different pages is an example of one such element. Obviously, creating the same element on each page is a hassle. To get around the problem, you can use frames, shared borders (explained earlier in this chapter), or Dynamic Web templates.

Dynamic Web templates have one advantage over shared borders: You can alter part of the page if you want. By designating part of a Web template as an *editable region,* you make it possible to change elements in the region without disturbing the layout of the page you're working on or any other page in the Web site. However, if you want to change the layout of all the pages, you can do so very quickly by changing the template on which the pages are based.

Creating a dynamic Web template

Follow these steps to create a dynamic Web template:

1. **On a new or existing Web page, insert the content that you want to appear on all the pages or several pages in your Web site.**

   For example, insert a navigation bar, company logo, or copyright information.

2. **Create table cells or layers for the editable region.**

   In other words, create space for material that will differ from page to page. Most of the time, this will be a single, empty table cell or layer.

3. **Choose Format⇨Dynamic Web Template⇨Manage Editable Regions and click Yes to save the page as a dynamic Web template.**

   You see the Save As dialog box.

4. **Enter a descriptive name for the template in the File Name text box and click the Save button.**

   You see the Editable Regions dialog box, shown in Figure 15-3. Commit to memory the name you choose: You will select it when you attach the template to a Web page.

5. **Enter a name for the region, click the Add button, and click Close.**

   Putting placeholder text or images inside the editable regions is a good way to show others who work on your Web site what kind of content or layout you want in the editable regions.

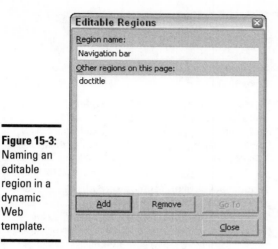

Figure 15-3:
Naming an editable region in a dynamic Web template.

Attaching a dynamic Web template to a Web page

After you've created a dynamic Web template, you can attach it to a new or existing page. The content on the template will appear on the page and move aside content in the editable region. Follow these steps to attach a dynamic Web template to a new or existing page:

1. **On a new page or an existing one, choose Format⇨Dynamic Web Template⇨Attach Dynamic Web Template.**

   You see the Attach Dynamic Web Template dialog box.

   To attach a dynamic Web template to more than one file, select the files in the Folders view before undertaking Step 1.

2. **Select the template you want to attach and click the Open button.**

3. **If you're attaching the template to an existing page, specify where to place existing content.**

   FrontPage is pretty good about placing existing content in the correct editable region, so you can probably just click OK in the Choose Editable Regions for Content dialog box. Alternatively, select a region from the old page, click the Modify button, select in which region (from the template) existing content should be placed, and then click OK.

4. **Add content to the editable regions.**

   Insert text, images, tables, and layers into the editable regions. As you do so, they expand to make room for the content you place in them (this is the only way to resize editable regions without modifying the attached dynamic Web template).

To detach a dynamic Web template from a Web page, choose Format⇨ Dynamic Web Template⇨Detach from dynamic Web template. Although FrontPage detaches the dynamic Web template, it leaves all content from the template on the Web page. You can delete this content or leave it.

A few words about frames

In effect, a *frame* is a mini-Web page that, together with other frames, forms a complete Web page. Frames permit you to display several Web pages in the same browser window. In most cases, one frame, a navigation bar, appears along the side of the window, and the rest of the Web site appears in another, larger frame. Frames were extremely popular several years back. You could hardly visit a Web site without encountering a frame or two.

However, frames make Web sites too complex — for the visitor and the designer. The designer must worry about what page goes in what frame. As for visitors, they never know quite which Web page they are looking at, which makes bookmarking Web pages difficult. Frames take longer to download.

They can look vastly different from one Web browser to the next.

For these reasons, I don't cover creating frames in FrontPage because I consider frames an out-of-date technology. If you want to experiment with frames, however, choose File⇨New, click the More Page Templates link in the New Task pane, select the Frames Pages tab, and then choose a frame design that you like. FrontPage creates the necessary frame structure. Your job is to create frames or specify which page should be loaded in each frame. After you've created your frames, test the pages carefully to make sure that hyperlinks open in the correct frame (that's the tricky part).

Making Sure Your Web Site Is Compatible with Different Web Browsers

To read your Web site, visitors must see it properly in their Web browsers. A *Web browser* is a software program for viewing Web pages and surfing the Internet. Being a Microsoft product, FrontPage creates Web pages that are optimized for viewing in Internet Explorer 6.0, the browser that comes with Windows. However, Internet Explorer is not the only browser out there. Although roughly 90 percent of computer users travel the Internet with Internet Explorer, the rest use Netscape Navigator, AOL, Mozilla, Opera, and Safari (an Apple creation). Most Web pages look fine in browsers apart from Internet Explorer, but complex pages that include tables, layers, or themes require a little tweaking in order to display properly.

The following subsections explain the three things that you can do to make sure that your Web pages appear properly in different browsers:

✦ Configure FrontPage to optimize its pages for different browsers.

✦ Use FrontPage's new Browser Compatibility tool to check pages for potential problems.

✦ Manually test your pages in a variety of browsers.

Because 90 percent of your Web site's visitors are likely to use Internet Explorer, as long as your Web site isn't too complicated, you can simply create your site for Internet Explorer and leave it at that. You will serve 90 percent of the people 100 percent of the time. Not bad, if I say so myself.

Optimizing pages for a particular browser

FrontPage gives you the opportunity to tailor Web pages for one or two Web browsers. Follow these steps to select the Web browsers that your target audience is most likely to use:

1. **Choose Tools➪Page Options.**

You see the Page Options dialog box.

2. **Select the Authoring tab.**

3. **From the Browsers drop-down list, select the Web browser with which you want to make your Web pages compatible.**

4. **From the Browser Versions drop-down list, select the browser version that you want to target.**

Depending on which browser you chose, FrontPage might disable certain Web technologies so that you don't include an element that the browser you chose can't handle. You can tell which elements are disabled by looking at the check boxes directly below the Browsers and Browser Versions drop-down lists.

Changing FrontPage's compatibility settings disables FrontPage features that are incompatible with the Web browsers you specify, and it changes the way that FrontPage creates the HTML code for layers and tables. However, it doesn't remove existing elements, even if they are incompatible with the browser.

You can use the Check Browser Behavior option to redirect visitors using an incompatible browser to a special version of your page designed to work with that browser. This page could simply tell users that they need a newer version of Internet Explorer, Netscape Navigator, or a compatible browser in order to properly view the Web site. Browser behaviors are discussed in Book VI, Chapter 18.

Checking for browser compatibility problems

Follow these steps to use the Browser Compatibility tool to check Web pages for Web browser compatibility problems:

1. **If you want to run the test on a handful of pages rather than all the pages in your Web site, open the pages or switch to Folders view and select the pages.**

Or, to run the test on a single page, simply open it.

2. **Choose Tools➪Browser Compatibility.**

You see the Browser Compatibility dialog box.

3. **Choose which pages to run the test on.**

Choose All Pages, Open Page(s), Selected Pages, or Current Page.

4. **Click the Check button.**

FrontPage checks the pages and displays a list of pages with compatibility errors, if any can be found. A summary of the error and the line on which it is found (in the HTML code) appear in the Browser Compatibility dialog box.

To create a Web page with a compatibility report, click the Generate HTML Report button.

You can create Web pages that are compatible with Internet Explorer and Netscape Navigator versions 4.0 and later without sacrificing nifty features such as themes and layers. If permitting all visitors to view your Web site is critical, use the 3.0 browsers and later settings, and then place a link on your home page to a text-only version of your Web site as well.

Manually testing pages in different browsers

Despite FrontPage's nifty tools for optimizing and testing pages for compatibility problems, the only reliable way to make sure pages look right in different browsers is to actually open the pages in different browsers. Here's what's what:

✦ **Download and install the browsers you want to test:** At minimum, test your Web pages in Microsoft Internet Explorer versions 5 or 6, and Netscape Navigator 7.1 (or Mozilla 1.*x*). Table 15-1 describes which versions to test and where to download Web browsers. Yes, you can download these browsers at no cost! To run Safari, however, you need a Macintosh computer.

Table 15-1	Different Web Browsers	
Web Browser	*Versions to Test*	*Download Site*
Microsoft Internet Explorer	6.*x* or 5.*x*	www.microsoft.com
Netscape Navigator	7.*x*, 4.7*x*, or 4.8	www.netscape.com
Mozilla	Newest released version	www.mozilla.com
Opera	7.*x*	www.opera.com
Apple Safari	1.*x*	www.apple.com/macosx

✦ **Preview your pages in each browser at different screen resolutions:** Open the pages in FrontPage, click the down arrow next to the Preview in Microsoft Internet Explorer button, and choose the browser and screen resolution.

✦ **Test your pages after you've published your site:** Sometimes pages look different when they're published on the Internet, especially if you're using features that require FrontPage Server Extensions. Book VI, Chapter 17 explains how to publish a Web site.

✦ **Test your pages on alternate platforms:** For bonus points, open your site on computers running Mac OS X and Linux, and watch out for fonts and colors that don't look right. If you don't have access to these types of computers, ask around for someone who has one. Also consider testing your site on TV-based browsing devices (such as WebTV) and hand-held computers.

When testing a Web page, look for tables and layers that aren't placed correctly, as well as interactive objects such as hover buttons, link bars, and forms that don't work right. While you're at it, make sure that visitors aren't required to scroll horizontally very far at the 640 x 480 or 800 x 600 screen resolutions. (Many developers believe that scrolling at 640 x 480 is acceptable.) Tables and layers shouldn't look strange at 1024 x 768, either.

The Check It Out section at the end of this chapter, "Viewing a Web Page at Different Resolutions," explains how you can quickly see Web pages at different resolutions in Page view.

You don't have to test your whole Web site every time you create a new page, but quickly testing pages in Netscape Navigator and Internet Explorer is recommended. Just to be on the safe side, test the entire Web site every once in a while and when a new browser or browser version is released.

Applying Themes and Background Colors to Web Pages

**Book VI
Chapter 15**

Laying Out a Web Page

FrontPage offers two ways to change the look of a Web page. You can choose a color or picture or you can visit the Theme task pane and select a full-blown design for the various elements — the headings, bulleted items, and hyperlinks, for example. Read on to see how to turn a simple Web page into a high-fashion boutique.

To apply a theme or background color to a handful of Web pages, select them first in Folders view.

Applying a color or shade to page backgrounds

Color backgrounds are a great way to "code" the various pages in a Web site. Visitors know they have come to a new page and are embarking on a new topic when they see a different background color. Just make sure the colors are similar to one another so that the contrast between one page and the next isn't too harsh.

To spruce up a Web page by giving it a color background or a picture background, start by choosing Format⇨Background. You see the Formatting tab of the Page Properties dialog box, as shown in Figure 15-4. Here are some ways to change the look of a Web page or Web pages:

✦ **Color background:** Select a color from the Background drop-down palette. If none of the colors tickles your fancy, select More Colors at the bottom of the menu and choose a color in the More Colors dialog box.

✦ **Picture background or logo:** Make sure that the Background Picture check box is selected and click the Browse button. In the Select Background Picture dialog box, select the picture you want for a background. You can use BMP, GIF, JPEG, or any other Windows-compatible graphic file as a background. GIF files are best for page backgrounds because they are smaller than graphics in other formats. Viewers don't have to wait long for the GIFs to appear. A background picture is *tiled* — that is, repeated across and down the page to fill the entire background. To make the picture appear faintly in the background, select the Make It a Watermark check box.

If you regret choosing a background for your Web page and you want to start all over, choose Format⇨Background and choose Automatic on the Background drop-down list.

Web-safe colors

When choosing colors for a Web page or theme, be careful which colors you choose. Not all colors appear the same on every platform (PCs, Macs, and Linux). Fortunately, FrontPage makes use of so-called *Web-safe colors* for all its themes. Web-safe colors are supposed to look the same on all platforms. To make it easy on you, FrontPage uses the Web-safe colors on main color wheels from which you choose colors.

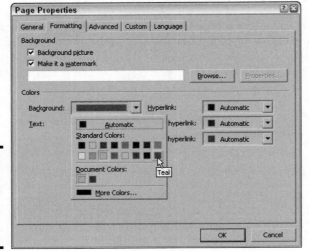

Figure 15-4: Choosing a background image or color for a Web page.

To borrow a background from a Web page you like, right-click it and choose Save Background As on the shortcut menu. If the background is copyrighted, however, you are obliged to obtain permission before you use the background image for your own purposes. (P.S.: You won't know whether it's copyrighted unless you ask.)

Applying a theme to different pages

A background theme is a "ready-to-wear" design. When you choose a background theme, all elements of the Web page are overhauled — the headings, bulleted items, and the background as well. If you created your Web site with the help of a template or the Web Page Wizard, you already know about themes, because templates come with a theme.

Follow these steps to choose a theme for your Web page:

1. **Choose Format➪Theme.**

The Theme task pane appears, as shown in Figure 15-5. Scroll through the themes and look for ones that catch your eye.

2. **Until you find one you like, click a few theme names to see what they do to your Web pages.**

When you select a theme, the Web page adopts it.

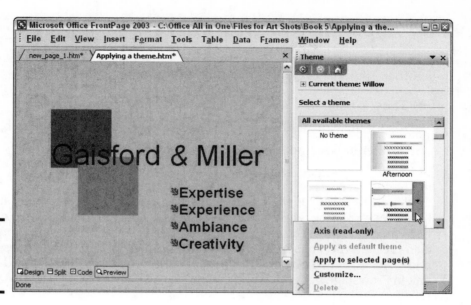

Figure 15-5: Choosing a theme for a Web page.

When you have found your theme, you can tweak it to your liking by selecting or deselecting the three check boxes at the bottom of the Theme task pane:

✦ **Vivid Colors:** Offers muted or vibrant variations of graphic elements in the theme.

✦ **Active Graphics:** Turns off and on the GIF animations or animated cartoons in the theme, if the theme includes animations.

✦ **Background Image:** Removes or restores the page background.

Theme files remain as part of your Web site when you abandon one theme for another. To remove these files and save hard drive or Web server space, choose View⇨Reports⇨Site Summary. Then, in the Site Summary window, click the Unused Themes link.

Style sheets for customizing themes

When you apply a theme to a Web site or page, FrontPage creates a separate file called a *style sheet* for storing the theme information. The style sheet file, which uses the industry standard Cascading Style Sheet (CSS) specification, is linked to all pages to which you apply the theme. Unless you want to create your own style sheets, though, you don't need to know this.

To create a style sheet, choose File⇨New, click More Page Templates in the New task pane, select the Style Sheets tab in the Page Templates dialog box, and then choose the style sheet template you want to use.

Including Hyperlinks in Web Pages

A *hyperlink* is an electronic shortcut from one place on the Internet to another. Hyperlinks can go from one Web page to

✦ The top of another Web page in the same Web site

✦ A spot apart from the top of another Web page in the same Web site

✦ A different spot on the same Web page

✦ A Web page in another Web site altogether

Clicking a hyperlink is the fastest way to go elsewhere. By convention, text hyperlinks are blue when first seen and purple after they have been clicked, but you can change the convention for your Web site if you want. You can also create hyperlinks from buttons, graphics, clipart images, shapes, layers, and other so-called objects. You can tell when you have encountered a hyperlink in FrontPage because when you move the pointer over it, a pop-up box tells where the link goes.

The next pages of this chapter explain how to create a hyperlink to the top of a different Web page, to the middle of a different Web page on your site, or to a Web page on the Internet. Finally, this section explains how to edit hyperlinks.

The rules of hyperlinking

Observe these rules about hyperlinking before you attempt to create a hyperlink:

✦ For a hyperlink to go to a page on another Web site, you must know the URL of the Web page. Each page on the Internet has an address, also known as a *URL,* or *Uniform Resource Locator.* You can tell the address of a Web page by looking in the Address bar in the Web browser. (Right-click the main menu in Internet Explorer and choose Address Bar if you don't see the Address bar.) For example, the URL of the Dummies Press is `http://www.dummies.com/WileyCDA`.

✦ For a hyperlink to go from one place to another on the same Web page or to a location apart from the top of another Web page in your site, the target of the link must be marked with a bookmark. Later in this chapter, the "Entering a bookmark on a Web page" section explains how to put a bookmark on a Web page.

Inserting a hyperlink

To insert a hyperlink, start by selecting the word, phrase, button, graphic, or other object that will form the hyperlink. Visitors to your Web site will activate the hyperlink when they click the thing you select. Then click the Insert Hyperlink button, press Ctrl+K, or choose Insert➪Hyperlink. You see the Insert Hyperlink dialog box, shown in Figure 15-6.

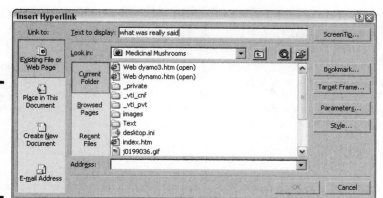

Figure 15-6:
The Insert
Hyperlink
dialog box,
where
hyperlinks
are born.

Enter the target of your hyperlink — the place where you want visitors to go when they click the link:

✦ **The top of a different page on your Web site:** Select the name of the Web page file. To find the file, click the Current Folder button, if necessary, and click folders to open them. If worse comes to worst and you can't find the file anywhere, click the Browse for File button to locate the Web page file in the Link to File dialog box.

✦ **A different place on the same page where the link is:** Click the Bookmark button. You see the Select Place in Document dialog box. Select the bookmark target of your hyperlink and click OK.

✦ **A place on another Web page apart from the top:** Select the name of the Web page file and then click the Bookmark button. Bookmark targets in the Web page you selected appear in the Select Place in Document dialog box. Select a bookmark and click OK.

✦ **A Web page in a different Web site:** Enter the address of the Web page in the Address text box. To enter it, use one of these techniques:

- Type the complete URL in the box. (Make sure that you include the http:// part.)

- Click the Browse the Web button and, in your Web browser, go to the Web page you want to link to. Its URL will appear in the Address box.

- Open the Address drop-down list and choose it from the list of URLs you entered recently in your browser's Address bar.

- Click the Browsed Pages button and select from the list of pages you visited in the last 90 days.

The next step is to click the ScreenTip button and enter a phrase or a short sentence in the Set Hyperlink ScreenTip dialog box that describes the who, the what, or the where of your hyperlink. When a visitor moves the pointer over the hyperlink you're creating, he or she will see the text you enter. This brief description will help the viewer decide whether the link is worth clicking. Without the ScreenTip, visitors see a cryptic pathname instead of a tidy description.

Changing the look of hyperlinks on a Web page

By convention, text hyperlinks are blue, links that have been visited are purple, and links that have been selected are red. Some people do not hold with convention and want to change this color scheme. Sometimes changing it is necessary to accommodate page backgrounds. On a blue page, for example, blue text hyperlinks don't show up well.

To change the hyperlink color scheme on a Web page, choose File⇨Properties in Design view and select the Formatting tab in the Page Properties dialog box. Then choose new colors on the Hyperlink drop-down palettes.

Test your hyperlink by clicking the Preview button, moving the mouse pointer over the link, and clicking. If all goes well, the page you linked to appears in FrontPage. You can also Ctrl+click a link in the Design window to test a hyperlink, but you can't read ScreenTips, the short descriptions of where a link takes you, in the Design window.

Editing and removing hyperlinks

For you and you only, here are techniques for editing and removing hyperlinks:

✦ **Editing a hyperlink:** Right-click the link in Design view and choose Hyperlink Properties. You see the Edit Hyperlink dialog box, which looks and works exactly the same as the Insert Hyperlink dialog box (refer to Figure 15-6). Change the link destination, change the ScreenTip, or do what you will and click OK.

✦ **Removing a hyperlink:** Right-click the link in Design view and choose Hyperlink Properties. In the Edit Hyperlink dialog box, click the Remove Link button. Removing a hyperlink does not delete the words or graphic that formed the link. Removing a link merely takes away the words' or graphic's hyperlink status.

Entering a bookmark on a Web page

To hyperlink to any part of a page except the top, it is necessary to place a bookmark on the page as a target for the hyperlink. When a visitor clicks the link, the Web page opens and scrolls to the bookmark's position. In long Web pages, targeting a hyperlink to a bookmark is essential. Without the bookmark, visitors have to search long and hard for the item they're looking for. Follow these steps to enter a bookmark:

1. **Click on the Web page where you want the bookmark target to be.**

2. **Choose Insert⇨Bookmark or press Ctrl+G.**

   The Insert Bookmark dialog box appears.

3. **Enter a name for the bookmark and click OK.**

   In Design view, the bookmark icon appears where bookmarks have been entered. Right-click this icon and choose Bookmark Properties to open the Bookmark dialog box and remove a bookmark.

Making It Easy for Visitors to E-Mail You

Usually, you will find the means to send an e-mail message to the person who maintains a Web site somewhere on the home page. Sometimes you see an e-mail address, but more often you see an e-mail icon. When a visitor clicks an address or e-mail icon, his or her default e-mail program opens. And if the person set up the address or icon correctly, the e-mail message is already addressed and given a subject line.

A hyperlink that opens an e-mail program is called a *mail-to hyperlink* or sometimes an *e-mail link*. Follow these steps to put a mail-to hyperlink on your home page so that others can get in touch with you:

1. **Select the words, graphic, or other object that will constitute the link.**

2. **Click the Insert Hyperlink button or choose Insert⇨Hyperlink.**

The Insert Hyperlink dialog box appears (refer to Figure 15-6).

3. **Under Link to, click the E-Mail Address icon.**

As shown in Figure 15-7, text boxes appear for entering an e-mail address and subject message.

Figure 15-7:
A mail-to hyperlink opens the default e-mail program.

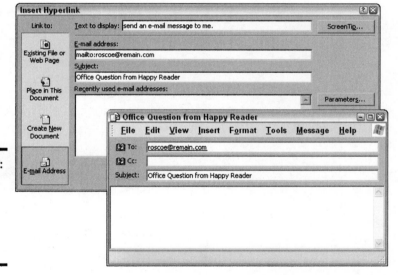

4. **Enter your e-mail address and a subject for the messages that others will send you in the text boxes.**

FrontPage inserts the word *mailto:* before your e-mail address as you enter it.

5. **Click OK.**

Test the link by clicking it. Your default e-mail program — probably Outlook — opens. The e-mail message is already addressed and given a subject.

CHECK IT OUT

Viewing a Web Page at Different Resolutions

Besides viewing Web pages in different Web browsers, people also view Web pages at different screen resolutions. Things are bigger and easier to see at low screen resolutions such as 640 x 480, but more items appear on-screen at higher resolutions such as 800 x 640. People whose eyesight isn't the best prefer low screen resolutions, whereas high screen resolutions are favored by people who like to put many programs on-screen and by people who have newer, larger monitors that display at 1024 x 768 pixels or higher.

As you construct your Web site, take a moment from time to time to see what your Web pages look like at different resolutions. People whose monitors display at low resolutions might have to scroll from side to side to see your Web pages if those pages are too wide. And your Web pages might look too small to people whose monitors display at high resolutions.

FrontPage offers two ways to quickly find out what pages look like at different resolutions:

- ✔ Choose View➪Page Size and an option on the submenu.

- ✔ Click the Page Size button on the Status bar and select an option from the drop-down list.

Chapter 16: Presenting the Content

In This Chapter

✔ **Placing and formatting text**

✔ **Choosing, inserting, and changing the size of images**

✔ **Changing an image's format**

✔ **Wrapping text around images**

✔ **Creating thumbnail images**

✔ **Putting horizontal rules on Web pages**

✔ **Creating and laying out a navigation bar**

✔ **Drawing an image map with hyperlinks**

*C*ontent is the droll term that Web site developers use to describe the text and images that are presented on a Web site. The person responsible for writing the text and choosing and creating the images is sometimes called the *content provider*. Don't let anyone tell you otherwise: Content is everything. People don't return to a Web site to see new Web technologies or marvel at page designs. They return because something on the Web site interests or intrigues them. If Web site developers spent more time putting interesting material on their Web sites and less time worrying about their Web sites' appearance, the Internet would be a much better place to visit.

This chapter is devoted to entering the content on a Web site. It explains how to lay out and enter text, choose images for a Web site, and insert the images. You also find out how to wrap text around images, handle thumbnail images, and create a *navigation bar* (a series of buttons that visitors can click to get from place to place quickly in your Web site). Finally, this chapter shows how to make a clickable image map.

Formatting and Positioning Text

When it comes to entering, editing, and positioning text, FrontPage works very much like its cousin, Microsoft Word. If you know your way around Word, you've got it made — you already know nearly everything there is to know about formatting and positioning text.

Formatting and aligning text

Here are techniques for handling text on Web pages:

✦ **Choosing fonts and fonts sizes:** Select the text and choose a font and font size from the Font and Font Size menus on the Formatting toolbar. You can also click the Increase Font Size and Decrease Font Size buttons to change the size of text.

Instead of fonts being measured in points, font sizes for Web pages are measured using a 1 to 7 scale. This way, no matter whether visitors change the size of text in their browsers, text and headings on your Web pages remain the same size relative to each other.

✦ **Choosing a font color for text:** Click the down arrow next to the Font Color button to select a color from the drop-down list. To change the default text color used throughout a Web page, choose File⇨Properties, select the Formatting tab in the Page Properties dialog box, and select a color from the Text drop-down list.

✦ **Choosing text effects:** Click the Bold, Italic, or Underline button to boldface, italicize, or underline text. You can also choose Format⇨Font and select from several text effects — strikethrough, superscript, and others — in the Font dialog box.

✦ **Aligning text:** Click the Align Left, Center, Align Right, or Justify button to align text relative to the margins of the Web page, the table cell, the layer, or whichever object the text is in.

✦ **Indenting text:** Click the Decrease Indent or Increase Indent button to move paragraphs further from or closer to the margin.

✦ **Making bulleted and numbered lists:** Click the Numbering or Bullets button. To change the look of bullets or choose a different numbering scheme, select the list, choose Format⇨Bullets and Numbering, and make choices in the List Properties dialog box.

✦ **Constructing a table:** Tables work the same way in Word as in FrontPage. The difference between FrontPage and Word tables, however, is that tables on a Web page can change shape to accommodate the browser window in which they're shown. To tell FrontPage to let tables stand or permit them to change shape, right-click your table and choose Table Properties. In the Table Properties dialog box, select the In Pixels option button if you want the table to always remain the same size; select the In Percent option button to permit the table to change shape.

To break a line before it reaches the right margin, click where you want the break to be and press Shift+Enter.

Formatting with paragraph styles

One way to change the look of text is to assign text a paragraph style. A *style* is a collection of formats that have been bundled under one name. Instead of assigning a font, font size, and font color, you can simply choose a style and be done with it. Styles help make headings and text consistent from Web page to Web page. You can change the look of text in one place on a Web site and rest assured that the text looks like text elsewhere that was assigned the same style.

To apply a style, click the text and select a style from the Style drop-down list on the Formatting toolbar, as shown in Figure 16-1. Note that styles apply to entire paragraphs.

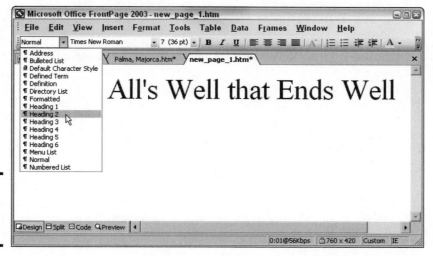

Figure 16-1:
Selecting a style for a heading.

I don't recommend altering a style because people can adjust text settings in their Web browsers. Substitute fonts in the form of HTML codes are a part of every style, but if you alter a style, you void those substitute fonts because no substitutes are built into the new style you created. As a result, a visitor to your Web site who doesn't have the proper font files on his or her computer for displaying the font you want might not see your font or a reliable substitute. What's more, if you adjust the font size when you alter the style, text that has been assigned the style can't resize if a visitor adjusts the text size in his or her browser. A visitor can't do this because fonts are assigned a 1-to-7 value on a relative scale, not a distinct point-size measurement.

Working with Images

A picture is worth a thousand words, or so they say, and a picture or two on a Web page is very attractive indeed. In fact, people expect to see pictures on Web pages. Following is advice for choosing Web page art, arranging pictures and images on Web pages, changing image formats, changing an image's size, and wrapping text around an image.

Advice for choosing Web page art

Here is some advice for choosing and using images:

✦ **Consider how long the image takes to download:** The Estimated Time To Download indicator on the status bar tells you how long it takes for a Web page to download. FrontPage considers a page slow if it takes 30 seconds to download over a 56K modem, but I believe 30 seconds is slower than slow. Pages should download faster than that. Try to keep download times under 16 seconds at 56K (30 seconds over a 28.8 Kbps modem).

✦ **Choose images that fit easily on the page:** Visitors have to scroll from side to side to see images that are too large to fit on the screen. If an image is larger than 320 x 240 pixels, create a thumbnail of it. (See the "Creating Thumbnail Images" section, later in this chapter.) Photo albums are an exception to the rule; the largest images in a photo album should be no larger than 760 x 420 (for display at 800 x 600 resolution), or 955 x 600 (for display at 1024 x 768 resolution).

✦ **Take image formats into consideration:** Use the JPEG image format for photographs; use the GIF format for small graphics such as buttons. The newer PNG (Portable Network Graphic) image format isn't widely compatible as of this writing. I recommend waiting a year or two to use PNG graphics.

✦ **Use animated GIFs sparingly:** Animated GIFs, the little graphics that dance on the page like bobble-head dolls, should be used sparingly if they are used at all. The little things can be distracting or even downright annoying.

Placing art on a Web page

Inserting a clipart image or picture file requires the same steps whether you're using Word, Excel, PowerPoint, Publisher, or FrontPage. Here are shorthand instructions for placing art on a Web page:

✦ **Inserting a graphic:** Click the Insert Picture from File button on the Drawing toolbar or choose Insert➪Picture➪From File. In the Picture dialog box, find and double-click the name of the graphic file whose image you want.

✦ **Inserting a clipart image:** Click the Insert Clip Art button on the Drawing toolbar or choose Insert➪Picture➪Clip Art. The Clip Art task pane opens. Find your image there and insert it.

Changing an image's size

Images are usually too large to fit on the Web page, and that's good because images retain their clarity better when they're shrunk than when they're enlarged. Whether you want to shrink or enlarge an image, do it the standard Office way — by dragging a selection handle on the image's border. Drag a corner to retain the image's proportions or drag a side to scrunch or stretch the image. You can also right-click the image, choose Picture Properties, and, in the Picture Properties dialog box, enter measurements in the Width and Height text boxes.

Don't specify the size of an image by percentage. Doing so causes the image to be pixilated, strangely proportioned, and the wrong size to boot.

Resampling to reduce download times

Reducing the size of an image shrinks the image on the page but doesn't shrink the file size of the image. Shrink a few large images, place them on a Web page, and pretty soon you have a bunch of small pictures that take forever to download.

To keep download times from growing too long, resample images after you resize them. Resampling

not only reduces the file size of an image but also usually improves the appearance of the image as well (resized images tend to look ragged and resampling prevents that). To resample an image, right-click it and choose Resample.

Positioning an image beside the text

FrontPage offers two techniques for positioning images on Web pages:

✦ **Putting the image in a layer:** As Book VI, Chapter 15 explains, a layer is a box that you can drag on-screen to any location on a Web page. To place an image in a layer, select it and click the Position Absolutely button on the Pictures toolbar. Now you can drag the image at will. Not all Web browsers can handle layers, so go this route only if you're certain that the people who will view your Web pages have advanced browsers.

✦ **Dragging the image:** Drag the image where you want it to go.

Wrapping text around an image

Unless you tell FrontPage to wrap text around an image, only one line of text appears next to an image before FrontPage wraps the text to a new line underneath the image. Follow these steps to choose precisely where text appears with respect to an image:

1. **Double-click the image (or right-click it and choose Picture Properties).**

   You see the Picture Properties dialog box, shown in Figure 16-2.

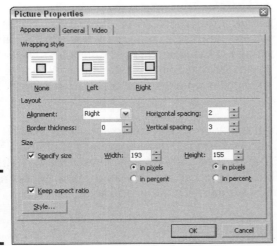

Figure 16-2:
Wrapping
text around
an image.

753

2. Choose a wrapping style — None, Left, or Right.

Wrapping styles determine where text goes when it runs into an image.

3. Select an option from the Alignment drop-down list.

Table 16-1 explains the Alignment options. These options determine where text falls horizontally with respect to the image.

4. In the Horizontal Spacing and Vertical Spacing text boxes, enter in pixels how close you want text to come to the image.

Be sure to leave some space between text and the image. Without the space, your Web page might suffer from claustrophobia.

5. Click OK.

Table 16-1	Alignment Options for Wrapping Text around Images
Option	*What It Does*
Left	Places the graphic on the left side of the browser window and wraps text around the right side of the graphic.
Right	Places the graphic on the right side of the browser window and wraps text around the left side of the graphic.
Top	Aligns the top of the graphic with the top of the tallest element on the same line.
Texttop	Aligns the top of the graphic with the top of the tallest character on the same line.
Middle	Aligns the middle of the graphic with the middle of the surrounding text.
Absmiddle	Aligns the middle of the graphic with the middle of the largest item on the current line.
Baseline and Bottom	Aligns the bottom of the graphic with the bottom of the surrounding text.
Absbottom	Aligns the bottom of the graphic with the bottom of the nearest line of text.
Center	Centers the graphic horizontally in the browser window.

Changing image formats

Two image formats are widely supported by Web browsers: JPEG (.jpg), which is used for photographs, and GIF (.gif), which is used for line art and graphics that are partially transparent. FrontPage also supports the higher-quality PNG (.png) file format, but PNG files are quite large and, moreover, not all Web browsers can handle them (in other words, don't use PNG files).

Use an image-editing program, such as Photoshop or Paint Shop Pro, to convert images to the JPEG or GIF format before you place them on a Web page, or else convert them with FrontPage. In fact, FrontPage converts files that aren't JPEG, GIF, or PNG to JPEG or GIF automatically. Follow these steps to change graphic file formats on your own in FrontPage:

1. **Right-click the image and choose Change Picture File Type.**

You see the Picture File Type dialog box, as shown in Figure 16-3.

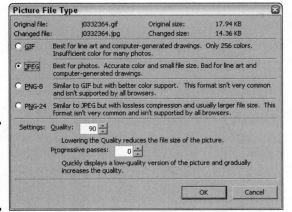

**Book VI
Chapter 16**

Presenting the Content

Figure 16-3:
Changing
the file
format of an
image.

2. **Choose an image format.**

Choose GIF for small, line-art images; otherwise choose JPEG. Don't use the PNG format unless your images need to be of exceptionally high quality and the audience for your Web site is likely to use the latest model of browsers.

3. **Click OK.**

Creating Thumbnail Images

When you're tempted to place an image larger than about 500 x 300 pixels on a Web page, consider using thumbnail images instead. A *thumbnail image* is a small image that a visitor can click to see the image in its entirety. To create thumbnails, as they're sometimes called, create small versions of each image and hyperlink each image to its full-sized version, or else use the Auto Thumbnail feature.

The Auto Thumbnail feature creates a second file from the original. The file is called by the name of the original followed by `_small`. The thumbnail file (for example, `cat_small.jpg`) appears on your Web page, and when a visitor clicks it, the original, full-sized image appears in its own Web page.

To create a thumbnail image with the Auto Thumbnail feature, select the image and click the Auto Thumbnail button on the Pictures toolbar or right-click the image and choose Auto Thumbnail. The image shrinks to the size of a thumbnail. You can adjust the thumbnail's size or position by dragging one of its corner handles and moving it as you would any image.

To adjust the default size of thumbnails created with the Auto Thumbnail feature, choose Tools⇨Page Options, select the Auto Thumbnail tab in the Page Options dialog box, and fiddle with the options there.

Inserting a Ruled Line

A ruled line is a horizontal line that separates one part of a Web page from another, as shown in Figure 16-4. Use ruled lines, also known as *dividers,* to let visitors know that you're changing subjects in the middle of a Web page. FrontPage offers two ways to draw a ruled line:

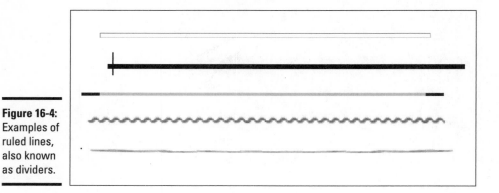

Figure 16-4: Examples of ruled lines, also known as dividers.

✦ **A plain horizontal line:** Choose Insert⇨Horizontal Line. To change the color or size of the line, double-click it or right-click it and choose Horizontal Line Properties. Then, in the Horizontal Line Properties dialog box, choose a new width, height, alignment, or color for the line.

✦ **A line from a clipart image:** Click the Insert Clip Art button on the Drawing toolbar or choose Insert⇨Picture⇨Clip Art. In the Clip Art task pane, enter the word **dividers** in the Search For text box and click the Go button. Then scroll in the task pane and select a divider that interests you. Change a divider's shape and position as you would any clip-art image.

Creating a Navigation Bar

A *navigation bar,* also known as a *link bar,* is a set of buttons or tabs that visitors can click to go quickly from page to page in a Web site. In reality, each button or tab is a hyperlink to a different Web page in the Web site. Figure 16-5 shows an example of two navigation bars, one composed of tabs and one composed of buttons. Typically, the first button or tab is called *Home* and takes you to the home page. Visitors can't get lost in a Web site with a navigation bar because they can always click a navigation bar button or tab to go where they want.

To create a navigation bar, you create the buttons — FrontPage calls them *interactive buttons* — one at a time and link them to different pages in your Web site. The easiest way to lay out a navigation bar is to start by creating a table for holding the buttons. To create a button, click in a table cell and choose Insert⇨Interactive Button. You see the Interactive Buttons dialog box, shown in Figure 16-6. Fashion your button in the dialog box's three tabs. As you go along, the Preview box shows precisely what your button will look like.

Navigation bar with buttons.

Navigation bar with tabs.

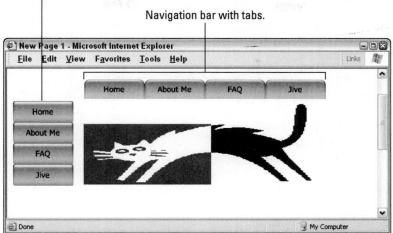

Figure 16-5:
Examples of navigation bars.

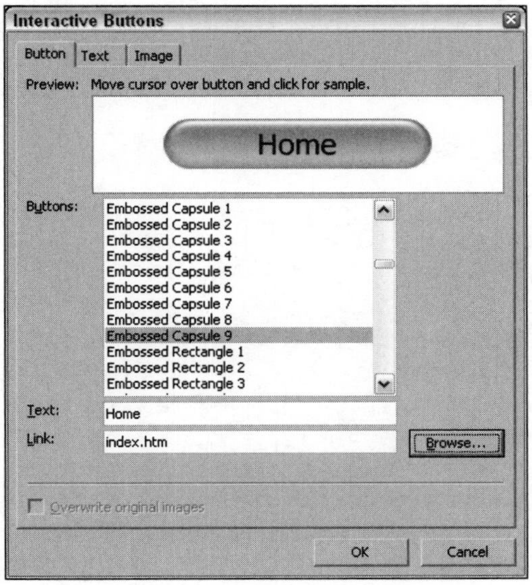

Figure 16-6:
Creating a button or tab for a navigation bar.

✦ **Button tab:** Choose a button or tab style in the Buttons list, enter the text in the Text box, and, in the Link box, enter the filename of the Web page that will open when visitors click the button. You can click the Browse button and select the filename in the Edit Hyperlink dialog box. (Book VI, Chapter 15 explains how to create hyperlinks, including hyperlinks between Web pages on the same site, in this dialog box.)

✦ **Text:** Choose a font and font size for the button or tab text. From the Font Color drop-down list, select what the button or tab will look like when it's idle, when the mouse pointer hovers over it, and when it's clicked. Click or move the pointer over the sample button or tab to see what your choices do. The alignment menus are for aligning text inside the button or tab.

✦ **Image:** Change the size of the button on this tab. You can also deactivate the hover or pressed mechanism.

To tinker with the button settings, double-click the button or tab or right-click it and choose Button Properties. Doing so opens the Interactive Buttons dialog box.

If you laid out your navigation bar inside a table, you probably need to adjust the amount of space between buttons and remove the table borders. To do so, right-click the table and choose Table Properties. In the Table Properties dialog box, enter **0** in the Size text box (under Borders) to remove the table borders. To adjust the amount of space between the buttons or tabs in the navigation bar, play with the Cell Padding and Cell Spacing measurements.

Creating an Image Map

An *image map* is a graphic that has links you can click in different places in the image to go to different Web pages. Often, image maps literally are maps. In Figure 16-7, for example, a visitor can click a number on the city map to go to a Web page with information about landmarks in a city. To create an image map, you insert the graphic that serves as the map, draw *hotspots* on it, and link the hotspots to different Web pages.

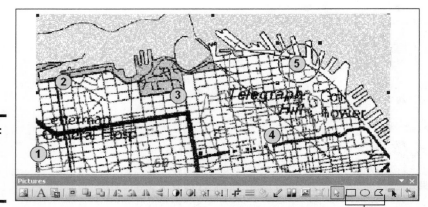

Figure 16-7: Drawing a hotspot on an image map.

Click a hotspot button and start drawing.

Make sure that the graphic you use for the image map is large enough to accommodate the hotspots. While you're at it, plan for hotspots that are large and easy to find. Scouring an image map for hotspots is an unpleasant experience. One way to help visitors recognize hotspots is to number them and simply create the hotspot on the number, as shown in Figure 16-7.

Creating a hotspot and hyperlink

Follow these steps to create a hotspot and a hyperlink to go with it:

1. **Insert the graphic.**

See the "Working with Images" section near the start of this chapter to find out how to insert a graphic on a Web page.

2. **Display the Pictures toolbar, if it isn't already displayed, and click one of the Hotspot buttons — Rectangular Hotspot, Circular Hotspot, or Polygonal Hotspot.**

The pointer changes into a pencil.

3. **Draw the hotspot on the graphic by dragging the pencil.**

To draw a perfect square or circle, hold down the Shift key as you drag.

If you want to draw an irregularly shaped hotspot, click the Polygonal Hotspot button. Rather than drag to create the hotspot, draw one line at a time. As you finish drawing each line, release the mouse button, click, and draw the next line. To enclose the polygon, return to the point where you started drawing and double-click.

When you finish drawing the hotspot, the Insert Hyperlink dialog box appears.

4. **Enter the hyperlink.**

Book VI, Chapter 15 explains how to insert a hyperlink and how the Insert Hyperlink dialog box works. Be sure to click the ScreenTip button and enter a description of what happens when you click the hotspot. This way, visitors to your Web site will understand that they can click the image and travel elsewhere.

Adjusting the hotspots

To adjust or delete a hotspot, start in Design view and click the image map to display its hotspots; then click the hotspot that needs changing. Boxes appear on the image to show you where the hotspots are. Here's how to move, resize, or delete a hotspot on an image map:

✦ **Moving a hotspot:** Click inside the hotspot and drag it to a new location.

✦ **Resizing a hotspot:** Click and drag a hotspot handle. If you're dealing with a polygonal hotspot, dragging a handle changes the hotspot's shape as well as its size.

✦ **Deleting a hotspot:** Press the Delete key.

If you have trouble finding a hotspot in an image, click the Highlight Hotspots button on the Drawing toolbar. The image will blank out and you'll clearly see where the hotspots are.

CHECK IT OUT

Artful Transitions for Web Pages

A *page transition* is a cinematic effect that appears as one page leaves the screen and another takes its place. Examples of page transitions include "wipe right" and "blend." FrontPage makes it easy to apply transitions to Web pages. To test-drive a page transition, choose Format⇨ Page Transition to open the Page Transitions dialog box. Then choose among these options:

- ✔ **Event:** Choose when the transition is to begin. Most people choose Page Enter to make the transition appear as the Web page lands on-screen.

- ✔ **Duration (Seconds):** Enter how long the transition occurs.

- ✔ **Transition Effect:** Choose a transition. (Choose No Effect to go without a page transition.)

Chapter 17: Publishing and Maintaining a Web Site

In This Chapter

✔ Generating a Site Summary report

✔ Recalculating and verifying the accuracy of hyperlinks

✔ Introducing FrontPage to your Web server

✔ Publishing and republishing a Web site

✔ Ideas for promoting a Web site

✔ Tracking visitors to your Web site

At last, the moment of truth has arrived. The work on your Web site is done. You have put together a little masterpiece. Now is the time to publish it on the Internet. This chapter explains how to do that and how to do the little chores that must be done before you publish. You will also find suggestions here for promoting a Web site and tracking the number of visitors to your site.

Getting Ready to Publish a Web Site

Before publishing a Web site to the Internet, check it over to make sure that everything is in its place and there is a place for everything. Checking for broken and invalid hyperlinks is vital, because nothing irks a Web site visitor more than clicking a hyperlink that goes nowhere. The following pages explain different ways to make sure that a Web site is ship-shape. Read on to discover how to run Site Summary reports, verify and fix hyperlinks, and check for unfinished tasks.

Running a Site Summary report

Run a *Site Summary report* to get an overview of your Web site and find out whether any problem will keep it from working properly. A Site Summary report is actually several reports, each dealing with a different aspect of your Web site. To run a Site Summary report, choose View⇨Reports⇨Site Summary. You see the Site Summary window, shown in Figure 17-1. Pay special attention to the following items shown in Table 17-1:

Table 17-1	Elements of a Site Summary Report
Report	What It Tells You
All Files	How many files are in your Web site and how much space they occupy. The number in the Size column cannot exceed the amount of server space your Web server provider grants for your Web site.

Table 17-1 *(continued)*

Report	*What It Tells You*
Slow Pages	The number of Web pages that take longer than 30 seconds to download over a 56 Kbps modem. Click the Slow Pages hyperlink to open slow pages and resize or delete some images.
Unverified Hyperlinks	The number of hyperlinks that haven't been tested.
Broken Hyperlinks	The number of hyperlinks to pages or files that no longer exist or have been moved.
Component Errors	The number of problems with any components (such as forms) that you've placed in your Web site.
Uncompleted Tasks	The number of uncompleted tasks in your Web site.

Click a link to see a report.

Click to verify hyperlinks.

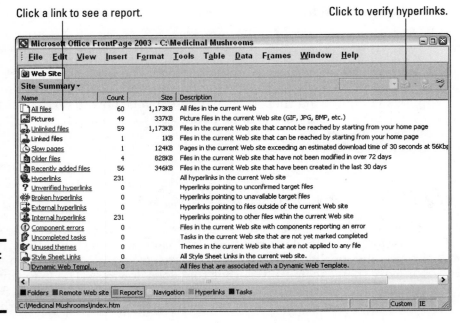

Figure 17-1:
A Site Summary report.

Recalculating the hyperlinks

Before you publish your Web site, recalculate all the hyperlinks. In FrontPage parlance, *recalculating* means to update all the hyperlinks that FrontPage creates automatically. (FrontPage creates hyperlinks automatically when you create navigation bars, create a photo album, or create thumbnail images.)

To recalculate the hyperlinks, choose Tools⇨Recalculate Hyperlinks and then click Yes.

Verifying and fixing hyperlinks

Especially if more than one person is working on a Web site, hyperlinks can get broken as files are moved. And if someone enters a URL for a hyperlink incorrectly, you get a dud hyperlink. Read on to discover how to generate a list of broken hyperlinks and, starting from the list, repair the broken links one at a time.

Generating a list of broken hyperlinks

Follow these steps to check all hyperlinks on your Web site and generate a list of the hyperlinks that are broken:

1. Choose View➪Reports➪Site Summary.

The Site Summary window appears (refer to Figure 17-1).

2. Click the Verifies Hyperlinks in Current Web button.

This hard-to-find button is located on the right side of the Site Summary title bar (refer to Figure 17-1). After you click it, you see the Verify Hyperlinks dialog box.

3. Select the Verify All Hyperlinks option button and click the Start button.

FrontPage methodically goes through your Web site, testing each and every hyperlink. Finally, if FrontPage finds links that don't work, you see a Hyperlinks report similar the one shown in Figure 17-2.

**Book VI
Chapter 17**

Publishing and
Maintaining a Web Site

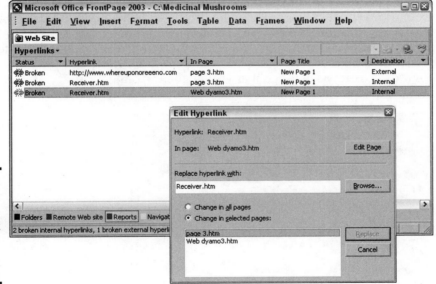

Figure 17-2:
To repair a broken link, double-click it in the Hyperlinks report.

Repairing a broken hyperlink

After you have generated a list of broken hyperlinks, select a hyperlink in the list and double-click it or click the Edit Hyperlink button to repair the link. You see the Edit Hyperlink dialog box, as shown in Figure 17-2. Starting here, you can fix the broken link in different ways:

✦ **Fix the link by going to its Web page:** Click the Edit Page button to open the Web page on your site where the hyperlink is found and fix it there.

✦ **Fix the link by entering a new target address:** Click the Browse button to open the Edit Hyperlink dialog box and fix the hyperlink there. Book VI, Chapter 15 explains how hyperlinking works.

✦ **Repair some instances of the hyperlink:** If a broken link to the same target is found in more than one place in your Web site, each page where the broken link appears is listed at the bottom of the Edit Hyperlink dialog box. If you want to repair some, not all, instances of the broken hyperlink, select the Change in Selected Pages option button and select the pages where you want to correct the link.

Check for uncompleted tasks

As Book VI, Chapter 14 explains, the Tasks list is a handy way to keep track of what needs to be done on your Web site. Before you publish your Web site, check to see whether any essential tasks still need completing. Choose View➪Tasks to examine the Tasks list.

Setting Up FrontPage to Work with Your Web Server

Before you can upload a Web site, you need to open the Remote Web Site Properties dialog box and tell FrontPage what kind of Web server will hold your Web pages and where the Web server is located. Figure 17-3 shows the Remote Web Site Properties dialog box. Before you open this dialog box, get the address of the Web server where you will upload your Web site from your Web server provider. And remember: Your Web server provider is obliged to help you upload Web pages, so don't hesitate to ask questions of it or seek its assistance if anything goes wrong.

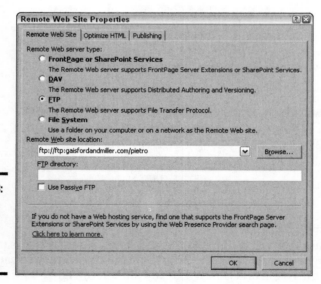

Figure 17-3: Telling FrontPage where to publish a Web site.

The Remote Web Site Properties dialog box appears automatically the first time you click the Publish Site button to try to publish a Web site. However, you can always return to the dialog box by following these steps:

1. **Choose View➪Folders.**

2. **Click the Remote Web Site button.**

You can find this button along the bottom of the Folders window next to Folders, Reports, Navigation, and the other buttons.

3. Click the Remote Web Site Properties button.

You can find this button in the middle of the FrontPage window. The Remote Web Site Properties dialog box appears.

Choose a Remote Web Server Type option to describe the Web server where you will publish your Web pages:

✦ **FrontPage or SharePoint Services:** If the FrontPage Server Extensions are installed on the Web server or you're using SharePoint Services (a topic not covered in this book), select this option button and enter the address that your Web server provider gave you in the Remote Web Site Location text box. Select the Encrypted Connection Required (SSL) check box if you're required to enter a password to publish your Web site.

✦ **DAV:** Distributed Authoring and Versioning (DAV or WebDAV) is an industry standard that makes it easy to track who is editing what Web page by way of a checkout and versioning scheme. If a Web server supports HTTP uploading, it most likely supports DAV. Enter a password and select the Encrypted Connection Required (SSL) check box if you're required to enter a password to publish the Web site.

✦ **FTP:** File Transfer Protocol (FTP) provides basic uploading capabilities and works fine for simple Web sites that don't use forms or other dynamic content. Enter the address of the Web server in the Remote Web Site Location text box. If your Web server provider requires you to enter an FTP directory, or if the Web server makes use of passive FTP to handle firewalls, enter the directory address and select the Use Passive FTP check box. (Your Web server provider will explain what these are and whether you need them.)

✦ **File System:** Select this option if you want to publish your Web site to another folder on your computer or on a network. Do this, for example, if you're creating a series of Web pages for a CD. Click the Browse button and, in the New Publish Location dialog box, select a folder on your computer or on a network.

After you click OK, the Publish Web site window appears. This is the same window you see when you click the Publish Web button and tell FrontPage to publish your Web site. Keep reading.

Publishing a Web Site

After you have done the preliminary work, you can upload your Web site to a remote Web server. Start out by clicking the Publish Web button, choosing File⇨Publish Site, or pressing Alt+P. You see the Publish Site window, as shown in Figure 17-4. The left side of the window lists the folders and files on your computer that make up your Web site. The right side shows the folders and files on the Web server that have already been published there. (If you have not yet published your Web site, no folders or files appear on the right side of the window.)

Files on your computer   Files on the Web server

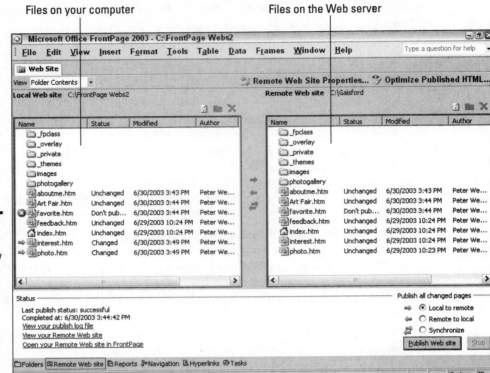

Figure 17-4:
The Publish
Site window
shows
which
folders and
files have
been
uploaded to
the Web
server.

Follow these steps to publish a Web site for the first time:

1. **Make sure that the Local to Remote option button is selected.**

You can find this option button under Publish All Changed Pages in the
lower-right corner of the Publish Site window.

2. **Click the Publish Web Site button.**

What happens next depends on your connection to the Internet and
whether you must enter a password to publish your Web pages.
However, the names of all files that are published successfully on the
Web server appear on the right side of the window.

Click the View Your Remote Web Site link (it's in the lower-left corner of
the window) to view your Web site in a Web browser.

Republishing a Web site

The Publish Site window (refer to Figure 17-4) is designed to help you
understand which files have been published already, which files have
changed and therefore need republishing, and which files are new and need
publishing for the first time. Look in the Status column on the left side of
the Publish Site window to find out where each file stands:

✦ **Unchanged:** These files are identical to files already published on the
Web server and don't need republishing.

✦ **Changed:** These files have been updated since the last time you published the Web site.

✦ **Unmatched:** These files didn't exist on your Web site the last time you published the site. They need to be published.

By default, only new files and files that have changed since the last time you published your Web site are sent to the Web server when you click the Publish Web Site button. However, you can decide for yourself which files are published by using these techniques:

✦ **Publishing a handful of files:** To save time, publish only the files you want to publish by Ctrl+clicking their names, right-clicking, and choosing Publish Selected Files.

✦ **Preventing files from being published:** Right-click a filename and choose Don't Publish. An X icon appears beside the names of files that aren't meant to be published. To see only not-to-be-published files in the window, open the View menu and choose Files Not to Publish.

Synchronizing files on your computer and the Web server

In computer lingo, *synchronizing* means to compare two files with the same name to see which one was saved more recently and then replace the older file with the newer one. If you copy files back and forth between your computer and the Web server, the files will need synchronizing now and then. To synchronize files, click the Synchronize option button in the Publish Site window (refer to Figure 17-4) and then click the Publish Web Site button.

Promoting Your Web Site

Obviously, you want your Web site to be more popular than Britney Spears, but it won't happen unless you promote your site. These pages look at various ways to promote a Web site. You discover how to ingratiate yourself with search engines, announce your site online, and promote your site the old-fashioned way — by pounding the proverbial pavement.

Helping search engines find your Web site

Search engines (Yahoo!, Lycos, Google, and the rest of them) are always scouring the Internet and recording information about Web pages. The search engines work a little differently in that some record information about every word on a Web page and some look only at titles and headings. The search engines store this information in enormous databases. When you conduct a search of the Internet, you're really searching a database that the search engine you're using maintains. Obviously, you should do all you can to help search engines find and index your Web site — and that is the subject of the next several pages.

Searchengines.com offers a superb explanation of search engines, how they work, and what they are. The Web site is located at this address: www.searchengines.com.

**Book VI
Chapter 17**

Publishing and
Maintaining a Web Site

The different types of search engines

Here's a quick rundown of the different kinds of search engines:

✦ **Crawler-based:** This type of search engines sends out a *crawler* (also known as a *spider*), an automated computer program that analyzes Web sites and captures pertinent information about Web sites for the search engine's database.

✦ **Directories:** This type of search engine works much like a card catalog at a library. Rather than rely on computer programs, people compile information about Web sites and store it in the search engine's database.

✦ **Hybrid:** This type of search engine combines the crawler-based and directory approach. A search is usually performed first in the directory, and if the results aren't satisfactory, the searcher is presented with information gathered by a crawler.

✦ **Meta-search:** This type of search engine rides piggyback on other search engines. It searches other search engines and returns summaries of the results it has found.

Providing meta information

Crawler-based search engines, when they record information about a Web page, record the meta information. The *meta information* — found in the HTML code — includes the Web page's title, its description, and the keywords that you provide. A *keyword* is a word that a person types in a search engine to look for information about a certain topic. Enter the keyword *Madagascar* in the Lycos.com search engine, for example, and you get Web pages that contain the word Madagascar. By entering keywords that describe your Web pages in the meta information, you help others find your Web pages.

FrontPage offers a special command for entering meta information without having to muck around with HTML tags. Follow these steps to enter meta information that helps people find your Web pages:

1. **Choose Format⇨Background.**

You see the Page Properties dialog box.

2. **Select the General tab.**

Figure 17-5 shows where to enter meta information in the General tab of the Page Properties dialog box.

3. **In the Title text box, enter a title for the Web page if you haven't already entered one.**

As I explain in Book VI, Chapter 14, the page title appears in the title bar of the Web browser. The title is the most important piece of meta information.

4. **In the Page Description text box, enter a description of the Web page.**

Some search engines display the description you enter, word for word, in the results of an Internet search, so enter the description carefully. Keep the description under 25 words.

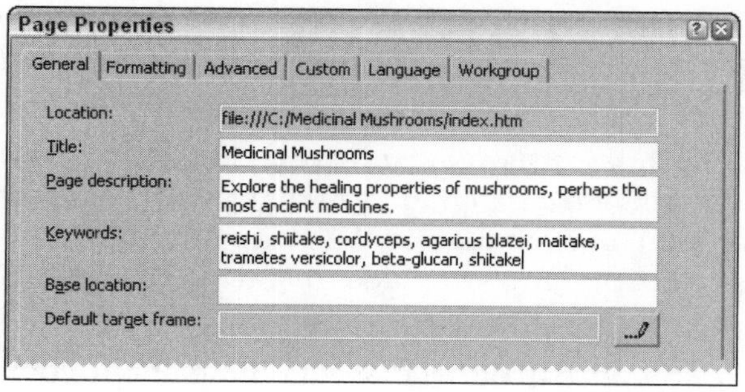

Page Properties

General | Formatting | Advanced | Custom | Language | Workgroup

Location: file:///C:/Medicinal Mushrooms/index.htm

Title: Medicinal Mushrooms

Page description: Explore the healing properties of mushrooms, perhaps the most ancient medicines.

Keywords: reishi, shiitake, cordyceps, agaricus blazei, maitake, trametes versicolor, beta-glucan, shitake|

Base location:

Default target frame:

Figure 17-5: Entering the meta information.

You can't check for spelling errors in the Page Properties dialog box, and the Page Description text box isn't a comfortable place to type a description. Try typing the description in Word, copying the spell-checked text, and pasting it into the text box. To paste the text in the text box, right-click in the text box and choose Paste.

5. **In the Keywords text box, enter some keywords.**

Put yourself in the place of someone searching the Internet and enter all keywords that people searching for a Web site like yours might enter when conducting a search. When someone enters a keyword that matches a keyword you enter, your site will appear in the search results.

People often make spelling errors or typos when they enter keywords. To help your site get found, enter misspelled words as well as correctly spelled words in the Keywords text box.

Submitting your Web site to search engines

Most search engines invite you to submit your Web site for inclusion in their catalog. Crawler-based search engines usually request the URL; directory-based engines usually request more information. Table 17-2 lists some search engines to which you can submit your site.

Table 17-2	Search Engines	
Name	*Type of Search Engine*	*Address*
Altavista	Hybrid using Open Directory	www.altavista.com
AOL Search	Hybrid using Open Directory and Google	http://search.aol.com
Google	Hybrid using Open Directory	www.google.com
Lycos	Hybrid using Open Directory	www.lycos.com
MSN Search*	Hybrid using Looksmart	www.msnsearch.com
Open Directory	Directory	www.dmoz.org
Teoma*	Crawler	www.teoma.com
Yahoo!	Hybrid using Google	www.yahoo.com

*You must pay a fee to submit to these search engines.

Book VI Chapter 17

Publishing and Maintaining a Web Site

Other ways to publicize a Web site

Here are some other ways to publicize a Web site:

✦ **Include your site in link exchanges and Web rings:** Link exchanges and Web rings are methods of exchanging hyperlinks with other Web sites, as long as you can find an exchange or Web ring that pertains to the topic your Web site covers. A good place to start looking for Web rings is www.webring.com.

✦ **Post your Web site on newsgroups:** Place a notice about your Web page on newsgroups where members might be interested in a Web site like yours. If you answer questions or post helpful and informative information to the newsgroup, the participants will appreciate it and probably come visit your site.

✦ **Link your site to other sites and hope they reciprocate:** Include a "Links" Web page on your site where hyperlinks to sites similar to yours are listed. Then send an e-mail message to the developer at each Web site to which your Web site is linked and hope that he or she reciprocates.

✦ **List your Web site address at the bottom of e-mail messages:** Add your Web site's URL to your e-mail signature. If you don't use an e-mail signature, casually enter a link to your Web site at the bottom of the e-mail messages you send. Doing so encourages more people to visit your site.

The Hit Parade: Keeping Track of Visitors

Obviously, you want to find out how many people are visiting your Web site. To obtain this information, you can take advantage of FrontPage Usage reports, examine site statistics from your Web server provider, or use a hit counter. Better keep reading.

FrontPage Usage reports

Find out whether your Web provider has installed FrontPage Server Extensions and whether FrontPage usage analysis has been enabled. If the answer is yes to both queries, you can use the various FrontPage Usage reports to track how many visitors are coming to your site.

To run these reports, choose Reports⇨Usage and then choose a report from the submenu. There are thirteen reports in all.

Site statistics provided by your Web host

Few Web providers support FrontPage's built-in usage analysis tools, but most can offer usage statistics for you. How you access these statistics varies from company to company, but the same information is there — hit counts, Web browser statistics, search engine terms, and more.

Placing a hit counter on a page

A *hit counter* keeps track of and displays the number of people who have visited a Web page. As long as your Web provider has installed the FrontPage Server Extensions, you can include a hit counter on a Web page by following these steps:

1. Click the Web Component button or choose Insert⇨Web Component.

You see the Insert Web Component dialog box.

2. Under Component Type, select Hit Counter.

Several hit counter styles appear on the right side of the dialog box.

3. Select a style and click the Finish button.

The Hit Counter Properties dialog box, shown in Figure 17-6, appears.

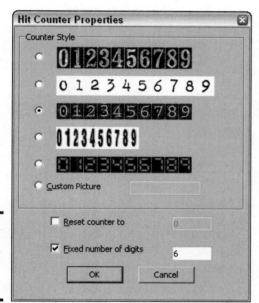

Figure 17-6:
Deciding what the hit counter looks like.

4. Select a style, enter the number of digits you want, and click OK.

To reset a hit counter, double-click it in Design view. You see the Hit Counter Properties dialog box. Select the Reset Counter To check box and enter **0** in the accompanying text box.

Chapter 18: Forms and Behaviors

In This Chapter

✔ Creating a user-input form for visitors to fill out

✔ Using preprogrammed behaviors to make your Web pages more compelling

This short chapter offers a little extra something to make your Web pages stand out in the crowd. It explains how to include a user-input form on a Web page and, in so doing, solicit information from the people who visit your Web pages. This chapter also explains how behaviors can make your Web pages more dynamic and exciting.

Creating User-Input Forms

As shown in Figure 18-1, a *user-input form* is a means of soliciting information from visitors to a Web page. After a visitor enters information in the form and clicks a button, the information is sent to the Web page developer. For conducting surveys and getting addresses and other types of useful information, user input forms can be invaluable.

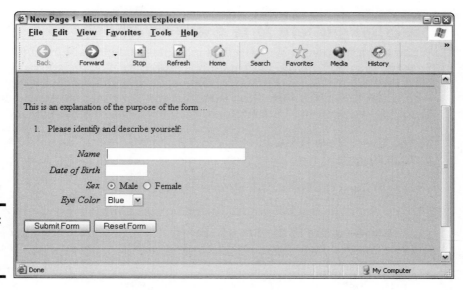

Figure 18-1:
A typical user-input form.

As long as the Web hosting service where your Web site is published has installed FrontPage Server Extensions or SharePoint Services, you can include user-input forms on your Web pages. Creating the forms is easy, although linking the forms to the Web server so that you can accept input from visitors and store the results can be a chore.

Creating the form

To create a form, you can choose Insert⇨Form and select an option on the submenu, or you can make use of the Form Page Wizard. I strongly suggest using the Form Page Wizard. This gizmo queries as to what kind of form you want and what kind of information you want to solicit, and it does all the layout work for you. Creating a form by using the Insert⇨Form command, on the other hand, is a sticky business. Here are instructions for creating a form:

✦ **With the Insert⇨Form command:** Choose Insert⇨Form and then choose a submenu option that describes how you want to solicit information. For example, choose Insert⇨Form⇨Checkbox to create a check box or choose Insert⇨Form⇨Textbox to create a text box that visitors to your Web site can type into. FrontPage inserts the item you selected. To enter the text or values in the item, double-click it and fill in the Properties dialog box.

✦ **With the Form Page Wizard:** Choose File⇨New and, in the New task pane, click More Page Templates. You see the Page Templates dialog box. Double-click Form Page Wizard and, in the Form Page Wizard dialog boxes, answer questions and keep clicking Next as you go along.

To alter any part of a form, double-click the text box, option button, check box, or whatever. You see a Properties dialog box for changing values, the size of the form field, and other things. To change the name of a button, double-click it in Design view and, in the Push Button Properties dialog box, enter a new name in the Value/Label text box.

Specifying where form data is stored

When a visitor to your Web site fills in a form and clicks the Submit or Submit Form button, the information is stored in a file called `formrslt.htm` (form result) in the _private folder. However, you can decide for yourself where and how the information is stored and, for that matter, you can tell FrontPage to send the information to you in an e-mail message.

Follow these steps to decide where information entered on a user-input form is stored:

1. **Right-click the form and choose Form Properties.**

You see the Form Properties dialog box, as shown in Figure 18-2.

2. **Enter the name of the file where you want to store form data in the File Name box.**

You can change the filename that FrontPage uses for form results if you want. Just be sure to leave the _private/ part.

3. **Optionally, enter an e-mail address where form data is to be sent in the E-Mail Address text box.**

While you're at it, you can click the Options button and, on the E-Mail Results tab of the Saving Results dialog box, choose a format and enter a subject line for the e-mail that will be sent to you.

4. **Click OK.**

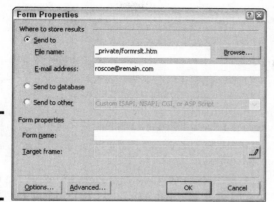

Figure 18-2:
Choosing
where form
data is
stored.

To retrieve form data stored on a Web server, use the Publish Web Site
window to copy form data from the remote server back to your local Web
site, and then open the file there.

Behaviors for More Dynamic Web Pages

If you've spent any time on the Internet, you've no doubt had the experience of seeing the screen come to life or a sound play when you move the
pointer over a part of a Web page. Almost certainly you've seen pop-up
boxes, usually advertisements, appear as you surf the Internet. To make
these kinds of things happen, programmers write scripts in the Java programming language. These scripts cause something to happen on the computer screen — a new browser window to open, a new Web page to appear,
a sound file to play — when a visitor, for example, moves the mouse pointer
over a graphic or presses a certain key.

Writing complex Java scripts is beyond the ability of most people who use
FrontPage, but that doesn't mean that you can't make dynamic things
happen on your Web pages. To make them happen, FrontPage offers behaviors and events. The following sections describe them.

Behaviors aren't compatible with Internet Explorer and Netscape Navigator
versions 3.*x* and earlier. However, few people still use these outdated
browser versions.

Behaviors and events

A *behavior* is a prewritten, canned piece of Java code that makes something
happen on-screen. Table 18-1 describes the different behaviors. Without
writing a lick of Java, you can make the actions in Table 18-1 happen on
your Web pages. (I tell you how in the next section.)

Table 18-1	Behaviors Available for Use in FrontPage
Behavior	*What It Does*
Call JavaScript	Executes the JavaScript code that you type.
Change Property	Changes the properties of the selected object (for example, you can change the font or hide a layer).
Change Property Restore	Restores the properties of an object back to the way it was before the Change Property Behavior was used.
Check Browser	Checks the visitor's Web browser type and version, and then loads a different page.
Check Plug-In	Checks what type of media plug-in the visitor's Web browser uses (Flash, QuickTime, and so on) and loads a different page.
Control Flash	Controls a Flash animation on the Web page.
Go To URL	Opens a new Web page in the visitor's Web browser.
Jump Menu	Creates a drop-down list with a number of options, each of which loads a different Web page. This is handy for a Table of Contents.
Jump Menu Go	Loads the URL associated with the specified Jump Menu entry.
Open Browser Window	Opens a new Web browser window with the desired dimensions, name, and URL.
Play Sound	Plays a sound file.
Popup Message	Displays a pop-up message box.
Preload Images	Preloads images (great for photo albums).
Set Text	Places the specified text in the frame, layer, status bar, or text field.
Swap Image	Replaces one image with another image.
Swap Image Restore	Restores the original image after a Swap Image behavior.

A behavior happens on-screen when the computer detects a certain kind of *event* occurring. Examples of events include a page appearing on-screen or a visitor moving the mouse pointer over a graphic. Table 18-2 lists the different events that can trigger a behavior. The section that follows describes how to get visitors to your Web pages to see a certain behavior when one of these events occurs.

Table 18-2	Some Events That Can Trigger Behaviors
Event	*Action That Triggers the Event*
onbeforeunload	The visitor closes the browser window, leaves the page, or clicks the Refresh button. This event occurs before the new page is loaded.
onblur	The visitor presses Tab on the keyboard to move to another object in the page, or switches to another application.
onchange	The visitor changes the text in a text box, or chooses a different option in a form, and then moves to another form field.
onclick	The visitor clicks the object.
ondlbclick	The visitor double-clicks the object.
onerror	A script error occurs, or an error occurs while downloading an object or image.

Event	Action That Triggers the Event
onfocus	The visitor clicks or moves the cursor to the object by pressing the Tab key.
onhelp	The visitor presses F1.
onkeydown	The visitor presses any key.
onkeypress	The visitor presses a key in the numeric keypad.
onkeyup	The visitor releases a key.
onload	The page loads in a Web browser.
onmousedown	The visitor presses a mouse button while the pointer is over an object.
onmousemove	The visitor moves the mouse pointer over an object.
onmouseout	The visitor moves the mouse pointer away from an object.
onmouseover	The visitor moves the mouse pointer over an object.
onmouseup	The visitor releases a mouse button while the pointer is over an object.
onresize	The visitor resizes the object or Web browser window.
onscroll	The visitor scrolls down, using the scroll bar or the keyboard.
onunload	The visitor closes the browser window, leaves the page, or clicks the Refresh button. This event occurs after the new page is loaded.

Making a behavior occur on a Web page

Follow these steps to make a behavior occur when a certain event transpires on a Web page:

1. **Choose Format⇨Behaviors.**

You see the Behaviors task pane, as shown in Figure 18-3.

2. **Select the text, image, or object to which you will assign a behavior.**

3. **Click the Insert button in the Behaviors task pane and, from the drop-down list, select the behavior that you want to insert.**

Table 18-1 explains these behaviors.

4. **In the dialog box that appears, describe how you want the behavior to unfold.**

Which dialog box you see depends on which behavior you chose. If you want to play a sound, for example, you will be asked to locate and select a sound file. If you want to display a pop-up message, you will be asked to enter the message.

5. **From the Events drop-down list, select the event that will trigger the behavior.**

Table 18-2 describes several of the different events. To begin with, onclick or onmouseover is usually the event, and the behavior is triggered when the user clicks or moves the mouse over the text, image, or object you chose in Step 2. However, you can open the Event drop-down list and choose a different event to trigger the behavior, as shown in Figure 18-3.

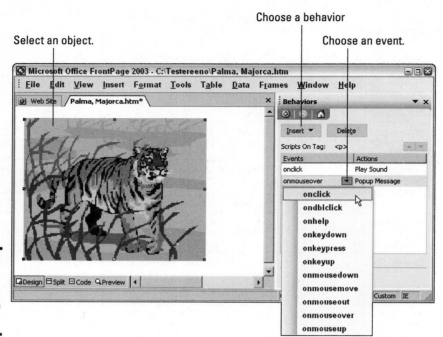

Choose a behavior

Select an object.

Choose an event.

Figure 18-3:
Assigning a
behavior
and event to
an object.

You can assign as many behaviors as you want to an object or a page. In
the Behaviors task plane, behaviors are listed in the order in which they
will occur. Just don't get carried away and enter too many behaviors. To
change the order in which behaviors occur, right-click in the Actions
column in the Behaviors task pane and choose Move Row Up or Move
Row Down.

To remove a behavior, right-click the Actions column in the Behaviors task
pane and choose Delete.

Chapter 19: Getting to Know Dreamweaver

In This Chapter

✓ Discovering the power of Dreamweaver

✓ Getting familiar with the Document window

✓ Examining a site with the Site window

✓ Choosing among Standard, Layout, and Expanded Tables modes

✓ Exploring toolbar buttons

✓ Using panels and Properties inspectors

*I*f you're looking for a Web design tool that's easy enough for beginners to use *and* sophisticated enough for Web design gurus, you have come to the right place. The powerful Dreamweaver MX 2004 from Macromedia enables you to create almost any type of Web page. This chapter covers the Dreamweaver basics and introduces you to some of the program's essential tools.

What Is Dreamweaver and What Can It Do?

Dreamweaver MX 2004 is the industry standard for professional Web site design, production, and maintenance. Whether you're interested in creating a site for fun (such as an online photo album or a site devoted to one of your hobbies) or for business (an online store, for example), the flexible Dreamweaver interface provides simultaneous graphical and HTML editing. In other words, using Dreamweaver, you can lay out pages like an artist and also fine-tune the associated code like a programmer. The built-in Dreamweaver FTP features enable you to upload your site to the Web in a snap so that you can share your masterpieces with the world. And using built-in support for server-side features, such as ColdFusion (for integrating Web pages with databases) and PHP (a server-side scripting language for creating dynamic Web pages), you can go beyond simple Web sites to create robust, full-fledged Web applications.

Introducing the Document Window

Your primary workspace in Dreamweaver MX 2004 is the Document window. The Document window appears automatically when you start Dreamweaver. You have two choices:

✦ **To work with an existing Web page:** Select a Web page from the option list that appears on the left side of the start-up page.

✦ **To create a new Web page:** Click Create New HTML from the option list that appears in the middle of the screen.

Figure 19-1 shows you the option list that appears when you start Dreamweaver. Figure 19-2 shows you an example of the Document window.

By default, the start-up page you see in Figure 19-1 appears when you open Dreamweaver for the first time. If you want to turn off the start-up page, choose Edit⇨Preferences, click the General category, and deselect the Show Start Page check box.

In the Document window, you construct your individual Web pages by using panels, inspectors, and dialog boxes to format your work. You can view the Document window in Design view to work in a completely graphical environment, as shown in Figure 19-2, or you can choose Split view, where you can view both the design layout and the HTML source code for your page at the same time. (To display the Split view, choose View⇨Code and Design.)

Option lists

Expand/Collapse button

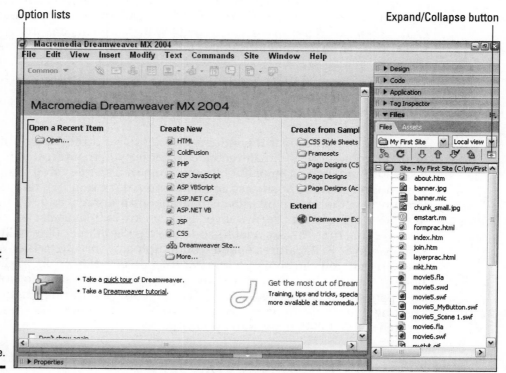

Figure 19-1:
Choose an option to create a new document or open an existing one.

The Standard toolbar — The Document toolbar

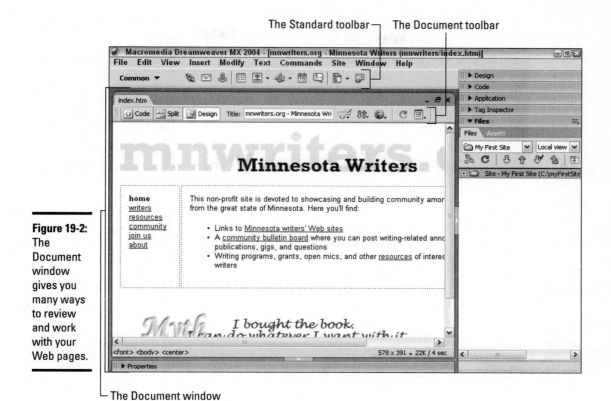

Figure 19-2: The Document window gives you many ways to review and work with your Web pages.

— The Document window

Examining Your Site with the Site Window

After you define a site in Dreamweaver (which I show you how to do in Book VI, Chapter 20), you can view that site in outline form by clicking the Site Map button that appears in the expanded Files panel. In Figure 19-3, you see the Expand/Collapse button you use to expand the Files panel and display the Site Map button; Figure 19-4 shows you an example of a site map.

As you can see in Figure 19-4, the Site window shows you a list of all the files in your site and a map of how those files connect. The Site window is also where you connect to the host server so that you can transfer, or *publish,* your site from your local computer to the Web. (You can find details in Book VI, Chapter 27 about publishing your site.) The Site window is just one built-in tool you can use in Dreamweaver. To see more tools, check out the following sections.

Expand/Collapse button

Figure 19-3:
Clicking the
Expand/
Collapse
button
displays
the Site
window.

Site Map button

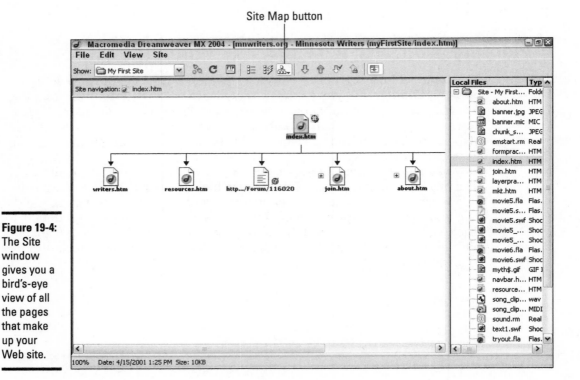

Figure 19-4:
The Site
window
gives you a
bird's-eye
view of all
the pages
that make
up your
Web site.

Choosing among Standard, Layout, and Expanded Tables Modes

You can work with content in your Document window using any of the following three modes (the first mode is good for general, all-purpose Web page design; the other two are useful for creating and editing HTML tables):

✦ **Standard mode:** This mode is the familiar — and only — WYSIWYG (What You See Is What You Get) graphical view through which you lay out pages in the Document window. To work in Standard mode, choose View⇨Table Mode⇨Standard Mode.

✦ **Layout mode:** This mode is specifically geared toward helping you use tables to design your Web page. The advantage of Layout mode is that it provides a simpler interface for drawing and editing tables and table cells. Using Layout mode, you can draw tables and individual table cells by choosing Insert⇨Layout Objects⇨Layout Table and Insert⇨Layout Objects⇨Layout Cell, respectively. To work in Layout mode, choose View⇨Table Mode⇨Layout Mode.

✦ **Expanded Tables mode:** In this mode, Dreamweaver displays your tables surrounded by nice crisp borders that make selecting, moving, and resizing your tables easier. To work in Expanded Tables mode, choose View⇨Table Mode⇨Expanded Tables Mode.

If you don't see the Layout mode or Expanded Tables mode buttons, choose View⇨Toolbars⇨Document to display the Document toolbar.

Exploring Toolbar Buttons

Dreamweaver provides you with two toolbars, the Standard toolbar and the Document toolbar, both of which are packed with useful buttons you can use to create and edit your Web pages quickly.

✦ **The Standard toolbar:** You can view the Standard toolbar by choosing View⇨Toolbars⇨Standard. This toolbar displays buttons you can use to create new Web pages, open existing Web pages, cut and paste text, and perform other common word-processing operations. Refer to Figure 19-2 to see what the Standard toolbar looks like.

✦ **The Document toolbar:** You can view the Document toolbar by choosing View⇨Toolbars⇨Document. (You can see an example of the Document toolbar in Figure 19-2.) You use the buttons in the Document toolbar to work with Dreamweaver Web documents. Table 19-1 gives you a run-down of the Document toolbar buttons.

Table 19-1	Documented-Related View Buttons
Name	*What You Can Do*
Show Code View button	View full-screen HTML page code
Show Code and Design View button	View HTML page code and Document window at the same time

(continued)

Table 19-1 *(continued)*

Name	What You Can Do
Show Design View button	View full-screen Document window
No Browser Check Errors button	Click and then select Check Browser Support and Show All Errors to specify target browser and view errors, respectively
File Management button	Click and then select Get to retrieve files from the Web site host or select Put to send files to the host
Preview/Debug in Browser button	Click and select to preview or debug in Internet Explorer or Netscape Navigator
Refresh button	Click to refresh (redisplay) the contents of the Document window
View Options button	Click and select to view visual drawing aids, such as rulers, grids, and more

Using Panels, Bars, and Properties Inspectors

You can use Dreamweaver panels, bars, and Properties inspectors to enter details about all aspects of your Web site. These interfaces offer areas where you can add and format page features, set up navigation and behaviors, and manage your workflow.

Panels and bars

Panels and bars typically provide information about all instances of a particular page feature. For example, you can use the Insert bar to add elements to your Web page quickly and easily. Using the Insert bar named Forms, you can click a button to add an HTML form to your Web page and then build your form by clicking buttons to add elements such as text fields, check boxes, and radio buttons until your form looks just the way you want it. In Figure 19-5, you see an example of the Forms bar.

You can choose Insert from the Dreamweaver main menu to insert any element you see displayed on the Insert bar. For example, you can choose Insert⇨Forms to insert form elements.

Dreamweaver offers several Insert bars, including the Common, Layout, Forms, HTML, and Application panels. In addition, Dreamweaver offers several additional panels. For example, in Figure 19-5, you see the Assets panel on the right side of the screen.

You can open panels and bars by choosing Window from the Dreamweaver main menu and then selecting the desired panel name (such as Insert, CSS Styles, Behaviors, Frames, or Layers) from the menu. To close a panel, you can right-click the panel and choose Close Panel Group from the shortcut menu that appears. To close all panels and bars, choose Window⇨ Hide Panels.

Click the arrow to see additional panels.

Forms panel

Forms-related buttons

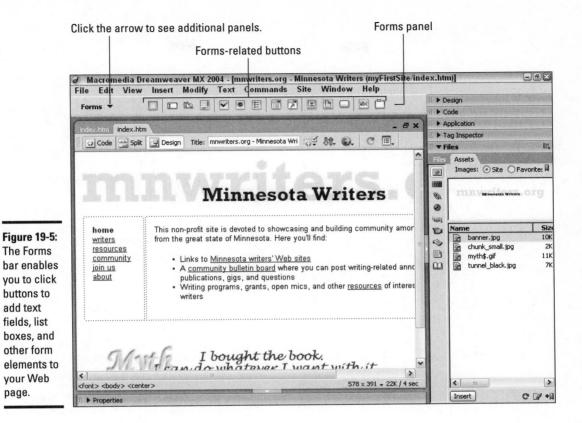

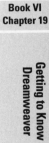

Figure 19-5:
The Forms bar enables you to click buttons to add text fields, list boxes, and other form elements to your Web page.

Properties inspectors

A Properties inspector is unique to the individual document object it represents, and it contains details on attributes of the object. For example, selecting text on a page opens the Properties inspector with options for formatting the text size, font, color, link, and other information. To make certain that the Properties inspectors are shown in the Document window, choose Window⇨Properties. You see an example of a Properties inspector showing options for formatting text in Figure 19-6.

Figure 19-6:
Use Properties inspectors to customize document objects.

Chapter 20: Creating Your First Web Site with Dreamweaver

In This Chapter

✔ **Starting Dreamweaver**

✔ **Creating a new site or document**

✔ **Adding content to your document**

✔ **Saving and previewing your document in a Web browser**

Developing a Web page from scratch is an easy task with Dreamweaver. In this chapter, you see a five-minute procedure for creating a simple Web page.

Starting Dreamweaver

Each time you start Dreamweaver, a list of options appears in the Document window — options you can click to open existing documents or create new documents. To start Dreamweaver, you do the following:

✦ **In Windows:** Choose Start⇨All Programs⇨Macromedia⇨Macromedia Dreamweaver MX 2004.

✦ **In Mac OS:** Click the Application button on the Launcher and click the Dreamweaver program icon.

Creating a New Site

In Dreamweaver, creating a new site means specifying a location where you want your documents (Web pages) and dependent files, called *assets* (such as images and audio files), to be stored. After you create a new site, you can use the powerful Dreamweaver site-related features, such as viewing a graphical site map and automatically checking site links.

To create a new site, follow these steps:

1. **Start Dreamweaver and choose Site⇨Manage Sites.**

The Manage Sites window appears.

2. **Click the New button in the Manage Sites window and then choose Site from the menu that appears.**

A Site Definition dialog box, similar to the one you see in Figure 20-1, appears. Note that the Advanced tab is displayed by default.

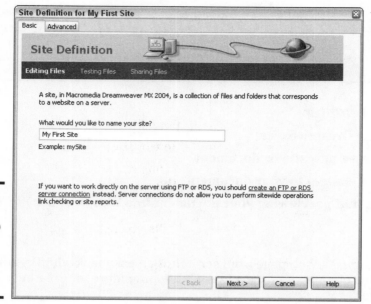

Figure 20-1:
Click the
Basic tab to
create a
new Web
site step
by step.

Click the Basic tab in the Site Definition dialog box to walk through the process of defining your site in a series of wizard-like steps.

3. In the Site Definition dialog box, enter a name for your site in the What Would You Like To Name Your Site? text box.

The name can contain spaces. For example, My First Site is a valid site name.

4. Click Next.

The Editing Files, Part 2 screen appears.

5. Choose Yes if you plan to add a server-side program (such as a database-accessing script written in PHP) to your Web site; otherwise, choose No.

If you choose Yes, a drop-down list appears. Choose the server-side technology you want to include in your Web site.

6. Click Next.

The Editing Files, Part 3 screen appears.

7. Choose whether you want to work with your files locally (on your computer) or remotely (on the Web server). After you choose, specify the location where you want to store your site files.

You can either type the fully qualified name of a folder in the text field provided or click the folder button and browse to locate an existing folder.

8. Click Next.

The Sharing Files screen appears.

9. Select a remote connection option, such as FTP, from the drop-down list.

Depending on the option you choose, additional options appear. For example, if you select FTP, additional options for that FTP address, remote folder, login, and password appear. Follow the instructions you see on the Sharing Files screen to make selections for all additional options that appear.

10. **Click Next.**

The Sharing Files, Part 2 screen appears.

11. **Choose whether you want to enable file check-in.**

Checking files in and out locks those files, preventing two people from making changes to the same file at the same time.

12. **Click Next.**

Book VI
Chapter 20

Creating Your First
Web Site with
Dreamweaver

A summary of the site definition details you specified in Steps 3 through 11 appears for your review.

If you want to make changes to the site definition details you see, you can click the Back button or the Advanced tab.

13. **Click Done.**

The Manage Sites dialog box reappears.

14. **Click the Done button in the Manage Sites dialog box.**

The folder (and existing files, if any) you specified in Step 7 appears in the Files panel, as shown in Figure 20-2.

15. **Click OK.**

The Manage Sites dialog box reappears.

16. **Click the Done button in the Manage Sites dialog box.**

Figure 20-2: After you define a site in Dreamweaver, site-related operations, such as getting and putting files, become available.

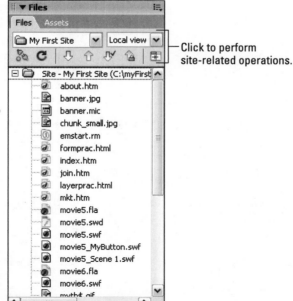

789

If you specified existing files in Step 7, you can view them in the Files panel by selecting Local View from the drop-down list in the Files panel.

You can specify much more information about your Dreamweaver site than the site's name and location. To specify additional information, such as the location of your Web server, choose Site➪Manage Sites, select the site name that you specified in Step 3, and then click the Edit button. In the Site Definition dialog box that appears, choose any of the categories you see on the left side of the screen (check out Figure 20-1 to see the categories) to specify additional site-related information.

Creating a New Document

Creating a new document means creating a new Web page or dependent file to save in your site folder. (Dreamweaver refers to Web pages and other separate files, such as scripts you include in your Web pages, as *documents*.) To create a new document, follow these steps:

1. **Choose File➪New.**

The New Document dialog box, as shown in Figure 20-3, appears.

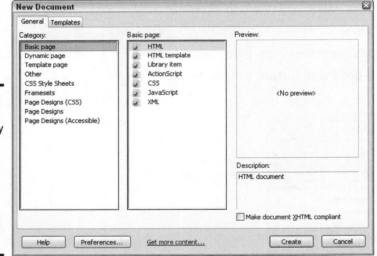

Figure 20-3: You can create many different types of Web documents by using the New Document dialog box.

2. **Select the type of document you want to create.**

To create a simple Web page, select Basic Page from the Category list and select HTML from the Basic Page list.

3. **Click the Create button.**

A new, untitled HTML document appears in the Document window.

Adding Content to a Document

After you start Dreamweaver, create a new site, and create a new document, you're ready to add content (such as text, links, or images) to that document, as shown in Figure 20-4.

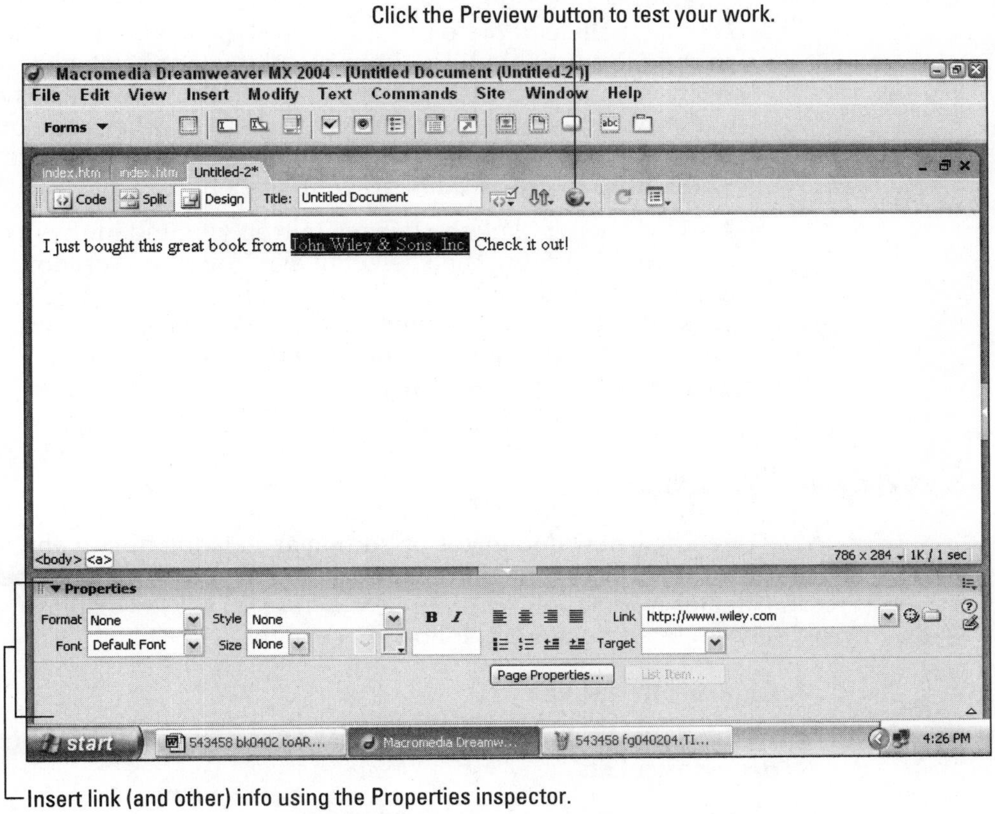

Click the Preview button to test your work.

Figure 20-4:
Inserting images and defining links in a Dreamweaver document is point-and-click easy.

Insert link (and other) info using the Properties inspector.

Chapters 21 through 25 of Book VI show you how to add many different kinds of cool content (including tables, frames, and animations) to your pages. To add content to a page, follow these steps:

1. **Switch to the untitled document.**

To switch in Windows, click the Untitled Document tab in the Document window. On a Macintosh, click the Untitled Document window.

2. **Add content and color to your page by doing as many (or as few) of the following procedures as you want:**

- **Choose a background color:** Choose Modify⊅Page Properties. Click the Appearance category and select a color from the Background color swatch palette. Click OK.

- **Specify a title:** Enter a title for your page in the Title text box at the top of the Document window. This title appears in the title bar of the browser window when your page is loaded.

- **Enter text:** Click your cursor in the Document window and start typing. Enter something compelling, riveting, or insightful; for example, "I just bought this great book from John Wiley & Sons, Inc."

- **Create a link:** Select the object (such as text or an image) you want to become the hyperlink; for example, select the text "John Wiley & Sons, Inc." A properties inspector appears at the bottom of the screen. (If it doesn't, choose Window⇨Properties.) In the Link text box, type the complete URL of the Web page you want the hyperlink to send the viewer to. For example, to have the link go to the John Wiley & Sons Web site, you would type **http://www.wiley.com** in the Link text box. If you want the link to go to another page on your site, enter the filename of the page in the Link text box; for example, enter **index.html** to create a link to your site's home page.

- **Add an image:** Click the Images button you find in the Insert Common panel and then select Image from the drop-down list that appears. Browse to find a GIF or JPEG image on your computer and click OK. (If the Insert Common panel isn't visible, choose Window⇨ Insert to display the Insert bar and then select Common from the Insert bar's drop-down list.)

Saving a Document

After opening a new document or editing an existing document, you must save your work. A document must be saved in your site folder before you can transfer it from your computer to a host server for display on the Web. To save an open document, follow these steps:

1. **Choose File⇨Save.**

2. **At the Save As dialog box, browse to your site folder in the Save In drop-down list.**

   This folder might already be selected.

3. **In the File Name area, enter a name for your document followed by the extension .html.**

4. **Click Save.**

To save a site, you simply save each document contained in the site. Also save all dependent files, such as images, that you use in your documents.

Previewing a Document in a Web Browser

After you create or modify a document, preview it in a Web browser to see how it will appear after you publish it. (For the steps on publishing your document, check out Book VI, Chapter 27.) To preview a document in a Web browser, follow these steps:

1. **Click the Preview in Browser button in the Document window.**

Alternatively, you can choose File➪Preview in Browser.

A list of installed browsers appears.

2. **From the list that appears, select the browser you want to use to preview the page.**

Dreamweaver launches the selected browser preloaded with your page.

3. **If you go online, you can click any links that you might have inserted to ensure that they open the appropriate Web site; click the Back button in your browser to return to your page.**

If the browser installed on your machine doesn't appear in the Preview in Browser list, choose File➪Preview in Browser➪Edit Browser List to display the Preferences dialog box. Then click the + you see next to Browsers and type the name and the fully qualified name of a browser-executable file in the Name and Application fields, respectively. Select either Primary Browser (if you want Dreamweaver to open the browser by default) or Secondary Browser (if the browser is just one of many browsers you want Dream-weaver to work with). When you finish, click OK to add the specified browser to the Preview in Browser list.

Book VI
Chapter 20

Creating Your First
Web Site with
Dreamweaver

Chapter 21: Creating Basic Web Pages

In This Chapter

✔ Adapting the Document window to your personal preferences

✔ Changing page properties

✔ Adding text and line breaks

✔ Working with images

✔ Using links and anchors

✔ Working with tables

The most significant (and, fortunately, the easiest) process in building a Web site is creating the individual pages that convey the site's content. Even if you plan to create an ultra-hip site chock-full of animation and interactive forms, the vast majority of your site-building efforts are spent constructing basic Web pages composed of words and images. This chapter shows you how to set up, color, and name individual Web pages. You also discover how to add basic elements, such as text, graphics, and tables, to your pages.

Customizing What You See in the Document Window

Dreamweaver offers you complete control over how you work in the Document window by providing two guide tools — rulers and a grid — to help you accurately lay out your work. You can customize a variety of guide tool attributes, such as ruler increments and grid snapping, to suit your personal preferences and speed Web page development.

You can customize almost all aspects of the Dreamweaver environment by specifying default settings in the Preferences dialog box. To open the Preferences dialog box, choose Edit➪Preferences.

Turning rulers on and off

Using rulers in the Document window can help you measure and numerically position page elements. Toggle the Ruler on and off by choosing View➪ Rulers➪Show.

Moving and resetting the origin

By default, the origin, or (0,0) coordinate, of a Dreamweaver ruler is set to the upper-left corner of the Document window. Reposition it to any coordinate in the Document window by clicking the origin cross hairs and dragging them to new coordinates. Reset the origin to its default position by choosing View➪Rulers➪Reset Origin.

Changing ruler measurement units

You can change the ruler's measuring increment by choosing View➪Rulers and then choosing Pixels, Inches, or Centimeters from the submenu.

Viewing the grid

Dreamweaver provides a Document window grid that can assist you in visually positioning and aligning page elements. You can toggle the grid on and off by choosing View➪Grid➪Show Grid.

Activating and deactivating grid snapping

The Document window grid offers a snapping feature that causes a page element to automatically align precisely with the snap-to points you define. You can toggle grid snapping on and off by choosing View➪Grid➪Snap to Grid.

You can adjust how the grid appears in the Document window through the Grid Settings dialog box. To do so, open the Grid Settings dialog box by choosing View➪Grid➪Grid Settings and changing any (or all) of the attributes that appear. When you finish, click Apply to view the effect of your changes. Click OK to accept the changes and close the dialog box.

Establishing Page Properties

The Page Properties dialog box provides you with control over several key page properties, grouped into five categories:

✦ Appearance

✦ Links

✦ Headings

✦ Title/Encoding

✦ Tracing Image

The kinds of page properties you can set by using the Page Properties dialog box include the title of the page, page background color, link colors, page margins, and much more. *Note:* Selections apply only to the current page, not the entire site.

Open a Page Properties dialog box similar to the one you see in Figure 21-1 by choosing Modify➪Page Properties or by clicking the Page Properties button that appears in the Properties inspector.

If you're working with a document containing frames, all five categories might not appear in the Page Properties dialog box.

As you see in Figure 21-1, the Appearance properties appear by default. Click the Links, Headings, Title/Encoding, or Tracing Image category to display (and edit) additional properties related to your Web site's appearance or to trace an existing image onto a Web page.

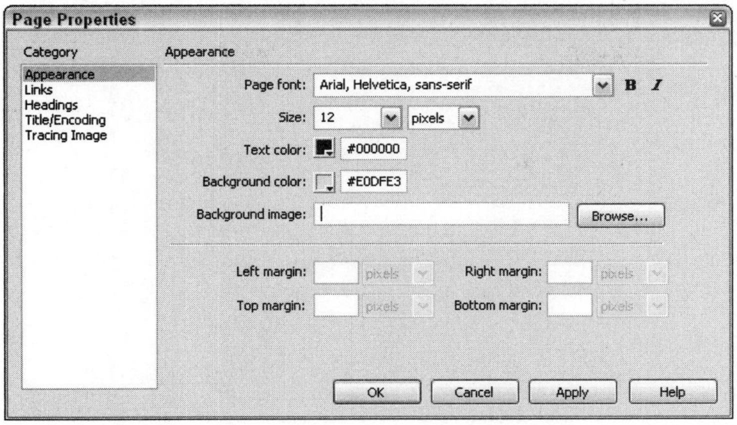

Figure 21-1: Use the Page Properties dialog box to specify settings such as background and font size.

Using the Page Properties dialog box, you can make changes to any of the following:

✦ **Appearance:** Click the Appearance category in the Page Properties dialog box (shown in Figure 21-1) to change font size and color, specify a background color and image, and define margins.

 • **Page Font:** Select a font from this drop-down list. Clicking the Bold or Italics button applies bold or italics formatting, respectively, to the selected font.

 • **Size:** Select a font size from this drop-down list; select a measurement (such as Pixels) from the drop-down list to the right.

 • **Text Color:** You can click the color box to select a text color by pointing and clicking, or you can enter a hexadecimal RGB value in the text box.

 • **Background Color:** You can click the color box to select a background color by pointing and clicking, or you can enter a hexadecimal RGB value in the text box.

 • **Background Image:** Click Browse (Windows) or Choose (Mac) to locate the image file that you want to appear as the Document window background. If the image is smaller than the available background area, it *tiles* (repeats in checkerboard fashion) to fill the background.

 • **Left Margin, Top Margin, Right Margin, Bottom Margin:** These Property text boxes set up margins that affect how your page appears in Microsoft Internet Explorer. Enter a whole number for the number of pixels of space you want on the left and top sides of your document.

✦ **Links:** Click the Links category in the Page Properties dialog box (shown in Figure 21-2) to define the way your links appear.

 • **Link Font:** Select a link font from this drop-down list. Click the Bold or Italics button to apply bold or italics formatting, respectively, to the selected font.

 • **Size:** Select the font size from this drop-down list; from the drop-down list to the right, select a measurement, such as pixels or inches (in).

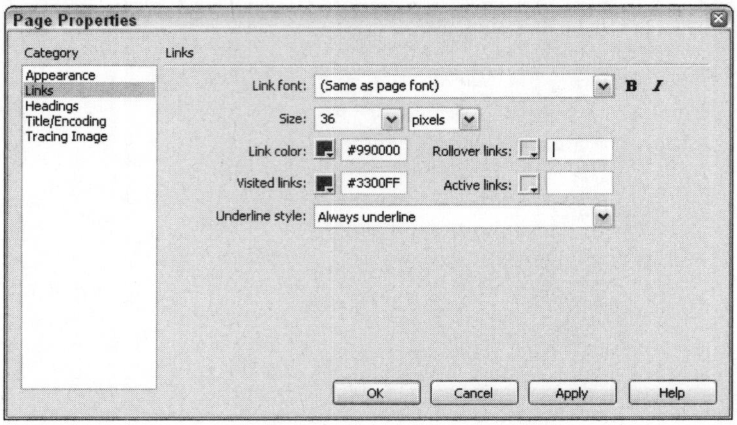

Figure 21-2:
The options in the Links category enable you to customize the way links appear in your pages.

- **Link Color, Visited Links, Rollover Links, and Active Links:** Click the color box to select a color from the color palette that appears. Alternatively, you might enter a hexadecimal RGB color code directly into any color text box.

- **Underline Style:** Use this drop-down list to select an underline style (such as Always Underline or Never Underline).

✦ **Headings:** Click the Headings category in the Page Properties dialog box (shown in Figure 21-3) to define the way that headings appear in your Web pages.

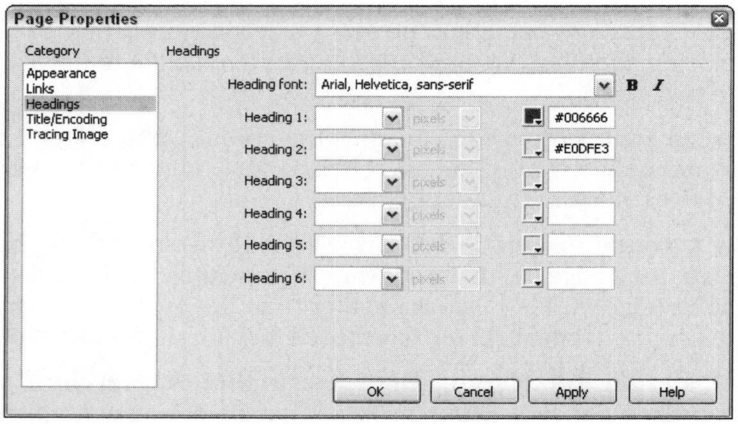

Figure 21-3:
The options in the Headings category enable you to customize headings in your pages.

- **Heading Font:** Select a font for your headings from this drop-down list. Click the Bold or Italics button to apply bold or italics formatting, respectively, to the selected font.

- **Heading 1 through 6:** For each individual heading level, from 1 to 6, you can select a different size and color. Click the Size drop-down list to select a font size for the heading; then click the drop-down list you find next to Size to specify a measurement, such as pixels or inches (in). To specify a color, you can click the color box or enter a hexadecimal RGB value in the text box.

✦ **Title/Encoding:** Click the Title/Encoding category in the Page Properties dialog box to specify a title for your Web page and to select a language for character encoding.

- **Title:** Enter a page title in the text box. This title appears in the title bar area of the window both during construction in Dreamweaver and when the page is viewed through a Web browser.

- **Encoding:** Select a language for character encoding of text on your page from this drop-down list. For example, if you want to create Web pages capable of displaying text in Korean, select Korean (EUC-KR); if you want to display text in English, select Western (Latin1). Click Reload to display the page with the changed encoding.

✦ **Tracing Image:** Select the Tracing Image category in the Page Properties dialog box to specify a helpful tracing image.

- **Tracing Image:** Click Browse (Windows) or Choose (Mac) to locate the image file you want to use as a guide for laying out your Web page in the Document window. This feature is handy for developers who prefer to mock up a portion of their Web page design in a graphics program and then re-create that design on their Web pages. Tracing images appear only in Dreamweaver as a pattern to help guide you in creating a Web page design; the tracing images never appear on the finished Web page.

- **Image Transparency:** Drag the slider to adjust the visibility level of the tracing image. At 0 percent, the tracing image is invisible; at 100 percent, the image is opaque.

Click Apply to view the effect of any property you change. Click OK to accept your changes and close the Page Properties dialog box.

Even if you choose to use a background image, select a complementary background color — the background color shows while the background image is downloading in the visitor's browser.

Entering Text

You can enter and manipulate text on a Web page in Dreamweaver by using similar procedures to those you use when working with a word-processing document.

Inserting text

To enter text on a page, click in the Document window and begin typing. Your mouse pointer appears as a blinking cursor that moves along with the text you enter. When you reach the end of a line, the text automatically wraps to the next line. Dreamweaver automatically adds the associated code for your new text to the HTML for the page.

Inserting a line break

When you want to start a new line in a word-processing program, you hit the Enter key. In Dreamweaver, you create a line break by pressing Shift+Enter or by choosing Insert➪HTML➪Special Characters➪Line Break. Alternatively, you might click the Characters button you find on the Insert HTML panel. Dreamweaver places the cursor at the start of the next line and creates the line break HTML code for the page.

If you want to view the Insert HTML panel, as shown in Figure 21-4, choose Window➪Insert➪HTML.

Figure 21-4: The Insert HTML panel allows you to add line breaks (and much more).

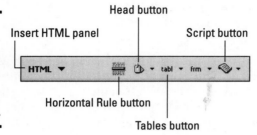

Head button

Insert HTML panel

Script button

Horizontal Rule button

Tables button

Deleting text and line breaks

To delete text and line breaks from a page, in the Document window, select the item that you want to delete and press Backspace or Delete on your keyboard.

Modifying text

You can modify how text appears on a page by editing its font, size, color, alignment, and other attributes.

To modify text in the Document window, drag your mouse to select the text you want to modify. The Properties inspector appears with options for formatting text, as shown in Figure 21-5. (If the Properties inspector doesn't show up, choose Window➪Properties to open it.) On the Properties inspector, modify any of the following properties:

✦ **Format:** Select a default text style from this drop-down list. These styles are relative, not absolute. Heading 1 is the largest style and Heading 6 is the smallest, but none of the headings correlates with a specific pixel size.

✦ **Font:** Select a font face from the drop-down list. Choosing Edit Font List from the font drop-down list allows you to add to the Font drop-down list any other fonts you might have installed on your computer.

✦ **Style:** Select a style sheet from the drop-down list. (None is the default.) You can create, edit, rename, or attach an existing style sheet to any portion of text by clicking the New, Edit, Rename, and Attach Style Sheet options, which appear at the bottom of the drop-down list.

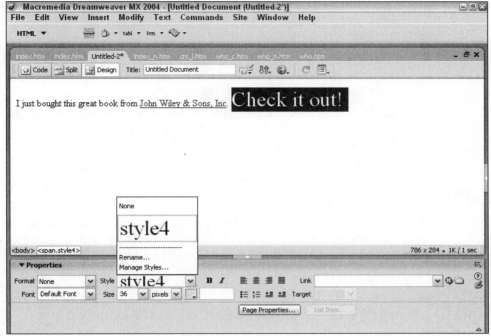

Figure 21-5:
You can change the format, color, and alignment of any text on your page using the Properties inspector.

✦ **Size:** Select a font size from the drop-down list. The options include specific font sizes (from 9 through 36), as well as descriptions ranging from xx-small (xx-small corresponds to 1 in previous versions of Dreamweaver) to xx-large (xx-large corresponds to 7 in previous versions of Dreamweaver). Choosing the Smaller font size setting displays text one font size smaller than the previously specified font size. Alternatively, choosing the Larger setting displays text one font size larger than the previously specified font size.

✦ **Color:** Click the color box that you find next to the Size drop-down list and select a text color from the Web-safe color palette that appears. Alternatively, you might enter a hexadecimal color code directly in any color code text box. (To set the default text color for a page, check out the section, "Establishing Page Properties," earlier in this chapter.)

✦ **Bold or Italic:** Click the Bold button to apply bold to your selected text. Click the Italic button to italicize your selected text. You can click either button or both.

✦ **Alignment:** Click an alignment button to align your text. Choices are Left, Center, Right, and Justify.

✦ **Link:** Type a URL in this text box to transform text into a hyperlink.

✦ **Target:** From the drop-down list, select one of the following: _blank (opens link in a new window), _parent (opens link in the parent of the currently opened window), _self (opens link in the opened window), and _top (opens link in the top-level window, replacing frames, if any).

✦ **List:** Click the Unordered List icon next to the Target text box to transform text into an unordered (bulleted) list; click the Ordered List icon to transform text into an ordered (numbered) list.

✦ **Placement:** Click the Text Outdent icon that you find next to the Ordered List icon to outdent (decrease the indent of) selected text; click the Text Indent icon to indent selected text.

✦ **List Item:** Click this button (which becomes active after you select a bulleted or numbered list item) to edit list properties such as the automatic starting number of a numbered list.

Manipulating Images

Next to entering text, manipulating images on a Web page is probably the most common Dreamweaver function you perform. You can add or delete an image and modify its properties to create an aesthetically pleasing layout that effectively conveys the information you want to deliver to the user.

To see how to place an image on the background of your page, check out the section, "Establishing Page Properties," earlier in this chapter.

Inserting an image

To insert an image on a page, follow these steps:

1. **Choose Insert⇨Image.**

Alternatively, you can click the Insert Image button from the Insert Common panel. (If the panel doesn't appear, display it by choosing Window⇨Insert and then clicking the Common tab.)

2. **In the Select Image Source dialog box (shown in Figure 21-6), click the image you want to insert.**

If the image is outside the current folder, click the arrow tab beside the Look In drop-down list and browse to select the file you want.

3. **Click OK to insert the image.**

Note: Every image you want to include on a Web page must reside within the folder of the current site. If you attempt to insert an image from another location, Dreamweaver asks whether you want to copy the image to the current site root. Click Yes. In the Copy File As dialog box, you can enter a new name for the image in the File Name text box or accept the current name, and then click Save.

Select the Preview Images check box at the bottom of the Select Image Source dialog box, as shown in Figure 21-6, to view a thumbnail image in the Image Preview area of the dialog box before you select the image for insertion. The preview area also tells you the size of the image and the expected download time.

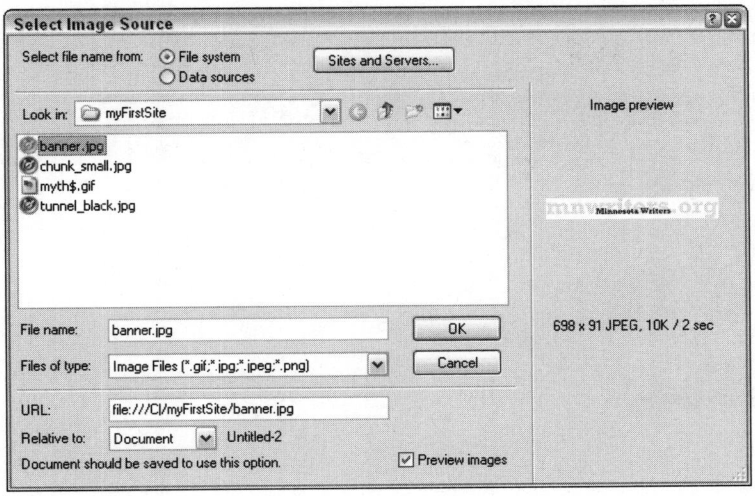

Select Image Source

Select file name from: ⦿ File system ○ Data sources   [Sites and Servers...]

Look in: 📁 myFirstSite

🔘 banner.jpg
🔘 chunk_small.jpg
🖼 myth$.gif
🔘 tunnel_black.jpg

File name: banner.jpg   [OK]

Files of type: Image Files (*.gif;*.jpg;*.jpeg;*.png)   [Cancel]

URL: file:///C|/myFirstSite/banner.jpg

Relative to: Document ▾ Untitled-2

Document should be saved to use this option.   ☑ Preview images

Image preview

Minnesota Writers

698 x 91 JPEG, 10K / 2 sec

Figure 21-6: Select an image to insert on your page from the Select Image Source dialog box.

Deleting an image

To delete an image from a page, click the image in the Document window to select it, and then press the Delete key on your keyboard.

Modifying an image

You can modify how an image appears on a page by editing its size and alignment, adding a border, and changing other attributes.

To modify an image, click the image in the Document window to select it. If the Properties inspector doesn't appear, choose Window⇔Properties to open it.

To see all the options for images that the Properties inspector offers, click the expand/contract arrow in the lower-right corner of the inspector. (Clicking the arrow a second time displays fewer options.) Alternatively, you can double-click anywhere on the inspector to display more or fewer options.

As shown in Figure 21-7, you can modify any of the following properties:

✦ **Name the image:** On the Image Properties inspector, enter a name in the text box next to the thumbnail image. (Naming an image is important if you want to refer to that image by using a scripting language, such as JavaScript.)

✦ **Resize the image:** Click and drag a sizing handle to change the dimensions of the image. To resize the image and maintain the same proportions, hold down the Shift key as you drag a sizing handle. Alternatively, you can change the numbers (representing pixels) you see in the W (width) and H (height) text boxes to change the image's size.

✦ **Change the image file:** On the Properties inspector, enter a different filename in the Src text box (or click the file icon to browse for image files).

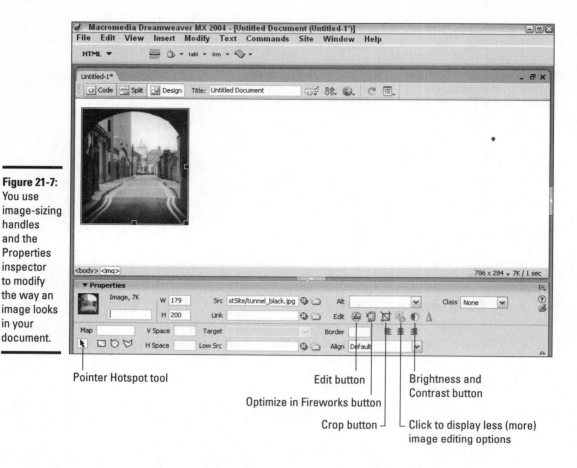

Figure 21-7: You use image-sizing handles and the Properties inspector to modify the way an image looks in your document.

Pointer Hotspot tool

Edit button

Optimize in Fireworks button

Crop button

Brightness and Contrast button

Click to display less (more) image editing options

✦ **Make the image a link:** On the Properties inspector, enter a URL in the Link text box. If you like, you can specify a target for the link by selecting an option from the Target drop-down list.

✦ **Specify alternative text for the image:** On the Properties inspector, enter alternative text in the Alt text box. (Specifying alternative text ensures that when viewers' browsers don't — or can't — display the image; some meaningful text appears instead.)

✦ **Edit the image:** On the Properties inspector, click the buttons you see next to Edit (check out Figure 21-7) to perform the following functions:

• **Edit:** Click the Edit button to edit the image by using an external image-editing program.

Dreamweaver doesn't enable you to edit images directly. Instead, clicking the Edit button opens the image-editing program that's installed on your computer. To specify a new image-editing program, choose Edit➪Edit with External Editor. In the Preferences dialog box that appears, choose File Types/Editors from the Category list. Choose an image extension (.gif, .jpg, or .png) from the Extensions list. Then choose a program from the Editors list and click the Make Primary button. You can add a new editor by clicking the add (+) button. Click OK to apply your changes and close the dialog box.

- **Optimize with Fireworks:** Click this button to reduce the image size by using Fireworks, an image-editing program from Macromedia. You must have Fireworks installed on your computer to use this feature.

- **Crop:** To crop a selected image, click this button, and then move and drag the dashed handles that appear over the image to specify which section of the image you want to crop. When you finish, click the Crop button again to crop the image to the specified dimensions.

- **Brightness and contrast:** Clicking this button allows you to adjust both the brightness and contrast of the image.

✦ **Create a hotspot:** A *hotspot* is a portion of an image that responds to a user's mouse click. To create a hotspot, click one of the hotspot tools (Rectangular, Oval, or Polygon). To create a hotspot on the image, click and drag the cross hair cursor that appears. In the Properties inspector, specify a link and a target.

Clicking the Pointer Hotspot Tool returns the cross hair pointer to a normal pointer, allowing you to move the hotspot around on the image.

✦ **Pad an image with spaces:** In the Properties inspector, enter a number in pixels in the V Space (V for vertical) text box for the space you want to appear at the top and bottom of the image; then enter a number in pixels in the H Space (H for horizontal) text box for the space you want to appear on either side of the image.

✦ **Specify a low source image.** Some Web designers like to specify a quick-loading, black-and-white "low source" version of each large image they work with. Doing so gives users a taste of what's to come while they wait for the real (large) image to download. To specify a low source image in the Properties inspector, enter in the Low Src text box the fully qualified name of an image file.

✦ **Add a border to the image:** On the Properties inspector, enter a number in the Border text box to add a border of that thickness to the image. Border thickness is measured in pixels.

✦ **Align the image:** On the Properties inspector, click an Alignment button to position the image on the page (or within a cell if the image is located in a table cell). Alignment button choices consist of Left, Center, and Right. To align an image with special word wrapping, select the image and choose one of the alignment options from the Align drop-down list, as shown in Table 21-1.

Table 21-1	Aligning an Image in Relation to Text
Alignment Option	*Effect on Image and Text Wrapping*
Browser Default	Same as Bottom alignment
Baseline	Same as Bottom alignment
Top	Aligns the image top with the highest other inline element
Middle	Aligns the image middle with the text baseline
Bottom	Aligns the image bottom with the text baseline

(continued)

Table 21-1 *(continued)*

Alignment Option	Effect on Image and Text Wrapping
Text Top	Aligns the image top with the text top
Absolute Middle	Aligns the image middle with the text middle
Absolute Bottom	Aligns the image bottom with the bottom of the text descenders
Left	Aligns the image flush left
Right	Aligns the image flush right

Dreamweaver doesn't offer image-editing functions, such as removing blemishes or red-eye, or adding drop shadows; you have to use a separate program, such as Macromedia Fireworks or Adobe Photoshop, to accomplish these tasks.

Working with Links

Linking your page to other Web pages enables you to direct visitors to related content on the Web. To insert a link, you must specify an image or some text to serve as the link; you must also specify the link location to which you want to send your visitors. The link can go to a page within your site or to a page elsewhere on the Web.

Inserting a link

To insert a link on a page, follow these steps:

1. **Select the text or image you want to make a link.**

   Doing so opens the Properties inspector for your text or image. If the Properties inspector doesn't appear, choose Window➪Properties to open it.

2. **In the Link text box of the Properties inspector, enter the target of the link (text or image) you created in Step 1.**

   The URL you specify can be any valid URL — for example, a Web page on your computer (`http://somePage.html`), on the Web (`www.someSite.com/somePage.html`), or even an e-mail address (`mailto:somebody@somewhere.com`).

   Alternatively, you might click the File Folder icon you see in the Properties inspector to display the Select File dialog box.

3. **Using the Select File dialog box, browse your computer to find a file, and then click Select to make that file the target of a link.**

To create an e-mail link quickly, click anywhere in your document and choose Insert➪Email Link. Specifying the same value for the Text and E-mail text boxes that appear allows folks who haven't configured their Web browsers to handle e-mail automatically to see the e-mail address on the page. Then, they can copy and paste the e-mail address information into their e-mail program of choice.

Deleting a link

To delete a link from a page, follow these steps:

1. **Select the text or image you want to remove the link from.**

   The Properties inspector for your text or image opens. If the Properties inspector doesn't appear, choose Window⇨Properties to open it.

2. **In the Properties inspector, delete the name of the link from the Link text box.**

Using named anchors

When you want to create a navigational link that connects users to not only a page but also a specific location on the page, you need to create a named anchor. *Named anchors* are frequently used for jumping to exact positions within large amounts of text so that users don't have to scroll through paragraph after paragraph to find the information they need. Setting up named anchors is especially useful when creating links from a directory or a table of contents to the content it presents.

Inserting a named anchor

Place an anchor anywhere on your Web page:

1. **In the Document window, click at the position you want to insert the named anchor.**

2. **Click the Named Anchor button on the Insert Common bar or choose Insert⇨Named Anchor.**

   If the Insert Common bar doesn't appear, open it by choosing Window⇨Insert⇨Common.

   The Insert Named Anchor dialog box appears.

3. **Type a name in the Anchor Name text box.**

4. **Click OK.**

You should insert the named anchor tag slightly above the actual position where you want the link to target. Doing so gives your targeted content a little padding on top. Otherwise, the top of your image or your first line of text appears flush with the top of the browser window.

Linking to a named anchor

To link to a named anchor, follow the procedure outlined in the section, "Inserting a link," earlier in this chapter, with the following modifications:

✦ **Linking to a named anchor on the current page:** In the Link text box of the Properties inspector, type a pound sign (#) followed by the anchor name.

✦ **Linking to a named anchor on a different page:** In the Link text box of the Properties inspector, type the HTML page name followed by a pound sign and then the anchor name.

As of this writing, the latest version of Netscape Navigator (version 7.1) supports linking to named anchors on the current page — but not on other pages.

Working with Tables

Adding a table to a Web page can help you lay out page elements more easily in the Document window. Tables consist of as many holding areas, or *cells,* as you like, and you can place virtually any Web element — such as text or an image — into a cell. Table cells are organized horizontally into *rows* and vertically into *columns.* Dreamweaver provides you with complete control over the size, position, color, and other attributes of your table. And you can edit these attributes at any time in the Properties inspector.

Inserting a table

To add a table, choose Insert⇨Table to open the Insert Table dialog box, shown in Figure 21-8. Alternatively, you might click the Insert Table button from the Insert Common panel. (If the panel doesn't appear, open it by choosing Window⇨Insert⇨Common.) Enter the following information in the Insert Table dialog box:

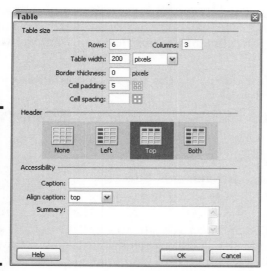

Figure 21-8: Use the Insert Table dialog box to specify which kind of table you want to add to your document.

✦ **Rows:** Enter a number in the text box for the number of rows in the table.

✦ **Columns:** Enter a number in the text box for the number of columns in the table.

✦ **Table Width:** Select Percent from the drop-down list and then enter a number (0–100) in the text box for the percentage of page width you want the entire table to occupy. Alternatively, select Pixels from the drop-down list and enter a number of pixels for the width of the entire table.

✦ **Border Thickness:** Enter a number in the text box for the width of the table borders in pixels. Entering 0 causes the borders to disappear.

✦ **Cell Padding:** Enter a number in the text box to specify how many pixels of padding you want between the inside edge of a cell and its contents.

✦ **Cell Spacing:** Enter a number in the text box to specify how many pixels of separation you want between cells.

✦ **Header:** Click an icon to enable row headings (Left), column headings (Top), both row and column headings (Both), or no headings (None).

✦ **Caption:** Enter text for a table caption.

✦ **Align Caption:** Use this drop-down list to select how you want your table caption aligned with respect to your table: top, bottom, left, right, or default (top).

✦ **Summary:** Enter text for an optional table summary. (Some devices, such as screen readers designed to help visually impaired folks surf the Web, don't display HTML tables; instead, they read and interpret summary information.)

Deleting a table

To delete a table from a page, click the border of the table to select it and then press the Backspace or Delete key. Dreamweaver removes the table from your page and deletes the associated code in the HTML for the page.

Storing Information in Table Cells

After you insert a table on a page, you can add or delete elements, such as text and images, in the table cells.

Adding an image to a cell

To add an image to a table cell, click to position the cursor in a table cell and choose Insert⇨Image. Browse and select an image you want to add to the cell and then click OK. (For more information on inserting images, flip to the section, "Inserting an image," earlier in this chapter.)

Adding text to a cell

To add text to a table cell, click to position the cursor in a table cell and type the text you want placed inside the cell.

Deleting an image from a cell

To delete an image from a table cell, select the image and press Backspace or Delete.

Deleting text from a cell

To delete text from a table cell, select the text and press Backspace or Delete.

CHECK IT OUT

Adjusting Page Size

When you design Web pages, you must consider how your target audiences will view them. People looking at your page might view it at any number of screen resolutions from 640 x 480 to 1024 x 768 (the standard factory-set resolution for many computers) or even higher. Your audience might also view your pages at low resolutions using WebTV or a hand-held computer. Because pages appear differently at different resolutions, Dreamweaver offers you the ability to build your pages for a variety of monitor resolutions. The higher the resolution, the larger the workspace appears in your Document window.

To size your pages, click the Window Size Indicator in the middle of the Status bar (which, in turn, is located along the bottom of the Document window) and select a standard size — for example, 640 x 480 — from the drop-down list. (Selecting the Edit Sizes option from the drop-down list allows you to specify any height and width dimensions you want.)

Chapter 22: Incorporating Interactive Images

In This Chapter

✔ Adding a link to an image

✔ Working with hotspots

✔ Adding color with Flash text

✔ Changing appearances with button rollovers (Flash buttons)

✔ Adding image rollovers

✔ Creating a navigation bar

*I*mages are great, but if you really want to add pizzazz to your Web site, consider adding interactive images to your pages. *Interactive images* are more than just pretty pictures: They change their appearance when users move their mouse pointers over them. The most popular types of interactive images, called *rollovers* and *hotspots,* serve as navigation buttons that enable users to move through the site.

Creating a Link from an Image

You can make an image interactive by simply making it a link. Clicking an image that's set up as a link causes the user to jump to another page in the site or on the Web. To create a link from an image, follow these steps:

1. **Select the image in the Document window.**

   The Properties inspector appears. (If the inspector doesn't appear, open it by choosing Window⇨Properties.)

2. **In the Properties inspector, click the Link folder to open the Select File dialog box.**

3. **Browse to select the page you want to link to.**

   If the link is outside the current folder, click the arrow tab beside the Look In drop-down list and browse to select the file you want. Alternatively, you can enter a Web address in the URL text box at the bottom of the Select File dialog box.

4. **Click OK.**

   The dialog box closes, and the link is activated.

Creating Clickable Hotspots

You can designate certain areas of an image as *hotspots* — active areas that a user can click to open a link to another Web page or activate some other behavior. Hotspots can be shaped like rectangles, circles, or polygons (irregular shapes).

Creating a hotspot

Use the following procedure to create a hotspot:

1. **Select the image to which you want to add a hotspot.**

The Properties inspector you see in Figure 22-1 appears. If the inspector doesn't appear, open it by choosing Window⇨Properties.

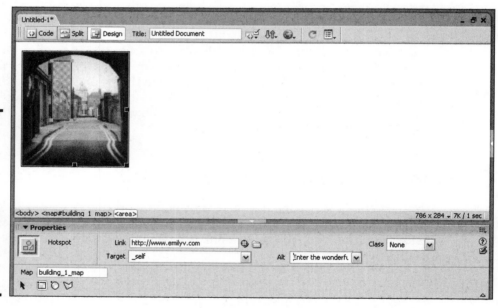

Figure 22-1: You can create hotspots anywhere on your image using the circle, rectangle, and polygon drawing tools.

If the bottom half of the Properties inspector isn't visible, click the Expand/Contract button (the arrow you see in the lower-right corner of Figure 22-1).

2. **In the Map area of the Properties inspector, click a Hotspot button for the shape you want to draw.**

You can choose from among a rectangle, circle, or polygon. Your mouse pointer becomes a cross hair cursor when you move it over the image.

3. **Draw the hotspot according to the shape you select:**

- **Circle or rectangle:** Click your cross hair cursor on the image and drag to create a hotspot. Release the mouse button when your hotspot reaches your desired dimensions. The area you draw is highlighted light blue.

- **Polygon:** Click your cross hair cursor on the image once for each point. Click the Arrow tool in the Properties inspector, if necessary, to close the shape. The area you draw is highlighted light blue.

4. **In the Properties inspector, supply the following information:**

- **Map:** Enter a unique name for the hotspot.

- **Link:** Enter a URL or the name of an HTML file you want to open when the user clicks the hotspot. Alternatively, you can click the folder and browse to select the link from your files.

  Completing this text box is optional. Instead, you might choose to attach a different kind of behavior to the hotspot.

  To attach a behavior other than a link to the hotspot, open the Behaviors panel by choosing Window⇨Behaviors. Then click the add (+) button in the Behaviors panel, which opens a menu of available behaviors, including Check Plug-In, Play Sound, Popup Message, Preload Images, and many others. Choose a behavior from the menu, complete the information in the dialog box that appears for your selected behavior, and click OK.

- **Target:** Select a target from the drop-down list if you entered a link in the Link text box. Your link appears in the selected target window. You can select from the following choices: _blank (opens a link in a new window), _parent (opens a link in the parent of the opened window), _self (opens a link in the opened window), and _top (opens a link in the top-level window, replacing frames, if any). If you have created frames, you can also select a frame name from this list.

- **Alt:** Enter the text you want to appear when the user moves the mouse pointer over the hotspot.

Modifying a hotspot

Use the following procedure to edit a hotspot:

1. **On an image in the Document window or table cell, click the hotspot you want to modify.**

   The Properties inspector appears. If the inspector doesn't appear, open it by choosing Window⇨Properties.

2. **Edit any information you want to change in the Properties inspector.**

3. **Reshape any hotspot by clicking the Arrow tool in the Properties inspector and dragging your mouse.**

4. **Delete a hotspot by clicking it and pressing the Delete key on your keyboard.**

Adding Text Rollovers (Flash Text)

A *text rollover* is text that changes colors when a user moves (rolls) the mouse pointer over it. One way to create text rollovers in Dreamweaver is by adding Flash text to your pages. *Flash text* and *Flash buttons* are so called because Dreamweaver implements these features using the same code that Flash — an animation program developed by Macromedia — uses.

Adding Flash text

To add Flash text, follow these steps:

1. **Click in the Document window on the part of the page or table cell where you want to add Flash text.**

2. **Click the Media button that you find on the Insert Common panel, shown in Figure 22-2, and then select Flash Text from the drop-down list that appears (or choose Insert⇨Media⇨Flash Text).**

   The Insert Flash Text dialog box appears. If the Insert Common panel doesn't appear, open it by choosing Properties⇨Insert and then selecting Common from the Insert bar drop-down list. Alternatively, you can choose Insert⇨Media⇨Flash Text.

Figure 22-2: Add a text rollover by selecting Flash Text from the Media drop-down list.

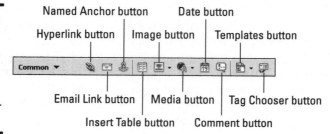

3. **In the Insert Flash Text dialog box, select a text font from the Font drop-down list.**

4. **Enter a point size for your text in the Size text box.**

5. **If you want, format the text.**

   You can click the Bold button and/or Italics button. You can also click an alignment button. Alignment choices are Left, Center, Right, and Justify.

6. **Select a color (initial color) and a rollover color (the color that the text changes to when the mouse cursor is over it) by clicking the color swatch in each area and selecting a color from the color palette that appears.**

7. **Enter your text in the Text box. Select the Show Font check box if you want to view the text you enter in your selected font.**

8. **In the Link text box, enter a URL or the name of the page that you want to appear when the user clicks the Flash text.**

   Alternatively, you can click the Browse button to select a page from your files.

9. **In the Target area, click the tab and select from the drop-down list a target window where the link will appear.**

   If you have created frames, you can select a frame name from this list, or you can select from the following choices: _blank (opens a link in a new window), _parent (opens a link in the parent of the currently opened window), _self (opens a link in the currently opened window), and _top (opens a link in the top-level window, replacing frames, if any).

10. **Select a background color by clicking the Bg Color swatch and selecting a color from the color palette that appears.**

    Your Flash text appears over the background color you choose.

11. **Enter a name for your Flash text component in the Save As text box or click the Browse button to select a name from your files.**

    Note: You must save Flash text with an `.swf` extension.

12. **Click OK to create your Flash text and close the dialog box.**

Changing Flash text

You can change a Flash text object you already created by simply double-clicking the object in the Document window. Doing so opens the Insert Flash Text dialog box where you can change your text as I describe in the section "Adding Flash text," a little earlier in this chapter. After you make changes to the Flash text object, you must resave the object.

Playing (previewing) Flash text

To play Flash text, select the text in the Document window to open the Properties inspector. In the Properties inspector, click the Play button to view your Flash text as it appears in the browser window. Click the Stop button when you finish.

Adding Button Rollovers (Flash Buttons)

Buttons that change appearance when a user moves the mouse pointer over them — called *button rollovers* — are so popular that Dreamweaver gives you a way to create them quickly and easily.

Adding a Flash button

To add a Flash button, follow these steps:

1. **Click in the Document window or table cell in which you want to add a Flash button.**

2. **Click the Media button that you find on the Insert Common panel (refer to Figure 22-2) and then select Flash Button from the drop-down list that appears.**

   An Insert Flash Button dialog box, similar to the one shown in Figure 22-3, appears.

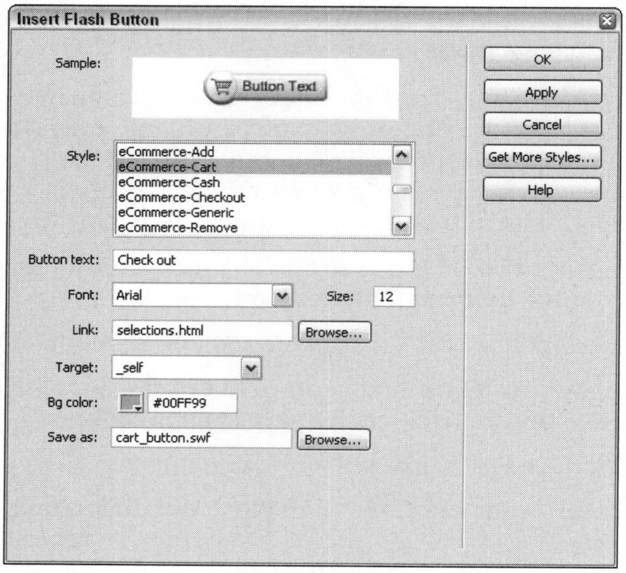

Figure 22-3:
You can add more than a dozen prebuilt rollover (Flash) buttons to your pages.

If the Insert Common panel doesn't appear, open it by choosing Properties⇨Insert and then selecting Common from the Insert bar drop-down list. Alternatively, you can choose Insert⇨Media⇨Flash Button.

3. **In the Insert Flash Button dialog box, scroll through the button selections in the Style list and click to select a style.**

   You can preview the style in the Sample area of the dialog box — just point to the sample with your mouse to see the Flash button play.

4. **If your selected button has a placeholder for text, enter in the Button Text box the text that you want to appear on the button.**

5. **Select a font for your Flash button text from the Font drop-down list.**

6. **Enter in the Size text box a point size for your text.**

7. **In the Link text box, enter a URL or the name for the page that you want to appear when the user clicks the Flash button.**

   Alternatively, you can click the Browse button to select a page from your files.

8. **Select a target window where the URL will appear from the Target drop-down list.**

   You can select from the following choices: _blank (opens a link in a new window), _parent (opens a link in the parent of the currently opened window), _self (opens a link in the currently opened window), and _top (opens a link in the top-level window, replacing frames, if any). If you have created frames, you can also select a frame name from this list.

9. **Select a background color by clicking the Bg Color swatch and selecting a color from the color palette that appears.**

   Your Flash button appears on top of the background color you select.

   Alternatively, you can enter a hexadecimal color code in the Bg Color text box.

10. **Enter a name for your Flash button in the Save As text box or click the Browse button to select a name from your files.**

    You must save the Flash button with an `.swf` extension.

11. **Click OK to create your Flash button and close the dialog box.**

You can download new Flash buttons from the Macromedia Dreamweaver Web site by clicking the Get More Styles button in the Insert Flash Button dialog box.

Changing a Flash button

To change a Flash button object that you have already created, simply double-click the object in the Document window. Doing so opens the Insert Flash Button dialog box where you can change your button as I describe in the section "Adding a Flash button," earlier in this chapter. After you make changes to the Flash button object, you must resave the object.

Modifying Flash button features

You can add additional features to a Flash button as follows:

1. **In the Document window, click to select the Flash button object that you want to enhance.**

   The Properties inspector appears. If the inspector doesn't appear, open it by choosing Window⇨Properties.

2. **In the Properties inspector, modify any of the available Flash button attributes.**

   For more information about Flash button attributes, check out the section, "Adding a Flash button," earlier in this chapter.

Playing (previewing) a Flash button

To see what a Flash button looks like in action, select the button in the Document window to open the Properties inspector. In the Properties inspector, click the Play button to view your Flash button as it appears in the browser window. Click the Stop button after you finish.

Inserting Image Rollovers

An *image rollover* (often just referred to as a *rollover*) is an image that changes whenever the user rolls the mouse pointer over it. Rollovers add interactivity to a Web page by helping users know what parts of the page link to other Web pages.

A rollover is actually two images — one for normal display on a page (the original image) and one that is modified for display when the image is rolled over (the rollover image). You can modify an image by changing the color or position, adding a glow or a shadow, or adding another graphic — such as a dog changing from sleeping to wide awake.

Insert a rollover by following these steps:

1. **Click inside the Document window or inside a table cell in which you want to insert the rollover.**

2. **Choose Insert⇨Image Objects⇨Rollover Image.**

The Insert Rollover Image dialog box, as shown in Figure 22-4, appears.

Figure 22-4:
Insert an
image
rollover.

3. **In the Insert Rollover Image dialog box, enter a name for the rollover in the Image Name text box.**

The rollover is referred to by this name in the HTML page code. Keep in mind that this rollover name refers to the combined original image/rollover image pair.

4. **Enter the name of the original image file in the Original Image text box or click the Browse button to select an image from your files.**

The original image appears on the page when the user's mouse pointer is *not* over the rollover.

5. **Enter the name of the Rollover Image file in the Rollover Image text box or click the Browse button to select an image from your files.**

The rollover image appears on the page when the user's mouse pointer is over the rollover.

6. **Select the Preload Rollover Image check box.**

This feature makes the rollover action appear without delay to users as they move the mouse pointer over the original image.

7. **In the When Clicked, Go to URL text box, enter a URL or the name of the page you want to appear when the user clicks the rollover.**

Alternatively, you can click the Browse button to select a page from your files.

8. **Click OK to accept your choices and close the dialog box.**

To check the rollover, preview your page in a browser by choosing File⇨ Preview in Browser or by clicking the Preview/Debug in Browser button that appears on the Document toolbar and using your mouse to point to the original image.

As with all images, you can't create the original image or the rollover image directly in Dreamweaver; you must use an image-editing program, such as Macromedia Fireworks or Adobe Photoshop.

Setting Up a Navigation Bar

A *navigation bar* is a group of buttons that users can access to move throughout your Web site. Buttons within a navigation bar might present users with options, such as moving backward, moving forward, returning to the home page, or jumping to specific pages within the site.

Each button in a navigation bar possesses properties similar to a rollover in that the button *changes state* — or appears differently — based on where the user is positioning the mouse pointer. However, a navigation bar button can possess as many as four different states:

Book VI
Chapter 22

Incorporating Interactive
Images

+ **Up:** The original state of the button.

+ **Over:** How the button appears when a user hovers the mouse pointer over it.

+ **Down:** How the button appears when a user clicks it.

+ **Over While Down:** How the button appears when the user moves the mouse pointer over it after clicking it.

A navigation bar differs from individual rollovers in that clicking a navigation bar button in the Down state causes all other buttons in the bar to revert to the Up state.

Creating a new navigation bar

To create a navigation bar, follow these steps:

1. **Select the Image button from the Insert Common panel and select Navigation Bar from the drop-down list that appears.**

If the panel doesn't appear, open it by choosing Properties⇨Insert and then selecting Common from the Insert bar drop-down list. Alternatively, you might choose Insert⇨Image Objects⇨Navigation Bar. The Insert Navigation Bar dialog box appears, shown in Figure 22-5.

2. **Enter a name for the first button in the Element Name text box.**

The new button appears in the Nav Bar Elements text box.

3. **For each state of the button — Up Image, Over Image, Down Image, and Over While Down Image — enter the name of the image file that you want to use in the associated text box.**

Alternatively, you can click the Browse button for each text box and select an image from your files. You must supply the Up Image. All other states are optional and can be left blank.

You don't need to use all four navigation bar button states — creating only Up and Down works just fine.

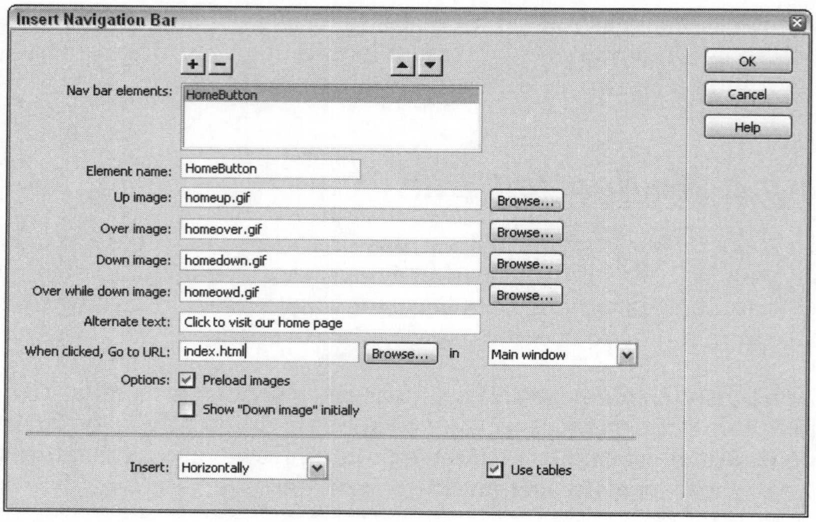

Insert Navigation Bar

OK
Cancel
Help

Nav bar elements: HomeButton

Figure 22-5:
You can
create as
many
buttons for
your
navigation
bar as you
want in the
Insert
Navigation
Bar
window.

Element name: HomeButton
Up image: homeup.gif — Browse...
Over image: homeover.gif — Browse...
Down image: homedown.gif — Browse...
Over while down image: homeowd.gif — Browse...
Alternate text: Click to visit our home page
When clicked, Go to URL: index.html — Browse... in Main window
Options: ☑ Preload images
☐ Show "Down image" initially

Insert: Horizontally ☑ Use tables

4. **In the When Clicked, Go to URL text box, enter a URL or the name for the page you want to appear when the user clicks the navigation bar button.**

   Alternatively, you can click the Browse button to select a page from your files.

5. **Select a target window where you want the URL to appear from the drop-down list.**

   If you aren't using frames, the only option is to use the Main window.

6. **Click the + button to add another navigation bar button.**

   Repeat Steps 2 through 5 to format the new button.

   Note: You can remove any button already created by clicking its name in the Nav Bar Elements text box and clicking the – button. Reorder the sequence of the buttons by clicking a button name in the Nav Bar Elements text box and clicking the up or down arrow.

7. **In the Options area, select the Preload Images check box if you want the rollover effects to appear without delay as soon as the page loads.**

8. **To set the current button to appear in the Down state when the user first sees the navigation bar, select the Show "Down Image" Initially check box in the Options area.**

9. **From the Insert drop-down list, select whether you want to position the navigation bar Horizontally or Vertically.**

10. **To set up the button images in a table format, select the Use Tables check box.**

11. **Click OK to accept your choices and close the dialog box.**

TIP

To check the navigation bar, you must preview your page in a browser. Choose File➪Preview in Browser or click the Preview/Debug in Browser button and use your mouse to point to the buttons.

Modifying a navigation bar

To change elements of a navigation bar that you already created, choose Modify⇨Navigation Bar, which opens the Modify Navigation Bar dialog box where you can make edits.

The Modify Navigation Bar dialog box is nearly identical to the Insert Navigation Bar dialog box (refer to Figure 22-5), except that you can no longer change the orientation of the navigation bar and the Use Tables check box is inactive.

Chapter 23: Adding Multimedia Objects

In This Chapter

✔ **Adding audio and video**

✔ **Embedding and linking video**

✔ **Incorporating other media (ActiveX controls, Java applets, and Flash movies)**

*I*f you want to understand and appreciate the power of adding video — streaming or downloadable — to your Web site, just take a peek at sites such as CNN (`www.cnn.com`). And for the talk-radio and music lovers among you, sites such as National Public Radio (`www.npr.org`) demonstrate how you can effectively use audio on your pages.

This chapter shows you how to incorporate both video and audio — as well as other multimedia objects, such as Java applets, Flash movies, and ActiveX controls — into your Web site using Dreamweaver. Keep in mind that Dreamweaver can't help you build the multimedia elements themselves; it can only make existing multimedia objects accessible to users who view your page.

Adding Audio and Video to Your Pages

You have two basic options for adding downloadable audio and video to your Web pages:

✦ **Embedding:** You embed an audio or video file to display a playback console on a Web page that users can use to play, rewind, and fast-forward the media file. (You can also embed an audio file and make it invisible to create a background audio effect.) Users must have an appropriate plug-in installed on their machines to play the embedded audio or video file.

✦ **Linking:** You link to an audio or video file to allow users the option of linking to that media file.

The following sections describe the two options.

Keep in mind that most audio and video files are large — large enough that many folks impatiently click the Stop button on their browsers before a Web page chock-full of audio or video effects has a chance to finish loading. Two basic rules help you use audio and video effectively in your Web pages:

✦ Use audio and video only when plain text just doesn't do the trick.

✦ Keep your audio and video clips as short (and corresponding file sizes as small) as possible.

Embedding an audio or video clip

You embed an audio file by following these steps:

1. In the Document window, click your page in the location where you want to add an embedded audio file.

2. Choose Insert⇨Media⇨Plugin.

Alternatively, you can click the Media button you find on the Insert Common panel. To display the panel, choose Window⇨Insert, and then select Common from the Insert bar drop-down list.

The Select File dialog box appears, as shown in Figure 23-1.

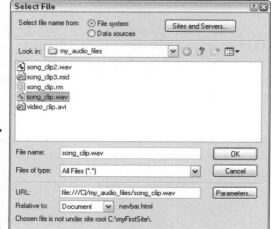

Figure 23-1: Embedding a media file by using the Select File dialog box.

3. In the File Name text box, enter the name of the audio file that you want to embed and click the OK button.

The Properties inspector appears with options for plug-ins.

If the file you enter is outside your Web site's root directory, Dreamweaver asks whether you want to copy the file to your site root. Click Yes.

4. In the Properties inspector, size the Audio Plugin placeholder to any dimensions you prefer.

You can either enter a width and height in the W and H text boxes in the Properties inspector or drag a handle on the placeholder to manually resize.

Entering a width of at least 144 pixels and a height of at least 60 pixels ensures that users can view all the audio playback controls in both Netscape Navigator and Internet Explorer.

Click the Play button in the Properties inspector to play your media file without previewing your page in a browser.

Streaming audio and video

RealPlayer, from RealNetworks, Inc., offers you the capability to stream audio and video files for user playback. *Streaming* files begin playing as soon as a browser transfers sufficient information to the user's computer to stay ahead of the remaining portion of the file as it downloads. Streaming enables the user to experience your audio or video clip much sooner than with a downloadable file. This option is especially useful for large audio files and all but the shortest video files. For helpful details on including streaming media files in your Web site, refer to *Dreamweaver MX 2004 Bible*, by Joseph W. Lowery (Wiley Publishing, Inc.).

Book VI
Chapter 23

Adding Multimedia Objects

To play an embedded media file, you must first install the appropriate plug-in media player.

To embed background music (music that plays automatically after the user opens a page), follow these steps:

1. **In the Document window, click your page in the location where you want to add an embedded audio file.**

2. **Choose Insert➪Media➪Plugin.**

   The Select File dialog box appears.

3. **In the File Name text box, enter the name of the audio file you want to embed and click the OK button.**

4. **Enter 2 for the width and height in the W and H text boxes in the Properties inspector.**

5. **Click the Parameters button to open the Parameters dialog box.**

6. **In the Parameters dialog box, click the Add (+) button to add a new parameter.**

7. **Click in the Parameter column and type** hidden.

8. **Press Tab to move to the Value column and type** true.

   Steps 7 and 8 hide the audio playback controls.

9. **Click OK to complete the process and close the dialog box.**

Linking to an audio or video clip

A simple and relatively trouble-free way to include audio and video clips on a Web page is to link the page to an audio or video file. Users can select the link if they want to hear or view the clip. This selection opens a player outside the browser where the user can control playback.

You follow the same steps to create a link to an audio or video file as you do to create a link to a Web page; the only difference is the file format you choose as the link target. For help with creating a link, see Book VI, Chapter 21.

Adding Other Media

Dreamweaver enables you to easily insert a number of other multimedia formats into your Web pages, including ActiveX, Java Applets, Flash, and Shockwave. After inserting any of the following media, you can set the control and playback features of the media in the Parameters dialog box. Additionally, you can fine-tune the media action on your page by using the Behaviors panel to create triggering actions that cause the media to play, stop, and execute other functions.

Follow these directions to insert other media in your Web page:

1. **In the Document window, click your page in the location where you want to add a multimedia file.**

2. **Choose Insert⇨Media and select from the drop-down list the media type that you want to use.**

3. **Enter the name of the media file you want to insert:**

    • **For Applet, Flash, and Shockwave files:** In the Select File dialog box, enter the path to the media and click the Select button. Your file is attached, and the associated Properties inspector appears. You can change the selected file in the Properties inspector by typing a new name in the Src text box or by browsing in the Src folder to select a file.

    • **For ActiveX:** An ActiveX placeholder is inserted, and the Properties inspector appears with options for ActiveX. Enter in the Class ID text box the name of the ActiveX file you want to play.

4. **In the Properties inspector for your selected media, enter dimensions in the W and H text boxes to size the Media placeholder to any dimensions you choose.**

5. **In the Properties inspector for your selected media, click the Parameters button to open the Parameters dialog box, where you can format the playback of your media file.**

See the manuals for Flash and other multimedia programs for details on formatting and playing files on your Web pages that you create with these programs.

Chapter 24: Punching Up Your Pages with Forms

In This Chapter

✔ Incorporating forms

✔ Adding text fields, buttons, and other form elements

*U*se forms to gather information and feedback from users who visit your Web pages. Forms are a great way to find out exactly who your readers or customers are. You can learn about them at the same time as they learn about you.

In this chapter, you find out how to work with powerful forms in Dreamweaver.

Incorporating Forms

Forms on the Web serve the same purpose as the paper-based forms you fill out — they provide a structured format for gathering specific information. The difference is that Web-based forms usually require less time for keyboard-savvy users to fill out (and using Web-based forms also saves a few trees otherwise destined for a paper mill). Dreamweaver offers you a number of handy tools for creating Web-based forms that you can easily include on your Web pages. You can incorporate everything from text boxes to radio buttons, and you can create surveys, gather user data, and conduct e-commerce.

Creating Web-based forms requires two steps:

1. Create the form that users see and interact with, which I demonstrate how to do using Dreamweaver in this chapter.

2. Create the processing program that accepts and processes form input. These processing programs — typically written in Perl or C and connected to Web-based forms through a protocol called CGI (Common Gateway Interface) — must be installed on a Web server and are beyond the scope of this book. For more information, check with your Web server provider (some allow you to use the simple form-processing programs on their Web servers for no extra charge) or check out a good book, such as *Perl For Dummies,* 4th Edition, by Paul E. Hoffman (Wiley Publishing, Inc.).

Adding a form

Before you can insert specific form objects, such as check boxes, on your Web page, you must first add a form to the page. You can add a form directly to the Document window or in a table cell.

To add a form to a page, click in the Document window where you want to add the form and choose Insert⇨Form⇨Form or click the Form button on the Insert Forms panel. (If the Insert Forms panel isn't open, choose Window⇨ Insert to open the panel and then select Forms from the Insert bar drop-down list.)

Dreamweaver adds the form to the page as indicated by the red dashed lines and also adds the associated form tag to your HTML page code. You can now insert form objects inside the red dashed lines of the form.

If you attempt to add a form element (such as a radio button) without first adding a form, a dialog box appears, asking whether you want to add a form tag. Click Yes to add both the form tag and the element to your page.

Specifying form properties

A form has several properties that you can set by using the Properties inspector: Form Name, Action, Method, Target, and Enctype (short for MIME encoded type). Click the form to open the Properties inspector. (If the Properties inspector doesn't appear, open it by choosing Window⇨ Properties.) Then specify the following properties:

+ **Form Name:** Enter an alphanumeric name in the empty text box. The advantage of naming your form is that you can use the name to reference the form in a scripting language that you use to retrieve, store, and manipulate the form data.

+ **Action:** Enter the address of the location that processes the form data. Alternatively, you can browse to the location by clicking the folder and making a selection in the Select File dialog box.

  You can select the following three common actions:

  • Enter the URL of a Common Gateway Interface (CGI) program that runs after the user submits the form. The action resembles the following:

    ```
    www.server.com/cgi-bin/formhandler.pl
    ```

  • Enter the JavaScript program that runs after the user submits the form. The action appears as follows:

    ```
    www.server.com/javascript:function()
    ```

    Here, `function` is your form handling function.

  • Enter a mailto: address where the form data goes after the user clicks Submit. A mailto: address appears similar to the following:

    ```
    mailto:gruntworker@formhandling.com
    ```

Data received at the specified mailto: address isn't formatted for easy reading. It appears as strings of code with the form data embedded within lots of ampersands and plus signs.

✦ **Method:** Select from the drop-down list a method for how the form data passes to the processing entity that you specified in the Action field. Choices are Default, GET, and POST. (Default and GET are the same.) GET sends the form data by appending it to the URL that the Action specifies. POST sends the form data as a separate entity. GET limits the amount of data that can pass along, but POST does not.

✦ **Target:** You can specify a target window where your returned form data will appear. Click the tab to select from the following choices: _blank (displays returned data in a new window), _parent (displays returned data in the parent of the currently opened window), _self (displays returned data in the currently opened window), and _top (displays returned data in the top-level window, replacing frames, if any). If you have created frames, you can also select a frame name from this list.

✦ **Enctype:** You use the Enctype drop-down list to specify the MIME encoding type of the form data you submit to the server for processing. (MIME, which stands for Multipurpose Internet Mail Extension, is simply a standard way to send non-ASCII data across the Internet.) You use the default setting of `application/x-www-form-urlencode` if you specify the POST method. If your form includes a file-upload field, however, you want to specify `multipart/form-data`.

**Book VI
Chapter 24**

Punching Up Your Pages with Forms

Labeling form objects

Dreamweaver enables you to provide labels for form elements (such as text fields) and provide the user with directions about how to complete the information requested for each option. To label form elements, simply position your cursor in the form and begin typing. Then insert the form element you want.

Using Text Fields

Text fields are blank text boxes that you can insert in your form to hold alphanumeric information that the user types. You can set up a text field as follows:

✦ **Single line:** Provides space for the user to enter a single word or short phrase.

✦ **Multiline:** Provides space for the user to enter a longer string of text. Appropriate for a comment box.

✦ **Password:** Provides space for the user to enter a password. An asterisk (Windows) or dot (Mac) appears on-screen for each character that the user types.

To add a text field, do the following:

1. **In the Document window, click where you want to add the text field and choose Insert⇨Form⇨Text Field or click the Text Field button on the Inset Form panel.**

   If the panel isn't open, choose Window⇨Insert to open the panel and select Forms from the Insert bar drop-down list.

   Dreamweaver adds a text field to your form, and a Properties inspector appears. If the Properties inspector doesn't appear, choose Window⇨ Properties to open the inspector.

2. **Fill in the following fields of the Properties inspector to format the text field:**

   - **TextField name:** Enter a name in the empty text box. The text field is referenced by this name in the HTML page code.

   - **Char Width:** Enter a whole number for the approximate visible width of the text field. (The actual size of the text field on the page is approximate because text characters in your form display differently according to users' browser settings.)

   - **Max Chars:** (Applies to Single line and Password only.) Enter a whole number to indicate the maximum number of characters that the user can enter in the field. Max Chars can be equal to or greater than Char Width.

   - **Num Lines:** (Applies to Multiline only.) Enter a whole number for the maximum number of lines that the user can enter in the text field.

   - **Type:** Select a radio button for Single line, Multiline, or Password.

   - **Init Val:** (Optional) Enter an alphanumeric word or phrase that occupies the text field when the user first encounters it. The user can enter his or her own information over the Init Val.

Setting Up Buttons

After a user enters data into a form, he or she must then perform some sort of task to transmit the data from his or her computer to another computer that can process the information. Dreamweaver offers you three buttons to use to activate your form: Reset, Submit, and Command:

✦ **Reset:** Clicking this button erases all data entered into the form, allowing the user to re-enter data into a fresh, clean form.

✦ **Submit:** After the user clicks this button, the form data scoots off to another computer based on the specified Action. (You see how to set the Action of a form in the section, "Specifying form properties," earlier in this chapter.)

✦ **Command:** After the user clicks this button, it executes the programming function that the Web designer assigned to it.

To insert a button, follow these steps:

1. **Click where you want to add the button in the Document window and choose Insert⇨Form⇨Button or click the Button button on the Insert Forms panel.**

If the panel isn't open, choose Window⇨Insert and then choose Forms from the Insert bar drop-down list.

Dreamweaver adds a button to your form, and a Properties inspector similar to the one in Figure 24-1 appears. If the Properties inspector doesn't appear, choose Window⇨Properties to open the inspector.

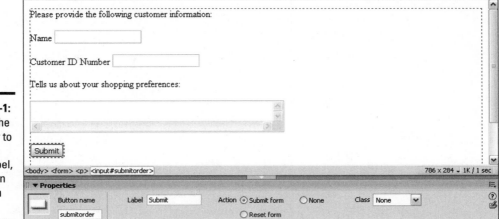

Figure 24-1: You use the inspector to specify a name, label, and action for a form button.

2. **Fill in the following fields of the Properties inspector to format the button:**

• **Button name:** Enter a name in the empty text box. This name identifies the button in the HTML code.

• **Label:** Enter the text that you want to appear on the button itself.

• **Action:** Select a radio button to indicate the function of the button. Choices consist of Reset form, Submit form, and None (Command).

You can create a graphical Submit button — a button created from a small image — by choosing Insert⇨Form⇨Image Field or by clicking the Image Field button on the Insert Forms panel. Then browse to the image file on your hard drive or type the name of the image file directly into the File Name field. When you finish, click OK to create the graphical Submit button.

Adding Form Elements

In addition to the text fields and buttons I describe in the sections, "Using text fields" and "Setting up buttons," earlier in this chapter, you can add a variety of form elements that help your users give you information. To insert any of the elements, follow these steps:

1. **Position your cursor in the area of the Document window where you want to add the element.**

2. **Click the appropriate button on the Insert Forms panel.**

If the panel isn't open, choose Window➪Insert to open the panel and then select Forms from the Insert bar drop-down list.

Dreamweaver adds the element to your form, and the appropriate inspector appears. (If the appropriate inspector doesn't appear, open it by choosing Window➪Properties.)

3. **Fill in the text boxes and make the appropriate selections in the inspector.**

4. **Click OK.**

Chapter 25: Laying Out Pages with Layers

In This Chapter

✓ Adding, selecting, and deleting a layer

✓ Placing objects in a layer

✓ Including a background image or color in a layer

✓ Naming a layer

✓ Nesting and aligning layers

✓ Changing the visibility of a layer

✓ Moving and resizing a layer or multiple layers

To precisely lay out the content of your Web page, you can use tables, or you can use the latest and greatest layout aid: layers. Layers in Dreamweaver work in much the same way as layers do in image-editing programs such as Macromedia Fireworks or Adobe Photoshop: Layers are like transparent sheets that you fill with content (images and text, for example) and then shuffle, stack, position, and overlap until your page looks exactly the way you want.

Adding a Layer

You can add a layer to the workspace of your Document window by using one of the following two methods:

✦ Choose Insert⇨Layout Objects⇨Layer. A new layer appears in the upper-left corner of your Document window.

✦ Click the Draw Layer button you see in the Insert Layout panel. (If the panel doesn't appear, open it by choosing Window⇨Insert, and then select Layout from the Insert bar's drop-down list.) Position the cross hair cursor anywhere in your Document window and click and drag until the layer obtains the dimensions you want. Release the mouse button.

After you add a layer, the Layers panel appears. If the Layers panel isn't displayed after you add a layer, choose Window⇨Layers.

Selecting a Layer

Selecting a layer enables you to identify which layer you want to change when executing a layer operation, such as moving or naming the layer. Use any of the following methods to select a layer:

- ✦ In the Document window, click the boundary of the layer.
- ✦ In the Document window, click the layer handle — the square enclosing a small grid located at the top-left corner of the layer.
- ✦ In the Document window, press the Shift key and click anywhere inside the layer.
- ✦ In the Layers panel, click the name of the layer.
- ✦ Click the layer's HTML tag in the tag selector of the Document window Status bar.

Selection handles appear on the boundary of the layer to indicate that you selected it.

Deleting a Layer

Deleting a layer removes the layer, the layer's contents, and the layer marker from the Document window. To delete a layer, select the layer and then press Delete or Backspace.

Don't delete a layer if you want to remove it from one page and add it to another. Instead, select the layer (see the preceding section, "Selecting a Layer") and choose Edit⇨Cut. Open the page where you want to add the layer and choose Edit⇨Paste.

Placing Objects in a Layer

To add an object to a layer, click inside the layer and follow the normal procedure for adding the object. For example, add text to a layer by clicking inside the layer and typing text or add other objects to a layer by clicking inside the layer and choosing Insert.

Including a Background Image or Color in a Layer

By default, an unnested layer has the same color or background image as the Document window in which it's drawn. (A nested *child* layer has the same color or background image as its *parent*. For more about nested layers, see the section, "Nesting Layers," later in this chapter.)

You can change the background of any layer by including a background image or color in the layer by following these steps:

1. Select the layer where you want to change the background.

If the Properties inspector doesn't appear, open it by choosing Window⇨Properties.

2. In the Properties inspector, change one of the following:

- • **Bg Image:** Click the folder to the right of the text box and browse to select a background image from the Select Image Source dialog box that appears. Click OK to accept your image choice and close the dialog box. The name of the background image appears in the Bg Image text box, and the image is added to the background of the layer.

- **Bg Color:** Click the color box and select a color from the color palette that appears. Alternatively, you can enter a color in the Bg Color text box. The new color appears in the background of the selected layer.

Naming a Layer

The first layer you add to a page is automatically named Layer 1; the second layer you add is named Layer 2; and so on. You can change these default names to other names that help you more easily distinguish layers when working with HTML and examining layers with the Properties inspector or Layers panel.

To name a layer by using the Layers panel, follow these steps:

1. **If the Layers panel doesn't appear, open it by choosing Window⇨Layers.**

2. **In the Layers panel, double-click the name of the layer whose name you want to change.**

The current name is selected.

3. **Enter a new name for the layer.**

Get in the habit of appropriately naming your layers as soon as you create them. The name *blueprint image map* helps you remember a layer's content much better than *Layer15*.

Nesting Layers

A *nested* layer has a dependent relationship with another layer. The nested layer is often referred to as a *child* layer, whereas the layer on which it depends is called the *parent* layer. A child layer can be drawn completely inside its parent (as shown in Figure 25-1), in an intersecting arrangement with its parent, or completely unattached to its parent, depending on the effect you want to achieve. A nested layer has or *inherits* the same visibility of its parent and moves with the parent when the parent layer is repositioned in the Document window.

Enabling nesting

To create nested layers in the Document window, you must first enable nesting. To do so, follow these steps:

1. **Choose Edit⇨Preferences to open the Preferences dialog box.**

2. **In the Preferences dialog box, select Layers in the category area.**

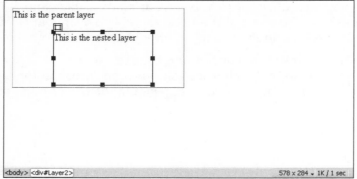

Figure 25-1:
A nested
layer can be
(but doesn't
have to be)
drawn
inside its
parent layer.

3. **Select the Nesting check box.**

4. **Click OK to banish the Preferences dialog box.**

5. **In the Document window, choose Window⇨Layers to open the Layers panel.**

6. **In the Layers panel, make sure that the Prevent Overlap check box is deselected.**

Creating a new nested layer

Use either of these methods to draw a nested layer:

✦ Click inside an existing layer and choose Insert⇨Layout Objects⇨Layer. A child layer of default size appears inside the parent layer. If the dimensions of the parent layer are smaller than the dimensions of the child layer, the child layer exceeds the boundaries of the parent.

✦ Click the Draw Layer button from the Insert Common panel and drag it into the parent layer. A child layer of default size appears inside the parent layer. If the dimensions of the parent layer are smaller than the dimensions of the child layer, the child layer exceeds the boundaries of the parent.

Changing the nesting of an existing layer

To change the nesting of an existing layer, follow these steps:

1. **Open the Layers panel by choosing Window⇨Layers.**

2. **In the Layers panel, press and hold the Ctrl key (Windows) or ⌘ key (Mac) while you drag the intended child layer on top of its new parent.**

   The child is in the correct position when you see a box appear around its intended parent layer.

3. **Release the mouse button.**

   The new child-parent relationship is shown in the Layers panel.

Dreamweaver draws the new child layer and updates the associated code for changed layer nesting in the HTML source code for your page.

Collapsing or expanding your view in the Layers panel

You can change how you view the names of nested layers in the Layers panel by collapsing or expanding your view, as shown in Figure 25-2.

✦ **To collapse your view:** Click the minus sign (-) in front of a parent layer. Names of nested child layers for that parent are hidden.

✦ **To expand your view:** Click the plus sign (+) in front of a parent layer. Names of nested child layers for that parent appear.

**Book VI
Chapter 25**

Laying Out Pages
with Layers

Visibility column

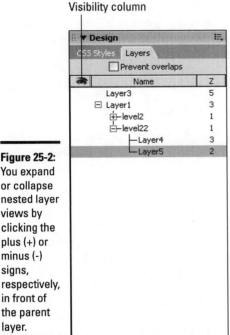

Figure 25-2:
You expand or collapse nested layer views by clicking the plus (+) or minus (-) signs, respectively, in front of the parent layer.

Aligning Layers

Aligning layers can help you precisely lay out visual content in the Document window. You can align layers with the top, left side, right side, or bottom. To align layers, select the layers you want to align by pressing and holding the Shift key and then clicking each layer in the Document window. Choose Modify⇨Align and choose one of the following options from the submenu that appears:

✦ **Left:** Assigns the x-coordinate of the leftmost selected layer to all selected layers.

✦ **Right:** Aligns the right side of all selected layers with the right side of the rightmost selected layer.

✦ **Top:** Assigns the y-coordinate of the topmost selected layer to all selected layers.

- ✦ **Bottom:** Aligns the bottom of all selected layers with the bottom of the bottommost selected layer.

- ✦ **Make Same Width:** Resizes layers to match the width of the layer selected last.

- ✦ **Make Same Height:** Resizes layers to match the height of the layer selected last.

Changing the Visibility of a Layer

You can specify whether a layer is visible or hidden when a Web page *loads* — first appears — and as a result of specific actions by the user. Visibility can change as many times as you want. Visibility options consist of

- ✦ **Default:** The layer's initial visibility is the default setting. (To edit layer default settings, choose Edit⇨Preferences and then, to display the layer default settings you can change, click Layers in the Preferences dialog box that appears.)

- ✦ **Inherit:** For a nested layer, the layer's initial visibility is the same visibility of its parent. For an unnested layer, selecting the Inherit option causes the layer to appear as visible.

- ✦ **Visible:** The layer's initial visibility is visible.

- ✦ **Hidden:** The layer's initial visibility is hidden.

You can also set layer visibility by using either the Properties inspector or the Layers panel. By setting layer visibility, you can create images that appear (or disappear) in response to user interaction. For example, you can create an image of a widget that appears on a Web page after a user clicks a link marked "Click here to see our top-of-the-line widget!"

To set the initial visibility of a layer by using the Properties inspector, select the layer in the Document window to open the Properties inspector. If the inspector doesn't appear, open it by choosing Window⇨Properties. Select a visibility option from the Vis drop-down list.

To set the initial visibility of a layer by using the Layers panel, click in the Visibility column (refer to in Figure 25-2) next to a layer's name to display an open eye (visible), closed eye (hidden), or no eye (inherited).

Layering Layers: Setting the Z-Index

The *z-index* of a layer indicates the layer's position in a stack of multiple layers. Z-indices are useful when you have a handful of layers — some containing transparent portions; some of different sizes — stacked one on top of the other. Changing the z-index of your layers lets you shuffle the layers — much as you shuffle a deck of cards — to create interesting visual effects.

Z-indices are measured in whole numbers and don't have to be consecutive — for example, you can have three layers with z-indices of 1, 3, and 7. The layer with the largest z-index sits on top of the layer stack, and the layer with the smallest z-index sits on the bottom of the layer stack. Layers with larger z-indices obscure those with smaller z-indices. You can change the z-index of a layer in either the Properties inspector or the Layers panel.

To assign the z-index of a layer by using the Properties inspector, first select the layer to open the Properties inspector. If the Properties inspector doesn't appear, open it by choosing Window⇨Properties. Then enter a new number in the Z-Index text box.

To assign the z-index of a layer by using the Layers panel (as shown in Figure 25-3), follow these steps:

1. **Select the layer to open the Layers panel.**

If the Layers panel doesn't appear, open it by choosing Window⇨Layers.

2. **Click the Z column for the layer whose z-index you want to change.**

The current z-index is selected.

3. **Enter a new z-index for the layer.**

The new number appears in the Z column for the selected layer.

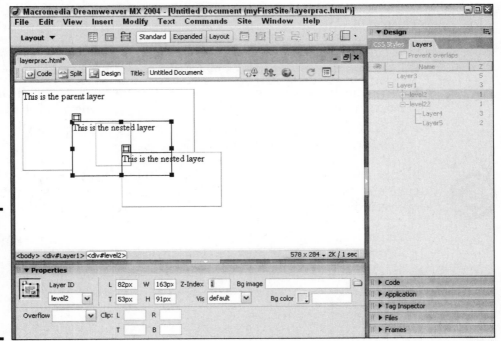

Figure 25-3:
You can set the z-index for your layers by using the Layers panel.

To assign relative z-indices to layers by reordering layers in the Layers panel, follow these steps:

1. **Open the Layers panel by choosing Window⇨Layers.**

   The Layers panel lists layers in order of descending z-index.

2. **Click the name of a layer for which you want to change the z-index.**

3. **Drag the layer name into a new list position and release the mouse button.**

   As you drag, the selected layer is indicated by a thick line.

Dreamweaver reorders the list in the Layers panel and renumbers layer z-indices to reflect your change. Also, Dreamweaver updates the associated code for the layers' z-indices in the HTML source code for your page.

 Because you don't have to number the z-index of layers consecutively, consider leaving gaps between indices in case you want to add new layers into the middle of the stack. For example, use only even numbers for your indices so that you can easily sandwich a new layer with an odd-numbered z-index in between old even-numbered layers.

Moving a Layer

You might choose to move a layer to a place in another location in the Document window or to a position relative to the grid or to other objects. To move a layer, select the layer in the Document window and then reposition your selection by using one of the following three methods:

✦ Click and drag the layer to a new location and release the mouse button.

✦ Press the arrow keys that you find on the numeric keypad on your keyboard to nudge the layer up, down, left, or right one pixel at a time.

✦ In the Properties inspector, enter a new value in the T and L text boxes to indicate the pixel coordinates of the layer's top-left corner.

 When moving layers, you can choose to enable or prevent layer overlap, depending on how you want the final image montage to appear. You enable or prevent layer overlap as the following list describes:

✦ **To prevent layer overlap:** Open the Layers panel by choosing Window⇨ Layers and select the Prevent Overlap check box.

✦ **To enable layer overlap:** Open the Layers panel by choosing Window⇨ Layers and deselect the Prevent Overlap check box.

Resizing a Layer

Resizing a layer means changing its height and width dimensions. To resize a layer, select the layer and perform one of the following tasks:

✦ Click and drag a selection handle — one of the large dots on the layer boundary — until the layer obtains the dimensions you desire.

✦ In the Properties inspector, enter a new width in pixels at the W text box and a new height in pixels at the H text box. If the Properties inspector doesn't appear, open it by choosing Window⇨Properties.

Resizing Multiple Layers at the Same Time

You can change the height and width dimensions of multiple layers at the same time as follows:

1. **Press and hold the Shift key while selecting each layer you want to resize.**

2. **If the Properties inspector doesn't appear, open it by choosing Window⇨Properties.**

3. **In the Properties inspector, enter a new width in pixels in the W text box and a new height in pixels in the H text box.**

Chapter 26: Using Templates for a Consistent Look

In This Chapter

✓ Finding out about templates

✓ Creating a template

✓ Adding an editable field to a template

✓ Using a template to create a Web page

Creating one or two Web pages by hand is easy to do. However, if you want to create a large site containing dozens (or even hundreds) of pages containing similar elements, such as your company logo or a nifty columnar layout, you quickly will find that hand-crafting each page takes a great deal of time. And because we humans tend to make mistakes from time to time, the more pages you create by hand, the more potential you have to make mistakes.

Fortunately, Dreamweaver helps solve this problem by providing a technique for creating templates. A *template* is a special kind of document that you can create to construct multiple Web pages, changing the content slightly with each Web page while keeping a specified portion (for example, your company logo and the navigation layout) static from page to page. Using templates saves you time (and frustration) as you create multiple Web pages with a consistent look and feel.

 Some Web development teams like to distinguish between *Web designers,* the folks who design the way Web pages look, and *Web content specialists,* the folks who keep the textual content of a Web site updated. Because using templates allows you to lock the design portion of your Web pages and specify text as editable, Web designers can create a great-looking Web site and then hand it over to Web content specialists to update — without fear! (Any updates that the Web content specialists make don't affect the locked design elements.)

About Templates

In Dreamweaver, a template is a special type of file you can use to create multiple Web pages that share certain design elements, such as navigation bars, images, colors, and links. Although templates resemble Web pages (as shown later in Figure 26-1), they have two important differences:

✦ **You can lock content on a template to create both fixed (non-editable) and editable regions.** Other developers using your template to create Web pages can change the editable regions of your template, but not the fixed regions. Locking content ensures that all Web pages created from a particular template contain at least some fixed, identical content. (The kinds of content that you typically want to appear identical from page to page include page layout, logos, copyright notices, and other design elements that contribute to the look and feel of the Web site.)

✦ **You save templates with a special file extension.** You save Web pages by using the `.html` or `.htm` extension; you save templates by using the `.dwt` (Dreamweaver template) file extension.

Creating and Using Templates

The steps you take to create a template are similar to those you use to create a Web page. In this section, I demonstrate how to save fixed content as a template; I then show you how to add editable regions to a template. Finally, you see how to use a template — one you create or one that already exists — to create a Web page.

Creating a template

Many prebuilt templates are available (for a price!). If you prefer to purchase a template rather than to create one from scratch, you might want to point your browser to a site that reviews third-party Dreamweaver templates, such as Dreamweaver-Templates.org (`www.dreamweaver-templates.org`).

Follow these steps to create a template:

1. **Create a new Web document or open an existing document.**

2. **Add any design elements you want to designate as fixed (non-editable) regions.**

   In Figure 26-1, you see a graphical logo across the top of the template, navigation links across the left side of the template, and an animation element at the bottom of the template.

Figure 26-1: You designate the fixed portion of a template in the Document window.

3. **Choose File⇨Save as Template.**

   The warning dialog box appears, as shown in Figure 26-2.

4. **Click OK to save the template and add editable regions later.**

   The Save as Template dialog box appears.

5. **Type a descriptive name for your template in the Save As text box.**

6. **Click Save.**

   Dreamweaver saves the template by using the `.dwt` file extension.

Adding an editable region

An *editable region* is the portion of a template you want to be able to change from Web page to Web page. You can specify as many editable regions in a template as you want.

Figure 26-2:
Click OK to save the template anyway.

In addition to editable regions, you can add other types of regions, such as repeating regions and optional regions, to your template. For more information about the regions you can add to your template, choose Help⇨Using Dreamweaver⇨Search to display the Search dialog box, type **templates** in the Keyword text box that you find in the Search dialog box, and click the Search button.

To add an editable region to a template, follow these steps:

1. **Open an existing template.**

2. **Select the area that you want to be editable and choose Insert⇨Template Objects⇨Editable Region.**

   The New Editable Region dialog box appears, as shown in Figure 26-3.

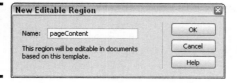

Figure 26-3:
Naming an editable region.

3. **Enter a name for the editable region in the Name text box and click OK.**

   A border appears around the editable region, as shown in Figure 26-4.

4. **Choose File⇨Save to save your changes.**

Figure 26-4:
Dreamweaver displays borders around editable regions.

Using a Template to Create a Web Page

To create a Web page using an existing template, follow these steps:

1. **Choose File⇨New.**

The New Document dialog box appears.

2. **Click the Templates tab that you see in the New Document dialog box.**

A New from Template dialog box appears, as shown in Figure 26-5.

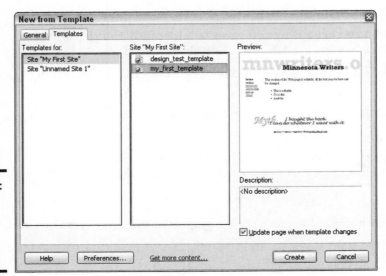

Figure 26-5:
Creating a Web page from an existing template.

3. **Select your site from the Templates For list; then select the template you want to use. When you finish, click Create.**

A new, untitled Web page based on the template you select appears in the Document window. Figure 26-6 shows you an example.

4. **Update the editable portion of the Web page.**

Notice that Dreamweaver doesn't allow you to update the fixed portion of the Web page.

5. **Choose File⇨Save to save the Web page.**

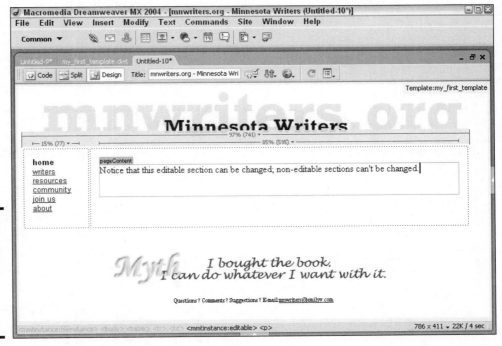

Figure 26-6:
Updating
the editable
portion of a
Web page
created
using a
template.

Chapter 27: Publishing and Maintaining Your Site

In This Chapter

✔ Defining remote host settings

✔ Connecting to a Web server

✔ Transferring files

✔ Collaborating on site revisions

✔ Measuring download time, monitoring links, and updating meta tags

To make your site available on the World Wide Web, you must sign up with a Web hosting service or have another method of accessing a Web server. You can then transfer a copy of your entire local site root to a folder on the Web server that hosts your site. You must transfer not only every HTML code page on your local site, but also every image, video, and sound (and all other files that you use on your site) to the remote host.

After your site is transferred, you and other collaborators can retrieve site pages, work on them locally, and upload the pages back to the host to keep the site updated. You can also fine-tune your site by setting up meta tags, measuring the download time that your site requires, and monitoring all the links on your site — quickly and easily — to ensure that users don't access any dead-end pages from your site.

Defining Remote Host Settings

Dreamweaver makes an easy task of transferring Web files from your local site to the remote host. But prior to transferring, or *uploading,* your first site to the host, you must tell Dreamweaver some basic information about the host, such as where it is located on the Web and what the access password is.

You define remote host attributes in the same dialog box that you use to define your local site — namely, the Site Definition dialog box — by following these steps:

1. **In Dreamweaver, choose Site⇨Manage Sites to open the Manage Sites dialog box.**

2. **From the Manage Sites dialog box, select the site that you want to work with and click the Edit button.**

    The Site Definition dialog box for your site opens, as shown in Figure 27-1.

3. **Select the Remote Info category.**

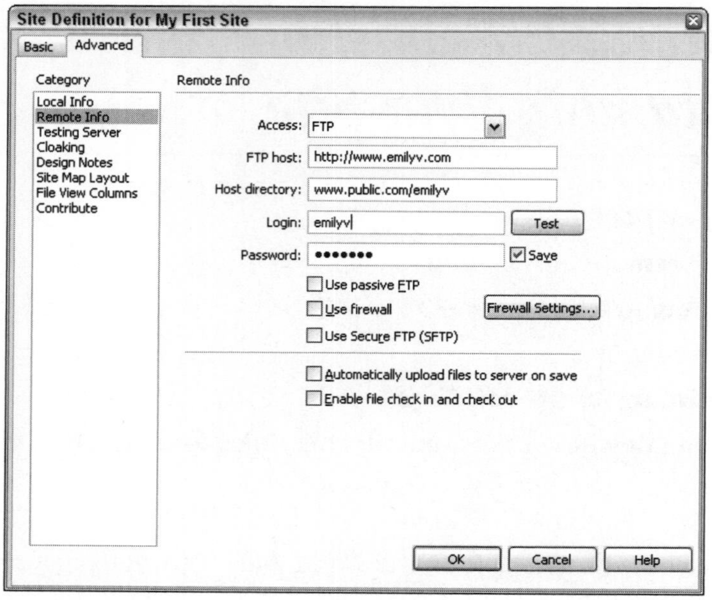

Figure 27-1:
You must
define the
settings for
your remote
host before
you can
transfer
your files.

4. **From the Access drop-down list, select a Web server access method from these options:**

   - **None:** Applicable only if you don't plan to upload your site to a remote server.

   - **FTP:** Select this option to transfer files to and from your server via File Transfer Protocol. Supply the requested information in the dialog box based on the information in Table 27-1.

Table 27-1	FTP-Related Settings in Dreamweaver
Item	*Description*
FTP Host	Enter the name of the FTP connection for your server, such as `www.domainname.com`.
Host Directory	Enter the name from which users will access your site, such as `www/public/yourID`.
Login	Enter your login identification for accessing the server and click the Test button if you want to test your FTP connection.
Password	Enter your password for accessing the server and select the Save check box if you want Dreamweaver to remember your password.
Use Passive FTP	Select this check box if your firewall requires that your local software establish the server connection instead of the remote host. (If you're not sure whether your computer configuration includes a firewall, ask your system administrator.)
Use Firewall	Select this check box if you connect to the host from behind a firewall; then click the Firewall Settings button to define a firewall host.
Use Secure FTP (SFTP)	Select this check box if your FTP host supports secure FTP.

Item	Description
Automatically Upload Files to Server on Save	Select this check box to upload files automatically every time you save your site in Dreamweaver.
Enable File Check In and Check Out	Select this check box to enable file check in and check out via the Files panel.

- **Local/Network:** Select this option if your local computer is also your Web server or if you connect to the Web server via a local area network. At the Remote Folder box, enter a folder name or browse to select the folder on the remote host where you store your site files. Select the Refresh Remote File List Automatically check box if you want to see the Remote Files pane of the Site window updated automatically as you transfer files to the remote server. Select the Automatically Upload Files to Server on Save check box to upload files automatically every time you save your site in Dreamweaver. Select the Enable File Check In and Check Out check box to enable file check in/check out (useful if many folks will be updating and maintaining your Web site pages).

- **RDS:** Select this option if you want to access ColdFusion Remote Development Services. Click the Settings button to display the Configure RDS Server dialog box and specify the host name, port, full host directory, user name, and password. Click OK to close the Configure RDS Server dialog box. Select the Automatically Upload Files to Server on Save check box to upload files automatically every time you save your site in Dreamweaver. Select the Enable File Check In and Check Out check box to enable file check in/check out (useful if many folks will be updating and maintaining your Web site pages). If you want to check out the files when you open the RDS server connection, select the Check Out Files When Opening check box and then specify a check out name and e-mail address.

- **SourceSafe Database:** Select this option if you want to access a SourceSafe database. Click the Settings button and complete the Open SourceSafe Database dialog box by typing (or browsing for) a database path, typing a project name, and providing your user name and password. When you finish, click OK to close the Open SourceSafe Database dialog box. Select the Automatically Upload Files to Server on Save check box if you want to upload files automatically every time you save your site in Dreamweaver. Select the Check Out Files When Opening check box if you want to check out the files when you open the SourceSafe database connection.

- **WebDAV:** Select this option if you want to make a WebDAV connection. (WebDAV, which is short for Web-based Distributed Authoring and Versioning, allows you to edit and manage files on remote Web servers collaboratively — in other words, to share files with other developers. For more information, visit www.webdav.org.) Click the Settings button and complete the WebDAV Connection dialog box by entering the server URL and providing your user name, password, and e-mail address; click OK to finish. Select the Automatically Upload Files to Server on Save check box to upload files automatically every time

Book VI
Chapter 27

Publishing and Maintaining Your Site

you save your site in Dreamweaver. Select the Enable File Check In and Check Out check box to enable file check in/check out (useful if many folks will be updating and maintaining your Web site pages).

5. **Click OK to close the Site Definition dialog box.**

6. **Click Done to close the Manage Sites dialog box.**

If you're confused about information regarding your Web server (and who isn't, at least at first?), contact your hosting service or your system administrator to find out the server name, directory, user name, password, and other details that you need to complete the Remote Info area of the Site Definition dialog box.

If you change hosting services or other remote server information, such as your password, you can edit your Remote Host attributes by returning to the Site Definition dialog box.

Connecting to a Web Server

To connect to your Web server, simply click the Connect to Remote Host button you see in the Files panel (and in Figure 27-2). If the Files panel doesn't appear, choose Window➪Files. If the Connect to Remote Host button doesn't appear in the Files panel, select a Dreamweaver site file from the Files panel and then choose Site➪Manage Sites. Then, in the Manage Sites dialog box that appears, select the site that you want to upload and click Done. The Site Management toolbar, including the Connect to Remote Host button, appears in the Files panel.

Connect to Remote Host

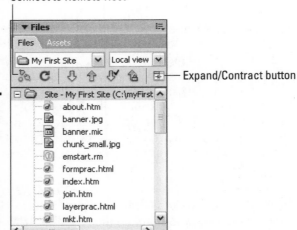

Expand/Contract button

Figure 27-2: Connecting to a Web server is as easy as clicking the Connect to Remote Host button.

To expand the Files panel and view the Site window, click the Expand/Contract button on the right side of the Files panel.

After you connect, as shown in Figure 27-3, your site files on the remote host appear in the *Remote Site pane* — the left pane of the Site window. Files in your local site root still appear in the right pane of the Site window.

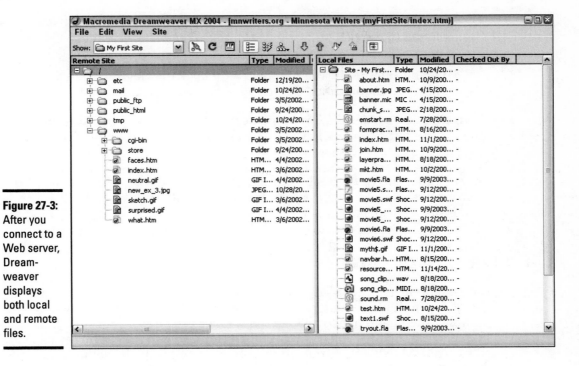

Figure 27-3: After you connect to a Web server, Dreamweaver displays both local and remote files.

When you're done working with your Web server, simply click the Disconnect from Remote Host button in the Site window.

Transferring Files

When you connect to the remote host, you can transfer files to and from the server. Just follow these steps:

1. **If you're not already at the Site window, switch to it by opening a Dreamweaver site file, choosing Window⇨Files, and clicking the Expand/Contract button.**

If the Site Management toolbar doesn't appear in the Files panel, choose Site⇨Manage Sites. Then, in the Manage Sites dialog box that appears, select the site that you want to upload and click Done. When the Site Management toolbar appears, click the Expand/Contract button to display the Site window.

2. **Select the files that you want to transfer.**

To select files that you want to send to the remote site: Click one or more files in the Local Files pane.

To select files that you want to retrieve from the remote site: Click one or more files in the Remote Files pane.

3. **Transfer the files.**

To send local files to the remote site: Click the Put button in the Site window or choose Site⇨Put from the Site window menu. Dreamweaver presents a dialog box that asks whether you want to include dependent files in the transfer. *Dependent files* are files, such as images, that are included in your HTML code pages. Click Yes to include these files or No to transfer only your selected files.

> **To bring remote files to the local site:** Click the Get button in the Site window or choose Site⇨Get from the Site window menu.

Your transferred files appear in the destination window pane. You can move files in and out of folders in their new location by using standard Windows procedures.

At any time, you can refresh your file lists to reread a directory of files. To refresh the selected file directory, just click the Refresh button in the Site window.

Collaborating on Site Revisions

Site maintenance can be an enormous task that you can accomplish best by giving multiple designers revision privileges for files on the site host. To simplify the maintenance task, Dreamweaver provides a check in/check out system that enables you to work collaboratively with others on revising site files. This system helps you and your team keep track of who has which file currently checked out so that revisers don't inadvertently duplicate editing efforts.

Enabling file check in/check out

Follow these steps to set up file check in/check out for a site:

1. **In Dreamweaver, choose Site⇨Manage Sites to open the Manage Sites dialog box.**

2. **From the Site list, select the site that you want to work on and click the Edit button.**

   A Site Definition dialog box for your site appears. (Refer to Figure 27-1 to see a similar dialog box.)

3. **Select the Remote Info category.**

4. **The options that you choose in this step depend on your access method.**

   If you select FTP or Local/Network for your Access method: Select the Enable File Check In and Check Out check box. After you do so, the additional options you see at the bottom of the Site Definition dialog box appear (refer to Figure 27-1).

   If you select SourceSafe Database or WebDAV for your Access method: Click the Settings button and complete the dialog box that appears.

5. **For all Access methods, select the Check Out Files When Opening check box.**

   The file is marked as checked out to you whenever you open it from the remote server.

6. **If you select FTP or Local/Network for your access method, enter a check out name and e-mail address.**

Any file that you check out shows this name and address listed in the Check Out column of the Remote Files pane of the Site window.

Checking files in and out

Follow these procedures to check files in and out for collaborative site editing:

✦ **To check files out:** In the Remote Files pane of the Site window, select the files that you want to check out. Then click the Check Out button at the top of the Site window or choose Site⇨Check Out. The Checked Out By column in the remote pane of the Site window identifies the person checking out the file. A check mark appears in front of the filename to indicate that it's checked out.

✦ **To check files in:** In the remote pane, select the files you want to check in. Then click the Check In button at the top of the Site window or choose Site⇨Check In. The Checked Out By column in the remote pane of the Site window removes the name of the person who had previously checked out the file. Also, the lack of a check mark in front of the filename indicates that its checked-out status is removed.

Maintaining Your Site

After you publish your site, you want to maintain and fine-tune it so that it always looks (and behaves) its very best. The maintenance tasks that you perform most often (other than updating content) include measuring download time, monitoring links, and updating meta tags.

Measuring download time

Download time is an important measurement for you as a Web designer because it tells you how long users must wait to view your entire page on their computers. Download time depends on the connection speed, or *bits per second* (bps), of a user's modem.

You can keep tabs on the expected download time for a page under construction by looking at the File Size/Download Time indicator in the Status bar at the bottom of the Document window, as shown in Figure 27-4.

Dreamweaver computes the estimated download time based on the connection speed specified in the Preferences dialog box. To change the default connection speed, choose Edit⇨Preferences to open the Preferences dialog box. At the Preferences dialog box, select the Status bar category and then choose a connection speed from the Connection Speed drop-down list. Choices consist of 14.4, 28.8, 33.6, 56, 64, 128, and 1,500 kilobits per second (Kbps).

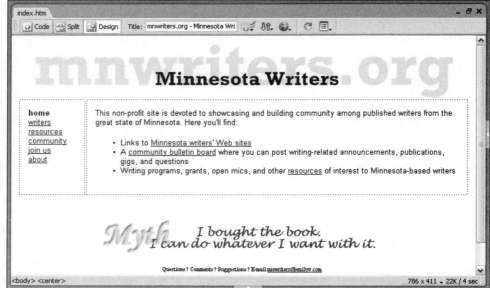

Figure 27-4:
File size and estimated download time appear at the bottom of the Document window as you work with a page.

Try minimizing download time for a page — by optimizing or reducing the images on your page, for example — to the greatest degree possible prior to uploading the page to the server. Then check the actual download time after the page goes online to determine whether you need to reduce the file size further.

Monitoring links

After constructing your site and putting it on the Web, you can monitor its currency by frequently ensuring that any external address links you set up still work as intended. URLs change frequently, and you don't want users to click links that don't open their intended destinations.

Setting your HTTP address

To assist Dreamweaver in checking link accuracy, you must provide the actual URL for your site on the Web. Dreamweaver uses this information to check whether links in your site refer to other pages in your site root or to absolute addresses external to your site. Follow these steps to set your HTTP address:

1. **In Dreamweaver, choose Site⇨Manage Sites to open the Manage Sites dialog box.**

2. **From the Site list, select the site that you want to work on and click the Edit button.**

   The Site Definition dialog box for your site opens.

3. **Select the Local Info category.**

4. **In the HTTP Address box, enter the URL for your site.**

   This URL is the actual Web address for your site — for example, `http://www.yoursite.com`.

5. Click OK to close the Site Definition dialog box.

6. Click Done to close the Manage Sites dialog box.

TIP

Select the Enable Cache check box in the Local Info category of the Site Definition dialog box. Enabling the cache causes file and assets information to be maintained in the site, which helps speed up site management tasks as you construct your site. You can rebuild the cache at any time by choosing Site⇨Advanced⇨Recreate Site Cache.

Updating links sitewide

The Dreamweaver Link Checker can tell you whether links in your site are functioning properly. If you do find an incorrect link, you can update the link throughout your site, whether it's a URL or a link to one of your own pages. To identify and update broken links, just follow this procedure:

1. If you're not already at the Site window, switch to it by opening a Dreamweaver site file, choosing Window⇨Files, and clicking the Expand/Contract button.

If the Site Management toolbar doesn't appear in the Files panel, choose Site⇨Manage Sites. Then, in the Manage Sites dialog box that appears, select the site whose links you want to check and click Done. When the Site Management toolbar appears, click the Expand/Contract button to display the Site window.

2. Choose Site⇨Check Links Sitewide from the Site window main menu.

A Results window similar to the one in Figure 27-5 appears, displaying broken links in your site. If you don't see the Results window, choose Window⇨Results from the Dreamweaver main menu and then choose Site⇨Check Links Sitewide from the Site window main menu.

Figure 27-5:
The broken links are displayed in a handy Results panel.

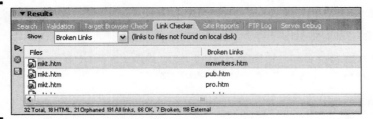

3. Choose Site⇨Change Link Sitewide from the Site window menu bar.

The Change Link Sitewide dialog box opens. Here you can replace the name of an old (broken) link with its new name.

4. In the Change All Links To text box, enter the current URL or internal page name or address that you want to change.

5. In the Into Links To text box, enter the URL or internal page of what you want the links to change to.

6. Click OK.

Setting up meta tags

Your goal in putting a Web site online is probably to make a certain body of information accessible to the public. Search engines can help users track down your site, but you can improve the likelihood of search engines listing your site by including special HTML code on your pages. This special code is contained in *meta tags* (tags defined using the <META> keyword) and consists of keywords and descriptions that you create to help search engines match user queries with your Web pages. (For more information about meta tags, see Chapter 7 of Book VI.)

Adding keyword <META> tags

To set up keyword <META> tags for a page, follow these steps:

1. **In the Document window, choose Insert⇨HTML⇨Head Tags⇨ Keywords.**

The Keywords dialog box appears.

2. **In the Insert Keywords dialog box, enter individual words or phrases that describe the content of your page and separate the entries with commas.**

Search engines use these keywords to index the page.

3. **Click OK.**

The dialog box closes and inserts your entries into the <META> tag in the HTML page code.

Adding a description <META> tag

To set up a description <META> tag for a page, follow these steps:

1. **In the Document window, choose Insert⇨HTML⇨Head Tags⇨ Description.**

The Insert Description dialog box appears.

2. **At the Insert Description dialog box, enter a sentence or paragraph that describes the content of your page.**

Search engines use this description to index the page.

3. **Click OK.**

The dialog box closes and inserts your entry into the <META> description tag and the HTML page code.

Index

Z